# Paleoindian Lifeways of the Cody Complex

# PALEOINDIAN LIFEWAYS OF THE CODY COMPLEX

edited by
Edward J. Knell and Mark P. Muñiz

THE UNIVERSITY OF UTAH PRESS
*Salt Lake City*

The Defiance House Man colophon is a registered trademark of the University of Utah Press. It is based on a four-foot-tall Ancient Puebloan pictograph (late PIII) near Glen Canyon, Utah.

17 16 15–14–13 1 2 3 4 5

LIBRARY OF CONGRESS CATALOGING-IN-PUBLICATION DATA

Paleoindian lifeways of the Cody Complex / edited by Edward J. Knell and Mark P. Muñiz.
p. cm.
Includes bibliographical references and index.
ISBN 978-1-60781-229-6 (cloth : alk. paper)
ISBN 978-1-60781-230-2 (ebook)
1. Paleo-Indians—Great Plains—Implement. 2. Paleo-Indians—Great Basin—Implement. 3. Paleo-Indians—Prairie Provinces—Implement. 4. Projectile points—Great Plains. 5. Projectile points—Great Basin. 6. Projectile points—Prairie Provinces. 7. Great Plains—Antiquities. 8. Great Basin—Antiquities. 9. Prairie Provinces—Antiquities.
I. Knell, Edward J., 1968– II. Muñiz, Mark P., 1973–
E78.G73P346 2012
978'.01—dc23

2012041902

Printed and bound by Sheridan Books, Inc., Ann Arbor, Michigan.

*I dedicate this book to my wife, Annie,*
*and children, Milo and Alice,*
*for their many years of support,*
*encouragement, and love.*
— Edward Knell

~

*My work in this book is dedicated*
*to Cara, Zea, and Aleatha;*
*thank you for your love, support,*
*and patience.*
— Mark Muñiz

# Contents

# Figures

# Tables

# I

# The Cody Complex

# 1

# Introducing the Cody Complex

Edward J. Knell and Mark P. Muñiz

Mention of the "Cody complex" usually evokes certain thoughts among those familiar with this cultural complex: late Paleoindian period, Great Plains, stemmed Eden and Scottsbluff points, Cody knife, early Holocene, large bison kills, and a handful of key sites (e.g., Finley, Horner, Olsen-Chubbuck, MacHaffie, and Scottsbluff). These perceptions of the Cody complex developed through work conducted during the last seven decades, mostly from individual site-based treatments of Cody sites. These perceptions are true and reasonably characterize the Cody complex; however, a more nuanced understanding of Cody complex lifeways has not been elucidated, in part because until now a detailed, wide-ranging, behavior-oriented synthesis devoted to the Cody complex has not been written. Several such syntheses exist for Clovis and Folsom (e.g., Amick 1999; Bonnichsen et al. 2005; Bradley et al. 2010; Clark and Collins 2002), but none for the Cody complex. The lack of such a synthesis for Cody is significant considering that it is one of the longest-lasting North American Paleoindian traditions (~2,800 calendar years) and is second only to Clovis in geographic expanse (extending from the Great Basin to the St. Lawrence River and from the Canadian plains to the Texas Gulf Coast; see Figure 1.2). The contributors to this book seek to remedy the situation for the Cody complex by offering behavior-oriented syntheses that significantly expand knowledge of Cody complex lifeways. This expanded understanding would not be possible without prior research on the Cody complex, and we recognize and summarize previous important contributions to establish a framework that allows the chapters in this book to highlight new insights about the Cody complex rather than recapitulate past findings.

This chapter begins by summarizing prior knowledge of Cody complex technology, chronology, geographic range, subsistence practices, land use, and worldview. Then the new contributions to the Cody literature contained in this book are briefly introduced, providing a road map for the chapters that follow.

### Lithic Technology and Chronology

Jepsen (1951:24) first coined the term "Cody complex" to describe the co-occurrence of Eden and Scottsbluff projectile points recovered from the Horner site near Cody, Wyoming. Previously, Eden and Scottsbluff points were subsumed under the broadly defined "Yuma" projectile point type (see discussion in Wormington 1957:103; also Wedel 1987). After Collateral Yuma points were found at the Finley site, located in the Eden Valley of Wyoming, and a second variety of Yuma point was found near Scottsbluff, Nebraska, called Scottsbluff Yuma, H. Marie Wormington (1948; also 1957:106) suggested dropping the term "Yuma" and simply renaming them "Eden" and "Scottsbluff," respectively. It was under this framework that in 1951 Jepsen suggested that the co-occurring Eden and Scottsbluff points at the

**FIGURE 1.1.** Primary projectile point styles comprising the Cody complex with site and catalog number: AC I = Alberta/Cody I; AC II = Alberta/Cody II; AL = Alberta; ED = Eden; SB I = Scottsbluff I; SB II = Scottsbluff II; FV = Firstview; KR = Kersey; CK = Cody knife. All photos are of original points, except Alberta point, which is a cast.

Horner site be considered part of a single cultural complex — the Cody complex. In 1957, Wormington further elaborated on the concept of a complex, which she defined as "a group of related traits or characteristics that combine to form a complete activity, process, or cultural unit. Lithic complexes are identified by the presence of several key implement or tool types in association" (p. 275). Wormington (1957) ultimately went on to identify the co-occurrence of Eden and Scottsbluff points and Cody knives as hallmark indicators of the Cody complex (Figure 1.1).

Since then, many researchers have considered the Alberta point type a distinct yet direct antecedent of the Cody complex (e.g., Agenbroad 1978; Bradley 1993, 2009, 2010; Frison 1991; Stanford 1999). However, results of detailed point production analyses (Bradley 1993, 2010; Bradley and Frison 1987) and the recognition that Alberta radiocarbon dates and geographic distribution overlap with Eden and Scottsbluff has led most archaeologists to include the Alberta point within the Cody complex (e.g., Agenbroad 1978; Amick, this volume; Bamforth 1991; Bradley 1993, 2009, 2010; Bradley and Frison 1987; Hofman and Graham 1998; Knell 2007; Muñiz 2005). For our purposes here, we consider the Cody complex to represent a taxonomic classification of early Holocene hunter-gatherers who shared distinctive projectile and knife technologies that set them apart from their contemporaries; these groups shared other important aspects of their lifeways, such as an emphasis on bison hunting and extensive long-term use of the Great Plains and Rocky Mountains. We make no assumptions about other cultural aspects such as language, ideology, or social organization, which may have varied between groups. Undoubtedly, smaller subdivisions of the Cody complex can be made depending on which characteristics are emphasized, and the researchers in this book may differ in their applications.

### *Projectile Point Technology*

In the decades following Wormington's seminal publication, researchers named many more "types" of Cody projectile points, generally basing the distinctions on variations in degree of shouldering, blade outline shape, length of stem, and final rounds of pressure flaking (Agenbroad 1978; Bamforth 1991; Beck and Jones 1997; Bradley and Frison 1987; Bradley and Stanford 1987; Forbis 1968; Frison 1991; M. G. Hill et al. 1995; Hofman and Graham 1998; Justice 1987; Mason 1997; Stanford 1999; Theler and Boszhardt 2003; Wheat 1972, 1979; also see Knudson, this volume; Bamforth, this volume). For example, Wheat (1972) added the Firstview type and provided a particularly informative description of the subtle differences between the Eden, Scottsbluff, Firstview, San Jon, and Milnesand types on the Great Plains. Hofman and Graham (1998) noted a potential association between Cody and Milnesand points from the southern Plains, and LaBelle (2002) documented a co-occurrence with James Allen points in eastern Colorado; however, we do not consider Milnesand or James Allen part of the Cody complex. Thus, the primary named point types associated with the Cody complex throughout the Great Plains, Rocky Mountains, and Great Basin are Alberta, Alberta/Cody I, Alberta/Cody II, Kersey, Firstview, Eden, Scottsbluff I, and Scottsbluff II (Figure 1.1). Other named Cody point variants include the enigmatic Scottsbluff III (Great Plains and Rocky Mountains), Eared Scottsbluff/Eden and Renier variants (western Great Lakes), San Jon (Llano Estacado region), and Texas Scottsbluff (southern Texas). The Hardin point type from the central Midwest is considered by many (Justice 1987; Mason 1997; Theler and Boszhardt 2003) to be either a stylistic variant or direct descendant of the Scottsbluff type. Some Holland points from the central Midwest have characteristic Cody point attributes (Holland 1971), but many researchers consider them Dalton variants (Justice 1987). Around the western Great Lakes, archaeologists have named several cultural phases and complexes (e.g., Interlakes composite, Lakehead complex, Minocqua phase, Reservoir Lakes complex) that include Cody points and variants (Fox 1975; Harrison et al. 1995; Ross 1997; Salzer 1974; Steinbring 1974). However, these complexes also include unrelated, nonfluted Paleoindian point styles (e.g., Agate Basin, Hell Gap, Angostura, and variants) that lack exclusively Cody traits.

Regardless of the specific named type, the basic Cody complex projectile point has a straight-sided (sometimes slightly expanding or contracting) squared base that may range from slightly convex to flat to slightly concave, squared to rounded shoulders that are occasionally subtle when ground or absent (e.g., Firstview), a lanceolate parallel-sided blade (that may range from convex to triangular) often with well-executed parallel collateral flaking (sometimes irregular), and a cross section ranging from biconvex (sometimes flattened) to median ridged (sometimes diamond shaped). In the Midwest, the Eared Scottsbluff/Eden type has small ears extending outward from the bottom of the base (as do some Holland points, to a much lesser extent), and Hardin points have broad corner-notches and a pronounced expanding stem.

### *Cody Knife*

The Cody knife is the other diagnostic artifact type for the Cody complex (Figure 1.1) and, like the projectile points, has a plethora of morphological varieties (Agenbroad 1978; Blackmar 1998; Bradley and Frison 1987; Bradley and Stanford 1987; Dick and Mountain 1960; Wormington 1957). Cody knives generally have square bases and asymmetrical blades, and are usually—but not always—stemmed on at least one margin. Blackmar (1998) noted that within the Great Plains, Colorado ($n = 15$) and Wyoming ($n = 15$) have the most frequent occurrence of the classic Cody knife as defined by Wormington. Furthermore, Blackmar found that the majority of knives recovered from the two states came from the Claypool site in Colorado ($n = 11$) and the Horner site in Wyoming ($n = 8$). More recently, three Cody knives were found at the Osprey Beach site, Yellowstone National Park, Wyoming (Johnson et al. 2004). Unlike the case of projectile points, our understanding of Cody knives remains somewhat enigmatic because this artifact type has received less discussion regarding its morphological variability or chronological or cultural implications. Recent high-magnification use-wear analyses by Muñiz (2005) on several Cody knives from the western and northwestern Plains identify these tools as butchering implements—a pattern consistent with their frequent recovery from bison kill sites.

### *Radiocarbon Chronology*

The chronometric relationship between the various projectile point styles is complex because of several factors: the paucity of radiocarbon dates associated with all the point styles except Eden and Scottsbluff, the implications of reversals and plateaus in the radiocarbon calibration curve, and variability in the morphological continuum exhibited by many of the point styles. With these limitations in mind, we briefly analyze chronological and geographic trends in the development

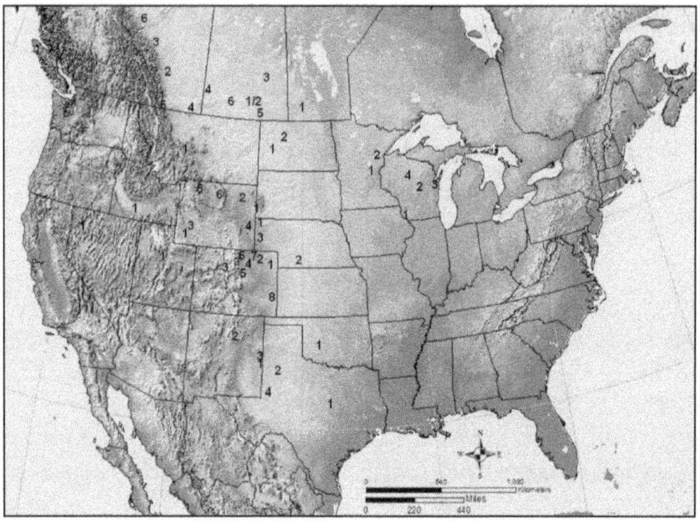

FIGURE 1.2. Map of selected Cody complex sites. Site names are listed in Table 1.2.

of Cody complex point styles. Radiocarbon dates are presented throughout this book, followed (in most cases) by the two standard error (95 percent confidence interval) calibrated year BP date range as appropriate. The radiocarbon dates were calibrated using CALIB 6.0.2 based on the INTCAL09 calibration curve (Reimer et al. 2009).

Several of the stemmed projectile point types from the Plateau and Great Basin have radiocarbon dates prior to 11,000 $^{14}$C yrs BP (see dates in Beck and Jones 2010), and may have been precursors to the stemmed point varieties on the Great Plains that appear around 10,000 $^{14}$C yrs BP (11,600–11,340 cal BP). The cultural and chronological relationships between Cody complex peoples from the Great Basin, Great Plains, Plateau, and Rocky Mountains are underresearched topics that hold great importance for understanding Cody complex origins (but see Amick, this volume), the stability of this early Holocene cultural tradition, and relationships with descendant early Archaic groups.

To explore the date range of the Cody complex, we provide summary data that include 64 radiocarbon dates from 41 Cody complex components at 31 sites (Table 1.1). We attempted to focus on single components as much as possible to reduce complications from mixed assemblages, although undoubtedly some components are mixed. The 31 sites we use to evaluate the Cody chronological record are generally located on the western Great Plains and Rocky Mountains, as most Cody complex research has been conducted there; the resulting analysis is probably affected by this bias. Despite the bias, the ten U.S. states and two Canadian provinces containing radiocarbon-dated sites (Figure 1.2, Tables 1.1 and 1.2) represent a wide swath of North America that should allow for the identification of temporal patterning resulting from large-scale geographical trends in occupation and possible colonization of territory by Cody groups.

A second potential source of bias in understanding time-space systematics for the Cody complex comes from the continuous nature of the technological attributes used to classify the diagnostic point styles. For example, identifying an extra round of pressure shaping or the emphasis a specific researcher places on degree of development and shape of shoulders may result in a slightly different point style classification. Generally, we relied on the typological classifications made by the original investigators with the understanding that different researchers may create slightly different groupings.

To assess the current state of the Cody chronology and to provide a chronological baseline for the chapters that follow, we developed a ranking system to organize the radiocarbon dates in Table 1.1. We included only those published radiocarbon dates that are most directly associated with each cultural deposit. The degree of association (from most to least associated) was ranked in the following tiers:

1. The dated material is in direct association with the cultural deposit in the form of a cultural feature (e.g., hearth, bonebed), and consists of charcoal, seed, or bone collagen (preferably dated in the mid-1990s or later due to advancements in bone dating techniques that occurred during this time).
2. The dated material is in indirect association with the cultural deposit because the sample is from the same stratum (either geologic or pedogenic) but spatially separated from the deposit and the dated material consists of charcoal, seed, or bone collagen (preferably dated in the mid-1990s or later).
3. The dated material is bulk sediment (e.g., humates, humic acid, "residue") in either direct or indirect association with the cultural deposit.

In order to better understand the chronological trends for specific point styles, we further analyzed the tier 1 and 2 dates (82.8 percent of the sample). The tier 3 samples lack direct association with the cultural deposit because they are bulk samples subject to the mixing effects of younger pedogenic processes; consequently, we excluded them from analysis. Also excluded were bracketing dates from super- or subjacent strata. Although Wheat's (1972) original date for Olsen-Chubbuck was made directly on bone from the bonebed, it was excluded both because of the very large standard error (500 years) and because the site was redated by Holliday and colleagues (1999) using better techniques.

Figure 1.3 illustrates the distribution of the 53 tier 1 and 2 uncalibrated radiocarbon dates by point style with a two-sigma error. When we consider single point styles from unmixed components, the Alberta/Cody components from the Horner II and Wallmann Bison sites (10,500–9620 $^{14}$C yrs BP; 12,590–10,870 cal BP) are oldest; however, this very small sample may not fully represent Alberta/Cody and must be considered cautiously. Alberta points are the next oldest, based on seven dates from five sites; when a two-sigma range is used, this point style dates from 10,065 to 8135 $^{14}$C yrs BP (11,720–9020 cal BP). The youngest date, from Swan Landing, Alberta, is an extreme outlier, and if it is removed, the range terminates at 9440 $^{14}$C yrs BP (ca. 10,655 cal BP). Following Alberta and Alberta/Cody is a florescence of point styles that include Eden, Scottsbluff, Firstview, and Kersey.

Two sites from Alberta, Canada—Fletcher and DjPm-1—provide data relevant to the termination of the Alberta phase and the initiation of Scottsbluff. The Fletcher site has a mixed Alberta and Scottsbluff component that was recently dated to 9540 ± 110 $^{14}$C yrs BP (11,185–10,575 cal BP) (see Dawe, this volume), a date that overlaps with the previously reported maximum bracketing age of 9380 ± 110 $^{14}$C yrs BP (10,265–11,072 cal BP) (Vickers and Beaudoin 1989). The new Fletcher date is also one of the earliest dates yet recorded for Scottsbluff. A minimum bracketing date of 9410 ± 95 $^{14}$C yrs BP (11,083–10,300 cal BP) was determined for the Alberta component at Locality I, Hell Gap (Haynes 2009) and provides further support for a terminal date for the Alberta style of about 9440 $^{14}$C yrs BP (ca. 10,655 cal BP). Site DjPm-16 produced two dates—9600 ± 210 and 9450 ± 230 $^{14}$C yrs BP—on a mixed Alberta and Scottsbluff component that average 9525 $^{14}$C yrs BP (see Dawe, this volume). Although large standard errors exist for the DjPm-16 dates, they provide further support for a pre-9500 $^{14}$C yr BP origin for the Scottsbluff style.

The earliest components with only Scottsbluff points occur at two sites in Alberta (EgPn-480, EkPu-8) and the Malin Fishing Hole site in Montana, which together range from 9910 to 9400 $^{14}$C yrs BP (11,320–10,580 cal BP). These sites are separated by 321 radiocarbon years (442 calendar years) from the remaining Scottsbluff component sites and possibly suggest that the Scottsbluff style originated in Alberta before spreading southward; more data are needed to evaluate this issue (see Dawe, this volume).

The four other sites with Scottsbluff-only components date from 9109 to 7500 $^{14}$C yrs BP (10,250–8330 cal BP). The youngest date, from MacHaffie, was run shortly after the advent of radiocarbon dating and has a large standard error (Forbis and Sperry 1952). As Figure 1.3 shows, several of the youngest Scottsbluff dates (MacHaffie, Red Rock Canyon) have large errors; we feel that a terminal date closer to 8000 $^{14}$C yrs BP (8990–8785 cal BP) is more likely.

The date range for single-component Eden occupations is much narrower than for Scottsbluff.

**TABLE 1.1.** Cody Complex Radiocarbon Dates Used for Spatio-Temporal Analysis.

| Site | Point Type[a] | Date | Error | Lab ID | Material | Tier | Reference |
|---|---|---|---|---|---|---|---|
| Benz, ND | AL | 9540 | 50 | UCR-3466 | charcoal | 2 | Root 1992, 1998 |
| | SB | 8910 | 70 | SMU-1271 | humates | 2 | Root 1992, 1998 |
| | SB | 8700 | 70 | SMU-1282 | humates | 2 | Root 1992, 1998 |
| Blackwater Draw, NM | FV | 8970 | 60 | SMU-1672 | humates | 2 | Holliday et al. 1999 |
| | FV | 8830 | 160 | Y-2488 | sediment organic residue | 2 | Holliday et al. 1999 |
| | FV | 8690 | 70 | SMU-1671 | humates | 2 | Holliday et al. 1999 |
| Blue Point, WY | AL | 9540 | 40 | Beta 133208 | charcoal | 1 | Johnson and Pastor 2003 |
| DjPm-16, Alberta | AL; SB | 9600 | 210 | AECV-746C | bone | 2 | Van Dyke et al. 1989 (in Dawe, this volume) |
| | AL; SB | 9450 | 230 | BIS-17 | bone | 2 | Van Dyke et al. 1989 (in Dawe, this volume) |
| EgPn-480, Alberta | SB | 9540 | 70 | Beta-127235 | bone | 1 | De Mille and Head 2001 (in Dawe, this volume) |
| EkPu-8, Alberta | SB | 9750 | 80 | TO-2999 | bison metacarpal | 2 | Ronaghan 1993 (in Dawe, this volume) |
| Finley, WY | ED; SB | 9026 | 118 | SMU-250 | bison apatite | 1 | Frison 1991 |
| | ED; SB | 8950 | 220 | RL-574 | bison apatite | 1 | Frison 1991 |
| Fletcher, Alberta | AL; SB | 9540 | 110 | CAMS-42980 | seed | 1 | Beaudoin et al. 2000 (in Dawe, this volume) |
| | AL; SB | 9380 | 110 | TO-1097 | seed | 3 | Vickers and Beaudoin 1989 |
| Frasca, CO | ED; SB | 8910 | 90 | SI-4848 | bone | 1 | Fulgham and Stanford 1982 |
| Hell Gap, Loc. I, WY | AL | 10,560 | 80 | AA-20545 | charcoal | 3 | Haynes 2009 |
| | AL | 9410 | 95 | AA-28774 | charcoal | 3 | Haynes 2009 |
| | ED; SB | 9120 | 490 | AA-27675 | charcoal | 2 | Haynes 2009 |
| Hell Gap, Loc. V, WY | ED | 9050 | 160 | A-753C3 | apatite | 1 | Haynes 1968, 2009; Knell et al. 2002 |
| | ED | 8890 | 110 | A-753A | apatite | 1 | Haynes 1968, 2009; Knell et al. 2002 |
| | ED | 8685 | 70 | A-35655 | bulk residue | 3 | Haynes 1968, 2009; Knell et al. 2002 |
| Heron Eden, Saskatchewan | ED | 9210 | 110 | S-3308 | bison bone | 1 | Corbeil 1995 |
| | ED | 8930 | 120 | S-3114 | bison bone | 1 | Corbeil 1995 |
| | ED | 8920 | 130 | S-3309 | bison bone | 1 | Corbeil 1995 |
| Horner I, WY | AC; ED; SB | 9390 | 75 | SI-4851 | charcoal | 3 | Frison 1987 |
| | AC; ED; SB | 8840 | 140 | UCLA-697A | bison bone | 1 | Frison 1987 |
| | AC; ED; SB | 8750 | 120 | UCLA-697A | bison bone | 1 | Frison 1987 |
| Horner II, WY | AC | 10,060 | 220 | I-10900 | charcoal | 2 | Frison 1987 |
| | AC | 9875 | 85 | SI-4851A | charcoal | 2 | Frison 1987 |
| Hudson-Meng, NE | AL | 9920 | 72.5 | 4 dates avg.[1] | charcoal | 2 | Todd and Rapson 1994 |
| | AL | 9820 | 160 | SMU-224 | charcoal | 2 | Agenbroad 1978 |
| | AL | 9675 | 70 | 2 dates avg.[2] | bone collagen | 1 | Todd and Rapson 1994 |

| | | | | | | | |
|---|---|---|---|---|---|---|---|
| | ED | 9539 | 55 | NZA 29717 | bone collagen | 1 | Muñiz 2008 |
| Jerry Craig, CO | ED; SB | 9310 | 50 | Beta-109467 | charcoal | 2 | Hill and Kornfeld 1999; Richings-Germain 2002 |
| Jim Pitts, SD | AL; SB; CK | 9390 | 65 | AA-23779 | wood | 3 | Sellet 2009 |
| Jurgens, CO | KR | 9070 | 90 | SI-3726 | charcoal | 2 | Wheat 1979 |
| Lamb Spring, CO | ED; SB | 8870 | 350 | M-1463 | bison collagen | 1 | Rancier et al. 1982; Stanford et al. 1981 |
| Lindenmeier, CO | AL | 9880 | 100 | TO-339 | charcoal | 2 | Haynes et al. 1992 |
| | ED; SB | 9690 | 60 | TO-341 | charcoal | 2 | Haynes et al. 1992 |
| Lubbock Lake, TX | FV | 8655 | 90 | SI-4177 | residue | 2 | Holliday et al. 1983 |
| | FV | 8210 | 240 | SMU-830 | humates | 2 | Holliday et al. 1983 |
| | FV | 7980 | 180 | SMU-827 | humates | 2 | Holliday et al. 1983 |
| MacHaffie, MT | SB | 8620 | 200 | GX-15152 | wood | 2 | Davis et al. 1991; Forbis and Sperry 1952 |
| | SB | 8280 | 120 | GX-15153-G | bone collagen | 1 | Davis et al. 1991; Forbis and Sperry 1952 |
| | SB | 8100 | 300 | L-578A | wood | 2 | Davis et al. 1991; Forbis and Sperry 1952 |
| Malin Fishing Hole, MT | CK | 8880 | 50 | n/a | n/a | 2 | Vivian 2005 |
| | SB | 9530 | 50 | Beta-196111 | n/a | 2 | Vivian 2005 |
| Mammoth Meadow, MT | ED; SB | 9390 | 90 | TO-1976 | charcoal | 2 | Bonnichsen et al. 1992 |
| Medicine Lodge Creek, WY | ED; AC? | 9360 | 380 | RL-150 | bone | 3 | Frison and Walker 2007 |
| | ED; AC? | 9030 | 470 | RL-439 | bone | 2 | Frison and Walker 2007 |
| | ED; AC? | 8830 | 470 | RL-446 | charcoal | 2 | Frison 1991; Frison and Walker 2007 |
| Nelson, CO | ED; SB | 9260 | 20 | UCIAMS-26939 | bone | 1 | Kornfeld et al. 2007 |
| | ED; SB | 7995 | 80 | SI-4898 | bone (bad date?) | 1 | Cassells 1997 |
| Olsen-Chubbuck, CO | FV | 10,150 | 500 | A-744 | bone collagen | 1[b] | Wheat 1972 |
| | FV | 9395 | 20 | 7 dates avg.[3] | bison bone gelatin | 1 | Holliday et al. 1999 |
| Osprey Beach, WY | ED; SB | 9360 | 60 | Beta-148567 | charcoal | 2 | Johnson et al. 2004 |
| Red Rock Canyon, Alberta | SB | 8220 | 260 | GX-1435 | charcoal | 2 | Dawe, this volume |
| San Jon, NM | FV | 8275 | 65 | A-7438.1 | humates | 2 | Holliday et al. 1999 |
| Scottsbluff, NE | SB | 8939 | 85 | AA-67443 | bison collagen | 1 | Hill 2008 |
| | SB | 8680 | 85 | AA-67442 | bison collagen | 1 | Hill 2008 |
| Swan Landing, Alberta | AL | 8675 | 270 | S-2178 | charcoal | 2 | Dawe, this volume |
| | AL | 8630 | 100 | AEVC-10cx | charcoal | 3 | Dawe, this volume |
| Wallmann Bison, NV | AC | 9770 | 50 | UCR-3782/CAMS 59156 | bison amino acids | 1 | Dansie and Jerrems 2004 (in Amick, this volume) |

[a] AC (Alberta/Cody), AL (Alberta), CK (Cody knife), ED (Eden), FV (Firstview), KR (Kersey), SB (Scottsbluff).

[b] Date (Wheat 1972) not used for this analysis because of very large standard error and redating of site by Holliday et al. 1999.

[1] Beta-64318; Beta-64320; Beta-65276; Beta-65277.

[2] CAMS-10364; CAMS-12841.

[3] NSRL-2801 CAMS-31812; NSRL-2797 CAMS-31813; NSRL-2797 CAMS-32682; NSRL-2799 CAMS-32683; NSRL-2798 CAMS24968; NSRL-2801 CAMS-32684; NSRL-2799 CAMS-31814.

**TABLE 1.2.** Key Cody Complex Sites Shown in Figure 1.2 by State/Province.

| State/Province | Site Name | Figure 1.2 Map # | Date? | Reference |
|---|---|---|---|---|
| Alberta | DjPm-16 | 1 | yes | Van Dyke et al. 1989 (in Dawe, this volume) |
| | EgPn-480 | 2 | yes | De Mille and Head 2001 (in Dawe, this volume) |
| | EkPu-8 | 3 | yes | Ronaghan 1993 (in Dawe, this volume) |
| | Fletcher | 4 | yes | Forbis 1968 |
| | Red Rock Canyon | 5 | yes | Reeves 1972 and Reeves and Bourges 2002 (in Dawe, this volume) |
| | Swan Landing | 6 | yes | Ball 1983, 1986 and Dawe 1983 (in Dawe, this volume) |
| Colorado | Claypool | 1 | no | Dick and Mountain 1960 |
| | Frasca | 2 | yes | Fulgham and Stanford 1982 |
| | Jerry Craig | 3 | yes | Richings-Germain 2002 |
| | Jurgens | 4 | yes | Wheat 1979 |
| | Lamb Spring | 5 | yes | Wedel 1963 |
| | Lindenmeier | 6 | yes | Wilmsen and Roberts 1978 |
| | Nelson | 7 | yes | Kornfeld et al. 2007 |
| | Olsen-Chubbuck | 8 | yes | Wheat 1972 |
| Idaho | Wilson Butte Cave | 1 | no | Gruhn 1961 |
| Manitoba | Carberry Plain | 1 | no | Pettipas 1970 |
| Minnesota | Bradbury Brook | 1 | yes | Malik and Bakken 1993, 1999 |
| | Reservoir Lakes | 2 | no | Harrison et al. 1995; Steinbring 1974 |
| Montana | MacHaffie | 1 | yes | Forbis and Sperry 1952 |
| | Mammoth Meadow | 2 | yes | Bonnichsen et al. 1992 |
| Nebraska | Hudson-Meng | 1 | yes | Agenbroad 1978 |
| | Medicine Creek Sites | 2 | no | Davis 1962; Bamforth 2007 |
| | Scottsbluff | 3 | yes | Barbour and Schultz 1932 |
| Nevada | Wallman Square-Base and Bison Site | 1 | yes | Amick, this volume |
| New Mexico | Blackwater Draw | 1 | yes | Hester 1972 |
| | R-6 | 2 | no | Stanford and Patten 1984 |
| | San Jon | 3 | yes | Roberts 1942 |
| North Dakota | Benz | 1 | yes | Root 1992 |
| | Max | 2 | no | Root et al., this volume |
| Oklahoma | Cedar Creek | 1 | no | Hofman 1990; see Blackmar and Hofman 1997 for distribution in Oklahoma |
| Ontario | Sheguiandah | 1 | yes | Julig 2002 |
| Saskatchewan | DjNf-8 | 1 | yes | Ebell 1975 |
| | Dunn | 2 | no | Ebell 1988 |
| | Haskey Area | 3 | no | Novecosky 2002 |
| | Heron Eden | 4 | yes | Corbeil 1995 |
| | McLeod | 5 | no | Joyes 1997, 2000 |
| | Niska | 6 | no | Meyer 1985 |
| South Dakota | Jim Pitts | 1 | yes | Sellet 2009 |
| Texas | Horn Shelter | 1 | no | Redder 1985 |
| | Lubbock Lake | 2 | yes | Johnson 1987 |
| | McFaddin Beach | 3 | no | Long 1977 |
| | Seminole Rose | 4 | no | Collins et al. 1997 |
| Utah | Martin | 1 | no | Janetski 2001 |

**TABLE 1.2.** (cont'd.) Key Cody Complex Sites Shown in Figure 1.2 by State/Province.

| State/Province | Site Name | Figure 1.2 Map # | Date? | Reference |
|---|---|---|---|---|
| Wisconsin | Bass | 1 | no | Stoltman 1997; Theler and Boszhardt 2003 |
| | Pope | 2 | no | Ritzenthaler 1972 |
| | Renier | 3 | no | Mason and Irwin 1960; Mason 1981 |
| | Robinson | 4 | no | Salzer 1974 |
| Wyoming | Blue Point | 1 | yes | Johnson and Pastor 2003 |
| | Carter/Kerr-McGee | 2 | no | Frison 1984 |
| | Finley | 3 | yes | Moss et al. 1951 |
| | Hell Gap | 4 | yes | Irwin-Williams et al. 1973; Knell 2009; Knell et al. 2009; Larson et al. 2009 |
| | Horner | 5 | yes | Frison and Todd 1987 |
| | Medicine Lodge Creek | 6 | yes | Frison and Walker 2007 |
| | Osprey Beach | 7 | yes | Johnson et al. 2004 |

Three sites (Hell Gap Locality V, Heron Eden, Hudson-Meng) with six single-component Eden occupations range in age from 9649 to 8660 $^{14}$C yrs BP (11,160–9525 cal BP). The raw dates (without errors) indicate that these components are generally older than single-component Scottsbluff sites, although there is considerable overlap. The oldest Eden date is from Hudson-Meng (9539 ± 55 $^{14}$C yrs BP; 10,679–11,105 cal BP) (Muñiz 2010) and is essentially identical to the oldest Scottsbluff dates. Although the sample size is small, the data lead to the hypothesis that Scottsbluff and Eden developed contemporaneously, with Scottsbluff to the north (southern Alberta and Montana) and Eden to the south (Nebraska–central High Plains).

Examples of both Eden and Scottsbluff projectile points in the same component occur in ten components at nine sites, and range from 10,100 to 8140 $^{14}$C yrs BP (11,760–9020 cal BP). The oldest date, from Locality I at Hell Gap, has a large standard error (Haynes 2009); thus, a more accurate estimate for the maximum date may be the 9810 $^{14}$C yr BP (11,240–11,220 cal BP) date from Lindenmeier (Haynes et al. 1992). As Figure 1.3 illustrates, the termination of the co-occurring Eden-Scottsbluff occupations appears to correlate with the end of Eden, since the Scottsbluff style continues for many centuries afterward.

Radiocarbon dates for eight Firstview components at four sites (Blackwater Draw, Lubbock Lake, Olsen-Chubbuck, San Jon) largely mirror those for the later Scottsbluff grouping. The majority (75 percent) of these dated components are from just two sites: Blackwater Draw and Lubbock Lake. The similarity in temporal range to the more northerly Scottsbluff sites may indicate distinct regional foci for groups making these styles (Firstview in the south; Scottsbluff in the north), as noted by Bamforth (1991) and Holliday (1997). If we take into consideration the temporal overlap at the end of Eden and beginning of Firstview, the lack of distinctive shouldering that typifies both styles, and the general southerly orientation in relation to Scottsbluff, the intriguing possibility is raised that Firstview evolved from an Eden precursor. Detailed technological analyses should be conducted to evaluate this possibility.

The final dated components in the sample include mixed deposits with Alberta/Cody, Eden, and Scottsbluff points, and the Kersey type as defined by Wheat (1979) at the Jurgens site. The mixed components at Horner I include Alberta/Cody, Eden, and Scottsbluff points that date to ca. 8800 $^{14}$C yrs BP (ca. 9905–9740 cal BP). Frison et al. (1987) noted the possibility that the Horner I deposit represents a palimpsest accumulation and that the Alberta/Cody points may date an older occupation. Otherwise, the Alberta/Cody component at Horner I is at least 500 $^{14}$C years younger than expected; however, the small Alberta/Cody sample may significantly bias this interpretation. The two dates from Medicine Lodge Creek are from a stratum with Eden and possibly Alberta/Cody points. The dates are more consistent with Eden, but as with Horner I, the lack of Alberta/Cody sites in the database may cause this

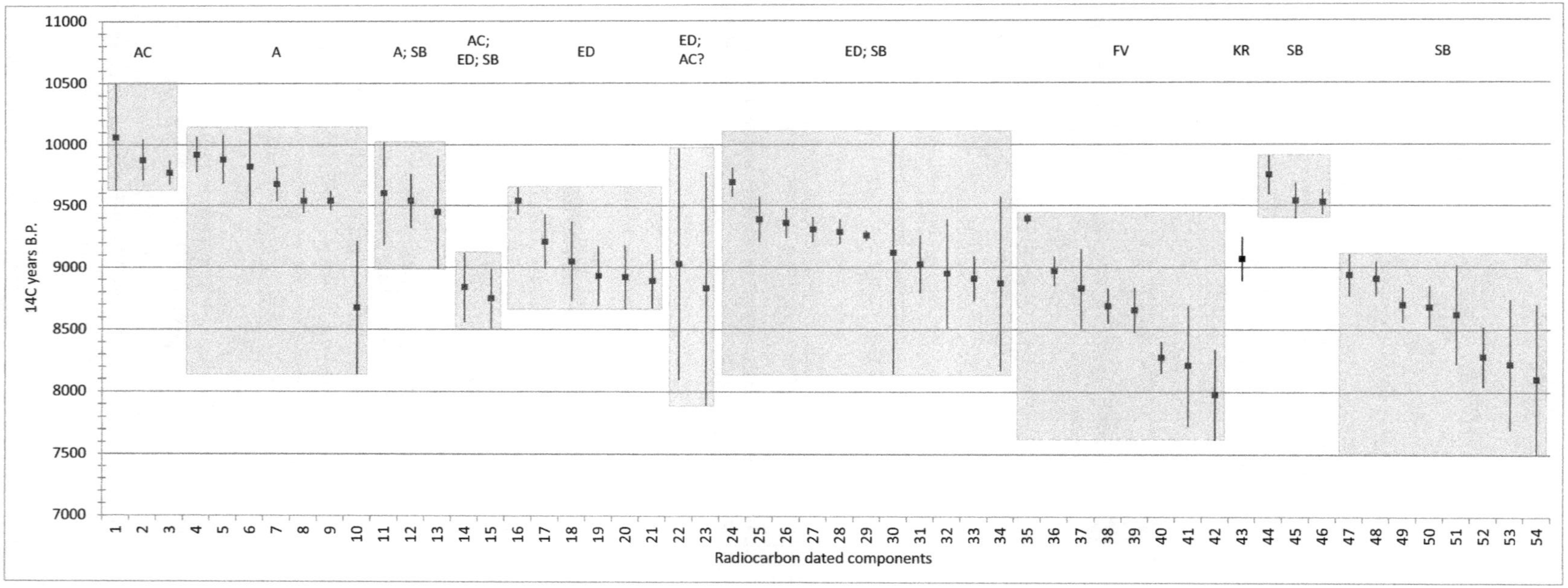


**FIGURE 1.3.** Cody complex radiocarbon dates: AC = Alberta/Cody; A = Alberta; ED = Eden; SB = Scottsbluff (I and II); FV = Firstview; KR = Kersey; combinations also indicated.

apparent anomaly. Finally, the radiocarbon date for the "Kersey component" at the Jurgens site fits well with both Eden and Scottsbluff dates and, as several researchers have noted (Bradley 1993, 2010; Muñiz 2005; Stanford 1999), represents a local stylistic variant rather than a separate cultural complex as originally proposed by Wheat (1979).

The Bradbury Brook site in east-central Minnesota was not included in this analysis but produced a date of 9220 ± 75 (10,568–10,240 cal BP) from charcoal in association with a Cody complex point base (Malik and Bakken 1999). The site has a dense lithic deposit with more than 125,000 artifacts from stone tool manufacturing, and represents the presence of Cody complex peoples in the upper Midwest woodlands. The projectile point (base and proximal blade fragment) was originally identified as Alberta (Malik and Bakken 1999) but could be Scottsbluff, which would make the radiocarbon date consistent with this attribution.

The Hardin point type occurs along the eastern Plains and southern Midwest and is estimated to date between 10,000 and 7500 $^{14}$C yrs BP (Justice 1987). Based on similarities in production strategy, flake scar patterns, and overall morphology, many Midwest researchers interpret the Hardin point style as deriving directly from Scottsbluff (Justice 1987; Mason 1997; Theler and Boszhardt 2003). If this is the case, then Hardin may be one of the final vestiges of the Cody complex and may represent an adaptation to the prairie-woodland environment of the lower Midwest that extended into the early Archaic period. However, the frequency of beveled blade edges through resharpening is reminiscent of southeastern early Archaic point styles; the cultural connection between Hardin points and the Cody complex thus remains enigmatic.

Generally, then, for the Great Plains and Rocky Mountain region, Alberta/Cody, Alberta, Eden, Scottsbluff, and Firstview depict temporal continuity between about 10,000 and 8000 $^{14}$C yrs BP, a period that spans some 2,815 calendar years (11,600–8785 cal BP), making it one of the longest known Paleoindian cultural traditions. If stemmed point sites from the Great Basin and Plateau, and Hardin sites from the Midwest, are added to this, the temporal range could expand at least another 700 radiocarbon years earlier (but see Amick, this volume) and perhaps another 600 radiocarbon years later.

Assuming that the many plateaus and reversals in the radiocarbon curve are not artificially structuring the chronological relationship of the various Cody point styles, it seems likely that for well over 2,500 years there were continuous Cody cultural "neighborhoods" or populations that covered vast territories and probably interacted with their surroundings in different ways. The use of different adaptive strategies by Cody peoples living in different environmental settings resulted in the unique and regionally specific mobility and subsistence strategies noted in the literature and in the chapters in this book.

The recognition that there were almost certainly contemporaneous groups making slightly different projectile points and practicing slightly different subsistence-settlement strategies (see Knudson, this volume) raises very important questions: how did Cody peoples vary their approaches to negotiating the social landscape and how did different settlement-subsistence strategies influence the development of social networks during the Cody era? Some of these issues are addressed below and in the chapters that follow.

## Geography

The Cody complex is a widespread cultural phenomenon; however, examination of Figure 1.2 (also see Table 1.2) makes clear that most excavated Cody sites are located in the Great Plains and Rocky Mountains. Cody sites occur on the grasslands/rolling hills and alluvial valleys of the Great Plains, extending from Alberta and Saskatchewan in the north to the Gulf Coast of Texas in the south, and from the Rocky Mountain Front Range on the west to Illinois on the east (e.g., Dawe, this volume; Frison et al. 1996; Hofman 1996; Hofman and Graham 1998; Justice 1987). Many other Cody sites occur in the foothills (mostly east of the Continental Divide) of the North, Central, and Southern Rocky Mountain Front Range as well as higher mountain zones (e.g., Brunswig 2007; Hill and Knell, this volume; Jodry 1999; Pitblado 2003). Outside the Great Plains, Cody projectiles and sites have been recovered from the Black Rock Desert in northern Nevada, in Idaho, and as far east as the Great Lakes woodlands of Minnesota, Wisconsin, southern Manitoba, and Ontario, as well as into New England (e.g., Amick, this volume; Beck and Jones 1997; Cox 2001; C.L. Hill 2007; M.G. Hill 1994; M.G. Hill et al. 1998; Julig 1994, 2002; Malik and Bakken 1999; Mason 1981; Mason and Irwin 1960; Pettipas 1970; Salzer 1974; Stoltman 1997; Theler and Boszhardt 2003; Wallman and Amick 1991). This geographic range is vast and encompasses considerable variation: in latitude and longitude and thus significant variability in temperature and precipitation; in elevation; in vegetation and fauna and how Cody peoples respond to environmental change; in availability of water, wood, and toolstone; and probably also in differential rates of population pressure. Cody complex sites occur across several biomes and throughout many ecozones with differing resource structure, which, as research has demonstrated time and again, influences Paleoindian subsistence and land-use strategies (e.g., Amick 1994; M.E. Hill 2007; Knell 2007, this volume; Knell and Hill 2012; LaBelle 2005). Consequently, it is not surprising that prior (e.g., Blackmar 2001; Johnson 1989; Knell 2007; Knell and Hill 2012; Muñiz 2005; Pitblado 2003) and current (Amick; Dawe; Hill; Hill and Knell; Muñiz; and Root et al., this volume) studies demonstrate considerable variability in Cody subsistence and land-use patterning across space.

The widespread distribution of Cody complex projectile points across much of North America is also fairly unique among Paleoindian cultural complexes. This distribution is on par with that of Clovis, making the Cody complex one of the most geographically expansive cultural complexes in the prehistory of North America. The reasons for this widespread distribution are not entirely understood; however, some authors in this book (Amick; Dawe; Muñiz [Chapter 2]) suggest that the expansion occurred as Cody peoples sought new niches during favorable times of the early Holocene.

### Subsistence

The extremely wide geographic expanse of Cody site distributions and the associated variability in plants and animals that must accompany such a geographic range indicate that Cody peoples developed successful subsistence strategies wherever they lived—whether the Great Basin, Rocky Mountains, Great Plains, Texas Hill Country, eastern prairies, Great Lakes region of the Upper Midwest, or Midwest woodlands. Common to the subsistence strategy in all these areas is an emphasis on bison, which clearly played an important part (but not an exclusive one, as we see below) in the Cody economic strategy.

To demonstrate this point, we acquired subsistence data from 23 Cody complex sites in the Rocky Mountains and greater northwestern and northern Great Plains (Table 1.3). Of these sites, all but one (Blue Point) has identifiable bison remains, and in all cases the minimum number of individual (MNI) bison is higher than for any other faunal type. The average bison MNI for these sites is 51.6 (excluding Hudson-Meng), a number that is skewed by some extremely large kill/processing sites on the grassland plains (e.g., Jurgens [$n$ = 68], Olsen-Chubbuck [$n$ = 190]). (This average estimate for bison MNI is very close to that reported by Hill [this volume] for a larger sample of Cody sites.) The average bison MNI drops drastically in the foothills-mountains and uplifts, where Jerry Craig has an MNI of seven (Richings-Germain 2002), as does Hell Gap Locality V (Knell et al. 2009); large, lower-elevation basins in the foothills-mountains zone seem to portray a different pattern, as indicated by the large bison kills at Horner I and II (Frison and Todd 1987). While the low MNI values at Jerry Craig and Hell Gap may not readily suggest an emphasis on bison, it is still the case that Cody people preferentially hunted bison in the mountains to a greater extent than did contemporary late Paleoindian groups (see Hill and Knell, this volume).

Little is said here regarding bison seasonality data obtained from analyses of bison maxillary and mandibular dentitions because Hill (this volume) covers this topic in considerably more detail. However, using the data in Table 1.4 and Figure 1.4, we briefly note some general trends. These data indicate that Cody hunter-gatherers dispatched bison throughout the year, with much of the hunting occurring in fall and early winter, and to some extent late summer. Cody subsistence strategies outside the Great Plains and Rocky Mountains are unknown; however, Hill's (this volume) finding that bison hunting patterns varied between the northern and southern Great

**TABLE 1.3.** Minimum Number of Individuals (MNI; bold) and Number of Identified Specimens (NISP; in parentheses) from Cody Complex Sites in the Northwestern and Northern Plains.

| Site | Environmental Zone | Bison | Pronghorn | Mule Deer | Deer sp. | Bighorn Sheep | Elk | Lagomorph | Canid sp. | Bird | Owl (horned) | Beaver | Marmot | Muskrat | Fish | Turtle | Species Richness |
|---|---|---|---|---|---|---|---|---|---|---|---|---|---|---|---|---|---|
| Benz | PGR | ? (1) | | | | | | | | | | | | | | | 1 |
| Blue Point | PGR | | | | | | | **2** (17) | | | | | | | | | 1 |
| Carter/ Kerr-McGee | PGR | **47** (?) | | | | | | | | | | | | | | | 1 |
| Claypool | PGR | X | | | | | | | | | | | | | | | 1 |
| Finley (Station B) | PGR | **82** (8,033) | | | | | | | | | | | | | | | 1 |
| Fletcher | PGR | X | | | | | | | | | | | | | | | 1 |
| Frasca | PGR | **56** (7,780) | | | | | | | X | | | | | | | | 1 |
| Hell Gap I (Alberta) | FHM | X | | | | | | | | | | | | | | | 1 |
| Hell Gap I (Cody) | FHM | X | | | | | | | | | | | | | | | 1 |
| Hell Gap V | FHM | **7** (334) | | ? (1) | | | | ? (1) | ? (7) | | | | | | | | 3 |
| Heron Eden | PGR | **37** (22,898) | ? (1) | | | | | | ? (2) | | | | | | | | 2 |
| Horner I | PAV | **100** (?) | **1** (3) | **2** (10) | | | | **1** (1) | | **1** (1) | **1** (2) | | | | | **1** (3) | 7 |
| Horner II | PAV | **65** (1,102) | **1** (5) | **2** (7) | | | | **1** (5) | **1** (3) | **2** (4) | | | | | | | 5 |
| Jerry Craig | FHM | **7** (55) | | | | | | | | | | | | | | | 1 |
| Jurgens 1–3 | PAV | **68** (5,497) | **9** (112) | **2** (12) | ? (1) | | **3** (5) | **3** (10) | **1** (4) | **3** (5) | | **1** (3) | **1** (1) | **1** (1) | **1** (3) | **1** (3) | 12 |
| Lamb Spring | PGR | **27** (1,990) | | | | | | | | | | | | | | | 1 |
| Lime Creek | PAV | 6 | 2 | | X | | 1 | 1 | 1 | 5 | | 5 | | | | 1 | 8 |
| MacHaffie | FHM | X | | X | | | | | X | | | | | | | | 2 |
| Nelson | PGR | **5** (212) | | | | | | | | | | | | | | | 1 |
| Niska | PGR | X | | | | | | | | | | | | | | | 1 |
| Olsen-Chubbuck | PGR | **190** (4,264) | | | | | | | | | | | | | | | 1 |
| Osprey Beach | FHM | X | | | X | X | | X | X | | | | | | | | 4 |
| Scottsbluff | PGR | 26 (1,461) | | | | | | | | | | | | | | | 1 |
| MNI Average | | 51.6 | 3.3 | 2 | — | — | 2 | 1.6 | 1 | 2.8 | 1 | 2 | 1 | 1 | 1 | 1 | |

*Note:* Species richness excludes canid remains. Environmental zone: FHM = foothills-mountains, PGR = plains grasslands, PAV = plains alluvial valleys.

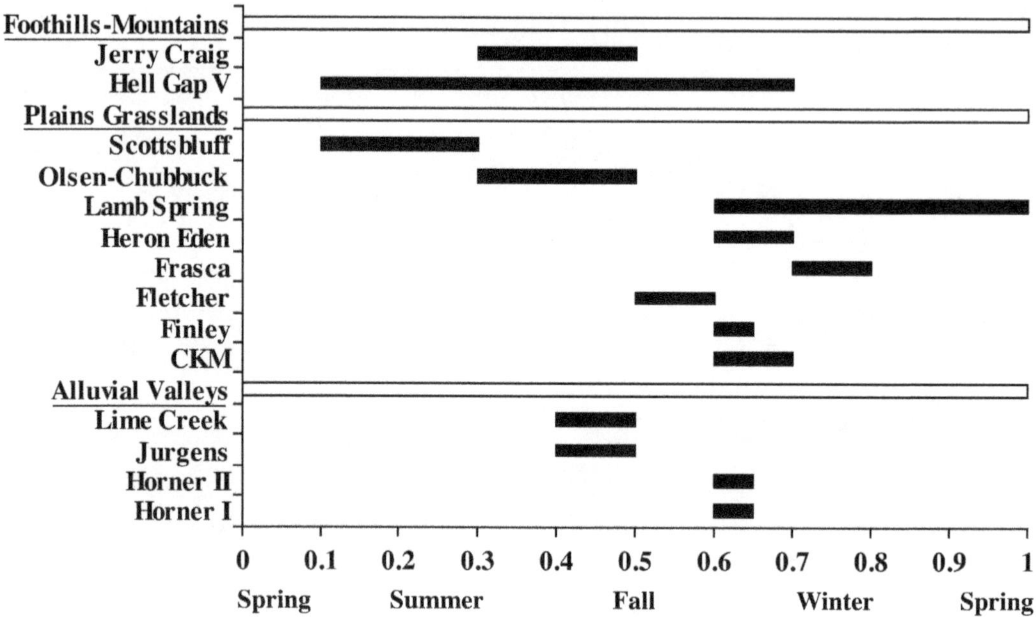


FIGURE 1.4. Bison season of death based on tooth eruption and wear patterns.

TABLE 1.4. Bison Seasonality Determinations.

| Site Name | Site Type | Season | Dental Age | Reference |
|---|---|---|---|---|
| Carter/Kerr-McGee | Processing | Early winter | .6–.7 | Frison 1984 |
| Finley (Station B) | Kill | Late fall–early winter | .6 | Todd et al. 1990 |
| Fletcher | Kill | Fall? | Unknown | Wilson and MacWilliams 1988 |
| Frasca | Kill | Early winter | Unknown | Fulgham and Stanford 1982 |
| Hell Gap V | Camp | Late spring–early winter | .1–.7 | Rapson and Niven 2009 |
| Heron Eden | Kill | Winter | .6–.7 | Corbeil 1995 |
| Horner I | Processing | Late fall–early winter | .6 | Todd and Hofman 1987 |
| Horner II | Processing | Late fall–early winter | .6 | Todd 1987 |
| Jerry Craig | Kill | Late summer–early fall | .3–.5 | Hill and Kornfeld 1999 |
| Jurgens | Processing | Fall | .4–.5 | Hill and Hill 2002 |
| Lamb Spring | Kill | Early winter–spring | Unknown | McCartney 1983 |
| Lime Creek | Camp | Fall | .4–.5 | Davis 1962; Jones 1999 |
| Nelson | Kill | Winter | .7–.8 | Kornfeld et al. 2007 |
| Olsen-Chubbuck | Kill | Late summer–early fall | .3–.5 | Frison 1991 |
| Scottsbluff | Unknown | Late spring–early summer | .1–.3 | Hill 2008; Todd et al. 1990 |

Plains suggests that differences between regions are likely.

Though bison figured prominently in the Cody subsistence strategy, many other nonbison species such as elk, pronghorn, and mule deer were hunted, along with smaller animals such as beaver, marmot, lagomorphs, and rodents (Table 1.3). Avian and aquatic species also occur in some Cody assemblages. If we consider species richness counts by environmental zone (Figure 1.5), a wider variety of animals was taken in the alluvial valleys compared with the plains grasslands, where bison, and particularly bison kills, dominate the patterning. While Cody complex peoples were obviously highly skilled bison hunters, understanding of their subsistence strategies remains incomplete until we better comprehend the role nonbison prey and plant resources played,

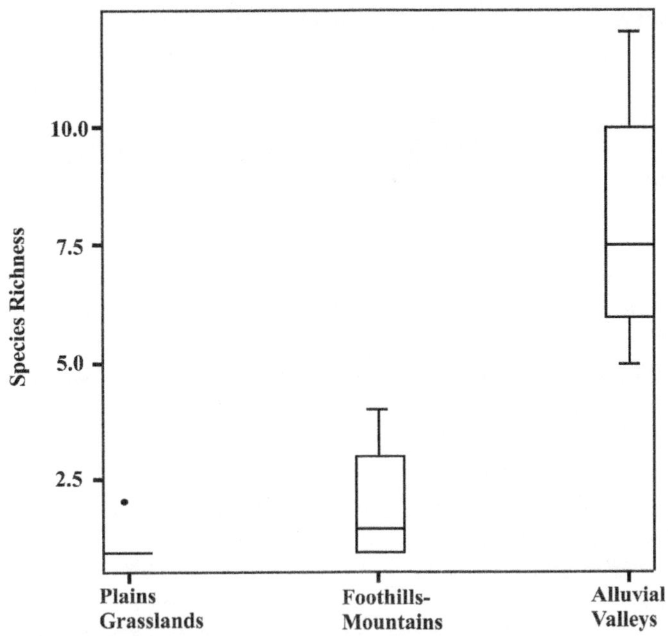


FIGURE 1.5. Boxplots of fauna species richness by environmental zone.

and until we identify a wider range of late winter through early summer occupations. Thus, the subsistence data mimic the projectile point data in terms of their defining influence on our understanding of the Cody complex. Despite the similarity among sites that show an emphasis on bison hunting, the variability around this trend indicates that Cody complex hunter-gatherers were dynamic and, above all, adaptable to local conditions. The ability to adjust to local conditions was critical to their survival, especially under the evolving climate and paleoenvironmental regimes they experienced during the early Holocene (see Muñiz, this volume [Chapter 2]; Widga, this volume) as well as changes in bison morphology and herd structure (increasing gregariousness; see Widga, this volume).

### Land Use

Prior studies of Cody land-use patterns also shed light on important characteristics of the complex. To date, four main Cody complex land-use strategies have been postulated. First is the apparent focus on local regions or ecozones for lengthy periods, sometimes as part of a seasonal round. Evidence for the focus on local regions usually comes from the predominance of local toolstone recovered at sites and seasonality data that depict a long-term or overwintering strategy. On the regional scale, Blackmar (2001) suggests this pattern for the southern Plains, as do Knell and Hill (2012) for the northern and northwestern Plains. At the site scale, Johnson et al. (2004) identify this pattern for the Osprey Beach site in Yellowstone National Park, Wyoming; Knell (2007, this volume) for the Hell Gap site; and Richings-Germain (2002) for the Jerry Craig site in Middle Park, Colorado. It thus appears that in some places and situations Cody complex peoples restricted their land use to specific ecozones for a considerable length of time.

Second, some Cody groups responded to variations in resource structure by preferentially exploiting the Rocky Mountain foothills habitats and the wider variety of resources available there during certain seasons (Amick 1994; Frison 1992; Frison and Bonnichsen 1996; Johnson et al. 2004; Knell and Hill 2012; also see Hill and Knell, this volume). Johnson et al. (2004) suggest, for example, that cold stress increased the likelihood that Cody complex hunter-gatherers exploited the more biotically diverse foothills and adjacent plains rather than high mountains during the cold season. Amick (1994) identified altitudinal variation in Cody complex sites and isolated projectile points in the Basin and Range versus plains of New Mexico. Isolated projectile points in this area occur, on average, 365 m higher than the residential sites, placing the isolated points in upland settings where solitary game lived. In contrast, residential sites generally occur in lower-elevation Basin and Range settings closer to wetlands and grasslands, which provided a higher diversity of resources. Frison (1992; Frison and Bonnichsen 1996) proposed that early Holocene climatic warming (environmental stress) affected the availability and distribution of resources, leading Cody complex groups to increasingly exploit foothills-mountains habitats when bison herd size dwindled on the plains grasslands. Cody complex settlement and subsistence strategies thus varied in accordance with the distribution of biotic resources, which demonstrates Cody hunter-gatherers' ability to adjust their land use to accommodate local variations in resource structure (also see Amick; Hill and Knell; Knell; and Root et al., this volume).

The third pattern depicts Cody groups as having maintained a seasonally transhumant land-use strategy (Blackmar 2001; Johnson et al. 2004). Blackmar (2001) found that Cody groups on the southern High Plains regularly incorporated marginal environments into their land-use strategy, likely during times of environmental stress (but see Johnson 1989). Despite suggestions of a seasonally transhumant land-use pattern, these studies are limited in scope and require additional large, regional-scale studies that more fully tie the patterning into variations in resource structure and bison seasonality data.

The fourth pattern of Cody land use occurs among High Plains sites older than 9000 $^{14}$C yrs BP (10,220–10,185 cal BP) that document long-distance travel from opposing directions across the western Plains and converge on large-scale bison kill sites during the fall. Muñiz (2005) interprets this convergent pattern as evidence for seasonal communal bison hunting on the western Plains at the Claypool, Jurgens, and Olsen-Chubbuck sites. Based on distance to lithic raw material sources, Muñiz documents that after 9000 $^{14}$C yrs BP, Cody groups reduced the maximum distance traveled (or traded) before a bison kill by 340 km on average; in addition, travel from opposite directions to a bison kill ceased. The post-9000 $^{14}$C yrs BP decrease in travel and trade probably reflects range restrictions on the western Plains in response to deteriorating grassland environments resulting from climate change (Muñiz 2005).

A significant gap exists in our understanding of Cody land-use strategies for the Great Lakes and Midwest. Sites such as Bradbury Brook (Minnesota); Robinson, Renier, and Pope (Wisconsin); Sheguiandah (Ontario); and areas with abundant isolated finds such as Reservoir Lakes (Minnesota) and Carberry Plain (Manitoba) indicate extensive use of the region by Cody groups. Researchers have noted general late Paleoindian movement between the Thunder Bay (Ontario) and Boundary Waters (Minnesota) regions along the north shore of Lake Superior (Fox 1975; Julig 1994; Ross 1997), and what appears to be extensive use of local aquatic and woodland resources in northern Wisconsin (Kuehn 1998; Salzer 1974). However, patterns specific to the Cody complex have not yet been clearly identified.

A theme commonly used to explain Cody land-use organization is macrogroup-level adaptation to variations in biotic resource structure, primarily adjustments to the distribution and availability of bison. These resource structure–based explanations fall into three types. The first includes those that view human and animal movements as responses to cold stress, with animals and thus humans congregating in lower-elevation foothills and basins during the cold season (e.g., Johnson et al. 2004; Pitblado 2003). The second group views climatic stress as influencing resource structure, with Cody complex hunter-gatherers responding to major fluctuations in grassland productivity and, ultimately, the distribution of bison (Amick, this volume; Blackmar 2001; Frison 1992; Frison and Bonnichsen 1996; Johnson 1989; Muñiz 2005; Stanford 1999). The third perspective uses optimal foraging theory, particularly diet breadth, to explain why Cody complex hunter-gatherers positioned their residential campsites closer to a wide, rather than narrow, diversity of resources (Amick 1994; Knell and Hill 2012). With the exception of Amick's and Knell and Hill's optimal foraging–based studies, these Cody land-use reconstructions lack an overtly theoretical explanatory framework. Several chapters in this book — Hill and Knell; Knell; Muñiz (Chapter 10); and Root et al. — seek to address this issue.

### Social Organization/Worldview

Little, if anything, concrete is known about Cody social organization or worldview. Nearly five decades ago, Mason and Irwin (1960) published a description of a Cody complex cremation burial in northeastern Wisconsin, called the Renier site. The Renier site contained the cremated remains of an adolescent that had been interred along a low sandy ridge overlooking the shore of modern Green Bay on the east coast of Wisconsin. In association with the cremated remains were 11 points — two Eden, eight Scottsbluff, and one St. Charles/Thebes — that were also badly burned. Another probable association between Scottsbluff and Eden points and a cremation burial comes from the Pope site in east-central Wisconsin (Ritzenthaler 1972).

The only clear example of Cody artwork comes from the Jurgens site. Wheat (1979:137–138) recovered a bison ulna with a series of linear and geometrical engravings that occur in pairs and triplets across the lateral and medial faces. The ulna was intentionally decorated, but unfortunately the image is unclear and one can only speculate as to its meaning.

Jurgens also produced the only known example of a Cody pipe (Wheat 1979:129). The implement was shaped from a naturally hollow iron silicate concretion that shows a high degree of polish from use. We can only guess what role a pipe may have played in the social or religious life of Cody people. The pipe demonstrates, however, that pipe smoking extends back to the Paleoindian period.

Aside from these brief glimpses of how Cody complex peoples treated their dead, created art, and used pipes, we have almost no understanding of their spirituality or ideology. The lack of emphasis in this direction naturally results from the unavailability of pertinent analogies, artifacts, and human remains, though there is no reason why researchers could not begin thinking along these lines. Comprehending the Cody worldview obviously would improve our understanding of Cody lifeways as a whole.

### Organization of the Book

The chapters in this book use behavior-oriented approaches to expand our current understanding of the Cody complex. While the Cody complex is one of the better-represented and geographically widespread Great Plains Paleoindian cultural complexes, this volume is the first major attempt at a synthesis. Before this book, the only major behavior-based analyses of the Cody complex were the dissertations by Muñiz (2005) and Knell (2007). Predating these dissertations, of course, is the Horner site monograph by Frison and Todd (1987), which is a detailed site report. We hope that the current volume places the Cody complex among the better-understood Paleoindian cultural complexes.

The first set of chapters, by Muñiz and Widga, reconstructs the early Holocene environment faced by Cody complex peoples and examines the impacts of climate on Cody lifeways. In reconstructing the early Holocene environment, these authors use multiple types of proxy data: fire frequency, gastropods, sand dune geomorphology, insects, isotopes, macrofossils, packrat middens, phytoliths, pollen, soil development, and sympatry of small mammalian assemblages. More specifically, Muñiz (Chapter 2) finds that the first half of the Cody era (~10,000–9000 $^{14}$C yrs BP; 11,600–10,185 cal BP) was generally conducive to abundant biotic production in a variety of ecozones throughout the central and northern U.S. Great Plains and adjacent Rocky Mountains. After about 9000 $^{14}$C yrs BP (10,220–10,185 cal BP), some regions began to dry out, and this trend became substantially amplified after 8500 $^{14}$C yrs BP (9530–9490 cal BP). Cody groups repeatedly selected for ecotonal settings that combined springs, streams, and riverbanks with grassland and foothill habitats. As many ecosystems substantially dried after 8500 $^{14}$C yrs BP (9530–9490 cal BP), the number of Cody sites also "dried up." This apparent correlation leads to the hypothesis that Cody complex peoples on the Great Plains and in the adjacent Rocky Mountains made significant adaptive changes to meet substantial environmental challenges.

Widga (Chapter 3) considers what the taxonomic diversity of small mammalian fauna indicates about past environments in the central and eastern United States between 21,000 and 8100

$^{14}$C yrs BP (25,000–9000 cal yrs BP), and what biometric analyses of bison crania and postcrania indicate about the physical and social evolution of bison populations on the Great Plains. His early Holocene paleoenvironmental reconstruction for the central and northwestern Great Plains indicates that the environment gradually warmed and precipitation decreased, leading to higher drought severity. In the Midwest, warmer and moister conditions persisted until ~8100 $^{14}$C yr BP (~9000 cal yr BP), after which it warmed and dried considerably. Concurrent with the warming and drying was the establishment of modern bison morphology and behavior. Changes in bison horn-core size and shape modified dominance patterns, resulting in increased gregariousness and larger herds. The changes in climate and bison had implications for Cody lifeways.

Following the two chapters on the environment and the impact it had on Cody lifeways is the contribution by Hill (Chapter 4), which considers the organization of Cody bison procurement. Hill addresses three main issues. The first is whether Cody bison hunts were fortuitous events or part of an integrated subsistence strategy. He finds that Cody hunters systematically pursued bison, and did so by adjusting their hunting strategies to seasonal shifts in bison biology and ethology. The second issue is whether variability exists in the preferred season(s) of bison hunting in the northern versus southern Great Plains. Seasonality data indicate that bison hunting occurred throughout the year but that bison kills in the north were larger than in the south and usually occurred during midsummer through early winter rather than primarily in the spring. The third issue concerns variability in bison herd size and composition and, like prior studies, suggests a preference for female-dominated herds throughout most of the year. This fresh examination of Cody bison hunting provides an important understanding of how Cody peoples organized pursuit of arguably their most important subsistence resource.

The next set of chapters—Root et al.; Dawe; Hill and Knell; Amick—provides important site and regional-scale reconstructions of land-use and technological organization in the Great Plains, Rocky Mountains, and northern Great Basin. These chapters address Cody complex lifeways in the key geographic areas inhabited by Cody peoples; however, additional research in the southern Great Plains and Midwest would considerably round out this understanding.

Root et al. (Chapter 5) test a model of Cody land-use organization in western North Dakota and southern Saskatchewan. Lithic-based variables from several key Cody sites from the Knife River flint (KRF) quarry area, the Missouri Coteau, and Glaciated Plains are evaluated and applied to the land-use model. Root et al. find that Cody groups tethered their movements to the KRF region for parts of the year but in late summer and fall geared up with KRF for rapid, long-distance movements north of the Missouri River to hunt bison. Such movements fit the expectations of the land-use model evaluated in this chapter.

Dawe (Chapter 6) provides a substantial overview of the Cody complex in Alberta, Canada. This data-heavy chapter not only summarizes many unpublished and hard-to-access reports, making it a gold mine for documenting the Cody occupation of Alberta, but also significantly improves our understanding of the lifeways of Cody groups in the northern limits of their geographic range. Dawe suggests, based on the spatial and temporal distribution of Cody sites, that a transition occurred from an early reliance on exotic lithic materials to a later reliance on local lithic raw materials. Based on ecological considerations, he interprets this pattern as resulting from the earliest Alberta/Cody inhabitants of Alberta being unfamiliar with the region and reducing risk by relying on nonlocal stones, with later Cody groups settling into Alberta and using the locally available resources. Dawe thus characterizes how Cody complex peoples colonized the northern latitudes of their geographic range.

Chapter 7, by Hill and Knell, is the first of two chapters that directly consider Cody lifeways beyond the grasslands and rolling hills of the Great Plains. While specifically evaluating Cody subsistence and land-use organization in the Rocky Mountains, the authors compare this patterning with Cody sites in the Great Plains as well as with contemporaneous Paleoindian complexes in the Rocky Mountains and Great Plains. As in some other chapters in this book, these patterns are considered within the framework of a land-use model. The analyses suggest that Cody foragers in the Rocky Mountains more narrowly focused on bison hunting than did contemporaneous groups in the mountains (particularly during the summer and fall), and restricted their movements to this area for long periods of time, but less so than their non-Cody mountain counterparts. By highlighting how Cody groups interacted with their contemporaries, this chapter offers significant insights about Cody adaptive strategies.

The chapter by Amick (Chapter 8) on Cody in the northwestern Great Basin is unique to the book in its examination of Cody evidence from outside the Great Plains/Rocky Mountains heartland. Amick considers two main issues. The first concerns the typological and chronological position of Cody-style projectiles in the northwestern Great Basin compared with those from the Great Plains. Despite a paucity of data, he concludes in part that Cody complex occupations are present but rare, occurred later in the Cody period, and likely reflect sporadic use of the northwestern Great Basin. The second issue concerns patterns of land use, mobility, and subsistence. Amick finds that Cody peoples were highly adaptable foragers who made range extensions from the Great Plains into the Great Basin during times of declining grassland productivity and bison population size. Amick's chapter complements Dawe's in the sense that Amick too considers Cody complex colonization, or more aptly range expansion, into an area beyond the traditionally identified Cody heartland.

The next set of chapters, by Knell, Muñiz, and Knudson, develop and test models of Cody land-use and technological organization and reconsider how the Scottsbluff projectile point evolved into a temporal diagnostic. These chapters are less site-oriented than the prior group and are somewhat more synthetic in their attempts to establish theoretical frameworks or models that explain Cody complex lifeways.

In Chapter 9, Knell evaluates and tests an optimal foraging–inspired model of land use that predicts how Cody peoples organized their movements across multiple zones of the northern portion of the Great Plains. This model has been tested elsewhere at the regional scale (Knell and Hill 2012), but here Knell tests the model at the local scale (at the Hell Gap site, Wyoming). The analyses indicate that Cody complex hunter-gatherers in biotically productive uplifts with high-quality toolstone sources, much like those in the Hartville Uplift where the Hell Gap site is located, optimally tethered their land use to these areas for reasonably long periods of time. When using such a strategy at Hell Gap, the Cody hunter-gatherers repetitively and intensively exploited the locally available Hartville Uplift resources for a protracted portion of the year. This chapter contributes to our understanding of Cody land-use dynamics by identifying the local-scale archaeological signatures for a restricted land-use strategy, and then explaining the conditions of resource structure under which Cody hunter-gatherers optimally employed this strategy.

Muñiz (Chapter 10) analyzes the technological organization strategies employed at Jurgens and Hell Gap Locality V using a risk management model. The predictions of the optimization-based model are compared with the actual decisions Cody people made regarding tool manufacture and maintenance, hunting, butchery, and hide working. High-magnification microwear analysis and independent lines of geological and biological evidence are used to evaluate the closeness of fit between the model predictions and observed behaviors. Muñiz identifies aspects of the technological strategy in which Cody people optimally managed risk, and explores reasons why their behaviors sometimes diverged from model predictions.

Knudson (Chapter 11) considers the historical development of the Cody complex based on the evolution of Scottsbluff point typology, our understanding of the Scottsbluff Bison Quarry site, and other contemporaneous Paleoindian sites on the central Plains. Recent analyses of the bison bone, the original excavators' notes, and current geomorphological evidence lead Knudson to conclude that the Scottsbluff Bison Quarry was probably a single-component bison kill event. The implications of the morphological variability in the projectile points used for this single kill event lead Knudson to some important considerations about the archaeological construct called the "Cody complex." This variability also leads her to suggest that as we define and refine Paleoindian typologies and culture histories, we be mindful of local scale patterns and the fluidity of the social groups we study.

Finally, Bamforth (Chapter 12) offers insightful discussions and thoughtful directions for future research that will further the aims of the studies presented in this book. Bamforth notes the bias that results from basing our concept of the Cody complex on a single *fossile directeur* (e.g., Cody point or knife) and the meaning this has for how we conceive of the actual groups of people who created the "Cody" archaeological record. For Bamforth, the lack of fit between how archaeologists currently define Cody groups and the original intent of the taxonomic categories used to shape the definition of the complex results in a late Paleoindian cultural construct without ethnographic parallels. Bamforth discusses the ambiguity stemming from defining late Paleoindian sites as Cody, and he identifies important directions for future research that should focus on understanding the actual social organization reflected by our archaeological constructs. Does Cody represent a cohesive group of people who shared a broadly similar culture, a technological horizon that moved through existing populations, or some variable combination of the two? While Bamforth unites many of the themes addressed in the contributed chapters, he also leaves the reader with several potent questions that will provide archaeologists fodder for subsequent research on the Cody and other late Paleoindian complexes.

Together the chapters in this book provide an integrated and wide ranging understanding of the Cody complex that significantly improves our understanding of the lifeways that comprise what archaeologists know as the Cody complex. The long-overdue synthesis of the Cody complex has finally arrived.

## References


Agenbroad, Larry D.
1978 *The Hudson-Meng Site: An Alberta Bison Kill in the Nebraska High Plains*. University Press of America, Washington, D.C.

Amick, Daniel S.
1994 *Folsom Diet Breadth and Land Use in the American Southwest*. Ph.D. dissertation, University of New Mexico, Albuquerque. University Microfilms, Ann Arbor, Michigan.
1999 *Folsom Lithic Technology: Explorations in Structure and Variation*. International Monographs in Prehistory Archaeological Series 12. Ann Arbor, Michigan.

Bamforth, Douglas B.
1991 Flintknapping Skill, Communal Hunting, and Paleoindian Projectile Point Typology. *Plains Anthropologist* 36:309–322.

Bamforth, Douglas B. (editor)
2007 *The Allen Site: A Paleoindian Camp in Southwestern Nebraska*. University of New Mexico Press, Albuquerque.

Barbour, E. H., and C. B. Schultz
1932 The Scottsbluff Bison Quarry and Its Artifacts. *Bulletin of the Nebraska State Museum* 1(34):283–286.

Beck, Charlotte, and George T. Jones
1997 The Terminal Pleistocene/Early Holocene Archaeology of the Great Basin. *Journal of World Prehistory* 11:161–236.
2010 Clovis and Western Stemmed: Population Migration and the Meeting of Two Technologies in the Intermountain West. *American Antiquity* 75:81–116.

Blackmar, Jeannette M.
1998 The Distribution of Cody Knives: A Distinctive Trait of the Cody Complex. *Current Research in the Pleistocene* 15:6–9.
2001 Regional Variability in Clovis, Folsom, and Cody Land Use. *Plains Anthropologist* 46: 65–94.

Blackmar, Jeannette M., and Jack L. Hofman
1997 Cody-Complex Artifacts in Oklahoma. *Current Research in the Pleistocene* 14:9–11.

Bonnichsen, Robson, Marvin Beatty, Mort D. Turner, Joanne C. Turner, and Diane Douglas
1992 Paleoindian Lithic Procurement at the South Fork of Everson Creek, Southwestern Montana: A Preliminary Statement. In *Ice Age Hunters of the Rockies*, edited by Dennis J. Stanford and Jane S. Day, pp. 285–321. University Press of Colorado, Niwot.

Bonnichsen, Robson, Bradley T. Lepper, Dennis Stanford, and Michael R. Waters
2005 *Paleoamerican Origins: Beyond Clovis*. Center for the Study of the First Americans. Texas A&M University Press, College Station.

Bradley, Bruce A.
1993 Paleo-Indian Flaked Stone Technology in the North American High Plains. In *From Kostenki to Clovis: Upper Paleolithic-*

Paleo-Indian Adaptations, edited by Olga Soffer and N. D. Praslov, pp. 251–262. Plenum Press, New York.

2009 Bifacial Technology and Paleoindian Projectile Points. In *Hell Gap: A Stratified Paleoindian Campsite on the Edge of the Rockies*, edited by M. L. Larson, M. Kornfeld, and G. C. Frison, pp. 259–273. University of Utah Press, Salt Lake City.

2010 Paleoindian Flaked Stone Technology on the Plains and in the Rockies. In *Prehistoric Hunters-Gatherers of the High Plains and Rockies*, 3rd ed., edited by Marcel Kornfeld, George C. Frison, and Mary Lou Larson, pp. 463–497. Left Coast Press, Walnut Creek, California.

Bradley, Bruce A., Michael C. Collins, and Andrew Hemmings

2010 *Clovis Technology*. International Monographs in Prehistory, Archaeological Series No. 17. Ann Arbor, Michigan.

Bradley, Bruce A., and George C. Frison

1987 Projectile Points and Specialized Bifaces from the Horner Site. In *The Horner Site: The Type Site of the Cody Cultural Complex*, edited by George C. Frison and Lawrence C. Todd, pp. 199–231. Academic Press, Orlando, Florida.

Bradley, Bruce A., and Dennis J. Stanford

1987 The Claypool Study. In *The Horner Site: The Type Site of the Cody Cultural Complex*, edited by George C. Frison and Lawrence C. Todd, pp. 405–434. Academic Press, Orlando, Florida.

Brunswig, Robert H.

2007 Paleoindian Cultural Landscapes and Archaeology of North-Central Colorado's Southern Rockies. In *Frontiers in Colorado Paleoindian Archaeology: From the Dent Site to the Rocky Mountains*, edited by Robert H. Brunswig and Bonnie L. Pitblado, pp. 261–310. University of Colorado Press, Boulder.

Cassells, E. Steve

1997 *The Archaeology of Colorado*. 2nd ed. Johnson Books, Boulder, Colorado.

Clark, John E., and Michael B. Collins (editors)

2002 *Folsom Technology and Lifeways*. Special Publication No. 4. Department of Anthropology, University of Tulsa. Tulsa, Oklahoma.

Collins, Michael B., Dennis J. Stanford, Jack L. Hofman, Margaret A. Jodry, Richard O. Rose, Lawrence C. Todd, Karl Kibler, and Jeannette M. Blackmar

1997 Cody Down South: The Seminole-Rose Site in West Texas. *Current Research in the Pleistocene* 14:15–18.

Corbeil, Marcel Ronald

1995 The Archaeology and Taphonomy of the Heron Eden Site, Southwestern Saskatchewan. Unpublished Master's thesis, Department of Anthropology, University of Saskatchewan, Saskatoon.

Cox, Stephen J.

2001 The Paleo-Indian Period. In *Twelve Thousand Years: American Indians in Maine*, edited by B. J. Bourque, pp. 13–36. University of Nebraska Press, Lincoln.

Davis, E. Mott

1962 *Archaeology of the Lime Creek Site in Southwestern Nebraska*. Special Publication No. 3. University of Nebraska State Museum, Lincoln.

Davis, Leslie B., John P. Albanese, Linda Scott Cummings, and John W. Fisher Jr.

1991 Reappraisal of the MacHaffie Site Paleoindian Occupational Sequence. *Current Research in the Pleistocene* 8:17–20.

Dick, Herbert W., and Bert Mountain

1960 The Claypool Site: A Cody Complex Site in Northeastern Colorado. *American Antiquity* 26:223–235.

Ebell, S. Biron

1975 A Cody Complex Site in South-Central Saskatchewan (DjNf-8). *Saskatchewan Newsletter* 49:1–6.

1988 The Dunn Site. *Plains Anthropologist* 33:505–530.

Forbis, Richard G.

1968 Fletcher: A Paleo-Indian Site in Alberta. *American Antiquity* 33:1–10.

Forbis, Richard G., and John D. Sperry

1952 An Early Man Site in Montana. *American Antiquity* 18:127–133.

Fox, William A.

1975 The Paleo-Indian Lakehead Complex. In *Canadian Archaeological Association: Collected Papers*, edited by P. Nunn, pp. 29–53. Historical Sites Branch Research Report No. 6. Ontario Ministry of Natural Resources, Toronto.

Frison, George C.

1984 The Carter/Kerr-McGee Paleoindian Site: Cultural Resource Management and Archaeological Research. *American Antiquity* 49: 288–314.

1987 The University of Wyoming Investigations at the Horner Site. In *The Horner Site: The Type Site of the Cody Cultural Complex*, edited by George C. Frison and Larry C. Todd, pp. 93–105. Academic Press, Orlando, Florida.

1991 *Prehistoric Hunters of the High Plains.* 2nd ed. Academic Press, San Diego.

1992 The Foothills-Mountains and Open Plains: The Dichotomy in Paleoindian Subsistence Strategies between Two Ecosystems. In *Ice Age Hunters of the Rockies*, edited by Dennis J. Stanford and Jane S. Day, pp. 323–342. University of Colorado Press, Niwot.

Frison, George C., and Robson Bonnichsen

1996 The Pleistocene-Holocene Transition on the Plains and Rocky Mountains of North America. In *Humans at the End of the Ice Age: The Archaeology of the Pleistocene-Holocene Transition*, edited by Lawrence G. Straus, Berit Valentin Eriksen, Jon M. Erlandson, and David R. Yesner, pp. 303–318. Plenum Press, New York.

Frison, George C., David Schwab, L. Adrien Hannus, Peter Winham, David Walter, and Robert C. Mainfort

1996 Archaeology of the Northwestern Plains. *In Archaeological and Bioarchaeological Resources of the Northern Plains*, edited by George C. Frison and Robert C. Mainfort, pp. 8–40. Arkansas Archaeological Survey Research Series No. 47. Fayetteville.

Frison, George C., and Lawrence C. Todd (editors)

1987 *The Horner Site: Type Site of the Cody Cultural Complex.* Academic Press, Orlando, Florida.

Frison, George C., Lawrence C. Todd, and Bruce A. Bradley

1987 Summary and Concluding Remarks. In *The Horner Site: Type Site of the Cody Cultural Complex*, edited by George C. Frison and Lawrence C. Todd, pp. 361–369. Academic Press, Orlando, Florida.

Frison, George C., and Danny N. Walker (editors)

2007 *Medicine Lodge Creek: Holocene Archaeology of the Eastern Big Horn Basin, Wyoming, Vol. 1.* Mark Mullins, Clovis Press.

Fulgham, Tommy, and Dennis J. Stanford

1982 The Frasca Site: A Preliminary Report. *Southwestern Lore* 48(1):1–9.

Gruhn, R.

1961 *The Archaeology of Wilson Butte Cave, South-Central Idaho.* Occasional Papers of the Idaho State College Museum No. 6. Pocatello.

Harrison, Christina, Elaine Redepenning, Christopher L. Hill, George Rapp Jr., Stanley E. Aschenbrenner, James K. Huber, and Susan C. Mulholland

1995 *The Paleo-Indian of Southern St. Louis County, Minnesota: The Reservoir Lakes Complex.* University of Minnesota–Duluth Interdisciplinary Archaeological Studies, University of Minnesota Monograph Series No. 4. Kendal/Hunt, Dubuque, Iowa.

Haynes, C. Vance, Jr.

1968 Radiocarbon: Analysis of Inorganic Carbon of Fossil Bone and Enamel. *Science* 161:687–688.

2009 Geochronology. In *Hell Gap: A Stratified Paleoindian Campsite on the Edge of the Rockies*, edited by M. L. Larson, M. Kornfeld, and G. C. Frison, pp. 39–71. University of Utah Press, Salt Lake City.

Haynes, C. Vance, Jr., Roelf P. Beukens, A. J. T. Jull, and Owen K. Davis

1992 New Radiocarbon Dates for Some Old Folsom Sites: Accelerator Technology. In *Ice Age Hunters of the Rockies*, edited by Dennis J. Stanford and Jane S. Day, pp. 83–100. University Press of Colorado, Niwot.

Hester, J.

1972 *Blackwater Locality No. 1: A Stratified, Early Man Site in Eastern New Mexico.* Fort Burgwin Research Center No. 8. Southern Methodist University, Dallas, Texas.

Hill, Christopher L.

2007 Geoarchaeology and Late Glacial Landscapes in the Western Lake Superior Region, Central North America. *Geoarchaeology* 22:15–47.

Hill, Matthew E., Jr.

2007 Causes of Regional and Temporal Variation in Paleoindian Diet in Western North America. Unpublished Ph.D. dissertation, Department of Anthropology, University of Arizona, Tucson.

2008 New Investigations of the Cody-Age Finley and Scottsbluff Bison Bone Beds. *Current Research in the Pleistocene* 25:90–93.

Hill, Matthew E., Jr., and Matthew Glenn Hill

2002 Season of Bison Mortality at the Jurgens Site, Weld County, Colorado. *Current Research in the Pleistocene* 19:104–106.

Hill, Matthew Glenn

1994 Paleoindian Projectile Points from the Vicinity of Silver Mound (47JA21), Jackson County, Wisconsin. *Midcontinental Journal of Archaeology* 19:223–259.

Hill, Matthew Glenn, Daniel S. Amick, and Thomas J. Loebel

1998 An Inventory of Wisconsin Paleoindian Projectile Points at the Milwaukee Public Museum. *Current Research in the Pleistocene* 15:18–20.

Hill, Matthew Glenn, Vance T. Holliday, and Dennis J. Stanford

1995 A Further Evaluation of the San Jon Site, New Mexico. *Plains Anthropologist* 40:369–390.

Hill, Matthew Glenn, and Marcel Kornfeld
1999 Inferring Season of Kill for a Cody-Complex Bonebed in Middle Park, Colorado. *Current Research in the Pleistocene* 16:30–32.

Hofman, Jack L.
1990 Cedar Creek: A Folsom Locality in Southwestern Oklahoma. *Current Research in the Pleistocene* 7:19–23.
1996 Early Hunter-Gatherers of the Central Great Plains: Paleoindian and Mesoindian (Archaic) Cultures. In *Archaeology and Paleoecology of the Central Great Plains*, edited by Jack L. Hofman, pp. 41–100. Arkansas Archaeological Survey Research Series No. 48. Fayetteville.

Hofman, Jack L., and Russell W. Graham
1998 The Paleo-Indian Cultures of the Great Plains. In *Archaeology on the Great Plains*, edited by W. Raymond Wood, pp. 87–139. University Press of Kansas, Lawrence.

Holland, Warren
1971 Dalton Type Cache Found. *Central States Archaeological Journal* 18(1):23–29.

Holliday, Vance T.
1997 *Paleoindian Geoarchaeology of the Southern High Plains*. University of Texas Press, Austin.

Holliday, Vance T., Eileen Johnson, Herbert Haas, and Robert Stuckenrath
1983 Radiocarbon Ages from the Lubbock Lake Site, 1950–1980: Framework for Cultural and Ecological Change on the Southern High Plains. *Plains Anthropologist* 28:165–182.

Holliday, Vance T., Eileen Johnson, and Thomas W. Stafford Jr.
1999 AMS Radiocarbon Dating of the Type Plainview and Firstview (Paleoindian) Assemblages: The Agony and the Ecstasy. *American Antiquity* 64:444–454.

Irwin-Williams, Cynthia, Henry T. Irwin, George A. Agogino, and C. Vance Haynes Jr.
1973 Hell Gap: A Paleo-Indian Occupation on the High Plains. *Plains Anthropologist* 18:40–52.

Janetski, Joel C.
2001 Late Paleoindian Artifacts from Utah Valley. *Utah Archaeology* 14(1):15–26.

Jepsen, Glenn L.
1951 Ancient Buffalo Hunters in Wyoming. *Archaeological Society of New Jersey Newsletter* 24:22–24.

Jodry, Margret A. B.
1999 Folsom Technological and Socioeconomic Strategies: Views from Stewart's Cattle Guard and the Upper Rio Grande Basin, Colorado. Unpublished Ph.D. dissertation, Department of Anthropology, American University, Washington, D.C.

Johnson, Ann, Brian Reeves, and Mack Shortt
2004 *Osprey Beach (Site 48YE409/410), Yellowstone National Park, Wyoming*. Lifeways of Canada. Submitted to Yellowstone Center for Resources, Yellowstone National Park, Cooperative Agreement No. CA-1268-1-9017 between Montana State University, Bozeman, and the National Park Service. Available from Yellowstone Center for Resources, Mammoth, Wyoming.

Johnson, David, and Jana Pastor
2003 *The Blue Point Site: Paleoindian/Archaic Transition in Southwest Wyoming*. Western Archaeological Services, Rock Springs, Wyoming.

Johnson, Eileen (editor)
1987 *Lubbock Lake: Late Quaternary Studies on the Southern High Plains*. Texas A&M University Press, College Station.

Johnson, LeRoy, Jr.
1989 *Great Plains Interlopers in the Eastern Woodlands during Late Paleo-Indian Times*. Texas Historical Commission, Office of the State Archaeologist, Report No. 36. Austin.

Jones, David Chadwick
1999 Late Paleoindian/Early Archaic Archaeology and Subsistence: A Taphonomic Analysis of the Lime Creek Site (25FT41), Southwest Nebraska. Unpublished Master's thesis, Colorado State University, Fort Collins.

Joyes, Dennis
1997 New Paleo-Indian Finds from Southern Saskatchewan. *Saskatchewan Archaeological Society Newsletter* 18:107–112.
2000 Cody Technology at the McLeod Site, Saskatchewan, Canada. *Current Research in the Pleistocene* 17:47–49.

Julig, Patrick J.
1994 *The Cummins Site Complex and Paleoindian Occupations in the Northwestern Lake Superior Region*. Ontario Archaeological Reports No. 2. Ontario Heritage Foundation, Toronto.
2002 *The Sheguiandah Site: Archaeological, Geological and Paleobotanical Studies at a Paleoindian Site on Manitoulin Island, Ontario*. Edited by Patrick J. Julig. Mercury Series, Archaeological Survey of Canada Paper No. 161. Canadian Museum of Civilization, Gatineau, Quebec.

Justice, Noel D.
1987 *Stone Age Spear and Arrow Points of the Midcontinental and Eastern United States: A Modern Survey and Reference*. Indiana University Press, Bloomington.

Knell, Edward J.
2007 The Organization of Late Paleoindian Cody Complex Land-Use on the North American Great Plains. Unpublished Ph.D. dissertation, Department of Anthropology, Washington State University, Pullman.
2009 Cody Complex at Locality I. In *Hell Gap: A Stratified Paleoindian Campsite on the Edge of the Rockies*, edited by M. L. Larson, M. Kornfeld, and G. C. Frison, pp. 180–194. University of Utah Press, Salt Lake City.

Knell, Edward J., and Matthew E. Hill Jr.
2012 Linking Bones and Stones: Regional Variation in Late Paleoindian Cody Complex Land Use and Foraging Strategies. *American Antiquity* 77:40–70.

Knell, Edward J., Matthew G. Hill, and Andrés Izeta
2009 The Locality IIIS/V Eden Complex Component. In *Hell Gap: A Stratified Paleoindian Campsite on the Edge of the Rockies*, edited by M. L. Larson, M. Kornfeld, and G. C. Frison, pp. 157–179. University of Utah Press, Salt Lake City.

Knell, Edward J., Matthew G. Hill, Andrés Izeta, Marcel Kornfeld, C. Vance Haynes Jr., and George C. Frison
2002 The Cody-Complex Component at Locality V of the Hell Gap Site, Wyoming. *Current Research in the Pleistocene* 19:49–52.

Kornfeld, Marcel, Mary Lou Larson, Craig Arnold, Adam Wiewel, Mike Toft, and Dennis Stanford
2007 The Nelson Site, a Cody Occupation in Northeastern Colorado. *Plains Anthropologist* 52:257–278.

Kuehn, Steven R.
1998 New Evidence for Late Paleoindian–Early Archaic Subsistence Behavior in the Western Great Lakes. *American Antiquity* 63:457–476.

LaBelle, Jason Mitchel
2002 Slim Arrow, the Long-forgotten Yuma-type Site in Eastern Colorado. *Current Research in the Pleistocene* 19:52–55.
2005 *Hunter-Gatherer Foraging Variability during the Early Holocene of the Central Plains of North America*. Ph.D. dissertation, Southern Methodist University, Dallas. University Microfilms, Ann Arbor, Michigan.

Larson, Mary Lou, M. Kornfeld, and George C. Frison (editors)
2009 *Hell Gap: A Stratified Paleoindian Campsite on the Edge of the Rockies*. University of Utah Press, Salt Lake City.

Long, Russell J.
1977 *McFaddin Beach*. Patillo Higgins Series of Natural History and Anthropology No. 1. Spindletop Museum, Lamar University, Beaumont, Texas.

Malik, Riaz, and Kent Bakken
1993 *Archaeological Data Recovery at the Bradbury Brook Site, 21ML42, Mille Lacs County, Minnesota*. Minnesota Trunk Highway Archaeological Reconnaissance Survey (MTHARS) Report, Agreement 67340. Minnesota Historical Society, St. Paul.
1999 Bradbury Brook (21ML42): A Late Paleoindian Lithic Workshop in East-Central Michigan. *Minnesota Archaeologist* 58:136–171.

Mason, Ronald J.
1981 *Great Lakes Archaeology*. Academic Press, New York.
1997 The Paleo-Indian Tradition. *Wisconsin Archaeologist* 78(1/2):78–110.

Mason, Ronald J., and Carol Irwin
1960 An Eden-Scottsbluff Burial in Northeastern Wisconsin. *American Antiquity* 26:43–57.

McCartney, Peter Howard
1983 Archaeological Analysis of Bison Remains from the Cody Paleo-Indian Site of Lamb Spring, Colorado. Unpublished Master's thesis, Department of Anthropology, University of Arizona, Tucson.

Meyer, David
1985 A Component of the Scottsbluff Tradition: Excavations at the Niska Site. *Canadian Journal of Archaeology* 9:1–37.

Moss, John H., Kirk Bryan, G. William Holmes, Linton Satterthwaite Jr., Henry P. Hanson, C. Bertrand Schultz, and W. D. Frankforter
1951 *Early Man in the Eden Valley*. University of Pennsylvania Museum Monographs No. 6. Philadelphia.

Muñiz, Mark P.
2005 The Cody Complex Revisited: Landscape Use and Technological Organization on the Northwestern Plains. Unpublished Ph.D. dissertation, Department of Anthropology, University of Colorado, Boulder.
2008 *Results of 2007 Archaeological Field Season, Hudson-Meng (25SX115), Sioux County, Nebraska*. Report submitted to Heritage Resources Program, Nebraska National Forest, Chadron.
2010 *Results of 2008 Archaeological Investigations at the Hudson-Meng Site (25SX115), Sioux County, Nebraska*. Report submitted to Heritage Resources Program, Nebraska National Forest, Chadron.

Novecosky, Brad
2002 The Haskey Area, a Cody-Complex Site from the Quill Lakes Region, Saskatchewan,

Canada. *Current Research in the Pleistocene* 19:73–74.

Pettipas, Leo

1970 Early Man in Manitoba. In *Ten Thousand Years: Archaeology in Manitoba*, edited by W. M. Hlady, pp. 5–28. Manitoba Centennial Corporation, Winnipeg.

Pitblado, Bonnie L.

2003 *Late Paleoindian Occupation of the Southern Rocky Mountains: Early Holocene Projectile Points and Land Use in the High Country.* University Press of Colorado, Boulder.

Rancier, James, Gary Haynes, and Dennis Stanford

1982 1981 Investigations of Lamb Spring. *Southwestern Lore* 48:1–17.

Rapson, David J., and Laura B. Niven

2009 Faunal Assemblage, 1960–1966. In *Hell Gap: A Stratified Paleoindian Campsite on the Edge of the Rockies*, edited by M. L. Larson, M. Kornfeld, and G. C. Frison, pp. 111–134. University of Utah Press, Salt Lake City.

Redder, Albert J.

1985 Horn Shelter Number 2: The South End; A Preliminary Report. *Journal of the Central Texas Archaeological Society* 10:37–65.

Reimer, P. J., M. G. L. Baillie, E. Bard, A. Bayliss, J. W. Beck, P. G. Blackwell, C. B. Ramsey, C. E. Buck, G. S. Burr, R. L. Edwards, M. Friedrich, P. M. Grootes, T. P. Guilderson, I. Hajdas, T. J. Heaton, A. G. Hogg, K. A. Hughen, K. F. Kaiser, B. Kromer, F. G. McCormac, S. W. Manning, R. W. Reimer, D. A. Richards, J. R. Southon, S. Talamo, C. S. M. Turney, J. van der Plicht, and C. E. Weyhenmeyer

2009 IntCal09 and Marine09 Radiocarbon Age Calibration Curves, 0–50,000 Years cal BP. *Radiocarbon* 51:1111–1150.

Richings-Germain, Sarah

2002 The Jerry Craig Site: A Paleoindian Bison Bonebed in the Colorado Rocky Mountains. Unpublished Master's thesis, Department of Anthropology, University of Wyoming, Laramie.

Ritzenthaler, Robert E.

1972 The Pope Site, a Scottsbluff Cremation in Waupaca County. *Wisconsin Archaeologist* 53:15–19.

Roberts, Frank H. H., Jr.

1942 *Archaeological and Geological Investigations in the San Jon District, Eastern New Mexico.* Smithsonian Miscellaneous Collections 103 (4). Smithsonian Institution, Washington, D.C.

Root, Matthew J.

1992 The Knife River Flint Quarries: The Organization of Stone Tool Production. Unpublished Ph.D. dissertation, Department of Anthropology, Washington State University, Pullman.

1998 Dating a Cody-Complex Occupation in the Knife River Flint Quarries. *Current Research in the Pleistocene* 15:62–64.

Ross, William

1997 The Interlakes Composite: A Re-definition of the Initial Settlement of the Agassiz-Minong Peninsula. *Wisconsin Archaeologist* 76:244–268.

Salzer, Robert J.

1974 The Wisconsin North Lakes Project: A Preliminary Report. In *Aspects of Upper Great Lakes Anthropology: Papers in Honor of Lloyd A. Wilford*, edited by E. Johnson, pp. 40–54. Minnesota Prehistoric Archaeology Series No. 11. Minnesota Historical Society, St. Paul.

Sellet, Frederic

2009 *The Jim Pitts Site: A Multi-component Paleoindian Campsite in the Black Hills of South Dakota.* University of Northern Colorado School of Social Sciences Anthropology Program, UNC Archaeology Laboratory Technical Series No. 3. Submitted to the South Dakota Archaeological Research Center, Rapid City.

Stanford, Dennis

1999 Paleoindian Archaeology and Late Pleistocene Environments in the Plains and Southwestern United States. In *Ice Age Peoples of North America: Environments, Origins, and Adaptations*, edited by Robson Bonnichsen and Karen L. Turnmire, pp. 281–339. Center for the Study of the First Americans. Oregon State University Press, Corvallis.

Stanford, Dennis, and Robert Patten

1984 R-6: A Preliminary Report of a Cody Site in North-Central New Mexico. Papers of the Philmont Conference on the Archaeology of Northeastern New Mexico. *New Mexico Archaeological Council Proceedings* 6(1):189–199.

Stanford, Dennis, Waldo R. Wedel, and Glenn R. Scott

1981 Archaeological Investigations of the Lamb Spring Site. *Southwestern Lore* 47:14–27.

Steinbring, Jack

1974 The Preceramic Archaeology of Northern Minnesota. In *Aspects of Upper Great Lakes Anthropology: Papers in Honor of Lloyd A. Wilford*, edited by E. Johnson, pp. 64–73. Minnesota Prehistoric Archaeology Series No. 11, Minnesota Historical Society, St. Paul.

Stoltman, James B.

1997 The Archaic Tradition. *Wisconsin Archaeologist* 78(1/2):112–139.

Theler, James L., and Robert F. Boszhardt
2003 *Twelve Millennia: Archaeology of the Upper Mississippi River Valley*. University of Iowa Press, Iowa City.

Todd, Lawrence C.
1987 Taphonomy of the Horner II Bone Bed. In *The Horner Site: The Type Site of the Cody Cultural Complex*, edited by George C. Frison and Lawrence C. Todd, pp. 107–198. Academic Press, Orlando, Florida.
1991 Seasonality Studies and Paleoindian Subsistence Strategies. In *Human Predators and Prey Mortality*, edited by Mary C. Stiner, pp. 217–238. Westview Press, Boulder, Colorado.

Todd, Lawrence C., and Jack L. Hofman
1987 Bison Mandibles from the Horner and Finley Sites. In *The Horner Site: The Type Site of the Cody Cultural Complex*, edited by George C. Frison and Lawrence C. Todd, pp. 493–539. Academic Press, Orlando, Florida.

Todd, Lawrence C., Jack L. Hofman, and C. Bertrand Schultz
1990 Seasonality of the Scottsbluff and Lipscomb Bison Bonebeds: Implications for Modeling Paleoindian Subsistence. *American Antiquity* 55:813–827.

Todd, Lawrence C., and David J. Rapson
1999 Formational Analysis of Bison Bonebeds and Interpretation of Paleoindian Subsistence. In *Le bison: Gibier et moyen de subsistance des hommes du Paléolithique aux Paléoindiens des Grandes Plaines*, edited by J. Brugal, F. David, J. G. Enloe, and J. Jaubert, pp. 479–499. APDCA, Antibes, France.

Todd, Lawrence C., and David J. Rapson (editors)
1994 *Hudson-Meng Bison Bonebed and Oglala National Grasslands 1993 Archaeological Research Design and Field Work Summary*. Report on file, Nebraska National Forest, Chadron.

Vickers, J. Roderick, and Alwynne B. Beaudoin
1989 A Limiting AMS Date for the Cody Complex Occupation at the Fletcher Site, Alberta, Canada. *Plains Anthropologist* 34:261–264.

Vivian, Brian C.
2005 Identifying a Cody Component at the Malin Fishing Hole Site (24YE353) in Yellowstone National Park. Paper presented at the 63rd Annual Plains Anthropological Conference, Edmonton, Alberta.

Wallman, S., and Daniel S. Amick
1991 Cody Complex Occupation in the Black Rock Desert, Nevada. *Current Research in the Pleistocene* 8:51–53.

Wedel, Waldo R.
1963 The High Plains and Their Utilization by the Indians. *American Antiquity* 29:1–16.
1987 History of the Princeton and Smithsonian Investigations at the Horner Site. In *The Horner Site: The Type Site of the Cody Cultural Complex*, edited by George C. Frison and Larry C. Todd, pp. 19–38. Academic Press, Orlando, Florida.

Wheat, Joe Ben
1972 *The Olsen-Chubbuck Site: A Paleo-Indian Bison Kill*. Memoirs of the Society for American Archaeology No. 26. Washington, D.C.
1979 *The Jurgens Site*. Memoir No. 15. Plains Anthropologist, Lincoln, Nebraska.

Wilmsen, Edwin N., and Frank H. H. Roberts Jr.
1978 *Lindenmeier, 1934–1974: Concluding Report on Investigations*. Smithsonian Contributions to Anthropology No. 24. Smithsonian Institution Press, Washington, D.C.

Wilson, Michael C., and Arthur C. MacWilliams
1988 Preliminary Geoarchaeological Studies at the Fletcher Paleo-Indian Bison Kill Site (Alberta/Scottsbluff), Southern Alberta. *Alberta Archaeological Review* 14:12–15.

Wormington, H. M.
1948 *A Proposed Revision of Yuma Point Terminology*. Proceedings of the Colorado Museum of Natural History 18(2). Denver, Colorado.
1957 *Ancient Man in North America*. 4th ed. Popular Series No. 4. Denver Museum of Natural History, Denver, Colorado.

# II

# Cody Complex Environment and Faunal Context

# 2

# Paleoenvironmental Change and Cultural Ecology of the Cody Complex on the Great Plains and Adjacent Rocky Mountains

Mark P. Muñiz

The Cody complex existed between two major environmental phenomena that have undergone a tremendous amount of research. The Younger Dryas, ~11,100–10,000 $^{14}$C yrs BP (~13,000–11,500 cal BP), represents a very rapid and dramatic reversal to glacial conditions during the transition to the interstadial Holocene (Cuffey and Clow 1997; Hughen et al. 2000; Murton et al. 2010; Yu 2000). The impact of this event on archaeological cultures in North America has been the subject of research for decades (e.g., Antevs 1955; Haynes 1970, 1993, 2008; Holliday and Meltzer 2009). Periods of increased temperature during the early to mid Holocene that were first identified as the Altithermal (Antevs 1953, 1955) have been untangled and redefined as the global "8.2 ka event" (~7600–7280 $^{14}$C yrs BP) (Alley and Ágústsdóttir 2005; Barber et al. 1999; Dean et al. 2002; Shuman et al. 2002) and the more complicated and time-transgressive Holocene Thermal Maximum (Kaufman et al. 2004). The period between these events (~10,000–8,000 $^{14}$C yrs BP) is when the Cody complex flourished, and its relatively stable climate has not attracted nearly the same amount of research as what preceded and followed. As a result, archaeologists have largely lacked a broad-scale synthesis of the environments used by the peoples who made up the Cody complex. The goal of this chapter is to provide a general paleoenvironmental context for the Cody complex on the Great Plains and adjacent Rocky Mountains based on 58 study sites that cover the time span from 10,000 to 8000 $^{14}$C yrs BP (11,600–8785 cal BP).

Many paleoenvironmental studies have focused on modeling climatic change since the Last Glacial Maximum, and the causes proposed for regional and subregional environmental trends are both numerous and complex. This chapter does not address causation but rather attempts to provide a wide-ranging synthesis of the effects paleoenvironmental change had on Cody lifeways. By describing how regional environmental changes affected the landscapes inhabited by Cody peoples, we can begin to understand the resource options available to them and the rate of change with which they had to contend. Combining data from Cody archaeological sites and nonarchaeological paleoenvironmental sites creates a clearer picture of the environmental characteristics Cody groups were selecting for, compared with a broad range of alternative options in surrounding areas. When these data are combined with observations of lithic raw material movement and season of occupation for Cody sites, we can begin to better understand Cody landscape use overall. Lithic resource data have been incorporated into a smaller subset of the paleoenvironmental sites included here (see Muñiz 2005) but are not addressed in this chapter.

An important consideration to make when we are describing the environments where Cody groups lived is the scale at which the data articulate with climate and rates of environmental change. Webb (1986) addressed the issue of how different spatial and temporal scales of analysis affect interpretations of vegetation response to climate change and cautioned that researchers need to consider both the spatial distribution of a species and its relative frequency. This is important because different floral species respond to climate change in different ways and at different rates. The Type A response is very quick, occurring on the order of decades (e.g., 50–80 years), and is focused at a subregional scale ($10^3$ to $10^4$ km$^2$) (Webb 1986:83–84). The Type A response does not require significant changes in regional soil development for local vegetation range extensions and increased species abundance to occur. The Type B response is much slower, requiring centuries (e.g., 1000 years) to develop, and is generally focused at a large regional scale ($10^4$ to $10^6$ km$^2$) (Webb 1986: 83–84). The Type B response results in new floral species colonizing diverse areas where they could not live before and thus requires significant soil development over a wide region in order for both species range expansion and increased abundance to occur (Webb 1986).

Webb's observations have important implications for the present study and for Paleoindian archaeologists generally. The Type A vegetative response correlates more closely to the scale of an individual human life span. Also, the region included ($10^3$ to $10^4$ km$^2$) is much closer to the range of total area covered by yearly residential mobility as recorded among historic hunter-gatherer cultures (Kelly 1995), although Paleoindian residential mobility may have been greater at times. The temporal and geographic scales of the Type B response, however, are more comparable to an entire Paleoindian phase (e.g., Folsom, Agate Basin, Hell Gap, Cody). This is an important distinction to make when we are evaluating human responses to floral resource availability at the scale of a single site occupation. While we may often think in terms of the Type B response, which broadly characterizes the Pleistocene-Holocene transition, human behavior responds more directly to Type A rates of change. When Paleoindian environments are characterized with a single overarching descriptor, subregional variation in biotic communities is obscured. For example, Greiser (1985:19–21) correlated the Cody period environment with the Boreal stage and characterized the floral communities on the central Plains during this time as receding woodlands yielding to short-grass plains. In addition to the large scale at which this biome shift occurred, the accompanying change in soil types (Ruhe 1970, 1983) exemplifies it as a Type B response. Focusing on the level of generalization Greiser used fails to account for the subregional Type A responses that affected species abundance and habitat distributions in ways that were more immediately relevant to Cody people on an annual basis.

We know that Cody hunters took other animals in addition to *Bison* spp. (bison). Animals such as *Cervus elephas* (elk), *Alces alces* sp. (moose), *Odocoileus* sp. (deer), *Antilocapra americana* (pronghorn), Leporidae (rabbit), Sciuridae (ground squirrel), *Marmota* sp. (marmot), *Castor canadensis* (beaver), Testudines (turtle), *Tympanuchus* sp. (grouse), waterfowl, and fish appear in Cody complex sites (Knell and Muñiz, this volume; Stanford 1999; Wheat 1979; Wormington 1957). While edible plants must have contributed important components to the Cody diet, direct evidence of which species were used is lacking. However, floral data (pollen, phytoliths, macrobotanical remains, isotopes) from areas where Cody people lived can be used to reconstruct the basic habitats that were relied on. By understanding trends in temperature, precipitation, and vegetative cover throughout the study area, we can model general degrees of quality and quantity for habitats utilized by Cody groups and hypothesize how they adapted to short-term (Type A) and long-term (Type B) environmental change.

## Methods

This chapter synthesizes data from a variety of paleoenvironmental studies that span the first 2000 radiocarbon years of the Holocene (10,000–8000 $^{14}$C yrs BP; 11,600–8785 cal BP). The reconstruction is based on 58 sites, primarily locations on the Great Plains of North and South Dakota, Nebraska, eastern Colorado, Kansas, and far western Oklahoma, as well as the southern Black Hills and portions of the central and southern Rocky Mountains of Wyoming and Colorado and the adjacent foothills and intermountain basins (Figure 2.1 and Table 2.1). The data used for this synthesis are drawn from a variety of studies that include invertebrates such as beetles, snails, and mollusks; macrobotanical plant remains, as well as pollen, phytolith, and isotopic signatures of decomposed flora; large and small mammals; and geomorphological studies of landscape evolution that focus on buried soils and periods of dune activation. Some of the data types used here record temperature while others record moisture, and some respond to local scale changes while others indicate wider, regional climate fluctuations. The use of a variety of data types is intended to provide complementary lines of observation that create a stronger interpretation than any single data type can provide. The studies used here are not exhaustive of the available literature but represent a thorough sample that summarizes the paleoecology of Cody occupations, provides broad coverage of the study area, and includes different data types.

The 58 sample localities include 234 individual "data type observations" made up of 13 kinds of data. Each data type observation consists of a specific data type (e.g., phytoliths) for a specific period (e.g., 10,000–9500 $^{14}$C yrs BP), which are unevenly distributed across the sample. For example, Temple Lake Valley, Wyoming, has a single data type observation (pollen) that characterizes the environment for the entire Cody period (10,600–<8000 $^{14}$C yrs BP), resulting in a single contribution to the study. Kettle Lake, North Dakota, has three data type observations (pollen, charcoal, mineralogy) that each apply to three temporal periods because of changes in the record (10,000–9500; 9500–8250; 8250–8000 $^{14}$C yrs BP), resulting in nine of the 234 sample contributions. The most common type of data is geomorphology (paleosols and dune activation studies), which makes up 25.6 percent of the sample ($n$ = 60) with pollen (20.9 percent, $n$ = 49) the second most common. The third through sixth most frequent data types are, respectively, macrobotanical (9.8 percent, $n$ = 23), isotopes (9.4 percent, $n$ = 22), diatoms (7.7 percent, $n$ = 18), and sediment geochemistry (7.7 percent, $n$ = 18). Fauna (6.0 percent, $n$ = 14) and phytoliths (5.1 percent, $n$ = 12) are seventh and eighth, and insects (2.6 percent, $n$ = 6), charcoal (1.7 percent, $n$ = 4), and gastropods round out the top 11. The least frequent data types are mineralogy (1.3 percent, $n$ = 3) and bivalves (0.4 percent, $n$ = 1). Table 2.1 provides summary data and references for each of the studies included here.

The paleoenvironmental sample used for this study is biased in terms of (1) the study locales (i.e., some regions are better represented than others); (2) the kinds of data available (i.e., preponderance of geomorphological and pollen data); and (3) the detail of preservation (i.e., differential preservation affecting data collection and interpretation). Considering that these biases are likely to be present in almost any kind of broad-scale synthetic paleoenvironmental reconstruction, the size of the sample and geographic distribution provide at least a baseline from which to identify trends and develop general interpretations.

It is beyond the scope of this chapter to provide background on the methods used by each analyst. The reader should consult the original publications and other sources such as Butzer (1971), Graham and Semken (1987), Hester and Schoenwetter (1964), Holliday (2004), Ruhe (1970, 1983), Semken and Graham (1987), Warner (1990), and many chapters in Wright and Frey (1965) and Wright (1983) for additional methodological background and examples of applications for specific methods.

## Early Holocene Regional Paleoenvironmental Reconstruction

The following paleoenvironmental reconstructions are presented in blocks of 500 radiocarbon years, beginning at 10,000 $^{14}$C yrs BP and ending at 8000 $^{14}$C yrs BP. The sample comprises 58 sites, but not all sites contribute data to each of the four 500-radiocarbon-year blocks. The map illustrating the locations of sites used in this reconstruction is divided into the major physical divisions of the study area (Figure 2.1). The presentation of results first summarizes paleoclimatic data for each region and then for Cody complex archaeological sites as appropriate. Values for precipitation, temperature, and habitat are given in relation to modern conditions; however, some studies describe trends over time that relate back to preceding

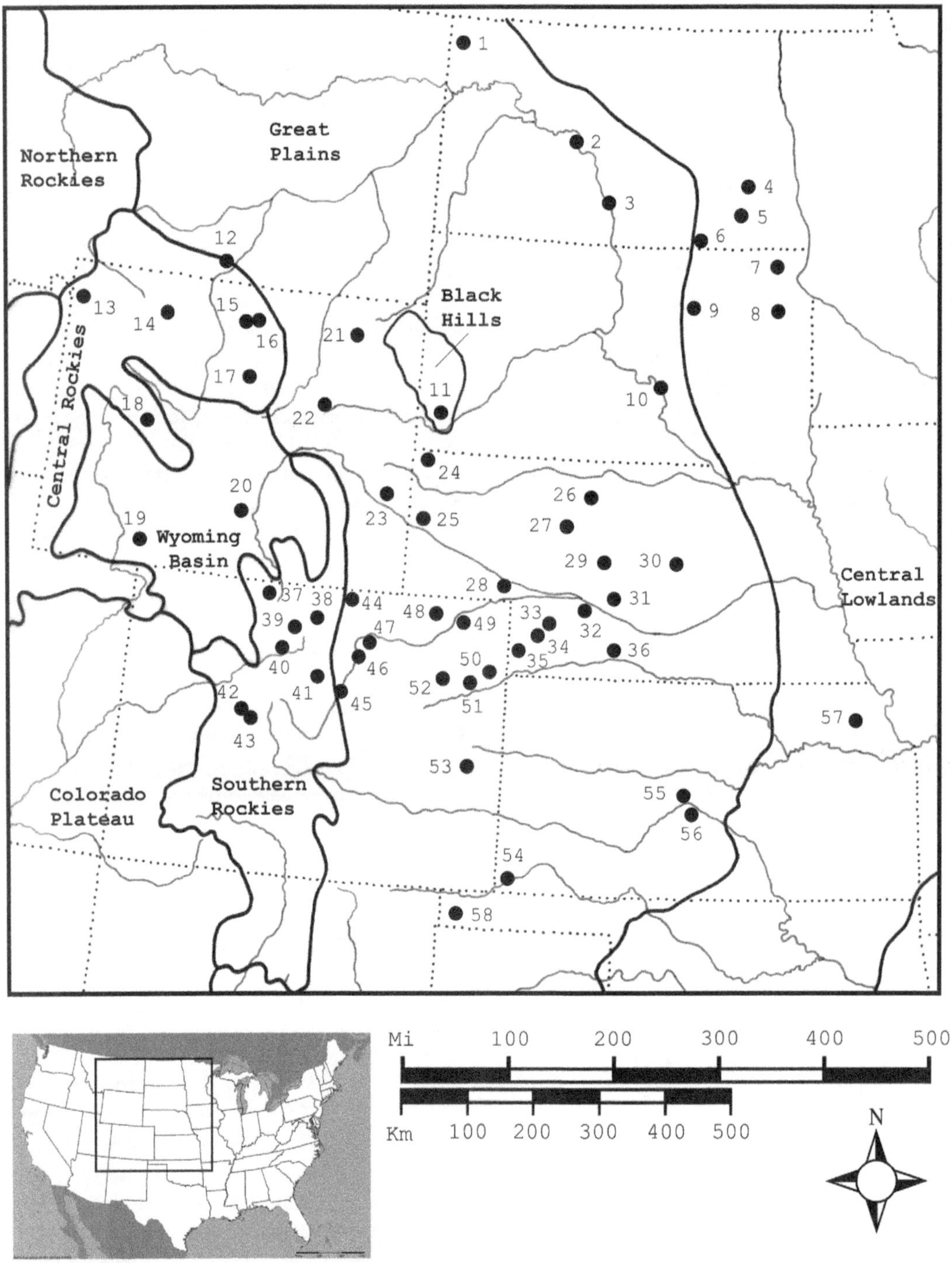


FIGURE 2.1. Total paleoenvironmental sample sites, 10,000–8000 $^{14}$C yrs BP (see Table 2.1 for corresponding site information).

**TABLE 2.1.** Paleoenvironmental Sample.

| Map # | Site | Dates ($^{14}$C BP)[a] | Data Types[b] | Paleoenvironmental Conditions (dates in $^{14}$C yrs BP) | Reference |
|---|---|---|---|---|---|
| 1 | Kettle Lake | 10,000–9500 | 2, 10, 12 | "Spruce parkland yielded to grassland under relatively moist conditions" with increasing temperature | Grimm et al. 2011:14 |
| 1 | Kettle Lake | 9500–8250 | 2, 10, 12 | Major drought early in period; abundant winter precipitation with warm dry summers; "severe but relatively brief droughts during an otherwise humid interval" occurring at 100–300-year intervals | Grimm et al. 2011:15 |
| 1 | Kettle Lake | 8250–8000 | 2, 10, 12 | "Megadrought" during this period culminating in the "driest interval of the Holocene" | Grimm et al. 2011:15 |
| 2 | Aggie Brown Coulee | 10,000–8500 | 1 | "Fairly cool and humid, not too different from today" | Clayton et al. 1976:12 |
| 2 | Aggie Brown Coulee | 8500–8000 | 1 | "Drier and a few degrees warmer than today" | Clayton et al. 1976:12 |
| 3 | Rattlesnake Buttes | 10,000–9300 | 1 | High effective moisture combined with decreased dust deposition as Missouri River valley was well vegetated | Mason et al. 2008 |
| 3 | Rattlesnake Buttes | 9300–8000 | 1 | Decreased effective moisture with a "relatively rapid shift toward a drier climate and much greater dust influx" | Mason et al. 2008:1781 |
| 4 | Moon Lake | 10,000–9500 | 2, 3, 4, 5, 6 | Deciduous hardwood parkland with high lake level stand | Yansa 2007 |
| 4 | Moon Lake | 9500–8500 | 2, 3, 4, 5, 6 | Grassland with lowering lake level | Yansa 2007 |
| 4 | Moon Lake | 8500–8000 | 2, 3, 4, 5, 6 | Grassland with peak aridity (indicated by *Ambrosia* pollen spike and peak salinity levels) beginning around 8000 BP and continuing afterward | Yansa 2007 |
| 5 | Wendel | 10,000–9500 | 2, 3, 4, 5, 6 | Deciduous hardwood parkland with lowering lake levels | Yansa 2007 |
| 5 | Wendel | 9500–9000 | 2, 3, 4, 5, 6 | Transition from deciduous hardwood parkland to grassland within first two centuries with continued lowering lake level | Yansa 2007 |
| 5 | Wendel | 9000–8000 | 2, 3, 4, 5, 6 | Grassland with lowering lake levels | Yansa 2007 |
| 6 | Coldwater Lake | 10,000–9500 | 2, 3, 4, 5, 6 | Deciduous hardwood parkland with high lake level stand | Yansa 2007 |
| 6 | Coldwater Lake | 9500–9000 | 2, 3, 4, 5, 6 | Deciduous hardwood parkland transitioning to grassland in final century accompanied by shift to lowering lake level | Yansa 2007 |
| 6 | Coldwater Lake | 9000–8000 | 2, 3, 4, 5, 6 | Grasslands with lowering lake level, peak aridity occurring ~8000 BP as indicated by *Ambrosia* pollen peak | Yansa 2007 |
| 7 | Pickerel Lake | 10,000–9500 | 2, 3, 4, 5, 6 | Deciduous hardwood parkland with high lake level stands | Yansa 2007 |
| 7 | Pickerel Lake | 9500–9000 | 2, 3, 4, 5, 6 | Shift from deciduous hardwood parkland to grassland very early followed by transition from high to low lake level stand | Yansa 2007 |
| 7 | Pickerel Lake | 9000–8000 | 2, 3, 4, 5, 6 | Grassland with low lake level stands throughout, culminating in high aridity just prior to 8000 BP as indicated by peaks in *Ambrosia* pollen and lake salinity | Yansa 2007 |
| 8 | Medicine Lake | 10,000–9500 | 2, 3, 4, 5, 6 | White spruce parkland transitions to deciduous hardwood parkland while lake stand remains high | Yansa 2007 |

**TABLE 2.1.** Paleoenvironmental Sample (continued).

| Map # | Site | Dates ($^{14}$C BP)[a] | Data Types[b] | Paleoenvironmental Conditions (dates in $^{14}$C yrs BP) | Reference |
|---|---|---|---|---|---|
| 8 | Medicine Lake | 9500–9000 | 2, 3, 4, 5, 6 | Deciduous hardwood parkland shifts to grassland midway through this period just after lake stand begins lowering | Yansa 2007 |
| 8 | Medicine Lake | 9000–8500 | 2, 3, 4, 5, 6 | Grassland aridity begins to peak with *Ambrosia* pollen spiking and lake levels continuing to lower | Yansa 2007 |
| 8 | Medicine Lake | 8500–8000 | 2, 3, 4, 5, 6 | Grassland setting remains while lake salinity begins to peak late in this period | Yansa 2007 |
| 9 | Cottonwood Lake | 10,000–9500 | 2, 3, 4, 5, 6 | Grassland with *Ambrosia* pollen peaking around 9500 BP indicating onset of local aridity | Yansa |
| 9 | Cottonwood Lake | 9500–8000 | 2, 3, 4, 5, 6 | Relatively arid grassland | Yansa 2007 |
| 10 | Crow Creek | 9345 | 1 | Soil development associated with cool and wet period with well-vegetated uplands; Leonard Paleosol may be resultant of riparian forest setting | Coogan 1987 |
| 11 | Wind Cave Nat'l. Park | 10,000–9500 | 4, 8 | Cooler than modern, dominated by $C_3$ grasses, analogous to modern conditions for central Alberta, Canada | Fredlund and Tieszen 1997 |
| 11 | Wind Cave Nat'l. Park | >9330–9000 | 4, 8 | Dominated by cooler $C_3$ grasses early on with $C_4$ grasses increasing throughout the period | Fredlund and Tieszen 1997 |
| 11 | Wind Cave Nat'l. Park | 9000–8500 | 4, 8 | Significant increase of $C_4$ grasses within a generally mixed $C_3/C_4$ environment, indicates warming | Fredlund and Tieszen 1997 |
| 12 | False Cougar Cave | 10,000 | 7, 9 | 2590 m elev.; January 5.6 to 10.4°C warmer than modern; July 2 to 4.5°C warmer than modern; boreal, reduced seasonality | Elias 1996; Graham et al. 1987 |
| 13 | Loon Lake | 10,500–9500 | 2 | Generally mesic but becoming drier | Whitlock et al. 1995 |
| 13 | Loon Lake | 9500–9000 | 2 | Drying trend increases significantly | Whitlock et al. 1995 |
| 13 | Loon Lake | 9000–8000 | 2 | Drying trend continues, becoming more arid | Whitlock et al. 1995 |
| 14 | *Horner* | 10,000–9500 | 1, 7, 8, 11 | Hydric to mesic, wooded and shrubby Horner II occupation dated 9875 ± 85 and 10,060 ± 220 BP | Evanoff 1987; Lewis 1987; Reider 1987; Walker 1987a |
| 14 | *Horner* | 9500–9000 | 1, 7, 11 | Very brief period of drying followed by return to wetter conditions and development of local pond | Evanoff 1987; Reider 1987; Walker 1987a |
| 14 | *Horner* | 8800 | 1, 7 | Mesic to hydric with shrubby-woody vegetation<br>Horner I occupation dated 8750 ± 120 and 8840 ± 140 BP | Reider 1987; Walker 1987a |
| 15 | *Medicine Lodge Creek* | 9590 ± 180 | 7 | 1463 m elev.; boreal and cooler than modern; Cody complex occupation dated 8830 ± 470, 9030 ± 470, and 9360 ± 380 BP | Walker 1987b; Frison 1991; Frison and Walker 2007 |
| 16 | *Laddie Creek* | 9500–9000 | 2 | Rapid shift from cool moist conditions before 9000 BP to drier conditions after; foothills-scrub vegetation throughout; later Cody occupation estimated 8800–8400 BP | Larson 1992; Walker 1987b |
| 17 | Bush Shelter | 9500–8730 | 7 | General shift from tundra-like environment to boreal | Walker 1987b |

| Map # | Site | Dates ($^{14}C$ BP)[a] | Data Types[b] | Paleoenvironmental Conditions (dates in $^{14}C$ yrs BP) | Reference |
|---|---|---|---|---|---|
| 18 | Temple Lake Valley | 10,600–<8000 | 2 | >3000 m elev.; summers warmer than modern by about 1.5°C | Fall et al. 1995 |
| 19 | *Finley* | 10,000–9500 | 1, 2 | Generally warmer and wetter than modern; evaporation rates increasing compared with earlier periods | Hansen 1951; Mayer 2003 |
| 19 | *Finley* | 9500–9000 | 1, 2 | Generally mesic but becoming drier; grasslands supporting bison still present | Hansen 1951; Mayer 2003 |
| 19 | *Finley* | 9000–8500 | 1 | Relatively stable mesic landscape becoming drier; Cody complex occupation dated 8950 ± 220 and 9026 ± 118 BP | Mayer 2003; Frison 1991 |
| 20 | Ferris Dune Field | 8800–8100 | 1 | Active eolian deposition beginning ~8800 BP; xeric, eolian deposition peaks around 8500 and continues until 8100 BP | Stokes and Gaylord 1993 |
| 21 | *Carter/ Kerr-McGee* | 9390–8750 | 1 | Mesic to hydric conditions; grasses, sedges, woodland along streams, sagebrush on uplands | Reider 1990 |
| 21 | *Carter/ Kerr-McGee* | 9000–8700 | 1 | Mesic to hydric with some lowering of the water table after 8700 BP, grasses, sedges, and perhaps broken woodland vegetation | Reider 1990 |
| 22 | Antelope Playa | 10,000–9500 | 2 | Substantially more mesic than modern; riparian trees stable | Markgraf and Lennon 1986 |
| 22 | Antelope Playa | 9500–9000 | 2 | Increasing moisture with stable floral communities | Markgraf and Lennon 1986 |
| 22 | Antelope Playa | 9000–8500 | 2 | Shift from mesic to drier vegetation | Markgraf and Lennon 1986 |
| 22 | Antelope Playa | 8500–8000 | 2 | Drying trend continues and increases; riparian trees disappear | Markgraf and Lennon 1986 |
| 23 | *Hell Gap* | 10,000–9500 | 8 | "Establishment of highly productive grassland community dominated by $C_3$ genera"; temperatures ~1°C cooler than modern; precipitation generally mesic with significant aridity spike around 9800; phytoliths indicate soil surface stability and high grassland productivity | Fredlund 2009:95–97 |
| 23 | *Hell Gap* | >10,000–9000 | 1, 7 | By 9500 BP comparable to modern environment; "a transition in environments from cool-wet to somewhat drier conditions or alternation of climatic regimes"; relatively moist and well-wooded<br>Cody complex occupations at Locality I; Scottsbluff dated 9120 ± 490; Alberta between 9410 ± 95 and 10,560 ± 80 BP | Miller and Goldberg 2009; Reider 2009:71; Walker 2009 |
| 23 | *Hell Gap* | 9000–8000 | 1, 7 | Very similar to modern, probably alternating between wet and dry conditions; drier conditions result in deposition of stratum F between 9000 and 8000 BP; Cody complex occupation at Locality V (Eden) dated 8890 ± 110 and 9050 ± 160 BP | Haynes 2009; Reider 2009; Walker 2009 |
| 24 | *Hudson-Meng* | 9800–9540 | 1, 2, 8, 11, 13 | Generally mesic with evidence for stable, well-vegetated soils, a relatively high water table, and plants such as sedge and hackberry; mid to tall grasses in valley bottoms with short grass predominant throughout surrounding uplands; Cody complex occupations dated 9820 ± 160, 9676 ± 35, and 9539 ± 55 BP | Agenbroad 1978; Lewis 1978; Muñiz 2007, 2008, 2010; Wu and Jones 1978; Young and Weedon 1978 |

**TABLE 2.1.** Paleoenvironmental Sample (continued).

| Map # | Site | Dates ($^{14}$C BP)[a] | Data Types[b] | Paleoenvironmental Conditions (dates in $^{14}$C yrs BP) | Reference |
|---|---|---|---|---|---|
| 24 | *Hudson-Meng* | 9440–9350 | 1, 8 | Shift to somewhat drier environment than previous; dominated by grasses but hackberry still present; soil A horizon development eventually outpaced by eolian deposition after ~9400 BP; probable Cody complex occupations dated 9444 ± 77 and 9355 ± 30 BP | Muñiz 2007, 2008, 2010; Born, pers. comm. 2010 |
| 25 | *Scottsbluff* | 9000–8500 | 7,11 | Estimated as similar to or wetter than modern conditions with locally available water and grasslands supporting bison; Cody complex occupation dated 8680 ± 85 and 8939 ± 85 BP | Schultz and Eiseley 1935; Hill 2008 |
| 26 | Merritt Reserv. | 10,200–9300 | 1 | Mesic, stable throughout interval | Forman et al. 2001 |
| 26 | Merritt Reserv. | 8800 | 1 | General region becoming drier with localized mesic to hydric catchment basins | Forman et al. 2001 |
| 26 | Merritt Reserv. | 8500–8000 | 1 | Stable dune surfaces | Forman et al. 2001 |
| 27 | Whitman Reserv. | 10,200–9300 | 1 | Mesic, stable throughout interval | Forman et al. 2001 |
| 27 | Whitman Reserv. | 8800 | 1 | General region becoming drier with localized mesic to hydric catchment basins | Forman et al. 2001 |
| 27 | Whitman Reserv. | 8500–8000 | 1 | Stable dune surfaces | Forman et al. 2001 |
| 28 | Dankworth Canyon | >10,000–8800 | 1 | Brady Soil characteristics indicate more effective precipitation than modern and likely dominated by grasslands with woody vegetation; infrequent fire regime; significant landscape stability and ecosystem productivity | Jacobs and Mason 2004 |
| 28 | Dankworth Canyon | 8500–<8000 | 1 | Climate drier than preceding period; possible increase in fire regime that discouraged woody vegetation; beginning of regional drought | Jacobs and Mason 2004 |
| 29 | Logan Road Cut | >10,000–8800 | 1 | Brady Soil characteristics indicate more effective precipitation than modern and likely dominated by grasslands with woody vegetation; infrequent fire regime; significant landscape stability and ecosystem productivity | Jacobs and Mason 2004 |
| 29 | Logan Road cut | 8500–<8000 | 1 | Climate drier than preceding period; possible increase in fire regime that discouraged woody vegetation; beginning of regional drought | Jacobs and Mason 2004 |
| 30 | Mirdan Canal | >10,000–8800 | 1 | Brady Soil characteristics indicate more effective precipitation than modern and likely dominated by grasslands with woody vegetation; infrequent fire regime; significant landscape stability and ecosystem productivity | Jacobs and Mason 2004 |
| 30 | Mirdan Canal | 8500–<8000 | 1 | Climate drier than preceding period; possible increase in fire regime that discouraged woody vegetation; beginning of regional drought | Jacobs and Mason 2004 |
| 31 | County Line Ranch | >10,000–8800 | 1 | Brady Soil characteristics indicate more effective precipitation than modern and likely dominated by grasslands with woody vegetation; infrequent fire regime; significant landscape stability and ecosystem productivity | Jacobs and Mason 2004 |

| Map # | Site | Dates ($^{14}C$ BP)[a] | Data Types[b] | Paleoenvironmental Conditions (dates in $^{14}C$ yrs BP) | Reference |
|---|---|---|---|---|---|
| 31 | County Line Ranch | 8500–<8000 | 1 | Climate drier than preceding period; possible increase in fire regime that discouraged woody vegetation; beginning of regional drought | Jacobs and Mason 2004 |
| 32 | Moran Canyon | >10,000–8800 | 1 | Brady Soil characteristics indicate more effective precipitation than modern and likely dominated by grasslands with woody vegetation; infrequent fire regime; significant landscape stability and ecosystem productivity | Jacobs and Mason 2004 |
| 32 | Moran Canyon | 8500–<8000 | 1 | Climate drier than preceding period; possible increase in fire regime that discouraged woody vegetation; beginning of regional drought | Jacobs and Mason 2004 |
| 33 | Cliff Dwellers Canyon | >10,000–8800 | 1 | Brady Soil characteristics indicate more effective precipitation than modern and likely dominated by grasslands with woody vegetation; infrequent fire regime; significant landscape stability and ecosystem productivity | Jacobs and Mason 2004 |
| 33 | Cliff Dwellers Canyon | 8500–<8000 | 1 | Climate drier than preceding period; possible increase in fire regime that discouraged woody vegetation; beginning of regional drought | Jacobs and Mason 2004 |
| 34 | Wauneta Road Cut | >10,000–8800 | 1 | Brady Soil characteristics indicate more effective precipitation than modern and likely dominated by grasslands with woody vegetation; infrequent fire regime; significant landscape stability and ecosystem productivity | Jacobs and Mason 2004 |
| 34 | Wauneta Road Cut | 8500–<8000 | 1 | Climate drier than preceding period; possible increase in fire regime that discouraged woody vegetation; beginning of regional drought | Jacobs and Mason 2004 |
| 35 | Hoover Blowout | 13,000–7900 | 1 | Xeric with active eolian deposition; NW prevailing wind after 9000 BP | Forman et al. 2001 |
| 36 | *Lime Creek site* | 10,030 ± 270–7910 ± 1000 | 2, 8 | Tall grasses much more abundant than present, probably resultant from higher water table early in period | Cummings et al. 2007 |
| 36 | Red Smoke site | 9820 ± 20 | 2, 8 | Mixed tall and short grasses with relatively moist water regime | Cummings et al. 2007 |
| 36 | Red Smoke site | 9220 ± 90 | 2, 8 | Tall grasses decline relative to short grasses, indicating slight drying trend; episodic spring–summer flooding | Cummings et al. 2007 |
| 36 | Red Smoke site | 8862 ± 230–8270 ± 80 | 2, 8 | Significant shift from tall grasses to short grasses, indicating drier summers than modern; episodic late spring–summer flooding | Cummings et al. 2007 |
| 36 | Medicine Creek and Lime Creek drainages (4 sites) | ca. 10,000–8000 | 2, 8 | Gallery forest with mixed prairie, abundant grasses and composites, occasional sedge, and other shrubs and herbs as well as hardwoods and possibly pine; upland prairie is mixed tall, short, and cool grasses with much more tall grass than today | Cummings et al. 2007 |
| 36 | Allen site | 9820 ± 190–8430 ± 80 | 10 | Mesic conditions supporting a gallery forest including mulberry, hackberry, and elm | Zalucha 2007 |
| 37 | LaPoudre Pass | 9850 ± 300 | 9 | 3100 m elev.; increased seasonality with colder winters (January ranged from −9.8 to +0.7°C) and moderately warmer summers (July 3.7 to 6.7°C warmer than modern) | Elias 1996 |

**TABLE 2.1.** Paleoenvironmental Sample (continued).

| Map # | Site | Dates ($^{14}$C BP)[a] | Data Types[b] | Paleoenvironmental Conditions (dates in $^{14}$C yrs BP) | Reference |
|---|---|---|---|---|---|
| 37 | LaPoudre Pass | 8800 ± 90 | 9 | 3100 m elev.; greater seasonality: January 13.6 to 1.3°C colder than modern and July 2.2 to 5.2°C warmer than modern | Elias 1996 |
| 38 | South St. Vrain Valley | 10,000–7600 | 2, 3 | 3100 m elev.; warmer and wetter than modern | Fall 1997 |
| 39 | *Jerry Craig* | 9310 ± 50 to 9290 ± 50 | 1, 2 | Moist wooded environment with active springs nearby | Cummings and Moutoux 1998; Richings-Germain 2002; Surovell et al. 2000 |
| 39 | *Jerry Craig* | 9000 to ~8500 | 2 | Shifting to drier conditions with fire evident | Cummings and Moutoux 1998; Richings-Germain 2002; Surovell et al. 2000 |
| 40 | Lake Isabelle Delta | 9000 ± 285 | 9 | 3323 m elev.; winters significantly colder than modern (January –23 to –6.8°C) while summers only somewhat warmer than modern (July 1 to 3.7°C warmer); seasonality increasing | Elias 1996 |
| 40 | Lake Isabelle Delta | 8500 | 9 | 3323 m elev.; January 15.3 to 7.8°C colder than modern, July 0.3°C colder to 2.2°C warmer than modern | Elias 1996 |
| 40 | Lake Isabelle Delta | 7800 ± 255 | 9 | 3323 m elev.; January 0.8 to 5.8°C colder than modern, July 0.2 to 2.2°C colder than modern | Elias 1996 |
| 41 | Arapaho Pass | 10,000–7250 | 1, 2, 3 | 3600 m elev.; increased summer rather than winter warmth, reduced seasonality, warmer summers than modern | Benedict 1985 |
| 42 | Ironbog | 9000 to 8000 | 2, 3 | 2900 m elev.; average annual temperature 1.6°C warmer, summers 1.9°C warmer, precipitation 8–11 cm greater than modern | Fall 1997 |
| 43 | Alkali Basin | 9000 to 8000 | 2, 3 | 2750 m elev.; average annual temperature 1.6°C warmer, summers 1.9°C warmer, precipitation 8–11 cm greater than modern | Fall 1997 |
| 44 | *Lindenmeier* | 9900 to 8300 | 1, 7 | Moist with wet meadow and nearby riparian environment; Cody complex occupation dated 9690 ± 60 and 9880 ± 100 BP | Graham 1987; Haynes and Agogino 1960; Haynes et al. 1992 |
| 45 | *Lamb Spring* | 8870 ± 350 | 1, 7 | Mesic to hydric with active spring flow and abundant vegetation | McCartney 1990; Rancier et al. 1982; Stanford et al. 1981 |
| 46 | Kersey Road | 13,500–9460 | 1 | Mesic with landscape stability for most of period; ending with eolian deposition before 9500 BP followed by return to stable soil development | Forman et al. 2001 |
| 46 | Kersey Road | 9460 ± 490 to ~8900 | 1 | Stable soil for about 300 years, followed by eolian deposition beginning about 8900 BP | Forman et al. 1992, 2001 |
| 46 | Kersey Road | ~8900 to 8000 | 1 | Xeric, increased drying with active eolian deposition, probable desertification | Forman et al. 1995 |

| Map # | Site | Dates ($^{14}$C BP)[a] | Data Types[b] | Paleoenvironmental Conditions (dates in $^{14}$C yrs BP) | Reference |
|---|---|---|---|---|---|
| 46 | Hudson Dune Field | 9000 to 8500 | 1, 2 | Shift from stable moisture regime to strong fluctuations and increased drying | Forman et al. 1995 |
| 46 | Hudson Dune Field | 8500 to 8000 | 1 | Generally dry with sporadic eolian deposition | Forman et al. 2001 |
| 47 | *Jurgens* | 9070 ± 90 | 2 | Open environment similar to modern with adjacent riverine resources available | Scott 1979 |
| 48 | *Frasca* | 8910 ± 90 | 7 | Estimated as probably similar to modern conditions with grasslands nearby | Fulgham and Stanford 1982 |
| 48 | *Nelson* | 9260 ± 20 | 7 | Estimated as at least similar to modern conditions with water in the drainage and grasslands on nearby uplands | Kornfeld et al. 2010 |
| 49 | Sterling Dune | 9500 to 9010 ± 100 | 1 | After stable moist period, eolian deposition resumes | Madole 1995 |
| 50 | Jones-Miller | 10,020 ± 320 | 7 | Cooler than modern with greater effective moisture; snowy winters and wet springs with drier summers and falls; increased seasonality | Stanford 1978 |
| 51 | Beecher Island | >10,000–8000 | 4 | Becoming warmer, shift from cool-season $C_3$ to warm-season $C_4$ grasses | Muhs et al. 1999 |
| 52 | *Claypool* | 9000 to 8000 | 1 | Much wetter than what followed in later Holocene and modern, probably abundant grassland | Reider 1990 |
| 53 | *Olsen-Chubbuck* | 9395 ± 20 | 2 | Mesic to hydric local environment fed by seeps with drier conditions and short grasses on the surrounding uplands | Leopold and Wheat 1972 |
| 54 | Winger | 9080 ± 90 | 1 | Mesic to hydric conditions | Mandel and Hofman 2003 |
| 54 | Winger | 9080 ± 90 to 8570 ± 60 | 1 | Alternating cycles of hydric conditions interrupted by stable soil development | Mandel and Hofman 2003 |
| 55 | Cheyenne Bottoms | 10,500–~9500 | 1 | Probably mesic, fully developed grasslands, relatively stable | Fredlund 1995 |
| 55 | Cheyenne Bottoms | 9500–8500 | 1 | Overall stable landscape with locally hydric conditions | Fredlund 1995 |
| 55 | Cheyenne Bottoms | 8500 to 8000 | 1, 2 | Drop in water table followed by landscape stability | Fredlund 1995 |
| 56 | Great Bend Sand Prairie | 10,000–9500 | 1 | Mesic, stable conditions | Forman et al. 2001 |
| 56 | Great Bend Sand Prairie | 9500–8000 | 1 | Overall stable landscape with locally hydric-mesic conditions | Forman et al. 2001 |
| 57 | Muscotah Marsh | 9930–8000? | 2, 3 | Generally mesic conditions; marsh-supported sedges; oak/hickory gallery forest and herbaceous prairie on adjacent uplands | Grüger 1973 |
| 58 | Nall | 10,000–9500 | 1 | Mesic and stable at 9645 BP but arid with eolian deposition before and after | LaBelle et al. 2003 |
| 58 | Nall | 9500 to 9000 | 1 | Period of aridity | LaBelle et al. 2003 |

*Note:* Map numbers correlate with Figures 2.1–2.5. Italics indicate sites that contain an archaeological Cody complex occupation.
[a] Dates provided in $^{14}$C years BP; exact dates with error provided when available; estimates and date ranges given as published.
[b] 1. Soils/geomorphology; 2. Pollen; 3. Macrobotanical; 4. Isotopes; 5. Diatoms; 6. Geochemistry; 7. Fauna; 8. Phytoliths; 9. Insects; 10. Charcoal; 11. Gastropods; 12. Mineralogy; 13. Bivalves.

intervals, and these different approaches are identified throughout.

### *10,000 to 9500 $^{14}$C yrs BP (11,600–10,710 cal BP)*

For the period 10,000 to 9500 $^{14}$C yrs BP, paleoenvironmental data are available from 41 sites in the study area (Figure 2.2, Table 2.1). The sample is composed of 11 sites in the Rocky Mountains, Black Hills, and intermountain basins with the remainder on the Plains. Of these 41 sites, Cody complex occupations are present in the Wyoming Rocky Mountains at Horner, in the Colorado foothills at Lindenmeier, and in Nebraska on the Pine Ridge at Hudson-Meng and along Medicine Creek at the Lime Creek site.

#### *Regional Summary*

Temperature data derived from fossil beetle assemblages at False Cougar Cave (Montana) and pollen from Temple Lake Valley (Wyoming) indicate that during this period winters in the Central Rockies were significantly warmer while summers were only slightly warmer than modern conditions (Elias 1996; Fall et al. 1995). Pollen samples collected from Loon Lake, also in the Central Rocky Mountains of Wyoming, indicated that conditions there were generally mesic but becoming drier (Whitlock et al. 1995). The Medicine Lodge Creek site is located in the Bighorn Mountains to the east of Horner and has both Cody and Paleoindian Foothill-Mountain components (Frison 1976, 1991). Walker (1987a) noted that in a non-Cody occupation level dated to 9590 ± 180 $^{14}$C yrs BP (11,389–10,301 cal BP), the small-mammal faunule suggested that a boreal forest environment may have extended to the site, which lies at an elevation of 1463 m. However, Walker cautioned that because *Ochotona* (pika), *Clethrionomys* (southern red-backed vole), and *Phenacomys* (heather vole) were recovered from a culturally derived deposit, they may represent the results of selective foraging in distant locales rather than the immediate local site environment. Regardless, it is apparent that a cool, boreal environment was in the vicinity. An Eden and possibly Alberta/Cody occupation occurred later at the site, between 9030 ± 470 and 9360 ± 380 $^{14}$C yrs BP (11,604–8994 and 11,743–9547 cal BP). These data indicate that in the northern high country overall, seasonality was less pronounced than modern conditions and precipitation was trending downward. It is unclear if the reduction in precipitation was in winter snowfall or warm-season rain.

Analysis of beetles, macrobotanical remains, pollen, and geomorphology from the southern Rocky Mountain sites of Arapaho Pass, La Poudre Pass, and South St. Vrain Valley in Colorado indicate a somewhat opposite trend to the one noted above. High-elevation winter temperatures ranged from slightly colder to about average with substantially warmer summers (Benedict 1985; Elias 1996; Fall 1997), indicating slightly increased seasonality compared with modern conditions. Macrobotanical and pollen data from South St. Vrain Valley (Fall 1997) also indicated wetter than modern moisture conditions.

At a lower elevation, geomorphology and pollen data from the Finley site indicated warmer and wetter conditions than modern in the Wyoming Basin (Hansen 1951; Mayer 2003). The pollen record from Antelope Playa in the Thunder Basin recorded substantially more mesic conditions than modern with a stable riparian habitat (Markgraf and Lennon 1986). In the southern Black Hills, Fredlund and Tieszen (1997) analyzed phytoliths and carbon isotopes to determine that cool-season $C_3$ grasses predominated in an environment that was analogous to modern central Alberta.

The Great Plains portion of the study area is generally characterized by a relatively homogeneous distribution of well-watered and wooded environments concentrated primarily along drainages and around lakes within an overall grassland landscape. Early on, the grasslands were primarily composed of cool-season $C_3$ grasses that began to shift to warm-season $C_4$ grasses in the southern portions of the study area closer to 9500 $^{14}$C yrs BP (10,770–10,710 cal BP) (Fredlund and Tieszen 1997; Muhs et al. 1999). Observations based on eight different data types for nine sites throughout central North Dakota and northeastern South Dakota (Table 2.1) record a well-watered grassland environment located on uplands with well-vegetated river valleys and deciduous hardwoods clustered around ponds and lakes (Clayton et al. 1976; Mason et al. 2008; Yansa 2007). Temperature data for these sites are very similar to modern. The last phase of the transition from

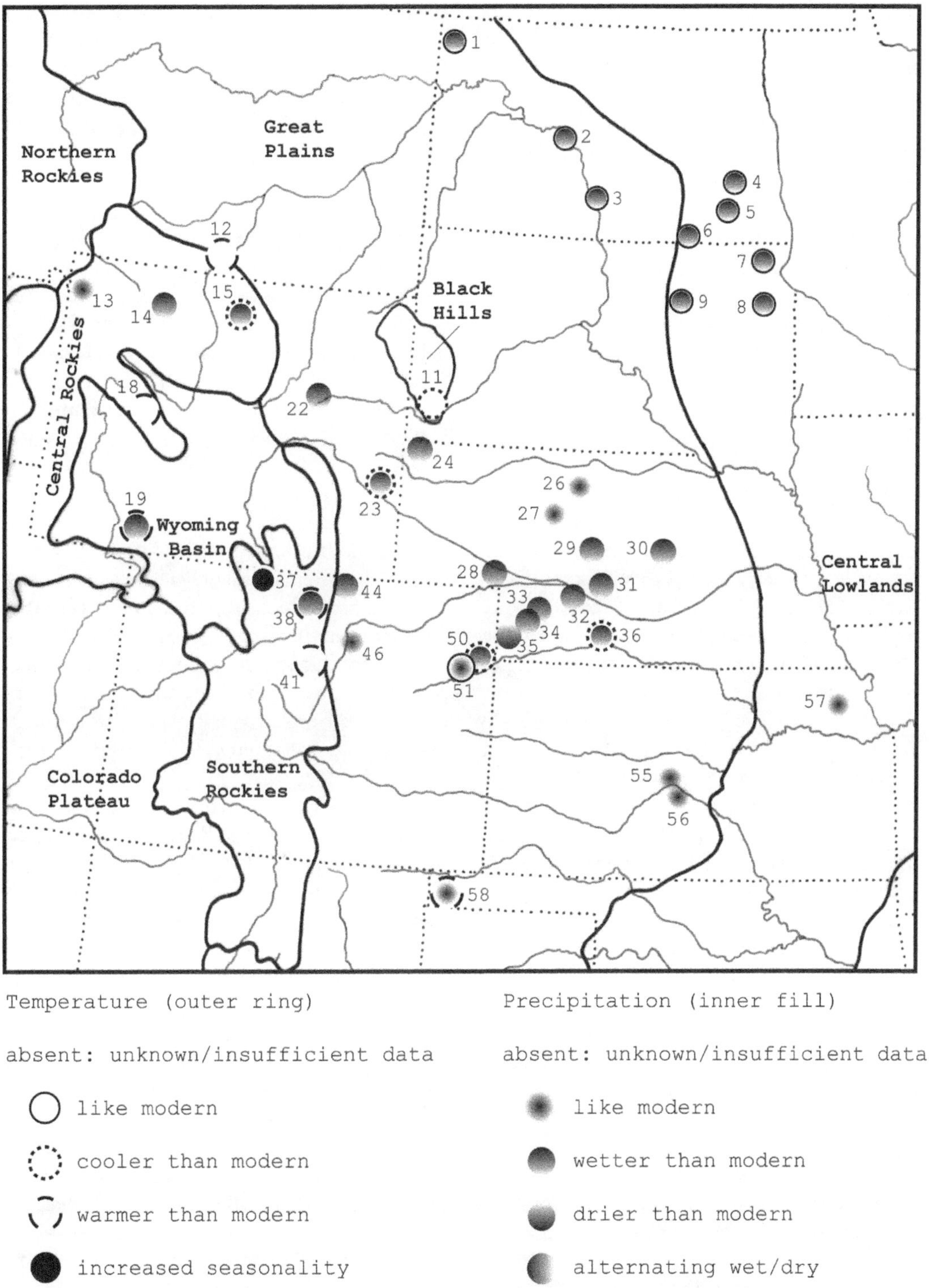


**FIGURE 2.2.** Paleoenvironmental precipitation and temperature sample: 10,000–9500 $^{14}$C yrs BP.

late Pleistocene spruce parkland to early Holocene grassland occurs at Kettle Lake in northwestern North Dakota during this period (Grimm et al. 2011).

Geomorphological data from two sites in northern Nebraska and central Kansas, along with pollen and macrobotanical data from Muscotah Marsh in northeast Kansas, record essentially modern conditions with mesic water regimes, gallery forests along bottomlands, and herbaceous prairie grasslands on the uplands (Forman et al. 2001; Fredlund 1995; Grüger 1973). Eight additional sites in central Nebraska record wetter than modern conditions that included abundant vegetation resulting in well-developed paleosols (Jacobs and Mason 2004).

Temperature data from Plains sites in the southern portion of the study area are somewhat mixed. The Medicine and Lime Creek drainages and Jones-Miller site recorded generally cool conditions for the early part of this interval (Cummings et al. 2007; Semken and Falk 1987; Stanford 1978). However, at the Beecher Island locale, Muhs and others (1999) documented a shift from cool-season $C_3$ grasses to warm-season $C_4$ grasses. Eolian deposition remained at least sporadically active at the Hoover Blowout (Forman et al. 2001), and at Nall a stable moist period around 9645 $^{14}$C yrs BP (10,885–11,165 cal BP) was preceded and followed by eolian deposition under drier conditions (LaBelle et al. 2003). Although a shift from cool-season to warm-season grasses could be caused by a combination of increasing temperature and decreasing moisture, the moisture data indicate steady precipitation throughout the Plains. This suggests that the expanding $C_4$ grasslands were responding to increasing average temperature that probably resulted in increased evaporation rates rather than a decrease in precipitation.

### *Cody Complex Occupations*

The Horner site is the type site for the Cody complex and was the location for two bison kills separated by about 1000 radiocarbon years. Horner II, dated to 9875 ± 85 and 10,060 ± 220 $^{14}$C yrs BP (11,701–11,157 and 12,522–10,895 cal BP), provides detailed data for environmental characteristics chosen by Cody peoples early in this period. Based on the faunal assemblage (Walker 1987b), snails (Evanoff 1987), phytoliths (Lewis 1987), and soils (Reider 1987), researchers determined that the Horner II occupation occurred within a moist, wooded, or shrubby habitat that was probably concentrated along a drainage, with mixed short grasses predominating throughout the surrounding uplands. Walker (1987b:343) stated: "Ecologically, the vertebrate remains suggest similar local environments at the site area during the deposition of both faunules [Horner I and Horner II]. The presence of the various microtine rodents and the thrush suggest a wooded, or shrubby, habitat surrounding the playa in which the site was deposited."

Evanoff (1987) reported that more than 8200 identifiable snail shells were collected from the Horner site, and concluded that overall they represent a moist wooded habitat. Lewis (1987) analyzed 10 soil samples for phytoliths and diatoms, and after noting discrepancies in phytoliths from the butchery and nonbutchery areas, she concluded that the high phytolith counts probably resulted from discarded digestive viscera rather than on-site vegetation. From this, Lewis interpreted the area surrounding the Horner site as composed of mixed grasses with short grasses predominating at about 9965 $^{14}$C yrs BP (11,390–11,290 cal BP).

Reider (1987) classified the soil horizon that contained the Horner II bonebed (soil 5) as an Aeric Calciaquoll. This type of soil generally forms around the margins of shallow intermittent ponds, on low stream terraces, or along floodplains (Reider 1987). Reider interpreted the presence of this soil to mean that during the Horner II occupation the climate was generally cooler and more humid than modern conditions. Overlying soil 5 is soil 4, which indicated improved drainage conditions following the Horner II occupation. Overlying soil 4 is soil 3, which formed during a period of brief surface stability and represents a shift to an even drier moisture regime than during the formation of soil 4. Soil 3 developed when the ground surface was well drained and there was a cessation of local ponding on the terrace. Finally, soil 2 developed sometime after 9400 $^{14}$C yrs BP (10,680–10,580 cal BP) and represents the surface on which the Horner I occupation/s eventually occurred. The soil data indicate that the Cody occupation at Horner II occurred during a wet moisture regime when the ground surface was stable and experiencing repeated inundations of water that probably collected in small ponded areas.

Overall, the soil, faunal, and terrestrial snail data all indicate a well-watered and somewhat wooded local setting. When combined with phytolith data, the local region appears as a mixed-grass environment dominated by short grasses in the surrounding uplands, with well-watered and wooded areas along the drainages. These reconstructions are consistent with the taphonomic observations of Todd (1987), who noted that the Horner II bonebed had good bone preservation, which may have resulted from a shaded depositional environment.

Just south of the Colorado-Wyoming border, the Lindenmeier site is located in the foothills of the Southern Rockies. Wilmsen and Roberts (1978) described what appeared to be two stratigraphically separate Cody occupations, evidenced by an intact hearth and Eden and probable Scottsbluff points, as well as two Alberta points recovered from an area of the site with disturbed strata. Unfortunately, evidence of the Cody occupations was "destroyed in the process of removing overburden in order to expose the Folsom occupations" (Wilmsen and Roberts 1978:60), and data on the occupations and almost all the artifacts are absent. Haynes and colleagues (1992) reported dates of 9690 ± 60 $^{14}$C yrs BP (10,788–11,231 cal BP) and 9880 ± 100 $^{14}$C yrs BP (11,110–11,753 cal BP) for the base of stratum D, which contained the Cody components, and a date of 8310 ± 70 $^{14}$C yrs BP (9092–9478 cal BP) for the top of this organically rich stratum. Haynes and Agogino (1960) interpreted the soil horizon that contained the Cody occupation level/s as developing under a moist climate associated with the formation of a wet meadow in the Lindenmeier valley. Graham (1987) described the Lindenmeier local environment during the early Holocene as predominantly grassland with riparian forest components.

The Hudson-Meng site in northwest Nebraska is located near a series of springs in a small drainage along the north-facing slope of the Pine Ridge. The site has been interpreted both as one of the largest Paleoindian bison kills in North America (Agenbroad 1978) and as a paleontological site that coincidentally contains Cody complex artifacts (Todd and Rapson 1991, 1999). Recently, multiple Paleoindian components associated with bison remains have been identified, and an Eden occupation overlying the Alberta component has been discovered (Muñiz 2007, 2008, 2010). The Cody complex deposits are contained within a well-developed Brady paleosol with two, at times welded, A horizons that contain multiple Cody complex occupations. Agenbroad (1978) reported a date of 9820 ± 160 $^{14}$C yrs BP (10,714–11,944 cal BP) for the Alberta component, and Muñiz (2010) dated the Eden level to 9539 ± 55 $^{14}$C yrs BP (10,679–11,105 cal BP). Muñiz (2010) has also dated cultural components in the paleosol sequence to 9676 ± 35 $^{14}$C yrs BP (10,812–11,204 cal BP), 9444 ± 77 $^{14}$C yrs BP (average of two dates) (10,444–11,082 cal BP), and 9355 ± 30 $^{14}$C yrs BP (10,500–10,670 cal BP). Most of the newly recognized cultural components currently lack diagnostic projectile points but date to within the first half of the Cody complex period. Bivalves, snails, phytoliths, pollen, and soil data provide paleoenvironmental information for the Cody period at the site.

The local setting for the Alberta occupation consisted of a moist, shrubby or wooded environment, with Rosaceae positively identified from a charcoal fragment (Lee Newsome, personal communication 2011). *Celtis* (hackberry) seed endocarps have been recovered from the paleosol and document this tree in the drainage by 9539 ± 55 $^{14}$C yrs BP (10,679–11,105 cal BP). Hackberry requires moist soil conditions to grow. Tall grasses were also present within the drainage basin, whereas short grasses dominated the surrounding uplands (Lewis 1978; Wu and Jones 1978; Young and Weedon 1978). Analysis of the stratigraphy 190 m south of the main bison bonebed has identified gleyed horizons indicative of prolonged groundwater inundation below the Brady paleosol, and recent phytolith analysis (Daniel Born, personal communication 2010) has identified freshwater sponge spicules from within the paleosol. These data reveal a well-watered local environment likely associated with a pond or wetland marsh derived from the nearby springs.

The Medicine Creek site complex in southwestern Nebraska contains the closely spaced Allen, Lime Creek, and Red Smoke Paleoindian sites. Analyses of small mammalian fauna (Semken and Falk 1987), freshwater mussels (Warren

2007), pollen, phytoliths (Cummings et al. 2007), and macrobotanical remains (Zalucha 2007) provide paleoenvironmental data for all three locales. All three sites are located within a 1.75-km stretch of Medicine Creek in southwestern Nebraska and demonstrate various types of Paleoindian utilization (e.g., camps, stone tool manufacture, quarry) between about 10,500 and 8000 $^{14}$C yrs BP (12,590–7972 cal BP) (Bamforth 2007). Although a diagnostic Cody complex occupation was identified only in Cultural Zone I at Lime Creek, data from the other two sites are presented here for the sake of continuity (however, see also Bamforth, this volume). The Cody occupation in Zone I at the Lime Creek site is bracketed by dates of 9960 ± 270 and 9060 ± 510 $^{14}$C yrs BP (10,700–12,414 and 8793–11,800 cal BP), and May (2007) provides an average of 9524 ± 450 $^{14}$C yrs BP (9560–12,370 cal BP) for the component. The Cody component at Lime Creek consists of a lithic quarry and workshop (Bamforth 2007; Hicks 2002).

Semken and Falk (1987) discussed the paleoenvironmental implications of small mammalian remains recovered at Lime Creek and noted that the presence of *Synaptomys cooperi* (southern bog lemming) and *Blarina spp.* (short-tailed shrew) in Zone I indicated mesic conditions for the local area between 9880 ± 670 and 9167 ± 600 $^{14}$C yrs BP (9560–12,964 and 8778–12,363 cal BP). Cummings and others (2007) analyzed pollen and phytoliths from both Lime Creek and Red Smoke. Samples at Lime Creek spanning the period from 10,030 ± 450 to 9960 ± 270 $^{14}$C yrs BP (10,297–12,700 to 10,700–12,414 cal BP) indicated that generally the area contained mixed prairie vegetation with the strongest signals from Cheno-Ams (goosefoot and amaranth families) and low-spine Asteraceae (ragweed, cocklebur, etc.), with only a minor signal from *Artemisia* (sagebrush) and high-spine Asteraceae (aster, rabbitbrush, snakeweed, sunflower, etc.) (Cummings et al. 2007:82–86). Arboreal pollen for this period included low amounts of *Alnus* (alder), *Fraxinus* (ash), *Picea* (spruce), *Pinus* (pine), *Salix* (willow), and *Ulmus* (elm) (Cummings et al. 2007:82–86). The researchers also noted that during the first half of the Cody complex there was a significant shift in the pollen record away from hardwood and arboreal species toward Graminae and composites. Although trees were in decline as grasses increased, small quantities of Betulaceae (birch), *Fraxinus*, *Juniperus* (juniper), *Pinus*, and *Ulmus* were present throughout the sequence. After 9960 $^{14}$C yrs BP (11,280–11,390 cal BP), *Picea* disappeared from the record completely. Cummings and colleagues noted that, in general, short-grass phytoliths (chloridoid forms) increased slightly during the early Holocene. However, phytoliths from cool-season grasses (festucoid) and tall grasses (panicoid) continued to remain prominent, especially when compared with the short-grass dominance of the area today.

Cummings and colleagues (2007) also analyzed samples from the Red Smoke site, which is located on Lime Creek about 0.3 km upstream from the Lime Creek site. The samples came from deposits dating 9820 ± 20 to 8270 ± 80 $^{14}$C yrs BP (11,206–11,247 to 9031–9442 cal BP). Cummings and colleagues illustrated *Pinus* pollen as the only arboreal pollen for the RS1 sample dated to 9820 ± 20 $^{14}$C yrs BP (11,220–11,240 cal BP). The nonarboreal pollen for this sample has the largest signal from low-spine Asteraceae, and also includes Cheno-Ams, *Artemisia*, high-spine Asteraceae, Liguliflorae (includes Chicory tribe), and *Ephedra nevadensis* (Mormon tea) in descending order (Cummings et al. 2007:87–89). The researchers found that the samples are dominated by pollen from short grasses and other species endemic to stream banks and floodplains. During the interval dating 9820 ± 20 to 9220 ± 90 $^{14}$C yrs BP (11,206–11,247 to 10,225–10,648 cal BP), the proportions of short, tall, and cool-season grasses were relatively balanced. As time progressed, the percentage of short-grass pollen increased and that of tall-grass pollen declined, with cool-season grasses peaking around 8830 ± 130 $^{14}$C yrs BP (9557–10,196 cal BP). Diatoms and sponge spicules present only in the lowest sample indicated abundant local moisture around 9820 ± 20 $^{14}$C yrs BP (11,220–11,240 cal BP). Based on various pollen characteristics throughout the samples, the researchers interpreted the deposits as largely resulting from summer floods. Overall, Cummings and colleagues (2007:96–97) described the Cody-aged paleoenvironment as "dominated by more tall and mid-grasses, more deciduous arboreal species, and a thicker understory along Medicine Creek than at present," and conclude that the upland prairie "would have provided an excellent habitat for a variety of game animals."

Of the three sites, the Allen site is located closest to the main channel of Medicine Creek. The Intermediate Zone (IZ) is estimated to date between roughly 10,000 and 9000 $^{14}$C yrs BP (11,600–10,185 cal BP). Warren (2007) noted that six primary species of freshwater mussels that indicate a relatively stable riverine environment were relatively evenly distributed throughout the three main levels at the Allen site (OL1, IZ, OL2) from 10,610 ± 620 to 8430 ± 80 $^{14}$C yrs BP (10,593–13,715 to 9157–9546 cal BP). Warren concluded that hydrological environments during the roughly two millennia represented by the mussels included both a perennial flowing stream with a sandy to gravelly substrate and mud-bottomed, shallow backwater sloughs or oxbow ponds located nearby. This sequence may indicate a possible shift in the stream channel and subsequent reduction in stream flow for the abandoned oxbow. Zalucha (2007) analyzed macrobotanical remains from the IZ at the Allen site and concluded that a mesic gallery forest with *Morus rubra* (red mulberry), *Ulmus* spp. (elm), and *Celtis/Morus/Ulmus* (probably hackberry) existed along Medicine Creek with a species diversity that was greater than what is present today.

*Summary*

Throughout the study area at this time there are some indications that seasonality was slightly more pronounced than modern conditions. The overall trends indicate that grassland and riparian species productivity was very good throughout the Rocky Mountain foothills and Plains and could have supported a diverse fauna. The floral resources present in well-developed riparian habitats and along drainages throughout the study area would have provided abundant plant and wood resources for Cody peoples. Cody sites at Horner II, Medicine Lodge Creek, Hudson-Meng, and Lime Creek all indicate a preference for mesic to hydric settings near freshwater and with (presumably) abundant plant and wood resources.

### *9500 to 9000 $^{14}$C yrs BP (10,770–10,185 cal BP)*

For the period 9500 to 9000 $^{14}$C yrs BP (10,770–10,185 cal BP), paleoenvironmental data are drawn from 48 sites with 12 located in foothills-mountain settings and the remainder on the Plains (Figure 2.3, Table 2.1). Of these sites, Cody occupations during this period occur at Medicine Lodge Creek, Hell Gap, Jurgens, Nelson, Olsen-Chubbuck, Jerry Craig, and probably Hudson-Meng. The Carter/Kerr-McGee site probably also dates to this period, although exact radiocarbon dates are lacking for the bonebed.

*Regional Summary*

Pollen data, supplemented with faunal analyses, for sites in the Central Rocky Mountains and intermountain basins of Wyoming indicate a generally mesic moisture regime that shifted to drier conditions during this interval with some indications that summers may have been slightly warmer than modern (Fall et al. 1995; Larson 1992; Walker 1987a; Whitlock et al. 1995). Geomorphology, fauna, and gastropod data from Horner record a brief drying period followed by a return to wetter conditions (Evanoff 1987; Reider 1987; Walker 1987b). Geomorphological and pollen studies at Finley established that grasslands that could support bison were still present (Hansen 1951; Mayer 2003).

High-elevation sites in the Southern Rocky Mountains of Colorado recorded generally wetter than modern conditions (Benedict 1985; Elias 1996; Fall 1997). Temperature data were not as internally consistent, as Arapaho Pass and the South St. Vrain sites indicated warmer average temperatures, but the Lake Isabelle Delta recorded much colder winters (Benedict 1985; Elias 1996; Fall 1997). The discrepancy may result from localized conditions recorded by the fossil beetles at Lake Isabelle Delta, conditions that were not recorded in the macrobotanical, pollen, and stratigraphic data at the other two sites.

At lower-elevation sites associated with the Front Range and intermountain basins of the Southern Rocky Mountains in Colorado, data generally indicate that conditions were wetter than modern and that local vegetation included shrubs and trees (Graham 1987; Haynes and Agogino 1960; Richings-Germain 2002; Surovell et al. 2000). The overall pattern for Rocky Mountain settings suggests that moisture was consistently available but that temperature trends may have fluctuated more rapidly during this 500-radocarbon-year period. Estimates for seasonality are difficult to derive based on somewhat

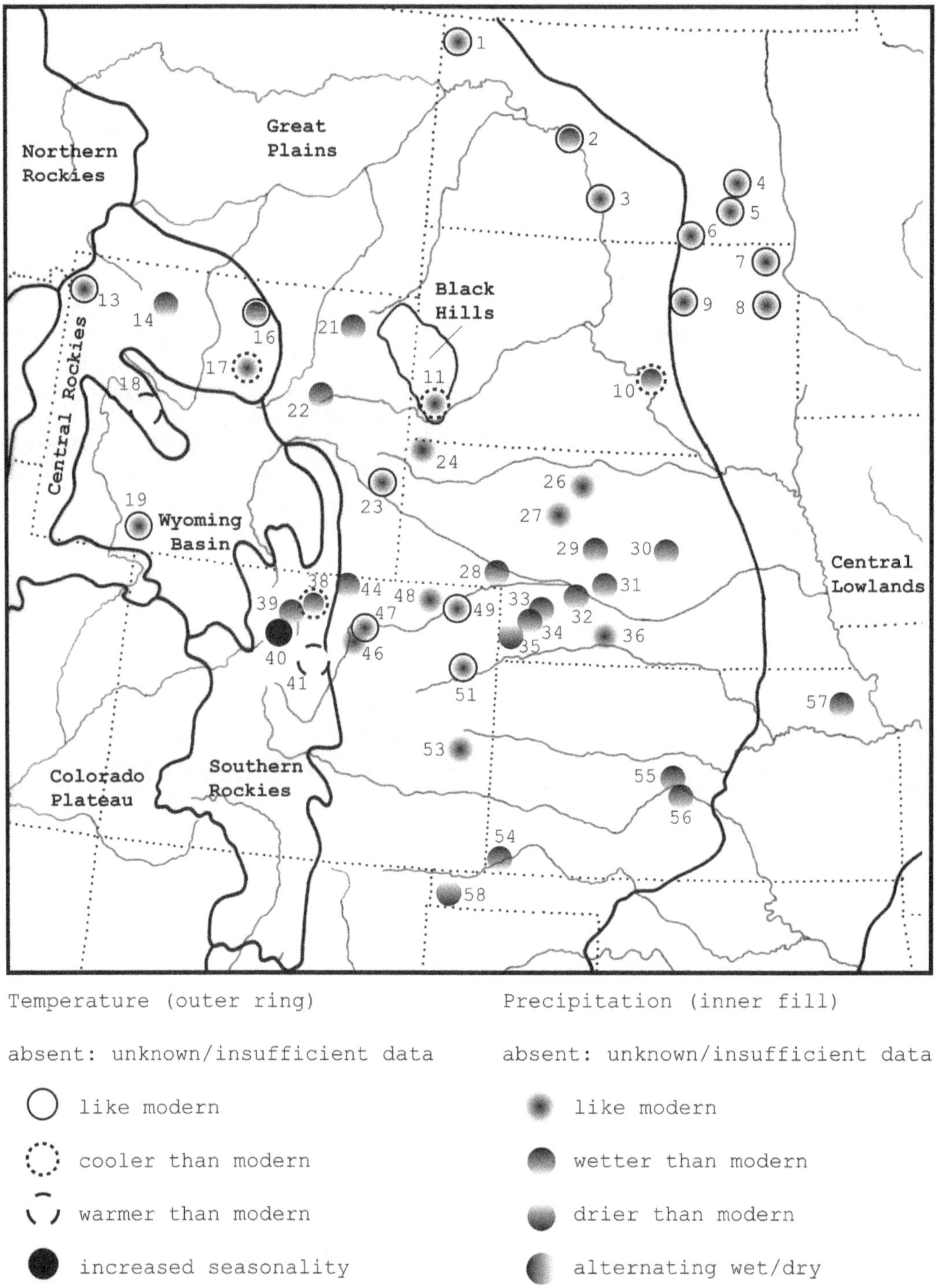


**FIGURE 2.3.** Paleoenvironmental precipitation and temperature sample: 9500–9000 $^{14}$C yrs BP.

mixed results. The data indicate that winter snowfall probably remained quite adequate to maintain streams fed with runoff for much of the year. This is important because adequate snowmelt runoff is required to maintain riparian ecosystems on the High Plains. Markgraf and Lennon (1986) noted that Antelope Playa documents increasing moisture with stable floral communities in the Thunder Basin. In the southern Black Hills, Wind Cave demonstrates predominantly cooler $C_3$ grasses with warmer-climate $C_4$ grasses increasing throughout the period (Fredlund and Tieszen 1997). The overall paleoenvironmental conditions indicate that generally floral and faunal resource availability for Cody groups was probably quite good in the foothill-mountain settings of the Colorado and Wyoming Rockies, but perhaps less so in the more arid southern Black Hills.

In the case of the Plains, the majority of sample locales recorded conditions that were similar to modern in terms of precipitation and temperature with many instances of increasing aridity as grasslands continued to expand. At Kettle Lake, Grimm and colleagues (2011) noted a major drought early in the period, although generally there was good evidence for abundant winter precipitation and warm dry summers. Mason and colleagues (2008:1781) document decreased effective moisture at Rattlesnake Buttes with a "relatively rapid shift toward a drier climate and much greater dust influx." A variety of data from pollen, macrobotanical remains, isotopes, diatoms, and geochemistry indicate that the cluster of lakes and ponds on the eastern side of North and South Dakota underwent lowering lake levels with increasing grasslands and decreasing deciduous tree stands during this interval (Yansa 2007). In contrast, the geomorphological data from both Aggie Brown Coulee and Crow Creek show evidence of a stable, aggrading soil likely resultant from consistently mesic conditions during this same time frame (Clayton et al. 1976; Coogan 1987).

Throughout central Nebraska and Kansas, geomorphological studies of the Brady soil (Jacobs and Mason 2004) document increased effective precipitation (compared with modern conditions) and grasslands with woody vegetation and infrequent fire regime. Pollen and macrobotanical analyses at Muscotah Marsh (Grüger 1973) also recorded mesic conditions with marsh and *Quercus-Carya* (oak-hickory) gallery forest in the lowland and an herbaceous prairie on the uplands. Other locales such as Merritt and Whitman reservoirs (Forman et al. 2001) and Lime Creek (Cummings et al. 2007) demonstrate stable grassland vegetation early in this period that presumably reflects relatively stable precipitation patterns that were probably similar to modern conditions.

Sites on the western Plains such as Kersey Road (Forman et al. 1992), Sterling Dune (Madole 1995), and Nall (Labelle et al. 2003) document oscillations between periods of aridity with eolian deposition and periods of surface stability with increased moisture resulting in soil development and ponded sediments. However, the sites that record significant aridity are in the minority and appear isolated compared with the region as a whole. Overall, water availability was generally good throughout the study area, and grassland productivity was consistently at a level that would have supported stable faunal populations throughout much of the Plains. At those locations that showed locally arid conditions, grassland productivity should have been relatively reduced. At sites that recorded the reactivation of dune fields, grassland productivity must have been extremely low and faunal and floral resources were probably not reliably available to Cody groups.

For the Plains locations with temperature data, cool-season grasses still predominated but warm-season species began to appear as far north as the southern Black Hills (Cummings et al. 2007; Fredlund and Tieszen 1997). This shift in grass types would have affected the nutritional quality of grassland forage for many Plains artiodactyls (Bamforth 1988).

Kutzbach and colleagues (1998) presented a general circulation model (CCM1) focused primarily on the Northern Hemisphere for the last 21,000 years. Although such a coarse-grained model is not capable of reflecting the subregional paleoenvironmental trends presented here, the results provide a modeled context for understanding the trends observed in the current study. Kutzbach and colleagues (1998) noted that during the Holocene the period of maximum summer insolation (resultant from orbital forcing) for North America occurred between 11,000 and 10,000 calendar years ago (~9560–8877 $^{14}$C yrs BP).

The CCM1 model estimated the maximum insolation at about 8 percent higher than modern conditions. At around 11,000 calendar years ago (~9560 $^{14}$C yrs BP), the CCM1 model (at 95 percent confidence) also estimated summer average temperatures for 30–60°N latitude between 2 and 4°C warmer than modern, with average winter temperatures 2–5°C colder than modern (Kutzbach et al. 1998:493). For these same latitudes at this time, CCM1 values for summertime Precipitation – Evaporation are generally lower than modern and significantly lower in July, resulting in less effective moisture. The reconstructed biome for this period does not differ significantly from modern, but the authors noted that for the mid-latitudes "warm grass/shrub expands at the expense of both forest biomes (implying a reduction in available moisture) and of cool grass/shrub (implying summer warming)" (Kutzbach et al. 1998:493).

Bartlein and colleagues (1998) used the CCM1 results to more carefully analyze the climatic history of North America. At 11,000 calendar years ago (~9560 $^{14}$C yrs BP), the researchers estimated that average January precipitation ranged from 10 to 50 mm throughout the study area with the lowest values in the Rocky Mountains, while July values ranged from 10 to 100 mm with the highest values in the central and northeastern Great Plains (Bartlein et al. 1998:556). January temperatures ranged from +5°C (41°F) in the southern part of the study area to -25°C (-13°F) in the northern; average July temperatures ranged from 20 to 35°C (68–95°F), with the hottest region located in the central and southern Great Plains (Bartlein et al. 1998:555). Compared with the summarized proxy data presented above, the modeled CCM1 temperature and precipitation values seem warmer and drier than expected. The timing of the trend described by the CCM1 model seems better reflected in the later datasets described below.

*Cody Complex Occupations*

The most northerly site in the Plains portion of the study area with a Cody occupation is the Carter/Kerr-McGee site (CKM), located in the Powder River Basin. Cody peoples hunted and butchered a group of bison here between 9390 and 8750 $^{14}$C yrs BP (10,660–9675 cal BP), and the site also includes Goshen, Folsom, and Hell Gap–Agate Basin levels (Frison 1984, 1991). Reider's (1990) analysis of the soil profile at the site indicated that from 9500 to 9000 $^{14}$C yrs BP (10,770–10,185 cal BP) the climate was so moist that local soils were often saturated with water. Reider also concluded that local vegetation was dominated by grasses, sedges, and perhaps even scattered woodland (possibly including aspen) along the streams with sagebrush predominating on the uplands.

To the south, at the Hell Gap site in eastern Wyoming, an Alberta occupation at Locality I was dated between 10,560 ± 80 and 9410 ± 95 $^{14}$C yrs BP (12,149–12,655 and 10,300–11,083 cal BP) while an Eden-Scottsbluff occupation overlying it was dated to 9210 ± 490 $^{14}$C yrs BP (9139–11,971 cal BP) (Haynes 2009). Walker's (2009) analysis of the rodent fauna from Locality I and geomorphological analyses of sediments throughout the site indicated that essentially modern environmental conditions were achieved by 9500 $^{14}$C yrs BP. Walker (2009) analyzed small mammals recovered from fine screening sediment samples from Locality I and reported that the fauna was dominated by such grassland species as *Microtus ochrogaster* (prairie vole) and *Lemmiscus curtatus* (sagebrush vole). These species indicate that environmental conditions after 11,000 $^{14}$C yrs BP were similar to today. Walker (2009:433) stated that while it was possible that forest cover may have been somewhat denser farther into the Hartville Uplift (away from Hell Gap) than it currently is, "the modern environment, habitat, and associated mammalian faunas were well established over the region before 11,000 yr BP [$^{14}$C yrs]. This wide-open view shed over the adjacent shortgrass prairie would have been present throughout the human occupation of the Hell Gap site."

Geomorphological analyses (Miller and Goldberg 2009; Reider 2009) at Localities I, II, and V at Hell Gap recognized four distinct paleosols at the site. The oldest was soil 5, which Reider reported as associated with the Folsom–Midland–Agate Basin occupations at Locality I. Soil 5 indicated the presence of a wet meadow that was fed by local springs in an environment that was much cooler and wetter than modern conditions. Overlying soil 5 are soils 4 and 3, each of which consists of weakly developed A horizons directly over parent C horizons. Soils 4 and 3 developed during and slightly after the Cody complex occupations, as indicated by the youngest radiocarbon date from soil 5 (10,360 ± 260 $^{14}$C yrs BP; 11,270–12,667 cal BP) and the presence of a Scottsbluff point recovered from the C horizon of soil 3. Reider identified soils 4 and 3 as Fluvent soils that developed in alluvial deposits and represent periods of brief stability during a relatively active period of sediment deposition at the site. Reider also noted a significant increase in alkalinity for soils 4 and 3 when compared with soil 5, and a prominent amount of sodium in soils 4, 3, and 2. This indicated to him that during the transition from soil 5 to soils 4 and 3, the local environment at Hell Gap was shifting from a cool wet meadow to a drier moisture regime, with the apex of the drying trend culminating in soil 2, which developed at about 6000 $^{14}$C yrs BP. Furthermore, the increased sodium deposits signified reduced spring activity, as the through-flow of water was not sufficient enough to leach the salts from the paleosols. Although the general trend exhibited by the Hell Gap paleosols indicated a shift from a cool-wet environment to a somewhat drier climate, Reider (2009:71) stated that the Cody-aged deposits may also mark the "alternation of climatic regimes." This is an important distinction because if the local environment alternated between wet and dry moisture regimes, the long-term faunal record might still record the relative stability noted by Walker (2009). Considering that the initial environment that created soil 5 was much cooler and wetter than modern conditions, the slight drying trend noted for the Cody period could still have approximated modern conditions. Miller and Goldberg (2009:86) noted that "the formation of an incipient calcic horizon and the evidence for a prairie fire suggest that by 9500 BP [$^{14}$C yrs] the Hell Gap valley was . . . probably comparable to the modern environment in Hell Gap." The Alberta occupants who likely visited the site between about 9500 and 9000 $^{14}$C yrs BP (10,770–10,185 cal BP) probably utilized a relatively moist, well-wooded environment that bordered extensive short-grass plains to the east.

Hudson-Meng has two or three archaeological components that date to the first half of this period and may belong to the Cody complex, but they currently lack culturally diagnostic artifacts. A comparison of data from Hudson-Meng in northwestern Nebraska with the Red Smoke and Lime Creek sites on Medicine Creek in southwestern Nebraska serves as an example of how precipitation patterns on the central Plains differed within the study area. The paleoenvironmental data at Medicine Creek indicated that the area experienced both seasonal flooding and an overall shift to drier conditions (Cummings et al. 2007). The phytoliths and stratigraphy at Hudson-Meng indicate a different pattern of precipitation. Hudson-Meng lacks alluvial or colluvial strata resultant from localized floods. Additionally, abundant tall grasses and festucoid (humid) grass phytoliths recovered at Hudson-Meng indicate that the area received adequate precipitation during the critical season of grass growth (Lewis 1978). The precipitation data from throughout the study area suggest that even though moisture was available at levels adequate to maintain productive grasslands throughout much of the Plains, the sources and timing of precipitation (e.g., snowmelt runoff from the Rocky Mountains, spring rain or snow, and summer rains) may have been quite variable.

The Jurgens site is located along the south margin of the South Platte River channel and had a large Cody occupation dated at 9070 ± 90 $^{14}$C yrs BP (9917–10,495 cal BP) (Wheat 1972). Wheat (1972) identified three areas at the site that record butchering of more than 60 bison and other ungulates and fur-bearing mammals, as well as areas of stone tool manufacture and maintenance and craft activities. Scott (1979) conducted a pollen analysis on four sediment samples collected from varying depths at Area 3, but only one contained enough pollen to reach a minimum 200 grain count. Scott listed *Ambrosia* (ragweed), *Artemisia*, Chenopodiaceae, Amaranthaceae, Compositae, Graminae (grass), *Opuntia* (prickly pear cactus), and *Umbelliferae* (cowslip) as constituting 90 percent of the pollen sample, with *Alnus*, *Betula* or *Corylus* (hazel), *Picea*, and *Pinus* making up a much smaller percentage that likely blew into the site from the nearby foothills to the west. Scott also observed *Populus* (poplar) pollen, which she felt was probably present at the time of the occupation since it does not preserve well when transported for any considerable distance. Scott (1979:151) interpreted the paleoenvironment at Jurgens as an "open habitat, exhibiting an environment very similar to that which existed prior to extensive cultivation in the area.... The pollen types present indicate not only open habitat-type environment, but also disturbance of the soil. The pollen types do not define whether the disturbance is due to man or natural factors." The strong presence of *Artemisia* and *Ambrosia* indicated that there was considerable soil moisture at some depth, which may have resulted from the South Platte River channel holding water and being close to the site. Finally, modern *Zea* (corn) pollen makes up 2 percent of the level-five sample, which was the deepest of all the samples, collected 83 cm below the unit datum. The presence of corn pollen at such a depth raises the question of contamination of the samples by modern pollen and is presented here as a caution to interpreting these data as directly representative of the Cody-age local environment.

The Nelson site is also located in northeastern Colorado and was dated to 9260 ± 20 $^{14}$C yrs BP (10,299–10,542 cal BP) (Kornfeld et al. 2010). Stanford (1999:321) described the hunting strategy at Nelson, where the bison herd was driven into a steep arroyo, as similar to that used at Frasca and Olsen-Chubbuck. Although the presence of a hunted bison herd at Nelson is at best indirect evidence of the paleoenvironment, it implies that grassland productivity in the region was sufficient to support bison. This pattern is consistent with other sites in the region such as Jurgens, Sterling Dune Field, and Dankworth Canyon.

Leopold and Wheat (1972) presented the results of a pollen analysis for the Olsen-Chubbuck bison kill, redated to 9395 ± 20 $^{14}$C yrs BP (10,571–10,690 cal BP) (Holliday et al. 1999). Although poor preservation severely hampered the interpretation of the paleoclimate, the authors were able to make some general observations. Regarding the sediment that filled the very bottom of the arroyo, and into which the deepest bison remains were deposited, Leopold and Wheat (1972:178–180) stated that it "suggested a very moist microenvironment, perhaps with mosses...fed by seeps" and that such small springs "probably are indicative of the general climatic pattern." Leopold and Wheat (1972:180) went on to write:

> It appears that pine pollen is relatively better represented at the site during the late Wisconsin than after the time of the bison kill, and than now. From our studies of modern pollen rain in eastern Colorado, this change may reflect the greater proximity of the foothill pine stands to the fossil site in Wisconsin time than since. On the other hand, selective preservation of the hardier types (pine) may have altered the original pollen assemblages.

The researchers concluded that while the site of the actual bison kill appeared to be consistently wet, the surrounding uplands were probably dominated by short grasses under a drier moisture regime.

Finally, soil (Richings-Germain 2002) and pollen (Cummings and Moutoux 1998; Richings-Germain 2002) analyses were conducted for the Jerry Craig site, which is a Cody bison kill located at 2475 m elevation in Middle Park, Colorado. The kill is dated to 9290 ± 50 and 9310 ± 50 $^{14}$C yrs BP (10,285–10,647 and 10,298–10,661 cal BP), and analysis of dentition determined that the bonebed represents at least five bison that were killed during the late summer or early fall (Hill and Kornfeld 1999; Richings-Germain 2002; Surovell et al. 2000). Analysts concluded that during or just after the Cody occupation, the slope where the bison kill was made was well wooded with spruce and oak and there was some pine and sagebrush present in the area as well. Overall, the local Middle Park environment was more humid than modern conditions with active springs and dense stands of pine, spruce, juniper, fir, oak, and sage (Richings-Germain 2002; Surovell et al. 2000).

In general, the distribution of primary resources for Cody peoples (water, wood, plants, and animals) was beginning to shift from what had been a relatively homogeneous distribution across the study area before 9500 $^{14}$C yrs BP (10,770–10,710 cal BP) to a slightly more heterogeneous one before 9000 $^{14}$C yrs BP (10,185–10,220 cal BP). A commonality for the Cody occupations during this period at CKM, Jurgens, Olsen-Chubbuck, Jerry Craig, probably Hudson-Meng, and possibly Hell Gap is that they all took advantage of well-watered and often wooded local environments that were adjacent to extensive grasslands. The fact that every one of these sites also contained evidence of bison hunting (with Jurgens containing a wide variety of other animals) underscores the fact that these ecotonal settings supported artiodactyl and small-game populations.

### *9000 to 8500 $^{14}$C yrs BP (10,220–9490 cal BP)*

For the period spanning 9000 to 8500 $^{14}$C yrs BP (10,220–9490 cal BP), paleoenvironmental data were compiled from 47 sites, 16 from the Rocky Mountains, foothills, and intermountain basins and the remainder in Great Plains settings (Figure 2.4, Table 2.1). Of the total sample, Cody occupations occur at Horner, Finley, Hell Gap, Claypool, Frasca, Lamb Spring, Scottsbluff, Lime Creek, and possibly CKM, given the range of dates.

#### *Regional Summary*

The drying trend that began during the previous period continued and intensified throughout much of the study area between 9000 and 8500 $^{14}$C yrs BP (10,220–9490 cal BP). In the Central Rocky Mountains of Wyoming, temperature data from Temple Lake Valley (Fall et al. 1995) indicated that summers were slightly warmer than modern. While the Loon Lake locale recorded a continued drying trend (Whitlock et al. 1995), the Horner site experienced wet conditions with abundant vegetation (Reider 1987; Walker 1987b). Data from the South St. Vrain Valley (Fall 1997), Arapaho Pass (Benedict 1985), Ironbog and Alkali Basin (Fall 1997), and Jerry Craig (Cummings and Moutoux 1998) in the Southern Rocky Mountains of Colorado all recorded warmer than modern temperatures. La Poudre Pass and Lake Isabel Delta, also in the Colorado Rocky Mountains, recorded slightly warmer than modern summer temperatures but much colder winters—as much as 13.6 to 15.3°C colder (Elias 1996). However, these colder temperatures were determined from fossil beetle assemblages that may have responded to localized conditions rather than larger regional trends. For example, Arapaho Pass indicated that at least some Front Range glaciers were not maintained over the summer months (Benedict 1985). While South St. Vrain Valley, Ironbog, and Alkali Basin all recorded wetter than modern conditions (Fall 1997), vegetation at the Jerry Craig site shifted to species that favored drier conditions (Cummings and Moutoux 1998; Richings-Germain 2002; Surovell et al. 2000).

For the intermountain basin and foothills settings in the western and central portions of the study area, Finley (Mayer 2003), Ferris Dune Field (Stokes and Gaylord 1993), Antelope Playa (Markgraf and Lennon 1986), Wind Cave National Park (Fredlund and Tieszen 1997), and Hell Gap (Haynes 2009; Reider 2009; Walker 2009) all recorded episodes of drying that generally occurred closer to 8500 $^{14}$C yrs BP (9490–9530 cal BP). However, because many of these locations began with moisture regimes that were wetter than modern conditions, the drying trend was a relative one and only the Ferris Dune Field documented active eolian deposition. The significant increase in warm-season $C_4$ grasses at Wind Cave National Park in the southern Black Hills (Fredlund and Tieszen 1997) is an important indication of the geographic shift in grassland composition as far north as South Dakota.

On the northern Plains the North Dakota study sites continued the general trend noted for the previous interval. Lakes and ponds on the eastern plains of this area demonstrated lowering lake levels with surrounding grasslands that in some locations became more arid (Yansa 2007). Merritt and Whitman reservoirs in north-central Nebraska (Forman et al. 2001) and the Red Smoke site in south-central Nebraska (Cummings et al. 2007) characterize the period as one of increasing aridity with localized mesic-hydric conditions in catchment basins and a significant shift from tall to short grasses, respectively. The cluster of seven sites between Whitman and Merritt reservoirs and Medicine Creek provide a different signal based on geomorphological data, as they maintain generally mesic conditions with stable grasslands and landscape stability (Jacobs and Mason 2004).

Paleoenvironmental conditions in the southern portion of the Plains study area were more mixed than the northern sites. Throughout Kansas there is good evidence for mesic to hydric conditions with landscape stability and soil development (Forman et al. 2001; Fredlund 1995; Grüger 1973; Mandel and Hofman 2003). On the western side of the Plains, Hoover Blowout (Forman et al. 2001) and Kersey Road (Forman et al. 1995) were very dry with active dune fields and eolian deposition. The Hudson Dune Field experienced fluctuations in the local moisture regime and eventually ended the period drier than it began (Forman

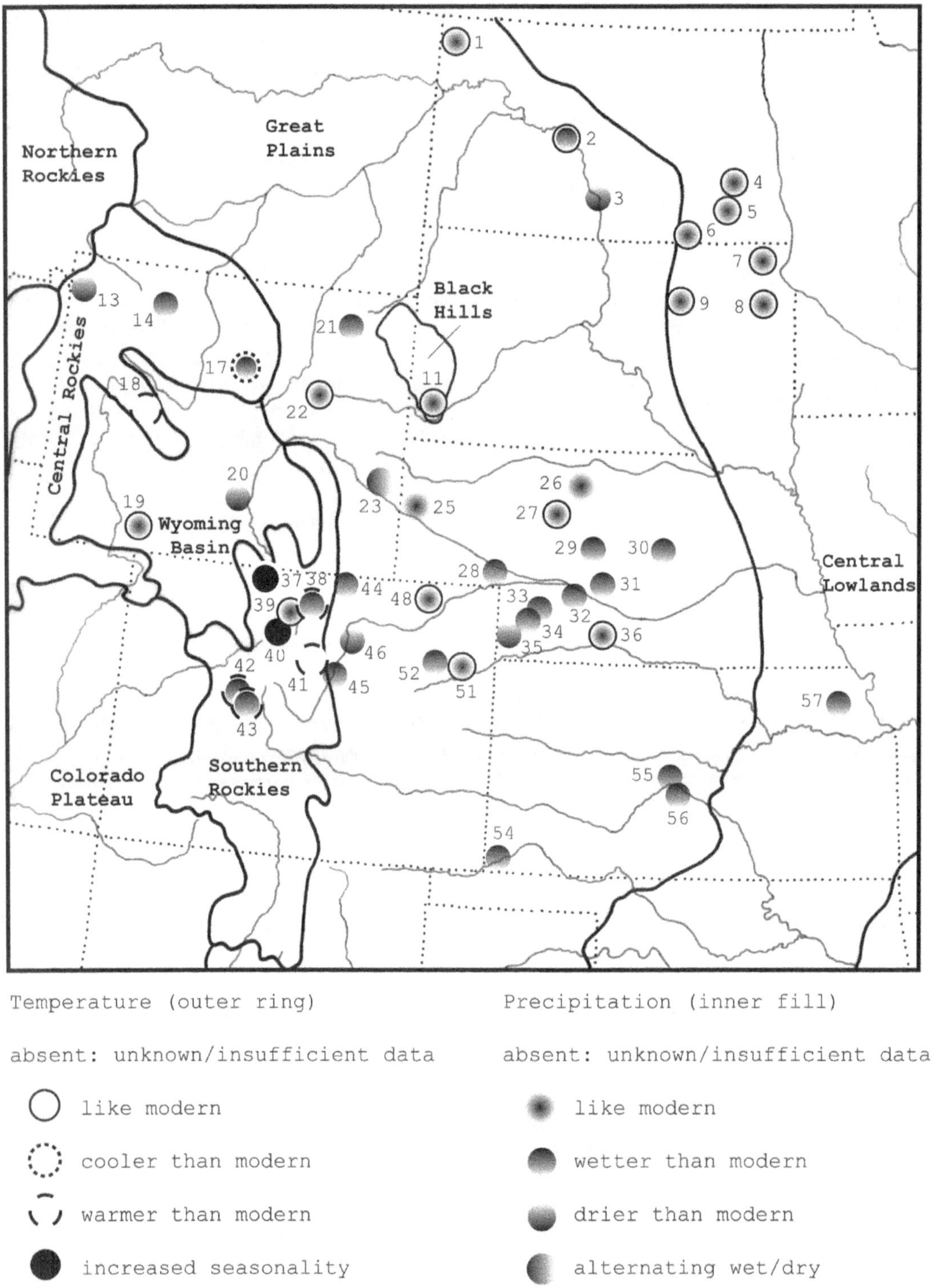


FIGURE 2.4. Paleoenvironmental precipitation and temperature sample: 9000–8500 $^{14}$C yrs BP.

et al. 1995). However, Claypool (Reider 1990) and Lamb Spring (Rancier et al. 1982; Stanford et al. 1981) documented conditions that were wetter than modern, and based on the faunal record, Frasca was probably relatively similar to modern conditions (Fulgham and Stanford 1982).

The paleoenvironmental reconstruction made by Forman and others (1995) at the Kersey Road locale is an instructive illustration of the positive feedback that can develop as a result of overgrazing by bison during periods of sustained aridity. Compared with historic droughts, Forman and others (1995) estimated that the degree of dune activation at Kersey Road indicated that repeated periods of drying and full drought conditions must have occurred on the order of a decade or greater between about 8900 and 8500 $^{14}$C yrs BP (10,165–9490 cal BP). The common presence of bison tracks in the eolian stratigraphy indicated that herds were active in the area during this time, and the researchers interpreted the resulting scenario as analogous to the process of desertification observed at the Jornada Experimental Range in New Mexico (Forman et al. 1995). The authors postulated that continued grazing by bison herds during this drying period accelerated and extended ground surface disturbance by trampling and overgrazing, which resulted in increased land surface heating, thus augmenting and maintaining locally arid conditions. With increased erosion of topsoil and loss of vegetation in the Hudson Dune Field local environment, a positive feedback was created in which precipitation was less effectively absorbed, further increasing surface sediment runoff and the removal of soil nutrients (Forman et al. 1995). While this detailed reconstruction was developed based on data from the Kersey Road site and the Jornada Experimental Range, the basic mechanism is applicable to other dune settings in the Plains and may have been more prevalent throughout the region than we currently have the data to document. The magnitude of the drying/drought conditions (>10 years) identified by the researchers would deter Cody use of the area during this period.

For Rocky Mountain settings, warmer temperatures combined with increased moisture may have resulted in early peak runoff for streams that drain the mountains across the Plains to the east. A lack of adequate snowpack maintained throughout the spring and summer results in steady declines in stream flow as runoff dries up during the summer months. While consistent summer rains may counteract reduced snowpack runoff, the paleoclimate data for the Plains suggests that summer rain did not fall evenly across the study area between 9000 and 8500 $^{14}$C yrs BP (10,220–9490 cal BP). The active dune fields in eastern Colorado and western Nebraska, and the consistent drying trend noted for many of the northern Plains locations, indicate that precipitation was becoming less frequent and more scattered throughout the region. However, data from the central and southern study sites indicate that mesic moisture regimes were maintained in many locations (Table 2.1, Figure 2.4).

*Cody Complex Occupations*

Reider (1987) analyzed soil 2 at Horner I, which is associated with the late fall to early winter Cody occupation dated at 8750 ± 120 and 8840 ± 140 $^{14}$C yrs BP (9540–10,157 and 9555–10,214 cal BP). Reider reported that the soil 2 characteristics were consistent with either a Haplaquoll or an Aquept, both of which form around the margins of ponds or wet meadows. This indicated that the Horner I environment was very similar to the older Horner II environment. The Horner I local setting was predominantly wooded or shrubby with increased moisture compared with modern conditions.

Frison (1991) reported two radiocarbon dates for Finley: 8950 ± 220 and 9026 ± 118 $^{14}$C yrs BP (9528–10,583 and 9744–10,495 cal BP). Mayer (2003) was unsure if the occupation occurred on a rather unconsolidated surface undergoing active sediment deposition or on a stable surface that was subsequently exposed to renewed deposition and soil development. Mayer (2003:63) noted "an increase in evaporation rates, resulting in the accumulation of carbonates, gypsum, and other soluble salts in the subsoil in and around interdunal areas," which likely resulted from decreased moisture, increased temperature, or a combination of the two. Even with this drying trend, Mayer (2003:64) noted that the overall moisture conditions at Finley were sufficient to maintain bison and human populations in the local area, and he stated that "while conditions were becoming increasingly dry, the early Holocene was probably moister than at present, perhaps the result of greater inland penetration of monsoonal flow." Overall, the stability in groundcover vegetation evidenced by Stratum 2, which contained the Cody occupation in its upper portion, appears to have continued throughout this period.

Reider's (1990) analysis of soils at the CKM site and throughout the Powder River Basin indicated that the general moisture level noted for the previous period was maintained after 9000 $^{14}$C yrs BP (10,185–10,220 cal BP) but eventually began to wane. Reider described the soils at the CKM site as Aquoll or Aquoll-like, often containing buried A horizons representing periods of surface stability associated with archaeological occupations, of which the Cody level is one. Aquoll soils generally occur in grasslands with organic-rich mineral surface horizons, frequently in low-lying areas where water collects, and can support a vegetation of grasses, sedges, and forbs (Reider 1990). Generally, Clovis- and Folsom-age Aquolls in the Powder River Basin are more strongly gleyed than Cody-age soils, which, as Reider explained, indicates that water tables were highest during these earlier times with some drying and lowering of water tables sometime after 8700 $^{14}$C yrs BP. The paleo-Aquoll soil that is the surface for the Cody occupation at CKM indicated that the area was water-saturated, and "dominant vegetation was probably grasses, sedges, and perhaps broken woodland, possibly with *Populus tremuloides* (aspen) along streams and sagebrush on uplands" (Reider 1990:337). These vegetation communities were maintained until about 8700 $^{14}$C yrs BP.

During this period at Hell Gap, an Eden occupation occurred at Locality V dated at 8890 ± 110 and 9050 ± 160 $^{14}$C yrs BP (9629–10,235 and 9675–10,642 cal BP) (Haynes 2009). As Walker (2009) noted for the previous millennium, the general environment was very similar to modern plant and animal communities and provided accessible water and wood with extensive grasslands nearby. Reider (2009) identified Fluvent soils that developed at Hell Gap during this period, representing alluvial deposition with brief periods of surface stability. Although the alluvial deposition implied flowing water, the alkaline nature of the soils and substantial sodium indicated to Reider that the local Hell Gap environment was becoming drier in general and may have been alternating between wet and dry moisture regimes. Miller and Goldberg (2009) noted that the Eden-Scottsbluff-bearing deposit of stratum $E_5$ was eventually buried by the following stratum F, which continued until about 8000 $^{14}$C yrs BP. Stratum F demonstrated more pronounced soil formation and may have represented a longer period of stability relative to the older Cody complex–aged surface.

Reider's (1990) analysis of the paleosols at Claypool provides some clues about the paleoenvironment in northeastern Colorado. Reider recognized a Cody-aged soil horizon which he estimated to date between 9000 and 8000 $^{14}$C yrs BP and which was related to soil development at other Cody sites:

> The strong development of the Cody-age soil at Claypool as measured by its dark, thick A horizon (77 cm) and compared to the weaker surface soil is evidence that the Cody-age soil formed under wetter conditions than those at the site currently or within the last several thousand years. Lush grasses could have stabilized late Pleistocene sheet sands and contributed to the formation of the thick, brown (10YR4/3, 6/3) A horizon. This probably happened somewhat during Cody occupation, but also following their occupation because the A horizon at Claypool lies above the cultural level, as does part of the Calciaquoll at the Horner site. The humid conditions and lush prairies implied by the Cody-age soil at Claypool may explain the existence of the large bison populations that these groups hunted. The climatic conditions appear to conform to the relatively humid conditions seen for Cody occupations at the Carter/Kerr-McGee site discussed previously, and for the Finley site as interpreted by Moss (1951) [Reider 1990:343].

Based on a region-wide model of climate and soil development, Reider suggested that the similarity between the soils at the three sites (Claypool, Finley, Horner) may narrow the timing of the Claypool occupation to between 9000 and 8500 $^{14}$C yrs BP, although the effects of local microenvironmental variability complicate this interpretation.

To the northwest of Claypool, the Frasca site offers only minimal data based on grassland requirements for bison herds. Fulgham and Stanford (1982:5) reported that the Frasca site contained two distinct bonebeds (Areas 1 and 2) that indicated the site was an early–midwinter Cody bison kill (Fulgham and Stanford 1982). The Area 1 bonebed contained the remains of at least 56 bison dated to 8910 ± 90 $^{14}$C yrs BP (9704–10,230 cal BP) (Fulgham and Stanford 1982:8). The site is located along the base of a dissected upland that borders Pawnee Creek. Based on conditions required to support a herd of bison during early to midwinter, the local habitat probably consisted of a well-developed grassland on the uplands with some water in Pawnee Creek. This interpretation is based on ecological assumptions rather than direct environmental data, however, and should be considered an estimate.

South of Denver, Colorado, at the Lamb Spring site, a Cody bison kill of at least 30 animals was dated at 8870 ± 350 $^{14}$C yrs BP (9034–11,068 cal BP) (McCartney 1990; Rancier et al. 1982:12; Stanford et al. 1981). Based on fetal bison remains, Stanford and others (1981) determined that the kill was made during the summer; however, analysis of bison dentition by McCartney (1990:112) indicated a range from early December to late April. Stanford and others (1981:24) described the depositional context of the bison kill as occurring in a channel fill adjacent to the spring, which contained a gleyed soil that "defined the bank of a shallow stream or pond," and went on to write that "gley soil in the channel would suggest boggy ground conditions." Rancier and others (1982:14) described the context of the Cody bison kill as "an early Holocene spring and outflow channel." The combination of gleyed stream or pond deposits and a well-developed, organic-rich buried A horizon just above (Rancier et al. 1982; Stanford et al. 1981) indicates that at the time of the Cody occupation and for some time afterward, Lamb Spring provided abundant water and vegetation that supported bison and probably many other species.

The Scottsbluff site in northwestern Nebraska was first investigated in the 1930s and is the type site for the Scottsbluff projectile point (Barbour and Schultz 1932; Schultz and Eiseley 1935; Wormington 1957). A recent analysis of the Cody-aged bison remains by Hill (2008) identified a minimum of 26 individuals and established dates of 8680 ± 85 and 8939 ± 85 $^{14}$C yrs BP (9500–10,115 and 9744–10,240 cal BP) for the kill event. As discussed by Knudson (this volume) and Schultz and Eiseley (1935), the geomorphology of the deposit indicated that the early Holocene creek bed did not differ greatly from the modern channel configuration. Schultz and Eiseley (1935:317) noted that there was a "definite progression from an abundance of fresh water forms [gastropods] in the bone horizon to an entirely land fauna in the upper layers... suggestive of a gradual climatic change tending toward greater aridity." At Scottsbluff, Cody hunters' use of a wet local environment surrounded by grasslands is consistent with patterns observed elsewhere throughout the region.

Even with the drying trend noted for this period, or perhaps because of it, Cody occupations at Horner, Finley, CKM, Hell Gap, Scottsbluff, Lime Creek, Claypool, and Lamb Spring consistently utilized places that were well watered and shrubby or wooded. The preference for occupying well-watered habitats appeared in the earliest Cody sites and was maintained throughout this period. By selecting locations with a good supply of water and abundant vegetation, Cody groups secured basic resources and accessed locations with greater biotic diversity than the surrounding grasslands. Generally, it appears that the overall distribution of plant, animal, and water resources for Cody peoples continued to become more heterogeneous between 9000 to 8500 $^{14}$C yrs BP (10,220–9490 cal BP) than it had been before. Reduced amounts of stream runoff, less predictable patterns of rainfall, and the reactivation of dune fields situated between otherwise stable and productive grasslands would have resulted in a patchy distribution of good-quality forage for artiodactyls. One outcome of this scenario for Cody groups would be the reduced predictability of bison herd locations and possibly increased mobility for humans (Bamforth 1988). While some resource areas were probably unaffected by these general changes, the overall landscape on the Plains at 8500 $^{14}$C yrs BP looked quite different than it had 500 radiocarbon years earlier.

### *8500 to 8000 $^{14}$C yrs BP (9530–8785 cal BP)*

For the final period in this study, 8500 to 8000 $^{14}$C yrs BP (9530–8785 cal BP), paleoclimate data are available from 37 sites, only nine of which are in

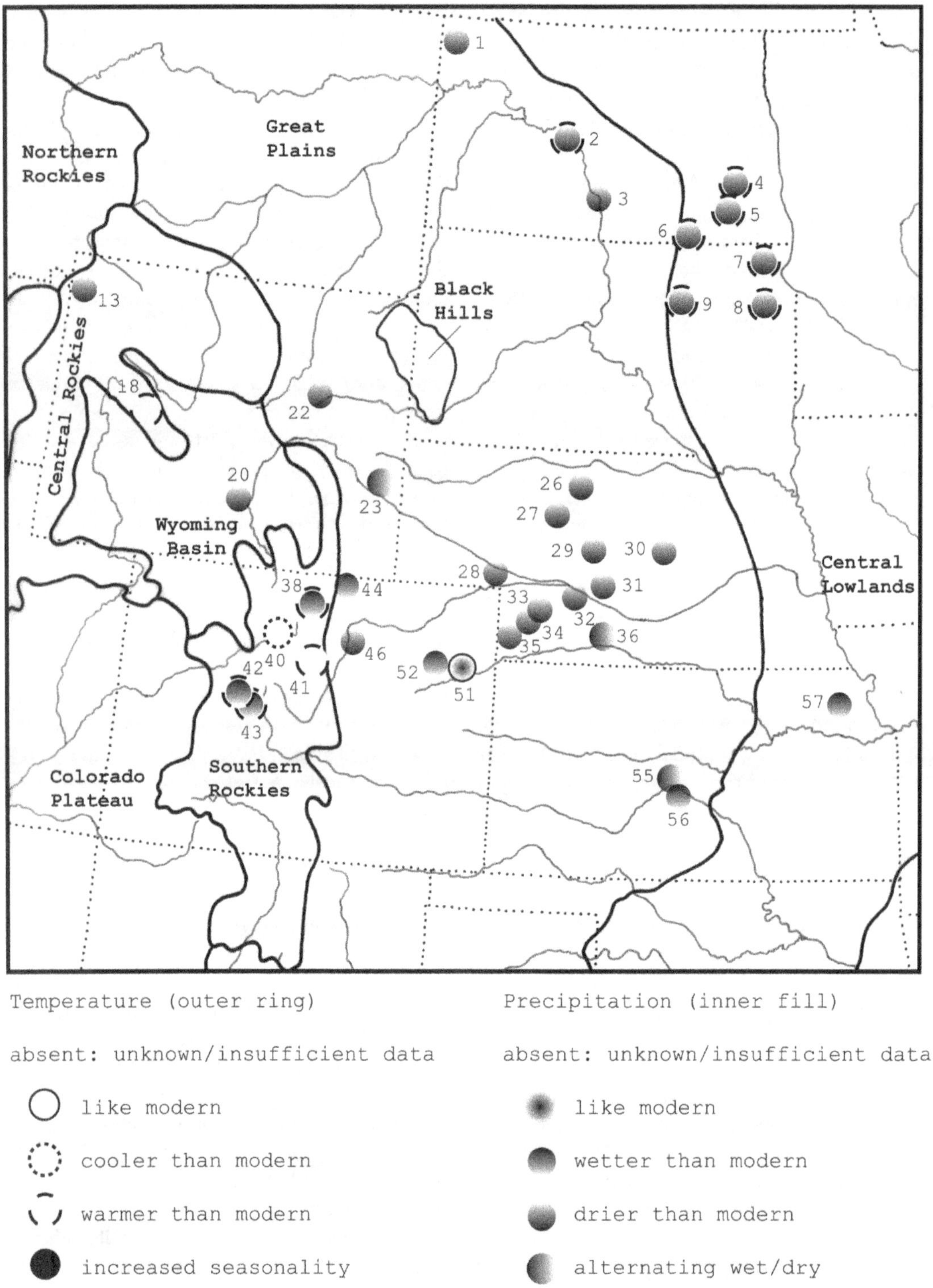


FIGURE 2.5. Paleoenvironmental precipitation and temperature sample: 8500–8000 $^{14}$C yrs BP.

the Rockies or intermountain basins (Figure 2.5, Table 2.1). There are no Cody complex sites dated to this period in the study area.

*Regional Summary*

Pollen data from Central Rocky Mountain sites in Wyoming recorded a continued drying trend (Whitlock et al. 1995) and summers that were somewhat warmer than modern conditions (Fall et al. 1995). In the Southern Rocky Mountains of Colorado, conditions were warmer and wetter at South St. Vrain Valley, Ironbog, and Alkali Basin (Fall 1997). However, on average, Lake Isabelle Delta had slightly colder winters and summers (Elias 1996). As noted earlier, the consistent temperature divergence recorded by the fossil beetle assemblages analyzed by Elias (1996) could possibly be the result of the localized habitat they occupied. The Lindenmeier site in the Front Range foothills recorded moist wet meadow conditions that maintained a thick soil until about 8300 $^{14}$C yrs BP (9400–9270 cal BP).

The Ferris Dune Field experienced dry conditions with active eolian deposition in the Wyoming Basin (Stokes and Gaylord 1993), and at Antelope Playa in the Powder River Basin riparian tree pollen disappeared as this locality became drier than it had been during the previous 1500 radiocarbon years (Markgraf and Lennon 1986). Hell Gap, on the Hartville Uplift, maintained an environment that was similar to modern, with alternating wetter and drier conditions (Haynes 2009; Reider 2009; Walker 2009).

In North Dakota, Grimm and colleagues (2011:15) identified evidence of a "megadrought" between 8250 and 8000 $^{14}$C yrs BP (9290–8785 cal BP) that culminated in the "driest interval of the Holocene" at Kettle Lake. Aggie Brown Coulee (Clayton et al. 1976) and Rattlesnake Buttes (Mason et al. 2008) recorded increasing aridity and temperature in central North Dakota. Yansa (2007) also documented peak aridity occurring just before 8000 $^{14}$C yrs BP (8990–8785 cal BP) for many of the lake sites she analyzed on the northeastern Plains. The significance of this marked aridity signal is underscored by the fact that it was identified by numerous researchers analyzing eight of the 13 different data types used in this study that represent both short-term and long-term responses.

The sites in Nebraska that had previously demonstrated consistent moisture and grassland productivity now show signs of drying. The Brady soil indicated a drier climate with a possible increase in fire regime culminating in the beginning of a regional drought (Jacobs and Mason 2004) near the end of this period. Many locations on the adjacent Colorado plains were dry as well. The Hoover Blowout, Hudson Dune Field, and Kersey Road were all dry with active dunes and eolian deposition (Forman et al. 1995, 2001).

Contrary to this drying trend, Cheyenne Bottoms (Fredlund 1995), Great Bend Sand Prairie (Forman et al. 2001), and Muscotah Marsh (Grüger 1973) in Kansas maintained good water levels and relatively stable vegetation with concomitant soil development. Merritt and Whitman reservoirs in north-central Nebraska have evidence of stabilized (in contrast to active) dune surfaces during this period (Forman et al. 2001). Reider (1990) interpreted the soil development at Claypool in northeastern Colorado as indicating that the site was much wetter than modern conditions and probably supported abundant grasslands.

Based on Rocky Mountain data, winters were generally warmer than they had been during the previous 500-radiocarbon-year period, while summer temperatures stayed about the same. This resulted in a relative decrease in seasonality compared with the previous period. The warmer winter temperatures may have affected high-elevation snowpack development. Predicted reductions in snowpack runoff noted for the previous interval (9000–8500 $^{14}$C yrs BP) would have continued during this period and may have become even more intensified. Rainfall may also have been more sporadic, as indicated by the widespread aridity throughout most of the Plains locations.

## Discussion

This chapter demonstrates that Cody hunter-gatherers regularly selected ecotonal settings that were mesic to hydric, and often spring-fed. Typical examples include an alluvial system or a spring within drier grassland or foothill environments. This observation highlights two important aspects of Cody cultural ecology. First, although bison would be attracted to these settings, such places would also support a wide variety of other faunal and floral subsistence resources. If

Cody hunter-gatherers were strictly bison specialists (also see Hill, this volume), we should expect kill sites to be more evenly dispersed across drier settings away from water sources — but they are not. The observed pattern suggests that we might answer Kornfeld's (2007) question — "Are [Cody complex] Paleoindians of the Great Plains and Rockies subsistence specialists?" — with a resounding "probably not." Second, the combination of bison kills near water sources may be indicative of something other than an ecological relationship between hunter and prey. While springs certainly attracted bison to drink, ready supplies of easily accessible water are also required for tanning their hides (Belitz 1973; Jodry 1999; Mooney 1910). Based on the transported distance of end scrapers and the time stress associated with hide working, I have previously identified this activity as one of the most important aspects of animal processing faced by Cody hunter-gatherers on the Great Plains (Muñiz 2005, this volume [Chapter 10]). The use of natural resources by Cody hunter-gatherers for technological purposes (e.g., hide working, tool making) rather than strictly subsistence pursuits is a critical aspect of their cultural ecology that should not be overlooked.

Overall, the paleoenvironmental data indicate that significant environmental changes began after 8500 $^{14}$C yrs BP (9530–9490 cal BP) that directly impacted Cody resource availability. Although some locales became slightly drier between 10,000 and 9000 $^{14}$C yrs BP (11,600–10,185 cal BP), the initial conditions were generally wetter than modern and many of the local habitats would have remained productive. As the degree of drying increased and the total number of locations that were becoming dry also increased, Cody peoples living after 9000 $^{14}$C yrs BP (10,220–10,185 cal BP) on the northern and central Plains had to deal with dropping lake levels and occasional active dune fields that began to have an impact on the total geographic distribution of edible plants and animals. Places like Kettle Lake, Rattlesnake Buttes, Hoover Blowout, Hudson Dune Field, and Kersey Road experienced decreasing biotic output as drought conditions repeatedly occurred and dunes began to move. Much larger areas of the Plains were still productive, however, and Cody peoples had many alternative subsistence options in adjacent habitats or completely different ecozones.

Between 8500 and 8000 $^{14}$C yrs BP (9530–8785 cal BP), drought conditions and active dunes became even more prominent throughout the northern and central Great Plains. Perhaps the most significant indicator of the severity of this environmental change is the widespread cessation of soil development. The end of Brady and Leonard soil development and resumption of loess deposition observed across much of the Great Plains by 8000 $^{14}$C yrs BP (8785 cal BP) indicates a significant long-term environmental change at a scale unlike any others witnessed by Cody complex groups. Compared with the conditions under which the Cody complex arose, this change could have required a major adaptive response.

Broughton and colleagues' (2008) analysis of early to mid-Holocene fluctuations of artiodactyl populations in the northern Great Basin has important implications for the current study. The researchers determined that artiodactyl populations (specifically *Ovis canadensis*, *Antilocapra americana*, *Odocoileus hemionus*, and *Bison bison*) were depressed because of increased early Holocene seasonality characterized by hot, dry summers and cold, wet winters. Under these conditions, artiodactyls are nutritionally stressed and physically weakened from short growing seasons and harsh winters. Furthermore, the probability of missing relatively short, seasonally determined windows for successful birthing is increased. Byers and Smith (2007) also noted that late Holocene low-amplitude fluctuations in aridity had a greater effect on bison than on pronghorn in the Wyoming Basin. The results of these studies indicate that Plains artiodactyl populations also likely experienced long-term population stress resulting from a period of increased seasonality (peaking around 9000 $^{14}$C yrs BP) followed by reduction in effective moisture after 8500 $^{14}$C yrs BP that activated dune fields and eventually shut down production of the Brady/Leonard soil. In many areas of the northern and central U.S. Great Plains, bison populations must have been affected quite severely by 8000 $^{14}$C yrs BP.

Bamforth's (1988:149) observations regarding the constancy of bison herd movements from season to season and year to year, and the ability of hunters to predict these future movements based on their immediate environmental conditions, offer predictions for what Cody groups on much of the Great Plains experienced beginning around 8500 $^{14}$C yrs BP (9530–9490 cal BP). Under conditions of low moisture availability and low forage production, Bamforth (1988:49–50, 84) predicted that bison herds should have been small (cf. Broughton et al. 2008) and seasonal ranges should have been large. The data reviewed here indicate that these conditions were met in the central and northern regions of the study area after 8500 $^{14}$C yrs BP (9530–9490 cal BP). Under these conditions, bison herd movements should have been more random from season to season and year to year, and compared with earlier times it would have been more difficult for Cody hunters to successfully predict future herd sizes and locations (Bamforth 1988:149). Areas experiencing reactivated dune fields may have even created barriers to movement across certain parts of the Plains. This trend continued and intensified closer to 8000 $^{14}$C yrs BP (8990–8785 cal BP).

The frequency of radiocarbon-dated Cody occupations (see Knell and Muñiz, this volume) shows a single peak occurring between 9500 and 9000 $^{14}$C yrs BP (10,000–9500 $^{14}$C yrs BP = 4; 9500–9000 $^{14}$C yrs BP = 11; 9000–8500 $^{14}$C yrs BP = 8; 8500–8000 $^{14}$C yrs BP = 1) with only MacHaffie dated after 8500 $^{14}$C yrs BP. There are no examples of well-dated Cody complex sites younger than 8000 $^{14}$C yrs BP. After 8500 $^{14}$C yrs BP (9530–9490 cal BP), Cody peoples may have been forced to avoid large areas of central Nebraska, central and southeastern North Dakota, northeastern South Dakota, and parts of northeastern Colorado. More productive resource areas such as the Hartville Uplift, Pine Ridge, Southern Rocky Mountains, central and northeastern Kansas, and southern Nebraska should have been favored instead. Following basic principles of optimal foraging theory, we might expect that after 8500 $^{14}$C yrs BP many Cody groups had to expand their diet breadth, increase return rates by improving some aspect of technology or social organization, or move to more productive resource patches. Did the selection of one or more of these adaptive strategies trigger formal cultural change that ultimately resulted in the disintegration of the Cody complex on the Plains? Are there Cody complex sites that represent a post-8000 $^{14}$C yrs BP adaptation on the northern and central Plains that are deeply buried and yet to be discovered? Do Eastern Woodland sites with Scottsbluff points (and variants) represent a post-8000 $^{14}$C yrs BP adaptation?

## Conclusion

From the data presented here, it is clear that changes in climate and environment were both varied and complex during the first 2800 calendar years of the Holocene. While some high-elevation locations experienced warmer than modern winters, other areas had much colder winters on average. Compared with modern measures of seasonality, early Holocene seasonality appeared to initially decrease between 10,000 and 9500 $^{14}$C yrs BP (11,600–10,710 cal BP), then increase until about 9000 $^{14}$C yrs BP (10,220–10,185 cal BP), and then steadily decrease again throughout the region. This pattern is generally consistent with CCM1 general circulation models (Bartlein et al. 1998; Kutzbach et al. 1998). While temperature certainly influences the environment in important ways, fluctuations in effective moisture may have had a greater impact.

Moisture regimes varied both geographically and temporally. Between 10,000 and 9000 $^{14}$C yrs BP (11,600–10,185 cal BP) most locations were characterized as either mesic or hydric with abundant floral productivity. The complex and continually changing conditions of when and where precipitation fell and how much of it evaporated away after 9000 $^{14}$C yrs BP would have made it increasingly difficult for Cody groups to make repeated long-term (i.e., seasonal to yearly) successful predictions regarding subsistence and mobility strategies. This is especially true after 8500 $^{14}$C yrs BP (9530–9490 cal BP), and as the Cody complex approached 8000 $^{14}$C yrs BP (8990–8785 cal BP) the biotic output for many large areas of the Great Plains was significantly reduced relative to earlier periods. The failure of the Brady and Leonard soils to continue accumulating an A horizon in many locations after 8000 $^{14}$C yrs BP (8990–8785 cal BP) is especially indicative of the immense scale of environmental change at this time. These significant environmental perturbations may have been sufficient to cause equally important technological and social changes to

Cody peoples that eventually resulted in the disintegration of the Cody complex. What is still very unclear, however, is why substantial environmental change on the Great Plains would affect Cody groups living in neighboring regions, such as the Rocky Mountains or Eastern Woodlands. Given the subsistence flexibility demonstrated by Cody peoples during the first 2100 calendar years of the complex, it is puzzling to think that the tradition could not have carried on in ecozones and biomes that were not adversely affected by widespread environmental change. This enigma leads to the possibility that the Great Plains served as a cultural heartland for the Cody complex (see Bamforth, this volume). As environmental change decreased the carrying capacity of large regions of the Plains, the ensuing strategies employed to adapt to new ecological situations may have irreversibly fragmented the previously cohesive cultural complex into a number of derivative archaeological cultures. Without chronological control on Cody (and Hardin) sites in the Eastern Woodlands, we cannot fully evaluate a hypothesis that proposes such a mechanism for the disintegration. Clearly, we need more research focused on this phenomenon to test the ideas presented here and provide a necessary conclusion to the long history of the Cody complex.

## Acknowledgments

Daniel Born analyzed phytoliths from Hudson-Meng for his Geography Master of Science thesis at St. Cloud State University in 2010; data and preliminary interpretations of the results reside in an unpublished manuscript in possession of the author. Lee Newsome kindly identified a charcoal fragment from Hudson-Meng in 2011 before the piece was submitted for radiocarbon dating; the written results are in possession of the author. Mary Lou Larson and Ed Knell offered constructive comments that strengthened the chapter. A very special thanks to my family for their patience and encouragement as I prepared this chapter.

## References

Agenbroad, L. D.
1978 *The Hudson-Meng Site: An Alberta Bison Kill in the Nebraska High Plains.* University Press of America, Washington, D.C.

Alley, R. B., and A. M. Ágústsdóttir
2005 The 8k Event: Cause and Consequences of a Major Holocene Abrupt Climate Change. *Quaternary Science Reviews* 24:1123–1149.

Antevs, E.
1953 Geochronology of the Deglacial and Neothermal Ages. *Journal of Geology* 61:195–230.
1955 Geologic-Climatic Dating in the West. *American Antiquity* 20:317–335.

Bamforth, D. B.
1988 *Ecology and Human Organization on the Great Plains.* Plenum Press, New York.

Bamforth, D. B. (editor)
2007 *The Allen Site: A Paleoindian Camp in Southwestern Nebraska.* University of New Mexico Press, Albuquerque.

Barber, D. C., A. Dyke, C. Hillaire-Marcel, A. E. Jennings, J. T. Andrews, M. W. Kerwin, G. Bilodeau, R. McNeely, J. Southon, M. D. Morehead, and J.-M. Gagnon
1999 Forcing of the Cold Event of 8,200 Years Ago by Catastrophic Drainage of Laurentide Lakes. *Nature* 400:344–348.

Barbour, E. H., and C. B. Schultz
1932 The Scottsbluff Bison Quarry and Its Artifacts. *Bulletin of the Nebraska State Museum* 1(34):283–286.

Bartlein, P. J., K. H. Anderson, P. M. Anderson, M. E. Edwards, C. J. Mock, R. S. Thompson, R. S. Webb, T. Webb III, and C. Whitlock
1998 Paleoclimate Simulations for North America over the Past 21,000 Years: Features of the Simulated Climate and Comparisons with Paleoenvironmental Data. *Quaternary Science Reviews* 17:549–585.

Belitz, L.
1973 *Brain Tanning the Sioux Way.* Hot Springs, South Dakota.

Benedict, J. B.
1985 *Arapaho Pass: Glacial Geology and Archaeology at the Crest of the Colorado Front Range.* Research Report No. 2. Center for Mountain Archaeology, Ward, Colorado.

Broughton, J. M., D. A. Byers, R. A. Bryson, W. Eckerle, and D. B. Madsen
2008 Did Climatic Seasonality Control Late Quaternary Artiodactyl Densities in Western North America? *Quaternary Science Reviews* 27:1916–1937.

Butzer, K. W.
1971 *Environment and Archaeology: An Ecological Approach to Prehistory.* 2nd ed. Aldine Atherton, Chicago.

Byers, D. A., and C. S. Smith
2007 Ecosystem Controls and the Archaeofaunal Record: An Example from the Wyoming basin, USA. *The Holocene* 17:1171–1183.

Clayton, L., S. R. Moran, and W. B. Bickley Jr.
1976 *Stratigraphy, Origin, and Climatic Implications of Late Quaternary Upland Silt in North Dakota*. Miscellaneous Series No. 54. North Dakota Geological Survey, Grand Forks.

Coogan, A. H.
1987 *Holocene Geomorphic and Stratigraphic Framework of Archaeological Sites along the Missouri River, Central South Dakota*. Report submitted to U.S. Army Corps of Engineers, Omaha District, Omaha, Nebraska.

Cuffey, K. M., and G. D. Clow
1997 Temperature, Accumulation, and Ice Sheet Elevation in Central Greenland through the Last Deglaciation. *Journal of Geophysical Research* 102:26383–26396.

Cummings, L. S., and T. E. Moutoux
1998 Pollen Analysis at the Jerry Craig (5GA639) and Lower Twin Mountain (5GA186) Sites and a Paleoenvironmental Summary of Paleoindian Period in Middle Park, Colorado. In *Early Prehistory of Middle Park: The 1997 Project and Summary of Paleoindian Archaeology*, edited by M. Kornfeld, pp. 95–100. University of Wyoming Technical Report No. 15a. Laramie.

Cummings, L. S., T. E. Moutoux, and R. A. Bryson
2007 Paleoenvironmental Interpretations of the Late Pleistocene and Early Holocene in Southwestern Nebraska: The Pollen and Phytolith Evidence. In *The Allen Site: A Paleoindian Camp in Southwestern Nebraska*, edited by D. B. Bamforth, pp. 77–97. University of New Mexico Press, Albuquerque.

Dean, W. E., R. M. Forester, and J. Platt Bradbury
2002 Early Holocene Change in Atmospheric Circulation in the Northern Great Plains: An Upstream View of the 8.2 ka Cold Event. *Quaternary Science Reviews* 21:1763–1775.

Elias, S. A.
1996 Late Pleistocene and Holocene Seasonal Temperatures Reconstructed from Fossil Beetle Assemblages in the Rocky Mountains. *Quaternary Research* 46:311–318.

Evanoff, E.
1987 Appendix 4: Fossil Nonmarine Snails from the Horner Site. In *The Horner Site: The Type Site of the Cody Cultural Complex* edited by G. C. Frison and L. C. Todd, pp. 443–450. Academic Press, Orlando, Florida.

Fall, P. L.
1997 Timberline Fluctuations and Late Quaternary Paleoclimates in the Southern Rocky Mountains, Colorado. *Geological Society of America Bulletin* 109:1306–1320.

Fall, P. L., P. T. Davis, and G. A. Zielinski
1995 Late Quaternary Vegetation and Climate of the Wind River Range, Wyoming. *Quaternary Research* 43:393–404.

Forman, S. L., A. F. H. Goetz, and R. H. Yuhas
1992 Large-Scale Stabilized Dunes in the High Plains of Colorado: Understanding the Landscape Response to Holocene Climates with the Aid of Images from Space. *Geology* 20:145–148.

Forman, S. L., R. Oglesby, V. Markgraf, and T. Stafford
1995 Paleoclimatic Significance of Late Quaternary Eolian Deposition on the Piedmont and High Plains, Central United States. *Global and Planetary Change* 11:35–55.

Forman, S. L., R. Oglesby, and R. S. Webb
2001 Temporal and Spatial Patterns of Holocene Dune Activity on the Great Plains of North America: Megadroughts and Climate Links. *Global and Planetary Change* 29:1–29.

Fredlund, G. G.
1995 Late Quaternary Pollen Record from Cheyenne Bottoms, Kansas. *Quaternary Research* 43:67–79.
2009 Phytolith Evidence for Vegetation and Climate Change during the Pleistocene-Holocene Transition. In *Hell Gap: A Stratified Paleoindian Campsite at the Edge of the Rockies*, edited by M. L. Larson, M. Kornfeld, and G. C. Frison, pp. 90–98. University of Utah Press, Salt Lake City.

Fredlund, G. G., and L. L. Tieszen
1997 Phytolith and Carbon Isotope Evidence for Late Quaternary Vegetation and Climate Change in the Southern Black Hills, South Dakota. *Quaternary Research* 47:206–217.

Frison, G. C.
1976 The Chronology of Paleo-Indian and Altithermal Cultures in the Big Horn Basin, Wyoming. In *Cultural Change and Continuity: Essays in Honor of James Bennett Griffin*, edited by C. E. Cleland, pp. 147–173. Academic Press, New York.
1984 The Carter/Kerr-McGee Paleoindian Site: Cultural Resource Management and Archaeological Research. *American Antiquity* 49: 288–314.
1991 *Prehistoric Hunters of the High Plains*. 2nd ed. Academic Press, San Diego.

Frison, G. C., and D. N. Walker (editors)
2007 *Medicine Lodge Creek Site.* Clovis Press, Avondale, Colorado.

Fulgham, T., and D. Stanford
1982 The Frasca Site: A Preliminary Report. *Southwestern Lore* 48(1):1–9.

Graham, M. A., M. C. Wilson, and R. W. Graham
1987 Paleoenvironments and Mammalian Faunas of Montana, Southern Alberta, and Southern Saskatchewan. In *Late Quaternary Mammalian Biogeography and Environments of the Great Plains and Prairies*, edited by R. W. Graham, H. A. Semken Jr., and M. A. Graham, pp. 410–459. Illinois State Museum Scientific Papers Vol. 22. Springfield.

Graham, R. W.
1987 Late Quaternary Mammalian Faunas and Paleoenvironments of the Southwestern Plains of the United States. In *Late Quaternary Mammalian Biogeography and Environments of the Great Plains and Prairies*, edited by R. W. Graham, H. A. Semken Jr., and M. A. Graham, pp. 24–86. Illinois State Museum Scientific Papers Vol. 22. Springfield.

Graham, R. W., and H. A. Semken Jr.
1987 Philosophy and Procedures for Paleoenvironmental Studies of Quaternary Mammalian Faunas. In *Late Quaternary Mammalian Biogeography and Environments of the Great Plains and Prairies*, edited by R. W. Graham, H. A. Semken Jr., and M. A. Graham, pp. 1–17. Illinois State Museum Scientific Papers Vol. 22. Springfield.

Greiser, S. T.
1985 *Predictive Models of Hunter-Gatherer Subsistence and Settlement Strategies on the Central High Plains.* Memoir No. 20. Plains Anthropologist, Lincoln, Nebraska.

Grimm, E. C., J. J. Donovan, and K. J. Brown
2011 A High-Resolution Record of Climate Variability and Landscape Response from Kettle Lake, Northern Great Plains, North America. *Quaternary Science Reviews.* doi:10.1016/j.quascirev.2011.05.015.

Grüger, J.
1973 Studies on the Late Quaternary Vegetation History of Northeastern Kansas. *Geological Society of America Bulletin* 84:239–250.

Hansen, H. P.
1951 Pollen Analysis of Pat Sections from Near the Finley Site, Wyoming. In *Early Man in the Eden Valley* by J. H. Moss, edited by L. C. Eiseley, pp. 111–118. University Museum, University of Pennsylvania, Philadelphia.

Haynes, C. V., Jr.
1970 Geochronology of Man-Mammoth Sites and Their Bearing on the Origin of the Llano Complex. In *Pleistocene and Recent Environments of the Central Great Plains*, edited by W. Dort Jr. and J. Knox Jones Jr., pp. 75–92. University of Kansas Special Publication No. 3. University of Kansas Press, Lawrence.
1993 Clovis-Folsom Geochronology and Climate Change. In *From Kostenki to Clovis*, edited by O. Soffer and N. D. Praslov, pp. 219–236. Plenum Press, New York.
2008 Younger Dryas "Black Mats" and the Rancholabrean Termination in North America. *Proceedings of the National Academy of Sciences* 105:6520–6525.
2009 Geochronology. In *Hell Gap: A Stratified Paleoindian Campsite at the Edge of the Rockies*, edited by M. L. Larson, M. Kornfeld, and G. C. Frison, pp. 39–52. University of Utah Press, Salt Lake City.

Haynes, C. V., Jr., and G. Agogino
1960 *Geological Significance of a New Radiocarbon Date from the Lindenmeier Site.* Denver Museum of Natural History Proceedings No. 9. Denver, Colorado.

Haynes, C. V., Jr., R. P. Beukens, A. J. T. Jull, and O. K. Davis
1992 New Radiocarbon Dates for Some Old Folsom Sites: Accelerator Technology. In *Ice Age Hunters of the Rockies*, edited by D. J. Stanford and J. S. Day, pp. 83–100. Denver Museum of Natural History and University Press of Colorado, Niwot.

Hester, J. J., and J. Schoenwetter (assemblers)
1964 *The Reconstruction of Past Environments.* Proceedings of the Fort Burgwin Conference on Paleoecology, 1962. Fort Burgwin Research Center Publication No. 3. Southern Methodist University, Dallas, Texas.

Hicks, K.
2002 Local Variability in Paleoindian Lifeways: A Comparison of the Lime Creek and Allen Site Worked Stone Assemblages, Southwest Nebraska. Unpublished Master's thesis, University of Colorado, Boulder.

Hill, M. E.
2008 New Investigations of the Cody-Age Finley and Scottsbluff Bison Bonebeds. *Current Research in the Pleistocene* 25:90–93.

Hill, M. G., and M. Kornfeld
1999 Inferring Season of Kill for a Cody-Complex Bison Bonebed in Middle Park, Colorado. *Current Research in the Pleistocene* 16:30–32.

Holliday, V. T.
2004 *Soils in Archaeological Research*. Oxford University Press, Oxford.

Holliday, V. T., E. Johnson, and T. W. Stafford Jr.
1999 AMS Radiocarbon Dating of the Type Plainview and Firstview (Paleoindian) Assemblages: The Agony and the Ecstasy. *American Antiquity* 64:444–454.

Holliday, V. T., and D. J. Meltzer
2009 The 12.9-ka ET Impact Hypothesis and North American Paleoindians. *Current Anthropology* 51:575–607.

Hughen, K. A., J. R. Southon, S. Lehman, and J. Overpeck
2000 Synchronous Radiocarbon and Climate Shifts during the Last Deglaciation. *Science* 290:1951–1954.

Jacobs, P. M., and J. A. Mason
2004 Paleopedology of Soils in Thick Holocene Loess, Nebraska, USA. *Revista Mexicana de Ciencias Geológicas* 21(1):54–70.

Jodry, M. A.
1999 Folsom Technological and Socioeconomic Strategies: Views from Stewart's Cattle Guard and the Upper Rio Grande Basin, Colorado. Unpublished Ph.D. dissertation, Department of Anthropology, American University, Washington, D.C.

Kaufman, D. S., T. A. Ager, N. J. Anderson, P. M. Anderson, J. T. Andrews, P. J. Bartlein, L. B. Brubaker, L. L. Coats, L. C. Cwynar, M. L. Duvall, A. S. Dyke, M. E. Edwards, W. R. Eisner, K. Gajewski, A. Geirsdóttir, F. S. Hu, A. E. Jennings, M. R. Kaplan, M. W. Kerwin, A. V. Lozhkin, G. M. MacDonald, G. H. Miller, C. J. Mock, W. W. Oswald, B. L. Otto-Bliesner, D. F. Porinchu, K. Rühland, J. P. Smol, E. J. Steig, and B. B. Wolfe
2004 Holocene Thermal Maximum in the Western Arctic (0–180°W). *Quaternary Science Reviews* 23:529–560.

Kelly, R. L.
1995 *The Foraging Spectrum: Diversity in Hunter-Gatherer Lifeways*. Smithsonian Institution Press, Washington, D.C.

Kornfeld, M.
2007 Are Paleoindians of the Great Plains and Rockies Subsistence Specialists? In *Foragers of the Terminal Pleistocene*, edited by R. B. Walker and B. N. Driskell, pp. 32–58. University of Nebraska Press, Lincoln.

Kornfeld, M., G. C. Frison, and M. L. Larson
2010 *Prehistoric Hunter-Gatherers of the High Plains and Rockies*. 3rd ed. Left Coast Press, Walnut Creek, California.

Kutzbach, J., R. Gallimore, S. Harrison, P. Behling, R. Selin, and F. Laarif
1998 Climate and Biome Simulations for the Past 21,000 Years. *Quaternary Science Reviews* 17:473–506.

LaBelle, J. M., V. T. Holliday, and D. J. Meltzer
2003 Early Holocene Paleoindian Deposits at Nall Playa, Oklahoma Panhandle, U.S.A. *Geoarchaeology: An International Journal* 18:5–34.

Larson, M. L.
1992 Site Formation Processes in the Cody and Early Plains Archaic Levels at the Laddie Creek Site, Wyoming. *Geoarchaeology: An International Journal* 7:103–120.

Leopold, E. B., and J. B. Wheat
1972 Appendix II: Palynology of the Olsen-Chubbuck Site. In *The Olsen-Chubbuck Site: A Paleo-Indian Bison Kill*, by J. B. Wheat, pp. 178–180. Memoirs of the Society for American Archaeology No. 26. Washington, D.C.

Lewis, R. O.
1978 Appendix III: Use of Opal Phytoliths on Paleo-Environmental Reconstruction at the Hudson-Meng Site. In *The Hudson-Meng Site: An Alberta Bison Kill in the Nebraska High Plains*, by Larry D. Agenbroad, pp. 211–215. University Press of America, Washington, D.C.

1987 Appendix 5: Opal Phytolith Studies from the Horner Site, Wyoming. In *The Horner Site: The Type Site of the Cody Cultural Complex*, edited by G. C. Frison and L. C. Todd, pp. 451–459. Academic Press, Orlando, Florida.

Madole, R. F.
1995 Spatial and Temporal Patterns of Late Quaternary Eolian Deposition, Eastern Colorado, U.S.A. *Quaternary Science Review* 14:155–166.

Mandel, R. D., and J. L. Hofman
2003 Geoarchaeological Investigations at the Winger Site: A Late Paleoindian Bison Bonebed in Southwestern Kansas, U.S.A. *Geoarchaeology: An International Journal* 18:129–144.

Markgraf, V., and T. Lennon
1986 Paleoenvironmental History of the Last 13,000 Years of the Eastern Powder River Basin, Wyoming, and Its Implications for Prehistoric Cultural Patterns. *Plains Anthropologist* 31:1–12.

Mason, J. A., X. Miao, P. R. Hanson, W. C. Johnson, P. M. Jacobs, and R. J. Goble
2008 Loess Record of the Pleistocene-Holocene Transition on the Northern and Central

Great Plains, USA. *Quaternary Science Reviews* 27:1772–1783.

May, D.

2007 Landforms, Alluvial Stratigraphy, and Radiocarbon Chronology at Selected Paleoindian Sites around Medicine Creek Reservoir. In *The Allen Site: A Paleoindian Camp in Southwestern Nebraska*, edited by D. B. Bamforth, pp. 17–46. University of New Mexico Press, Albuquerque.

Mayer, J. H.

2003 Paleoindian Geoarchaeology and Paleoenvironments of the Western Killpecker Dunes, Wyoming, U.S.A. *Geoarchaeology: An International Journal* 18:35–69.

McCartney, P. H.

1990 Alternative Hunting Strategies in Plains Paleoindian Adaptations. In *Hunters of the Recent Past*, edited by L. B. Davis and B. O. K. Reeves, pp. 111–121. Unwin Hyman, London.

Miller, C. E., and P. Goldberg

2009 Micromorphology and Paleoenvironments. In *Hell Gap: A Stratified Paleoindian Campsite at the Edge of the Rockies*, edited by M. L. Larson, M. Kornfeld, and G. C. Frison, pp. 72–89. University of Utah Press, Salt Lake City.

Mooney, J.

1910 Skin and Skin Dressing. In *Handbook of American Indians North of Mexico, Part 2*, edited by F. W. Hodge, pp. 591–594. Bureau of Ethnology Bulletin No. 30. Smithsonian Institution, Washington, D.C.

Muhs, D. R., J. N. Aleinikoff, T. W. Stafford Jr., R. Kihl, J. Been, S. A. Mahan, and S. Cowherd

1999 Late Quaternary Loess in Northeastern Colorado: Part I — Age and Paleoclimatic Significance. *Geological Society of America Bulletin* 111(12):1861–1875.

Muñiz, M. P.

2005 The Cody Complex Revisited: Landscape Use and Technological Organization on the Northwestern Plains. Unpublished Ph.D. dissertation, Department of Anthropology, University of Colorado, Boulder.

2007 *Report of 2006 Archaeological Excavation at Hudson-Meng (25SX115), Sioux County, Nebraska*. Report submitted to Mammoth Site and Heritage Resources Program, Nebraska National Forest, Chadron.

2008 *Results of 2007 Archaeological Field Season, Hudson-Meng (25SX115), Sioux County, Nebraska*. Report submitted to Mammoth Site and Heritage Resources Program, Nebraska National Forest, Chadron.

2010 *Results of 2008 Archaeological Investigations at the Hudson-Meng Site (25SX15), Sioux County, Nebraska*. Report submitted to Heritage Resources Program, Nebraska National Forest, Chadron.

Murton, J. B., M. D. Bateman, S. R. Dallimore, J. T. Teller, and Z. Yang

2010 Identification of Younger Dryas Outburst Flood Path from Lake Agassiz to the Arctic Ocean. *Nature* 464:740–743.

Rancier, J., G. Haynes, and D. Stanford

1982 1981 Investigations of Lamb Spring. *Southwestern Lore* 48(2):1–17.

Reider, R. G.

1987 Soil Formation and Paleoenvironmental Interpretation at the Horner Site, Park County, Wyoming. In *The Horner Site: The Type Site of the Cody Cultural Complex*, edited by G. C. Frison and L. C. Todd, pp. 347–360. Academic Press, Orlando, Florida.

1990 Late Pleistocene and Holocene Pedogenic and Environmental Trends at Archaeological Sites in Plains and Mountain Areas of Colorado and Wyoming. In *Archaeological Geology of North America*, edited by N. P. Lasca and J. Donahue, pp. 335–360. Centennial Special Volume 4. Geological Society of America, Boulder, Colorado.

2009 Soil Development. In *Hell Gap: A Stratified Paleoindian Campsite at the Edge of the Rockies*, edited by M. L. Larson, M. Kornfeld, and G. C. Frison, pp. 53–71. University of Utah Press, Salt Lake City.

Richings-Germain, S.

2002 The Jerry Craig Site: A Paleoindian Bison Bonebed in the Colorado Rocky Mountains. Unpublished Master's thesis, Department of Anthropology, University of Wyoming, Laramie.

Ruhe, R. V.

1970 Soils, Paleosols, and Environment. In *Pleistocene and Recent Environments of the Central Great Plains*, edited by W. Dort Jr. and J. K. Jones Jr., pp. 37–52. Department of Geology, University of Kansas, Special Publication No. 3. University Press of Kansas, Lawrence.

1983 Aspects of Holocene Pedology in the United States. In *Late-Quaternary Environments of the United States, Volume 2: The Holocene*, edited by H. E. Wright Jr., pp. 12–25. University of Minnesota Press, Minneapolis.

Schultz, C. B., and L. Eiseley

1935 Paleontological Evidence for the Antiquity of the Scottsbluff Bison Quarry and Its Associated Artifacts. *American Anthropologist* 37:306–319.

Scott, L.

1979 Appendix 1: Jurgens Site Palynological Analysis. In *The Jurgens Site*, by Joe Ben Wheat, pp. 149–151. Memoir No. 15. Plains Anthropologist, Lincoln, Nebraska.

Semken, H. A., Jr., and C. R. Falk

1987 Late Pleistocene/Holocene Mammalian Faunas and Environmental Changes on the Northern Plains of the United States. In *Late Quaternary Mammalian Biogeography and Environments of the Great Plains and Prairies*, edited by R. W. Graham, H. A. Semken Jr., and M. A. Graham, pp. 176–313. Illinois State Museum Scientific Papers Vol. 22. Springfield.

Semken, H. A., Jr., and R. W. Graham

1987 Summary: Environmental Analysis and Plains Archaeology. In *Late Quaternary Mammalian Biogeography and Environments of the Great Plains and Prairies*, edited by R. W. Graham, H. A. Semken Jr., and M. A. Graham, pp. 474–480. Illinois State Museum Scientific Papers Vol. 22. Springfield.

Shuman, B., P. Bartlein, N. Logar, P. Newby, and T. Webb III

2002 Parallel Climate and Vegetation Responses to the Early Holocene Collapse of the Laurentide Ice Sheet. *Quaternary Science Reviews* 21: 1793–1805.

Stanford, D. J.

1978 The Jones-Miller Site: An Example of Hell Gap Bison Procurement Strategy. In *Bison Procurement and Utilization: A Symposium*, edited by L. B. Davis and M. Wilson, pp. 90–97. Memoir No. 14. Plains Anthropologist, Lincoln, Nebraska.

1999 Paleoindian Archaeology and Late Pleistocene Environments in the Plains and Southwestern United States. In *Ice Age Peoples of North America: Environments, Origins, and Adaptations of the First Americans*, edited by R. Bonnichsen and K. L. Turnmire, pp. 281–339. Oregon State University Press, Corvallis.

Stanford, D., W. R. Wedel, and G. R. Scott

1981 Archaeological Investigations of the Lamb Spring Site. *Southwestern Lore* 47(1):14–27.

Stokes, S., and D. R. Gaylord

1993 Optical Dating of Holocene Dune Sands in the Ferris Dune Field, Wyoming. *Quaternary Research* 39:274–281.

Surovell, T., N. M. Waguespack, S. Richings-Germain, M. Kornfeld and G. C. Frison

2000 *1999 Investigations at the Barger Gulch and Jerry Craig Sites, Middle Park, Colorado.* University of Wyoming Technical Report No. 18a. Laramie.

Todd, L. C.

1987 Taphonomy of the Horner II Bonebed. In *The Horner Site: The Type Site of the Cody Cultural Complex*, edited by G. C. Frison and L. C. Todd, pp. 107–198. Academic Press, Orlando, Florida.

Todd, L. C., and D. J. Rapson

1991 1991 Excavations at the Hudson-Meng Bison Bonebed: Aspects of the Formational History. Paper prepared for the 49th Plains Anthropological Conference, Lawrence, Kansas. Submitted to the USDA Forest Service, Nebraska National Forest, Chadron.

1999 Formational Analysis of Bison Bonebeds and Interpretation of Paleoindian Subsistence. In *Le bison: Gibier et moyen de subsistance des hommes du Paléolithique aux Paléoindiens des Grandes Plaines*, edited by J.-Ph. Brugal, F. David, J. G. Enloe, and J. Jaubert, pp. 479–499. Éditions APDCA, Antibes, France.

Walker, D. N.

1987a Late Pleistocene/Holocene Environmental Changes in Wyoming: The Mammalian Record. In *Late Quaternary Mammalian Biogeography and Environments of the Great Plains and Prairies*, edited by R. W. Graham, H. A. Semken Jr., and M. A. Graham, pp. 334–392. Illinois State Museum Scientific Papers Vol. 22. Springfield.

1987b Horner Site Local Fauna: Vertebrates. In *The Horner Site: The Type Site of the Cody Cultural Complex*, edited by G. C. Frison and L. C. Todd, pp. 327–345. Academic Press, Orlando, Florida.

2009 Small Mammals from Locality I: A Paleoenvironmental Reassessment. In *Hell Gap: A Stratified Paleoindian Campsite at the Edge of the Rockies*, edited by M. L. Larson, M. Kornfeld, and G. C. Frison, pp. 429–434. University of Utah Press, Salt Lake City.

Warner, B. G. (editor)

1990 *Methods in Quaternary Ecology*. Geoscience Canada, Reprint Series No. 5. Geological Association of Canada, Department of Earth Sciences, Memorial University of Newfoundland, St. John's.

Warren, R. E.

2007 Cultural and Paleoenvironmental Implications of Freshwater Mussels from the Allen Site. In *The Allen Site: A Paleoindian Camp in Southwestern Nebraska*, edited by D. B. Bamforth, pp. 47–68. University of New Mexico Press, Albuquerque.

Webb, T., III
1986 Is Vegetation in Equilibrium with Climate? How to Interpret Late-Quaternary Pollen Data. *Vegetation* 67:75–91.

Wheat, J. B.
1972 *The Olsen-Chubbuck Site: A Paleo-Indian Bison Kill*. Society for American Archaeology Memoir No. 26. Washington, D.C.
1979 *The Jurgens Site*. Memoir No. 15. Plains Anthropologist, Lincoln, Nebraska.

Whitlock, C., P. J. Bartlein, and K. J. Van Norman
1995 Stability of Holocene Climate Regimes in the Yellowstone Region. *Quaternary Research* 43:433–436.

Wilmsen, E. N., and F. H. H. Roberts Jr.
1978 *Lindenmeier, 1934–1974: Concluding Report on Investigations*. Smithsonian Contributions to Anthropology No. 24. Smithsonian Institution Press, Washington, D.C.

Wormington, H. M.
1957 *Ancient Man in North America*. 4th ed. Popular Series No. 4. Denver Museum of Natural History, Denver.

Wright, H. E., Jr. (editor)
1983 *Late-Quaternary Environments of the United States, Volume 2: The Holocene*. University of Minnesota Press, Minneapolis.

Wright, H. E., Jr., J. C. Almendinger, and J. Grüger
1985 Pollen Diagram from the Nebraska Sandhills and the Age of the Dunes. *Quaternary Research* 24(1):115–120.

Wright, H. E., Jr., and D. G. Frey (editors)
1965 *The Quaternary of the United States: A Review Volume for the VII Congress of the International Association for Quaternary Research*. Princeton University Press, Princeton, New Jersey.

Wu, S.-K., and C. Jones
1978 Appendix II: Molluscs from the Hudson-Meng Site. In *The Hudson-Meng Site: An Alberta Bison Kill in the Nebraska High Plains*, by Larry D. Agenbroad, pp. 193–210. University Press of America, Washington, D.C.

Yansa, C. H.
2007 Lake Records of Northern Plains Paleoindian and Early Archaic Environments: The "Park Oasis" Hypothesis. *Plains Anthropologist* 52:109–144.

Young, L. W., and R. R. Weedon
1978 Appendix IV: Vegetation and Flora of the Hudson-Meng Bison Kill. In *The Hudson-Meng Site: An Alberta Bison Kill in the Nebraska High Plains*, by Larry D. Agenbroad, pp. 217–225. University Press of America, Washington, D.C.

Yu, Z.
2000 Ecosystem Response to Lateglacial and Early Holocene Climate Oscillations in the Great Lakes Region of North America. *Quaternary Science Reviews* 19:1723–1747.

Zalucha, L. A.
2007 Early Holocene Vegetation of the Central Great Plains Based on Paleobotanical and Paleoethnobotanical Remains from the Medicine Creek Area. In *The Allen Site: A Paleoindian Camp in Southwestern Nebraska*, edited by D. B. Bamforth, pp. 98–108. University of New Mexico Press, Albuquerque.

# 3

# Evolution of the High Plains Paleoindian Landscape

## The Paleoecology of Great Plains Faunal Assemblages

Chris Widga

The study of climate change is a persistent and prominent part of Paleoindian studies. Changes in climate undoubtedly affected how Cody hunter-gatherers interacted with landscape elements and had concomitant effects on the social, technological, and subsistence practices of Cody groups. This chapter explores the transition from Pleistocene to Holocene ecosystems through analyses of small-mammal faunal assemblages from central and eastern North America, as well as the physical and social evolution of bison populations in the Great Plains.

Understanding how the transition between Late Glacial and modern conditions impacted human groups in North America has been challenging, to say the least. Indeed, there is enough ambiguity in the timing and degree of landscape changes during the Paleoindian period that it is difficult to tell whether cultural changes coincide with certain landscape changes or occur independently of such changes (Martin and Klein 1984). This ambiguity is due, in part, to differences in the scale of processes acting at a landscape level (Storch and Bissonette 2003). Cultural groups adjust to landscape changes at one scale (e.g., a human lifetime), while climate changes are resolved at many different scales (e.g., seasonal, decadal, millennial). To further complicate matters, we are dealing with not only the temporal aspects of the archaeological record but synchronic differences in space as well. Recent discussions of time averaging and space averaging in fossil assemblages illustrate the challenges inherent in interpreting any regional record of landscape and lifeways (e.g., Lyman 2003; Martin 1999:186).

Despite these issues, it is clear that basic climate characteristics such as relative temperature and precipitation influence hunter-gatherer group organization at some level (Binford 2001; Kelly 1995:66). These groups also respond to climate variability (e.g., seasonality, drought, winter severity) through various cultural mechanisms such as explicit risk management behavior (e.g., storage), mobility, or diet breadth decisions.

Prey behavior also affects hunter-gatherer organization. Bison were a key Paleoindian resource in the Great Plains. Although we traditionally interpret the fossil bison record through the lens of modern bison observations (e.g., Frison 2004), the range of behavioral and ecological variability in fossil bison is not necessarily reflected in contemporary populations, owing to modern constraints on animal mobility, diet, and predator pressure. Paleoecological studies of bison population dynamics are critical to understanding the decisions of human groups that relied on these herds, especially during the Pleistocene/Holocene transition, when ecosystems, including large faunal populations, were in flux.

Previous studies of proxy climate records for the Pleistocene/Holocene boundary in North America indicate that the transition was by no means smooth (Strong and Hills 2005; Webb et al. 1983; Yu and Eicher 1998). Lake sediments in the northern Great Plains suggest a sequence (Grimm et al. 2011; Laird et al. 1998) that went from a cold, dry period dominated by spruce (>13,000–12,000 cal BP) to temperate deciduous parkland (Moon Lake, 12,150–11,250 cal BP) or grassland (Kettle Lake, 11,930–10,730 cal BP), followed by a more mesic (but droughty) early Holocene (10,730–9250 cal BP). According to the Kettle Lake record, conditions overall were drier and droughts more frequent and severe by ~9250 cal BP in northwestern North Dakota. At Moon Lake in eastern North Dakota, elm is absent by ~8900 cal BP, but oak remained on the landscape until 7800 cal BP.

The Great Lakes lake sediment record is slightly more robust than that of the northern Plains. There is evidence for at least two broad-scale climate oscillations interspersed with short-term events (Yu 2000): a warm Bølling-Allerød (14,600–12,800 cal BP) with possible evidence for a brief Gerzensee/Killarney event (~13,000 cal BP), a cold Younger Dryas (12,800–11,500 cal BP), and a brief Pre-Boreal Oscillation (11,000 cal BP) during early Holocene warming (<11,500 cal BP). The lake record at Crystal Lake in northeastern Illinois suggests warm/wet conditions throughout the Bølling-Allerød with a colder Younger Dryas (Gonzales and Grimm 2009). In this lake, the beginning of the Younger Dryas lagged behind ice-core records by up to 300 years. Gill et al. (2009) suggest a decline in the coprophilus fungi *Sporomiella* (a proxy for megafaunal populations) in the southern Great Lakes beginning ~16,000 cal BP. Levels of *Sporomiella* are reduced to Holocene levels by ~13,500 cal BP.

While the general trends of these paleoenvironmental records are similar, they highlight the difficulty of reconstructing climate patterns during the Pleistocene/Holocene transition. First, the records at Kettle and Moon Lakes measure local landscape changes at a different scale than the geochemistry of small ponds in the Great Lakes region. Second, although these records span roughly the same time period, there is an obvious geographic component to reconstructed paleoenvironmental conditions: vegetation changes in the relatively arid western sites are more sensitive to changes in precipitation and fire frequency than temperature. Finally, both regions provide a paleoenvironmental context only for the last 15,000 years and cannot speak to landscape conditions south of the ice in the Midwest and Great Plains before this period.

Faunal records of landscape changes have similar problems in interpretation (Graham and Semken 1987). However, there are a number of assemblages distributed throughout the Great Plains and Midwest that offer insight into changing climate conditions during the late Quaternary. In periglacial areas during the Last Glacial Maximum (LGM), fossil faunules are valuable assets in paleoenvironmental reconstruction (e.g., Baker et al. 1986). When these are combined with additional high-resolution climate-proxy records, we can better understand landscape changes affecting human groups, the flora they gathered, and the fauna they hunted.

## Methods

The Pleistocene/Holocene transition on the Great Plains was very dynamic. Not only was the landscape changing rapidly, but human populations were expanding and increasingly successful at procuring targeted faunal and floral resources. This overview of the paleoenvironmental changes that took place during the Pleistocene/Holocene transition relies on three major datasets: (1) taxonomic diversity in small fauna from a series of 33 paleontological and archaeological faunal assemblages dating between 25,000 and 6000 cal BP (21,000 to 5000 $^{14}$C yr BP), (2) biometrics of bison postcrania (metacarpal size) as a proxy for animal body size, and (3) biometrics of bison crania as a proxy for selective pressures on bison breeding populations. These datasets are used to address changes in paleoenvironmental conditions and keystone landscape elements (i.e., bison populations) during the late Quaternary in the Great Plains and eastern United States.

Chronometric information is calibrated to calendar years before present (cal BP) with Oxcal 3.1 for Windows (Bronk Ramsey 2005) and the IntCal09 calibration dataset (Reimer et al. 2009). Oxcal models are used to combine $^{14}$C age estimates and to constrain large date ranges from stratigraphic sequences where appropriate. Two sigma errors are used for all calibrated age estimates.

### *Quantitative Bioclimatic Models*

Small fauna are important for an understanding of local paleoenvironmental conditions. To help visualize climate conditions, researchers have developed a number of tools that characterize taxa represented in a locality (Graham and Semken 1987). One of the most common tools used to glean paleoenvironmental information from fossil faunas is a graphical technique that looks at the overlap between geographic ranges of different species on the modern landscape (i.e., sympatry). Once an area of sympatry is identified, the moisture and temperature restrictions operating within a particular fossil faunal community can be defined.

There are some limitations to this graphical technique, however. The method does not necessarily provide quantitative data compatible with climate modeling efforts, nor does it deal effectively with disharmonious paleofaunas, a relatively common situation in the late Pleistocene of North America (Semken et al. 2010; Stafford et al. 1999). To bypass some of these issues, this study utilizes a series of predictive equations developed by Hernández Fernández and Peláez-Campomanes (2005) for use on fossil mammal assemblages.

Each faunal assemblage (fossil or modern) has a unique association of taxa, and each taxon within this faunule has a unique profile of presence/absence data across a series of nine world biomes (Figure 3.1). Some taxa have geographic ranges that are exclusive to one or two biomes (e.g., plains pocket gopher), while others are almost universally distributed (e.g., cottontail rabbit). In essence, this technique characterizes a faunal assemblage as a series of weighted averages in which the presence of a species with limited bioclimatic distribution (i.e., lives in only one or two biomes) has a heavier weight than those with a larger bioclimatic distribution (i.e., spread across many different biomes). This series of weighted averages is quantified as the Climate Restriction Index (CRI) (Hernández Fernández 2001), and can be defined as

$$CRI_i = 1/n,$$

where $n$ is the number of biomes inhabited by a species and $i$ is the biome in which the species occurs. High CRI values characterize taxa with a limited distribution across the world biomes while low CRI values characterize widely distributed taxa.

Within an assemblage, summing CRI values creates a unique "bioclimatic component" (BC) (Hernández Fernández and Peláez-Campomanes 2005) for each faunal assemblage:

$$BC_i = (\Sigma CRI_i)100/S.$$

In this formula, $i$ is a particular climate zone and $S$ is the number of species in the locality.

The CRI and BC are relative measures that gauge the fit of a particular paleofaunal assemblage with the modern faunal community of a biome. Climatic parameters (e.g., mean annual temperature, drought length) can be further estimated from the BC with the predictive equations developed by Hernández Fernández and Peláez-Campomanes (2005) (see Table 3.3 below). These equations were constructed by means of multiple linear regressions between more than 50 globally distributed, modern mammal faunas with associated climatic data (Table 3.1). Error estimates are 95 percent confidence intervals of the mean using standard errors in Hernández Fernández and Peláez-Campomanes (2005: Table 4).

The construction of the bioclimatic component is illustrated for the taxa present in Cheek Bend Cave, Tennessee (Table 3.2). Qualitatively, the taxonomic makeup of this assemblage is weighted toward the temperate (biome VI) and cold-temperate (boreal; biome VIII) biomes (sensu Hernández Fernández and Peláez-Campomanes 2005). The predictive equations based on the BC quantify the climate parameters acting on this assemblage (Table 3.3). In this example, the annual temperature (T) is estimated to be 4.12 ± 3.5°C while annual precipitation (P) is 945 ± 30 mm.

Bioclimatic components are calculated for 33 different paleofaunal assemblages from the Rocky Mountains, central High Plains, and eastern United States (Figure 3.2). The taxonomic structure of these assemblages is derived wholly from published sources (Table 3.4). Profiles were constructed from the modern ranges of 280 extant North American rodent taxa. Extinct species were not used since, by definition, the modern

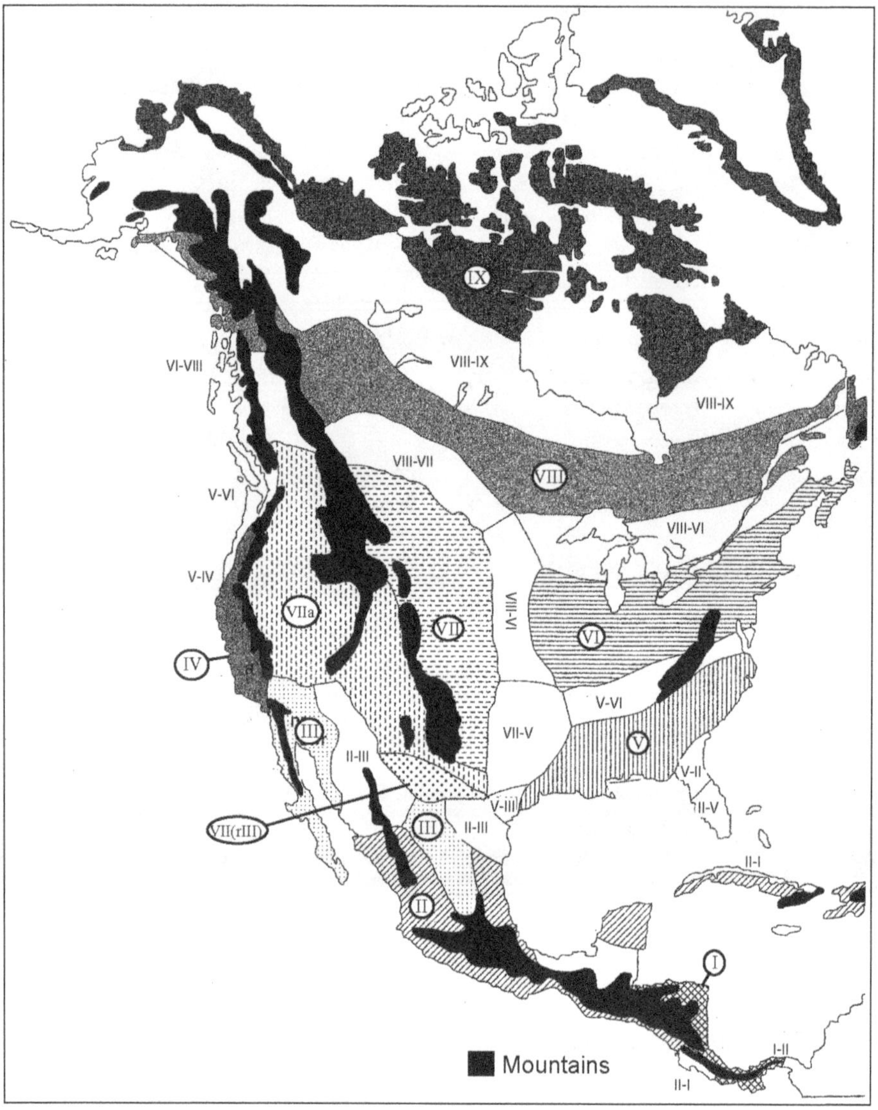


FIGURE 3.1. North American biomes, from Walter (2002) as modified by Hernández Fernández (2001): Evergreen tropical rain forest (I), tropical deciduous forest (II), savanna (II–III), subtropical desert (III), sclerophyllous woody plants (IV), temperate evergreen forest (V), nemoral broadleaf-deciduous forest (VI), steppe to cold desert (VII), boreal coniferous forest (VIII), tundra (IX).

geographic range of these taxa cannot be determined and climatic parameters cannot be estimated. Finally, paleoclimatic constraints of each paleofaunal sample are estimated by means of the multiple regression equations in Hernández Fernández and Peláez-Campomanes (2005: Table 3) for moisture (e.g., annual precipitation, drought length), temperature (e.g., annual temperature, mean annual thermal amplitude), and growing season (e.g., vegetation activity period). By necessity, these assemblages are drawn from a large area and have the potential for autocorrelation with landscape features; however, annual mean temperature (T) does not correlate with either latitude ($p$ = -0.335; sig. = 0.110) or elevation ($p$ = -0.317; sig. = 0.132).

As with most biological systems, the trends within this dataset are rarely clear cut; however,

**TABLE 3.1.** Climate Variables Used in This Study.

| Climatic Factor | Explanation | Unit |
|---|---|---|
| Annual mean temperature (T) | Average of mean monthly temperatures | °C |
| Annual positive temperature (Tp) | Sum of the monthly mean temperature of those months whose average temperature is higher than 0°C. | °C |
| Mean temperature of the warmest month (Tmax) | | °C |
| Mean temperature of the coldest month (Tmin) | | °C |
| Mean thermal amplitude (Mta) | Continentality index. Mta expresses the range between the average temperatures of the warmest and coldest months of the year (Mta = Tmax – Tmin). | °C |
| Thermicity index (It) | Measures the intensity of winter cold (It = 10(T + Tmin)). | |
| Compensated thermicity index (Itc) | Designed to equilibrate the cold "excess" that occurs during winter in the continental climates or the excessively mild winter in the oceanic regions so that these index values can be significantly compared. | |
| Winter length (W) | Period in which t < 0°C | months |
| Vegetative activity period (VAP) | Period in which t > 7°C. Estimates length of plants' winter dormancy and spring-summer growing periods. | months |
| Free vegetative activity period (FVAP) | Since vegetation growth stops during the dry season, this index gives the length of the period in which both the temperature and the humidity allow the normal growing of vegetation (FVAP = VAP – D) | months |
| Annual precipitation (P) | Total annual precipitation | mm |
| Drought length (D) | Period in which P < 2T. Estimates length of the dry period. | months |

*Note:* After Table 1 in Hernández Fernández and Peláez-Campomanes (2005).

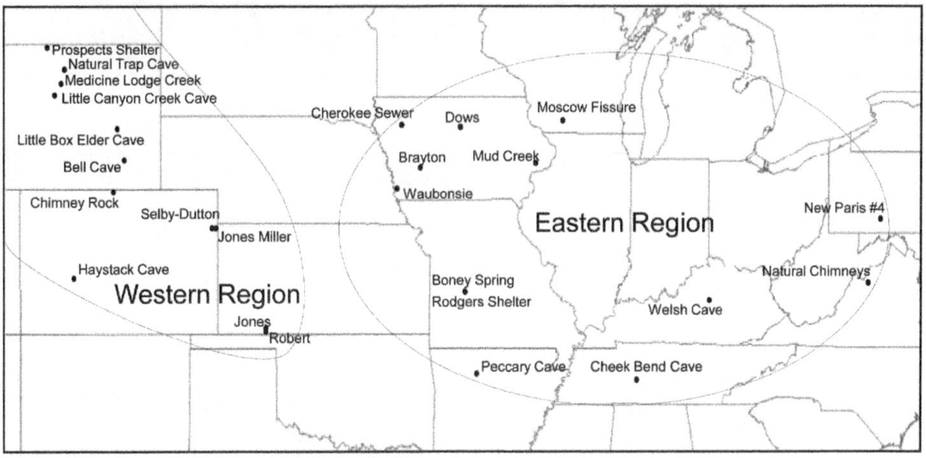


**FIGURE 3.2.** Locality map for bioclimatic models.

there are consistent, general changes that characterize the evolving High Plains landscape through time. As always, when more data become available or site chronologies are better refined, these trends may change; however, this technique offers a paleoclimatic picture that is internally consistent and complements other proxy records of landscape change such as lake core records from the Midwest and northern Great Plains and the chronology of glacial recession.

### *Bison Biometrics*

Bison were an important subsistence resource for Cody groups, as is evident in numerous multi-animal kill sites in the High Plains (see Hill, this volume). While nonbison fauna were certainly

**TABLE 3.2.** Construction of the Bioclimatic Component from Horizon II, Cheek Bend Cave, Tennessee.

| Species | Biome I | Biome II | Biome II/III | Biome III | Biome IV | Biome V | Biome VI | Biome VII | Biome VIII | Biome IX |
|---|---|---|---|---|---|---|---|---|---|---|
| *Glaucomys sabrinus* | 0 | 0 | 0 | 0 | 0 | 0 | 0 | 0 | 1 | 0 |
| *Microtus xanthognathus* | 0 | 0 | 0 | 0 | 0 | 0 | 0 | 0 | 1 | 0 |
| *Sorex arcticus* | 0 | 0 | 0 | 0 | 0 | 0 | 0 | 0 | 1 | 0 |
| *Sorex palustris* | 0 | 0 | 0 | 0 | 0.333 | 0 | 0 | 0.333 | 0.333 | 0 |
| *Phenacomys intermedius* | 0 | 0 | 0 | 0 | 0 | 0 | 0 | 0.5 | 0.5 | 0 |
| *Erethizon dorsatum* | 0 | 0 | 0.2 | 0.2 | 0 | 0 | 0.2 | 0.2 | 0.2 | 0 |
| *Clethrionomys gapperi* | 0 | 0 | 0 | 0 | 0 | 0 | 0.333 | 0.333 | 0.333 | 0 |
| *Microtus pennsylvanicus* | 0 | 0 | 0 | 0 | 0 | 0 | 0.333 | 0.333 | 0.333 | 0 |
| *Sorex hoyi* | 0 | 0 | 0 | 0 | 0 | 0 | 0.333 | 0.333 | 0.333 | 0 |
| *Synaptomys cooperi* | 0 | 0 | 0 | 0 | 0 | 0 | 0.333 | 0.333 | 0.333 | 0 |
| *Tamiasciurus hudsonicus* | 0 | 0 | 0 | 0 | 0 | 0 | 0.333 | 0.333 | 0.333 | 0 |
| *Condylura cristata* | 0 | 0 | 0 | 0 | 0 | 0 | 0.5 | 0 | 0.5 | 0 |
| *Napaeozapus insignis* | 0 | 0 | 0 | 0 | 0 | 0 | 0.5 | 0 | 0.5 | 0 |
| *Blarina brevicauda* | 0 | 0 | 0 | 0 | 0 | 0 | 0.5 | 0.5 | 0 | 0 |
| *Geomys bursarius* | 0 | 0 | 0 | 0 | 0 | 0 | 0.5 | 0.5 | 0 | 0 |
| *Spermophilus tridecemlineatus* | 0z | 0 | 0 | 0 | 0 | 0 | 0.5 | 0.5 | 0 | 0 |
| *Peromyscus sp.* | 0 | 0.125 | 0.125 | 0.125 | 0.125 | 0.125 | 0.125 | 0.125 | 0.125 | 0 |
| *Sylvilagus floridanus* | 0.143 | 0.143 | 0.143 | 0.143 | 0 | 0.143 | 0.143 | 0.143 | 0 | 0 |
| *Cryptotis parva* | 0 | 0.25 | 0 | 0 | 0 | 0.25 | 0.25 | 0.25 | 0 | 0 |
| *Ondatra zibethicus* | 0 | 0 | 0 | 0 | 0 | 0.25 | 0.25 | 0.25 | 0.25 | 0 |
| *Zapus hudsonius* | 0 | 0 | 0 | 0 | 0 | 0.25 | 0.25 | 0.25 | 0.25 | 0 |
| *Tamias striatus* | 0 | 0 | 0 | 0 | 0 | 0.333 | 0.333 | 0.333 | 0 | 0 |
| *Sorex fumeus* | 0 | 0 | 0 | 0 | 0 | 0.5 | 0.5 | 0 | 0 | 0 |
| *Sorex longirostris* | 0 | 0 | 0 | 0 | 0 | 0.5 | 0.5 | 0 | 0 | 0 |
| Climate restriction index | 0.143 | 0.518 | 0.468 | 0.468 | 0.458 | 2.351 | 6.716 | 5.549 | 7.323 | 0 |
| Bioclimatic component | 0.596 | 2.158 | 1.95 | 1.95 | 1.908 | 9.796 | 27.9833 | 23.121 | 30.513 | 0 |

*Note:* Data from Klippel and Parmalee (1982). Climate restriction index and bioclimatic component defined in Hernández Fernández and Peláez-Campomanes (2005).

**TABLE 3.3.** Transfer Functions for Rodent Faunas from Hernández Fernández and Peláez–Campomanes (2005).

| Climatic Factor | b | aII | aII/III | aIII | aIV | aV | aVI | aVII | aVIII | aIX |
|---|---|---|---|---|---|---|---|---|---|---|
| T | 26.686 | 0.024 | −0.029 | −0.024 | −0.074 | −0.12 | −0.135 | −0.217 | −0.404 | −0.386 |
| Tp | 3205.394 | 2.657 | −3.408 | −3.762 | −8.691 | −12.934 | −23.194 | −22.625 | −30.897 | −32.036 |
| Tmax | 26.219 | 0.07 | 0.021 | 0.02 | 0.031 | −0.032 | −0.113 | −0.037 | −0.121 | −0.287 |
| Tmin | 27.538 | −0.033 | −0.096 | −0.08 | −0.175 | −0.212 | −0.141 | −0.418 | −0.71 | −0.465 |
| Mta | −1.319 | 0.103 | 0.117 | 0.1 | 0.206 | 0.18 | 0.027 | 0.381 | 0.589 | 0.178 |
| It | 817.614 | −0.421 | −2.199 | −1.846 | −4.242 | −5.435 | 0.027 | 0.381 | 0.589 | 0.178 |
| Itc | 726.156 | 0.267 | −1.497 | −1.583 | −2.949 | −3.973 | −5.752 | −7.092 | −11.409 | −13.014 |
| W | −0.013 | 0.002 | −0.004 | −0.006 | −0.004 | 0.006 | −0.034 | 0.049 | 0.11 | 0.09 |
| VAP | 12.075 | −0.007 | 0.002 | 0.003 | 0.01 | 0.027 | −0.055 | −0.066 | −0.107 | −0.131 |
| FVAP | 13.137 | −0.05 | −0.139 | −0.187 | −0.099 | 0.055 | −0.03 | −0.117 | −0.114 | −0.146 |
| P | 2978.195 | −21.237 | −27.563 | −33.05 | −32.648 | −6.678 | −5.076 | −28.4 | −33.109 | −25.98 |
| D | −1.064 | 0.043 | 0.141 | 0.189 | 0.11 | −0.027 | −0.027 | 0.053 | 0.006 | 0.014 |

*Note:* See Table 3.1 for definitions of climatic factors.

**TABLE 3.4.** Locality List for Small-Fauna Assemblages Used in Bioclimatic Modeling.

| Paleolocality | Period[a] | Region | Calibrated BP age range (2 sigma) | Number of taxa | Reference |
|---|---|---|---|---|---|
| Little Canyon Creek Cave | H | West | 6790–6490 | 11 | Walker 1987 |
| Mud Creek | H | East | 7310–7150 | 14 | Semken and Falk 1987 |
| Cherokee Sewer (Hzn 1) | H | East | 7420–7160 | 11 | Semken 1980 |
| Cherokee Sewer (Hzn 2b) | H | East | 8150–7940 | 10 | Semken 1980 |
| Cherokee Sewer (Hzn 3a) | H | East | 8350–8060 | 9[b] | Semken 1980 |
| Cherokee Sewer (Hzn 2c) | H | East | 8360–8200 | 12 | Semken 1980 |
| Rodgers Shelter (9) | H | East | 9250–8770 | 10 | Parmalee et al. 1976 |
| Little Box Elder Cave (Late) | H | West | 11,100–10,150 | 22 | Walker 1987 |
| Dows | H | East | 11,100–10,300 | 11 | Semken and Falk 1987 |
| Medicine Lodge Creek | H | West | 11,190–10,700 | 16 | Walker 1987 |
| Jones Miller | YD | West | 12,250–11,050 | 26 | Graham 1987 |
| Natural Trap (Terminal Pleistocene) | YD | West | 13,250–12,400 | 9[b] | Walker 1987 |
| Robert | B-A | West | 13,450–12,650 | 15 | Davis 1987 |
| Chimney Rock | B-A | West | 14,050–13,650 | 9[b] | Graham 1987 |
| Bell Cave | B-A | West | 14,750–13,750 | 18 | Walker 1987 |
| Brayton | B-A | East | 14,800–14,100 | 9[b] | Semken and Falk 1987 |
| New Paris #4 | B-A | East | 15,130–12,550 | 25 | Guilday et al. 1964; Semken et al. 2010 |
| Prospects Shelter (Terminal Pleistocene) | Sta | West | 15,650–14,550 | 12 | Walker 1987 |
| Natural Chimneys | Sta | East | 15,870–13,780 | 33 | Guilday 1962; Semken 1988; Semken et al. 2010 |
| Cheek Bend Cave (Hzn 2) | Sta | East | 17,350–16,740 | 24 | Klippel and Parmalee 1982; Semken et al. 2010 |
| Waubonsie (Waubonsie) | Sta | East | 18,750–16,650 | 21 | Rhodes 1984 |
| Haystack Cave | Sta | West | 18,650–17,050 | 11 | Emslie 1986 |
| Selby Dutton (Peoria Loess) | Sta | West | 19,450–18,990 | 7[b] | Graham 1987 |
| Boney Spring bonebed | Sta | East | 19,810–15,650 | 15 | Saunders 1977 |
| Peccary Cave (Unit C) | Sta | East | 19,830–19,570 | 34 | Semken 1988; Semken et al. 2010 |
| Moscow fissure | Sta | East | 22,250–18,750 | 21 | Foley 1984 |
| Natural Trap (Full glacial) | Sta | West | 22,900–22,350 | 14 | Walker 1987 |
| Waubonsie (Craigmile) | Sta | East | 23,850–22,650 | 24 | Rhodes 1984 |
| Welsh Cave | Sta | East | 24,100–18,900 | 15 | Guilday et al. 1971; Semken et al. 2010 |

*Note:* Regions defined and localities shown in Figure 3.2.
[a] H = Holocene, YD = Younger Dryas, B-A = Bølling-Allerød, Sta = Stadial.
[b] Assemblage with a small number of taxa; results are the same regardless of inclusion or exclusion of these data points.

important in some contexts for Cody groups, we must study the population dynamics and behavioral ecology of bison herds if we are to understand Cody land-use and subsistence decisions. From a paleobiological point of view, bison have the added benefit of entering the fossil record in large numbers as the result of catastrophic (or nearly so) kill operations. The fossil record of bison gives us a unique window into how one species tracks landscape changes throughout the Pleistocene/Holocene transition.

Temporal changes in bison skeletal morphology have interested archaeologists and paleontologists since the nineteenth century (Leidy 1852; McDonald 1981). Changes in cranial traits during the Pleistocene/Holocene transition are complicated by the presence of long-horned, Pleistocene taxa that show a high degree of inter- and intraspecies variability (e.g., *Bison latifrons*, *Bison alaskensis*, *Bison crassicornis*). However, among the short-horned species (e.g., *B. antiquus antiquus*, *B. antiquus occidentalis*, *B. bison bison*, *B. bison athabascae*) there is more consistency within the genus. Previously, researchers used bison biometric datasets to infer a gradual decrease in body size throughout the late Pleistocene and Holocene (McDonald 1981; Wilson 1975). However, recent research shows that this diminution tracks overall landscape changes fairly closely and is neither gradual nor unidirectional (Hill et al. 2008).

It is important to note that bison body size and the evolution of cranial traits may change independently of each other (Guthrie 1980). Body size is directly affected by the quality and quantity of forage ingested by an animal. Size of an animal is best estimated through examination of postcranial, load-bearing elements such as metapodials, calcanei, or other limb bones (Hill et al. 2008). Alternatively, cranial traits such as horn-core size and shape are a function of successful social behaviors within a bison population (Guthrie 1980). Horn-core curvature, compression, length, and other characteristics will vary depending on the frequency and severity of dominance contests in both male and female bison.

Biometric studies of bison remains are relatively standard in zooarchaeological analyses in the Great Plains. Often these studies are used to gain information about the demographic structure of a herd in a kill site (e.g., Todd 1987) or to determine taxonomic identity (e.g., Wilson 1974). However, bison biometrics also reflect basic biological information such as body size and successful evolutionary traits. When examined within a long-term chronological context, they provide valuable information on nutritional status and intraspecific competition, both of which have some bearing on animal density and the availability of good-quality forage on the landscape.

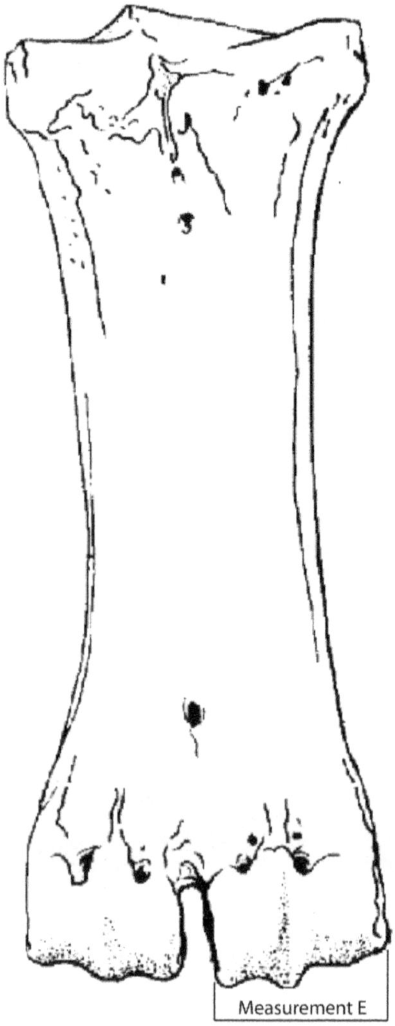


FIGURE 3.3. Location of measurement E on distal medial condyle of *Bison* metacarpals.

A number of skeletal elements have been used as proxies for bison body size (Hill 1996; Hill et al. 2008; Hofman and Todd 2001; Speth 1983). Presumably the most accurate reflection of body size is preserved in load-bearing elements such as long bones and, in this analysis, metacarpals. The metacarpal dataset used in the current study is a portion of a larger dataset spanning North America throughout the late Pleistocene and Holocene. Previous analyses of bison metacarpals indicate that measurements such as distal condyle breadth successfully distinguish males from females, are sensitive to chronological changes in bison body size, and are minimally influenced by habitat variability (Widga 2006a, 2006b). For this study, I focus exclusively on breadth of the distal medial condyle (Figure 3.3). This measurement is highly correlated with other measures of metacarpal size and reflects overall trends in bison body size (Speth 1983; Widga 2006a).

Bison cranial traits are often used for examining the evolutionary dynamics of bison (McDonald 1981; Skinner and Kaisen 1947; Wilson 1975); however, recent work also emphasizes their utility for understanding broad-scale biogeographic patterns in bison social behaviors (Widga 2006a, 2006b). Measurements used in this analysis fol-

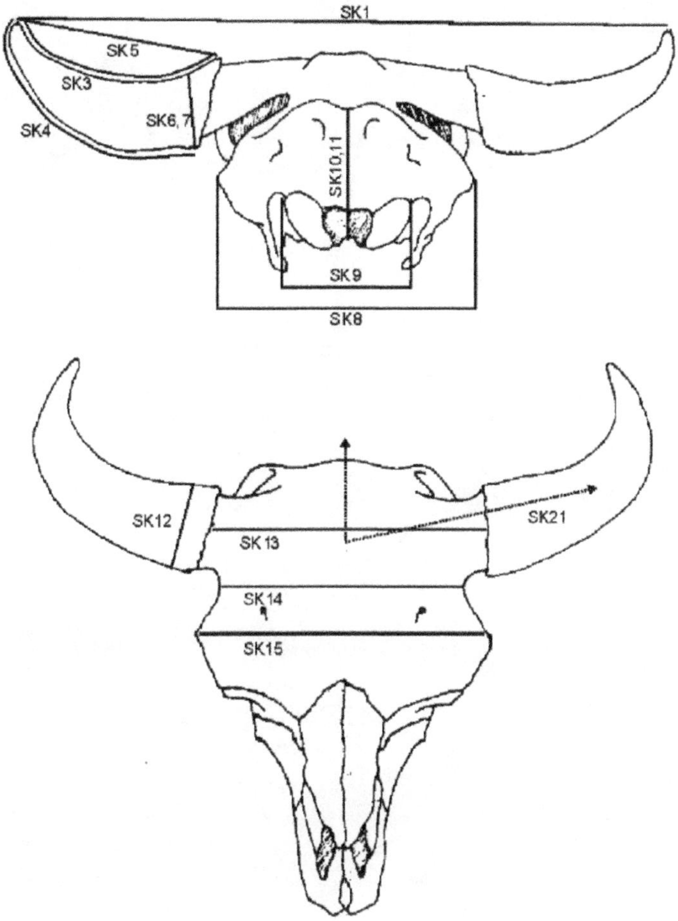


**FIGURE 3.4.** Locations of measurements on *Bison* crania. Numbers prefixed by "SK" refer to measurements codified by Skinner and Kaisen (1947).

low Wilson (1975) and McDonald (1978) (Figure 3.4). The horn-core indices were codified by Skinner and Kaisen (1947), with the exception of the index of horn-core curvature, which is modified here to increase sample size (Table 3.5).

### A Rodent's View of Landscape Evolution

Despite low data density during some periods (including the Cody period), faunal data from the Great Plains and eastern United States successfully reflect the broad outlines of landscape changes that occurred after the Late Glacial Maximum (LGM) in North America. Further, they provide semi-quantitative paleoenvironmental information in areas where alternative climate proxies are unavailable (Table 3.6a, Table 3.6b, and Figure 3.5).

**TABLE 3.5.** Horn-Core Shape Indices.

| Index | Description[a] |
|---|---|
| Horn-core curvature[b] | (Horn-core length on upper curve (SK3)/Core tip to burr (SK5))100 |
| Horn-core compression | (Vertical diameter of core at base (SK6)/Transverse diameter of core at base (SK12))100 |
| Horn-core proportion | (Core length on upper curve, tip to burr (SK3)/Circumference of core at base (SK7))100 |
| Horn-core length | (Length of core on upper curve, tip to burr (SK3)/postcranial width of skull (SK14))100 |

[a] SK refers to numbered measurements in Skinner and Kaisen (1947).
[b] Modified from Skinner and Kaisen (1947). As originally defined, this index used the length of horn core along the lower curve (SK4) rather than the upper curve (SK3).

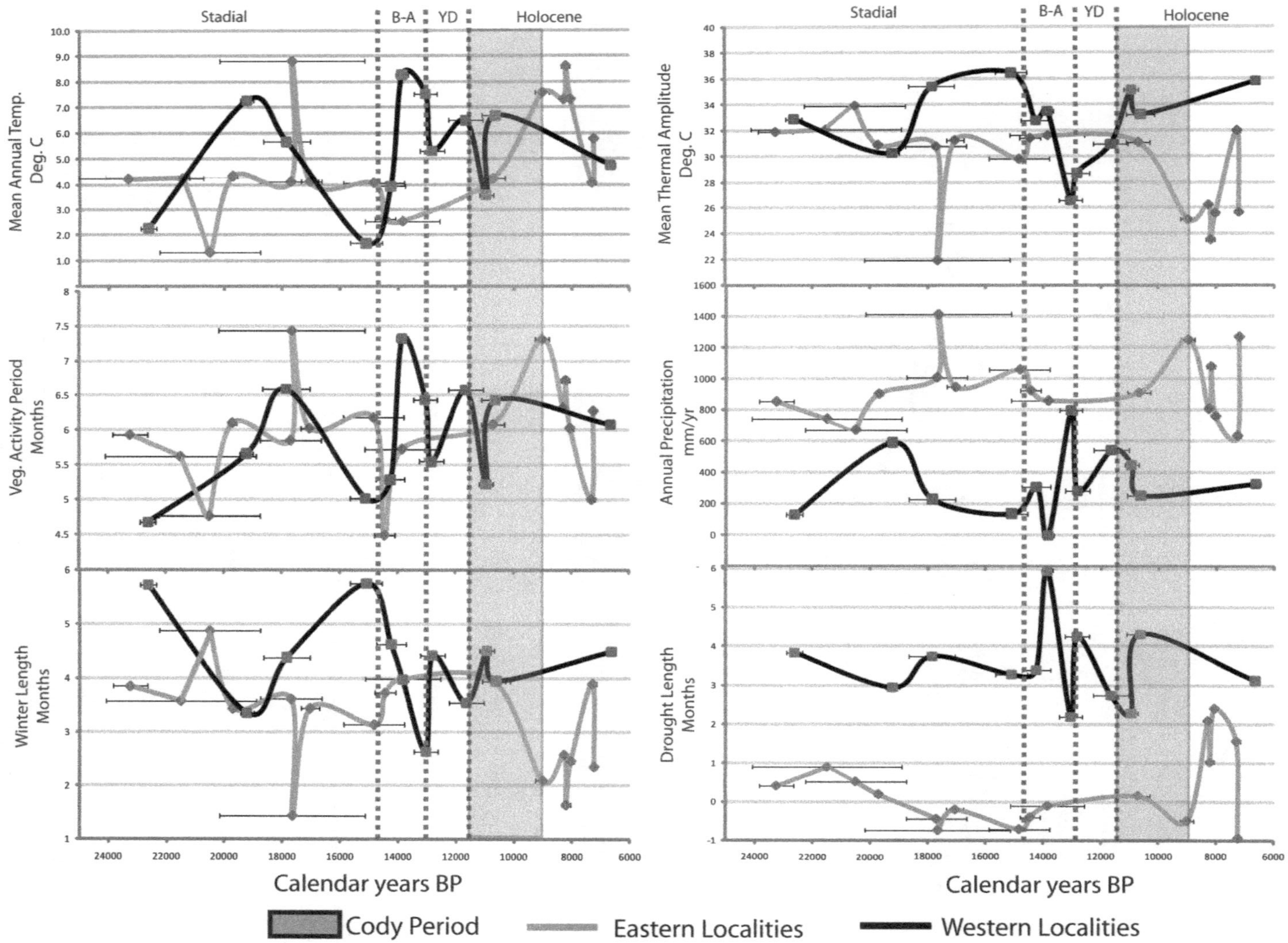


FIGURE 3.5. Paleoclimatic trends inferred from rodent faunas.

**TABLE 3.6A.** Bioclimatic Indices from Small-Fauna Assemblages.

| Paleolocality | Biome I | Biome II | Biome II/III | Biome III | Biome IV | Biome V | Biome VI | Biome VII | Biome VIII | Biome IX |
|---|---|---|---|---|---|---|---|---|---|---|
| Mud Creek | 0.000 | 0.893 | 0.893 | 0.893 | 0.893 | 15.171 | 33.614 | 30.043 | 15.764 | 1.786 |
| Cherokee Sewer (Hzn 1) | 0.000 | 2.436 | 2.436 | 2.436 | 2.436 | 1.136 | 24.400 | 42.582 | 19.855 | 2.273 |
| Cherokee Sewer (Hzn 2b) | 0.000 | 2.680 | 4.350 | 6.850 | 6.850 | 1.250 | 29.340 | 29.340 | 16.840 | 2.500 |
| Cherokee Sewer (Hzn 3a) | 0.000 | 1.589 | 1.589 | 4.367 | 6.589 | 8.700 | 33.433 | 33.433 | 10.289 | 0.000 |
| Cherokee Sewer (Hzn 2c) | 0.000 | 2.233 | 3.625 | 5.708 | 5.708 | 5.900 | 26.533 | 34.867 | 13.342 | 2.083 |
| Rodgers Shelter (9) | 1.430 | 3.100 | 1.430 | 1.430 | 3.670 | 17.590 | 29.250 | 25.920 | 16.160 | 0.000 |
| Dows | 0.000 | 1.136 | 1.136 | 1.136 | 4.164 | 6.436 | 20.818 | 23.845 | 29.909 | 2.273 |
| New Paris #4 | 0.000 | 1.740 | 2.540 | 2.540 | 2.408 | 10.496 | 25.196 | 17.864 | 33.200 | 4.000 |
| Brayton | 0.000 | 0.000 | 0.000 | 0.000 | 0.000 | 3.700 | 32.389 | 37.944 | 23.133 | 2.778 |
| Welsh Cave | 0.000 | 1.947 | 2.167 | 2.167 | 4.167 | 4.167 | 26.600 | 32.153 | 26.600 | 0.000 |
| Natural Chimneys | 0.000 | 1.191 | 1.545 | 1.545 | 2.555 | 12.470 | 30.424 | 19.818 | 29.670 | 0.758 |
| Cheek Bend Cave (Hzn 2) | 0.596 | 2.158 | 1.950 | 1.950 | 1.908 | 9.796 | 27.983 | 23.121 | 30.513 | 0.000 |
| Waubonsie (Waubonsie) | 0.000 | 1.390 | 0.595 | 0.595 | 1.390 | 8.924 | 25.981 | 28.362 | 26.781 | 1.190 |
| Boney Spring bonebed | 0.953 | 4.687 | 1.907 | 1.907 | 2.067 | 18.167 | 33.560 | 24.673 | 12.060 | 0.000 |
| Peccary Cave (Unit C) | 0.000 | 1.744 | 2.088 | 2.088 | 2.479 | 10.729 | 26.097 | 28.156 | 25.856 | 0.735 |
| Moscow fissure | 0.000 | 0.000 | 1.748 | 1.748 | 2.381 | 2.776 | 20.786 | 27.133 | 32.690 | 5.952 |
| Waubonsie (Craigmile) | 0.000 | 1.217 | 0.521 | 2.604 | 2.604 | 7.808 | 22.733 | 30.371 | 26.904 | 1.042 |
| Little Canyon Creek Cave | 0.000 | 1.136 | 2.955 | 2.955 | 5.982 | 5.982 | 10.827 | 54.764 | 15.373 | 0.000 |
| Little Box Elder Cave (Late) | 0.000 | 2.355 | 3.264 | 7.809 | 8.941 | 2.127 | 12.123 | 47.345 | 16.014 | 0.000 |
| Medicine Lodge Creek | 0.000 | 0.000 | 2.294 | 2.294 | 3.125 | 3.644 | 16.869 | 53.325 | 16.869 | 1.563 |
| Jones Miller | 0.000 | 3.115 | 2.154 | 6.000 | 7.281 | 7.050 | 16.892 | 39.646 | 16.892 | 0.962 |
| Natural Trap (Terminal Pleistocene) | 0.000 | 5.756 | 5.756 | 5.756 | 6.678 | 2.978 | 8.533 | 48.344 | 5.089 | 11.111 |
| Robert | 0.000 | 1.907 | 3.020 | 6.353 | 5.240 | 7.060 | 25.233 | 37.453 | 12.060 | 1.667 |
| Chimney Rock | 0.000 | 2.978 | 2.978 | 8.533 | 15.933 | 2.978 | 2.978 | 54.822 | 8.789 | 0.000 |
| Bell Cave | 0.000 | 0.000 | 2.039 | 4.817 | 7.406 | 3.239 | 12.222 | 52.033 | 11.294 | 6.944 |
| Prospects Shelter (Terminal Pleistocene) | 0.000 | 4.317 | 4.317 | 4.317 | 5.008 | 2.233 | 6.400 | 40.425 | 24.650 | 8.333 |
| Haystack Cave | 0.000 | 2.818 | 2.818 | 2.818 | 10.391 | 5.845 | 7.364 | 54.327 | 13.636 | 0.000 |
| Selby Dutton (Peoria Loess) | 0.000 | 2.386 | 0.000 | 7.143 | 2.386 | 2.386 | 21.429 | 57.143 | 7.143 | 0.000 |
| Natural Trap (Full glacial) | 0.000 | 4.893 | 3.700 | 3.700 | 5.486 | 3.107 | 3.107 | 53.700 | 8.036 | 14.286 |

**TABLE 3.6B.** Paleoclimatic Data from Small–Fauna Assemblages.

| Paleolocality | T | Tp | Tmax | Tmin | Mta | It | Itc | W | VAP | FVAP | P | D |
|---|---|---|---|---|---|---|---|---|---|---|---|---|
| Mud Creek | 5.77±3.0 | 872±24 | 18.58±2.2 | −7.09±3.7 | 25.62±2.5 | −83±28 | 23±39 | 2.4±1.3 | 6.3±0.7 | 7.3±1.0 | 1268±26 | −0.9±2.6 |
| Cherokee Sewer (Hzn 1) | 4.07±3.5 | 866±24 | 19.94±2.1 | −12.09±2.9 | 31.97±2.2 | −198±18 | −5±82 | 3.9±1.0 | 5.0±0.8 | 3.5±1.4 | 633±37 | 1.6±2.0 |
| Cherokee Sewer (Hzn 2b) | 7.32±2.6 | 1104±21 | 20.22±2.1 | −5.39±4.3 | 25.56±2.5 | −31±46 | 75±21 | 2.5±1.2 | 6.0±0.8 | 3.7±1.4 | 758±34 | 2.4±1.6 |
| Cherokee Sewer (Hzn 3a) | 8.61±2.4 | 1084±22 | 20.45±2.1 | −3.11±5.6 | 23.51±2.6 | 26±50 | 98±19 | 1.6±1.5 | 6.7±0.7 | 5.8±1.1 | 1079±28 | 1.0±2.5 |
| Cherokee Sewer (Hzn 2c) | 7.31±2.6 | 1090±22 | 20.44±2.1 | −5.81±4.1 | 26.20±2.5 | −40±40 | 75±21 | 2.6±1.2 | 6.3±0.7 | 4.3±1.3 | 805±33 | 2.1±1.8 |
| Rodgers Shelter (9) | 7.57±2.6 | 1096±22 | 20.18±2.1 | −4.93±4.5 | 25.07±2.5 | −21±56 | 92±19 | 2.1±1.3 | 7.3±0.7 | 7.9±0.9 | 1250±26 | −0.5±3.6 |
| Dows | 4.24±3.5 | 1010±22 | 19.63±2.1 | −11.48±2.9 | 31.06±2.3 | −186±19 | 28±35 | 3.9±1.0 | 6.1±0.8 | 6.0±1.1 | 907±31 | 0.2±6.6 |
| New Paris #4 | 2.53±4.5 | 849±24 | 18.30±2.2 | −13.35±2.7 | 31.60±2.2 | −240±17 | −29±34 | 4.0±1.0 | 5.7±0.8 | 5.9±1.1 | 857±32 | −0.1±7.7 |
| Brayton | 2.61±4.4 | 643±28 | 18.03±2.2 | −13.42±2.7 | 31.39±2.2 | −242±16 | −64±23 | 3.7±1.0 | 4.5±0.9 | 5.0±1.2 | 923±30 | −0.4±4.0 |
| Welsh Cave | 4.25±3.5 | 897±24 | 20.17±2.1 | −11.96±2.9 | 32.08±2.2 | −194±18 | 11±56 | 3.6±1.0 | 5.6±0.8 | 4.8±1.2 | 740±34 | 0.9±2.7 |
| Natural Chimneys | 4.06±3.5 | 869±24 | 18.91±2.1 | −10.93±3.0 | 29.79±2.3 | −177±19 | 4±89 | 3.1±1.1 | 6.2±0.7 | 6.9±1.0 | 1059±28 | −0.7±3.0 |
| Cheek Bend Cave (Hzn 2) | 4.12±3.5 | 909±24 | 19.63±2.1 | −11.65±2.9 | 31.23±2.2 | −190±19 | 13±51 | 3.4±1.0 | 6.0±0.8 | 6.3±1.0 | 945±30 | −0.2±5.7 |
| Waubonsie (Waubonsie) | 4.11±3.5 | 904±24 | 19.38±2.1 | −11.44±2.9 | 30.76±2.3 | −186±19 | 10±57 | 3.6±1.0 | 5.9±0.8 | 6.4±1.0 | 1008±29 | −0.4±3.9 |
| Boney Spring bonebed | 8.80±2.4 | 1160±21 | 20.15±2.1 | −1.81±7.4 | 21.92±2.7 | 56±34 | 121±17 | 1.4±1.6 | 7.4±0.7 | 8.2±0.9 | 1410±25 | −0.7±3.0 |
| Peccary Cave (Unit C) | 4.3±3.4 | 911±24 | 19.69±2.1 | −11.25±3.0 | 30.88±2.3 | −180±19 | 14±49 | 3.4±1.0 | 6.1±0.8 | 6.0±1.1 | 900±31 | 0.2±5.9 |
| Moscow fissure | 1.3±6.2 | 768±26 | 17.95±2.2 | −16.02±2.5 | 33.90±2.2 | −307±15 | −68±23 | 4.9±0.9 | 4.8±0.9 | 4.3±1.3 | 671±36 | 0.5±3.5 |
| Waubonsie (Craigmile) | 4.3±3.4 | 953±23 | 20.02±2.1 | −11.91±2.9 | 31.88±2.2 | −194±18 | 20±42 | 3.9±1.0 | 5.9±0.8 | 5.6±1.1 | 851±32 | 0.4±4.0 |
| Little Canyon Creek Cave | 4.7±3.3 | 989±23 | 22.17±2.0 | −13.69±2.7 | 35.78±2.1 | −225±17 | 32±33 | 4.5±0.9 | 6.1±0.8 | 3.1±1.5 | 327±51 | 3.1±1.4 |
| Little Box Elder Cave (Late) | 6.7±2.8 | 1188±21 | 23.01±1.9 | −10.28±3.1 | 33.22±2.2 | −136±22 | 89±20 | 4.0±1.0 | 6.4±0.7 | 2.3±1.7 | 252±58 | 4.3±1.2 |
| Medicine Lodge Creek | 3.6±3.8 | 827±25 | 20.60±2.1 | −14.58±2.6 | 35.11±2.1 | −256±16 | −18±44 | 4.5±0.9 | 5.2±0.8 | 3.1±1.5 | 449±44 | 2.3±1.7 |
| Jones Miller | 6.5±2.8 | 1151±21 | 21.92±2.0 | −9.09±3.3 | 30.95±2.3 | −113±24 | 80±21 | 3.5±1.0 | 6.6±0.7 | 3.9±1.3 | 542±40 | 2.8±1.5 |
| Natural Trap (Terminal Pleistocene) | 5.3±3.1 | 1139±21 | 19.96±2.1 | −8.81±3.4 | 28.71±2.3 | −116±24 | 31±33 | 4.4±0.9 | 5.6±0.8 | 1.4±2.2 | 281±55 | 4.1±1.2 |
| Robert | 7.5±2.6 | 1105±21 | 20.75±2.0 | −5.87±4.1 | 26.56±2.4 | −40±41 | 81±21 | 2.6±1.2 | 6.4±0.7 | 4.3±1.3 | 795±33 | 2.2±1.7 |
| Chimney Rock | 8.3±2.5 | 1374±19 | 24.79±1.9 | −8.77±3.4 | 33.49±2.2 | −89±27 | 142±16 | 4.0±1.0 | 7.3±0.7 | 1.5±2.1 | 0±0 | 5.9±1.1 |
| Bell Cave | 3.9±3.6 | 906±24 | 19.88±2.1 | −12.94±2.8 | 32.75±2.2 | −219±17 | −19±43 | 4.6±0.9 | 5.3±0.8 | 2.0±1.8 | 307±53 | 3.4±1.4 |
| Prospects Shelter (Terminal Pleistocene) | 1.7±5.5 | 956±23 | 19.87±2.1 | −16.64±2.4 | 36.45±2.1 | −311±14 | −37±30 | 5.8±0.8 | 5.0±0.8 | 1.9±1.9 | 137±79 | 3.3±1.4 |
| Haystack Cave | 5.7±3.0 | 1118±21 | 23.12±1.9 | −12.36±2.8 | 35.41±2.1 | −187±18 | 68±23 | 4.4±0.9 | 6.6±0.7 | 3.0±1.5 | 227±61 | 3.7±1.3 |
| Selby Dutton (Peoria Loess) | 7.3±2.6 | 1069±22 | 22.18±2.0 | −8.16±3.5 | 30.27±2.3 | −87±27 | 75±21 | 3.4±1.0 | 5.7±0.8 | 2.9±1.5 | 591±38 | 2.9±1.5 |
| Natural Trap (Full glacial) | 2.3±4.8 | 949±23 | 18.83±2.1 | −14.11±2.7 | 32.88±2.2 | −254±16 | −50±26 | 5.7±0.8 | 4.7±0.9 | 1.0±2.6 | 131±81 | 3.8±1.3 |

*Note:* See Table 3.1 for definitions of climatic factors.

### *Stadial: >25,000–14,650 cal BP (21,000–12,500 $^{14}$C yr BP)*

The general outline of climatic parameters derived from rodent assemblages dating to this period is consistent with the known glacial chronology. In western assemblages (Figure 3.2), annual temperature estimates increase until ~19,000 cal BP, then decrease to 14,600 cal BP. Precipitation also increases to ~600 mm/yr by ~19,000 cal BP before stabilizing at ~200 mm/yr by ~18,000 cal BP. Indeed, there is a shift from warmer-wetter conditions with moderate thermal amplitude, winter length, and vegetation activity period in the Selby-Dutton assemblage (~19,000 cal BP) to more severe stadial conditions with the advance of the Des Moines and James lobes in the central and eastern Plains.

With two exceptions (see below), the eastern assemblages show relatively stable annual temperature, thermal amplitude, and winter length estimates. Moisture variables are also steady throughout this time (e.g., annual precipitation, drought length). The Waubonsie (Iowa) assemblage, dating to the Last Glacial Maximum, indicates cold stadial conditions, as does Peccary Cave (Arkansas). Interestingly, estimates of thermal amplitude at this time are as high as, or higher than, those of the early Holocene.

The Moscow Fissure (Wisconsin) and Boney Springs (Missouri) assemblages are exceptions to this general pattern. Moscow Fissure is located in the Driftless Area of southwestern Wisconsin, and the faunal assemblage dates to a time when the locality would have been close to the glacial margin (20,500 cal BP). The small-mammal fauna from this locality reflects this extreme environment, and reconstructed conditions were very cold and moderately dry.

The Boney Springs annual temperature, precipitation, and vegetation activity period estimates are much higher than other assemblages dating to this time period, and its thermal amplitude and winter length estimates are much lower. It is unlikely that these patterns are due to biogeographic variability since other assemblages from the region (Peccary Cave, Arkansas, and Wabonsie, Iowa) show expected stadial conditions at this time (~17,500 cal BP). However, it is possible that the relatively low taxonomic diversity of small mammals in the Boney Springs assemblage (15 taxa) is the cause of these anomalous patterns. It is also possible that the predictive equations do not deal well with the particular nature of late Pleistocene disharmonious faunas in the western Ozarks.

These trends are broadly consistent with the deglaciation sequence proposed by Dyke and colleagues (2003; Dyke 2004). Although LGM ice covered the Great Lakes from 22,000 to 19,100 cal BP, there is a brief recession ~18,500 cal BP when open water is present in the southern Great Lakes. Ice still covered much of this region until ~16,800 cal BP, when the southern Laurentide ice sheet underwent a series of retreats and readvances. Major advances of both the James lobe in the Dakotas and the Des Moines lobe in the eastern Plains between 18,000 and 14,600 cal BP strongly affected the biogeographic distribution of small-mammal taxa. Pollen records also indicate cool, dry spruce parkland in the northern Plains and Midwest (Gonzalez and Grimm 2009; Grimm and Jacobson 2004; Yansa 2007).

### *Bølling-Allerød: 14,650–12,900 cal BP (12,500–11,000 $^{14}$C yr BP)*

The Bølling-Allerød is represented by only three assemblages in the High Plains and two in the eastern United States. The beginning of the Bølling chronozone is very cold and exhibits relatively short vegetation activity periods. Temperatures generally increase throughout the Bølling-Allerød. In the western localities, thermal amplitude and winter length decrease dramatically. Precipitation initially increases slightly over late stadial conditions, then dry conditions are present ~14,000 cal BP, followed by increases in moisture toward the end of the Allerød.

Eastern assemblages at the beginning of the Bølling suggest that annual temperatures were cooler than the preceding late stadial but similarly dry. The nature of Allerød temperature and precipitation parameters based on eastern faunules is unknown.

Glacial records indicate increasing temperatures and general recession of the Laurentide ice sheet during this period. The James and Des Moines lobes retreat for the last time by 14,100 cal BP, and all but the northernmost Great Lakes are open water (Dyke et al. 2003). Open spruce parkland is maintained in the northern Plains

(Grimm et al. 2011; Yansa 2007), while black ash and other deciduous species dominate the region surrounding the deglaciated Great Lakes (Gonzalez and Grimm 2009).

### *Younger Dryas: 12,900–11,700 cal BP (11,000–10,100 $^{14}$C yr BP)*

Two High Plains assemblages are available from the Younger Dryas, one from the early Younger Dryas (Natural Trap Cave, Wyoming) and one late in this chronozone (Jones-Miller, Colorado). There are no well-dated assemblages from the eastern United States to represent this time period. The early Younger Dryas is generally cooler and drier than the peak of Bølling-Allerød warming, although not to the extent of the preceding stadial. The late Younger Dryas assemblage may represent the onset of Holocene conditions because it exhibits a return to warmer conditions with more precipitation.

At a larger landscape scale, deglaciation proceeds rapidly during this period, and by 11,600 cal BP Lake Superior and the St. Lawrence River are ice free (Dyke et al. 2003). Open spruce parkland transitions into grassland (western) or deciduous parkland (eastern) in the northern Plains (Grimm et al. 2011; Yansa 2007), and there is a decline of deciduous taxa and a resurgence of spruce in the Great Lakes. This supports the inference for cold-dry conditions, particularly in the latter half of the Younger Dryas (Gonzalez and Grimm 2009).

### *Early Holocene (Cody Period): 11,700–9000 cal BP (10,100–8100 $^{14}$C yr BP)*

Both regions exhibit low data density for the Cody period, so only a coarse approximation of paleoenvironmental parameters is possible. Data from two Great Plains assemblages from the early part of the Cody period and two eastern assemblages spanning the Cody period are available. Elevated temperatures and decreasing moisture levels are present in the Great Plains and Rocky Mountains at the beginning of this period. Temperature reconstructions from Medicine Lodge Creek suggest a possible cold event at the beginning of the Holocene, ~11,000 cal BP. Little Box Elder Creek Cave has warmer temperature estimates, similar to the end of the Younger Dryas, but with increased seasonal amplitude and less moisture. No data are available for the second half of the Cody period in the western assemblages.

In the eastern United States, there is a warming trend accompanied by increased moisture; however, the resolution of this trend is coarse due to low data density for the period. The subsequent post-Cody period (<9000 cal BP) shows continued warming and a decrease in moisture until ~7500 cal BP, when there is abrupt cooling and increased precipitation.

Pollen records from the northern Plains also suggest warming and drying. The nonarboreal component of the landscape increases, passing ~50 percent of the total pollen assemblage at Coldwater Lake (North Dakota) by ~11,500 cal BP (Yansa 2007). There is a prominent, permanent shift to drier conditions at ~9250 cal BP in the western northern Great Plains (Grimm et al. 2011). In the Great Lakes, deciduous taxa typical of the Holocene (e.g., elm, oak) rapidly dominate the local pollen rain after 11,000 cal BP (Gonzalez and Grimm 2009).

### *Paleoenvironmental Summary*

Overall, quantitative bioclimatic models derived from rodent paleofaunas indicate a series of oscillating climate episodes between ~25,000 and 6000 cal BP (Table 3.7). It is important to note that reconstructed climate parameters in the Great Plains and eastern North America do not necessarily proceed in lockstep. Mid-to-high-elevation localities in the Rocky Mountains and the High Plains show climatic changes that generally correlate with glacial activity. Assemblages in the eastern United States show less overall variability, however, particularly with respect to moisture variables, and a relative insensitivity to glacial activity in the Great Lakes area.

#### *Western Assemblages*

In the High Plains and Rocky Mountains, the LGM was very cold and dry at ~23,000 and 14,600 cal BP. However, between ~19,000 and 18,500, conditions were significantly warmer with more effective precipitation. The Bølling-Allerød was a period of increasing temperatures and variable precipitation, while the Younger Dryas was cooler (compared with the Bølling-Allerød) with variable precipitation. Longer droughts and reduced rainfall characterize the early part of the

**TABLE 3.7.** Summary of Landscape Changes Evident in Faunal Proxy Data during the Late Quaternary in the High Plains and Eastern North America.

| Time Period | Bioclimatic Component Trends | Metacarpal Trends | Horn-Core Trends |
|---|---|---|---|
| 25,000–14,650 cal BP<br>Stadial | Temperature: Cold<br>Precipitation: Dry<br>Drought severity: High<br>*Relatively warm/moist between ~19,000–18,500 cal BP | No data | No data |
| 14,650–12,900 cal BP<br>Bølling-Allerød | Temperature: Increasing<br>Precipitation: Variable<br>Drought severity: Increasing<br>Winter severity: Decreasing (west); increasing (east) | No data | Small sample size |
| 12,900–11,700 cal BP<br>Younger Dryas | Temperature: Decreasing<br>Precipitation: Increasing (west)<br>Drought severity: Decreasing<br>Winter severity: Decreasing (west); increasing (east) | Relatively stable | Curvature: Increasing<br>Compression: Increasing<br>Proportion: Stable |
| 11,700–9000 cal BP<br>Early Holocene (Cody) | Temperature: Increasing?<br>Precipitation: Decreasing (west); increasing (east)<br>Drought severity: Increasing (west); decreasing (east)<br>Winter severity: Stable (west); decreasing (east) | Decreasing size | Curvature: High, then decreasing<br>Compression: High<br>Proportion: Decreasing |
| 9000–6000 cal BP<br>(post-Cody) | Temperature: Increasing<br>Precipitation: Decreasing<br>Drought severity: High<br>Winter severity: Increasing | Stable | Curvature: Decreasing<br>Compression: Variable<br>Proportion: Stable |

*Note:* Faunal proxy data include small-mammal faunal assemblage, bison metacarpal size, and bison horn-core shape.

Cody period. Temperature-based parameters (e.g., mean annual temperature, vegetative activity period, winter length) are more or less stable throughout the early Holocene.

Thermal amplitude is high during the Late Glacial (18,500–14,600 cal BP) and decreases to a low at the beginning of the Younger Dryas (12,900 cal BP), then increases again into the early Holocene. This indicates increasing seasonality into the early Holocene. Significantly, thermal amplitude levels at this time never reach those of the Late Glacial.

*Eastern Assemblages*

In eastern North America, the LGM is cold and dry. The warm, wet conditions that characterize Boney Springs occur simultaneously with the relatively warm and wet conditions in the High Plains; however, it is also possible that these conditions are a methodological artifact (see above). Conditions in the Driftless Area of the Midwest during this time were extremely cold and somewhat dry, as would be expected. The beginning of the Bølling is very cold and moderately dry; however, no assemblages are available from this region for the Allerød or Younger Dryas. Temperature and moisture estimates increase throughout the early Holocene Cody period to a high ~9000 cal BP, then precipitation decreases and drought length increases dramatically. A decrease in temperature lags behind the initiation of this dry period by ~1000 years.

Thermal amplitude in the eastern assemblages remains relatively steady until the early Holocene (~9000 cal BP). Thereafter, it decreases significantly, perhaps resulting in permanent changes to the Holocene landscape.

## Bison during the Pleistocene/Holocene Transition

Biometric data were recorded on 272 bison metacarpals from 15 stratigraphic contexts dating between 13,000 and 6000 cal BP. Summary data are presented in Table 3.8. Breadth measurements provide the best measure of gross body size. Figure 3.6 shows temporal changes in the breadth of the distal medial condyle. While there is an overall trend toward body-size diminution, this trend is by no means gradual or even linear. A similar pattern has recently been demonstrated in *Bison* calcanei and humeri (Hill et al. 2008). Based on these metacarpal data, bison body size was

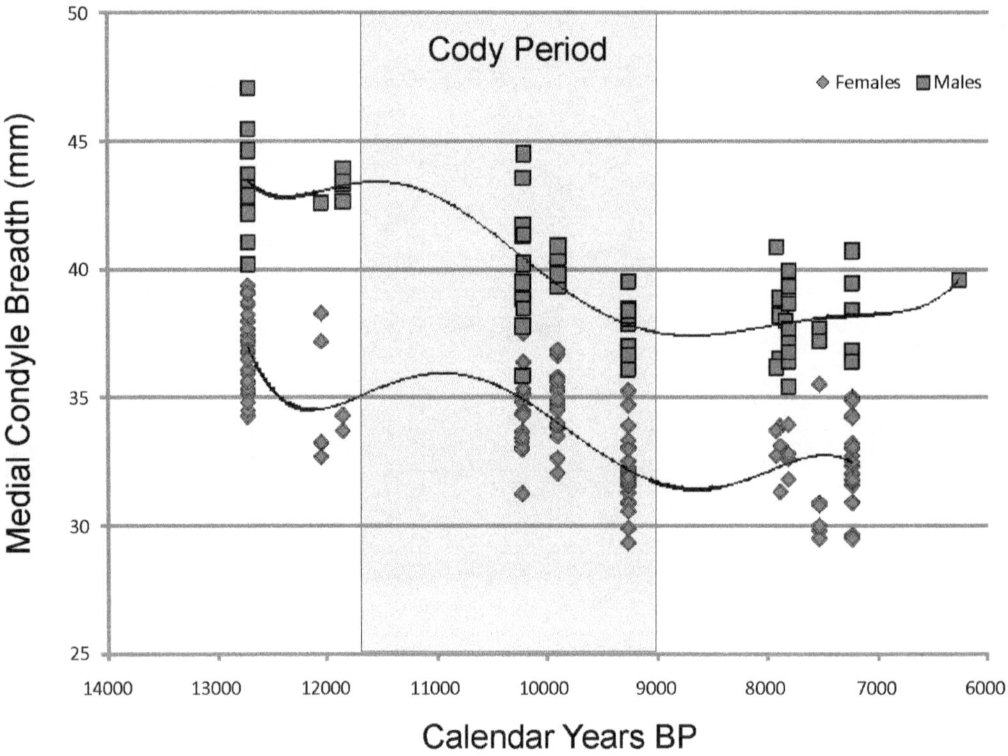


**FIGURE 3.6.** Bison body size change as measured by width of the medial distal condyle.

relatively stable between 13,000 and 11,500 cal BP. During Eden-Scottsbluff times (~10,600–9600 cal BP), bison underwent a relatively rapid decrease in body size before stabilizing during the early part of the middle Holocene (9000–6000 cal BP). Body-size changes in both males and females occur synchronously. This rapid, early Holocene decrease in body size corresponds to a period of landscape warming and drying, as is evident in the small-fauna bioclimatic models (see above) and other proxy records from the High Plains.

The late Pleistocene/early Holocene bison crania dataset includes 139 specimens from 24 dated contexts (Table 3.9). While trends are highly variable, crania and horn-core size decreased gradually throughout the late Pleistocene and Holocene. Horn-core shape characteristics, on the other hand, do not follow crania size in lockstep (Figure 3.7). Beginning ~12,000 cal BP, compression indices increase to a peak ~10,000 cal BP and remain high afterward. Both male and female curvature values are variable during the Cody period, with slightly above average values in male crania. The proportion indices of all animals generally decrease over the same time period. These trends have often been interpreted in terms of the northern *B. occidentalis* morphotype successfully replacing the *B. antiquus* morphotype in postglacial North America. However, recent aDNA studies suggest that bison south of the ice sheets were a single breeding population (Shapiro et al. 2004). Thus, these changes in horn-core characteristics are better interpreted as evolutionarily successful traits in bison of the postglacial landscape. In this case, we are potentially seeing the success or failure of specific traits in response to ecological pressures.

Overall, bison show a decrease in body size and horn-core proportion during the Cody period, and an increase in horn-core compression. Curvature in male animals is only slightly higher during this period. These changes occur during relatively moderate changes in landscape conditions. Overall, temperatures were slightly cooler and the region was drier with longer droughts.

**TABLE 3.8.** Summary Data of Late Pleistocene/Early Holocene Bison Metacarpals.

| Locality | Sex | Cal Years BP (2 sig.) | *N* | Mean (SD) | Reference |
|---|---|---|---|---|---|
| Coffey | Male | 6500–6000 | 1 | 39.6 | Schmits 1978 |
| Interstate Bog | Female | 7580–7470[a] | 7 | 32 (3.2)[a] | Pond 1937 |
| | Male | | 3 | 37.4 (0.3)[a] | |
| Cherokee 1a | Female | 7530–7020 | 10 | 32.7 (1.3) | Anderson and Semken 1980 |
| | Male | | 4 | 38.9 (1.6) | |
| Logan Creek B | Female | 7600–6850 | 12 | 32.4 (1.7) | Kivett 1962; Mandel 1995 |
| | Male | | 1 | 36.4 | |
| Simonsen, level 7 | Female | 7930–7680 | 4 | 32.8 (0.9) | Agogino and Frankforter 1960 |
| | Male | | 11 | 37.9 (1.6) | |
| Itasca | Female | 7970–7790 | 3 | 32.8 (1.3) | Shay 1971 |
| | Male | | 3 | 37.9 (1.2) | |
| Logan Creek C | Female | 8000–7670 | 1 | 32.7 | Kivett 1962; Mandel 1995 |
| | Male | | 1 | 38 | |
| Logan Creek D | Female | 8160–7670 | 2 | 33.2 (0.7) | Kivett 1962; Mandel 1995 |
| | Male | | 2 | 38.5 (3.3) | |
| Milburn | Female | 9490–9030 | 34 | 32 (1.2) | Hillerud 1970 |
| | Male | | 14 | 37.7 (1) | |
| Scottsbluff | Female | 10,200–9600 | 17 | 34.7 (1.3) | Hill 2007; Schultz and Eisley 1935 |
| | Male | | 4 | 40.1 (0.7) | |
| Clary Ranch | Female | 10,250–10,180 | 9 | 35.5 (1) | Myers et al. 1981; Hill 2005 |
| | Male | | 4 | 41.2 (2.5) | |
| Burntwood Creek | Female | 10,550–9900 | 6 | 34.4 (1.1) | Hill et al. 1992 |
| | Male | | 5 | 39.6 (3) | |
| 12 Mile Creek | Female | 12,450–11,250 | 2 | 34 (0.4) | Hill 2002 |
| | Male | | 4 | 43.4 (0.5) | |
| Allen | Female | 12,950–11,150 | 5 | 34.9 (2.6) | Bamforth 2007; Holder and Wike 1949 |
| | Male | | 1 | 42.6 | |
| Lipscomb | Female | 13,100–12,350 | 30 | 37 (1.5) | Schultz 1943; Hofman 1995 |
| | Male | | 11 | 43.5 (2) | |

[a] Data courtesy of Matthew G. Hill, Iowa State University.

Thermal amplitude was relatively high when compared with the Younger Dryas. These landscape changes were not extreme and do not support interpretations of intense environmental pressure on early Holocene bison populations. Perhaps the largest landscape change leading to increased numbers of bison in Cody archaeological sites was the extinction of other megafauna. Increased intrataxonomic competition likely had a concomitant negative impact on animal nutrition, thus decreasing animal body size (Hill et al. 2008).

Changes in horn-core morphology can be linked to changes in bison dominance behavior (McDonald 1981). Horn-core morphology in the extant large Bovidae can be visualized as a spectrum with "hook-and-roll" fighters on one end (*Bubalus* sp.) and "clash-and-release" fighters on the other (*Bison bison*). Species with hook-and-roll strategies tend to have simple dominance hierarchies due to smaller herd sizes, whereas clash-and-release taxa live in larger groups with more rigid social hierarchies. Increases in bison horn-core compression and decreases in horn-core proportion are both morphological adjustments to the clash-and-release fighting style that characterizes modern bison, which navigate highly structured social relationships. Thus, at an intrataxonomic level, these trends may indicate an increased frequency of dominance contests and competition for mates, a pattern suggesting larger social groups.

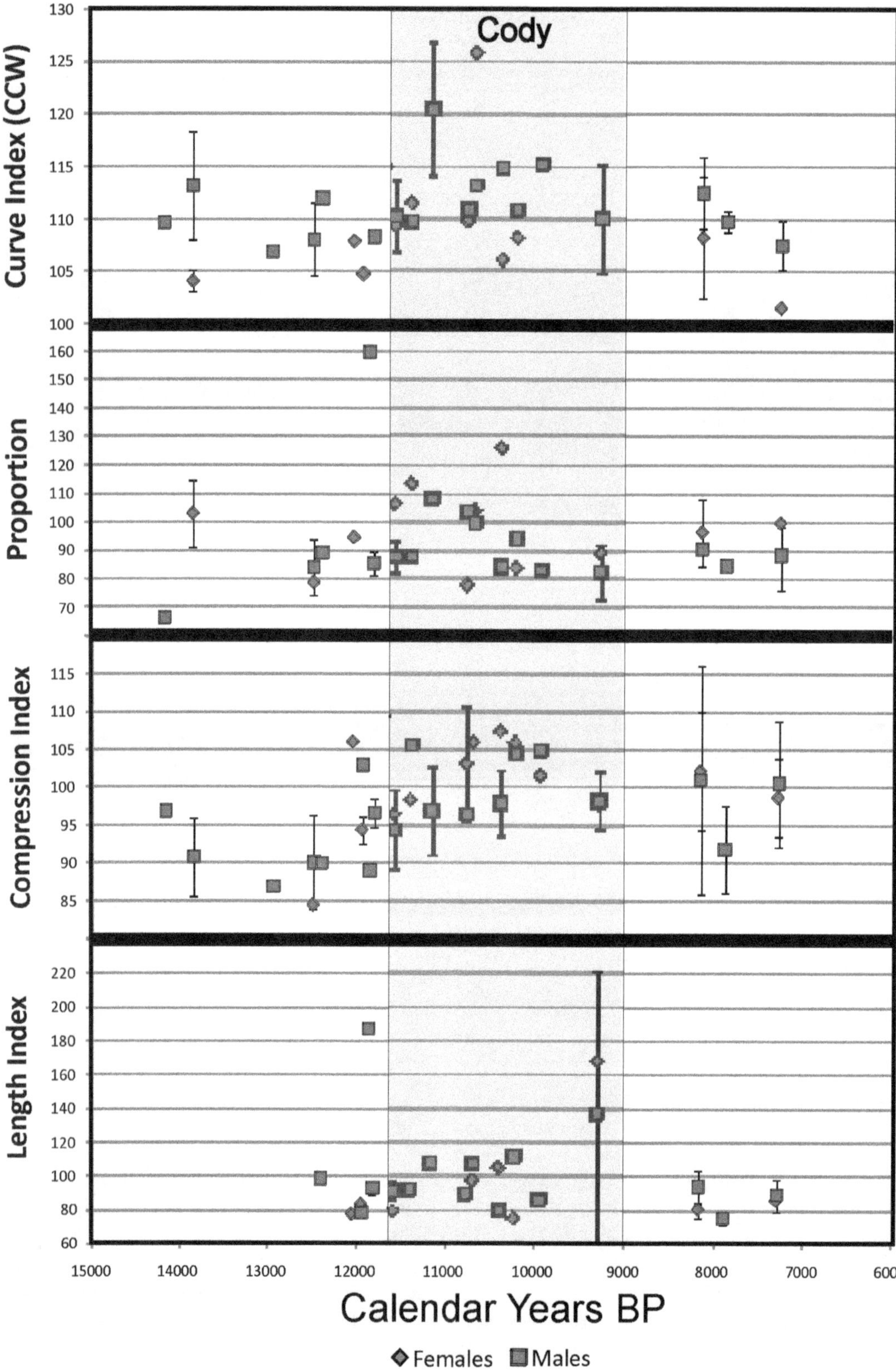


FIGURE 3.7. Changes in bison horn-core traits. Error bars are 1 standard deviation.

TABLE 3.9. Summary Data of Late Pleistocene/Early Holocene Bison Horn-Core Indices.

| Locality | Calibrated BP Age Range (2 sigma) | Sex | Lower Curve Index (SD) | Upper Curve Index (SD) | Compression Index (SD) | Proportion Index (SD) | Length Index (SD) | Data Source | Site Reference |
|---|---|---|---|---|---|---|---|---|---|
| Hughes Bog (IA) | 5950–5300 | Male | | 113.31 | 92.71 | 111.31 | 107.51 | McDonald 1978 | Hall 1972 |
| Hawken (WY) | 7440–7150 | Male | 125.96 (3.8) | 107.6 (2.3) | 100.6 (8.3) | 88.46 (12.4) | 88.78 (9.7) | Wilson 1975 | Frison et al. 1976 |
| | | Female | | 101.54 | 98.73 (5.2) | 99.71 (1.1) | 85.34 | | |
| Itasca (MN) | 7945–7845 | Male | 130.74 (4.9) | 109.81 (1) | 91.87 (5.8) | 84.86 (1.2) | 75.25 (3.6) | this study | Shay 1971 |
| Duffield (Alberta) | 8310–8030 | Male | 135.89 (6.8) | 112.53 (3.4) | 101.03 (15.1) | 90.67 (6.1) | 93.82 (9.8) | Hillerud 1970 | Hillerud 1966 |
| | | Female | 129.93 (25.1) | 108.26 (5.8) | 102.2 (7.8) | 96.4 (12) | 80.22 (4.5) | | |
| Milburn (NE) | 9440–9130 | Female | 134.65 | 110.09 | 97.78 | 89.01 | 168.46 | Hillerud 1970 | Hillerud 1970 |
| | | Male | 141.1 (14.2) | 110.04 (5.1) | 98.23 (3.9) | 82.53 (9.5) | 137.02 (84.3) | | |
| Scottsbluff (NE) | 10,120–9700 | Male | 143.46 | 115.19 | 104.95 | 83.23 | 85.85 | Hillerud 1970 | Hill 2007; Schultz and Eisley 1935 |
| | | Female | | | 101.62 (0.1) | | | | |
| Treesbank (Manitoba) | 10,490–10,180 | Female | | 106.13 | 107.41 | 125.7 | 105.14 | McDonald 1978 | Hay 1924 |
| | | Male | | 114.84 | 97.88 (4.4) | 84.27 | 79.77 | | |
| Kerr-McGee, Walker Pit (WY) | 10,550–9800 | Female | 118.68 | 108.24 | 105.92 | 83.83 | 74.62 | Wilson 1975 | Frison 1984 |
| | | Male | 130.59 | 110.86 | 104.49 (0.3) | 94.13 | 111.22 | | |
| Rex Rodgers (TX) | 10,740–10,500 | Female | | 125.73 | 105.97 | 103.86 | 97.29 | McDonald 1978 | Speer 1978 |
| | | Male | | 113.23 | | 99.72 | 107.34 | | |
| Dows Bog (IA) | 11,100–10,300 | Male | | 110.87 | 96.43 | 103.66 | 89.16 | McDonald 1978 | Hudak 1984 |
| | | Female | | 109.8 | 103.17 (7.6) | 77.78 | | | |
| Milan (Alberta) | 11,400–10,750 | Male | | 120.47 (6.4) | 96.91 (5.8) | 108.22 (1.2) | 107.38 | McDonald 1978 | Shackleton and Hills 1977 |
| Lubbock Lake (TX) | 11,600–11,350 | Female | | 109.3 | 96.43 | 106.21 | 78.99 | McDonald 1978 | Johnson 1987 |
| | | Male | | 110.3 (3.4) | 94.47 (5.3) | 87.76 (5.4) | 91.35 (5.4) | | |
| Casper (WY) | 11,760–11,400 | Female | 135 | 115 | 109.38 | | 80.54 | Wilson 1975 | Frison 1974 |
| A&R Gravel Pit (Alberta) | 12,100–11,640 | Male | | | 89.15 | 159.66 | 186.89 | McDonald 1978 | McDonald 1978 |
| Plainview (TX) | 12,150–10,450 | Female | | 111.46 | 98.36 | 113.23 | | McDonald 1978 | Sellards et al. 1947; Broeker and Kulp 1957 |
| | | Male | | 109.78 | 105.56 | 87.83 | 92.1 | | |
| Athabasca (Alberta) | 12,250–11,400 | Male | | 108.38 | 96.63 (1.8) | 85.49 (4.2) | 92.48 (3.4) | McDonald 1978 | McDonald 1978 |
| Folsom (NM) | 12,600–12,390 | Female | | | 84.51 | 78.67 | | McDonald 1978 | Figgins 1927; Meltzer 2006 |
| | | Male | | 108.07 (3.4) | 90.13 (6.2) | 84.04 (9.8) | | | |
| Olsen-Chubbuck (CO) | 12,650–11,250 | Male | | | 103 | | 77.92 | McDonald 1978 | Wheat 1972 |
| | | Female | | 104.79 | 94.4 (1.8) | | 83.12 | | |
| Agate Basin (WY) | 12,950–11,150 | Female | 126.32 | 107.89 | 106.06 | 94.47 | 77.36 | Wilson 1975 | Frison and Stanford 1982 |
| Lindenmeier (CO) | 13,300–12,600 | Male | | 106.96 | 87.04 | | | McDonald 1978 | Wilmsen and Roberts 1978 |
| Palo Duro Canyon (TX) | 13,550–11,250 | Male | | 112.01 | 90 | 89.3 | 98.45 | McDonald 1978 | McDonald 1978 |
| Fairbanks (AK) | 13,960–13,740 | Female | | 104.11 (1) | | 102.86 (11.7) | | McDonald 1978 | McDonald 1978 |
| | | Male | | 113.2 (5.2) | 90.85 (5.2) | | | | |
| Aucilla River (FL) | 14,270–14,050 | Male | | 109.73 | 96.88 | 66.56 | | Webb et al. 1984 | Webb et al. 1984 |
| Dome Creek (AK) | 21,650–20,250 | Male | | 116.76 (5.6) | 91.36 (8) | 125.47 (8.1) | 139.85 (19.6) | McDonald 1978 | McDonald 1978 |
| | | Female | | 109.56 | 99.31 (3.3) | 130.33 | 113.64 | | |

*Note:* Horn-core indices are defined in Table 3.5.

### Summary and Implications for Cody Hunter-Gatherers

North American landscapes underwent rapid changes throughout the Cody period. Bioclimatic models derived from paleofaunal assemblages indicate relatively warm and moist conditions at the inception of the Alberta-Cody complex in the western localities, with a possible cold-dry event ~11,000 cal BP (i.e., Medicine Lodge Creek, Wyoming). However, as the Cody period progressed in the western Great Plains and Rocky Mountains, precipitation decreased as part of an overall trend toward middle Holocene conditions (Grimm et al. 2011; Yansa 2007). These landscape changes complement interpretations of bison behavior derived from changes in cranial and postcranial anatomy, which suggest the intensified selection for morphological traits that heralded larger and more socially structured herds.

The patterns presented in these datasets are, like many biological patterns, inherently noisy. However, the combined analyses of paleoenvironmental and bison morphological changes produce results that are internally consistent and suggest that bison populations responded to regional landscape changes at both a morphological and a behavioral level. This discussion produced a hypothesis of bison evolution between ~12,000 and 6000 years ago that is amenable to further testing and refinement as more data become available.

During the Cody period, modern bison morphology and behavior emerged. Before this time, bison formed small groups, possibly with a more fluid and flexible herd structure. During the late Cody period (<10,600 cal BP), general patterns in horn-core morphology suggest a change in dominance behavior that led to the success of large herds, which clearly are present in the archaeological record of Cody bison kill sites (Hill, this volume). Larger regional bison populations would have increased encounter rates for bison, a highly ranked prey resource, thereby making communal hunting efforts more profitable.

### Acknowledgments

Thank you to the editors of this book — Ed Knell and Mark Muñiz — for both the invitation to contribute and insightful comments on early versions of the chapter. I also thank Matthew E. Hill Jr., Eric Grimm, Jeff Saunders, Bonnie Styles, and two reviewers for their feedback during various phases of this project.

### References

Agogino, G. A., and W. D. Frankforter
1960 A Paleo-Indian Bison-Kill in Northwestern Iowa. *American Antiquity* 25:414–415.

Anderson, D. C., and H. A. Semken Jr. (editors)
1980 *The Cherokee Excavations: Holocene Ecology and Human Adaptations in Northwestern Iowa.* Academic Press, New York.

Baker, R. G., R. S. Rhodes III, D. P. Schwert, A. C. Ashworth, T. J. Frest, G. R. Hallberg, and J. A. Janssens
1986 A Full-Glacial Biota from Southeastern Iowa, USA. *Journal of Quaternary Science* 1: 91–107.

Bamforth, D. B. (editor)
2007 *The Allen Site: A Paleoindian Camp in Southwestern Nebraska.* University of New Mexico Press, Albuquerque.

Binford, L. R.
2001 *Constructing Frames of Reference: An Analytical Method for Archaeological Theory Building Using Ethnographic and Environmental Datasets.* University of California Press, Berkeley.

Broecker, W. S., and J. L. Kulp
1957 Lamont Natural Radiocarbon Measurements IV. *Science* 126:1324–1334.

Bronk Ramsey, C.
2005 Oxcal 3.10. http://c14.arch.ox.ac.uk. Accessed August 5, 2011.

Davis, L. C.
1987 Late Pleistocene/Holocene Environmental Changes in the Central Plains of the United States: The Mammalian Record. In *Late Quaternary Mammalian Biogeography and Environments of the Great Plains and Prairies,* edited by R. W. Graham, H. A. Semken Jr. and M. A. Graham, pp. 88–143. Scientific Papers Vol. 22. Illinois State Museum, Springfield.

Dyke, A. S.
2004 An Outline of North American Deglaciation with Emphasis on Central and Northern Canada. In *Quaternary Glaciations — Extent and Chronology, Part II: North America,* edited by J. Ehlers and P. L. Gibbard, pp. 373–424. Elsevier, Amsterdam.

Dyke, A. S., A. Moore, and L. Robertson
2003 *Deglaciation of North America.* Open File

1574. Geological Survey of Canada, Ottawa, Ontario.

Emslie, S. D.

1986 Late Pleistocene Vertebrates from Gunnison County, Colorado. *Journal of Paleontology* 60:170–176.

Figgings, J. D.

1927 The Antiquity of Man in America. *Natural History* 27:229–239.

Foley, L.

1984 *Late Pleistocene (Woodfordian) Vertebrates from the Driftless Area of Southwestern Wisconsin: The Moscow Fissure Local Fauna.* Report of Investigations No. 39. Illinois State Museum, Springfield.

Frison, G. C.

1974 *The Casper Site: A Hell Gap Bison Kill on the High Plains.* Academic Press, New York.

1984 The Carter/Kerr-McGee Paleoindian Site: Cultural Resource Management and Archaeological Research. *American Antiquity* 49: 288–314.

2004 *Survival by Hunting: Prehistoric Human Predators and Animal Prey.* University of California Press, Berkeley.

Frison, G. C., and D. J. Stanford

1982 *The Agate Basin Site: A Record of the Paleoindian Occupation of the Northwestern High Plains.* Academic Press, New York.

Frison, G., M. Wilson, and D. Wilson

1976 Fossil Bison and Artifacts from an Early Altithermal Period Arroyo Trap in Wyoming. *American Antiquity* 41:28–57.

Gill, J. L., J. W. Williams, S. Jackson, K. B. Lininger, and G. S. Robinson

2009 Pleistocene Megafaunal Collapse, Novel Plant Communities, and Enhanced Fire Regimes in North America. *Science* 326:1100–1103.

Gonzalez, L. M., and E. C. Grimm

2009 Synchronization of Late-Glacial Vegetation Changes at Crystal Lake, Illinois, USA with the North Atlantic Event Stratigraphy. *Quaternary Research* 72:234–245.

Graham, R. W.

1987 Late Quaternary Mammalian Faunas and Paleoenvironments of the Southwestern Plains of the United States. In *Late Quaternary Mammalian Biogeography and Environments of the Great Plains and Prairies*, edited by R. W. Graham, H. A. Semken Jr. and M. A. Graham, pp. 24–87. Scientific Papers Vol. 22. Illinois State Museum, Springfield.

Graham, R. W., and H. A. Semken Jr.

1987 Philosophy and Procedures for Paleoenvironmental Studies of Quaternary Mammalian Faunas. In *Late Quaternary Mammalian Biogeography and Environments of the Great Plains and Prairies*, edited by R. W. Graham, H. A. Semken Jr. and M. A. Graham, pp. 1–17. Scientific Papers Vol. 22. Illinois State Museum, Springfield.

Grimm, E. C., J. J. Donovan, and K. Brown

2011 A High-Resolution Record of Climate Variability and Landscape Response from Kettle Lake, Northern Great Plains, North America. *Quaternary Science Reviews* 30:2626–2650.

Grimm, E. C., and G. L. Jacobson Jr.

2004 Late Quaternary Vegetation History of the Eastern United States. In *The Quaternary Period in the United States*, edited by A. R. Gillespie, S. C. Porter, and B. F. Atwater, pp. 381–302. Elsevier, Amsterdam.

Guilday, J. E.

1962 The Pleistocene Local Fauna of the Natural Chimneys, Augusta County, Virginia. *Annals of the Carnegie Museum* 36:87–122.

Guilday, J. E., H. W. Hamilton, and A. D. McCrady

1971 The Welsh Cave Peccaries (*Platygonus*) and Associated Fauna, Kentucky Pleistocene. *Annals of the Carnegie Museum* 43:249–320.

Guilday, J. E., P. S. Martin, and A. D. McCrady

1964 New Paris No. 4: A Late Pleistocene Cave Deposit in Bedford County, Pennsylvania. *National Speleological Society Bulletin* 26(4): 121–194.

Guthrie, R. D.

1980 Bison and Man in North America. *Canadian Journal of Anthropology* 1:55–73.

Hall, S. A.

1972 Holocene Bison Occidentalis from Iowa. *Journal of Mammalogy* 53:604–606.

Hay, O. P.

1924 *The Pleistocene of the Middle Region of North America and Its Vertebrated Animals.* Carnegie Institute of Washington, Publication No. 322a. Washington, D.C.

Hernández Fernández, M.

2001 Bioclimatic Discriminant Capacity of Terrestrial Mammal Faunas. *Global Ecology and Biogeography* 10:189–204.

Hernández Fernández, M., and P. Peláez-Campomanes

2005 Quantitative Palaeoclimatic Inference Based on Terrestrial Mammal Faunas. *Global Ecology and Biogeography* 14:39–56.

Hill, M. E., Jr.

2002 The Folsom-Age 12 Mile Creek Bison Bonebed in Western Kansas. In *Institute for Tertiary-Quaternary Studies—TerQua*

*Symposium Series* 3, pp. 53–70. University of Kansas, Lawrence.
2007 Causes of Regional and Temporal Variation in Paleoindian Diet in Western North America. Unpublished Ph.D. dissertation, Department of Anthropology, University of Arizona.

Hill, M. E., Jr., M. G. Hill, and C. Widga
2008 Late Quaternary Bison Diminution on the Great Plains of North America: Evaluating the Role of Human Hunting versus Climate-Change. *Quaternary Science Reviews* 27:1752–1771.

Hill, M. E., Jr., J. L. Hofman, and L. D. Martin
1992 A Reinvestigation of the Burntwood Creek Bison Bonebed. *Current Research in the Pleistocene* 9:99–102.

Hill, M. G.
1996 Size Comparison of the Mill Iron Site Bison Calcanea. In *The Mill Iron Site*, edited by G. C. Frison. University of New Mexico Press, Albuquerque.
2005 Late Paleoindian (Allen/Frederick Complex) Subsistence Activities at the Clary Ranch Site, Ash Hollow, Garden County, Nebraska. *Plains Anthropologist* 50:249–263.

Hillerud, J. M.
1966 The Duffield Site and Its Fossil Bison, Alberta, Canada. Unpublished Master's thesis, University of Nebraska, Lincoln.
1970 Subfossil High Plains Bison. Unpublished Ph.D. dissertation, Department of Geology, University of Nebraska, Lincoln.

Hofman, J.
1995 Dating Folsom Occupations on the Southern Plains: The Lipscomb and Waugh Sites. *Journal of Field Archaeology* 22:421–437.

Hofman, J., and L. Todd
2001 Tyranny in the Archaeological Record of Specialized Hunters. In *People and Wildlife in Northern North America: Essays in Honor of R. Dale Guthrie*, edited by S. C. Gerlach and M. S. Murray. BAR International Series No. 944. British Archaeological Reports, Oxford.

Holder, P., and J. Wike
1949 The Frontier Culture Complex. *American Antiquity* 14:260–266.

Hudak, C. M.
1984 Paleoecology of an Early Holocene Faunal and Floral Assemblage from the Dows Local Biota of North-Central Iowa. *Quaternary Research* 21:351–368.

Johnson, E.
1987 *Lubbock Lake: Late Quaternary Studies on the Southern High Plains*. Texas A&M University Press, College Station.

Kelly, R. L.
1995 *The Foraging Spectrum: Diversity in Hunter-Gatherer Lifeways*. Smithsonian Institution Press, Washington, D.C.

Kivett, M.
1962 The Logan Creek Complex. Paper presented at the 20th Plains Anthropological Conference, Lincoln, Nebraska.

Klippel, W. E., and P. W. Parmalee
1982 *The Paleontology of Cheek Bend Cave, Maury County, Tennessee: Phase II Report to the Tennessee Valley Authority*. Report on file, Tennessee Valley Authority, Knoxville.

Laird, K. R., S. C. Fritz, B. F. Cumming, and E. C. Grimm
1998 Early-Holocene Limnological and Climatic Variability in the Northern Great Plains. *The Holocene* 8:275–285.

Leidy, J.
1852 *Memoir on the Extinct Species of American Ox*. Smithsonian Contributions to Knowledge 5(3). Smithsonian Institution, Washington, D.C.

Lyman, R. L.
2003 The Influence of Time Averaging and Space Averaging on the Application of Foraging Theory in Zooarchaeology. *Journal of Archaeological Science* 30:595–610.

Mandel, R.
1995 Geomorphic Controls of the Archaic Record in the Central Plains of the United States. In *Archaeological Geology of the Archaic Period in North America*, Special Paper No. 297, edited by E. A. Bettis III, pp. 37–66. Geological Society of America, Boulder, Colorado.

Martin, P. S., and R. G. Klein (editors)
1984 *Quaternary Extinctions*. University of Arizona Press, Tucson.

Martin, R. E.
1999 *Taphonomy: A Process Approach*. Cambridge Paleobiology Series No. 4. Cambridge University Press, Cambridge.

McDonald, J. N.
1978 The North American Bison: A Revised Classification and Interpretation of Their Evolution. Unpublished Ph.D. dissertation, University of California, Los Angeles.
1981 *North American Bison: Their Classification and Evolution*. University of California Press, Berkeley.

Meltzer, D. J. (editor)
2006 *Folsom: New Archaeological Investigations of a Classic Paleoindian Bison Kill*. University of California Press, Berkeley.

Myers, T. P., R. G. Corner, and L. G. Tanner

1981 Preliminary Report on the 1979 Excavations at the Clary Ranch Site. *Transactions of the Nebraska Academy of Sciences* 9:1–7.

Parmalee, P. W., R. B. McMillan, and F. B. King

1976 Changing Subsistence Patterns at Rodgers Shelter. In *Prehistoric Man and His Environments*, edited by R. B. McMillan and W. R. Wood, pp. 141–162. Academic Press, New York.

Pond, A.

1937 Wisconsin Joins Ranks of Oldest Inhabited Areas in America. *Wisconsin Archeologist* 17(3):51–54.

Reimer, P. J., M. G. L. Baillie, E. Bard, A. Bayliss, J. W. Beck, P. G. Blackwell, C. B. Ramsey, C. E. Buck, G. S. Burr, R. L. Edwards, M. Friedrich, P. M. Grootes, T. P. Guilderson, I. Hajdas, T. J. Heaton, A. G. Hogg, K. A. Hughen, K. F. Kaiser, B. Kromer, F. G. McCormac, S. W. Manning, R. W. Reimer, D. A. Richards, J. R. Southon, S. Talamo, C. S. M. Turney, J. van der Plicht, and C. E. Weyhenmeyer

2009 Intcal09 and Marine09 Radiocarbon Age Calibration Curves, 0–50,000 Years cal BP. *Radiocarbon* 51:1111–1150.

Rhodes, R. S.

1984 Paleoecology and Regional Paleoclimatic Implications of the Farmdalian Craigmile and Woodfordian Waubonsie Mammalian Local Faunas, Southwestern Iowa. Report of Investigations No. 40. Illinois State Museum, Springfield.

Saunders, J. J.

1977 *Late Pleistocene Vertebrates of the Western Ozark Highland, Missouri.* Report of Investigations No. 33. Illinois State Museum, Springfield.

Schmits, L. J.

1978 The Coffey Site: Environment and Cultural Adaptation at a Pairie-Plains Archaic Site. *Midcontinental Journal of Archaeology* 3:69–185.

Schultz, C. B.

1943 Some Artifact Sites of Early Man in the Great Plains and Adjacent Areas. *American Antiquity* 8:242–249.

Schultz, C. B., and L. Eisley

1935 Paleontological Evidence for the Antiquity of the Scottsbluff Bison Quarry and Its Associated Artifacts. *American Anthropologist* 37: 306–319.

Sellards, E. H., G. L. Evans, and G. E. Meade

1947 Fossil Bison and Associated Artifacts from Plainview, Texas. *Geological Society of America Bulletin* 58:927–954.

Semken, H. A., Jr.

1980 Holocene Climatic Reconstructions Derived from the Three Micromammal Bearing Cultural Horizons at the Cherokee Sewer Site, Northwestern Iowa. In The *Cherokee Excavations: Holocene Ecology and Human Adaptations in Northwestern Iowa*, edited by D. C. Anderson and H. A. Semken Jr., pp. 67–100. Academic Press, New York.

1988 Environmental Interpretations of the "Disharmonious" Late Wisconsinan Biome of Southeastern North America. In *Late Pleistocene and Early Holocene Paleoecology and Archeology of the Eastern Great Lakes Region*, edited by R. S. Laub, N. G. Miller, and D. W. Steadman, pp. 185–194. Buffalo Society of Natural Sciences, Buffalo, New York.

Semken, H. A., Jr., and C. R. Falk

1987 Late Pleistocene/Holocene Mammalian Faunas and Environmental Changes on the Northern Plains of the United States. In *Late Quaternary Mammalian Biogeography and Environments of the Great Plains and Prairies*, edited by R. W. Graham, H. A. Semken Jr. and M. A. Graham, pp. 176–313. Scientific Papers Vol. 22. Illinois State Museum, Springfield.

Semken, H. A., Jr., Graham, R. W., and T. W. Stafford Jr.

2010 AMS $^{14}C$ Analysis of Late Pleistocene Non-analog Faunal Components from 21 Cave Deposits in Southeastern North America. *Quaternary International* 217(1–2):240–255.

Shackleton, D. M., and L. V. Hills

1977 Post-glacial Ungulates (Cervus and Bison) from Three Hills, Alberta. *Canadian Journal of Earth Sciences* 14:963–986.

Shapiro, B., A. J. Drummond, A. Rambaut, M. C. Wilson, P. E. Matheus, A. V. Sher, O. G. Pybus, M. T. P. Gilbert, I. Barnes, J. Binladen, E. Willerslev, A. J. Hansen, G. F. Baryshnikov, J. A. Burns, S. Davydov, J. C. Driver, D. G. Froese, C. R. Harington, G. Keddie, P. Kosintsev, M. L. Kunz, L. D. Martin, R. O. Stephenson, J. Storer, R. Tedford, S. Zimov, and A. Cooper

2004 Rise and Fall of the Beringian Steppe Bison. *Science* 306:1561–1565.

Shay, T.

1971 *The Itasca Bison Kill Site: An Ecological Analysis.* Minnesota State Historical Society, St. Paul.

Skinner, M. F., and O. C. Kaisen

1947 The Fossil Bison of Alaska and Preliminary Revision of the Genus. *Bulletin of the American Museum of Natural History* 89:123–256.

Speer, R.

1978 Bison Remains from the Rex Rodgers Site. In

*Bison Procurement and Utilization: A Symposium*, edited by L. B. Davis and M. Wilson, pp. 113–127. Memoir No. 14. Plains Anthropologist, Lincoln, Nebraska.

Speth, J. D.
1983 *Bison Kills and Bone Counts.* University of Chicago Press, Chicago.

Stafford, T. W. J., H. A. J. Semken, R. W. Graham, W. F. Klippel, A. Markova, N. G. Smirnov, and J. Southon
1999 First Accelerator Mass Spectrometry 14C Dates Documenting Contemporaneity of Nonanalog Species in Late Pleistocene Mammal Communities. *Geology* 27:903–906.

Storch, I., and J. A. Bissonette
2003 The Problem with Linking Scales in the Use of Indicator Species in Conservation Biology. In *Landscape Ecology and Resource Management: Linking Theory with Practice*, edited by J. A. Bissonette and I. Storch. Island Press, Washington, D.C.

Strong, W. L., and L. V. Hills
2005 Late-Glacial and Holocene Palaeovegetation Zonal Reconstruction for Central and North-Central North America. *Journal of Biogeography* 32:1043–1062.

Todd, L. C.
1987 Analysis of Kill-Butchery Bonebeds and Interpretation of Paleoindian Hunting. In *The Evolution of Human Hunting*, edited by M. Nitecki and D. Nitecki, pp. 225–266. Plenum Press, New York.

Walker, D.
1987 Late Pleistocene/Holocene Environmental Changes in Wyoming: The Mammalian Record. In *Late Quaternary Mammalian Biogeography and Environments of the Great Plains and Prairies*, edited by R. W. Graham, H. A. Semken Jr. and M. A. Graham, pp. 334–393. Scientific Papers Vol. 22. Illinois State Museum, Springfield.

Walter, H.
2002 *Walter's Vegetation of the Earth: The Ecological Systems of the Geo-Biosphere.* 4th ed. Translated by S. Breckle. Springer, New York.

Webb, S. D., J. T. Milanich, R. Alexon, and J. S. Dunbar
1984 A Bison Antiquus Kill Site, Wacissa River, Jefferson County, Florida. *American Antiquity* 49:384–392.

Webb, T., III, E. J. Cushing, and H. E. Wright Jr.
1983 Holocene Changes in the Vegetation of the Midwest. In *Late-Quaternary Environments of the United States*, edited by H. E. Wright, pp. 142–165. University of Minnesota Press, Minneapolis.

Wheat, J. B.
1972 *The Olsen-Chubbuck Site: A Paleo-Indian Bison Kill.* Society for American Archaeology, Memoir No. 26. Washington, D.C.

Widga, C.
2006a Bison, Bogs, and Big Bluestem: The Subsistence Ecology of Middle Holocene Hunter-Gatherers in the Eastern Great Plains. Ph.D. dissertation, Department of Anthropology, University of Kansas, Lawrence.
2006b Niche Variability in Late Holocene Bison: A Perspective from Big Bone Lick, KY. *Journal of Archaeological Science* 33:1237–1255.

Wilmsen, E. N., and F. H. H. Roberts Jr.
1978 *Lindenmeier, 1934–1974: Concluding Report on Investigations.* Smithsonian Contributions to Anthropology No. 24. Smithsonian Institution Press, Washington, D.C.

Wilson, M.
1974 The Casper Local Fauna and Its Fossil Bison. In *The Casper Site: A Hell Gap Bison Kill on the High Plains*, edited by G. C. Frison, pp. 125–172. Academic Press, New York.
1975 Holocene Fossil Bison from Wyoming and Adjacent Areas. Unpublished Master's thesis, Department of Anthropology, University of Wyoming, Laramie.

Yansa, C. H.
2007 Lake Records of Northern Plains Paleoindian and Early Archaic Environments: The "Park Oasis" Hypothesis. *Plains Anthropologist* 52: 109–144.

Yu, Z.
2000 Ecosystem Response to Lateglacial and Early Holocene Climate Oscillations in the Great Lakes Region of North America. *Quaternary Science Reviews* 19:1723–1747.

Yu, Z., and U. Eicher
1998 Abrupt Climate Oscillations during the Last Deglaciation in Central North America. *Science* 282:2235–2238.

# 4

# Sticking It to the Bison

## Exploring Variation in Cody Bison Bonebeds

Matthew E. Hill Jr.

This chapter addresses how Cody hunters structured and organized bison hunts, and compares their hunting strategies with those of other Paleoindian groups. I try to answer three basic questions about Cody large-game hunting. First, was bison hunting an occasional event, contributing random windfalls of food and raw material to foragers, or was it a predictable part of a larger regular resource procurement system? Second, are there regional differences in the size and seasonal timing of Cody bison kills? Finally, given that the size of bison herds changes seasonally, does kill size reflect these natural shifts? In exploring each of these issues, I compare data from Cody sites with information from early and late Paleoindian bison bonebeds to see how similar the hunting strategies used by Cody hunters were to those of other Paleoindians.

My approach here is to compare empirical observations of bison remains from Cody (and other Paleoindian) assemblages with ecological models that outline how environmental variation influences bison condition, behavior, and herd size. These ecological models were used to establish a set of expectations concerning how noncultural variables (e.g., climate, forage quality, and forager abundance) would influence bison biology and behavior. Once we understand the degree to which the variability observed in Cody bison use reflects noncultural processes, we can better understand how cultural factors (e.g., human demography, subsistence strategies, labor organization) influence bison hunting.

Because this chapter's focus is limited to bison exploitation, I consider only one aspect of the larger subsistence regime employed by Cody groups. The potentially important nutritional and technological contributions that small game and plant resources made to the Cody diet is acknowledged but not discussed further here (however, see Knell and Hill 2012; Hill and Knell, this volume). Therefore, this research only indirectly contributes to the debate over whether Cody and other Paleoindian foragers relied on bison and other large-bodied game to satisfy the bulk of their basic subsistence and technological needs, or instead satisfied those needs using smaller-bodied taxa and plant resources (e.g., Cannon and Meltzer 2004; Kornfeld 2007; Kornfeld and Larson 2008; Meltzer 1988, 1995; Waguespack and Surovell 2003).

I begin by briefly reviewing previous research concerning Paleoindian bison procurement strategies to identify key themes and important variables of study. I then develop testable hypotheses related to kill composition, kill size, and season of mortality using the wildlife biology literature on bison ethology and biology. Next I review the nature and condition of bison assemblages from Great Plains Cody sites. Finally, I compare the ecologically inspired predictions with data from Cody period bison assemblages to evaluate their explanatory value.

As discussed below, problems with small sample size and the combined effects of excavation and preservation biases limit my ability to draw many statistically rigorous conclusions. However, as further outlined in the discussion and conclusion section, several findings from this study may help shape our understanding of Cody hunting and serve as a guide for future research. First, while all Cody bison hunters preferentially scheduled kills during seasons when bison would be in good physical condition, Cody hunters in the northern Plains followed a different hunting schedule than those in the southern Plains. Second, although the seasonal variation in Paleoindian bison kill size usually reflected natural shifts in bison herd size, Cody bison hunters were unique in making significantly larger kills than other Paleoindian groups, especially during the late fall/winter. Finally, this study supports earlier findings that Cody bison hunters preferentially preyed on female-dominated herds, which were likely more visible on the landscape and represented a more valuable prey target than did the smaller bull herds.

### Previous Interpretations

It is important to place this study of Cody bison exploitation within the context of previous explanations of Paleoindian hunting strategies. In this section, I position the current study within the historical context of research on this issue, highlighting a few areas where I believe this project can advance our basic understanding of Paleoindian subsistence practices.

Over the last few decades, research into Paleoindian bison hunting has focused on which time(s) of the year bison hunts occurred, what factors influenced the size of kills, and whether hunters' goals were directed toward procuring particular individuals or groups of bison. The most commonly used analytical variables include estimates of the season of mortality, minimum number of individuals (MNI), and composition of kills (i.e., proportion of bulls, cows, and calves).

For most of the twentieth century, it was assumed that Paleoindian bison procurement was organized in the same way as historic or late prehistoric period communal bison hunts (e.g., Branch 1929; Catlin 1841; Gilmore 1931; Schoolcraft 1856; Wissler 1920). Paleoindian bonebeds were therefore thought to represent large communal kills in the late summer/early fall, timed to occur when bison herds were very large and the individual animals were in peak physical condition (Dibble and Lorrain 1968; Moss 1951; Sellards et al. 1947; Wheat 1972:85). The goal of Paleoindian bison hunting, just as with late Holocene hunters, was seen as cooperative hunting by multiple households to provide groups with a windfall of meat, fat, and skins that could be stored for later use during the winter or traded with neighboring populations.

Beginning in the 1980s, Frison (1982) and others (Bamforth 1988, 2011; Todd 1987a; Todd et al. 1992) began to question the assumed similarities to historic bison hunters. Studies of the season of bison mortality suggest that Paleoindian kills occurred during all seasons (Todd et al. 1992, 1996). Hunters focused on prey in peak condition and aggregated into large herds, but also pursued small and scattered herds and animals in subprime condition. Second, not all Paleoindian kills were large; many represented the killing of a single animal or a small group (Amick 1994; Bamforth 1985; Johnson 1987). Finally, hearth features and intensive bone breakage, which indicate carcass processing for extraction of skeletal fats, are missing from Paleoindian sites (Bamforth 2011; Byers 2002; M. G. Hill 2008; Jodry and Stanford 1992; LaBelle 2005; Todd 1987a, 1991). In total this evidence strongly suggests differences in the goals and perhaps the organization of Paleoindian bison hunters compared with those of later times (see Bamforth 2011).

Alternatively, Frison (1982), using seasonality studies from a number of northern Plains bison kills, argued that Paleoindian hunters made large kills primarily during the winter to take advantage of natural refrigeration to store meat until the next round of hunting the following year. Frison's model does not fit all Paleoindian-age kills (see Todd 1991), however. Paleoindian kills at Lipscomb and Scottsbluff, for example, likely occurred during the summer, when freezing carcasses following the kill was not possible.

Todd (1991; Todd et al. 1990) and others (Hofman 1996; Hofman and Todd 2001; Kelly and

Todd 1988) instead argue that Paleoindian hunters killed bison year-round, with no preferred season. A key reason for this lack of a preferred season is that many bison kills, especially large mass kills, were opportunistic events in which hunters took advantage of chance encounters with bison under conditions favorable to make a kill (M. G. Hill 2008:101; Hofman 1994:359; however, see Bamforth 2007:246 and this volume for arguments that large bison kills were intentional communal undertakings). Given that most kills were fortuitous accidents, hunters were likely ill-prepared in terms of available labor to intensively process the carcasses or conduct extended camping activities to take full advantage of the kill. As a result, it seems that hunters spent very little time (perhaps a day or two) at a kill after minimally utilizing choice portions of the carcasses (Bamforth 2011; Bamforth et al. 2005; M. G. Hill 2008). Kills of all sizes may have been made, but after satisfying immediate needs, hunters abandoned the kill locality and left any remaining food value of the partially butchered carcasses to move on to new opportunities. Under this hypothesis, one has the impression that Paleoindian hunters moved continuously from kill event to kill event (Hofman 1992:198).

Bement (2003) and McCartney (1990) both developed models correlating bison hunting strategies with seasonal variation in bison behavior and condition. McCartney (1990) argued that Paleoindian hunting preferentially focused on animals in or near peak condition. During the fall, hunting focused on nursery herds with higher biomass and higher fat content than bull herds, which are in poor condition following the summer rut. During the late winter and spring, the deleterious effects of pregnancy and subsequent lactation meant that small bull herds became more attractive to hunters (see also Speth 1983).

Recently, Bement (2003) hypothesized that a dichotomy exists in the way Folsom period bison hunting was organized on the southern High Plains (see also Bamforth 1985, 2007; Johnson 1989; Wheat 1978). Small kill sites occur during all seasons and resulted from ambushing small groups of animals near water sources. Large kills, which used natural features like arroyos to trap the bison, occurred only during the late summer or early fall, when bison naturally aggregate into large herds. According to this model, kill size is also correlated with the intensity of carcass butchery. At small kill sites carcasses received extensive butchery, whereas at large kill sites carcasses underwent only light butchery (see Bamforth 2007; Johnson 1989).

While the described models make important contributions to the Paleoindian literature, their impact is often limited because they (1) do not consider regional or long-term variation in bison procurement patterns, (2) are based on the analysis of just a handful of sites, or (3) make vague or unexplained assumptions about seasonal changes in bison behavior and physiology. The rest of this chapter attempts to overcome these problems, first by using clearly defined ecological models from wildlife biology research on bison behavior and bioenergetics and then by empirically comparing these models with zooarchaeological data from a large number of Cody and other Paleoindian assemblages.

### *Bison Ethology and Biology*

This review of bison ethology and biology considers the relationship between environmental conditions and bison behavior and biology under current conditions across the Great Plains. A fuller discussion of this literature is in M. E. Hill (2007). My presentation here is limited to predictions about the actions of Paleoindian hunters who behave optimally with respect to energetic efficiency. Four basic predictions can be made about the size, composition, and seasonality of Cody kills based on modern bison behavior.

First, when planning an unselective (mass) kill, hunters are likely to consider the overall economic potential of the group of prey being targeted. Because nursery (cow/calf) herds are larger than bull herds and cows are in better condition than bulls for most of the year (Berger and Cunningham 1994; McHugh 1958; Melton et al. 1989), cows are a preferable food choice. An exception occurs during spring and early summer, immediately before and after cows give birth, when bull condition is superior to that of cows (Blaxter 1957; Green 1986; Green and Rothstein 1991; Speth 1983; Speth and Spielmann 1983). In general, the sexual composition of most mass kill sites should be biased toward cows and calves over bulls. On the other hand, hunters are likely to preferentially focus on the individual's condition when planning to selectively kill just a single animal or small number of animals, especially during spring or early summer. As a result, the larger body size of bulls (Berger and Cunningham 1994; McHugh 1958; Soper 1941) probably makes them more attractive individual targets than cows or calves. Male bison should be more preferentially represented in assemblages resulting from hunting of individual animals, especially during spring and early summer.

Second, because the size of bison herds changes seasonally and regionally, the potential size of mass kills should reflect, at least in part, natural fluctuations in bison herd size (Berger and Cunningham 1994; McHugh 1958; Melton et al. 1989). Irrespective of region, very large mass kills are generally only possible during late summer and early fall, when multiple bison herds aggregate for mating, and forage quality and quantity is superior (Speth 1983). Herds will presumably decrease in size through late fall and early winter as individuals and groups of bison scatter across the landscape in search of forage. Because forage quality and quantity is the poorest during late winter through early spring (Speth 1983), herd size likely reaches its minimum at this time of year.

Third, a strong climate gradient across the Great Plains influences grassland productivity, composition, nutrition, and palatability. For example, the southern and eastern Plains grasslands are dominated by warm-season ($C_4$) grasses whereas the northern and western grasslands are covered by mixed cool-season ($C_3$) and warm-season ($C_4$) grasses (Epstein et al. 1997; Tieszen et al. 1997). This gradient means that compared with northern forage, southern grasses have lower nutritional values (less protein, nitrogen, and phosphorous; more starch), shorter and later onset of the growth period, lower spring and fall net productivity, and lower digestibility (higher levels of lignin, hemicellulose, and cellulose) (Caswell et al. 1973; Tieszen et al. 1997). Because bison population size is influenced by forage quantity and quality, more bison can be supported in northern regions than in southern areas (Bamforth 1988:84; 2011:33). Therefore, all other factors being equal, mass kills in northern areas should be larger than those in the south.

Finally, the climatically induced environmental changes following the end of the Pleistocene likely affected bison hunting through time (M. E. Hill 2007, 2008a). Bison genetic studies (Rambaut et al. 2009; Shapiro et al. 2004) suggest a long-term population decline from the terminal Pleistocene through middle Holocene. However, these changes were not necessarily immediately detrimental for human hunters. Because early Paleoindian human population density was still likely quite low during this period, bison hunting was probably quite rewarding (Amick 1996; Hofman 1999; MacDonald 1998). By the late Paleoindian period, the continued increase in mean temperature and decline in effective precipitation across the midcontinent of North America (Baker et al. 2000; Davis et al. 1986; Holliday 1997; Neck 1995; Olson and Porter 2002) probably resulted in a decline in bison populations to a point where it influenced human subsistence patterns, at least in some locations, such as the Rocky Mountains and far western areas (e.g., Byers et al. 2005; Hughes 2003; MacDonald 1981). Even in the Great Plains, the continued decline in bison population size probably affected both the probability that hunters would encounter bison to hunt and the size of the bison group being hunted. Through time, bison would have become less frequently encountered and, when found, would be in smaller, more dispersed herds.

## The Record for Cody Complex Bison Bonebeds

Bison remains have been reported from 30 Cody (i.e., Alberta, Eden, Firstview, and Scottsbluff) assemblages in the project area (Figure 4.1, Table 4.1). Detailed information on size of the excavation area, season(s) of occupation, the minimum number of individuals, or the percentage of male and female/immature animals is available from 27 of those assemblages. Not surprisingly, given that bison prefer grassland settings, most of the Cody bison assemblages occur in grassland plains/rolling hill settings ($n = 21$), with fewer in alluvial valley ($n = 4$) and foothill/mountain ($n = 5$) habitats. Also, the regional distribution is highly biased toward northern Plains ($n = 21$) over southern Plains ($n = 9$) sites.

Although the association of bison remains with chipped stone artifacts does not unambig-

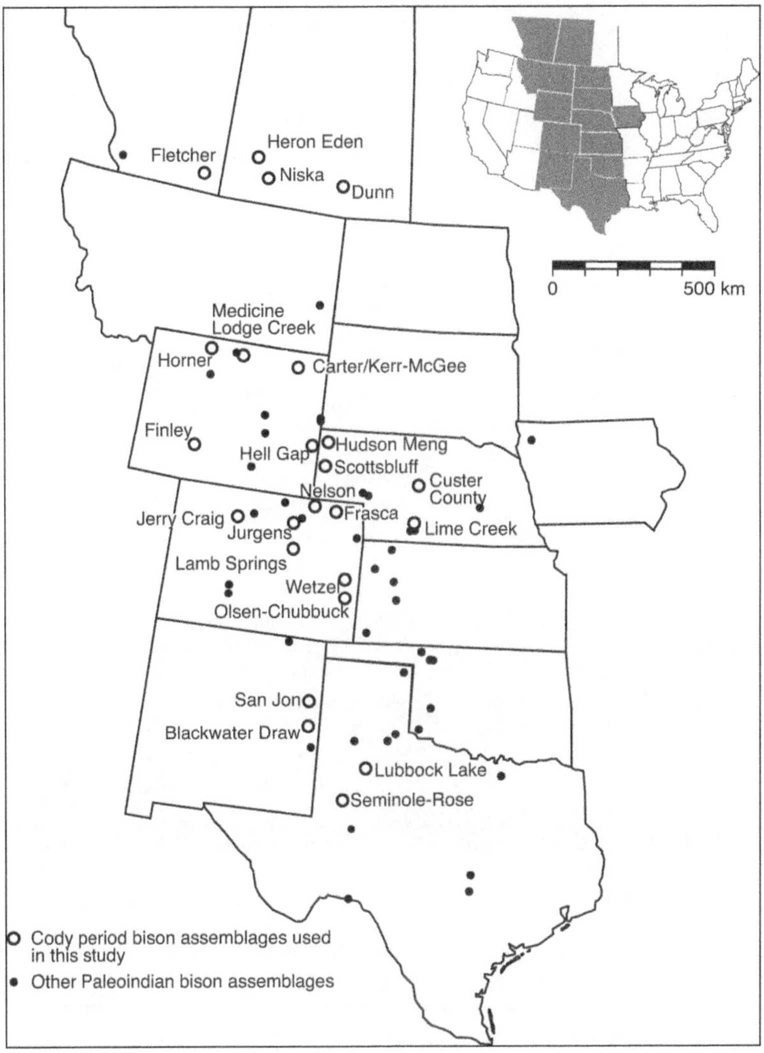


**FIGURE 4.1.** Map of the Great Plains of North America showing Cody period and other Paleoindian period bison bonebeds used in this analysis.

uously indicate a kill or procurement event (see Kornfeld 2007:39), prior studies suggest that the majority of localities considered here represent kill/processing assemblages ($n = 18$) with relatively few ($n = 7$) representing short-term camps. The site function for an additional five localities is unreported. The site type function bias is not considered to be a significant problem because the primary focus of this analysis is on understanding seasonal and long-term variation in bison predation.

While the focus is on Cody period bison assemblages, for comparison purposes I use data from 46 early Paleoindian (>10,000 $^{14}$C years BP, >11,470 cal BP) and 31 non-Cody late Paleoindian (10,000–8500 $^{14}$C years BP, 11,470–9510 cal BP) period sites (Table 4.2).

### *Taphonomy/Assemblage Condition*

Using published information to make comparisons among large numbers of assemblages can be problematic. Sites often have different degrees of bone preservation and unequal excavation areas, levels of analysis, and detailed reporting of results. Researchers commonly acknowledge these problems and attempt to overcome some of them by conducting their own high-quality taphonomic analyses of multiple assemblages, generally

**TABLE 4.1.** Summary of Excavation Area Size, Site Functional Interpretation, and Bonebed Condition and Preservation for Cody Sites Used in This Study.

| Site | Excavation Area ($m^2$) | Level of Investigation | Bone Condition | Skeletal Articulations | Backdirt Screened? |
|---|---|---|---|---|---|
| Blackwater Draw: Loc. 4E | 116 | Unknown portion of bonebed excavated but biased recovery of faunal remains | Palimpsest deposit with bone trampling and weathering | A few articulated axial and lower limb units | No |
| Carter/ Kerr-McGee | 80 | Significant portion of bonebed excavated | Poor preservation with extensive carbonate coating | Numerous articulated units | Not reported |
| Custer County | 11 | Unknown portion of bonebed excavated | Poor preservation with extensive carbonate coating | None reported | No |
| Dunn | 6 | Mostly surface site, limited subsurface testing | Extremely poor preservation of highly fragmented bone and teeth | None reported | Not reported |
| Finley: Station A | 79 | Entire bonebed excavated or damaged by looters | Moderately good preservation but high degree of breakage from excavators | None reported | Yes |
| Finley: Station B | 200 | Entire bonebed excavated or damaged by looters | Good preservation but high degree of breakage from looters | Several articulated limb units | Yes |
| Fletcher | 24 | Unknown portion of bonebed excavated | Poor preservation and high degree of breakage | None reported | Not reported |
| Frasca: Area 1 | 28 | Significant portion of bonebed excavated | Poor preservation | 561 articulated units | Yes |
| Hell Gap: Loc. IIIS/V | 47 | Significant portion of bonebed excavated | Poor bone preservation | None reported | Yes |
| Heron Eden | 82 | Most or all of bonebed excavated | Poor bone preservation with heavy weathering and high degree of breakage | None reported | Yes |
| Horner I | 770 | Most or all of bonebed excavated | Poor bone preservation with heavy weathering and root etching | Several articulated axial and lower limb units | Yes |
| Horner II | 130 | Most or all of bonebed excavated | Very good bone preservation | Numerous articulated units | Yes |
| Hudson-Meng | 600 | Approximately 60% of bonebed excavated | Extensive carbonate coating and carnivore gnawing | Six complete carcasses, numerous limb and axial units | Yes |
| Jerry Craig | 18 | Limited excavation | Bone condition not reported | None reported | Yes |
| Jurgens: Area 1 | 112 | Most or all of bonebed excavated | Moderately good preservation but numerous pieces discarded in field | Seventy articulated axial and lower limb units | Yes |
| Jurgens: Area 2 | 52 | Most or all of bonebed excavated | Moderately good preservation but numerous pieces discarded in field | Very few (5) articulated units | Yes |
| Jurgens: Area 3 | 88 | Most or all of bonebed excavated | Moderately good preservation but numerous pieces discarded in field | Numerous articulated units (850 bones) | Yes |

**TABLE 4.1.** (cont'd.) Summary of Excavation Area Size, Site Functional Interpretation, and Bonebed Condition and Preservation for Cody Sites Used in This Study.

| Site | Excavation Area ($m^2$) | Level of Investigation | Bone Condition | Skeletal Articulations | Backdirt Screened? |
|---|---|---|---|---|---|
| Lamb Spring: Cody | 108 | Large portion of bonebed excavated | Poor bone preservation with evidence of density mediated destruction | None reported | Not reported |
| Lime Creek: Zone I | 137 | Large portion of bonebed excavated | Moderately good bone preservation | None reported | No |
| Lubbock Lake: FA5-8/10 | 70 | Large portion of bonebed excavated | Bone condition not reported | None reported | Yes |
| Lubbock Lake: FA6-3 | 120 | Large portion of bonebed excavated | Good bone preservation | Mostly disarticulated elements | Yes |
| Lubbock Lake: GA5-2 | Not reported | Unknown portion of bonebed excavated | Bone condition not reported | None reported | Yes |
| Medicine Lodge Creek: Cody Level | Not reported | Unknown portion of bonebed excavated | Bone condition not reported | None reported | Yes |
| Nelson | 1 | Very limited excavation | Poor preservation with heavy weathering and root etching | None reported | Yes |
| Niska | 22 | Limited test excavation of unknown portion of bonebed | Very poor bone preservation with abundant breakage and burning | None reported | Yes |
| Olsen-Chubbuck | 78 | Most or all of bonebed excavated | Good bone preservation but some pieces discarded in field | Mostly articulated units | Yes |
| San Jon: Area 2 | 62 | Unknown portion of bonebed excavated | Poor preservation with heavy carbonate coating on bone | Several articulated limb units | No |
| Scottsbluff | 10 | Entire bonebed excavated | Good bone preservation but evidence of fluvial sorting | Thirteen articulate limb and axial units | No |
| Seminole-Rose | 16 | Unknown portion of bonebed excavated | Poor bone preservation with abundant breakage | None reported | Unknown, surface obscured |
| Wetzel | None | Mostly surface site, limited subsurface testing | Very poor | None reported | No |

ignoring published data from other assemblages (e.g., M. G. Hill 2008; Todd 1987b). These studies contribute much to the literature on Paleoindian use of bison, but many more assemblages that can potentially expand our knowledge of the past have not undergone comparable analyses.

This study uses as large a sample of bison assemblages as possible, thereby including high-quality data (well-preserved assemblages with well-studied site formational history) and low-quality data (poorly preserved assemblages subject to limited taphonomic analysis). I briefly and qualitatively evaluate the data used in this study by considering excavation area size, screening of back dirt, and general assemblage condition and bone preservation (see Table 4.1).

Eighteen (60 percent) of the 30 Cody assemblages underwent extensive or nearly complete excavation of the bonebed. For these sites, either large areas (>50 $m^2$) were excavated or the excavated areas included most of the known bone deposit. Several Cody sites, such as Custer County, Dunn, Jerry Craig, Nelson, Niska, and Seminole Rose, have undergone very limited testing and/or limited recovery of faunal remains. Of those components with large excavation areas, 12 (Finley Station A and B, Heron Eden, Horner I and II, Hudson-Meng, Jurgens Areas 1–3, Lubbock Lake

**TABLE 4.2.** Other Paleoindian Sites with Bison Remains Used in This Study.

| Site | Reference |
|---|---|
| **Early Paleoindian Sites (>10,000 $^{14}$C years BP, >11,470 cal BP)** | |
| 12 Mile Creek | M.E. Hill 2002a |
| Agate Basin (Areas 1, 2 & 3) | M.G. Hill 2008 |
| Allen (Level 1) | Bamforth 2007 |
| Aubrey | Ferring 2001 |
| Blackwater Draw (Loc. 7A, 11, 12C, & 15F) | Hester 1972; Johnson and Holliday 1997 |
| Bonfire Shelter (A and B/C) | Byerly et al. 2005; Dibble and Lorrain 1968 |
| Carter/Kerr-McGee (Folsom) | Frison 1984 |
| Casper | Frison 1974 |
| Cattle Guard | Jodry 1999a |
| Cooper | Bement 1999 |
| Folsom | Meltzer 2006 |
| Hanson | Amick 1994; Frison 1991 |
| Hell Gap (Loc. I, II, III) | Larson et al. 2009 |
| Hot Tub | Meltzer et al. 2006 |
| Howard Gully | Hurst et al. 2010 |
| Jake Bluff | Bement and Carter 2010 |
| Jones Miller | Stanford 1999 |
| Lake Theo (Folsom) | Baxevanis 1997 |
| Levi Rockshelter (Zone II) | Alexander 1963 |
| Lindenmeier | Wilmsen and Roberts 1984 |
| Linger | Jodry 1999b |
| Lipscomb | Todd et al. 1992 |
| Lubbock Lake (FA2-2, FA6-15, FA6-8, GA12-5) | Johnson 1987; Johnson and Holliday 1989 |
| Marks Beach | LaBelle and Meltzer 1996 |
| Mill Iron | Frison 1996 |
| Rattlesnake Pass | Smith and McNees 1990 |
| Sheaman | Frison and Stanford 1982 |
| Upper Twin Mountain | Kornfeld and Frison 2000 |
| Waugh | Hill and Hofman 1997 |
| Wilson Leonard (Units Isi, Isi/Icl, Igl/Isi, Isi/Isi-c, Isi/Icl/Isi-c) | Collins 1998 |
| **Non-Cody Late Paleoindian Sites (10,000–8500 $^{14}$C years BP, 11,470–9510 cal BP)** | |
| Allen (Intermediate Zone, Level 2) | Bamforth 2007 |
| Big Lake | Turpin et al. 1997 |
| Burntwood Creek | Hill et al. 1992 |
| Cherokee Sewer (IIIa) | Whittaker 1997 |
| Clary Ranch | M.G. Hill 2008 |
| Frazier | Borresen 2002 |
| Helen Lookingbill (Layer 2/4 & 7/9) | Kornfeld et al. 2001; Kornfeld and Larson 2008 |
| Hell Gap (Locality I) | Larson et al. 2009 |
| James Allen | Berman 1959 |
| Laird | Hofman and Blackmar 1997 |
| Levi Rockshelter (Zone IV) | Alexander 1963 |
| Lime Creek (Zone II & III) | Jones 1999 |
| Lubbock Lake (FA5-3, FA5-7/GA5-3, FA5-12, FA5-17, FA6-11, & FA9-1) | Johnson 1987; Johnson and Holliday 1989 |
| Medicine Lodge Creek (Pryor stemmed & deep deer faunule) | Walker 2007 |
| Merserve | Widga 2007 |
| Milnesand | M.E. Hill 2002b |
| Mona Lisa (Locality A) | Wilson 1974 |
| Norton | Hofman et al. 1995 |
| OV Clary | M.G. Hill et al. 2008 |
| Perry Ranch | Hofman and Todd 1997 |
| Plainview | M.E. Hill 2010a |
| Rex Rodgers | M.E. Hill 2010b |
| Winger | Mandel and Hofman 2003 |

FA5-8/10 and FA6-3, and Olsen-Chubbuck) also had the back dirt systematically screened.

Finally, differences in intensity and quality of previous analyses mean that detailed information on site formational history, skeletal element frequency, seasonality, and bone preservation are available from relatively few Cody assemblages (e.g., Hell Gap, Heron Eden, Horner II, Lime Creek, San Jon, and Olsen-Chubbuck). For most other Cody assemblages, even those intensively investigated (e.g., Jurgens, Hudson-Meng, Carter/Kerr-McGee, Frasca, Lubbock Lake, Finley, and Blackwater Draw), little is known about the site formational histories or assemblage composition.

Qualitative assessments of 19 of the 30 (63 percent) assemblages used here suggest that bone preservation and assemblage condition was either not reported or described as poor. Published accounts of these sites commonly describe the condition of the faunal remains as poor, highly fragmented, heavily weathered, or having undergone extensive trampling, fluvial action, looter's damage (e.g., bone breakage and removal of specimens), or carnivore damage. Claims for very good faunal preservation or assemblage integrity are reported for only a handful of assemblages (e.g., Horner II, Lubbock Lake FA6-3, Olsen-Chubbuck, and Lime Creek). In at least four instances (Blackwater Draw, Carter/Kerr-McGee, Lamb Spring, Heron-Eden; also probably Hudson-Meng and Scottsbluff) it is fairly clear that the Cody bison assemblage is a palimpsest of multiple kill events.

This study, like most other comparative studies in faunal analysis, is not without problems when it comes to uneven assemblage condition, bone preservation, and data reporting. Due to poor bone preservation, overprinting of multiple kill events, and incomplete analyses, we can expect that relevant information on MNI, seasonality, and herd composition will be available from only a few sites, and even these data may not perfectly reflect the original composition. Nonetheless, if we limit analyses to just the best-preserved and most completely documented assemblages (i.e., Horner II, Lubbock Lake FA6-3, Lime Creek, and Olsen-Chubbuck), we will have only a partial view of what bison exploitation was like during the Cody period. Even with the preliminary results given here, subject to the vagaries of uneven preservation and collection bias, I believe that it is still possible to make robust statements concerning the structure of Cody period bison use. This is true even though it is not always possible to demonstrate statistically significant patterns.

## Results

In this section I address the three questions about Cody bison procurement outlined in the introduction. First, during which season(s) did bison hunting occur? Second, what factors influence the size of Cody bison assemblages from a locality? Third, what is the sexual composition of Cody bison assemblages? Each is discussed in turn below.

### *Seasonality of Kill*

If we want to understand whether Cody bison hunting was an occasional event or part of a regular procurement system, we need to understand how hunters responded to the variability in bison condition and herd size. Chance encounter hunting would likely not be directly correlated with predictable seasonal shifts in bison biology or behavior. However, hunters operating under an optimizing strategy would try to maximize their returns (e.g., access to greater numbers of animals or access to animals in superior physical condition) by preferentially hunting bison during certain times of year and avoiding bison at other times of year. Specifically, the late winter and spring is a poor time of year for hunting, with hunters encountering few animals in generally poor condition. Alternatively, the late summer and early fall is anticipated to be a good time to hunt because large herds of bison would be in top physical condition. The late fall through early winter would also be a good period for hunting, although perhaps not as optimal as late summer/early fall. Also, while regional differences in overall forage and bison populations are expected between the northern and southern Plains, these differences should not affect the preferred timing of bison hunting; therefore, foragers in these two areas should follow a similar hunting schedule.

Season of animal mortality is inferred from mandibular tooth eruption and occlusal attrition patterns (Frison 1978, 1982; Todd et al. 1996). These data often permit accurate assessments of the season in which an animal died. Dental age

**TABLE 4.3.** Summary Information on Cody Sites Used in This Analysis.

| Site | Site Function | Dental Age | Bison MNI | %Male | %Female/ Young | Bison NISP | Reference |
|---|---|---|---|---|---|---|---|
| Blackwater Draw (Locality 4E) | Unknown | | 3 | | | 9 | Hester 1972 |
| Carter/Kerr-McGee | Processing Loci | .6–.7 | 47 | | | | Frison 1984 |
| Custer County | Kill | | 1 | | | | Schultz 1932 |
| Dunn | Kill | | | | | | Ebell 1988 |
| Finley (Station A) | Processing Loci | .6–.9 | 77 | | | 3417 | Schultz 1951; Miller 1987 |
| Finley (Station B) | Kill/ Process | .6 | 83 | 38 | 62 | 8121 | This chapter; Todd et al. 1990 |
| Fletcher | Kill/ Process | .5–.6 (est.) | | | | | Wilson and MacWilliams 1987 |
| Frasca (Area 1) | Processing Loci | .7–.8 (est.) | 63 | 29.4 | 70.6 | 7531 | Fulgham and Stanford 1982; M.G. Hill 2008 |
| Hell Gap (Locality V Cody) | Camp | .1–.7 | 7 | | | | Knell et al. 2002 |
| Heron Eden | Kill/ Process | .6–.7 | 37 | 53.7 | 46.3 | 2676 | Corbeil 1995 |
| Horner I | Camp | .6 | 158 | | | 1025 | Frison and Todd 1987 |
| Horner II | Kill | .6 | 65 | 20 | 80 | 7097 | Frison and Todd 1987 |
| Hudson-Meng | Kill/ Process | .2–.4 | 474 | 10 | 90 | | Agenbroad 1978; Todd and Rapson 1999 |
| Jerry Craig | Kill/ Process | .3–.5 | 7 | | | 55 | Hill and Kornfeld 1999 |
| Jurgens (Area 1) | Kill/ Process | .4–.5 | 37 | 14 | 86 | 2448 | Hill and Hill 2002; Wheat 1979 |
| Jurgens (Area 2) | Camp | | 2 | | | 94 | Hill and Hill 2002; Wheat 1979 |
| Jurgens (Area 3) | Kill/ Process | .4–.5 | 36 | 10 | 90 | 3028 | Hill and Hill 2002; Wheat 1979 |
| Lamb Spring | Kill | .6–.0 | 28 | 70 | 30 | 1220 | McCartney 1983, 1990 |
| Lime Creek (Zone 1) | Camp | .4–.5 | 3 | 0 | 100 | 47 | Jones 1999 |
| Lubbock Lake (FA5-8/10) | Kill/ Process | | 2 | 0 | 100 | | Johnson 1987; Johnson and Holliday 1989 |
| Lubbock Lake (FA6-3) | Camp | .9–1.1 (est.) | 7 | 0 | 100 | | Johnson 1987; Johnson and Holliday 1981 |
| Lubbock Lake (GA5-2) | Kill/ Process | | 1 | | | | Johnson 1987; Johnson and Holliday 1989 |
| Medicine Lodge Creek | Temporary Camp | | 1 | | | 2 | Walker 1975 |
| Nelson | Unknown | .7–.8 | 5 | | | | Kornfeld et al. 2007 |
| Niska | Unknown | | | | | | Meyer 1985 |
| Olsen-Chubbuck | Kill | 0.4 | 190 | 24 | 76 | 5370 | Wheat 1972; Frison 1991 |
| San Jon (Area 2) | Unknown | | 5 | | | 231 | Hill et al. 1995 |
| Scottsbluff | Kill | .1–.3 | 26 | 14 | 86 | 1461 | M.E. Hill 2008b |
| Seminole-Rose | Kill | .1 | 5 | | | | Collins et al. 1997 |
| Wetzel | Unknown | | | | | | Cassells 1983 |

group values from 20 Cody sites are presented in 0.1-year increments starting with a presumed middle of spring (i.e., late April) birth pulse (N) (Table 4.3).

The distribution of dental age patterns from multiple sites was estimated using the technique developed by Todd (1991). In this system a frequency of occurrence per 0.1-year segments was tabulated by counting the number of assemblages spanning each increment (Todd 1991:219). For example, for the Horner I and II bonebeds, the dental age estimate is a single 0.1-year interval

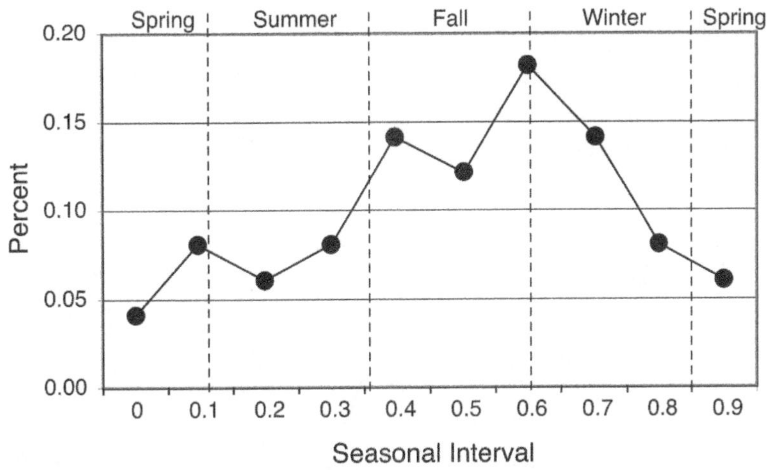


**FIGURE 4.2.** Cumulative season of death of 20 Cody period bison assemblages, based on frequency of occurrence across 0.1-year increments.

(N + 0.6), so only that interval is counted. However, where dental ages span multiple increments, such as at Jerry Craig (N + 0.3 to 0.5), each 0.1 increment is counted. Thus, the N + 0.3, N + 0.4, and N + 0.5 intervals are counted individually for Jerry Craig.

Figure 4.2 depicts the seasonal distribution of kill events for the 20 Cody sites with seasonality estimates. Bison hunting clearly occurred during all times of the year, although as predicted, more assemblages are represented in the late summer through early winter periods (stages N + 0.4–0.7) than during late winter through early summer (stages N + 0.8–0.3). Despite this visual pattern, no statistically significant difference exists between the observed distribution and the one expected if all intervals were equally represented (Kolmogorov-Smirnov D = .14, $p$ > .10). The insignificant difference may in part result from grouping all Cody sites together, which might obscure regional differences in the timing of bison hunting.

As discussed above, one would not predict differences in the timing of northern and southern kills; however, the data suggest there are potentially regional and possibly temporal differences in the timing of hunts (Figure 4.3). For example, as expected, northern kills occur most frequently between late summer and early winter (stages N + 0.4–0.7). Surprisingly, for southern sites, spring kill events are the most common. Unfortunately, neither north nor south distributions differ significantly from each other (Kolmogorov-Smirnov D = .35, $p$ > .10), which likely is a function of the small sample of southern Cody sites ($n$ = 4).

The analysis of the early Paleoindian and late non–Cody complex Paleoindian seasonality data suggest results similar to those presented above (Figure 4.4). In general, when site location is not considered, bison hunting appears most frequent during fall through winter, a slightly later time in the year than the model predicts but not entirely at odds with the expectations. However, when northern and southern sites are considered separately, the distribution of kills differs regionally, although not necessarily in ways analogous to the Cody distribution. For example, during the early Paleoindian period there was a significant difference (Kolmogorov-Smirnov D = .39, $p$ < .01) in the seasonal distribution of kills. For northern sites, summer kills were infrequent, while fall through early winter kills were common. For southern sites, the pattern was nearly the reverse: low numbers of kills during the fall and winter and high numbers during the summer. Unfortunately, this difference was not statistically significant (Kolmogorov-Smirnov D = .25, $p$ > .10).

Overall, the model used here had mixed results explaining seasonal scheduling of bison hunting. In general, Cody foragers appear to follow the predicted schedule of all late Paleoindian bison hunters. As the model predicts, northern groups took bison most frequently during the summer through winter and less commonly at

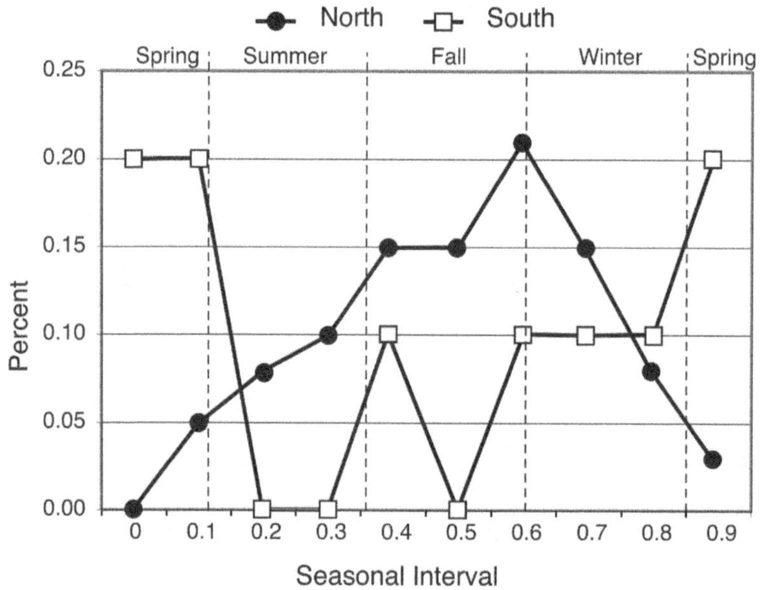


FIGURE 4.3. Cumulative season of death comparison for 16 northern and 4 southern Cody period bison assemblages, based on frequency of occurrence across 0.1-year increments.

other times of the year. Unexpectedly, southern groups focused their bison hunting mostly during the spring.

There was also an unanticipated temporal shift in the timing of bison hunting. Early Paleoindians appear to have practiced a different schedule: northern groups infrequently took bison in the summer but did a lot of fall and winter hunting. Early Paleoindian hunters in the south did a lot of hunting during the summer but less during the fall and winter.

### *Bison Abundance: MNI Values*

This section examines variation in the abundance of bison (as measured by MNI) at Cody sites. As described above, there are three predictions based on the size of bison kills: (1) through time, bison kills should decrease in size, (2) northern kills should be larger than southern kills, and (3) kill size should vary throughout the year, being largest in late summer/early fall and smallest in late winter/early spring.

For the sites considered here, Cody bison MNI varies between 1 and 474 (see Table 4.3). Admittedly, due to problems associated with bone preservation and collection bias discussed above, published MNI values are not necessarily the most accurate indicators of the original number of animals killed. Likewise, MNI estimates do not always reflect the total number of animals used for food (see Wheat 1972). However, despite these problems, a few general conclusions can be drawn from the bison MNI data.

First, against the expectations outlined above, Cody sites generally have larger bison assemblages than do other Paleoindian assemblages. If measured using either mean MNI or median MNI values, Cody kills tend to be twice as large as early Paleoindian kills and three to four times the size of late Paleoindian sites (Table 4.4).

Unfortunately, because of potential problems with sample bias and uncertainty concerning the relationship between the sample of MNI values and the underlying population of Paleoindian bison kills, it is difficult to make statistically meaningful comparisons between the size of kills from different periods or regions. To investigate the variability in MNI values, I used a nonparametric bootstrapping, or resampling, technique (Diaconis and Efron 1983; Sokal and Rohlf 1995). The bootstrapping simulation method uses the existing MNI data for the Cody, early Paleoindian, and late Paleoindian period sites as the populations of study. Then a fictional sample was

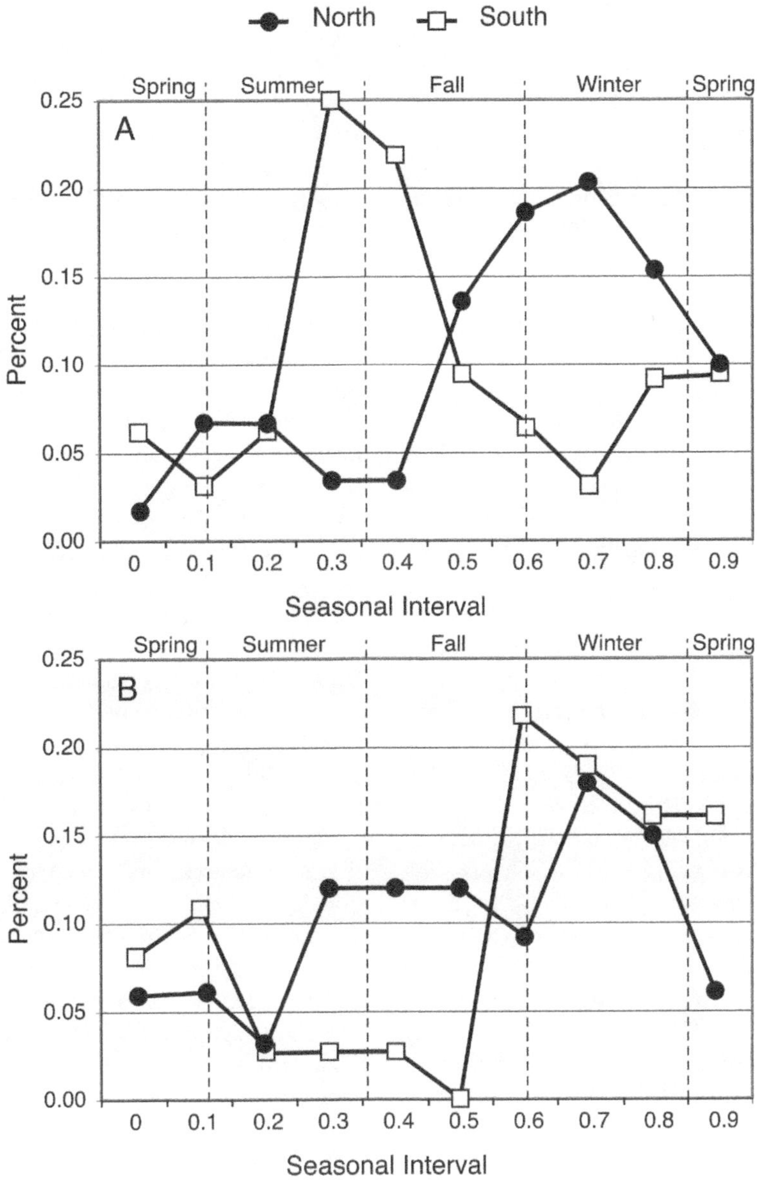


**FIGURE 4.4.** Cumulative season of death comparison for northern and southern bison bonebeds for 31 (north $n = 16$; south $n = 15$) early Paleoindian bison assemblages (A) and 22 (north $n = 8$; south $n = 14$) late Paleoindian (B) period bison assemblages, based on frequency of occurrence across 0.1-year increments.

**TABLE 4.4.** Resampled Frequency Distribution for MNI Values with Associated 95% Confidence Intervals (CI) Using Nonparametric Bootstrapping, or Resampling, Technique.

| Time Period | Early Paleoindian | Cody | Cody w/o Hudson-Meng | Late Paleoindian |
|---|---|---|---|---|
| Minimum | 1 | 1 | 1 | 1 |
| 1st quartile (95% CI) | 3 (2–4.5) | 3 (1–7) | 3 (1.5–7.0) | 2 (1–4) |
| Median (95% CI) | 7 (4–14) | 16.5 (5–42) | 7 (5–37) | 5 (2.5–7.0 |
| Mean (95% CI) | 20.4 (10.9–34.5) | 52.7 (23.2–96.0) | 35.8 (18.8–57.4) | 12.6 (5.9–21.4) |
| 2nd Quartile (95% CI) | 22 (13–34) | 63.50 (30.3–158.0) | 55 (27–83) | 9.5 (6–33) |
| Outlier boundary (>1.5 × interquartile range) | >50.5 | >154.3 | >125 | >20.8 |
| Maximum | 250 | 474 | 190 | 100 |

created by randomly resampling (with replacement) from the observed MNI values. This process was repeated 5000 times. With the results from resampling, it is possible to accurately estimate a 95 percent confidence interval (CI) for any statistical measure (e.g., mean, median, 2nd quartile) we want to consider. Statistically speaking, CI values that do not overlap at the 95 percent intervals are unlikely to originate from populations with a similar distribution (Sokal and Rohlf 1995).

As a result, the data suggest that while median MNI values for the three time periods cannot be statistically differentiated with a high level of confidence, the mean MNI values for the Cody period were significantly larger than the penecontemporary late Paleoindian kills, but overlap with the early Paleoindian kills. The uneven results produced from the analysis of mean and median MNI values might hint at an important aspect of Cody-age kills.

Specifically, this does not mean that the "normal" size of a Cody kill is substantially different than kills from other time periods. This is because the "average" kill for all Paleoindian hunters is small (usually less than 7 animals). As seen in Table 4.4, the distribution of MNI values of Cody-age kills is skewed toward large kills, having larger median and 2nd quartile values for MNI values than either of the other time periods. The Cody period appears to have a greater contribution of large kills than other Paleoindian groups. In general, we should reconsider the significance of the concept of "average" kill size. The distribution of kill sizes is not a normal distribution, and therefore a measure of the central tendency of kill size might not be a useful measure when MNI values are compared.

Of course, large kills occurred during the early Paleoindian period (i.e., Agate Basin-Agate Basin MNI = 53, Lipscomb MNI = 56, Casper MNI = 75, Jones-Miller MNI = 250) and late Paleoindian (i.e., Burntwood Creek MNI = 32, Milnesand MNI = 33; Clary Ranch MNI = 41, Frazier-Plainview MNI = 100). But statistically speaking, all these kills are outliers compared with the size of the other kills during these periods. I define outlier here as a value 1.5 times the interquartile range of the sample that value is drawn from (Hartwig and Dearing 1979:23–24). In comparison, while Cody has eight very large kills (i.e., Carter/Kerr-McGee MNI = 47, Frasca MNI = 63, Horner II MNI = 65, Finley-Station A MNI = 77, Finley-Station B MNI = 83, Horner I MNI = 158, Olsen-Chubbuck MNI = 190, Hudson-Meng MNI = 474), all but Horner I, Olsen-Chubbuck, and Hudson-Meng should not be considered outliers.

Before completing this discussion, I must acknowledge that Todd and Rapson (1999) question whether the Hudson-Meng site is even a human-induced kill. While Agenbroad (1978; also Largent 2007) strongly supports the role of humans in the Hudson-Meng bison kill, there are still many unresolved questions about the formation history of the site. As shown in Table 4.4, even if Hudson-Meng is dropped from consideration, the Cody time period is still skewed toward large kills, especially compared with the late Paleoindian periods. These differences are not necessarily statistically significant, however.

Finding that Cody bison kills are larger than those from other time periods does not explain what factors contribute to more bison being present. It is important to consider the various site formation, environmental, and cultural factors that might influence MNI values.

One factor that many archaeologists would probably assume to be key in influencing kills is excavation area. The logic is that all things being equal, larger excavation areas result in the recovery of more bones and thus larger kill assemblages. However, I believe that one would be mistaken to assume that the relation is linear (i.e., larger excavation area equals larger MNI). Obviously, because of the large body size of bison, when a kill consists of a large number of complete carcasses, a big excavation area is needed to uncover those remains. However, a number of taphonomic, behavioral, and recovery strategy factors also affect this relationship.

Figure 4.5 has scatter plots of square-root-transformed bison MNI values and natural-log-transformed excavation area for Cody assemblages. The data were transformed because of the very large range of variation, and the transformation would assist in highlighting a linear relationship between the two variables if one exists.

The distributions in Figure 4.5 form a triangular distribution (Beaver 2004). This follows because the dependent value (bison MNI) is limited but not determined by the independent variable (excavation area). For example, small excavation areas may correspond to low MNI values, medium-sized excavations may correspond with both low and moderate MNI values, and large excavation areas can be associated with a full range of MNI values. Therefore, large excavation areas are necessary, but not sufficient, for large MNI.

A nonparametric analysis of the excavation area and MNI shows a significant correlation ($r_s$ = .48, $p$ < .001); however, because of the relatively low $r_s$ value, much of the variation in MNI is not explained by excavation area (Figure 4.5a). This is apparent visually in Figure 4.5a, where 11 of the 24 Cody assemblages used in this analysis fall outside the 95 percent CI range for a linear regression between the two variables. Consequently, recognizing that excavation area explains only part of the variation in MNI forces one to look for other variables that help explain kill size.

Not surprisingly, site function is an important variable affecting MNI values. As shown in Figure 4.5b, when excavation area is considered, campsites tend to have smaller MNI values than kill assemblages, although the difference is not statistically significant (Mann Whitney U = 25, $p$ = .10).

Where a kill occurs also seems to influence the size of the kill. Cody kill/processing localities in the north tend to be larger than those in the south (Figure 4.5c). An obvious outlier to this pattern is the huge Olsen-Chubbuck kill, which is located south of 40° N but is nonetheless a very large kill of 190 animals. However, due to the fact that the southern Plains Olsen-Chubbuck site is a significant outlier, the geographic difference in kill size is not statistically significant (Mann Whitney U = 47, $p$ = .18).

As discussed above, another variable that influences bison MNI values is the time of year the kill occurred. Because of small sample size, only three seasonal intervals were used: spring/early summer (stages N + 0.9–0.2), late summer/early fall (stages N + 0.3–0.5), and late fall/winter (stages N + 0.6–0.8).

Figure 4.6a depicts a box plot for MNI values for each seasonal category during the Cody period. This figure does not include data from the problematic site of Hudson-Meng. Based on this graph, we see that seasonal changes in Cody kill size do not fit expectations. While the MNI values are lowest at spring/early summer sites ($n$ = 3) and

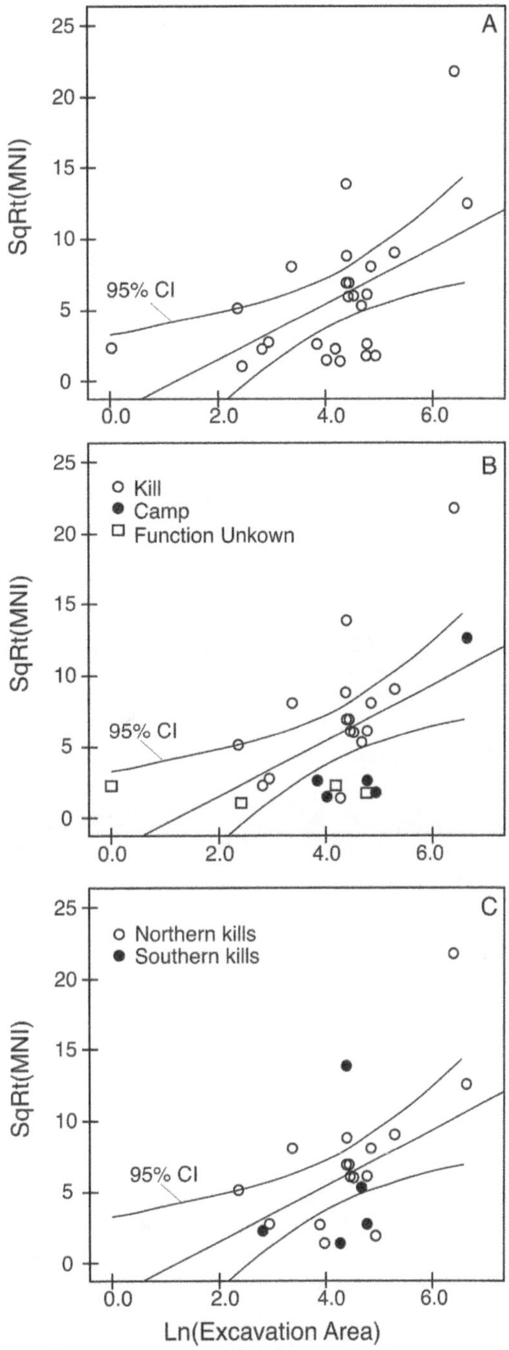


FIGURE 4.5. Cross plot for all Cody period bison assemblages of square-root-transformed minimum number of individual (SqRt[MNI]) estimates over natural-log-transformed excavation areas (Ln[Excavation Area])(A), with kill and camp assemblages (B), and northern and southern kill assemblages depicted separately (C).

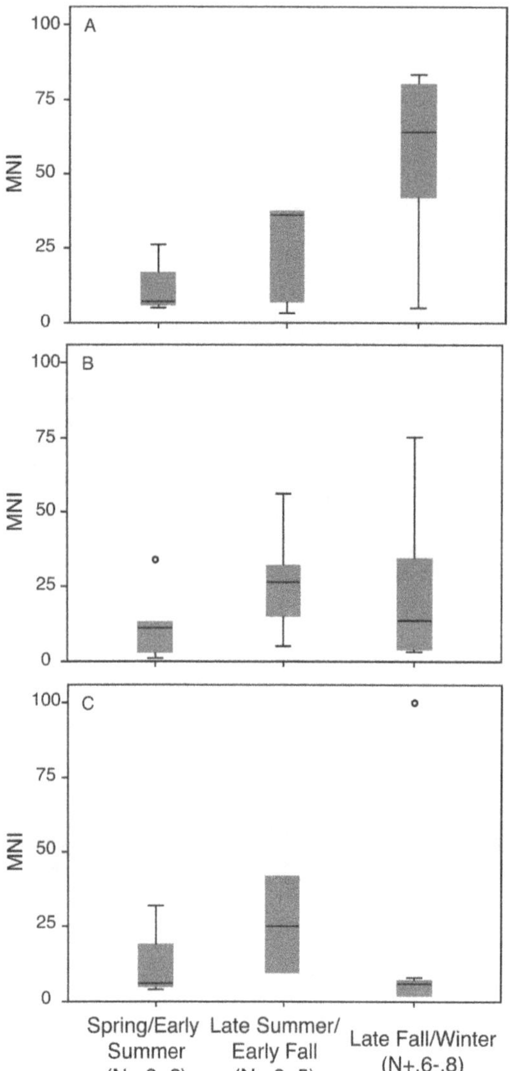


**FIGURE 4.6.** Box plots of median seasonal minimum number of individual (MNI) estimates for Cody period bison assemblages (excluding Hudson-Meng) (A), early Paleoindian (>11,500 cal BP) bison assemblages (B), and late Paleoindian (11,500–9500 cal BP) bison assemblages (C).

higher at late summer/early fall sites ($n = 5$), the largest MNI value occurs unexpectedly during the late fall/winter ($n = 8$). This is a time of year when one would normally expect kill size to decline over late summer/early fall peak sizes. Unfortunately, these seasonal differences in MNI values are not statistically significant (Kruskal-Wallis H = 3.54; $df = 2$; $p = .17$), probably because of small sample size for some of the seasonal intervals (e.g., spring/early summer).

Interestingly, compared with Cody sites, the seasonal variation in kill size for early and late Paleoindian sites fits the model expectations better (Figures 4.6b and 4.6c). For both early and late sites, the median kill sizes are smallest during the spring/early summer and fall/winter and higher during the late summer/early fall.

As discussed above, the evidence for Cody kills being larger than kills during other periods likely relates to Cody's unusually large late fall/winter kills. The difference in kill size through time is not statistically significant for either the spring/early summer or the late summer/early fall sites. However, Cody kills are significantly (Kruskal-Wallis H = 9.07; $df = 2$; $p = .01$) larger than early and late Paleoindian period kills during the late fall/winter. As outlined above, the large size of kills during this period is unexpected because this is normally a time when herds disperse and individual and small groups of bison scatter across the landscape.

### *Herd Composition*

Estimates of herd composition (i.e., proportion of bulls to cows and calves) are available for 13 Cody assemblages (see Table 4.3). Because data are available from so few sites, this study does not separate sites into different regions but instead groups all sites together. Many of these assemblages seem to represent single-event, multi-animal kills, and thus the abundance of females and immature animals probably reflects predation focused on nursery herds.

Cow/calf-dominated assemblages are represented in all seasons of the year. The only Cody sites in which the proportion of bulls approaches or exceeds that of cows and immature animals are Heron Eden (fall/winter) and Lamb Spring (fall through spring). Both sites are thought to represent palimpsests of both a large kill from a bull herd and a smaller kill from a cow/calf herd (Corbeil 1995; McCartney 1990). The Finley site was previously reported as a bull-dominated Cody assemblage (Haspel and Frison 1987), but a recent reanalysis of the assemblage suggests this is not the case (M. E. Hill 2008b).

The preference for cow/calf herds seemingly extends to the entire Paleoindian period. Cows and calves outnumber bulls in all but a handful of sites. Bull-dominated assemblages occur either as small to medium-sized late winter/early spring kills (Waugh and 12 Mile Creek) or as assemblages likely representing multiple mortality events (Plainview and Lindenmeier). In this latter group, the seasonality estimate for Plainview (N + 0.6–0.9) does not preclude the possibility that a bull herd was preyed on during the late winter or early spring, as at Waugh and 12 Mile Creek.

### Discussion and Conclusions

The findings of this analysis generally agree with many of the predictions outlined above, although they differ in some significant ways. The findings strongly suggest that seasonality and regional differences in grassland conditions influenced the timing, size, and composition of Cody bison bonebeds. Therefore, Cody hunters were not randomly hunting bison whenever they were encountered. Instead, hunters followed a systematic strategy that took into account predictable seasonal shifts in bison biology and behavior.

The available data suggest that bison hunting occurred throughout the year. However, the frequency of hunting was probably not uniform during the year, but varied by season, by region, and possibly through time. In this case, bison hunting was a predictable event, not so much in terms of how often it occurred but during which season it was most likely to occur. Further, the results raise the possibility that the timing and size of bison kills differed in the northern and southern Great Plains. Kills in the north generally were larger and occurred more frequently during midsummer through early winter, whereas in the south kills were generally smaller and spring kills more abundant.

There are probably many reasons for these differences. Undoubtedly, sample size biases affect the results presented here, and likely explain why many of the statistical analyses could not identify significant differences. Data from many more sites will be needed before we can demonstrate that statistically significant regional differences exist in hunting schedules.

However, it would not be surprising if such differences actually existed. Conditions in the south would have been significantly warmer and drier than in the north (Baker et al. 2000; Ferring 1995; Holliday 1997). Consequently, the south had poorer quality and quantity of forage, which would have supported many fewer bison and those bison were likely in poorer condition. However, during winter the south likely had less snow cover and milder temperatures. Northern Cody hunters may have responded to the harsh late winter and early spring climate by making large kills before the onset of these conditions, and then remained fairly sedentary, surviving on stores of meat and fat, until conditions improved (see Frison 1982). In the south, conditions probably would not allow for cold storage of meat, but the lack of deep snow would permit hunters to make at least occasional kills, even if that meant their prey were in suboptimal or even poor condition.

This study also indicates that archaeologists need to think more about what a "typical" bison kill actually means. For a long time, the very large multi-animal kill assemblages such as Olsen-Chubbuck and Hudson-Meng were perceived as "typical" Paleoindian kills, even though most bison kills are actually fairly small (i.e., <7 animals). We probably need to think of bison hunting as resulting in a bimodal distribution of kill sizes: mostly small kills but some large kills.

In fact, the Cody complex is probably different from other Paleoindian complexes in that there is a greater emphasis on large kills. Specifically, it is shown that Cody kills during the late fall/winter are significantly larger than in other time periods. These kills are actually larger than expected given our knowledge of the natural fluctuations in bison herd size.

The seasonal and regional differences in kill size patterning suggest that Cody hunters likely relied on communal hunting more than other Paleoindian groups. The minimum number of hunters and support personnel (e.g., carcass butchers and haulers of meat) necessary to successfully conduct a small kill is probably quite modest. A single household or extended family likely could accomplish such a task. As a result, it is not surprising that small kills occur in all settings and seasons. The decision to undertake a small kill likely occurred when the need or desire arose in a family group.

In contrast, large kills could occur only during certain seasons and likely required the cooperative efforts of multiple households or even multiple foraging groups (see Bamforth 2011; however, see alternative view in Hofman 1994). The timing of these events was certainly constrained by seasonally determined herd conditions: there must be enough animals on the landscape to make up the large kills. In order to make a large kill, hunters also had to organize and coordinate the labor of a large enough group to aggregate and direct large numbers of animals to move toward the kill site and then to actually kill the animals.

It is important to mention here, however, that due to incomplete butchery and carcass processing evident at many large Cody period kills (Todd 1987a, 1987b), the increase in predation efficiency may not necessarily result in a comparable increase in total dietary caloric returns. Simply put, while more than 100 animals may perish at a large kill event, only a small portion of those animals are probably used for food if butchery is incomplete. That said, even incomplete butchery of a very large bison kill would probably produce substantially more meat and hides than the complete processing of a "normal" kill, which is usually just a few animals.

Finally, this analysis supports the earlier findings of McCartney (1990), who suggested that Paleoindians preferentially preyed on female-dominated herds throughout most of the year. Hunting of the comparatively small male herds was relatively rare, and seems to have occurred only during or just before the calving season. This period co-occurs with the time when pregnant or lactating females were in their poorest condition. It seems that for most of the year, the significantly large size of cow/calf herds, especially when cows were in equivalent or better condition than bulls, represented a more attractive target for Paleoindian hunters.

Clearly, then, much variability exists in the Cody period regarding the size of bison kills and the seasonal timing of those kills. Natural variation in grassland conditions and bison population likely explains some of the seasonal and regional differences in bison kills and composition. However, the strategies of Cody bison hunters are different in a few important ways from those of earlier and contemporary Paleoindian bison hunters. In particular, Cody groups repeatedly made larger kills, especially during the late fall through winter, a pattern that cannot easily be explained based on our current understanding of environmental conditions. This might mean that Cody groups used different social strategies, such as greater reliance on communal based hunts, or technological approaches, such as greater use of surrounds or arroyo traps to confine large numbers of animals, than other Paleoindian foragers. Future research should be directed at understanding the important technological and social factors that made Cody bison hunting so successful.

## Acknowledgments

Thanks to Ed Knell and Mark Muñiz for inviting me to contribute to this book. Data used in this study came from my own analysis of museum collections; I am grateful to Fred Lange, Diana Leonard, and Deborah Confer of the University of Colorado Museum (Jurgens); Larry Martin of the University of Kansas Museum of Natural History (12 Mile Creek and Burntwood Creek); George Corner of the Nebraska State Museum (Finley, Scottsbluff); Jack Hofman of the University of Kansas Department of Anthropology (Norton and Waugh); Jeff Indeck and Rolla Shaller of the Panhandle-Plains Historical Museum (Rex Rodgers); Ernest Lundelius and Melissa Winans of the Texas Archaeological Research Laboratory and University of Texas Vertebrate Paleontology Laboratory (Bonfire Shelter, Milnesand, and Plainview); and Judy Brown, George Frison, Marcel Kornfeld, Martha Rodgers, and Danny Walker of the University of Wyoming (Finley). Financial support for various stages of this research was provided by the University of Iowa, the Carroll D. Clark Fund of the Department of Anthropology at the University of Kansas, the Haury Fund of the Department of Anthropology at the University of Arizona, and the George C. Frison Institute of the University of Wyoming. This chapter was improved based on comments received from Margaret Beck, Ed Knell, Mark Muñiz, and two anonymous reviewers.

## References

Agenbroad, Larry D.
1978 *The Hudson-Meng Site: An Alberta Bison Kill in the Nebraska High Plains.* University Press of America, Washington, D.C.

Alexander, H. L., Jr.
1963 The Levi Site: A Paleo-Indian Campsite in Central Texas. *American Antiquity* 28:510–528.

Amick, Daniel S.
1994 Folsom Diet Breadth and Land Use in the American Southwest. Unpublished Ph.D. dissertation, Department of Anthropology, University of New Mexico, Albuquerque.
1996 Regional Patterns of Folsom Mobility and Land Use in the American Southwest. *World Archaeology* 27:411–426.

Baker, Richard G., Glen Fredlund, Rolfe Mandel, and Elmer A. Bettis III
2000 Holocene Environments of the Central Great Plains: Multi-proxy Evidence from Alluvial Sequences, Southern Nebraska. *Quaternary International* 67:75–88.

Bamforth, Douglas B.
1985 The Technological Organization of Paleo-Indian Small-Group Bison Hunting on the Llano Estacado. *Plains Anthropologist* 30: 243–258.
1988 *Ecology and Human Organization on the Great Plains*. Plenum Press, New York.
2011 Origin Stories, Archaeological Evidence, and Post-Clovis Paleoindian Bison Hunting on the Great Plains. *American Antiquity* 76:24–40.

Bamforth, Douglas B. (editor)
2007 *The Allen Site: A Paleoindian Camp in Southwestern Nebraska*. University of New Mexico Press, Albuquerque.

Bamforth, Douglas B., Mark Becker, and Jean Hudson
2005 Intrasite Spatial Analysis, Ethnoarchaeology, and Paleoindian Land-Use on the Great Plains: The Allen Site. *American Antiquity* 70:561–580.

Baxevanis, Susan E.
1997 Collection Management and Analysis of the Lake Theo Folsom Bone Assemblage. Unpublished Master's thesis, Department of Anthropology, Texas Tech University, Lubbock.

Beaver, Joseph E.
2004 Identifying Necessity and Sufficiency Relationships in Skeletal-Part Representation Using Fuzzy-Set Theory. *American Antiquity* 69:131–140.

Bement, Leland C.
1999 *Bison Hunting at Cooper Site: Where Lightning Bolts Drew Thundering Herds*. University of Oklahoma Press, Norman.
2003 Constructing the Cooper Model of Folsom Bison Kills on the Southern Plains. *Great Plains Research* 13:27–41.

Bement, Leland, and Brian Carter
2010 Jake Bluff: Clovis Bison Hunting on the Southern Plains of North America. *American Antiquity* 75:907–933.

Berger, Joel, and Carol Cunningham
1994 *Bison: Mating and Conservation in Small Populations*. Columbia University Press, New York.

Berman, Jack E.
1959 Bison Bones from the Allen Site, Wyoming. *American Antiquity* 25:116–117.

Blaxter, K. L.
1957 The Effects of Defective Nutrition in Farm Livestock. *Proceedings of the Nutrition Society* (England and Scotland) 16:52–58.

Borresen, Jennifer A.
2002 Faunal Analysis of the Frazier Site, an Agate Basin–Age Bison Kill-Butchery Site in Northeastern Colorado. Unpublished Master's thesis, Department of Anthropology, University of Tennessee, Knoxville.

Branch, E. Douglas
1929 *The Hunting of the Buffalo*. D. Appleton, New York.

Byerly, Ryan M., Judith R. Cooper, David J. Meltzer, Matthew E. Hill, and Jason M. LaBelle
2005 On Bonfire Shelter (Texas) as a Paleoindian Bison Jump: An Assessment Using GIS and Zooarchaeology. *American Antiquity* 70:595–629.

Byers, David A.
2002 Paleoindian Fat-Seeking Behavior: The Hell Gap Site Locality II Agate Basin Faunal Assemblage. *Plains Anthropologist* 47:359–377.

Byers, David A., C. S. Smith, and J. M. Broughton
2005 Holocene Artiodactyl Population Histories and Large Game Hunting in the Wyoming Basin, USA. *Journal of Archaeological Science* 32:125–142.

Cannon, Michael D., and David J. Meltzer
2004 Early Paleoindian Foraging: Examining the Faunal Evidence for Large Mammal Specialization and Regional Variability in Prey Choice. *Quaternary Science Review* 23:1955–1987.

Cassells, E. Steve
1983 *The Archaeology of Colorado*. Johnson Books, Boulder, Colorado.

Caswell, Hal, Frank Reed, S. N. Stephenson, and Patricia A. Werner
1973 Photosynthetic Pathways and Selective Herbivory: A Hypothesis. *American Naturalist* 107:465–480.

Catlin, George
1841 *Letters and Notes on the Manners, Customs, and Conditions of North American Indians*. 2 vols. Reprint. Dover, New York.

Collins, Michael B. (editor)
1998 *Wilson-Leonard: An 11,000-Year Archaeological Record of Hunter-Gatherers in Central*

*Texas*. Studies in Archaeology No. 31. Texas Archaeological Research Laboratory and Archaeological Studies Program Report No. 10. Texas Department of Transportation, Austin.

Collins, Michael B., Dennis J. Stanford, Jack L. Hofman, Margaret A. Jodry, R. O. Rose, Lawrence C. Todd, K. Kilber, and Jeannette M. Blackmar

1997 Cody Down South: The Seminole-Rose Site in West Texas. *Current Research in the Pleistocene* 14:15–18.

Corbeil, Marcel R.

1995 The Archaeology and Taphonomy of the Heron Eden Site, Southwestern Saskatchewan. Unpublished Master's thesis, Department of Anthropology and Archaeology, University of Saskatchewan, Saskatoon.

Davis, Owen K., J. C. Sheppard, and S. Robertson

1986 Contrasting Climatic Histories for the Snake River Plains, Idaho, Resulting from Multiple Thermal Maximum. *Quaternary Research* 26: 321–339.

Diaconis, P., and B. Efron

1983 Computer-Intensive Methods in Statistics. *Scientific American* 248:96–108.

Dibble, D. S., and D. Lorrain

1968 *Bonfire Shelter: A Stratified Bison Kill Site, Val Verde County, Texas*. Miscellaneous Paper No. 1. Texas Memorial Museum, University of Texas, Austin.

Ebell, S. B.

1988 The Dunn Site. *Plains Anthropologist* 33:505–530.

Epstein, H. E., W. Laurenroth, I. C. Burke, and D. P. Coffin

1997 Productivity Patterns of $C_3$ and $C_4$ Functional Types in the U.S. Great Plains. *Ecology* 78: 722–731.

Ferring, C. Reid

1995 Middle Holocene Environments, Geology, and Archaeology in the Southern Plains. In *Archaeological Geology of the Archaic Period in North America*, edited by E. Arthur Bettis III, pp. 21–35. Special Paper No. 297. Geological Society of America, Boulder, Colorado.

2001 *The Archaeology and Paleoecology of the Aubrey Clovis Site (41DN479) Denton County, Texas*. Submitted to U.S. Army Corp of Engineers, Fort Worth District, Fort Worth, Texas.

Frison, George C.

1974 *The Casper Site: A Hell Gap Bison Kill on the High Plains*. Academic Press, New York.

1978 Animal Population Studies and Cultural Inference. *Plains Anthropologist* 15:44–52.

1982 Paleo-Indian Winter Subsistence Strategies on the High Plains. In *Plains Indian Studies: A Collection of Essays in Honor of J. C. Ewers and Waldo Wedel*, edited by D. H. Ubelaker and H. J. Viola, pp. 193–201. Smithsonian Contributions to Anthropology No. 30. Smithsonian Institution Press, Washington, D.C.

1984 The Carter/Kerr-McGee Paleoindian Site: Cultural Resource Management and Archaeological Research. *American Antiquity* 49: 288–314.

1991 *Prehistoric Hunters of the High Plains*. 2nd ed. Academic Press, San Diego.

Frison, George C. (editor)

1996 *The Mill Iron Site*. University of New Mexico Press, Albuquerque.

Frison, George C., and Dennis J. Stanford

1982 *The Agate Basin Site: A Record of Paleoindian Occupation of the Northwestern High Plains*. Academic Press, New York.

Frison, George C., and Lawrence C. Todd (editors)

1987 *The Horner Site: The Type Site of the Cody Cultural Complex*. Academic Press, Orlando, Florida.

Fulgham, T., and Dennis J. Stanford

1982 The Frasca Site: A Preliminary Report. *Southwestern Lore* 48:1–9.

Gilmore, Melvin R.

1931 Methods of Indian Buffalo Hunts. *Papers of the Michigan Academy of Science, Arts, and Letters* 16:17–32.

Green, Wendy C. H.

1986 Age-Related Difference in Nursing Behavior among American Bison Cows (*Bison bison*). *Journal of Mammalogy* 67:739–741.

Green, Wendy C. H., and Aron Rothstein

1991 Trade-Offs between Growth and Reproduction in Female Bison. *Oecologia* 18:521–527.

Hartwig, Frederick, and Brian E. Dearing

1979 *Exploratory Data Analysis*. Sage University Papers, Beverly Hills, California.

Haspel, Howard, and George C. Frison

1987 The Finley Site Bison Bone. In *The Horner Site: The Type Site of the Cody Cultural Complex*, edited by G. C. Frison and L. C. Todd, pp. 475–491. Academic Press, Orlando, Florida.

Hester, J. J.

1972 *Blackwater Locality No. 1: A Stratified, Early Man Site in Eastern New Mexico*. Fort Burgwin Research Center Publication No. 8. Southern Methodist University, Dallas, Texas.

Hill, Matthew E., Jr.
2002a The Folsom-Age 12 Mile Creek Bison Bonebed in Western Kansas. In *TER-QUA Symposium Series, Volume 3*, edited by Wakefield Dort Jr., pp. 53–70. Institute for Tertiary-Quaternary Studies, University of Kansas, Lawrence.
2002b The Milnesand Site: Site Formation Study of a Paleoindian Bison Bonebed in Eastern New Mexico. *Plains Anthropologist* 47:323–337.
2007 A Moveable Feast: Variations in Faunal Resource Use among Central and Western North American Paleoindian Sites. *American Antiquity* 72:417–438.
2008a Variation in Paleoindian Fauna Use on the Great Plains and Rocky Mountains of North America. *Quaternary International* 191:34–52.
2008b New Investigations of the Cody-Age Finley and Scottsbluff Bison Bone Beds. *Current Research in the Pleistocene* 25:90–93.
2010a Season of Bison Mortality at the Plainview Type Site (41HA1). *Current Research in the Pleistocene* 27:93–96.
2010b Analysis of Site Formation Processes at the Rex Rodgers Bison Bonebed. *Plains Anthropologist* 55:3–24.

Hill, Matthew E., Jr., and Matthew G. Hill
2002 Season of Bison Mortality at the Jurgens Site, Weld County, Colorado. *Current Research in the Pleistocene* 19:104–106.

Hill, Matthew E., Jr., and Jack L. Hofman
1997 The Waugh Site: A Folsom-Age Bison Bonebed in Northwestern Oklahoma. *Plains Anthropologist* 42:63–83.

Hill, Matthew E., Jr., Jack L. Hofman, and Larry D. Martin
1992 A Reinvestigation of the Burntwood Creek Bison Bonebed. *Current Research in the Pleistocene* 9:99–102.

Hill, Matthew G.
2008 *Paleoindian Subsistence Dynamics on the Northwestern Great Plains: Zooarchaeology of the Agate Basin and Clary Ranch Sites*. BAR International Series No. 1756. Archaeopress, Oxford.

Hill, Matthew G., Vance T. Holliday, and Dennis J. Stanford
1995 A Further Evaluation of the San Jon Site, New Mexico. *Plains Anthropologist* 40:369–390.

Hill, M. G., and M. Kornfeld
1999 Inferring Season of Kill for a Cody-Complex Bison Bonebed in Middle Park Colorado. *Current Research in the Pleistocene* 16:3–32.

Hill, Matthew G., David W. May, David J. Rapson, Andrew R. Boehm, and Erik Otárola-Castillo
2008 Faunal Exploitation by Early Holocene Hunter/Gatherers on the Great Plains of North America: Evidence from the Clary Ranch Sites. *Quaternary International* 191:115–130.

Hofman, Jack L.
1992 Recognition and Interpretation of Folsom Technological Variability on the Southern Plains. In *Ice Age Hunters of the Rockies*, edited by D. J. Stanford and J. S. Day, pp. 193–224. University Press of Colorado, Niwot.
1994 Paleoindian Aggregations on the Great Plains. *Journal of Anthropological Archaeology* 13:341–370.
1996 Early Hunter-Gatherers of the Central Great Plains: Paleoindian and Mesoindian (Archaic) Cultures. In *Archaeology and Paleoecology of the Central Great Plains*, edited by Jack Hofman, pp. 41–100. Research Series No. 48. Arkansas Archeological Survey, Fayetteville.
1999 Unbounded Hunters: Folsom Bison Hunting on the Southern Plains circa 10,500; The Lithic Evidence. In *Le bison: Gibier et moyen de subsistance des hommes du Paléolithique aux Paléoindiens de Grandes Plaines*, edited by J.-P. Brugal, F. David, J. G. Enloe, and J. Jaubert, pp. 383–416. Éditions APDCA, Antibes, France.

Hofman, Jack L., and Jeanette M. Blackmar
1997 The Paleoindian Laird Bison Bone Bed in Northwestern Kansas. *Kansas Anthropologist* 18:45–58.

Hofman, Jack L., Matthew E. Hill Jr., William C. Johnson, and Dean T. Sather
1995 Norton: An Early-Holocene Bison Bone Bed in Western Kansas. *Current Research in the Pleistocene* 12:19–21.

Hofman, Jack L., and Lawrence C. Todd
1997 Reinvestigation of the Perry Ranch Plainview Bison Bonebed, Southwestern Oklahoma. *Plains Anthropologist* 42:101–117.
2001 Tyranny in the Archaeological Record of Specialized Hunters. In *People and Wildlife in Northern North America: Essays in Honor of R. Dale Guthrie*, edited by S. C. Gerlach and M. S. Murray, pp. 200–215. BAR International Series No. 944. Archaeopress, Oxford.

Holliday, Vance T.
1997 *Paleoindian Geoarchaeology of the Southern High Plains*. University of Texas Press, Austin.

Hughes, Susan S.
2003 Beyond the Altithermal: The Role of Climate Change in the Prehistoric Adaptation of Northwestern Wyoming. Unpublished Ph.D. dissertation, Department of Anthropology, University of Washington, Seattle.

Hurst, Stance, Brian J. Carter, and Nancy Beavan Athfield
2010 Investigation of a 10,214 Year Old Late Paleoindian Bison Kill at the Howard Gully Site in Southwestern Oklahoma. *Plains Anthropologist* 55:25–37.

Jodry, Margaret A.
1999a Folsom Technology and Socioeconomic Strategies: Views from Stewart's Cattle Guard and the Upper Rio Grande Basin, Colorado. Unpublished Ph.D. dissertation, Department of Anthropology, American University, Washington, D.C.
1999b Paleoindian Stage. In *Colorado Prehistory: A Context for the Rio Grande Basin*, edited by M. A. Martorano, T. Hoefer III, M. A. Jodry, Vince Spero, and M. L. Taylor, pp. 45–114. Colorado Council of Professional Archaeologists, Denver.

Jodry, Margaret A., and Dennis J. Stanford
1992 Stewart's Cattle Guard Site: An Analysis of Bison Remains in a Folsom Kill-Butchery Campsite. In *Ice Age Hunters of the Rockies*, edited by D. J. Stanford and J. S. Day, pp. 11–168. University Press of Colorado, Niwot.

Johnson, Eileen (editor)
1987 *Lubbock Lake: Late Quaternary Studies on the Southern High Plains*. Texas A & M University Press, College Station.

Johnson, Eileen, and Vance T. Holliday
1981 Late Paleoindian Activity at the Lubbock Lake Site. *Plains Anthropologist* 26:173–193.
1989 Lubbock Lake: Late Quaternary Cultural and Environmental Change on the Southern High Plains, USA. *Journal of Quaternary Science* 4:145–165.
1997 Analysis of Paleoindian Bonebeds at the Clovis Site: New Data from Old Excavations. *Plains Anthropologist* 42:329–352.

Johnson, LeRoy, Jr.
1989 *Great Plains Interlopers in the Eastern Woodlands during Late Paleo-Indian Times*. Office of State Archeologist Report No. 36. Texas Historical Commission, Austin.

Jones, D. Chad
1999 Late Paleoindian/Early Archaic Archaeology and Subsistence: A Taphonomic Analysis of the Lime Creek Site (25ST41), Southwestern Nebraska. Unpublished Master's thesis, Department of Anthropology, Colorado State University, Fort Collins.

Kelly, Robert L., and Lawrence C. Todd
1988 Coming into the Country: Early Paleoindian Hunting and Mobility. *American Antiquity* 53:231–244.

Knell, Edward J., and Matthew E. Hill Jr.
2012 Linking Bones and Stones: Regional Variation in Late Paleoindian Cody Complex Land Use and Foraging Strategies. *American Antiquity* 77:40–70.

Knell, Edward J., Matthew G. Hill, A. Izeta, Marcel Kornfeld, C. Vance Haynes Jr., and George C. Frison
2002 The Cody-Complex Component at Locality V of the Hell Gap Site, Wyoming. *Current Research in the Pleistocene* 19:49–52.

Kornfeld, Marcel
2007 Are Paleoindians of the Great Plains and Rockies Subsistence Specialists? In *Foragers of the Terminal Pleistocene in North America*, edited by Renee B. Walker and Boyce N. Driskell, pp. 32–58. University of Nebraska Press, Lincoln.

Kornfeld, Marcel, and George C. Frison
2000 Paleoindian Occupation of the High County: The Case of Middle Park, Colorado. *Plains Anthropologist* 45:129–153.

Kornfeld, Marcel, and Mary Lou Larson
2008 Bonebed and Other Myths: Paleoindian to Archaic Transitions on North American Great Plains and Rocky Mountains. *Quaternary International* 191:18–33.

Kornfeld, Marcel, Mary Lou Larson, Craig Arnold, Adam Wiewel, Mike Toft, and Dennis Stanford
2007 The Nelson Site: A Cody Occupation in Northeastern Colorado. *Plains Anthropologist* 52:257–278.

Kornfeld, Marcel, Mary Lou Larson, D. Rapson, and G. C. Frison
2001 10,000 Years in the Rocky Mountains: The Helen Lookingbill Site. *Journal of Field Archaeology* 28:307–324.

LaBelle, Jason M.
2005 Hunter-Gatherer Foraging Variability during the Early Holocene of the Central Plains of North America. Unpublished Ph.D. dissertation, Department of Anthropology, Southern Methodist University, Dallas.

LaBelle, Jason M., and David J. Meltzer
1996 Reinvestigation of Marks Beach: A Possible Early/Middle Holocene Campsite on Blackwater Draw. *Current Research in the Pleistocene* 13:31–33.

Largent, Floyd
2007 Is It or Isn't It? The Quiet Controversy of

the Hudson-Meng Site. *Mammoth Trumpet* 22:14–16, 20.

Larson, Mary Lou, Marcel Kornfeld, and George Frison (editors)

2009 *Hell Gap: A Stratified Paleoindian Campsite on the Edge of the Rockies*. University of Utah Press, Salt Lake City.

MacDonald, Douglas H.

1998 Subsistence, Sex, and Cultural Transmission in Folsom Culture. *Journal of Anthropological Archaeology* 17:217–239.

MacDonald, J. N.

1981 *North American Bison: Their Classification and Evolution*. University of California Press, Berkeley.

Mandel, Rolfe D., and Jack L. Hofman

2003 Geoarchaeological Investigations at the Winger Site: A Late Paleoindian Bison Bonebed in Southwestern Kansas, U.S.A. *Geoarchaeology* 18:129–144.

McCartney, Peter H.

1983 An Archaeological Analysis of Bison Remains from the Cody Paleo-Indian Site of Lamb Spring. Unpublished Master's thesis, Department of Anthropology, University of Arizona, Tucson.

1990 Alternative Hunting Strategies in Plains Paleoindian Adaptation. In *Hunters of the Recent Past*, edited by L. B. Davis and B. O. K. Reeves, pp. 111–121. Unwin Hyman, Boston.

McHugh, Thomas

1958 Social Behavior of the American Buffalo (*Bison bison bison*). *Zoologica* 43:1–40.

Melton, D. A., N. C. Larter, C. C. Gates, and J. A. Virgil

1989 The Influence of Rut and Environmental Factors on the Behavior of Wood Bison. *Acta Theriologia* 34:179–193.

Meltzer, David J.

1988 Late Pleistocene Human Adaptations in Eastern North America. *Journal of World Prehistory* 2:1–52.

1995 Clocking the First Americans. *Annual Review of Anthropology* 24:21–45.

2006 *Folsom: New Archaeological Investigations of a Classic Paleoindian Bison Kill*. University of California Press, Berkeley.

Meltzer, David J., John D. Seebach, and Ryan M. Byerly

2006 The Hot Tubb Folsom-Midland Site (41CR10), Texas. *Plains Anthropologist* 51:157–184.

Meyer, D.

1985 A Component in the Scottsbluff Tradition: Excavation at the Niska Site. *Canadian Journal of Archaeology* 9:1–37.

Miller, Mark E.

1987 *Data Recovery and Mapping in the Finley Site Area, 1987*. Report prepared for U.S. Bureau of Land Management. On file at the Office of the Wyoming State Archaeologist, Laramie.

Moss, John H.

1951 *Early Man in the Eden Valley*. University Museum, University of Pennsylvania, Philadelphia.

Neck, R. W.

1995 Molluscan Remains. In *Stratigraphy and Paleoenvironments of Late Quaternary Valley Fills on the Southern High Plains*, by Vance T. Holliday, pp. 59–67. Geological Society of America Memoir No. 186. Boulder, Colorado.

Olson, C. G., and D. A. Porter

2002 Isotopic and Geomorphic Evidence for Holocene Climate, Southwestern Kansas. *Quaternary International* 87:29–44.

Rambaut, A., S. Y. W. Ho, A. J. Drummond, and B. Shapiro

2009 Accommodating the Effects of Ancient DNA Damage on Inferences of Demographic Histories. *Molecular Biological Evolution* 26:245–248.

Schoolcraft, Henry

1856 *Information Respecting the History, Conditions, and Prospects of the Indian Tribes of the United States*. J. B. Lippincott, Philadelphia.

Schultz, C. Bertrand

1932 Associations of Artifacts and Extinct Mammals in Nebraska. *Bulletin of Nebraska State Museum* 33(1):271–282.

1951 A Preliminary Report on the Bison Remains in the Finley Site (Eden Bison Quarry). In *Early Man in the Eden Valley*, edited by L. C. Eiseley, pp. 121–124. University Museum, University of Pennsylvania, Philadelphia.

Sellards, E. H., Glen L. Evans, and Grayson E. Meade

1947 Fossil Bison and Associated Artifacts from Plainview, Texas. *Bulletin of Geological Society of America* 58:927–954.

Shapiro, B., A. J. Drummond, A. Rambaut, M. C. Wilson, P. E. Matheus, A. V. Sher, O. G. Pybus, M. T. Gilbert, I. Barnes, J. Binladen, E. Willerslev, A. J. Hansen, G. F. Baryshnikov, J. A., Burns, S. Davydov, J. C. Driver, D. C. Froese, C. R. Harington, G. Keddie, P. Kostintsev, M. L. Kunz, L. D. Martin, R. O. Stephenson, J. Storer, R. Tedford, S. Zimov, and A. Cooper

2004 Rise and Fall of the Beringian Steppe Bison. *Science* 306:1561–1565.

Smith, Craig S., and Lance M. McNees

1990 Rattlesnake Pass Site: A Folsom Occupation in South Central Wyoming. *Plains Anthropologist* 35:273–289.

Sokal, Robert R., and F. James Rohlf

1995 *Biometry: The Principles and Practice of*

*Statistics in Biological Research.* W. H. Freeman, New York.

Soper, J. Dewey
1941 History, Range, and Home Life of the Northern Bison. *Ecological Monographs* 11:347–412.

Speth, John
1983 *Bison Kills and Bone Counts.* University of Chicago Press, Chicago.

Speth, John D., and Katherine Spielmann
1983 Energy Source, Protein Metabolism, and Hunter-Gatherer Subsistence Strategies. *Journal of Anthropological Archaeology* 2:1–31.

Stanford, D. J.
1999 Analysis and Interpretation of Hell Gap Hunting Strategies at the Jones-Miller Site. In *Le bison: Gibier et moyen de subsistence des hommes du Paléolithique aux Paléoindiens des Grandes Plaines*, edited by J.-P. Brugal, F. David, J. G. Enloe, and J. Jaubert, pp. 437–454. Éditions APDCA, Antibes, France.

Tieszen, Larry L., Bradley C. Reed, Norman B. Bliss, Bruce K. Wylie, and Donovan D. DeJong
1997 NDVI, C3 and C4 Production and Distribution in Great Plains Grassland Land Cover Classes. *Ecological Applications* 7:59–78.

Todd, Lawrence C.
1987a Analysis of Kill-Butchery Bonebeds and Interpretation of Paleoindian Hunting. In *The Evolution of Human Hunting*, edited by M. Nitecki and D. Nitecki, pp. 225–266. Plenum Press, New York.
1987b Taphonomy of the Horner II Bone Bed. In *The Horner Site: The Type Site of the Cody Cultural Complex*, edited by G. C. Frison and L. C. Todd, pp. 107–198. Academic Press, Orlando, Florida.
1991 Seasonality Studies and Paleoindian Subsistence Strategies. In *Human Predators and Prey Mortality*, edited by M. C. Stiner, pp. 215–238. Westview Press, Boulder, Colorado.

Todd, Lawrence C., Jack L. Hofman, and C. Bertrand Schultz
1990 Seasonality of the Scottsbluff and Lipscomb Bison Bonebed: Implications for Modeling Paleoindian Subsistence. *American Antiquity* 55:813–827.
1992 Faunal Analysis and Paleoindian Studies: A Reexamination of the Lipscomb Bison Bonebed. *Plains Anthropologist* 37:137–165.

Todd, Lawrence C., and David J. Rapson
1999 Formational Analysis of Bison Bonebeds and Interpretation of Paleoindian Subsistence. In *Le bison: Gibier et moyen de subsistance des hommes du Paléolithique aux Paléoindiens de Grandes Plaines*, edited by J.-P. Brugal, F. David, J. G. Enloe, and J. Jaubert, pp. 479–499. Éditions APDCA, Antibes, France.

Todd, Lawrence C., David J. Rapson, and Jack L. Hofman
1996 Dentition Studies of the Mill Iron and Other Early Paleoindian Bison Bonebed Sites. In *The Mill Iron Site*, edited by G. C. Frison, pp. 145–176. University of New Mexico Press, Albuquerque.

Turpin, Solveig, Leland C. Bement, and Herbert H. Eling Jr.
1997 Stuck in the Muck: The Big Lake Bison Kill Site (41RG13), West Texas. *Plains Anthropologist* 42:119–133.

Waguespack, Nicole M., and Todd Surovell
2003 Clovis Hunting Strategies, or How to Make Out on Plentiful Resources. *American Antiquity* 68:333–352.

Walker, Danny N.
1975 A Cultural and Ecological Analysis of the Vertebrate Fauna from the Medicine Lodge Creek Site (48BH499). Unpublished Master's thesis, Department of Anthropology, University of Wyoming, Laramie.
2007 Vertebrate Fauna. In *Medicine Lodge Creek: Holocene Archaeology of the Eastern Big Horn Basin, Wyoming*, edited by G. C. Frison and D. N. Walker, pp. 177–226. Clovis Press, Santa Fe, New Mexico.

Wheat, Joe B.
1972 *The Olsen-Chubbuck Site: A Paleoindian Bison Kill.* Society for American Archaeology, Memoir No. 26. Washington, D.C.
1978 Olsen-Chubbuck and Jurgens Sites: Four Aspects of Paleo-Indian Economy. In *Bison Procurement and Utilization: A Symposium*, edited by L. B. Davis and M. Wilson, pp. 84–89. Memoir No. 14. Plains Anthropologist, Lincoln, Nebraska.
1979 *The Jurgens Site.* Memoir No. 15. Plains Anthropologist, Lincoln, Nebraska.

Whittaker, William E.
1997 The Cherokee Excavations Revisited: Prehistoric Adaptation and Change in the Eastern Great Plains. Unpublished Master's thesis, Department of Anthropology, University of Iowa, Iowa City.

Widga, Chris
2007 Ongoing Investigations of the Merserve Type Locality in Central Nebraska. *Current Research in the Pleistocene* 24:145–147.

Wilmsen, Edwin N., and Frank H. H. Roberts Jr.
1984 *Lindenmeier, 1934–1974: Concluding Report on Investigations*. Smithsonian Contribution to Anthropology No. 24. Smithsonian Institution Press, Washington, D.C.

Wilson, Michael
1974 Fossil Bison and Artifacts from the Mona Lisa Site, Calgary, Alberta, Part 1: Stratigraphy and Artifacts. *Plains Anthropologist* 19:34–45.

Wilson, M. C., and A. C. MacWilliams
1987 Preliminary Geoarchaeological Studies at the Fletcher Paleo-Indian Bison Kill Site (Alberta/Scottsbluff), Southern Alberta. *Alberta Archaeological Review* 14:12–15.

Wissler, Clark
1920 *North American Indians of the Plains*. 2nd ed. Handbook Series No. 1. American Museum of Natural History, New York.

# III

# The Cody Complex in Site and Regional Context

5

# Cody Complex Land Use in Western North Dakota and Southern Saskatchewan

Matthew J. Root, Edward J. Knell, and Jeb Taylor

Nonlocal toolstones are common components of Cody complex chipped stone assemblages, especially Knife River flint (KRF) (e.g., Agenbroad 1978:72–77; Frison 1987:277; Knudson 1983:66, 83; Muñiz 2005; Wheat 1972:126). Whether these nonlocal tools were introduced to the western North Dakota and southern Saskatchewan sites under study by direct acquisition followed by long-distance transport or by long-distance or down-the-line exchange remains an important research question (e.g., Muñiz 2005). We consider this question in relation to land-use patterns in western North Dakota and southern Saskatchewan.

Using general principles of optimal foraging and temporal resource predictability theories, Knell (2007, this volume; Knell and Hill 2012) developed and tested a land-use model for the northwestern Plains that untangles questions of group mobility. We propose that economically minded hunter-gatherers would tether their land use for part of the year to places that provided the following: (1) high caloric returns (as measured in kcal/ha), (2) temporally predictable plant and animal resources, and (3) good toolstone sources. We call such places "core areas," and we call such tethered land-use strategies "regionally focused." When hunter-gatherers occupied areas with low caloric returns and temporally unpredictable resources, they increased their residential mobility and rapidly passed through these places. We call such land-use strategies, which are not focused on restricted regions and which used short-term occupations with high residential mobility, "nonregional strategies."

Testing this land-use model in the grasslands and rolling hills of the northwestern and High Plains indicated that Cody groups generally used nonregional strategies (Knell 2007, this volume; Knell and Hill 2012). The Missouri Slope Upland, Coteau Slope, and Missouri Coteau of western North Dakota and the Glaciated Plains of north-central North Dakota and southern Canada are physiographic regions (see Figure 5.2) with relatively unpredictable biotic resources and comparatively low kcal/ha returns. These regions generally have few sources of good toolstones, and toolstones frequently occur in widely scattered secondary geologic deposits, such as glaciated tills (e.g., Low 1996; Root et al. 1999:50–57). The Missouri Slope Upland lies south and west of the Missouri River. The Coteau Slope is just north and east of the Missouri River. The Missouri Coteau is north and east of the Coteau Slope and consists of hummocky, irregular glacial plains. The Glaciated Plains region lies north of the Coteau and is characterized by a low rolling landscape with generally less than 30 m of local relief (Bluemle 1991).

These areas typically have (1) a low kcal/ha resource abundance (i.e., low caloric returns), (2) plant and animal resources that are seasonally unpredictable, and (3) a paucity of high-quality toolstones. The land-use model further proposes

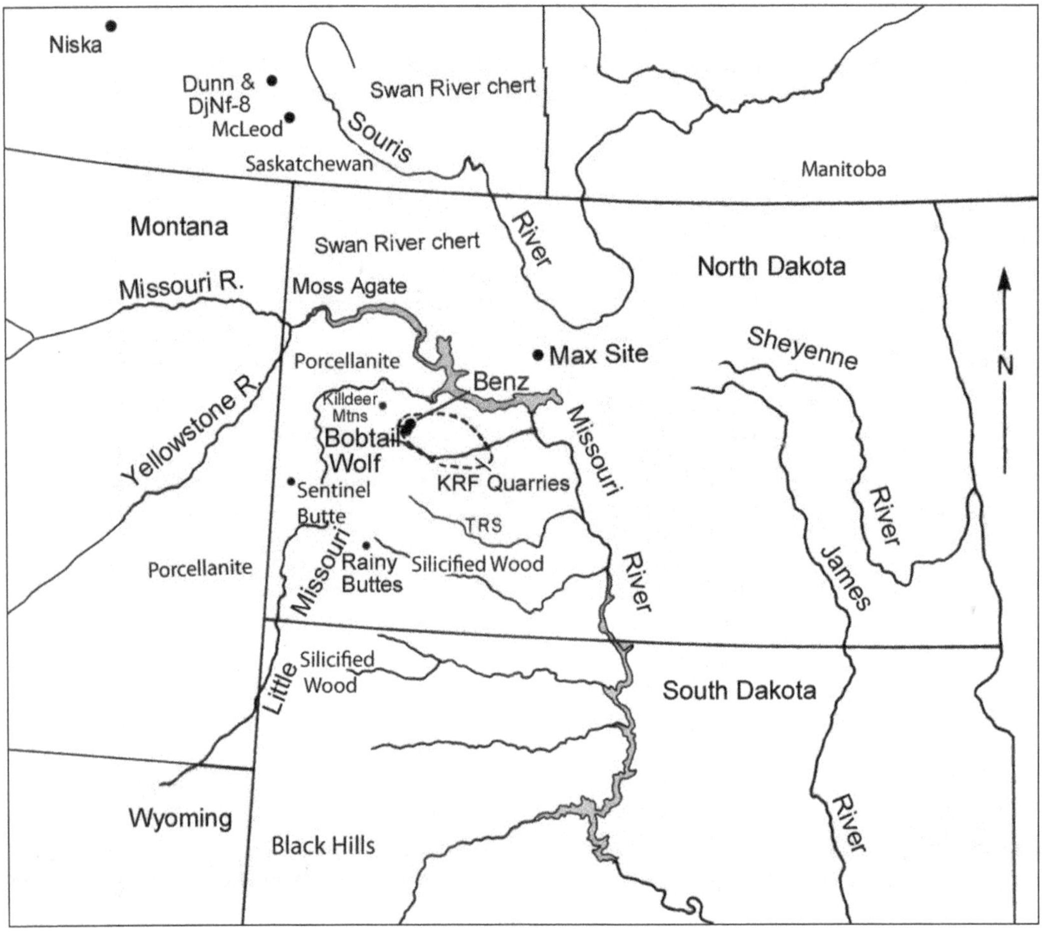


FIGURE 5.1. Map of the northern Plains showing site locations and selected toolstone sources.

that areas with high-quality toolstones in the grasslands (such as the KRF quarry area) drew repeated occupation by Cody groups. The model further predicts that hunter-gatherers used the grassland plains with a nonregional strategy during all seasons, with the possible exception of summer.

### The Open Plains Modern Environment of Western North Dakota and Southern Saskatchewan

The Missouri Coteau, Coteau Slope, and Glaciated Plains north of the Missouri River, and the Missouri Slope south and west of the Missouri River (Bluemle 1991:3–5), are generally homogeneous regions of relatively low ecological productivity. Wood (for tools, fuel, and shelters) and drinking water are limited in these areas today. Food plants and animals are seasonally limited as well. The large river valleys such as the Missouri and Souris valleys, and areas elevated above the plains (e.g., Killdeer Mountains, Rainy Buttes, and Cypress Hills), are more heterogeneous, with more wood, water, and higher ecological productivity (e.g., Osborn 2003; Osborn and Kornfeld 2003). Furthermore, the Coteau and Glaciated Plains have few sources of high-quality toolstones. Outside of the KRF quarry area, the Missouri Slope contains only a few concentrated toolstone sources, such as Rainy Buttes silicified wood (Loendorf et al. 1984) and White River Group chert on Sentinel Butte (Huckell and Kilby 2009) (Figures 5.1 and 5.2).

The KRF quarries in North Dakota are in a mixed-grass prairie region (Whitman and Wali 1975:53). Small marshes and sloughs support wetland vegetation and draw game to water. Govern-

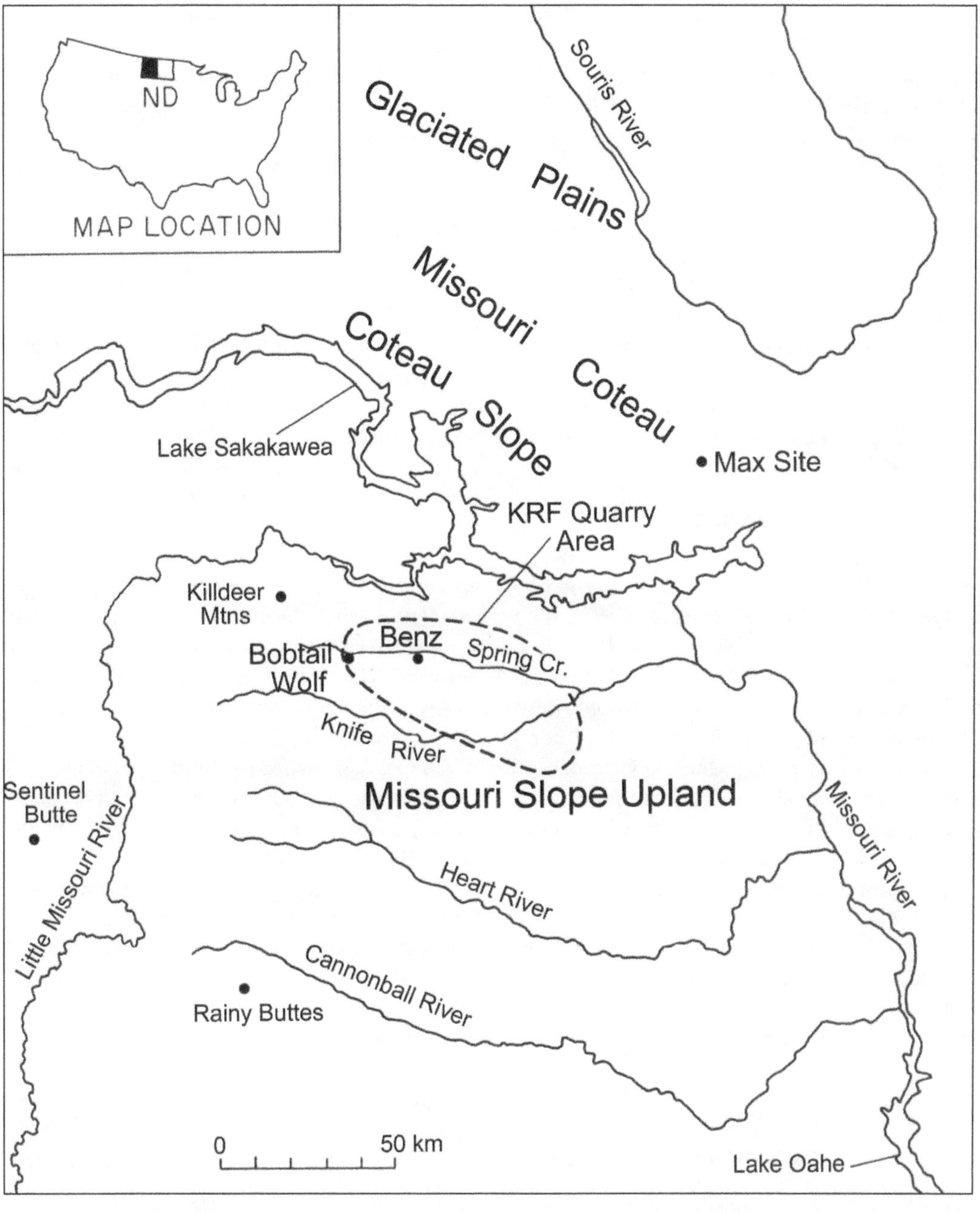


FIGURE 5.2. Knife River flint quarry area and physiographic regions of western North Dakota.

ment Land Office maps compiled from 1893 to 1899 show no trees in most of the region at that time. Exceptions include the large river valleys and high buttes, such as the Killdeer Mountains, where native stands of timber grew. Important plant foods in the northern prairie included Jerusalem artichoke (*Helianthus tuberosus*), prickly pear cactus (*Opuntia fragilis*), chokecherry (*Prunus viginiana*), and prairie turnip (*Psoralea esculenta*) (Dodds 1979; Stevens 1963).

Historically, animals in this vast expanse of prairie included deer, pronghorn, elk, jackrabbit, cottontail, muskrat, weasel, mink, coyote, and raccoon, as well as birds such as hawks, grouse, and prairie chickens. The most important animal in Cody times (Hill, this volume; Knell 2007;

Muñiz 2005) as well as later was, of course, bison. The prairie offered good grazing land for bison and pronghorn. Wooded areas, such as the high buttes and the deep draws in the Little Missouri Badlands and Missouri Breaks, provided good habitat for mule deer, elk, and small game (Bailey 1926).

Paleoindian groups frequently used Rainy Buttes silicified wood and White River Group chert (found on and around Sentinel Butte) (e.g., Huckell and Kilby 2009; Root et al. 2000), each of which occurs on prominent buttes with many biotic resources. The early discovery of such toolstone sources likely occurred because pioneering populations were drawn to the buttes as productive hunting and gathering locations.

### Paleoclimate

Paleoenvironmental studies in the region suggest that there were few trees in the area after 10,000 $^{14}$C yrs BP (11,470 cal BP). By 10,000 $^{14}$C yrs BP, prairie replaced spruce forests in southern Saskatchewan and Manitoba, as well as forest and parkland in the eastern Dakotas and southwestern and central South Dakota (Barnosky, Anderson, and Bartlein 1987; Barnosky, Grimm, and Wright 1987; Wendland 1978). Pollen records at Guardipee and Lost Lakes, northwestern Montana, suggest that extensive woodland was not present there at the close of the Pleistocene (Barnosky 1989).

Study of fossil diatoms, pollen, and sediments at Moon Lake, eastern North Dakota, suggests that spruce (*Picea* sp.) forest was present until 10,300 $^{14}$C yrs BP, when it was replaced by a parkland of mixed elm (*Ulmus* sp.), oak (*Quercus* sp.), and open grassland. During Cody times and thereafter, from 10,000 to 7300 $^{14}$C yrs BP (11,470–8103 cal BP), there was a major change from a wet to a dry climate (Laird et al. 1996). Paleolimnological research at Coldwater Lake, eastern North Dakota, indicates a wet period during the late Pleistocene and beginning of the early Holocene. At 8900 $^{14}$C yrs BP (10,043 cal BP), a predominantly dry period began that lasted until 5000 $^{14}$C yrs BP (5730 cal BP) (Bryson and Bryson 1996).

At the Mill Iron site, several hundred kilometers southwest of the KRF quarries in Montana, no evidence exists in the pollen or phytolith records for spruce. Pine pollen (*Pinus* sp.) is present, but the landscape was apparently sagebrush steppe or mixed grassland. During the Goshen occupation (ca. 11,000 $^{14}$C yrs BP, 12,825 cal BP), sagebrush (*Artemisia* sp.) dominated the site area. From 11,000 to 8000 $^{14}$C yrs BP (12,825–8888 cal BP), there may have been an increase in summer drought and a reduction in effective moisture (Cummings 1996).

Pollen and phytolith analyses at the Alkali Creek site in the KRF quarry area indicate important climatic changes about 10,000 $^{14}$C yrs BP (11,470 cal BP) (Cummings 1995), near the beginning of the Cody complex and the end of the Younger Dryas. During the Goshen-Plainview occupation of Alkali Creek (ca. 11,000 $^{14}$C yrs BP, 12,825 cal BP), the high terraces along Spring Creek were dominated by sage and grass. Junipers (*Juniperus* sp.) were apparently more abundant than today in draws, which also supported hazelnut (*Corylus* sp.), birch (*Betula* sp.), and alder (*Alnus* sp.). Pine pollen was more abundant than in later samples, suggesting that pine was more abundant on ridges than in the Holocene; however, there is no evidence of widespread forest (Cummings 1995). The Leonard Paleosol at Alkali Creek likely formed under grass after ca. 10,000 $^{14}$C yrs BP (11,470 cal BP), though soil formation began before this date (Van Nest 1995). The Leonard Paleosol is widespread in western North Dakota (e.g., Haynes 2008; Kuehn 1997; Root et al. 1986) and contains the abundant remains of Cody complex occupations in the KRF quarry area (Root 1992).

Studies of pollen, plant macrofossils, lithostratigraphy, and sediments from the Kettle Lakes on the Missouri Coteau in the Dakotas and southern Saskatchewan indicate widespread and increasing aridity during Cody complex times. White spruce trees were generally gone by ca. 10,000 $^{14}$C yrs BP (11,470 cal BP). The demise of spruce was followed by a colonization of deciduous trees. By 9300–9000 $^{14}$C yrs BP (10,530–10,200 cal BP), all deciduous trees were gone and vegetation was exclusively grassland. From 9000 to 8000 $^{14}$C yrs BP (10,200–8888 cal BP), low and fluctuating lake levels across the region indicate increasing aridity (Clark et al. 2001; Dean and Schwalb 2000; Laird et al. 1996; Last et al. 1998; Yansa et al. 2007).

The widespread development of the Leonard Paleosol in the KRF quarry area suggests that the region supported a healthy mixed-grass prairie during the early Holocene (Kuehn 1997; Root et al. 1986). The percentage of organic matter in the Leonard Paleosol often exceeds that of the modern prairie soil, attesting to the thick prairie cover throughout the early Holocene (Clayton et al. 1976; Root 1992:170–172).

In general, the paleoenvironmental data indicate a moist period at the onset of the early Holocene followed by a drying trend through the rest of early Holocene and beyond (also see Muñiz [Chapter 2], Widga, this volume). The study area supported a rich mixed-grassland prairie as suggested by paleosol development, with parkland largely confined to elevated areas. Prairie grasslands are comparatively homogeneous landscapes in terms of plant and animal availability, not to mention the paucity of toolstone across much of the study area. The land-use model indicates that homogeneous environments with poor toolstone availability were efficiently exploited by nonregionally focused Cody hunter-gatherers (Knell 2007; Knell and Hill 2012). Thus, people probably moved quickly through the open plains.

An exception to this expected pattern may be the use of the KRF quarry area. Most Great Plains Cody bison kills were late summer to fall events (Hill, this volume; Muñiz 2005:252). Cody groups may have tethered their settlement to the quarry area during the late summer or early fall before moving out to hunt bison elsewhere on the Missouri Slope and northward to the Coteau and Glaciated Plains. Regardless of the length of individual occupations, people likely made repeated annual visits to the quarries to gear up before large hunts. The data presented below test this proposition.

### Knife River Flint in Cody Complex Toolkits

Knife River flint occurs in many Cody complex sites across the Plains, often far from the source area (e.g., Horner in Wyoming [Frison 1987:277], Olsen-Chubbuck in Colorado [Wheat 1972], Hudson-Meng in Nebraska [Agenbroad 1978:72–77], and Jurgens in Colorado [Muñiz 2005]). The widespread distribution of KRF is consistent with analysis of Cody tool production in the KRF quarries that indicates Cody flintknappers produced bifacial blanks well beyond the needs of individual family groups (Root 1992, 1997). This suggests that knappers made large bifacial blanks for exchange while at the KRF quarries. Many of the KRF tools found in Cody sites far from the source area, such as those in Wyoming, Nebraska, and Colorado, were probably trade items, perhaps passed through several trading partners (e.g., Bamforth 2009). We demonstrate a different pattern, however, in the Missouri Couteau and Glaciated Plains.

We investigate the Benz and Bobtail Wolf sites in the KRF quarry area, four sites in the Canadian Glaciated Plains, and the Max site on the Missouri Coteau. The Canadian sites and the Max site are far north of the quarry area, yet each has a projectile point assemblage dominated by KRF. Only the Niska site in southern Saskatchewan has artifacts other than KRF points that are definitely associated with Cody complex occupations. The large proportion of KRF weapons suggests that hunters obtained most of their KRF points through direct acquisition, though some may have been obtained via exchange (Meltzer 1989). This suggests that groups of Cody hunters geared up at workshops in the KRF quarries before moving northward. We propose that such northward movements were probably for bison hunting in late summer to early winter, though few good data exist on the seasons of these Cody complex occupations. We propose that these hunts were part of a pattern of short-term occupations with high residential mobility following nonregional land-use strategies. After these hunts, Cody groups likely retreated from the open plains to sheltered river valleys or wooded buttes to overwinter.

### Test Implications

The proportion of local to nonlocal toolstone can be used to distinguish between regional and nonregional land-use strategies (e.g., Bamforth 2002a, 2002b; Gardner 1983; Knudson 2002; Smith 1990, 1991; Stanford 1999). Other factors, such as raw material richness and transport distances (Brantingham 2003, 2006) and the number of tool-depleting events (Ingbar 1994; Surovell 2009: 67–70), also influence the proportion of raw materials. Generally, a large ratio of local to nonlocal toolstone signifies a tethered or regional land-use strategy.

Conversely, a large ratio of nonlocal toolstone indicates a nonregional strategy. This expectation is inherently weak, however, because the amount of on-site tool production can inflate the proportion of local to nonlocal toolstone in assemblages from lithic workshops. The cutoff between local and nonlocal toolstone is 40 km (after Gould and Saggers 1985; Meltzer 1989).

The proportion of long use-life tools (projectile points, bifacial knives, and end scrapers) manufactured from local and nonlocal toolstone provides a more robust measure. These tools typically remain in toolkits for long periods, increasing the likelihood that people transported them over long distances and carried them from nonlocal sources. Thus, highly mobile hunter-gatherers who rapidly move through a region are more likely to discard a larger proportion of long use-life tools of nonlocal toolstone than groups that remain tethered to a region.

The need to replenish toolstone was one factor that structured Cody hunter-gatherer mobility patterns. Where high-quality toolstone is located near a site, regionally restricted groups should repeatedly replenish their toolkits with the local stone. This results in the discard of a large proportion of manufacturing debris of local stone as people gear up (Surovell 2009:77–78).

Nonregional Cody groups would replenish their toolkits with local stone to meet any on-site needs and to gear up. Uncertainty about the ability to replenish toolkits in the future, however, would lead to off-site gearing up. It was probably more efficient for nonregional hunter-gatherers to deplete any surplus of transported, nonlocal stone, producing debitage of nonlocal stone.

We expect that regionally restricted hunter-gatherers would regularly replenish their toolstone with local materials. As they moved around toolstone source areas, they would, by attrition, discard many previously manufactured tools of local stone along with the debitage from the associated tool maintenance. We expect that large proportions of the worn-out, discarded tools that were transported to a site would be of local stone. There should be evidence for resharpening and reworking tools of local materials.

Conversely, groups that rapidly moved between regions would transport and maintain finished tools acquired in previously occupied regions. Thus, nonregional groups would discard moderate to large proportions of worn-out, transported tools of nonlocal stone. There should be debitage from maintaining those nonlocal tools.

The longer a group was tethered to a region with sources of toolstone, the more likely it was to encounter and collect toolstone from many formations and outcrops. This increases the frequency of sources represented and the variety of toolstone types. Nonregional groups rapidly passed through these locales and thus did not have time to exploit more than a few sources. Thus, regionally focused hunter-gatherers exploited a wider variety of individual sources, resulting in a higher diversity of lithic materials than nonregional groups that spent less time in one area.

Thus, nonregional strategies should produce lithic assemblages with the following characteristics (Carr 2005; Carr and Boszhardt 2010; Knell 2007, this volume):

1. large to moderate proportions (>25 percent) of long use-life tools are from nonlocal toolstones;
2. large to moderate proportions (>25 percent) of production debris (e.g., biface thinning flakes, shatter, broken blanks) are from nonlocal toolstones from on-site flaking of imported tools, cores, and blanks;
3. most flake debris from local toolstones (>50 percent) is from manufacture of tool blanks for transport and use elsewhere (e.g., biface thinning debris), with a minority from on-site manufacture of tools to meet immediate needs (e.g., uniface retouch flakes);
4. moderate to large proportions (>25 percent) of worn-out, discarded tools are of nonlocal stone; and
5. there is a low diversity of toolstone types, resulting from occupation in the region for a short period.

In contrast, lithic assemblages resulting from regionally focused strategies should have the following characteristics:

1. 80 percent or more of the technologically finished long use-life tools (i.e., not blanks or cores) are of local stone;
2. 80 percent or more of production debris is local material;
3. flake debris of local toolstone is a mix of tool manufacture for transport off-site and repair of existing implements;

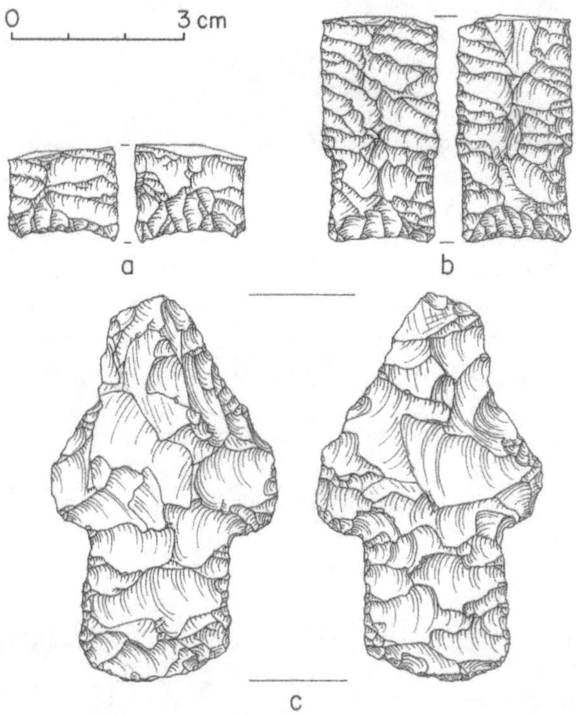


**FIGURE 5.3.** Cody complex points from the Benz site: (a) Scottsbluff point from 60–70 cm below surface; (b) Scottsbluff point from 75 cm; (c) reworked Alberta point from 64 cm.

4. a large proportion (>80 percent) of tools of local stone are discarded; and
5. there is a high diversity of toolstone types, resulting from prolonged regional occupation and procurement from different point sources (though these could be from the same geologic stone type).

Using these expectations, we test whether the Cody complex hunter-gatherers in western North Dakota and southern Canada had high residential mobility and were nonregionally focused, or whether they were seasonally tethered to the KRF quarry area.

## Testing the Land-Use Model

### *Knife River Flint Quarry Area*

#### *The Benz Site*

The Benz site (23DU452A) is in the KRF quarry area in North Dakota (Figure 5.1) and is a stratified lithic workshop and camp with several layers of Cody artifacts spread through 40 vertical centimeters (see Root et al. 1985; Root 1992:168–198, 1997, 1998). Quarry pits are several hundred meters from the workshop-camp, but the age of those quarries is unknown. Cody complex artifacts were recovered from an 11-m$^2$ area in an excavation trench. Cody artifacts and features are vertically stratified between 70 cm and 110 cm below surface in the early Holocene, Leonard Paleosol. This clearly indicates multiple occupations. One Scottsbluff point from 60–70 cm (Figure 5.3a) and one from 75 cm below surface (Figure 5.3b) were recovered, both in the upper half of the paleosol (Root et al. 1985; Root 1992:168–198).

Uncalibrated radiocarbon ages on base-soluble humates from the Leonard Paleosol in the trench are stratigraphically consistent, ranging from 8590 ± 55 $^{14}$C yr BP (SMU-1488) (9486–9679 cal BP) at the top of the buried A horizon (the 2Ab soil horizon) to 9320 ± 60 $^{14}$C yr BP (SMU-1487) (10,297–10,691 cal BP) near the bottom of the buried A horizon. A small basin-shaped hearth (Feature 19) located 10 cm above the base of the buried A horizon yielded a base-soluble age of 8600 ± 40 $^{14}$C yr BP (9502–9669 cal BP) from sediment in the hearth. This is stratigraphically inconsistent with the other ages from the

**TABLE 5.1.** Radiocarbon Dates from the Benz Site.

| Lab Number | Radiocarbon Age ($^{14}$C yr BP) | Material Dated | Provenience | Stratigraphic Context |
|---|---|---|---|---|
| SMU-1500 | 2210 ± 40 | base-soluble humates | XU12, F.6, hearth, 30–39 cm | hearth in late Archaic level |
| SMU-1307 | 8000 ± 80 | base-soluble humates | XU3, 69–77 cm | upper Leonard Paleosol |
| SMU-1300 | 8400 ± 55 | base-soluble humates | XU3, 81–88 cm | lower Leonard Paleosol |
| SMU-1488 | 8590 ± 55 | base-soluble humates | XU8, 52–57 cm | top of Leonard Paleosol |
| SMU-1282 | 8700 ± 70 | base-soluble humates | XU6, 65–70 cm | middle Leonard Paleosol |
| SMU-1271 | 8910 ± 70 | base-soluble humates | XU6, 75–80 cm | lower Leonard Paleosol |
| SMU-1487 | 9320 ± 60 | base-soluble humates | XU8, 78–84 cm | lower Leonard Paleosol |
| SMU-1390 | 8600 ± 40 | base-soluble humates | XU18, F.19, 87–99 cm | hearth in lower Leonard Paleosol |
| UCR-3466 | 9540 ± 50 | 9 mg, wood charcoal | XU18, F.19, 87–99 cm | hearth in lower Leonard Paleosol |

**TABLE 5.2.** Total of Stone Tools and Cores from the Benz Site Listed by Cody Component.

| Tool Class | Upper Scottsbluff | Lower Scottsbluff | Alberta |
|---|---|---|---|
| Projectile points | 1 (1.1%) | 1 (0.9%) | 0 (0.0%) |
| Flake tools | 6 (6.7%) | 8 (7.5%) | 7 (7.5%) |
| End scrapers | 2 (2.2%) | 0 (0.0%) | 0 (0.0%) |
| Finished bifacial tools | 0 (0.0%) | 1 (0.9%) | 0 (0.0%) |
| Hammerstones, manuports | 1 (1.1%) | 1 (1.1%) | 0 (0.0%) |
| Unfinished bifacial blanks | 48 (53.9%) | 53 (50.0%) | 51 (54.8%) |
| Cores | 16 (18.0%) | 19 (17.9%) | 27 (29.0%) |
| Tested cobbles | 15 (16.9%) | 23 (21.7%) | 8 (8.6%) |
| **Total** | 89 (100%) | 106 (100%) | 93 (100%) |

Leonard Paleosol. An AMS age on 9 mg of unidentifiable wood charcoal from the hearth was dated to 9540 ± 50 $^{14}$C yr BP (10,697–11,097 cal BP) and is consistent with the other dates from the trench. The date on base-soluble humates from the hearth certainly represents contamination by younger material. Two radiocarbon ages from the Leonard Paleosol in an isolated excavation unit (XU3) 110 m east of the trench are younger than the ages from the trench. These samples were probably contaminated with younger soluble humates (Root 1992:168–198, 1998). The locations of radiocarbon samples, diagnostic artifacts, and the Leonard Paleosol in the trench are shown in Figures 5.4 and 5.5. Radiocarbon dates are listed in Table 5.1.

An Alberta point was recovered from 64 cm below surface in a disturbed part of the excavation area (Figure 5.3c). The AMS date from the nearby hearth (9540 ± 50 $^{14}$C yr BP) is consistent with an Alberta occupation (Root 1992, 1998). Therefore, it is likely that the occupations represented in the lower part of the paleosol are Alberta. The Scottsbluff and Alberta sequence was divided into four analytic units, corresponding to 10-cm excavation levels (Figure 5.5). Within single analytic units, features are vertically stratified, indicating that more than one occupation is represented in each analytic unit. The upper two analytic units contain Scottsbluff points, and the lower two units date to Alberta times; however, no diagnostic artifacts were recovered from the lower levels. Only a few artifacts were in the lowest level, some of which may have been displaced downward by pedoturbation. Therefore, we combine the lower two analytic units (9 and 10) for this analysis.

The Scottsbluff and Alberta levels have the same basic structure and artifact content. They contain large concentrations of KRF flakes and have tool collections dominated by cores and unfinished bifacial blanks that knappers broke during percussion thinning (Table 5.2). The largest flake debris concentration (Feature 16) is in the lower Scottsbluff unit and contains 32,899 flakes. These flake debris features represent in situ knapping areas. The upper Scottsbluff unit contains 89 tools

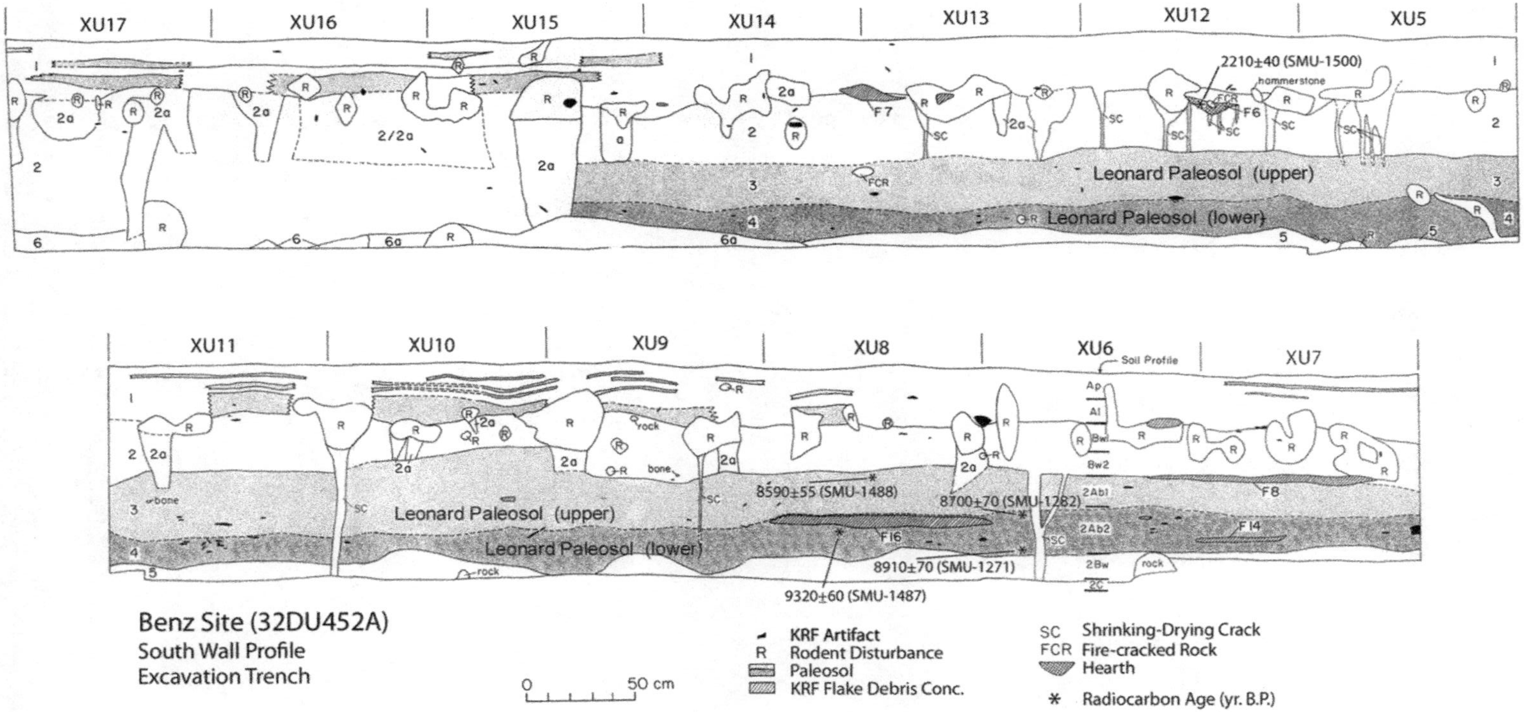


**FIGURE 5.4.** Stratigraphic profile of the excavation trench at the Benz site.

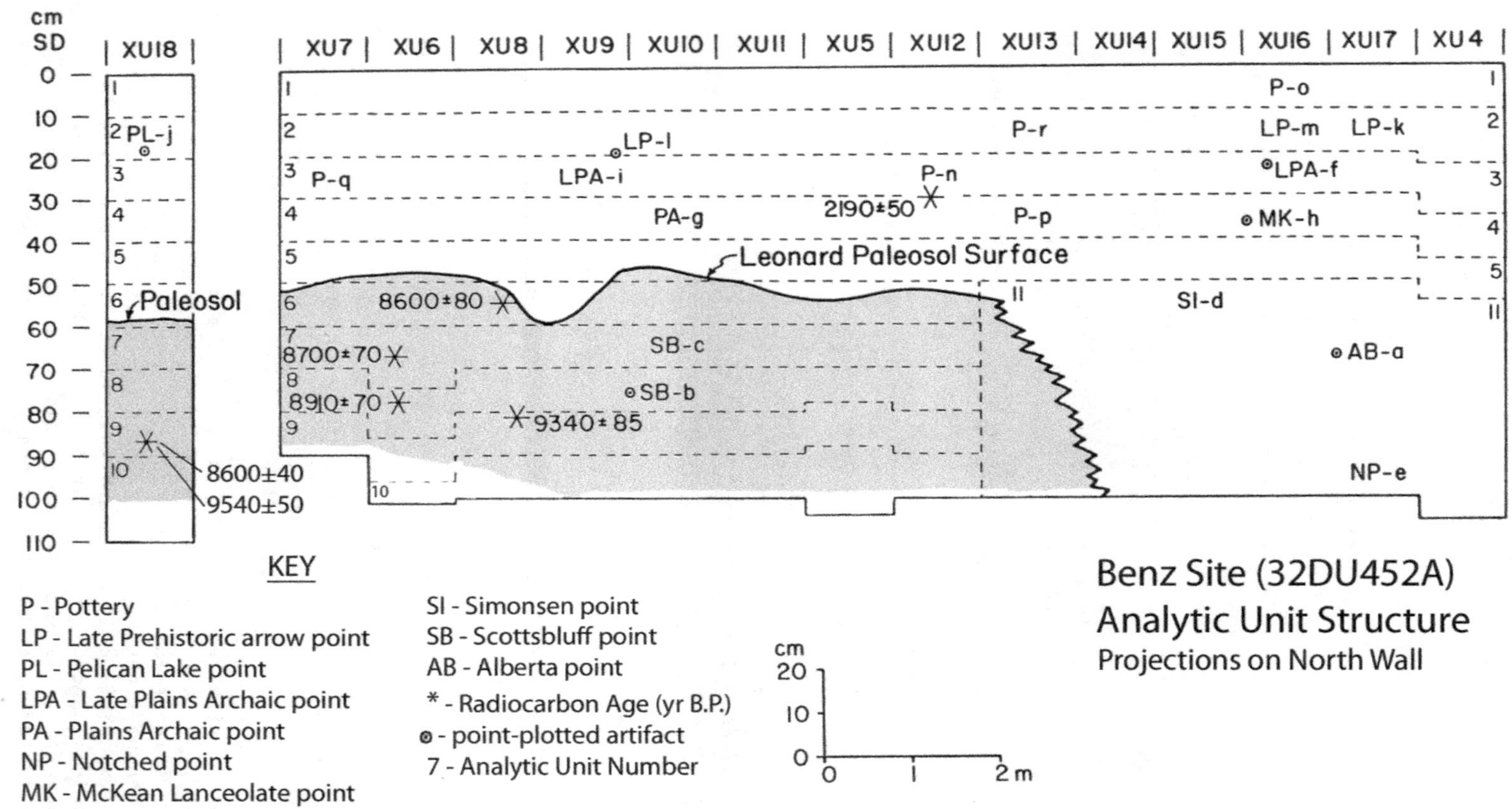


FIGURE 5.5. Schematic diagram of analytic unit structure showing radiocarbon dates and time-diagnostic artifacts at the Benz site.

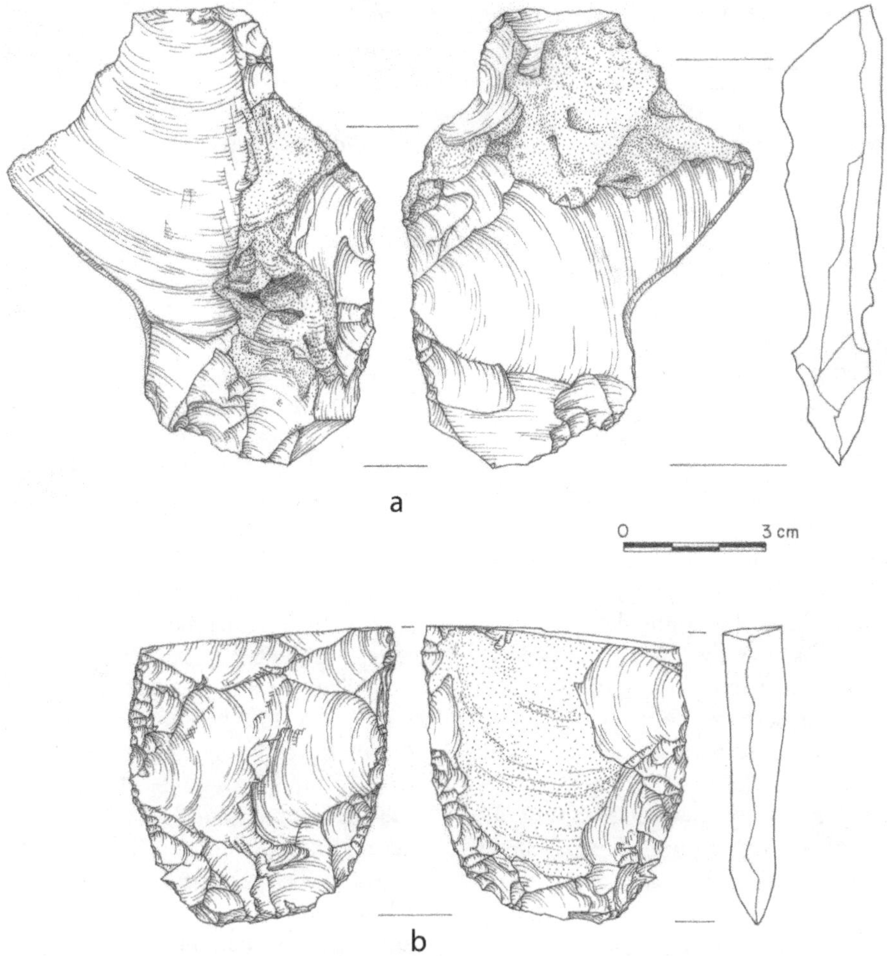


FIGURE 5.6. (a) bifacial core from the Alberta unit, Benz site; (b) biface blank broken in manufacture from the upper Scottsbluff unit, Benz site.

and cores, the lower Scottsbluff unit contains 106 tools and cores, and the Alberta unit contains 93 tools.

The tool and core collections from each analytic unit contain (1) more than 50 percent broken biface blanks, (2) between 18 and 29 percent cores, and (3) from 9 to 21 percent tested tabular or blocky cobbles (pieces that broke during the first few percussion blows) (Table 5.2). Thus, about 90 percent of the stone tools in each analytic unit are debris discarded during manufacture. The remaining tools consist of a few retouched flakes, end scrapers, and projectile point fragments (Table 5.2).

Working wood and bone rapidly depletes stone tools, making it likely that these activities took place where toolstone was abundant (Crabtree and Davis 1968). Therefore, some of the tools used to work hard materials (e.g., wood or bone) may reflect manufacture and repair of tool hafts made of wood or bone, or manufacture of wood and bone tools (based on low-power use-wear analysis; see Root et al. 1985 and Root 1992).

Cody knappers made large bifacial blanks directly from high-quality, tabular flint cobbles. These blanks were suitable for manufacture into any of the Cody complex dart point forms or into large bifacial butchering implements. The bifacial blanks have a very different design than the prepared cores and were not bifacial cores (Figure 5.6; see also Root 1992:Figures 5.16, 5.17). Prepared cores were designed with bifacial platforms and with shaped core faces so that large flakes could be detached that traveled the entire length of the

**TABLE 5.3.** Benz Site Flake Debris by Toolstone Type and Cody Complex Component.

| Toolstone | Upper Scottsbluff | Lower Scottsbluff | Alberta |
|---|---|---|---|
| Knife River flint | 53,617 | 79,325 | 65,427 |
| Porcellanite | 2 | 25 | 107 |
| Translucent chert | 0 | 6 | 3 |
| Silicified wood | 0 | 1 | 0 |
| Opaque chert | 0 | 0 | 1 |
| Tongue River silcrete | 1 | 0 | 0 |
| Local silcrete | 0 | 0 | 1 |
| Local metaquartzite | 0 | 8 | 65 |
| **Total** | 53,620 | 79,365 | 65,604 |

core. Biface blanks had much smaller flakes detached that are slightly transmedial. These were designed to shape and thin the blanks for tool manufacture, not to detach large flakes for tool blanks. Though bifacial thinning flakes were occasionally used as tools, they were produced as a by-product of tool shaping and thinning rather than designed blank production.

Estimates of the number of tools produced on the site, based on the amount of debitage, indicate that Cody knappers exported a substantial number of percussion-thinned biface blanks from the site. Production estimates of the largest features indicate that they contain debris equivalent to the manufacture of more than 100 bifaces (Root 1992:Table 7.2; 1997). There is no evidence that knappers finished KRF tools on the site (i.e., there are no pressure-flaked preforms that broke during manufacture and no KRF biface pressure flakes). It is clear that Cody complex groups produced percussion-flaked blanks for subsequent manufacture into bifacial tools and points, but they carried these from the quarry-workshop for finishing and use elsewhere.

Only two tools from the Cody levels are not KRF: a Phosphoria chert flake tool and a granite hammerstone. The Phosphoria tool consists of two cross-mended fragments of a large retouched flake, which was made on a blank from a prepared core. One piece is from the lower Scottsbluff unit and one is from the Alberta unit (with a 12-cm vertical separation), indicating that some mixing has occurred. Phosphoria chert is available far to the southwest in Wyoming, though similar stone occurs as secondary gravels in the high Pleistocene terraces along the Yellowstone River in eastern Montana and in the Goose Egg formation in the Black Hills of South Dakota. Granite cobbles are abundant in the local glacial till.

Flake debris is overwhelmingly KRF (Table 5.3). The two Scottsbluff components contain 53,617 and 79,325 KRF flakes, and the Alberta component contains 65,427 KRF flakes. One Tongue River silcrete and two porcellanite flakes are from the upper Scottsbluff horizon. The lower Scottsbluff unit contains 25 porcellanite, six chert, one silicified wood, and eight metaquartzite flakes. The Alberta horizon contains 107 porcellanite, four chert, one silcrete, and 65 metaquartzite flakes. Of the porcellanite, 91 flakes are the same gray toolstone from one feature. These are mostly biface pressure flakes and small nondiagnostic fragments that probably represent a single tool-making or maintenance event. The 177 non-KRF flakes in the Alberta unit comprise only 0.27 percent of the collection.

Porcellanite is available in the Little Missouri Badlands 30 km to the north but is also present in surface deposits to the west and south within 100 km of the quarries. Chert, silicified wood, metaquartzite, and silcrete are all locally available in glacial till and secondary lag deposits. Nonlocal sources of chert and silicified wood are widely scattered in western North Dakota. Distinguishing local from nonlocal toolstones of these materials is difficult for small flakes, and these artifacts are of unknown origin. Tongue River silcrete is certainly nonlocal, with sources 100 km to the southwest. The small number of flakes of these materials and the occurrence of a single non-KRF tool suggests that the debris is from on-site tool maintenance, not manufacture.

In total, we recovered 49.9 g of bone from the Cody levels, of which 1.1 g is burned. The only identified bone includes a bison horn-core fragment from the upper Scottsbluff unit, a bison petrous temporal bone from the Alberta unit, and fragments of bison dental enamel from the upper Scottsbluff and Alberta levels. These levels also contain scattered pieces of unidentified large mammal bone. These data provide evidence of occasional procurement of bison during the Cody occupations (Root et al. 1985:123–131).

The season of occupation is unknown, but if knappers gathered stone from even shallow

**TABLE 5.4.** Bobtail Wolf Site Stone Tools by Toolstone Type and Functional Class.

| Toolstone | Cores, Test Cobbles, Blanks | Projectile Points | Finished Knives, End Scrapers | Retouched Flakes, Incising, Woodwork | Hammers, Core Tools |
|---|---|---|---|---|---|
| KRF | 63 | 2[a] | 4 | 49 | 0 |
| Local chert | 1 | 0 | 1 | 0 | 0 |
| Local silcrete | 0 | 0 | 0 | 0 | 1 |
| Local basaltic | 0 | 0 | 0 | 0 | 2 |
| Silicified wood | 0 | 0 | 0 | 1 | 0 |
| Rainy Buttes silicified wood | 0 | 0 | 0 | 2 | 0 |
| Orthoquartzite | 0 | 1[b] | 0 | 0 | 0 |
| **Total** | 64 | 3 | 5 | 52 | 3 |

[a] Folsom.
[b] Scottsbluff.

quarry pits, they could have done so only during the warm seasons. The ground is frozen from late fall through early spring, and even digging with metal hand tools is not feasible. Though scattered flint cobbles are available on the surface and in stream gravels, personal experience shows that gathering stone when the ground and streams are frozen is difficult, especially with snow cover.

*The Bobtail Wolf Site*

The Bobtail Wolf site, located at the western edge of the KRF quarry area, has a deposit of mixed Folsom and Cody artifacts. One orthoquartzite Scottsbluff point comes from the mixed Folsom-Cody deposit, and one ostracod fossil–bearing, brown chert Alberta/Cody I point is from the surface. The orthoquartzite Scottsbluff point is similar to material from the Hartville Uplift, Wyoming. The ostracod-bearing chert is similar to materials from the Green River Basin, Wyoming, 750 km to the southwest; it is certainly nonlocal (Root et al. 2000).

The mixed deposits contain Cody and Folsom artifacts, and it is not possible to isolate Cody artifacts other than the points. The mixed collection, however, is dominated by KRF tools (116 of 124 [93.5 percent]) and flakes (34,781 of 34,834 [99.8 percent]). Most of the non-KRF artifacts are locally available stones. There is one small, nondiagnostic flake of ostracod-bearing chert, which may be related to the Cody occupation. Other nonlocal materials include Swan River chert ($n$ = 2), porcellanite ($n$ = 5), Rainy Buttes silicified wood ($n$ = 7), and nonlocal chert ($n$ = 3).

Just over half of the tool collection consists of cores ($n$ = 10), tested cobbles ($n$ = 21), and biface blanks broken during manufacture ($n$ = 32). There is also one unmodified KRF cobble that must have been carried to its recovery context. Thus, workshop activities dominate (Table 5.4). In contrast to the Benz site, Bobtail Wolf has much larger proportions of retouched flakes ($n$ = 32, 25.8 percent), incising tools ($n$ = 8, 6.5 percent), finished knives ($n$ = 4, 3.2 percent), and woodworking tools ($n$ = 9, 7.3 percent). Manufacture of biface blanks designed for transport from the site was important, though more tools were used in maintenance activities here than at Benz. The mixing of Cody and Folsom artifacts, however, makes it impossible to determine exactly which of the tools are Cody and which are Folsom (Root 2000; Root et al. 2000).

### *Summary: Cody Land Use in the Knife River Flint Quarry Area*

The implications of Knell's (2007; Knell and Hill 2012) land-use model are divided in their application to the Benz and Bobtail Wolf sites. Regionally focused land use is evident from the following: (1) most technologically finished tools are KRF, (2) almost all debitage is local KRF, (3) most discarded finished tools are KRF, and (4) the small amount of non-KRF flake debris suggests limited on-site maintenance of tools that were manufactured elsewhere. In contrast, production debris of KRF is almost exclusively from blank manufacture and core reduction. Most KRF tools were clearly made for transport from the area. There is a low diversity of toolstones, with over 99 percent of the flake debris and all but a few tools made of

**TABLE 5.5.** Cody Complex Projectile Points from the Max Site by Type and Raw Material.

| Raw Material | Eden | Scottsbluff | Alberta/Cody I | Total |
|---|---|---|---|---|
| Knife River flint | 17 (56.7%) | 6 (50.0%) | 2 (66.7%) | 25 (55.6%) |
| Porcellanite | 10 (33.3%) | 4 (33.3%) | 0 (0.0%) | 14 (31.1%) |
| Silicified wood | 2 (6.7%) | 1 (8.3%) | 0 (0.0%) | 3 (6.7%) |
| Brown chert | 0 (0.0%) | 0 (0.0%) | 1 (33.3%) | 1 (2.2%) |
| Rainy Buttes silicified wood | 0 (0.0%) | 1 (8.3%) | 0 (0.0%) | 1 (2.2%) |
| Tongue River silcrete | 1 (3.3%) | 0 (0.0%) | 0 (0.0%) | 1 (2.2%) |
| **Total** | 30 (100%) | 12 (100%) | 3 (100%) | 45 (100%) |

KRF. It is a homogeneous material, without variation in different point sources. Therefore, it is difficult to meaningfully apply the diversity implication to the KRF quarry area. The emphasis on tool production for off-site purposes is expected at a workshop, especially one located at the dominant, naturally occurring toolstone source for over 50 km in all directions. The emphasis on production suggests elements of a nonregional land-use strategy.

Thus, the Benz and Bobtail Wolf sites probably represent a mix of warm-season, regionally and nonregionally focused use of the open plains in the KRF quarry area. The collection from Benz clearly represents many occupations, and the Bobtail Wolf collection contains debris from different Folsom and Cody occupations. Strategies may have changed with different occupations due to many external factors, such as game availability. The Cody occupations represent episodes of retooling and gearing up, probably before hunts in toolstone-poor areas such as those to the north. People likely geared up for overwintering, when toolstone procurement was difficult as well.

### *The Missouri Coteau and Glaciated Plains*

The sample of Cody artifacts from the Coteau and the Glacial Plains of southern Saskatchewan consists primarily of surface-collected projectile points. Therefore, results must be viewed cautiously. Hunters generally used projectile points for one activity, and these weapons were not used and discarded in the same ways as other kinds of tools. As Bamforth (2009) explicates, weapon tips made from exotic materials may have been obtained by individuals or small groups of hunters (e.g., MacDonald 1999), or through exchange networks. Therefore, atlatl dart tips made of exotic toolstones do not, ipso facto, indicate that entire residential groups traveled to quarries and then out to hunting grounds. As described above, analysis of large samples of debitage and tools rejected at the Benz KRF workshop indicates that Cody knappers made tool blanks for exchange (Root 1992, 1997). Therefore, reliable analysis of residential mobility and land use requires samples of all tool classes and debitage, not just surface-collected points.

#### *The Max Site*

The Max site is located in the Missouri Coteau in an area of closed drainages formed by dead-ice moraines (Figures 5.1, 5.2). The Coteau is characterized by thousands of closed depressions, now filled with small sloughs and kettle lakes. Some stagnant glacial ice persisted in this region until 9000 $^{14}$C yrs BP (10,203 cal BP) (Bluemle 1991:30; Clayton 1967), or throughout most of Cody times. The Max site is about 20 km north of the Missouri River, on the divide between the Missouri and Souris Rivers.

The site is on private land, and we analyzed a collection made by the landowner from a low rise above a small pothole slough. The collection, from an eroding, sandy slope at the slough margin, consists of 47 projectile points and one flake tool. Flakes were apparently not collected. Forty-five of the points are Cody complex types, one is Plainview, and one is a base fragment of a lanceolate point of undetermined type. Many of the points are broken, and the counts (below) tally refit specimens as one point (Table 5.5).

Of the Cody specimens, 30 are Eden points (Figure 5.7), 12 are Scottsbluff (Figure 5.8c, d), and 3 are Alberta/Cody I (Figure 5.8a, b; using the types of Bradley and Frison [1987]). Twenty-five points are Knife River flint, 14 are porcellanite, and 3 are silicified wood; there are single spec-

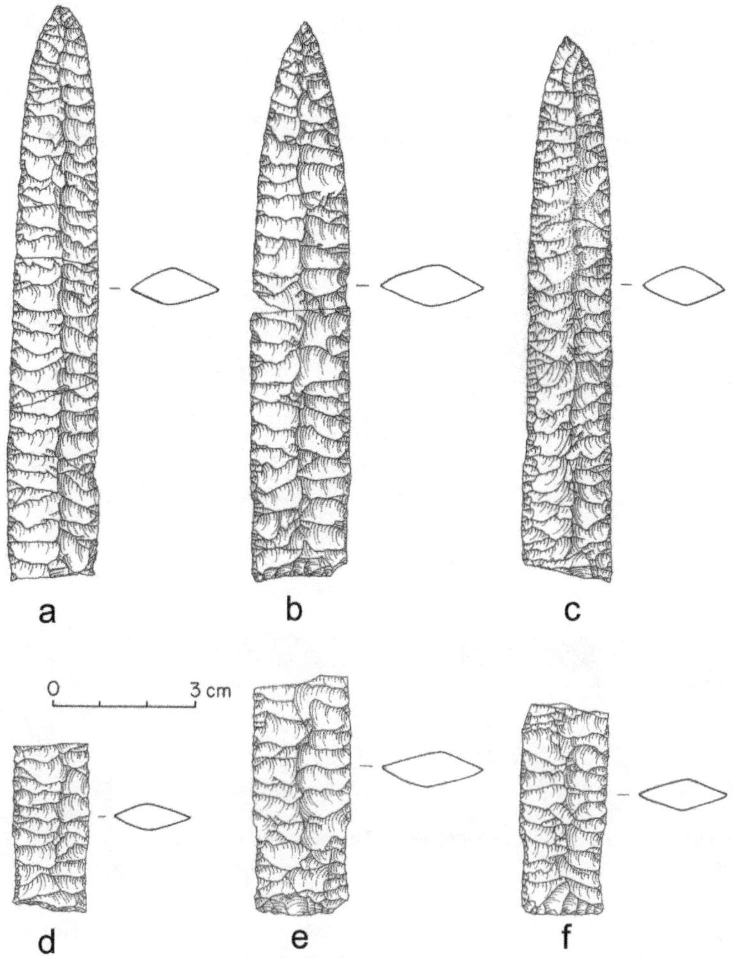


**FIGURE 5.7.** Eden points from the Max site.

imens of Rainy Buttes silicified wood, Tongue River silcrete, and a brown translucent chert (which resembles Knife River flint but is not) (Table 5.5). The translucent brown chert may be derived from the local till, and the remainder are definitely nonlocal. Though Knife River flint occurs in the Missouri River valley, tabular cobbles large enough and of sufficient quality to make the large Eden points at the Max site do not occur in the Missouri valley (at least in our experience). The other raw materials occur well south of the Missouri River, with Rainy Buttes silicified wood occurring 200 km to the southwest and Tongue River silcrete occurring 120 km to the south. At least half of the Eden, Scottsbluff, and Alberta/Cody points are made of Knife River flint, and one-third of the Eden and Scottsbluff points are made of porcellanite (Table 5.5).

Twenty of the points have definite impact fractures, and most others have bend fractures that likely resulted from impact. The large flake tool is KRF and was made on a thin flake (Figure 5.8e) struck from a prepared core. The retouched edge displays flaking and polish under low magnification, with wear types that are consistent with use as a butchering implement.

The presence of point tips, midsections, and four cross-mended specimens (with tips or midsections fitted to bases) indicates that this is a kill and perhaps butchery location. The largest of the refit Eden points are well over 100 mm long and were finished by comedial, serial pressure flaking.

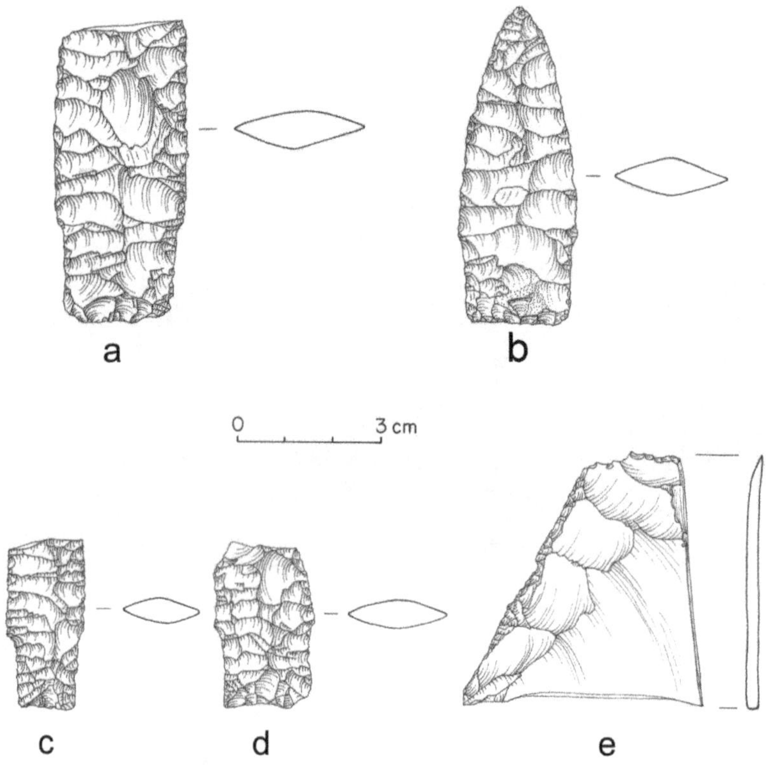


**FIGURE 5.8.** Tools from the Max site: (a, b) Alberta Cody I points; (c, d) Scottsbluff points; (e) flake tool.

Most have no signs of reworking or resharpening. Thus, hunters came well equipped to the Coteau for hunts. They apparently stopped in the Knife River flint source area to gear up, but they came with many weapons made of porcellanite as well. Porcellanite occurs in widely scattered sources across western North Dakota and eastern Montana. The closest sources to Max are in the Little Missouri Badlands, situated between the Knife River flint quarries and the Max site.

The presence of one Plainview point and the three Alberta/Cody I points indicates that multiple occupations took place here. Though we do not know how many kill events are represented by the collection, several large kills are possible.

### *The McLeod Site*

The McLeod site is in the Glaciated Plains of southern Saskatchewan about 300 km north-northwest of the KRF quarries (Joyes 1997, 2000) (Figure 5.1). The site consists entirely of surface specimens. There are 76 Cody complex points, including 28 Scottsbluff, 10 Eden, 2 Scottsbluff II, and 36 untyped fragments. Sixty of the Cody complex points (79 percent) are KRF, with seven porcellanite (9.2 percent), eight chert or chalcedony (10.5 percent), and one metamorphic slate (1.3 percent). There are also five Cody knives, 18 end scrapers (four are spurred), and symmetrical knives that Joyes tentatively associated with the Cody component (though Agate Basin and Hell Gap points are also present). All of these tools are KRF.

Joyes (1997) inferred that the McLeod site was a kill and processing location. As with the Max site, KRF is the dominant toolstone with smaller numbers of porcellanite points. The chert and chalcedony could be locally derived, though their sources are not specified. Twenty-two points are resharpened, and some heavily reworked blades are about as long as the stems. Toolstones from far to the south dominate the collection, indicating south-to-north movements through western North Dakota and surrounding regions before the kills.

*The Dunn Site (DjNf-1) and Site DjNf-8*

The Dunn site and DjNf-8 are located 6 km from each other on the Canadian Glaciated Plains; both are above small sloughs and kettle lakes (Ebell 1975, 1988). They are about 50 km southeast of the McLeod site (Figure 5.1). The Dunn site contains 77 projectile points and 155 flakes. The points were divided into reduction stages, but they all appear to be Scottsbluff and Eden points. The stems of even the earliest stage 1 points are ground, and all appear to be finished projectile points. The later-stage points are reworked, with several points exhibiting impact fractures. Ebell (1975, 1988) inferred that four of the artifacts were knives, one of which was made on a cortical flake.

Seventy-five of the points are classified as KRF. All are brown microcrystalline stone, but some have white inclusions described as "fern-like." These points may be made of a KRF look-alike. Brown translucent cherts are common in eastern Montana, and we have collected materials that superficially resemble KRF from glacial gravels in the Canadian Plains, though those materials were not large enough for Scottsbluff or Eden point manufacture. Regardless, the majority of points are apparently KRF.

There are 107 flakes from the surface and 48 flakes from limited excavations. None are unambiguously associated with the Cody occupations. Thirty-five flakes were classified as petaloid flakes, which are pressure flakes that could be from the final stage of point manufacture or from maintenance. Twenty-one of the 35 petaloid flakes are KRF, seven are red jasper, three are porcellanite, and four are obsidian, suggesting that some final pressure flaking or maintenance took place. The raw materials of the other flakes are not reported. There is no evidence that percussion-flaked blanks were worked into projectile points or other finished tool forms. Ebell inferred that the site was a kill and processing location.

Eleven Eden and Scottsbluff points were surface collected from site DjNf-8. Only three of the 11 are KRF, with the other eight made from various types of chert. The sources of the chert points are unknown, and they are probably nonlocal. Regardless, the presence of the three KRF points is similar to other Cody complex occupations in the region. Ebell (1975) suggested that this hilltop occupation may have been a lookout, related to kill and processing sites such as Dunn.

*The Niska Site*

The Niska site, located almost 500 km northwest of the KRF quarry area, is above a glacial meltwater channel in the Old Wives Lake Plain, east of the Cypress Hills (Figure 5.1). Unlike the other sites in the Glaciated Plains of southern Saskatchewan, Niska is inferred to be a base or residential camp, not a kill-processing area (Meyer 1985). Excavation of two small blocks revealed a Cody complex component in a well-developed paleosol but recovered few artifacts. The blocks were located only 10 m apart and probably exposed the same occupation horizon (Meyer 1985).

The western block contained only 176 flakes, 70 percent of which ($n$ = 124) are probably KRF. (Artifacts are labeled "brown chalcedony" but are described as being "almost certainly Knife River flint" [Meyer 1985:32]). One stem from a Cody knife or point, one end scraper, and one core, all KRF, were recovered. The eastern block contained 349 flakes, 234 of which (67 percent) are KRF. This block also contained 76 porcellanite flakes (21.8 percent). Most of the flakes are small biface thinning flakes and edge retouch flakes (biface pressure flakes?). There are a few core reduction flakes. Tools from the eastern block include two perforators, two point stem fragments, and four end scrapers; all are KRF.

Surface-collected tools include five projectile points: three are porcellanite, one is KRF, and one is red-brown chert. There are also five Cody knives, all of which are KRF. Thus, nine of the ten Cody complex points and knives from the surface are porcellanite or KRF. There are 12 surface-collected end scrapers, and though all may not be associated with the Cody complex occupation, nine are KRF.

Niska is similar in toolstone proportions to other southern Saskatchewan sites and the Max site. Unlike those kill-processing sites, however, Niska shows evidence of some core reduction and tool manufacture, suggesting that bifacial implements and projectile points may have been finished from imported preforms. People made flake

TABLE 5.6. Summary of Land-Use Strategies by Site.

| | Expectation 1 | Expectation 2 | Expectation 3 | Expectation 4 | Expectation 5 |
|---|---|---|---|---|---|
| Benz | R | R | NR | R | NR |
| Bobtail Wolf | R | R | NR | R | NR |
| Max | NR | — | — | NR | R |
| McLeod | NR | — | — | NR | NR |
| Dunn | NR | NR | — | NR | |
| Dj-NF-8 | NR | — | — | NR | R |
| Niska | NR | NR | — | NR | NR |

*Note:* R = regional; NR = nonregional.

tools from transported cores. It is at such residential sites that we expect to find the final stages of tool manufacture using imported stone in preparation for hunts.

### *Summary: Cody Land Use in the Coteau and Glaciated Plains*

Testing Knell's (2007; Knell and Hill 2012) land-use model with data from sites on the open plains north of the Missouri River suggests that Cody hunter-gatherers employed a nonregional land-use strategy. Though only Niska has an excavated sample of Cody artifacts, most of the recovered debitage is KRF and porcellanite, indicating final manufacture or maintenance of imported tools. Most of the long use-life tools (projectile points, Cody knives, and end scrapers) are KRF. These were initially flaked far to the south, probably at sites like Benz and Bobtail Wolf. The small amount of debris that is possibly from local materials indicates only occasional on-site manufacture of tools for immediate use. There is a lack of toolstone diversity at McLeod, Dunn, and Niska, where most stone consists of nonlocal KRF and porcellanite. The Max site exhibits large raw material diversity: just over half of the points are of KRF, about one-third are of porcellanite, and the remainder are of chert, Rainy Buttes silicified wood, Tongue River silcrete, and silicified wood. The small collection from Dj-NF-8 is relatively diverse with KRF and points described as various types of chert.

## Conclusions

We propose that Cody groups used the open plains north of the Missouri River in western North Dakota and southern Saskatchewan during the late summer and fall in a nonregional land-use pattern. A summary of test expectations is in Table 5.6. People occupied areas for short periods to hunt bison, moving to other areas following kills. There are many timbered upland "islands"—such as the Turtle Mountains in North Dakota and the Cypress Hills in Saskatchewan—that are potential overwintering areas. The major river valleys, such as the Missouri and Souris, also provide adequate timber and shelter for overwintering.

The dominance of KRF at the Benz and Bobtail Wolf sites fits the pattern expected for regionally focused land use (Table 5.6). Benz and Bobtail Wolf are principally lithic workshops, however, and the by-products of tool production from KRF overwhelm the few by-products of nonlocal toolstone use. By comparison, we note that the Folsom occupations at Bobtail Wolf—a flint-procurement, workshop, and camp site—contain a substantial proportion of nonlocal toolstones (Root et al. 2000), suggesting a nonregional land-use strategy during Folsom times.

The dominance of KRF in the Cody debitage samples at Benz and Bobtail Wolf conforms to the pattern expected for regionally focused land use. There are few exhausted tools of nonlocal stone; instead, most technologically finished tools are KRF, as expected in a regional strategy. The pattern of Cody knappers making bifacial blanks (in excess of household needs at Benz) for transport from the workshops for subsequent manufacture into finished tools, like the many Eden and Scottsbluff points at the Max site some 100 km northward, fit the nonregional pattern, however. There is a low diversity of toolstone types, which also corresponds to the expectations for nonregional land use.

Thus, Benz and Bobtail Wolf most likely represent a pattern of occupations somewhat tethered to the KRF source area, followed by movement out of the quarry area after groups geared up with new tools. While the groups were in the quarry area, however, data indicate a mix of the patterns expected for both regional and nonregional strategies. Land-use strategies are not dichotomous classes but vary continuously (e.g., with occupation span). Therefore, we should not expect all sites, especially those with multiple occupations like Benz, to exhibit clear-cut patterns.

The dominance of nonlocal toolstones in southern Saskatchewan and the Missouri Coteau indicates a nonregional land-use pattern. That is, Cody groups moved northward to the Missouri Coteau and Glaciated Plains, most likely for bison hunts. They did not stay in these locations for long periods but moved through relatively quickly. The small proportions of even potentially local toolstones indicate that Cody groups carried stocks of transported, high-quality toolstones, especially KRF, with smaller numbers of porcellanite weapons.

The dominance of KRF and the large amounts of porcellanite at all sites but DjNf-8 (with a collection of only 11 points) suggest that people geared up in the KRF quarry area and at other toolstone sources south of the Missouri River during the warm seasons, probably late summer to early fall. The presence of KRF debitage and tools at Niska, in addition to projectile points, suggests that residential groups moved northward from the KRF source area to hunt with replenished supplies of stone and newly refurbished toolkits. Though long-distance residential mobility is suggested, some exotic stone likely reached the Canadian Plains through movements of small task groups or exchange. Patterns of group movements and exchange are likely complex, and a single strategy probably did not exist through the entirety of Cody times.

Most sites north of the Missouri River are kill sites that contain finished but impact-fractured and destroyed projectile points. All artifacts are from the surface or shallow excavations and are poorly dated. There is little evidence for tool manufacture at the kill and processing locations. Niska, the lone base or residential camp, contains KRF and porcellanite debris from maintenance or final-stage manufacture.

Though this test of the land-use model for western North Dakota and southern Saskatchewan suggests nonregional strategies, results for the KRF quarry area are ambiguous. Hunters apparently carried unfinished bifacial blanks from the Benz site, not finished points or tools. Cody hunters possessed many large, finished Eden and Scottsbluff points when they reached the Max site, 100 km from the quarries. If this pattern was the predominant mode of working in the KRF quarries, then there must be knapping areas at camps where people finished weapons and other tools either in the quarry area or just beyond. We need to find more camps associated with quarries, field camps related to kills and procurement of other resources, and winter residential camps to fully evaluate Cody land use in the open plains of western North Dakota and southern Saskatchewan.


## Acknowledgments

Excavations at the Benz site were funded through a federal matching grant administered by the State Historical Society of North Dakota, with matching funds provided by the University of North Dakota (UND). Marvin Kay was the first to conduct test excavations at the site with a UND field school. A subsequent UND field school under the direction of M. Root carried out additional excavations. Stan Ahler was the principal investigator, and M. Root was the co-principal investigator and project director. Julieann VanNest drew the stratigraphic profiles, and Carl Falk identified the bone from the Benz site. We wish to dedicate this chapter to the memory of Sarah Moore, who illustrated all of the artifacts and drew the maps. These are among her last illustrations.


## References


Agenbroad, Larry D.

1978 *The Hudson-Meng Site: An Alberta Bison Kill in the Nebraska High Plains.* University Press of America, Washington, D.C.

Bailey, V.

1926 *A Biological Survey of North Dakota.* Bureau of Biological Survey, North American Fauna No. 49. Government Printing Office, Washington, D.C.

Bamforth, D. B.
2002a High-Tech Foragers? Folsom and Later Paleoindian Technology on the Great Plains. *Journal of World Prehistory* 16:55–98.
2002b The Paleoindian Occupation of the Medicine Creek Drainage, Southwestern Nebraska. In *Medicine Creek: Seventy Years of Archaeological Investigations*, edited by Donna C. Roper, pp. 54–83. University of Alabama Press, Tuscaloosa.
2009 Projectile Points, People, and Plains Paleoindian Perambulations. *Journal of Anthropological Archaeology* 28:142–157.

Barnosky, C. W.
1989 Postglacial Vegetation and Climate in the Northwestern Great Plains of Montana. *Quaternary Research* 31:57–73.

Barnosky, C. W., P. M. Anderson, and P. J. Bartlein
1987 The Northwestern U.S. during Deglaciation: Vegetational History and Paleoclimatic Implications. In *North America and Adjacent Oceans during the Last Deglaciation*, edited by W. F. Ruddiman and H. E. Wright, pp. 289–321. Geology of North America, Vol. K-3. Geological Society of North America, Boulder, Colorado.

Barnosky, C. W., E. C. Grimm, and H. E. Wright Jr.
1987 Towards a Postglacial History of the Northern Great Plains: A Review of the Paleoecologic Problems. *Annals of Carnegie Museum* 56:259–273.

Bluemle, J. P.
1991 *The Face of North Dakota*. Rev. ed. Educational Series No. 21. North Dakota Geological Survey, Bismarck.

Bradley, B. A., and G. C. Frison
1987 Projectile Points and Specialized Bifaces from the Horner Site. In *The Horner Site: The Type Site of the Cody Cultural Complex*, edited by G. C. Frison and L. C. Todd, pp. 199–231. Academic Press, Orlando, Florida.

Brantingham, J.
2003 A Neutral Model of Stone Raw Material Procurement. *American Antiquity* 68:487–509.
2006 Measuring Forager Mobility. *Current Anthropology* 47:435–459.

Bryson, R. U., and R. A. Bryson
1996 An Archaeoclimatic Reconstruction of the Holocene Climate of Lake Ilo, North Dakota. Ms. on file, Department of Anthropology, Washington State University, Pullman.

Carr, D. H.
2005 The Organization of Late Paleoindian Lithic Procurement Strategies in Western Wisconsin. *Midcontinental Journal of Archaeology* 30:3–36.

Carr, D. H., and R. Boszhardt
2010 The Organisation of Lithic Procurement at Silver Mound, Wisconsin: Source of Hixton Silicified Sandstone. In *Ancient Mines and Quarries: A Trans-Atlantic Perspective*, edited by Margaret Brewer-LaPorta, Adrian Burke, and David Field, pp. 132–141. Oxbow Books, Oxford.

Clark, J. S., E. C. Grimm, J. Lynch, and P. G. Mueller
2001 Effects of Holocene Climate Change on the $C_4$ Grassland/Woodland Boundary in the Northern Plains. *Ecology* 82:620–636.

Clayton, L.
1967 Stagnant-Glacier Features on the Missouri Coteau in North Dakota. In *Glacial Geology of the Missouri Coteau and Adjacent Areas*, edited by L. Clayton and T. R. Freers, pp. 25–46. North Dakota Geological Survey, Miscellaneous Series No. 30. Grand Forks.

Clayton, L., S. R. Moran, and W. B. Bickley Jr.
1976 *Stratigraphy, Origin, and Climatic Implications of Late Quaternary Upland Silt in North Dakota*. North Dakota Geological Survey, Miscellaneous Series No. 54. Bismarck.

Crabtree, D. E., and E. L. Davis
1968 Experimental Manufacture of Wooden Implements with Tools of Stone. *Science* 159: 426–428.

Cummings, L. S.
1995 Stratigraphic Pollen and Phytolith Analysis at the Alkali Creek Site. In *Alkali Creek: A Stratified Record of Prehistoric Flint Mining in North Dakota*, edited by M. D. Metcalf and S. A. Ahler, pp. 111–131. Submitted to USDA Soil Conservation Service, Contract No. 53-6633-0-7, Bismarck, North Dakota. Metcalf Archaeological Consultants, Eagle, Colorado.
1996 Paleoenvironmental Interpretation for the Mill Iron Site: Stratigraphic Pollen and Phytolith Analysis. In *The Mill Iron Site*, edited by G. C. Frison, pp. 177–193. University of New Mexico Press, Albuquerque.

Dean, W. E., and A. Schwalb
2000 Holocene Environmental and Climatic Change in the Northern Great Plains as Recorded in the Geochemistry of Sediments in Pickerel Lake, South Dakota. *Quaternary International* 67:5–20.

Dodds, D. L.
1979 *Common Grasses and Sedges in North Dakota*. USDA Cooperative Extension Service, North Dakota State University, Fargo.

Ebell, S. B.

1975 A Cody Complex Site in South-Central Saskatchewan (DjNf-8). *Saskatchewan Archaeological Society Newsletter* 49:1–6.

1988 The Dunn Site. *Plains Anthropologist* 33:505–530.

Frison, G. C.

1987 The Tool Assemblage, Unfinished Bifaces, and Stone Flaking Material Sources for the Horner Site. In *The Horner Site: The Type Site of the Cody Cultural Complex*, edited by G. C. Frison and L. C. Todd, pp. 233–278. Academic Press, Orlando, Florida.

Gardner, W. M.

1983 Stop Me if You've Heard This One Before: The Flint Run Paleoindian Complex Revisited. *Archaeology of Eastern North America* 11:49–64.

Gould, R. A., and S. Saggers

1985 Lithic Procurement in Central Australia: A Closer Look at Binford's Idea of Embeddedness in Archaeology. *American Antiquity* 50: 117–136.

Haynes, C. V., Jr.

2008 Younger Dryas "Black Mats" and the Rancholabrean Termination in North America. *Proceedings of the National Academy of Sciences* 105(18):6520–6525.

Huckell, B. B., and J. D. Kilby

2009 Beach: A Clovis Cache in Southwestern North Dakota. *Current Research in the Pleistocene* 26:68–70.

Ingbar, E. E.

1994 Lithic Raw Material Selection and Technological Organization. In *The Organization of North American Prehistoric Chipped Stone Tool Technologies*, edited by Philip J. Carr, pp. 45–56. International Monographs in Prehistory Archaeological Series No. 7. Ann Arbor, Michigan.

Joyes, D. C.

1997 New Paleoindian Finds from Southern Saskatchewan. *Saskatchewan Archaeological Society Newsletter* 18(6):107–112.

2000 Cody Technology at the McLeod Site, Saskatchewan, Canada. *Current Research in the Pleistocene* 17:47–49.

Knell, E. J.

2007 The Organization of Late Paleoindian Cody Complex Land-Use on the North American Plains. Unpublished Ph.D. dissertation, Department of Anthropology, Washington State University, Pullman.

Knell, Edward J., and Matthew E. Hill Jr.

2012 Linking Bones and Stones: Regional Variation in Late Paleoindian Cody Complex Land Use and Foraging Strategies. *American Antiquity* 77:40–70.

Knudson, R.

1983 *Organizational Variability in Late Paleo-Indian Assemblages*. Washington State University Laboratory of Anthropology Reports of Investigations No. 60. Pullman.

2002 Medicine Creek Is a Paleoindian Cultural Ecotone: The Red Smoke Assemblage. In *Medicine Creek: Seventy Years of Archaeological Investigations*, edited by Donna C. Roper, pp. 84–141. University of Alabama Press, Tuscaloosa.

Kuehn, D. D.

1997 A Geoarchaeological Assessment of Bison Kill Site Preservation in the Little Missouri Badlands. *Plains Anthropologist* 42:319–328.

Laird, K. R., S. C. Fritz, E. C. Grimm, and P. G. Mueller

1996 Century-Scale Paleoclimatic Reconstruction from Moon Lake, a Closed-Basin Lake in the North Great Plains. *Limnology and Oceanography* 41:890–902.

Last, W. M., R. E. Vance, S. Wilson, and J. P. Smol

1998 A Multi-proxy Limnologic Record of Rapid Early-Holocene Hydrologic Change on the Northern Great Plains, Southwestern Saskatchewan, Canada. *Holocene* 8:503–520.

Loendorf, L. L., D. D. Kuehn, and N. F. Forsman

1984 Rainy Buttes Silicified Wood: A Source of Lithic Raw Material in Western North Dakota. *Plains Anthropologist* 29:335–338.

Low, B. D.

1996 Swan River Chert. *Plains Anthropologist* 41:165–174.

MacDonald, D.

1999 Modeling Folsom Mobility, Mating Strategies, and Technological Organization in the Northern Plains. *Plains Anthropologist* 44:141–161.

Meltzer, D. J.

1989 Was Stone Exchanged among Eastern North American Paleoindians? In *Eastern Paleoindian Lithic Resource Use*, edited by C. J. Ellis and J. C. Lothrop, pp. 10–39. Westview Press, Boulder, Colorado.

Meyer, D.

1985 A Component in the Scottsbluff Tradition: Excavations at the Niska Site. *Canadian Journal of Archaeology* 9:1–37.

Muñiz, M. P.

2005 The Cody Complex Revisited: Landscape Use and Technological Organization on the Northwestern Plains. Unpublished Ph.D. dissertation, Department of Anthropology, University of Colorado, Boulder.

Osborn, A. J.
2003 "Places Where They Kill Deer": Moisture Islands, Winter Climate, and Ungulate Ecology in the Northwestern Great Plains. In *Islands on the Plains: Ecological, Social, and Ritual Use of Landscapes*, edited by M. Kornfeld and A. J. Osborn, pp. 193–219. University of Utah Press, Salt Lake City.

Osborn, A. J., and M. Kornfeld
2003 Biogeographical Islands and Ecological Patches: Seeing the Great Plains from the Inside Out. In *Islands on the Plains: Ecological, Social, and Ritual Use of Landscapes*, edited by M. Kornfeld and A. J. Osborn, pp. 1–18. University of Utah Press, Salt Lake City.

Root, M. J.
1992 *The Knife River Flint Quarries: The Organization of Stone Tool Production*. Ph.D. dissertation, Washington State University, Pullman. University Microfilms, Ann Arbor, Michigan.
1997 Production for Exchange at the Knife River Flint Quarries, North Dakota. *Lithic Technology* 21:33–50.
1998 Dating a Cody-Complex Occupation in the Knife River Flint Quarries. *Current Research in the Pleistocene* 15:32–64.
2000 Excavations on the Central Rise: Blocks 1, 3, and 5. In *The Archaeology of the Bobtail Wolf Site: Folsom Occupation of the Knife River Flint Quarry Area*, edited by M. J. Root, pp. 51–84. Washington State University Press, Pullman.

Root, M. J. (editor)
2000 *The Archaeology of the Bobtail Wolf Site: Folsom Occupation of the Knife River Flint Quarry Area*. Washington State University Press, Pullman.

Root, M. J., S. A. Ahler, C. R. Falk, J. E. Foss, H. Haas, and J. A. Artz
1986 *Archeological Investigations in the Knife River Flint Primary Source Area, Dunn County, North Dakota: 1982–1986 Program*. Submitted to the State Historical Society of North Dakota, Bismarck. Department of Anthropology, University of North Dakota, Grand Forks.

Root, M. J., S. A. Ahler, J. Van Nest, C. R. Falk, and J. E. Foss
1985 *Archeological Investigations in the Knife River Flint Primary Source Area, Dunn County, North Dakota: The Benz Site, 32DU452*. Submitted to the State Historical Society of North Dakota, Bismarck. Department of Anthropology, University of North Dakota, Grand Forks.

Root, M. J., S. A. Ahler, J. D. William, and A. J. Osborn
1999 Methods and Techniques of Stone Tool and Core Analysis. In *Field and Laboratory Methods and Techniques for the Lake Ilo Archaeological Project*, edited by M. J. Root, pp. 17–68. Submitted to U.S. Fish and Wildlife Service, Denver, Cooperative Agreement No. 14-48-0010-93-901. Contributions in Cultural Resource Management No. 60. Center for Northwest Anthropology, Washington State University, Pullman.

Root, M. J., J. D. William, and A. M. Emerson
2000 Stone Tools and Flake Debris. In *The Archaeology of the Bobtail Wolf Site: Folsom Occupation of the Knife River Flint Quarry Area*, edited by M. J. Root, pp. 223–308. Washington State University Press, Pullman.

Smith, E. E., Jr.
1990 Paleoindian Economy and Settlement Patterns in the Wyandotte Chert Source Area, Unglaciated South-Central Indiana. In *Early Paleoindian Economies of Eastern North America*, edited by Kenneth B. Tankersley and Barry L. Isaac, pp. 217–258. Research in Economic Anthropology, Supplement No. 5. JAI Press, Greenwich, Connecticut.
1991 *Paleo-Indian Settlement and Lithic Procurement Patterns in the Karstic Region of South-central Indiana*. Ph.D. dissertation, Indiana University, Bloomington. University Microfilms, Ann Arbor, Michigan.

Stanford, Dennis
1999 Paleoindian Archaeology and Late Pleistocene Environments in the Plains and Southwestern United States. In *Ice Age Peoples of North America: Environments, Origins, and Adaptations*, edited by Robson Bonnichsen and Karen L. Turnmire, pp. 281–339. Center for the Study of the First Americans. Oregon State University Press, Corvallis.

Stevens, O. A.
1963 *Handbook of North Dakota Plants*. North Dakota Institute for Regional Studies, Fargo.

Surovell, T. A.
2009 *Toward a Behavioral Ecology or Lithic Technology: Cases from Paleoindian Archaeology*. University of Arizona Press, Tucson.

Van Nest, J.
1995 Geology of the Alkali Creek Site. In *Alkali Creek: A Stratified Record of Prehistoric Flint Mining in North Dakota*, edited by M. D. Metcalf and S. A. Ahler, pp. 51–109. Sub-

mitted to USDA Soil Conservation Service, Contract No. 53-6633-0-7, Bismarck. Metcalf Archaeological Consultants, Eagle, Colorado.

Wendland, W.
1978 Holocene Man in North America: The Ecological Setting and Climatic Background. *Plains Anthropologist* 23:273–287.

Wheat, J. B.
1972 *The Olsen-Chubbuck Site: A Paleo-Indian Bison Kill.* Society for American Archaeology, Memoir No. 26. Washington, D.C.

Whitman, W. C., and M. K. Wali
1975 Grasslands of North Dakota. In *Prairie: A Multiple View*, edited by M. K. Wali, pp. 53–73. University of North Dakota Press, Grand Forks.

Yansa, C. H., W. E. Dean, and E. C. Murphy
2007 Late Quaternary Paleoenvironments of an Ephemeral Wetland in North Dakota, USA: Relative Interactions of Ground-Water Hydrology and Climate Change. *Journal of Paleolimnology* 38:441–457.

# 6

# A Review of the Cody Complex in Alberta

Robert J. Dawe

This chapter provides an overview of the Cody complex in Alberta, the data for which are summarized in Appendix 6.1. Such an overview is necessary because discussions of the Cody complex in Plains literature usually focus on site distributions from the Plains of the American Midwest, often showing the Fletcher site (DjOw-1) at the northwest end of the area under discussion. The physiographic region of the Great Plains extends in a broad swath across the province of Alberta, and based on this review it is apparent that Cody peoples initially exploited most of this area, ultimately forming an entrenched population of considerable duration. Any comprehensive understanding of the Cody complex in the Great Plains is incomplete without a consideration of this northern distribution.

The Alberta/Cody complex has been described as the first intensive human occupation of the province of Alberta (Adams 1976:105; Vickers 1986:39; Wormington and Forbis 1965:185). For this reason, it seems appropriate that this province lent its name to the projectile point type that is now recognized as the harbinger of the Cody complex—the first of a series of projectile points persisting for over a thousand years in Alberta. "Cody complex" hereafter refers to assemblages that include any of the Alberta, Scottsbluff, Eden, or Cody knife artifact types.

The Archaeological Survey of Alberta (2011) has amassed a database of more than 37,000 sites. These data are largely the product of 40 years of legislated cultural resource management (CRM) activity. Other contributions to this database were culled from surveys by the Glenbow Museum starting in the 1950s, and in the following decade by the University of Calgary, the University of Alberta, and the Provincial Museum of Alberta (now the Royal Alberta Museum). More recently, and critical to this compilation, were some excellent systematic regional surveys of private collections (Boag 1989; Hjermstad 1991; Peace River Archaeology Society 1996; Red Deer and District Museum 1983; Wood 1991; Wood et al. 1993; Wormington and Forbis 1965). Collectors have aided our understanding of the distribution of Cody material in Alberta, but this resource is diminishing because the demographic of the typical collector in these studies is an aging farmer who enjoyed the collecting heyday of yesteryear.

Collectively from these various sources, Cody material has been reported from 331 discrete sites (Figure 6.1, Appendix 6.1), and more than 1000 Cody complex projectile points have been documented. Of this total, Cody artifacts are reported in situ in a subsurface context in only 22 sites. The lack of stratigraphy has clearly hampered both our ability to date this occupation and our understanding of what constitutes a Cody assemblage.

## Setting the Stage

The province of Alberta is located between 49 and 60 degrees north latitude and 110 and 120 degrees west longitude, bordering the east flank of the

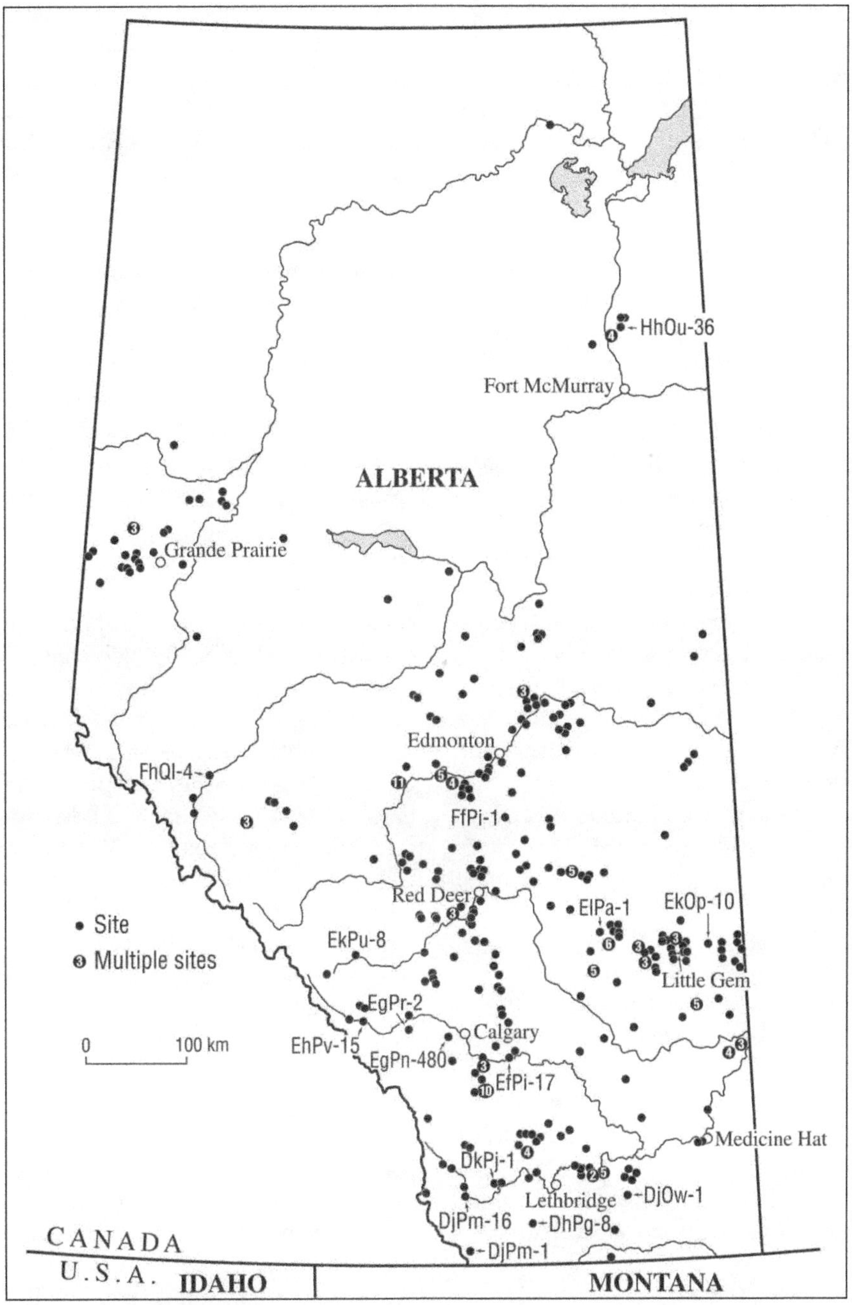


FIGURE 6.1. Distribution of Cody sites in Alberta.

Rocky Mountains. At the end of the Pleistocene, Alberta figured prominently as a north-south conduit, the "ice-free corridor," for the movement of people and animals as soon as Cordilleran and Laurentide ice receded sufficiently. The immediate postglacial landscape of Alberta consisted of vast treeless tracts of well-watered glacial disintegration terrain blanketed by nutrient-rich loess and interspersed with flat, clay-lined, proglacial lake basins. The colonizing steppe tundra in the north and grasslands in the south (Beaudoin and Oetelaar 2003; Dyke 2005) would have been a highly desirable habitat for herd animals, and consequently attracted humans who preyed on them.

Current evidence suggests that Alberta was first occupied by people who used fluted points. Eugene Gryba (1988) and John W. Ives (2006; personal communication 2012) have documented approximately 250 fluted projectile points from Alberta. These earliest sites are typically located on elevated landforms associated with a body of water, whether along lake or river margins or in knob-and-kettle topography. The postglacial landscape not only provided ample pasture for ungulates but was well suited for spotting and ambushing prey.

The interval between the fluted point users and later Cody complex peoples is comparably poorly represented in the archaeological record of Alberta. The impression is that at the onset of the Holocene the population in Alberta was small. The numbers of sites and artifacts attributed to Agate Basin and Hell Gap groups, for example, collectively pale in comparison to the succeeding Cody complex. The temporal gap between the time period that should represent the fluted point occupation in Alberta and that of the later Cody complex coincides partly with the Younger Dryas climatic event (Rutter et al. 2000). At this time there are not enough data to evaluate whether a cooling trend during the Younger Dryas contributed to an apparent low population at the end of the Pleistocene.

By approximately 10,000 $^{14}$C years ago (11,470 cal BP), the landscape had stabilized. Forests were established in the north and occupied much of the current distribution of what is now boreal forest, and extensive open areas of graminoid vegetation covered much of the south half of the province (Beaudoin and Oetelaar 2003). This was the landscape that the first people using Cody technology wandered into, leaving behind the traces of more than a thousand years of occupation.

### Typology

Our understanding of the Cody complex in Alberta began as a consequence of erosion during the "dirty Thirties." Vast expanses of land, particularly in southeastern Alberta, were pockmarked with blowouts that stripped as much as several meters of topsoil from cultivated fields and sandy dune areas. Under these conditions the first large assemblage of Cody material was collected by a farmer, Russell A. Johnston, in the Little Gem area of southeastern Alberta (Johnston 1975; Pettipas 1980; Wormington and Forbis 1965). Careful collection of surface material from blowouts at 22 sites led Johnston to be the first person to postulate an association of Eden, Scottsbluff, and Cody knives (Wormington and Forbis 1965:56). Had he published his copious and extremely detailed observations in 1939, the Little Gem complex might have been the name for what we now call the Cody complex.[1]

The next major development in our understanding of the Cody complex in Alberta was the chance discovery of the Fletcher site (DjOw-1) in 1963 (Wormington and Forbis 1965; also see Forbis 1968). This (apparent) single-component site sparked considerable interest because of the association of *Bison antiquus* with both Scottsbluff and Alberta projectile points.

From these first observations of the Cody complex it was clear that considerable typological diversity existed, even in single-component sites. Discrepancies between the various Cody projectile point types have been refined, but some gray area remains in terms of what constitutes an Alberta point and a Scottsbluff point, and distinctions between Scottsbluff and Eden points (also see Knudson, this volume). Wormington (1957:134) proposed the Alberta type name to account for points similar to Scottsbluff but larger and with longer stems, and further discriminated two styles each of Scottsbluff points and Eden points (Wormington 1957:137, 267). As the sample of Cody materials increased, the Alberta point type was inferred to predate later Scottsbluff and Eden types. Frison (1991) presented a succession of cultural complexes in the High Plains that began with an Alberta occupation approximately 9800 radiocarbon years ago (11,220 cal BP), followed by a hybrid point form called Alberta/Cody, and then Cody, which subsumes both Scottsbluff and Eden types (see Frison 1991:62, 63). Bradley and Frison further subdivided Alberta/Cody types into Alberta/Cody I and Alberta/Cody II based on manufacturing differences (Bradley and Frison 1987:207, 219; Frison 1991:63).

Such typological distinctions are a luxury in Alberta, where only rarely can two Cody points be demonstrated to be associated or anything distal to the stem is present in an excavated context. Here archaeologists rely on the overall outline

**TABLE 6.1.** Radiocarbon Dates from Cody Sites in Alberta.

| Site | Site Type | Dated Material | Date ($^{14}$C Yr BP) | Calibrated Date (Cal BP) |
|---|---|---|---|---|
| Red Rock Canyon (DgPm-1) | Scottsbluff and Agate Basin point in buried concentration of artifacts | Date on charcoal from buried hearth associated with Scottsbluff point | 8220 ± 260 (GX1435) | 8447–9728 |
| Fletcher (DjOw-1) | Deeply buried Bison antiquus bonebed with associated Alberta and Scottsbluff points, other lithic tools | AMS dates on seeds from below (TO-1097) and in bonebed (CAMS-42980) | 9380 ± 110 (TO-1097) 9540 ± 110 (CAMS-42980) | 10,265–11,072 10,575–11,185 |
| DjPm-16 | Deeply buried campsite with Alberta point fragment and possible Scottsbluff base, lithic tools, debitage, and variety of fauna | Date on bone from paleosol | 9600 ± 210 (AECV-746C) 9450 ± 230 (BIS-17) | 10,272–11,601 11,171–11,336 |
| EgPn-480 | Probable Scottsbluff point fragment with other lithic material and unidentifiable bone in buried campsite | Date on bone from occupation level | 9540 ± 70 (Beta-127235) | 10,607–11,140 |
| EkPu-8 | Base of apparent Scottsbluff point, with other tools, cores, and debitage in stratified multicomponent campsite | Date on bone from base of occupation level | 9750 ± 80 (TO-2999) | 10,787–11,319 |
| Swan Landing (FhQl-4) | Alberta point and a few pieces of debitage from very deeply buried site | Date on charcoal at same depth as point | 8675 ± 270 (S-2178) | 9029–10,388 |

morphology and dimensions to discriminate between Alberta and Scottsbluff points. Only with Eden points is there some sort of a consensus, where often just a midblade will be confidently classified as an Eden point (see Ronaghan 1983). Clearly, before any harmony can be achieved in Cody typology, a bigger sample of discrete dated components containing large assemblages is required. This may not happen soon in Alberta. The Cody complex here is manifest as a widespread distribution of often fine specimens recovered on the surface, lacking both context and chronology. The six sites that provide us with dates each have only a single Cody component (Table 6.1).

An example of the frustration the archaeologist faces in trying to interpret this record is provided by a recent donation of two large, complete Cody points of Knife River flint (KRF) to the Royal Alberta Museum (Figure 6.2:n, o). The Small family recovered the two points in adjacent cultivated fields shortly after the land was broken more than 60 years ago on a farm northeast of Edmonton (see Appendix 6.1:GaPg-3 and 4). According to the two brothers who brought in the artifacts, no other cultural material has shown up in either field since the two points were first recovered.

One specimen could be considered a "classic" Alberta point except it has diminutive barbed shoulders that are both tight to the stem and narrower than the midblade. The second point is what Wormington (1957:267) refers to as a "Type 2" Scottsbluff point. It has a long triangular blade and a short, slightly expanding stem with well-developed angled shoulders.

Both points were complete when lost, extremely well made, symmetrical, and aesthetically appealing. Both are made of heat-treated KRF, have a greasy luster, and have a patina on one face. Many questions are posed by this find: for example, are the specimens contemporary and associated, and are they functional? It seems too coincidental that these two essentially perfect specimens, more than 1000 km from the KRF source area, could have been left in close proximity in the absence of any other cultural material without being associated. How they even ended up in the archaeological record is a mystery. Their function as grave goods cannot be ruled out. The pronounced grinding on the lateral stem edges suggests that at one time these were both at least hafted if not used. Despite the fact that they are stylistically quite different types and not found in context, it is hard to imagine how they can not be associated. Such a lack of context is the curse of Paleoindian research in Alberta.

A further problem is that our sample of Cody material is vastly biased by what is probably a very

FIGURE 6.2. Cody artifacts from Alberta. (a) GdOo-16; (b) GjQh; (c) DkPj-1 (Head-Smashed-In); (d) FhQl-4; (e, f) Bower Collection (FP); (g, h) FfPi-1 (Fullerton); (i) GfPt-13; (j, k) HhOu-36 (Nezu); (l, m) GlQl (Poohkay Collection); (n) GaPg-3 (Small Collection); (o) GaPg-4 (Small Collection).

small representation of the material culture left by Cody people: projectile points. In most cases this is the only artifact type in a disturbed context that can be confidently attributed to this complex. Were the archaeologists of the future to consider only the shotgun shell as the artifact diagnostic of our culture, one wonders what wonky interpretations regarding our distribution and diet this would render. In a few instances, discrete Cody assemblages have been observed in Alberta; these are summarized in the following section.

### Selected Site Descriptions

#### *Fletcher (DjOw-1)*

The Fletcher site was brought to the attention of Richard Forbis in 1963 by a collector, Armin Dyck, who observed bone and lithic artifacts exposed in a cattle dugout south of Taber in south-central Alberta (Forbis 1968; Wormington and Forbis 1965: 120, 121). Subsequent excavations by Forbis and Reeves in 1963 and 1964 yielded *Bison antiquus* remains and associated lithic materials in buried clay (Vickers 1986:41). Paleoenvironmental studies indicate that the site was on the margin of a freshwater marsh and may have been a bison trap. The site is located south of a low ridge in an otherwise featureless prairie setting, and were it not for the fortuitous exposure provided by the dugout, it is unlikely that this deeply buried site would have been found by conventional archaeological survey methods.

The site has yielded a considerable diversity of projectile points in terms of morphology, scale, and lithology (Figure 6.3). Of the projectile points reported by Forbis (1968), the four he described as Alberta were all found in the bonebed, whereas the four identified as Scottsbluff were found in the dugout spoil pile. Despite further excavations by Quigg in 1975 (1976a) and Vickers in 1987 and 1988 (Vickers and Beaudoin 1989; Wilson et al. 1991), the association of Alberta and Scottsbluff points could not be verified. Quigg (1976a) distinguished two closely spaced living floors 2–5 cm apart, but subsequent investigations suggest that the Fletcher site is a single-component kill site (Rod Vickers, personal communication 2001).

FIGURE 6.3. Fletcher site (DjOw-1) projectile points.

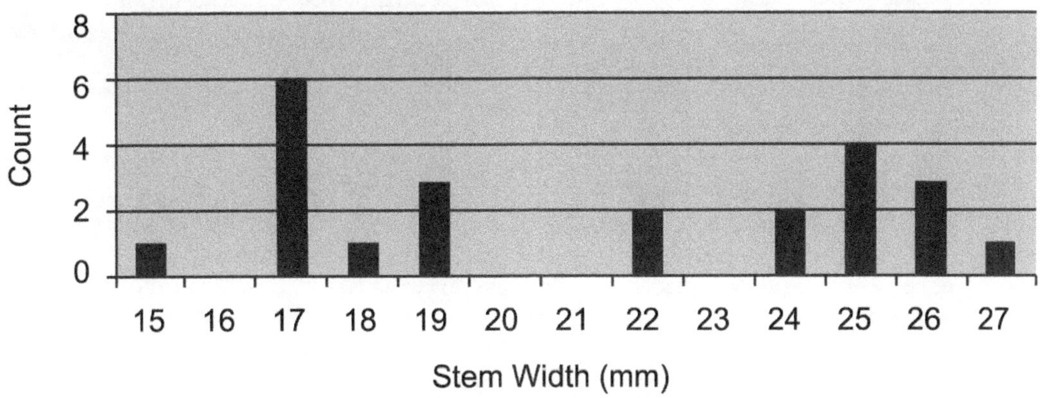


FIGURE 6.4. Fletcher Cody point stem widths.

If the Alberta and Scottsbluff points are in fact associated, why do these two somewhat distinct styles co-occur? Some question exists as to whether these points even represent two types. Where Forbis (1968) and Vickers (1986) identify both Alberta and Scottsbluff points in the assemblage, Huckell (1978:187) sees no reason to describe the Fletcher points as anything but Alberta, based on the lack of "even collateral pressure flaking" typical of Scottsbluff points. If these points are considered a single type, they certainly represent a fairly liberal interpretation of a mental template by their makers.

When we compare the stem width dimensions of the 13 Cody complex points illustrated by Forbis (1968:4–5) and those of an additional 10 specimens obtained from Armin Dyck, an apparent bimodal distribution is observed (Figure 6.4). Stem widths clustering at approximately 18 mm and 25 mm, respectively, seemingly indicate two shaft sizes. It is unknown whether this represents the dichotomy of dart versus spear or projectile versus knife. It should be noted, however, that the bimodality of stem widths was observed on artifacts classified as both Alberta and Scottsbluff.

The Fletcher assemblage included various other tool types: a Cody knife, gravers, side scrapers, an end scraper on a flake, a reamer, spokeshaves, bifaces, a pitted hammerstone/anvil, a burinated Hell Gap point base, and a possibly intrusive grooved maul fragment. The raw materials used for the projectile points and other small flaked tools include exotic cherts, basalt, "welded tuff," porcellanite, locally available cherts, quartzite, and argillite. A side scraper made on what looks like the distal end of a blade is KRF. The heavier tools are made of locally available quartzite.

Two AMS dates were obtained on seeds from this site. One sample was recovered just below the bonebed and dates to 9380 ± 110 BP (TO-1097; Vickers and Beaudoin 1989) (10,265–11,072 cal BP); the other was in the bonebed and dates to 9540 ± 110 BP (CAMS-42980; Beaudoin et al. 2000) (10,575–11,185 cal BP). These dates overlap at one sigma and thus give an approximate date for the Cody occupation.

### *Red Rock Canyon (DgPm-1, 762R)*

Two Cody points were recovered from Red Rock Canyon, a multicomponent, buried site in Waterton-Glacier Park (Reeves 1972; Reeves and Bourges 2002). Reeves (1972) suggests that although several living floors may have contributed to the concentration, they probably were laid down in a short time period. Among the artifacts recovered were a reworked Scottsbluff point and an Agate Basin point base that Reeves incorporated into the Red Rock Canyon phase. A date on charcoal from a hearth associated with the artifact concentration is 8220 ± 260 BP (GX1435) (8447–9728 cal BP).

### *Wally's Beach (DhPg-8)*

Wally's Beach covers a large area (approximately 1.5 by 2 km) inside what is normally the lakebed of St. Mary's Reservoir in southern Alberta. In the winter of 1999 a unique set of circumstances exposed much of the reservoir basin. The drawdown of the reservoir for maintenance coupled with drought conditions and subsequent water and wind erosion stripped up to 2 m off the lakebed, exposing ancient paleosols that had not seen the light of day since, in some cases, the late Pleistocene. Lithic and faunal material and the recognition of tracks of extinct Pleistocene fauna (McNeil et al. 2005) attest to the intermittent use of this valley by both people and animals for the last 11,000 radiocarbon years (12,825 calendar years). Paleoindian material is represented by approximately 100 projectile points including those identified as Clovis, Goshen, Plainview, Agate Basin, Hell Gap, Alberta, Scottsbluff, and Eden.

Pertinent to this study, Tolman (2001) identified 30 Alberta, four Eden, and two Scottsbluff points, and what he describes as an Alberta cache. The majority of the Cody lithic material is exotic: one Eden point and 16 Alberta points are KRF. Other Cody points are basalt, chert, jasper, siltstone, argillite, and quartz. Tolman observes that KRF is present throughout the archaeological record at Wally's Beach, but its use "peaked in terms of quantity and exquisitely produced artifacts during the Cody complex era" (Tolman 2001:104). The Alberta cache includes four end scrapers, two large Alberta points, and six flakes (four are heavily patinated KRF) from the site surface (Tolman 2001:106).

### *DjPm-16*

Two chert point fragments were recovered from a buried paleosol in a small campsite 10 m above the Oldman River (Van Dyke et al. 1990, 1991). One point fragment made of Top-of-the-World chert is tentatively classified as an Alberta point; the other is a point base that looks like Scottsbluff or Pryor Stemmed (Van Dyke et al. 1991:35). Each point was associated with a debitage concentration. Other artifacts include a uniface on a reworked point, an end scraper, a spokeshave, "six retouched flakes, five core tools, two bifaces, an elongate pebble and 1,118 pieces of debitage" (Van Dyke et al. 1991:37). The lithic raw materials come from a variety of local and nonlocal sources from the south, southeast, and west (Van Dyke et al. 1991:39). A bone in the paleosol associated with the projectile points yielded a date of 9600 ± 210 BP (AECV-746C) (10,272–11,601 cal BP). A date of 9450 ± 230 BP (BIS-17) (11,171–11,336 cal BP) on bone from the later of two closely spaced paleosols apparently relates to this occupation as well (Van Dyke et al. 1989:138). Associated faunal remains include bison, deer, canid, rabbit or hare, and ground squirrel. Three pieces of freshwater clam shell were also recovered.

### *Head-Smashed-In Buffalo Jump (DkPj-1)*

Boyd Wettlaufer (1949) of the University of New Mexico conducted the first extensive excavations at Head-Smashed-In buffalo jump near Fort Macleod, Alberta. His investigations recovered two Scottsbluff projectile point bases (one obsidian and one KRF; see Figure 6.2c), the large square base of what is probably an Alberta point of obsidian, and a potlidded chert point midsection from what may be an Eden point. All these points were recovered from fill previously excavated in the process of digging a dugout for cattle in the processing area. X-ray fluorescence of the obsidian Scottsbluff specimen suggests that it is from Burns, Oregon (Godfrey-Smith 1988), and the Alberta point of obsidian is from American Falls, Idaho (Skinner 2007).

No intact deposits of Paleoindian age have been identified at Head-Smashed-In. These artifacts represent at least one Cody component, and potentially three or more, from a deep gully at the foot of a natural spring. This location may have been a campsite, or a site that offered opportunities for trapping or ambushing game. The fill damming the spring channel on the downhill side of the dugout likely covers intact deposits that could answer this question. A mass of bone was exposed in this channel during construction of an interpretive trail that removed much of the dam fill (Brink and Dawe 1989:17). The unresolved question is whether the gully was itself a trap or whether it exposed preexisting earlier deposits relating to the use of the cliff as a jump. In a deep geological trench cut through the slump block on which the known kill site deposits sit, Reeves observed bone fragments under the slip plane of the slump (1978:161). The small amount of subslump bone recovered at that time was insufficient for a radiocarbon date.

### *EkOp-10*

EkOp-10, a Cody occupation with 206 lithic items, was identified in a buried paleosol on a gentle rise overlooking an outwash channel. The lone projectile point is a resharpened Scottsbluff Type 1, probably made of Swan River chert. Other artifacts included four end scrapers, one side scraper, one bifacial knife, five heavy stone tools, 45 pebble cores of local pebble cherts, and 145 pieces of debitage (Brumley and Brumley 1977).

### *Little Gem Complex*

During the 1930s Russell A. Johnston collected thousands of artifacts from 182 wind-eroded sites in the vicinity of the towns of Little Gem and Helmsdale, southeastern Alberta. At least 22 of these sites contained Cody material (Figure 6.5), 96 artifacts of which have been described as Cody points or point fragments. Unfortunately, the various descriptions of this collection (Adams 1976; Pettipas 1980; Wormington and Forbis 1965) have yielded little harmony in the classification of the point types. Problems with attempting to sort out the discrepancies in the published data have been exacerbated by the use of different, and in some cases wrong, site designations.

The close association of Cody diagnostics with a variety of other tool forms, including "Plainview-like" and "Milnesand-like" points, led Johnston to introduce the term "Little Gem Complex" (Pettipas 1980). Pettipas regarded Little Gem as a regional co-phase, along with Cody, of a larger Scottsbluff tradition (Pettipas 1980:12). Johnston included a corner-tanged knife and microblades with the Little Gem assemblages (Johnston 1975; Pettipas 1980:10). Johnston (1975) observed that in the blowouts from which he recovered the Paleoindian material, cultural material was associated with a distinctive black soil horizon 2.5 to 3 inches thick.

Johnston indicated that the majority of the Cody material in his collection was KRF and that only a minor amount of the Little Gem material was local stone. Johnston also described opaque obsidian as one of the distinctive Little Gem raw materials. Unfortunately, 11 obsidian artifacts from his collection were lost when sent for obsidian hydration dating.

None of the demonstrably Cody material from the Johnston collection was recovered in a dated context, but a blowout at EeOp-56 yielded a KRF artifact in close association with bone that has recently been dated at 9380 ± 50 BP (Beta 254976, Brink 2011) (10,442–10,734 cal BP). The artifact is a large, atypical, corner-removed projectile point

FIGURE 6.5. Johnston collection Cody material. (a, f, g, h, i, p, q, r) EkOs-1; (c, e) EkOs-2; (j) EkOt-2; (b) EhOq-7; (d) EgOv-1; (l, m, n, o) EjOs-1; (k) EhOr-4.

or knife of patinated KRF, with a ground base and notched edges, and one shoulder was modified into a graver spur. There is nothing Cody-like about the diminutive tang on this point, but Brink (2011:9) believes the date, coupled with the use of KRF and the Paleoindian trait of fashioning one of the shoulders into a graver spur, may indicate a Scottsbluff or Alberta affiliation.

### *EfPi-17*

The multicomponent site EfPi-17 occurs on two long, linear slump blocks detached from a valley wall high above the Bow River. The west block has two buried cultural components: the upper has a Pelican Lake and the lower a Cody complex occupation. The 299 lithic artifacts recovered from the lower component include six projectile point fragments, two bifaces, one scraper, one scraper/graver, and 16 expedient tools. Three unidirectional, conical quartzite cores indicate the production of large blade-like flakes, though such flakes were not observed in the assemblage. Local quartzite dominates the lithic assemblage; however, chert, chalcedony, petrified wood, basalt, and obsidian make up 20 percent of the lithic items. Exotic material includes Montana cherts, 14 pieces of heavily patinated KRF, and obsidian sourced to Bear Gulch, Idaho (Hanna 2002:69, 75). Cortex is uncommon on both tools and debitage, suggesting that most of the assemblage was transported from elsewhere.

Three of the point fragments are identified as Eden point bases, two of which are made of chert and one of siliceous siltstone. All three points are impact fractured (Hanna 2002:78). Stratigraphic separation exists between the two prehistoric components; however, soil cracks from slumping and rodent disturbance caused some admixture of assemblages. A Pelican Lake point in the lower layer probably was intrusive, an inference supported by two pieces of bone in the lower component submitted for radiocarbon dating and yielding a date consistent with the Pelican Lake occupation. Overall, contamination of the early component with later materials was considered insignificant.

### EgPn-480

EgPn-480 is a multicomponent site in a basin on top of the Elbow River valley edge (De Mille and Head 2001). A heavily ground, well-made Scottsbluff point base was recovered in Component 1 below two pre-Mazama paleosols. The latter of two bone dates from this component—9540 ± 70 (Beta 127235) (10,607–11,140 cal BP) and 5850 ± 40 BP (Beta 127236) (6549–6776 cal BP)—was rejected. None of the recorded bones was identifiable to species. The lithic assemblage in Component 1 includes 181 items, of which 20 were tools or cores. The assemblage was dominated by quartzite (80 percent) and to a lesser extent silicified siltstone (11 percent), with chert, chalcedony, and quartz present in small amounts. The chalcedony is possibly KRF. Besides the silicified siltstone point fragment, four bifaces, two end scrapers, a uniface, and a bifacially retouched tool were recovered. The tools are evenly represented by quartzite, silicified siltstone, and chert; however, eight of the 10 cores are sandstone and two are limestone.

### Sibbald Creek (EgPr-2)

EgPr-2 is a multicomponent site with an extensive record of use packed into a thin deposit on the Sibbald Flat meadow adjacent to Sibbald Creek (Gryba 1983a). The solitary siltstone Scottsbluff base was found at the same depth below surface as two fluted points, two Mount Albion points, a Midland point, an Agate Basin point, and other tools. No visible stratigraphy was apparent; however, a sequence of radiocarbon dates indicates that some stratigraphic integrity exists.

### Norquay (EhPv-15 or 156R)

The Norquay site straddles the Trans-Canada Highway, whose construction destroyed more than half the site in 1958. An Alberta point was recovered in a stratified deposit below Mazama ash in occupation 4 (Fedje 1988; Fedje and White 1984). A similar stratigraphic position elsewhere at the site had a considerable number of lithic artifacts, but their association with the Alberta point is uncertain. Two dates from charred bone below the Mazama ash were rejected because they postdate the Mazama event (Fedje 1988). Fedje assigns the Alberta occupation to the Norquay subphase in the Banff cultural sequence, which dates between 9500 and 9000 radiocarbon years BP (10,740–10,203 cal BP) (Langemann and Perry 2002).

### EkPu-8

EkPu-8 is a stratified site with at least four pre-Mazama ash occupation levels situated on a sheltered bench overlooking a grassy meadow in the James Pass, just inside the front range of the Rocky Mountains (Ronaghan 1993). The base of a silicified siltstone Scottsbluff projectile point was one of 3357 lithic artifacts recovered from Cultural Unit 7 (CU-7). CU-7 is about 10 cm below a uniform deposit of Mazama ash, and may contain a series of closely spaced occupations rather than a discrete single component. A date from a distal bison metacarpal at the base of CU-7 is 9750 ± 80 BP (TO-2999) (10,787–11,319 cal BP).

Apart from the point base, one projectile point tip, 14 mostly fragmentary small bifacial knives, three end scrapers, one thick bifacial chopper, one beaked graver, two spokeshaves, 41 marginally retouched flake tools, 19 cores including a large boat-shaped core, and 3274 pieces of debitage were recovered. The lithic assemblage is almost entirely local material, mostly silicified siltstone with significantly less quartzite and a poor-quality local chert. A few flakes of exotic chert were found, including Madison formation chert and Swan River chert. Of the tools, only a green pebble chert end scraper and the very fine agatized wood beaked graver could be considered nonlocal material. Exotic lithic material of any kind was extremely rare in any component at this site. The only KRF artifact found at EkPu-8, an end scraper, was attributed to the next lower occupation (CU-8), near and at the same depth as the Scottsbluff point base.

### Scapa Ribstone (ElPa-1)

The Scapa Ribstone site is a deeply stratified multicomponent site on a prominent ridge overlooking Sullivan Lake. Three buried campsite components occur below Mazama ash; the middle component was attributed to the Cody complex. Artifacts from this level include one KRF Scottsbluff point, two bifaces, one scraper, one uniface fragment, 17 marginally retouched tools, 23 cobble cores, and 852 pieces of debitage of which 5.5 percent were exotic stone. No identifiable bone was recovered; however, blood residue analysis on the point tested positive for antelope, and two other tools tested positive for bison (Hanna and Neal 1992:106).

### *Fullerton (FfPi-1)*

Fullerton is a large, multicomponent site excavated by Fraser Taylor in the Peace Hills near Wetaskiwin (Taylor 1969). The site occupies the top of a large sand dune overlooking a knob-and-kettle landscape with numerous sloughs. Cultural material was exposed by road construction to a depth of 1.5 m. No natural stratigraphy was discernible; however, the relative depths of the temporally diagnostic materials (including some 143 projectile points representing almost the whole spectrum of northern Plains culture history) indicated that cultural stratigraphy was inherent in the deposit. Three Scottsbluff points were found: one "recycled" quartzite specimen (Figure 6.2h) in a Late Prehistoric context, and the other two (one each of chalcedony and KRF; Figure 6.2g) buried in the deepest arbitrary excavation level (Level G). Three obsidian microblades, an Oxbow point, five corner-notched points, and two lanceolate projectile points (one is Plainview) also occurred at this depth.

### *Swan Landing (FhQl-4)*

One extensively resharpened siliceous mudstone Alberta point (Figure 6.2d) and a few pieces of debitage were recovered subsurface from a stratified, multicomponent eolian sand deposit at Swan Landing on the west side of Brule Lake (Ball 1983, 1986; Dawe 1983). A sample of charcoal from just above the point yielded a date of 8630 ± 100 BP (AEVC-10CX), (9442–10,114 cal BP), and a charcoal sample from the same depth as the projectile point yielded a date of 8675 ± 270 BP (S-2178) (9029–10,388 cal BP).

### *Nezu Complex*

In the Fort McMurray vicinity, northeastern Alberta, oil sands development has generated an unprecedented amount of archaeological investigation. A number of assemblages that share attributes of both Cody and Northern Plano material have been described as the Nezu complex (Saxberg and Reeves 2003) (Figure 6.1). This complex has been dated to 9400–8500 radiocarbon years BP (10,630–9510 cal BP) through the linking of Nezu sites to a chronological model using the Lower Athabasca River elevations (Saxberg and Reeves 2003). Stemmed projectile points that look very similar to Scottsbluff and Eden have been described as variants of the classic Cody complex (Figure 6.2j, k). The type site — the Nezu site (HhOu-36) — also contained two points described as Jimmy Allen and an eastern Plano type, along with numerous bifaces, scrapers, drills, and some 8000 pieces of debitage. The vast majority of this material is local Beaver River silicified sandstone (BRSS). The small amount of calcined bone was unsuitable for dating. Faunal analyses indicate utilization of bison, moose, rabbit, deer, and caribou. Cody material has been documented from four other Nezu complex sites: Scottsbluff material from HhOv-123, and Eden points from HhOv-4, HhOv-159 and HhOv-196 (Saxberg and Reeves 2003:300–301).

Apart from subtle morphological differences, the confidence with which some Nezu points are classified as Cody is constrained by an absence of radiocarbon dates, a paucity of stratigraphy, and the lack of exotic lithic material (especially KRF) that forms the hallmark of the Cody occupation elsewhere in the province. Adding to the confusion is the marked similarity of more recent middle and early Taltheilei points (roughly 1300–2500 years old) found near Lake Athabasca to the north (see Gordon 1996).

## Lithic Raw Materials

The province of Alberta is poorly endowed with sources of high-quality lithic raw material suitable for flintknapping. The most commonly used raw material is quartzite, which has a widespread distribution in river gravels and till deposits and is ubiquitous in most precontact artifact assemblages. Cobbles of Swan River chert are available on the east margin of Alberta that when heat-treated can be a fine raw material. The Rocky Mountains provide sources of fine-grained siliceous mudstones and siltstones, as well as outcrops of what are generally poor-quality, highly fractured cherts. The bedrock source of the very fine quality Peace River chert common in the northwest corner of Alberta has not been located. Small, typically black, pebble cherts of variable quality occur in most river gravels and some till deposits.

**TABLE 6.2.** Raw Materials of Cody Complex Projectile Points in Alberta.

| | Alberta | | Scottsbluff | | Eden | | Cody Knife | | Total | |
|---|---|---|---|---|---|---|---|---|---|---|
| **Raw Material** | *n* | % | *n* | % | *n* | % | *n* | % | *n* | % |
| Knife River flint | 47 | 42.7 | 69 | 25.6 | 14 | 21.9 | 7 | 43.8 | 137 | 28.8 |
| Chert | 8 | 7.3 | 50 | 18.5 | 16 | 25.0 | 1 | 6.3 | 75 | 15.8 |
| Quartzite | 7 | 6.4 | 51 | 18.9 | 10 | 15.6 | 1 | 6.3 | 69 | 14.5 |
| Swan River chert | 2 | 1.8 | 25 | 9.3 | 7 | 10.9 | 1 | 6.3 | 35 | 7.4 |
| Siliceous siltstone/Siltstone | 7 | 6.4 | 22 | 8.1 | 4 | 6.3 | 1 | 6.3 | 34 | 7.2 |
| Montana (Madison formation) chert | 3 | 2.7 | 18 | 6.7 | 1 | 1.6 | 3 | 18.8 | 25 | 5.3 |
| Chalcedony/Brown chalcedony (KRF?) | 4 | 3.6 | 17 | 6.3 | 3 | 4.7 | 1 | 6.3 | 25 | 5.3 |
| Basalt | 14 | 12.7 | 5 | 1.9 | 2 | 3.1 | | | 21 | 4.4 |
| Obsidian/Volcanic | 4 | 3.6 | 12 | 4.4 | | | | | 16 | 3.4 |
| Porcellanite | 2 | 1.8 | 4 | 1.5 | 2 | 3.1 | | | 8 | 1.7 |
| Silicified sandstone/BRSS | | 0.0 | 5 | 1.9 | 2 | 3.1 | | | 7 | 1.5 |
| Siliceous mudstone/ Mudstone | 1 | 0.9 | 3 | 1.1 | 2 | 3.1 | | | 6 | 1.3 |
| Peace River chert | 2 | 1.8 | 1 | 0.4 | | | | | 3 | 0.6 |
| Silicified wood | 1 | 0.9 | 2 | 0.7 | | | | | 3 | 0.6 |
| Argillite | 2 | 1.8 | | | | | | | 2 | 0.4 |
| Quartz | 1 | 0.9 | | | | | | | 1 | 0.2 |
| Top-of-the-World | 1 | 0.9 | | | | | | | 1 | 0.2 |
| Other | 4 | 3.6 | 1 | 0.4 | 1 | 1.6 | 1 | 6.3 | 7 | 1.5 |
| **Total** | 110 | | 285 | | 64 | | 16 | | 475 | |

A distinctive fine siliceous sediment called Beaver River silicified sandstone (BRSS) dominates lithic assemblages in the Fort McMurray region in the northeast corner of Alberta. Southern Alberta offers some fine but fairly soft argillites. The dearth of good material in central Alberta resulted in the use of often very poor quality silicified wood.

The raw material types of individual Cody complex projectile points recovered in Alberta are summarized in Table 6.2. Although more than a thousand artifacts potentially could have contributed to the sample, the raw materials of only 475 artifacts were reported; this sample consequently represents less than half the known Cody material in the province. In many cases the raw material type was not reported, particularly in some surface collections and early CRM reports. Moreover, if a collection or assemblage contained a raw material description for a sample of the Cody points or the description was ambiguous, it was excluded from this analysis.

KRF is the most abundant raw material, accounting for 28.8 percent of all Cody points and knives, and is the dominant material except for Eden points, which are more frequently made of chert (Table 6.2). KRF is by far the most common raw material for Alberta points, at 42.7 percent. The high proportion of Alberta points made from basalt come primarily from Wally's Beach (DhPg-8). Otherwise, an Alberta point in this province is almost six times as likely to be made of KRF as any other material.

Quartzite and chert were more commonly used for Scottsbluff and Eden points than for earlier Alberta points. Swan River chert, a raw material ubiquitous in later assemblages along the east side of the province, was used for only two of the Alberta points, with a relative increase of use in Scottsbluff and Eden points. Montana chert, porcellanite, Top-of-the-World chert, and argillite were restricted to southern Alberta; BRSS and Peace River chert were limited to the north.

Although exotic materials are rare in northeastern Alberta, obsidian and a few KRF specimens were recovered from the northwest, notably the Grande Prairie area. Trace element analyses conducted on two obsidian Scottsbluff points from this area yielded different results:

one from Anaheim in British Columbia (Figure 6.2m; Hughes 2008), and the other likely from Bear Gulch, Idaho (Bailey 1992). In southern Alberta, Hanna (2002) similarly reports Bear Gulch, Idaho, as the source for the specimen from EfPi-17. Obsidian from Big Southern Butte, Idaho, was the source of material for all three Scottsbluff points from EdPk-3 (Hughes 2010; Wilson et al. 2011). Two Cody artifacts of obsidian from Head-Smashed-In (DkPj-1) have also been sourced: one from American Falls, Idaho (Hughes 2008; Skinner 2007), and the other from Burns, Oregon (Godfrey-Smith 1988). Again, obsidian would figure more prominently in Table 6.2 were it not for the 11 specimens lost from the Russell Johnston collection.

Why is so much KRF recovered from Cody assemblages in Alberta? Furthermore, why the apparent early reliance on KRF and other exotic materials with a gradual shift toward local materials when we compare Alberta, Scottsbluff, and Eden projectile points (Table 6.2)? It appears that Alberta was initially occupied by people unfamiliar with local lithic resources who geared up with familiar lithics and curated a toolkit from the region where they originated (see Root et al., this volume, for southern Saskatchewan). The scant utilization of Swan River chert to make Alberta points does not resemble the usage expected of flintknappers familiar with local resources for retooling. Over time, with growing familiarity of the distribution of local material, the functional demand for exotic material diminishes for a population of residents or frequent visitors. This inference remains speculative.

Trade is a possible agent of distribution for some of the exotic raw material and probably had a role in bringing exotic stone into Alberta. However, the particularly diverse suite of exotic materials from discordant directions represented at each of DjPm-16, Head-Smashed-In (DkPj-1), and Fletcher (DjOw-1) might be easier to explain in the context of an "aggregation of groups from distant areas" (Bamforth 2002:86) than as the migration of a single cohesive group. Such an aggregation could explain the considerable formal variation in point types at both Head-Smashed-In and Fletcher, should these both prove to be single-component events.

Initially, though, a migration of people from the south and southeast across Alberta has to be considered. The use of vast amounts of KRF in Alberta by Cody peoples, between 700 km and 1500 km from the source area, is unprecedented, and bespeaks of a heavily curated toolkit. Muñiz (2005) documents at several Plains Cody sites the distribution of KRF points that were transported particularly long distances from the quarry area: 940 km to Olsen-Chubbuck, 800 km to Claypool, and 775 km to Jurgens. Only Olsen-Chubbuck comes close to the dominant use of KRF observed in Alberta, however.

In contrast to the bias for using exotic stone to make Alberta projectile points, the considerable numbers of fluted points that predate the arrival of Cody are almost exclusively made of local material (Ives 2006). Most of the fluted points in Alberta are considered Clovis; Folsom points are rare, and what should be temporally sequent Agate Basin and Hell Gap types are poorly represented both in CRM projects and in private collections. Exotic material of any kind from the pre-Cody period is rare, not just KRF. The initial Cody complex occupation represents a marked departure from earlier occupations in the province, especially in sheer numbers of artifacts and the influx of exotic lithic materials.

The dependence on curated toolkits by the initial Alberta Cody occupants is in accordance with the situation postulated by Kelly and Todd (1988: 234). In their view, Paleoindian peoples who lack local knowledge in unfamiliar and unpopulated territory would depend on hunting as a relatively predictable resource. They would characteristically have "a lifeway of high residential, logistical, and range mobility" (Kelly and Todd 1988:235). These people could be expected to utilize a lithic toolkit "designed to be transportable, have long-term utility, and be of use in areas where only a limited number of stone sources might have been known" (Kelly and Todd 1988:238).

The appearance of Cody technology in Alberta coupled with the unprecedented reliance on exotic raw material for the first time suggests that the initial Cody occupation was by newcomers. Kelly and Todd (1988:233) speculate that resource stress could stimulate emigration, which may explain the initial Cody occupation in Alberta, which has all the earmarks of a foreign intrusion. These first Cody peoples can be viewed as "strangers in a strange land" if the landscape offered an unknown distribution of lithic resources and an unfamiliar distribution of alternate subsistence resources such as plants. By the end of the Cody occupation, when a shift toward local lithic materials is evident, a shift toward a more diverse subsistence base may have occurred when the mysteries of resource distribution were solved.

This model supports an interpretation of a late-term Cody occupation in the northeastern part of Alberta. Elsewhere in the province, even in the northwest "Peace Country," large Cody assemblages typically contain exotic materials (notably KRF). With the exception of some end scrapers and possibly one obsidian point base,[2] the Fort McMurray specimens are almost exclusively made of the local BRSS, which begs the question: if Cody assemblages are typified by exotic materials and occur in the northwest, then why not in the northeast? The Nezu complex depicts a population reliant on local resources; these people may have either used up or lost access to a supply of exotic material, and ultimately did not need it. In the Fort McMurray region the situation is somewhat different from elsewhere in Alberta, as the region has an abundant supply of reasonably good quality toolstone (BRSS). A visitor to this location would soon become familiar with this resource and could depend on retooling here, as attested by the ubiquitous presence of BRSS in archaeological assemblages.

While there is no apparent influx of raw material into the Fort McMurray region during the Cody term, there appears to be movement staged from this area. Artifacts made from BRSS have been found in Great Plains sites to the south, indicating some type of interaction or movement during the Cody period. An Eden point made from BRSS was observed in a collection from the Barrhead vicinity, some 200 miles south of Fort McMurray (Fenton and Ives 1990:124), and Saxberg and Reeves (2003:310) report a Scottsbluff point made from this material at the Heron Eden site in Saskatchewan (Linnamae and Corbeil 1993).

### Site Distribution

The distribution of documented Cody sites in Alberta is illustrated in Figure 6.1. What this distribution represents must be tempered with consideration of disproportionate current land use, modern population density, and archaeological activity. This distribution is expressed in Figure 6.6 as the count and percentage of Cody sites in each major Borden block[3] as compared with the total count and percentage of all sites documented from all time periods in Alberta. Where significant differences are observed between the values for Cody sites compared with the values for the total number of sites in any given region, this should indicate that factors other than the postdepositional ones described above have influenced these distributions.

Because greater than 95 percent of the sites in Alberta are from time periods later than Cody, the differences observed in the distribution of sites in Figure 6.6 reflect changes between the Cody and later occupations. It is argued here that much of the difference in distribution was driven by environmental changes under way during the Cody tenure.

When we compare the relative frequency of Cody sites with all other sites in the different Borden blocks in the province, we find that the Grande Prairie area (GQ block) and the area just southwest of Edmonton (FP block) have disproportionately high amounts of Cody material. The bias of Cody material in the Grande Prairie area is particularly noticeable. As a northern pocket of open parkland in an area otherwise dominated by boreal forest, this region is still something of an anomaly today. It is probable that up to 9000 radiocarbon years ago (10,203 cal BP) this region was open forest and provided suitable bison habitat.

Given that most of the Cody sites in Alberta are surface finds, it is expected that areas with high modern population density will exhibit a higher recovery rate of artifacts. This may be the case in central Alberta. The concentration of sites in the almost linear distribution from just northeast of Edmonton to just south of Calgary apparent in Figure 6.1 coincides with the zone of highest population density today. But since much of this latter area occurs on the parkland edge and is a resource-rich ecotone (Losey 1978), it is expected to have had a high level of prehistoric usage. In a study of the Canadian Prairie ecozone, this swath of land features prominently as a zone of high ecological diversity and uniqueness, factors

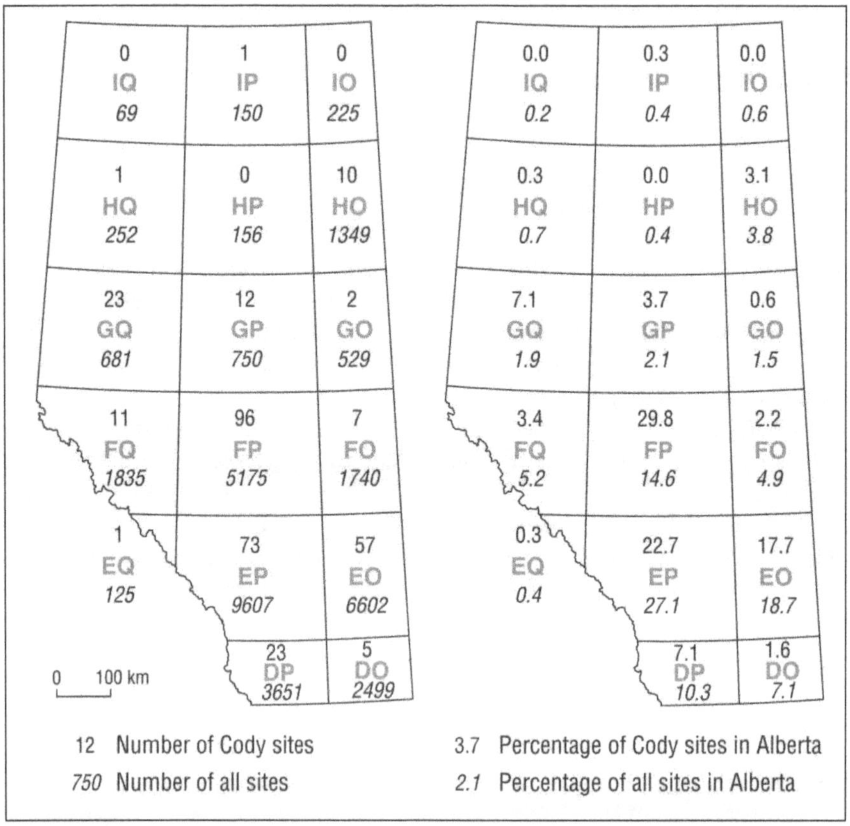


**FIGURE 6.6.** Cody site count and relative percentage by Borden block compared with all sites in Alberta.

that coincide with high archaeological site density across the prairies (Wiseman and Graham 2007).

Another region with very high Cody site density is near Little Gem in southeastern Alberta (EO block). This region is sparsely populated, so a high site density here does not simply reflect current population or land use. However, a disproportionately high amount of erosion during periods of drought coupled with very determined collecting activity in this region may account for the high archaeological site density.

Two areas stand out as having little representation of Cody material: the boreal forest in the north half and the extreme southeast corner of Alberta. While the lack of Cody material in the north may partly be a consequence of limited site visibility due to factors such as heavy forest cover, minimal cultivation and development, and low population, this should not be the case in the southeast. Sites in the southeast may be buried too deep to be exposed, such as at the Fletcher site, where cultural material was almost 2 m deep, or aridity may have been too great during the Cody occupation. Part of the southeast tip of Alberta is occupied by the Cypress Hills (an ecotonal zone of considerable biodiversity), which curiously has not produced Cody material.

Most of the Cody material found in Alberta occurs in areas currently under cultivation, including the Grande Prairie region. It is evident that most of the Cody distribution occurs in areas that supported grassland, parkland, or open forest during the early Holocene; virtually all of it would have been bison habitat. The evidence suggests that Cody peoples here were principally bison hunters. Consequently, it is not surprising that Cody material is scarce west of Alberta.[4]

Beaudoin and Oetelaar (2003:196) produced a preliminary map of the distribution of postglacial vegetation in southern Alberta and Saskatchewan. This map approximates the limits of open vegetation at 11,000 $^{14}$C BP (12,825 cal BP) and then at 9000 $^{14}$C BP (10,203 cal BP). The 11,000 $^{14}$C BP (12,825 cal BP) vegetation plots effectively bracket the maximum position of open vegetation when Alberta was first populated by Cody peoples, and the 9000 $^{14}$C BP (10,203 cal BP) limit represents the range of grassland that is similar to what we can expect at the end of the Cody term. At this early time, the zone of open vegetation is not grassland per se, but rather mixed graminoid vegetation including grasses, sedges, and low herbaceous shrubs. The progressive encroachment of forests into this zone of open vegetation would have effectively reduced the habitat utilized by bison. When the distribution of Cody projectile points is compared with the distribution of what was open vegetation according to the vegetation limits presented by Beaudoin and Oetelaar (2003), the Cody distribution neatly conforms to this zone (Figure 6.7). Differences in the distribution of Alberta, Scottsbluff, and Eden points, respectively, also conform to this changing pattern of vegetation cover. If we assume that the projectile point distribution represents the range of the people who made them, we see some interesting changes in the areas utilized by Cody people during the Cody complex.

These data suggest that the distribution of bison habitat has significant bearing on the distribution of the Cody complex. As the forests gradually in-filled northwestern Alberta, the distribution of Cody artifacts from Alberta through Eden times shifted toward the southeast. This trend is demonstrated in Figure 6.8, which compares relative projectile point densities from a northwest-to-southeast sample of artifacts from three Borden blocks that fall in this zone of open vegetation.

Figure 6.8 indicates that the percentage of each Cody point type drops off from the southeast to the northwest. If we assume the Cody complex was ultimately derived from an influx of people from the southeast, we would expect this drop-off in artifact numbers as the distance from the point of origin increases. The frequencies between the point types are different, however, which I interpret as a function of time and concomitant changes in environment. More than 11 percent of all Alberta points in Alberta are found in the northwest GQ block, compared with only 3 percent of all Eden points. In contrast, 22 percent of Alberta points and 32 percent of Eden points are found in the southeastern EO Borden block.

The distribution differences shown in Figures 6.7 and 6.8 suggest a gradual reduction in the utilization of the Grande Prairie (GQ block) area through time, and the apparent abandonment of mountain valleys and meadows as forests encroached. Alternatively, in the Fort McMurray area in northeast Alberta (HO block), Scottsbluff or Nezu peoples did not appear until the later part of the Cody term. A late arrival might indicate that conditions for a suitable habitat were not met until after the early Holocene "tsunami" outwash event of Glacial Lake Agassiz between 9900 and 9400 $^{14}$C BP (11,280–10,630 cal BP) (Fisher 2007; Fisher and Smith 1994; Lowell et al. 2005; Rayburn and Teller 2007). This catastrophic event would have scoured the Athabasca River basin and opened the forest to create a broad swath of bison habitat.

## Discussion and Conclusion

The Cody complex persisted for over a thousand years in Alberta. Early in the Cody period the consistent utilization of exotic lithic material from the south, sometimes at the exclusion of local material, is suggestive of an initial population movement from the south, particularly the southeast, into what is now the province of Alberta. The movement of people, rather than trade, seems to be the best explanation for how KRF was dispersed, especially by the makers of Alberta points, who used this stone for almost half of their spearheads (see Root et al., this volume, for southern Saskatchewan). At such a great distance from the source area, between 500 km and 1500 km, it seems implausible that any group would rely on trade to sustain a critical component of a tool inventory. Also compelling about a migration hypothesis is that the Alberta point users introduced not only a new lithic suite but also a brand-new technology. It is unlikely they traded for that.

Agenbroad (1978:91–95) suggests that the Alberta assemblage at Hudson-Meng, Nebraska, has closer technological similarities to Clovis assemblages than the intervening Hell Gap and Agate Basin toolkits. Although he offers the disclaimer that he does not "favor postulated 'invasions' of cultural groups through time" (Agenbroad 1978:

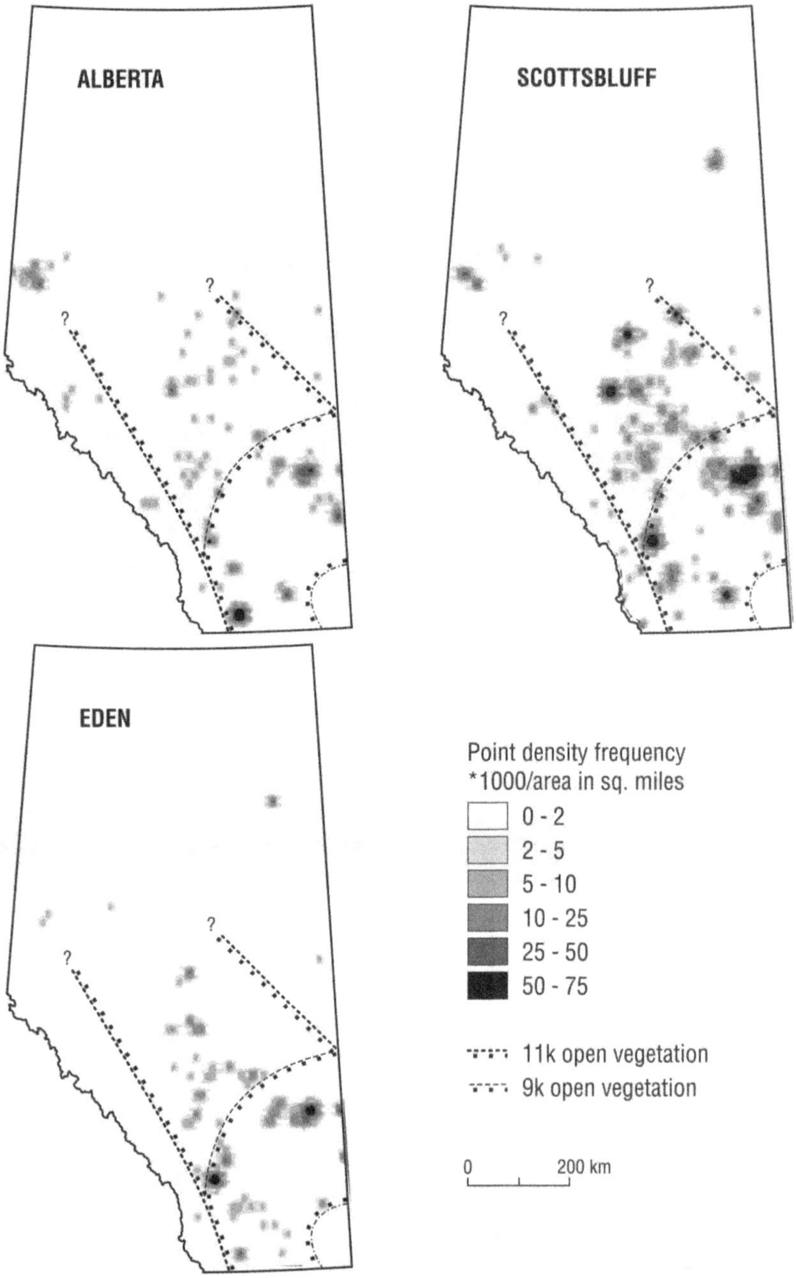


**FIGURE 6.7.** Cody point frequencies in Alberta.

95), the evidence supports such an "invasion" in the case of Alberta artifacts at Hudson-Meng. Here, too, KRF is the dominant raw material, although at 512 km from the Knife River quarries Hudson-Meng is considerably closer to the source than any of the Cody sites in the province of Alberta.

A similar "cultural invasion" potentially occurred again in Alberta some 7000 years after the Cody people first arrived. The almost exclusive use of KRF in the Besant assemblages at Muhlbach (FbPf-1; Gruhn 1969) and the Swainson site (FeOw-3; Varsakis 2006) in central Alberta points to a migration of people from the southeast.

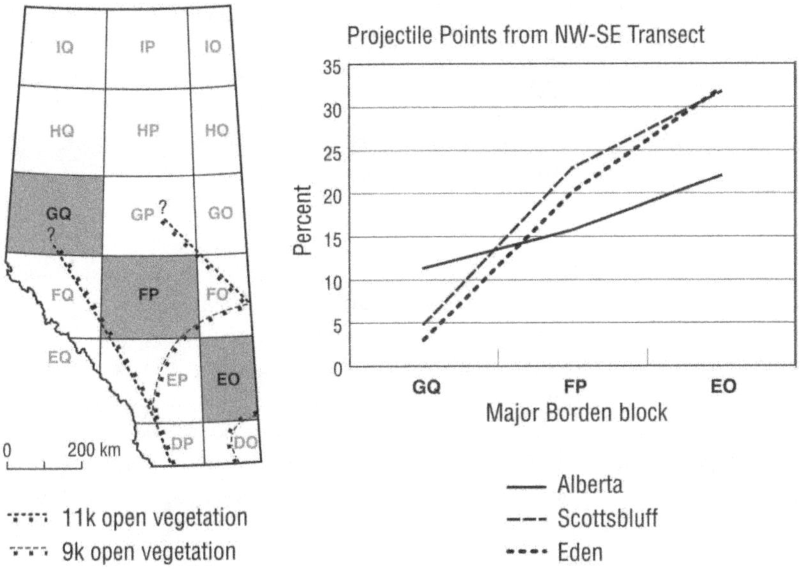


FIGURE 6.8. Sample of Cody point frequencies by type in northwest-southeast transect.

Another possibility is that the Cody complex people participated in a very long range seasonal round. In the Late Prehistoric period, winter camps were frequently situated in the parkland to take advantage of shelter and also the wood required as fuel (Vickers and Peck 2004). A further attraction of the parkland in winter may have been game. Both Losey (1978) and Peck (2001) provide compelling historic and ethnographic evidence to indicate that the parkland in Alberta, as a winter refuge for bison, was exploited by bison hunters most successfully in the coldest of winter months (January, February, and March). In the first few millennia of the Holocene, the parkland was probably not established as we now know it but instead was a buffer zone between the forest and open vegetation. This forest transition ecotone may have provided a winter refuge to people and herbivores that is analogous to the later parkland. It might be speculated that if users of Cody points anticipated overwintering in the Alberta forest transition zone, they would gear up with a curated toolkit rather than chance being able to locate stone in a snow-covered landscape. Huckell (1978:183, 185) proposed a reduction sequence for Alberta points based on the assemblage from Hudson-Meng, a sequence that, in terms of raw material use, was highly efficient and "characteristic of a group which expected to be away from its favored material sources for a long period of time" (Huckell 1978:183). If it is further speculated that users of Cody points geared up with KRF, either by direct or indirect procurement, and followed the bison herds to the forest transition zone to overwinter, the residual archaeological assemblages would be biased toward KRF, much as we see in the earliest Cody assemblages in Alberta. We do not have sufficient seasonality data at this time from Cody sites to evaluate whether the Alberta forest transition zone could have figured in such a seasonal round, but this possibility should not be overlooked.

The distribution of Cody material conforms to the area of the province occupied by open vegetation in the early Holocene, an area dominated by the graminoid vegetation interpreted here as bison habitat. The Cody people in Alberta were conspicuously bison hunters, for where there is an association of fauna in a Cody archaeological context, bison remains are usually present. Since most of the documented sites involve a slough or water body (usually) adjacent to a hill, the circumstantial evidence indicates a hunting strategy of miring or ambushing bison.

It is therefore easy to characterize Cody people as bison hunters. Kornfeld (2003:3) cautions that we fall into the trap of labeling Paleoindians bison hunters with the implicit assumption that they were specialists in an eternal quest for bison. He notes that Klein (1989:367) observed that single-species dominance of bones from Upper Paleolithic sites in Europe often represent disparate fauna that dominated the particular site environs, and hence targeted fauna should not be considered a hunting specialization but rather an environmental exploitation. From this perspective, Cody people could have been generalists exploiting a plains grassland environment, and as the dominant biomass is bison, Cody people were de facto bison hunters. Whether they are bison hunters by design or default, bison clearly were an important prey species. Evidence here suggests a diet augmented by other ungulates including deer, moose, caribou, and antelope, and possibly also including bear, canid, lagomorphs, ground squirrels, and even freshwater clams. A lack of evidence for avian, fish, or vegetal utilization is probably more a function of poor preservation than dietary omission.

In summary, the Cody complex represents a significant and widespread occupation in early Holocene Alberta. Temporal trends in both the distribution of sites and the utilization of lithic raw materials have been observed. The distribution of Cody sites through time is synchronous with the diminishing distribution of the zone of open vegetation, which can be regarded as bison habitat. A shift from a bias toward exotic lithic material by users of Alberta points, to a later bias of local material by the users of Eden points, is also evident. This shift in raw material utilization toward local materials occurs despite the fact that the concomitant shift in site distribution in later times is closer to the source of the exotic lithic of choice: Knife River flint. The interpretation presented here is that the first Cody occupation of Alberta was by a new population unfamiliar with the distribution of resources who offset risk by carrying a curated toolkit. Through time, as familiarity with local resources increased, the need for exotic stone decreased. The continued use of significant, if somewhat reduced, amounts of KRF near the end of the Cody term by users of Eden points indicates continual direct or indirect access to the source area.

Despite the increase in CRM activities since the establishment of the Archaeological Survey of Alberta in 1973, subsurface Cody materials have not been recovered in the proportions that might be expected based on the Cody material found in surface collections. Several factors contribute to this discrepancy. Paleoindian sites of any kind can be deeply buried, reducing the likelihood of recovery even during CRM activities that have a near-surface sampling bias. In contrast, Cody artifacts tend to be more conspicuous than many other artifact types in surface contexts. Cody points are often relatively large and tend to be made of exotic materials that make them stand out; hence they are more likely to be picked up than artifacts made of local rocks. This sampling bias of picking up unusual or nice-looking rocks by collectors is evident when assemblages excavated by professionals are compared with those recovered from the surface by untrained collectors. A situation thus exists in Alberta in which Cody surface material is ubiquitous in much of the province but the lack of stratified Cody sites limits our ability to understand this phenomenon.

It has now been 50 years since the discovery of the Fletcher site, and despite the documentation of some 37,000 archaeological sites in the province since that time, the Fletcher site still stands out as the best example of a stratified Cody site in Alberta, and the only one with a considerable amount of associated faunal material. Clearly, other buried sites are out there, somewhere.

## Acknowledgments

I thank Alwynne Beaudoin for her comments on things paleoenvironmental; George Chalut, who provided help with the raw material analysis; Joan Damkjar and Barry Newton for contributing site data and a plethora of map revisions; Marsha Mickalyk and Sylvie LeBlanc, who did piles of legwork; Wendy Johnson and Michael Semenchuk for the drafting; Rod Vickers for discussions on the Fletcher site; Dixon Christie for help with photos; Nancy Saxberg and Lifeways of Canada for permission to use the Nezu point images; Darryl Bereziuk for the GfPt-13 point image; Rena Varsakis for help with Parks Canada records; Wendy Unfreed for last-minute editing assistance; and Jack Brink, Edward Knell, Mark Muñiz, and Heinz Pyszczyk for comments on this chapter. I would be remiss if I did not thank Les Davis for getting me started.

## Notes

1. The environmental conditions that exposed the Little Gem material were not peculiar to Alberta. Seebach (2006) has documented the results of considerable collecting opportunities during episodes of drought and erosion across the Great Plains, particularly starting in the 1930s. The disproportionately large representation of artifacts and sites recovered under these circumstances of severe erosion may have actually biased our understanding of how and where these ancient people lived (Seebach 2006).
2. A fragment of what might be part of a Cody complex point base was recovered from site HhOv-271 in the Fort McMurray vicinity. This artifact has been sourced to Bear Gulch, Idaho (Hughes 2008).
3. Borden blocks are the grid units based on latitude and longitude in the Borden site designation system used across Canada (Borden 1952).
4. A Scottsbluff point, probably Peace River chert, was recovered in a shallow deposit at Pink Mountain (HhRr-1). It apparently is the only Cody point recovered in a buried context in British Columbia (Wilson 1989 and 1996). Pink Mountain, in northeastern British Columbia, is in the foothills on the east side of the Rockies. Reeves and Bourges (2002:17) mention an Eden point in the Rocky Mountain Trench near Windermere, and a few other Cody-like materials have been observed in collections from the British Columbia interior (Stryd and Rousseau 1996:181; Wilson 1989:57). I was shown a photograph of an apparent KRF Alberta point collected on the Fraser River valley, and recent investigations at the Stave Lake Reservoir 65 km east of Vancouver near the Fraser River yielded at least one good candidate for a Scottsbluff point (Eldridge and McLaren 1998).

## Appendix: Cody Site Summary for Alberta

| | Site Name | Point Type | Lithic Type | Site Type | Notes | Reference |
|---|---|---|---|---|---|---|
| 1 | Fletcher (DjOw-1) | AB(>5) SB(>14) CK(1) | porc, bas, tuff, cht, krf, chal, mc | buried kill/ campsite | 9380 ± 110 (TO-1097) 9540 ± 110 (CAMS-42980) | Reeves 1964; Wormington and Forbis 1965; Forbis 1968; Knudson 1971; Quigg 1976a; Vickers 1986; Vickers and Beaudoin 1989; Wilson et al. 1991; Beaudoin et al. 2000 |
| 2 | Arnold (Dick) Hudson Collection (DO block) | AB(2) SB(2) | AB: obs, cht; SC: bas, cht | surface collection | | Wood 1991 |
| 3 | Frank Brewin Collection (DkOx block) | AB(1) | bas | surface collection | Purple Springs | Wood 1991 |
| 4 | Irene Hudson Collection (DO block) | AB(1) | bas | surface collection | | Wood 1991 |
| 5 | Lawrence Halmrast Collection (DhOx block) LH14 | ED(1) | mud | surface collection | beside ephemeral lake | Wood 1991 |
| 6 | Red Rock Canyon (DgPm-1, 762R) | SB(2) | bas(1) | multicomponent buried campsite | 8220 ± 210 (GX-1435) on charcoal from hearth associated with artifact concentration, 10–20 cm above till in alluvial deposit, 100 cm below surface | Reeves 1972; Reeves and Bourges 2002 |

## Appendix: Cody Site Summary for Alberta (continued)

| | Site Name | Point Type | Lithic Type | Site Type | Notes | Reference |
|---|---|---|---|---|---|---|
| 7 | Wally's Beach (DhPg-8) | AB(30) ED(4) SB(2) | AB: krf(16), bas(10?), arg, mc, oth(2); SC: oth(2); ED: krf(1), silt(1), cht(1), oth(1) | multicomponent surface scatter | eroded reservoir basin | Tolman 2001 |
| 8 | DjPm-16 | AB(1) SB(1?) | cht(2) | deeply buried campsite | 9600 ± 210 (AECV-746C), on second terrace of Crows-nest River | Van Dyke et al. 1989 and 1990 |
| 9 | Crowsnest Valley Campsite (DjPp-8) | SB(1) | | multicomponent campsite | north side of Crowsnest River at exit from lake | Driver 1983 |
| 10 | DkPc-2 | CK(1) | | scatter | blowout | Glenbow Museum 1962 |
| 11 | DkPh-1 | SB(1) | | campsite | | U of Calgary 1969 |
| 12 | Head-Smashed-In Buffalo Jump (DkPj-1) | AB(1) SB(2) | AB: obs SC: krf, obs | large multicom-ponent campsite; kill site | in spring channel at foot of cliff | Brink and Dawe 1989; Wettlaufer 1949; Reeves 1978 |
| 13 | Schamp (DkPj-38) | SB | | multicomponent campsite | blowout | Arch. Survey Alberta 2011 et seq. (Permit 92-066) |
| 14 | Poulsen (DkPm-14) | AB | | multicomponent lithic scatter | elevated area beside ephemeral slough | McCullough and Reeves 1978 |
| 15 | Coulee View (DlPd-5) | SB | | multicomponent campsite | overlooking Oldman River | Glenbow Museum 1957 |
| 16 | Cranford (DlPb-13) | CK(3) | krf, silt, mc | multicomponent campsite surface collection | upper south terrace of Oldman River | Wood et al. 1993, Armin Dyck collection |
| 17 | Chanticlear (DlPh-17) | SB(3) ED(1) | | multicomponent collection | | Hjermstad 1991 |
| 18 | DlPh-21 | SB(1) | | isolated find; collection | | Hjermstad 1991 |
| 19 | Old Toboggan Blow (DlPh-23) | SB | | multicomponent campsite; kill site | on blowouts near rise | Hjermstad 1991 |
| 20 | Dennis Home-stead (DlPn-2) | ED(1) | | multicomponent scatter | on high terrace overlooking Oldman River | U of Alberta 1966 |
| 21 | DlPo-59 | SB(1) | krf | campsite | Scottsbluff or Eden blade in disturbed gravel pit on ter-race overlooking abandoned Old-man Dam channel | Gryba 1983b |
| 22 | Armin Dyck Col-lection (DP block) Meyer's | CK(1) | src | surface collection | from Meyer's River Land | Wood et al. 1993 |
| 23 | Darwin Lund Collection (DkPc block) DL1 | ED(1) | bas | surface collection | 4 miles north of Chin elevators | Wood 1991 |
| 24 | Darwin Lund Collection (DkPa block, Taber) DL3 | ED(1) | bas | surface collection | point midsection, Taber area | Wood 1991 |

| | Site Name | Point Type | Lithic Type | Site Type | Notes | Reference |
|---|---|---|---|---|---|---|
| 25 | Elsie Kitchener Collection (DP block) EK10 | AB(1) | silt | surface collection | on blowout | Wood 1991 |
| 26 | John Reti Collection (DlPa block) JR7 | SB(1) | cht | surface collection | Taber area | Wood 1991 |
| 27 | Ken Fisher Collection (DlPa block) | CK(1) SB(1) | cht | surface collection | sandhills, east of Taber, were blown out to base then cultivated | Wood 1991 |
| 28 | Lawrence Halmrast Collection (DjPa block) LH10 | CK(1) | mc | surface collection | on blown-out land | Wood 1991 |
| 29 | EaOq-11 | SB/ ED(1) | | campsite | one Cody point, no data in report, just a notation in site description, on first terrace of South Saskatchewan River | Quigg 1980 |
| 30 | EaOq-12 | SB/ ED(1) | | buried campsite | blowout | Dau and Brumley 1980 (ASA 79-084) |
| 31 | EbOp-42 | SB(1) | | scatter | | Brumley and Willis 1977 |
| 32 | EbOv-1 | CD | | campsite; collection | | Hjermstad 1991 |
| 33 | EeOn-13 | SB(1) | mc | multicomponent scatter; collection | | Boag 1989 |
| 34 | EeOn-15 | SB(1) | silt | multicomponent scatter; collection | | Boag 1989 |
| 35 | EeOn-16 | SB(1) | cht | multicomponent scatter; collection | | Boag 1989 |
| 36 | EfOm-52 | SB(1) ED(2) CK(1) | SC: silt; ED: krf(2); CK: mc | multicomponent scatter; collection | | Boag 1989 |
| 37 | EfOm-53 | SB(1) | mud | multicomponent scatter; collection | | Boag 1989 |
| 38 | Johnston Locality 17 (EgOq-1) | SB(1) | | | Johnston site "FL" | Glenbow Museum 1965; Wormington and Forbis 1965; Johnston 1975; Pettipas 1980 |
| 39 | Johnston Locality 28 (EgOr-1) | AB(1) SB(4) | | collection | Johnston site "Q"; 25 artifacts of which 18 appear to be KRF | Glenbow Museum 1965; Johnston 1975; Pettipas 1980 |
| 40 | Johnston Locality 15 (EgOv-1) | SB(2) | krf(2) | scatter; collection | in blowouts, Johnston site "DP" | Glenbow Museum 1965; Wormington and Forbis 1965; Johnston 1975; Pettipas 1980; McCullough 1988 |
| 41 | EhOo-2 | AB(1) CK(1) | | multicomponent collection | beside Armitage Lake | Hjermstad 1991 |
| 42 | EhOq-4 | SB(1) | | | Johnston site "FK" | Glenbow Museum 1965; Johnston 1975; Pettipas 1980 |

## Appendix: Cody Site Summary for Alberta (continued)

| | Site Name | Point Type | Lithic Type | Site Type | Notes | Reference |
|---|---|---|---|---|---|---|
| 43 | EhOq-5 | SB(5) | | | Johnston site "D" | Glenbow Museum 1965; Johnston 1975; Pettipas 1980 |
| 44 | Johnston Locality 16 (EhOq-7) | AB(1) SB(1) | krf(2) | scatter; collection | Johnston site "DV" | Glenbow Museum 1965; Wormington and Forbis 1965; Johnston 1975; Pettipas 1980 |
| 45 | Johnston (EhOr-4) | AB(1) | krf | | Johnston site "BG" | Johnston 1975 |
| 46 | EiOx-11 | SB | | multicomponent collection | beside lake | Hjermstad 1991 |
| 47 | Johnston Locality 3 (EjOr-1) | SB(2) | qtzte, src | multicomponent collection | blowouts beside slough, Johnston site "DL" | Glenbow Museum 1965; Wormington and Forbis 1965; Johnston 1975 |
| 48 | Johnston Locality 2 (EjOs-1) | CK(1) AB(1) ED(4) SB(7) | AB: krf(1); SC: krf(1), cht(2), silt(1); ED: krf(1), src(1), cht(1), porc(1); CK: chal(1) | lithic scatter | beside dry slough, Johnston site "BJ" | Glenbow Museum 1965; Wormington and Forbis 1965; Johnston 1975; Pettipas 1980 |
| 49 | Schowalter (EjOs) | AB(1) | krf | isolated surface find | on prominent drumlin | Royal Alberta Museum, Tim Schowalter Collection |
| 50 | Johnston Locality 10 (EjOt-1) | SB(5) | | surface collection | Johnston site "GI" | Glenbow Museum 1965; Wormington and Forbis 1965; Johnston 1975; Pettipas 1980 |
| 51 | Johnston Locality 8 (EjOt-2) | SB(1) ED(1) AB(1) | AB(krf) | multicomponent (Clovis and Cody) collection | Johnston site "GC" | Glenbow Museum 1965; Wormington and Forbis 1965; Johnston 1975; Pettipas 1980; Head 1989 |
| 52 | Johnston Locality 9 (EjOu-1) | ED(1) SB(5) | "local" | collection | Johnston site "GH" | Glenbow Museum 1965; Wormington and Forbis 1965; Johnston 1975; Pettipas 1980 |
| 53 | EjOu-11 | ED | | multicomponent collection | | Hjermstad 1991 |
| 54 | EjOu-20 | SB(1) | | multicomponent collection | | Hjermstad 1991 |
| 55 | EkOm-3 | SB AB ED | | multicomponent isolated find | on sandy hill | Boag 1989 |
| 56 | EkOm-4 | SB AB ED | | multicomponent scatter; collection | | Boag 1989 |
| 57 | EkOm-5 | ED(2) SB(5) | | multicomponent scatter; collection | sandy hills | Boag 1989 |
| 58 | EkOn-5 | CK(1) | | multicomponent collection | | Hjermstad 1991 |

| | Site Name | Point Type | Lithic Type | Site Type | Notes | Reference |
|---|---|---|---|---|---|---|
| 59 | EkOp-10 | SB(1) | src? | buried multicomponent workshop/campsite | on gently sloping rise overlooking outwash channel | Brumley 1977 |
| 60 | Johnston Locality 4 (EkOr-1) | SB(35) ED(13) AB(3) | AB: krf(1), cht(1); SC: src(3), cht(2), mc(2); ED: src(5), krf(1), cht(1) | multicomponent campsite; collection | near slough, Johnston site "FR" | Glenbow Museum 1965; Wormington and Forbis 1965; Johnston 1975; Pettipas 1980 |
| 61 | Johnston Locality 5 (EkOr-2) | CK(1) SB(3) ED(4) | SC: krf(1); ED: krf(2), chal(2); CK: krf(1) | workshop; collection | blowout on high ground beside slough, Johnston site "DR"; 25 of 37 artifacts apparently krf | Glenbow Museum 1965; Wormington and Forbis 1965; Johnston 1975; Pettipas 1980 |
| 62 | Johnston Locality 6 (EkOr-3) | SB(6) | | collection | blowout on gravel knoll, Johnston site "FS" | Glenbow Museum 1965; Wormington and Forbis 1965; Johnston 1975; Pettipas 1980 |
| 63 | Johnston Locality 32 (EkOr-4) | AB/ SB(3) | | | Johnston site "DK" | Glenbow Museum 1965; Johnston 1975; Pettipas 1980 |
| 64 | Johnston Locality 1 (EkOs-1) | AB(2) ED(4) SB(10) CK(3) | AB: cht(1), krf(1); SC: src(3), krf(3), cht(1); silt(1); ED: krf(2), src(1), cht(1); CK: krf(1) | multicomponent collection | on hill beside dry lake, assemblage includes a tanged krf pendant and microblade, Johnston site "DJ" | Glenbow Museum 1965; Wormington and Forbis 1965; Johnston 1975; Pettipas 1980 |
| 65 | Johnston Locality 7 (EkOs-2) | AB/ SB(3) | krf(2), obs(1) | | Johnston site "FX" | Glenbow Museum 1965; Wormington and Forbis 1965; Johnston 1975; Pettipas 1980 |
| 66 | EkOs-4 | SB(1) | krf | scatter; collection | | Boag 1989 |
| 67 | Johnston Locality 11 (EkOt-2) | AB(2) | krf, cht | multicomponent (Hell Gap and Cody) collection | Johnston site "GK" | Glenbow Museum 1965; Wormington and Forbis 1965; Johnston 1975; Pettipas 1980 |
| 68 | Johnston Locality 14 (EkOt-3) | SB(2) | | | Johnston site "GL" | Glenbow Museum 1965; Wormington and Forbis 1965; Johnston 1975 |
| 69 | Johnston Locality 13 (EkOt-4) | AB/ SB(1) | | multicomponent collection | Johnston site "GM" | Glenbow Museum 1965; Wormington and Forbis 1965; Johnston 1975 |
| 70 | Johnston Locality 12 (EkOu-1) | SB(7) | | | Johnston site "GO" | Glenbow Museum 1965; Wormington and Forbis 1965; Johnston 1975; Pettipas 1980 |
| 71 | EkOu-4 | SB(1) ED(1) | | multicomponent collection | | Hjermstad 1991 |

## Appendix: Cody Site Summary for Alberta (continued)

| | Site Name | Point Type | Lithic Type | Site Type | Notes | Reference |
|---|---|---|---|---|---|---|
| 72 | EkOx-17 | SB | | multicomponent scatter; collection | | Boag 1989 |
| 73 | EkOx-18 | SB | | multicomponent scatter; collection | | Boag 1989 |
| 74 | EkOx-19 | AB<br>SB<br>ED | | multicomponent scatter; collection | | Boag 1989 |
| 75 | EkOx-22 | ED | | multicomponent collection | bank of Berry Creek tributary | Hjermstad 1991 |
| 76 | ElOw-2 | SB(2) | | multicomponent scatter; collection | | Boag 1989 |
| 77 | ElOw-3 | AB<br>SB<br>ED | | multicomponent scatter; collection | | Boag 1989 |
| 78 | ElOw-4 | AB<br>SB<br>ED | | multicomponent scatter; collection | | Boag 1989 |
| 79 | ElOx-7 | AB<br>SB<br>ED | | multicomponent scatter; collection | | Boag 1989 |
| 80 | ElOx-9 | CK(1) | chal | multicomponent scatter; collection | | Boag 1989 |
| 81 | Bill Woods Collection (EO block) | AB(2) | chal, arg | multicomponent scatter; collection | | Wood et al. 1993 |
| 82 | Brad Wuerfel Collection (EeOo block) | CK(1) | krf | surface collection | near Cavendish | Wood et al. 1993 |
| 83 | Doug Meloney Collection (EO block) | AB | | surface collection | Sandy Point | Wood et al. 1993 |
| 84 | Doug Meloney Collection (EgOn block) | AB(1) | chal | surface collection | Acadia Valley | Wood et al. 1993 |
| 85 | George Woods Site (EO block) | SB(1)<br>ED(1) | src | surface collection | | Wood et al. 1993 Bill Woods Collection |
| 86 | Robin Woods Collection (EfOn block) | AB(5)<br>SB(2) | AB: src(1), krf(3), chal(1), SB: porc(1), qtzte(1) | surface collection | between Bindloss and Empress | Wood et al. 1993 |
| 87 | EaPc-4 | ED | | multicomponent collection | | Hjermstad 1991 |
| 88 | EaPe-39 | ED(1) | | isolated find; collection | in dried-up slough | Hjermstad 1991 |
| 89 | EaPg-25 | ED | | multicomponent collection | blowout on hillside | Hjermstad 1991 |
| 90 | EaPg-31 | AB(1)<br>SB(1) | | multicomponent collection | | Hjermstad 1991 |
| 91 | Yogi Bear Blow (EaPh-6) | SB(1)<br>ED(1) | | multicomponent collection | blowouts | Hjermstad 1991 |
| 92 | Alberta Blow (EaPh-9) | AB(2) | | multicomponent scatter; collection | blowouts beside Little Bow valley | Hjermstad 1991 |

| | Site Name | Point Type | Lithic Type | Site Type | Notes | Reference |
|---|---|---|---|---|---|---|
| 93 | Old Toboggan Blowouts (EaPh-20) | SB(2) | | multicomponent collection | blowouts | Hjermstad 1991 |
| 94 | EaPh-27 | AB(1) | | multicomponent collection | | Hjermstad 1991 |
| 95 | EaPm-9 | SB(1) | | scatter | | Arch. Survey Alberta 2011 et seq. (Permit 86-039) |
| 96 | EaPm-33 | SB(1) | | buried kill site | on terrace; associated bone was described as much bigger than modern bison | Vivian et al. 2006 (ASA Permit 02-051) |
| 97 | EbPf-32 | ED(1) | | isolated find; collection | | Hjermstad 1991 |
| 98 | EcPp-29 | SB(1) | silt | buried | upper terrace of Highwood River | Youell 2007 |
| 99 | Little Pasture, South (EdPk-3) | SB(15)<br>ED(>2) | SB: chal?(9), obs(4), qtzte(2) | scatter | on ridge overlooking Frank Lake | Glenbow Museum 1958; Wilson et al. 2011 |
| 100 | Little Bow, Fraser (EdPk-4) | SB<br>ED | | campsite | north bank of Little Bow River | Glenbow Museum 1958 |
| 101 | Noble NE (EdPk-5) | AB<br>SB | | multicomponent campsite | edge of Little Bow valley | Glenbow Museum 1957 and 1958 |
| 102 | MacLeod North (EdPk-6) | ED | | campsite | flat area near sloughs | Glenbow Museum 1958 |
| 103 | MacLeod Centre (EdPk-7) | ED | | campsite | flat area near sloughs | Glenbow Museum 1958 |
| 104 | Little Pasture (EdPk-9) | SB | | campsite | flat ridge above Frank Lake | Glenbow Museum 1958 |
| 105 | Calahan North (EdPk-11) | SB<br>ED | | campsite | | Glenbow Museum 1957 and 1958 |
| 106 | High River Eden (EdPk-17) | ED | | scatter; campsite | blowout on high land | Glenbow Museum 1957; Arch. Survey Alberta 2011 et seq. |
| 107 | EdPk-37 | SB(1) | | multicomponent campsite | surface find on ridge | Balcom 1985; Landals 1996 |
| 108 | EdPk-45 | AB(1)<br>SB(24)<br>ED(10) | | multicomponent collection | blowouts | Hjermstad 1991 |
| 109 | EdPl-15 | SB? | | multicomponent campsite | dubious, on slight rise | Balcom 1985 |
| 110 | EdPl-39 | AB(1) | | multicomponent collection | blowouts | Hjermstad 1991 |
| 111 | EePk-74 | SB(1) | | campsite; kill site | on hummocky moraine beside Kettle Lake | U of Calgary 1971 |
| 112 | Highwood Burial Coop's Hill (EePk-272) | SB | | multicomponent campsite | surface on high terrace overlooking Highwood River | McCullough 1988 |
| 113 | EePl-138 | SB or ED(1) | | campsite | Highwood River valley edge | U of Calgary 1971 |
| 114 | Rye (EePl-195) | AB(1) | | campsite | | U of Calgary 1972 |
| 115 | EePn-82 | ED | | multicomponent collection | | Hjermstad 1991 |

**Appendix: Cody Site Summary for Alberta (continued)**

| | Site Name | Point Type | Lithic Type | Site Type | Notes | Reference |
|---|---|---|---|---|---|---|
| 116 | Three Boulder Blow (EfPi-9) | ED | | multicomponent scatter; collection | blowout in dry slough beside hill | Hjermstad 1991 |
| 117 | EfPi-17 | ED(3) CD(1?) | ED: cht(2), silt(1); CD: qtzte(1) | buried, stratified multicomponent campsite | Cody material 35–50 cm deep at base of sandy silt above lacustrine deposit | Hanna 2002 |
| 118 | Garriott (EfPj-13) | SB(1) | | multicomponent scatter; collection | on knoll | Hjermstad 1991 |
| 119 | EfPk-4 | SB(1) | | campsite; kill site | on Bow River Valley edge | U of Calgary 1971 |
| 120 | M.C.C. (EfPl-173) | AB | | multicomponent scatter; campsite | on first terrace of Bow River | Arch. Survey Alberta 2011 et seq. |
| 121 | Anita's Knoll (EgPi-6) | ED | | multicomponent collection | on knoll | Hjermstad 1991 |
| 122 | EgPn-480 | CD(1) | silt | multicomponent campsite | point base, 9540 ± 70 (Beta-127235) | De Mille and Head 2001 |
| 123 | Sibbald Creek (EgPr-2) | SB(1) | silt | buried multicomponent campsite in meadow beside creek | Cody point found 40–45 cm below surface; at same depth as other Paleoindian points and tools | Gryba 1983a |
| 124 | Eden Blow (EhPj-8) | ED | | multicomponent scatter; collection | in blowout | Hjermstad 1991 |
| 125 | Bad Weather Blow (EhPj-19) | SB(1) | | multicomponent collection | in blowout | Hjermstad 1991 |
| 126 | Lake Minnewanka (EhPu-1 or 349R) | AB/ SB(3) | | buried stratified multicomponent campsite | surface finds from eroding stratified site | Christensen 1971 |
| 127 | Norquay (EhPv-15 or 156R) | AB(1) | | multicomponent buried campsite | | Fedje and White 1984; Fedje 1988 |
| 128 | EhPw-2 | SB(1) | | campsite | eroded out of surface on high bench overlooking Bow River | Christensen 1971 |
| 129 | EiPc-23 | CD?(1) | src | isolated find | distal point portion, in knob-and-kettle terrain near tributary of Red Deer River | Gryba and Stirling 2001 |
| 130 | Hump Hill (EiPj-4) | SB | | multicomponent collection | on hill beside dry lake, other early types also | Hjermstad 1991 |
| 131 | Spike Blow (EiPj-5) | AB(2) SB(2) | | multicomponent collection | blowout | Hjermstad 1991 |
| 132 | EjPa-8 | ED | | multicomponent scatter; collection | on top of hill | Hjermstad 1991 |
| 133 | EjPa-9 | ED | | multicomponent collection | | Hjermstad 1991 |
| 134 | EjPa-17 | AB(1) | | multicomponent collection | | Hjermstad 1991 |
| 135 | EjPa-22 | SB(1) | | multicomponent collection | | Hjermstad 1991 |
| 136 | EjPb-5 | SB(1) | | multicomponent (Folsom and Cody) collection | | Hjermstad 1991 |

|  | Site Name | Point Type | Lithic Type | Site Type | Notes | Reference |
|---|---|---|---|---|---|---|
| 137 | EjPb-6 | ED |  | multicomponent collection | rolling land | Hjermstad 1991 |
| 138 | Walking Crow (EjPj-19) | SB(1) |  | multicomponent collection |  | Hjermstad 1991 |
| 139 | New House Blow (EjPj-8) | ED |  | multicomponent collection | blowout | Hjermstad 1991 |
| 140 | EjPo-36 | CK(1) |  | campsite | cultivated field | Duncan and Murray 1971; Reeves and McCullough 1976 |
| 141 | EjPo-116 | CD(1) |  | campsite | on ridge | U of Calgary 1971 |
| 142 | EjPo-141 | AB(1) |  | multicomponent collection | on top of hill | Hjermstad 1991 |
| 143 | EjPo-144 | ED |  | multicomponent collection |  | Hjermstad 1991 |
| 144 | Waterstreets Knoll (EjPp-40) | ED |  | collection | on knoll beside creek | Hjermstad 1991 |
| 145 | EkPa-3 | ED(1) | krf | collection |  | Boag 1989 |
| 146 | EkPb-4 | SB |  | scatter; collection |  | Boag 1989 |
| 147 | Alberta Bob (EkPj-12) | AB(1) |  | multicomponent collection |  | Hjermstad 1991 |
| 148 | EkPn-6 | AB(1)<br>SB(1)<br>ED(2) |  | multicomponent collection | beside slough | Hjermstad 1991 |
| 149 | EkPp-2 | AB(1) |  | campsite |  | McFee 1979 (ASA Permit 78-075) |
| 150 | EkPu-8 | SB(1) | silt | multicomponent buried site | on bench overlooking mountain meadow | Ronaghan 1993, Arch. Survey Alberta 2011 et seq. |
| 151 | Scapa Ribstone (ElPa-1) | SB(1) | krf | deeply stratified multicomponent campsite | on ridge overlooking Sullivan Lake basin to the east | Hanna and Neal 1992; Head 1997 |
| 152 | ElPa-17 | SB |  | multicomponent scatter; collection |  | Boag 1989 |
| 153 | ElPk-2 | SB(1) |  | grass circle | described as "Yuma"; on drumlin overlooking Knee-hills Lake | Glenbow Museum 1961 |
| 154 | Rosebud Hill, East (ElPl-10) | SB(3) |  | multicomponent scatter; kill site | on hill | Hjermstad 1991 |
| 155 | Native Camp (ElPm-4) | AB/ SB(1) | krf | multicomponent scatter; collection |  | Boag 1989 |
| 156 | Armin Dyck Collection (EbPd block) | SB(1) | chal | surface collection | Travers | Wood et al. 1993 |
| 157 | Elsie Kitchener Collection (EP block) EK15 | AB(1) | cht | surface collection | on eroding hill | Wood 1991 |
| 158 | Tom MacPhail Collection (EePc block) TMP2 | SB(1) | cht | surface collection | point base, Bassano | Wood 1991 |
| 159 | Gordon Dibble Collection (EP block) GD1 | SB(1) | KRF | surface collection | Eagle Valley | Boag 1989 |

## Appendix: Cody Site Summary for Alberta (continued)

| | Site Name | Point Type | Lithic Type | Site Type | Notes | Reference |
|---|---|---|---|---|---|---|
| 160 | Mary McMurty Collection (EkPq block) MM1 | SB(4) | mc(2), krf, silt | collection | Bearberry Valley | Boag 1989 |
| 161 | Hugh Bower Collection (EP block) | AB(1)<br>SB(2) | | | Carstairs/ Nier vicinity | Wormington and Forbis 1965 |
| 162 | EjQa-5 | CD ?(1) | | collection | alpine bench beside stream | Arch. Survey Alberta 2011 et seq. |
| 163 | FaOr-10 | AB(1)<br>SB(2)<br>ED(1) | AB: krf;<br>SC: cht(2);<br>ED: qtzte | multicomponent scatter; collection | | Boag 1989 |
| 164 | FcOx-17 | SB(8)<br>CK(1)<br>ED(n=?) | SC: src(4), cht(2), mc(1), krf(1);<br>CK: krf | scatter; collection | large multicomponent surface scatter | Boag 1989 |
| 165 | FeOs-46 | SB(1) | cht | multicomponent campsite | high-quality chert, surface find on high hill top | McCullough and Landals 1995 |
| 166 | Fluney (FiOp-1) | AB(1) | | campsite; workshop | | Prov. Museum of Alberta 1973 |
| 167 | FiOp-13 | SB | | multicomponent scatter; collection | | Boag 1989 |
| 168 | FiOq-6 | SB | | multicomponent scatter; collection | | Boag 1989 |
| 169 | Todd Ree Collection (FiOr block) | AB(1) | krf | surface | in Vermilion 1 km from glacial outwash channel | Royal Alberta Museum files |
| 170 | Lee Ahlstrom Collection (FkOu block) | AB(1) | krf | surface | near Beauvallon adjacent to slough | Royal Alberta Museum files |
| 171 | Merland (FlOt-2) | SB(1) | | scatter; campsite | adjacent to slough | Newton and Fedirchuk 1982 |
| 172 | FaPc-2 | AB?(1) | | multicomponent scatter; collection | | Boag 1989 |
| 173 | FaPl-8 | SB | | multicomponent scatter; collection | | Boag 1989 |
| 174 | FaPl-11 | SB(1) | qtzte | multicomponent scatter; collection | on terrace | Boag 1989 |
| 175 | FaPl-12 | SB(1) | cht | multicomponent scatter; collection | | Boag 1989 |
| 176 | Blair Marshall's Land (FaPl-30) | AB(1) | agate | campsite; collection | | Red Deer and District Museum 1983 |
| 177 | FaPm-4 | SB(1)<br>ED(1) | SC: mud;<br>ED: cht | multicomponent scatter; collection | | Boag 1989 |
| 178 | FaPm-5 | ED | | multicomponent scatter; collection | on sandy ridge | Boag 1989 |
| 179 | FaPn-83 | ED(1) | qtzte | multicomponent scatter; collection | on terrace | Boag 1989 |
| 180 | FaPo-24 | SB(1) | krf | scatter; collection | | Boag 1989 |
| 181 | FaPo-25 | AB(1) | | multicomponent collection | beside slough | Hjermstad 1991 |
| 182 | FaPq-10 | SB(1)<br>ED(1) | SC: krf;<br>ED: cht | multicomponent scatter; collection | on sandy ridge | Gorham 1997; Boag 1989 |

| | Site Name | Point Type | Lithic Type | Site Type | Notes | Reference |
|---|---|---|---|---|---|---|
| 183 | FaPq-17 | AB(1) | | multicomponent collection | on top of knoll near spring | Hjermstad 1991 |
| 184 | Wilfort (FbPe-1) | SB<br>ED(3) | | collection | blowouts on sandy knolls | U of Alberta 1965; Royal Alberta Museum files, Graham Collection |
| 185 | Alberta Gas Ethylene Plant (FbPj-23) | SB(1) | | isolated find | at base of large hill | Red Deer and District Museum 1983 |
| 186 | Bower Home (FbPk-1) | SB | | campsite; collection | cultivated high land near creek | Glenbow Museum 1959 |
| 187 | Hugh Bower Collection (FP block) | AB(1)<br>SB(4)<br>ED(1)<br>CK(1) | | | | Wormington and Forbis 1965 |
| 188 | Big Knife (FbPm-5) | SB(1) | | multicomponent collection | | Hjermstad 1991 |
| 189 | FcPb-5 | CK(1) | krf | campsite | on surface of plowed ridge NW of Paint-Earth Creek | Arch. Survey Alberta 2011 et seq. (Permit 75-002) |
| 190 | FcPb-19 | AB(1) | krf | scatter; campsite | high ridge beside slough | Boag 1989 |
| 191 | FcPb-29 | ED | | multicomponent scatter; collection | beside creek | Boag 1989 |
| 192 | Red Willow (FcPc-1) | SB | | scatter; campsite | on ridge beside creek | Boag 1989 |
| 193 | FcPc-4 | AB(1) | | multicomponent scatter; collection | flat terrain | Boag 1989 |
| 194 | FcPc-6 | AB ?(1) | | multicomponent scatter; collection | on knobby hill beside creek | Boag 1989 |
| 195 | FcPc-7 | SB(1) | | multicomponent scatter; collection | on flat sandy ridge | Boag 1989 |
| 196 | FcPc-11 | SB(2) | qtzte, wood | multicomponent scatter; collection | | Boag 1989 |
| 197 | FcPd-2 | SB(1)<br>ED(3) | SC: krf;<br>ED: cht(2), src(1) | multicomponent scatter; collection | large amounts of krf debitage observed | Boag 1989 |
| 198 | FcPf-17 | ED | | campsite?; collection | possible point cache | Red Deer and District Museum 1983 |
| 199 | FcPk-34 | ED(1) | qtzte | multicomponent scatter; collection | | Boag 1989 |
| 200 | FcPl-10 | ED | | multicomponent collection | | Hjermstad 1991 |
| 201 | FcPo-7 | SB(1)<br>ED(1) | SC: cht;<br>ED: mud | multicomponent scatter; collection | | Boag 1989 |
| 202 | FcPo-10 | SB(1) | cht | multicomponent scatter; collection | | Boag 1989 |
| 203 | Boss Hill (FdPe-4) | ED(1)<br>CD?(1) | CD: krf | multicomponent kill site, campsite | surface finds near prominent hill | Kidd 1978; Doll 1980 |
| 204 | FdPk-9 | ED | sand | scatter; collection | | Boag 1989 |
| 205 | FdPg-23 | SB(2) | src, silt | multicomponent scatter; collection | on rise overlooking Gadsby Lake | Boag 1989 |
| 206 | FdPh-17 | SB(2)<br>ED(2) | SC: cht(2);<br>ED: silt, qtzte | multicomponent scatter; collection | | Boag 1989 |

## Appendix: Cody Site Summary for Alberta (continued)

| | Site Name | Point Type | Lithic Type | Site Type | Notes | Reference |
|---|---|---|---|---|---|---|
| 207 | FdPh-19 | AB(1) | silt | multicomponent scatter; collection | | Boag 1989 |
| 208 | FdPk-1 | SB(1) | krf | multicomponent scatter; collection | | Boag 1989 |
| 209 | FdPl-13 | SB(1) | | isolated find; collection | | Hjermstad 1991 |
| 210 | FdPp-1 | SB(1) | quartzite | multicomponent campsite; collection | beside high ridge and outwash channel | Royal Alberta Museum files |
| 211 | FdPr-4 | CK(1) | | collection | | Boag 1989 |
| 212 | FdPr-5 | ED(1) | qtzte | collection | | Boag 1989 |
| 213 | FdPu-2 | SB(1) | cht | campsite | on sandy knoll overlooking two meadows, near Baptiste River | Gryba 1983b |
| 214 | FePg-19 | SB(4) | qtzte(3), cht | multicomponent scatter; collection | slough area | Boag 1989 |
| 215 | FePk-6 | AB/ SB(1) | krf | scatter; collection | | Boag 1989 |
| 216 | FePn-6 | AB(1) SB(2) ED(1) | AB: silt; SC: silt, qtzte; ED: cht | multicomponent scatter; collection | | Boag 1989 |
| 217 | Driedmeat Hill (FfPe-1) | CD(1) | | campsite; workshop | point base on high hill (kame) overlooking lake | Quigg 1978 |
| 218 | Brown (FfPe-6) | SB(1) | krf | isolated find | sloughs nearby | Royal Alberta Museum files |
| 219 | Fullerton (FfPi-1) | SB(3) | qtzte, krf, chal | stratified multicomponent campsite | on hilltop | Taylor 1969; Gibson 1987 |
| 220 | FgPl-4 | SB(1) | chal | multicomponent scatter; collection | | Boag 1989 |
| 221 | FhPh-5 | SB(1) | | multicomponent collection | in coulee | Hjermstad 1991 |
| 222 | Nacuk (FhPl-10) | SB(2) ED(2) | SC: sand, qtzte; ED: mc, src | multicomponent scatter; collection | | Boag 1989 |
| 223 | Lawrence (FhPm-1) | SB(2) ED(1) | SC: krf, qtzte; ED: qtzte | scatter; campsite | hummocky terrain | Boag 1989 |
| 224 | FhPm-16 | ED(1) | | multicomponent scatter; collection | | Boag 1989 |
| 225 | FhPm-24 | SB(2) | chal, cht | multicomponent scatter; collection | | Boag 1989 |
| 226 | FhPn-21 | SB(1) | | campsite | beside large kettle bog | Damp and Reeves 1981 |
| 227 | FhPn-75 | SB(1) | cht | campsite | ridge top | Van Dyke and Damp 1981 |
| 228 | Bruce Morden (FhPn-137) | SB(1) ED(2) | SC: cht; ED: krf, src | scatter | beside Strawberry Creek | Boag 1989 |
| 229 | FhPn-176 | SB(1) | src | scatter; collection | | Boag 1989 |
| 230 | Ackland (FhPr-6) | SB(2) | | collection | | Heitzmann 1980 |
| 231 | Cameron (FhPr-9) | AB(>3) SB(>5), ED | AB: krf(1); SC: silt(2), qtzte(1) | campsite; workshop | on slope overlooking creek | Prov. Museum of Alberta 1976 |

| | Site Name | Point Type | Lithic Type | Site Type | Notes | Reference |
|---|---|---|---|---|---|---|
| 232 | Urkevich Oilwell (FhPr-10) | SB(4) | | campsite | on large hill facing North Saskatchewan River | Prov. Museum of Alberta 1975 |
| 233 | Brooks (FhPr-11) | SB | | multicomponent campsite; collection | beside creek | Smith 1993 |
| 234 | FhPr-14 | SB(2) | | collection | beside creek | Prov. Museum of Alberta 1976 |
| 235 | McCullagh (FhPr-16) | SB(1) | krf | multicomponent collection | | Prov. Museum of Alberta 1976 |
| 236 | Distrohoft (FhPr-20) | SB(2) | arg(silt?), cht | multicomponent collection | beside creek | Prov. Museum of Alberta 1975 |
| 237 | Thomas (FhPr-21) | SB(4) | cht(2) | collection | | Prov. Museum of Alberta 1976 |
| 238 | Urkevich (FhPs-2) | SB | | campsite | low hill beside slough | Prov. Museum of Alberta 1971 |
| 239 | Romanchuk (FhPs-3) | SB(2) | qtzte, cht | collection | | Prov. Museum of Alberta 1976 |
| 240 | FhPs-6 | SB(1) | obs | collection | | Prov. Museum of Alberta 1976 |
| 241 | FhPs-7 | ED | | collection | | Prov. Museum of Alberta 1976 |
| 242 | FiPg-10 | AB(1) | krf | isolated find | | Quigg 1976b |
| 243 | FiPk-5 | SB(1) | | isolated find | | ASA site files |
| 244 | Wensentaylo site (FiPk-76) | SB(1) | | surface collection | | ASA site files, Todd Stiles private collection 1995 |
| 245 | FiPk-81 | AB(1) | krf | | top of broad knoll | Cameron and Kowal 2007 (ASA Permit 07-190) |
| 246 | FiPn-31 | SB(1) | silt | campsite | | Damp and Reeves 1981 |
| 247 | FiPn-194 | AB(1) | | lithic scatter | point base, site on knob | Ronaghan 1983 |
| 248 | FiPo-32 | AB(1) | cht | campsite | on large knoll beside slough | Wright 1978 and 1979 |
| 249 | FiPo-207 | ED | | lithic scatter | | Ronaghan 1983 |
| 250 | FiPo-215 | ED | | multicomponent lithic scatter | on knob | Ronaghan 1983 |
| 251 | FiPo-222 | SB(1) | | multicomponent lithic scatter | on knob | Ronaghan 1983 |
| 252 | FiPr-1 | AB | | campsite | side hill beside ravine | Glenbow Museum 1958 |
| 253 | FjPc-11 | AB(1) | src | isolated find | in field near slough | Wondrasek et al. 1999 |
| 254 | FjPk-29 | AB(1) | | isolated find | prairie level near North Saskatchewan River | McCullough 1991b |
| 255 | FjPt-2 | SB(1) | qtzte | buried multicomponent campsite | beside river | Forner and Brenner 2008 |
| 256 | Kliachik Bison (FkPd-10) | SB(1) | | kill site; collection | | Arch. Survey Alberta 2011 et seq.; Todd Stiles private collection 1995 |

**Appendix: Cody Site Summary for Alberta (continued)**

| | Site Name | Point Type | Lithic Type | Site Type | Notes | Reference |
|---|---|---|---|---|---|---|
| 257 | FkPg-91 | AB/ SB(1) | qtzte | campsite | point base, on sandy rise near creek | Gorham 1996 |
| 258 | FkPg-108 | SB(1) | chert | scatter | in level field | Unfreed and Tischer 2002 |
| 259 | FkPh-2 | SB(1) | | collection | | Prov. Museum of Alberta 1969 |
| 260 | FkPh-47 | AB(1) | krf | scatter | | Kowal and Cameron 2003 (ASA Permit 03-064) |
| 261 | Topolinsky (FlPc-2) | SB(2) | | collection | | U of Alberta 1964; Prov. Museum of Alberta 1972 |
| 262 | FlPc-7 | SB(2) | | multicomponent collection | sand dune blowouts | Hjermstad 1991 |
| 263 | Avonlea (FlPd-3) | SB(1) | | surface collection | | Prov. Museum of Alberta, Todd Stiles private collection 1995 |
| 264 | FlPe-2 | AB/ SB(2) | cht(1) | campsite | | U of Alberta 1964 |
| 265 | Lekochinski (Victoria Trail) site FlPf-27 | CK(1) | | surface collection | Cody knife blade | Prov. Museum of Alberta, Todd Stiles private collection 1995 |
| 266 | Lakusta site (FlPg-69) | SB(1) | krf | surface collection | basal half | Prov. Museum of Alberta, Todd Stiles private collection 1995 |
| 267 | FlPo-6 | SB(1) | | scatter | | Arch. Survey Alberta 2011 et seq. |
| 268 | Rilling (FlPp-2) | AB | qtzte | campsite | | Prov. Museum of Alberta Archaeological Survey 1971 |
| 269 | Wade Collection (FiPi block) | SB(1) | krf | surface collection | Ellerslie | Prov. Museum of Alberta, Wade Collection |
| 270 | Braseau Clovis site (FfQd-8) | SB?(1) | cht | surface | elevated knob (kame?) | Meyer 2007 (ASA Permit 05-472) |
| 271 | FfQh-24 | | | multicomponent workshop with krf debitage interpreted as Cody | elevated bench between two creeks | Meyer et al. 2007 |
| 272 | FfQh-26 | AB or SB(4) | cht(1) krf(3) | campsite | point base, on prominent hill at confluence of several creeks with McLeod River | Landals et al. 1998; Meyer et al. 2007 |
| 273 | FfQh-27 | SB or AB(1) | | large buried multicomponent campsite/ workshop | possible failed Scottsbluff point, on high terrace at confluence of two creeks | Kulle and Neal 1998 |
| 274 | Palisades Paleoindian (FfQm-56) | AB/ CD(1) | | scatter | beside bog | Pickard 1985 |

|  | Site Name | Point Type | Lithic Type | Site Type | Notes | Reference |
|---|---|---|---|---|---|---|
| 275 | Lovettville (FgQe-3) | SB(1) |  | scatter; campsite | on alluvial fan terrace beside Lovett River | Reeves 1976 |
| 276 | FgQf-62 | Nezu/ CK(1) | qtzte | workshop |  | Meyer and Reeves 2002 (ASA Permit 01-296) |
| 277 | Shane's site (FgQg-70) | AB/ SB(1) | cht |  | terrace overlooking Macleod River | Meyer and Roe 2006 (ASA Permit 05-206) |
| 278 | FgQm-6 | AB(1) | mud/silt | campsite | lower terrace on west side of Athabasca River | Elliott 1970–71 |
| 279 | Swan Landing (FhQl-4) | AB(1) | silt | buried campsite | 8675 ± 270 (S-2178) | Ball 1983 |
| 280 | 2211R (FQ Block) | SB ?(1) | quartz crystal | buried campsite | mountain terrace overlooking valley | Parks Canada site files 2007 |
| 281 | GcOo-3 | ED(1) | cht | kill site | point tip, surface find near creek | Heitzmann 1980 |
| 282 | Duckett (GdOo-16) | SB(1)<br>AB(1)<br>CD(1) |  | multicomponent campsite; workshop | surface finds at north end of Ethel Lake | Landals et al. 1998; McCullough 1981; Reeves and McCullough 1978 |
| 283 | GaPg-3 | AB(1) | krf | isolated find |  | Royal Alberta Museum, Mike and Peter Small Collection |
| 284 | GaPg-4 | SB(1) | krf | isolated find |  | Royal Alberta Museum, Mike and Peter Small Collection |
| 285 | GaPq-1 | SB | chal | scatter |  | U of Alberta 1964, A. Schlitter donation |
| 286 | GaPq-4 | ED<br>SB(2 or 3) |  | scatter | low ridge | U of Alberta 1964 |
| 287 | GbPl-2 | SB |  | isolated find |  | Prov. Museum of Alberta 1972 |
| 288 | Fisher (GbPo-1) | AB(1)<br>SB(14)<br>ED(4)<br>CK | AB: silt;<br>SC: krf(5), qtzte(5), cht(2), bas(1), chal(1);<br>ED: krf, brss, silt, qtzte | surface scatter; collection | large multicomponent site area on elevated terrain on east side of Shoal Lake, near Barrhead | Boag 1989 |
| 289 | Turkawski (GcPg-1) | AB(1) |  | isolated find | on drumlin-like hill beside marsh | Arch. Survey Alberta 2011 et seq. |
| 290 | GdPf-4 | AB(1)<br>SB(5) | AB: krf;<br>SC: krf, mc, prc, silt, qtzte | multicomponent scatter; collection |  | Boag 1989 |
| 291 | Sid Alexander Collection (GdPf-6) | AB(1),<br>SB(4) | AB: krf;<br>SC: krf(1), prc(1), mc(1), sand(1) | multicomponent collection | Boyle | Boag 1989 |
| 292 | Kaliel (GdPm-1) | AB |  | multicomponent campsite | blowouts on dunes near French Creek | Arch. Survey Alberta 2011 et seq. (Permit 77-104) |
| 293 | Dmitruk (GfPf-1) | AB(1) | krf | isolated find |  | Le Blanc 1983 |

**Appendix: Cody Site Summary for Alberta (continued)**

| | Site Name | Point Type | Lithic Type | Site Type | Notes | Reference |
|---|---|---|---|---|---|---|
| 294 | GfPt-13 | AB(1) | qtzte | subsurface scatter | upper of two terraces | Cloutier 2006 (ASA Permit 05-378) |
| 295 | Joe Papastasis Cabin (GdQm-1) | CD(1) | qtzte | scatter | on high hill with year round spring | Fedirchuk et al. 1998 (ASA Permit 96-063) |
| 296 | GgQo-3 | CD | | multicomponent kill site (Bison) | on dune beside lake | Arch. Survey Alberta 2011 et seq. (Permit 92-049) |
| 297 | GgQt-10 | AB CD?(3) | qtzte, cht(2) | multicomponent campsite | on dunes beside large slough; points described as "crude" | Fedirchuk and Bailey 2002 |
| 298 | GhQr-2 | ED(1) | | surface | | Arch. Survey Alberta 2011 et seq. (Permit 97-062) |
| 299 | GhQt-5 | AB/ SB?(1) | | isolated find | point base, beside slough | McCullough 1991a |
| 300 | GhQu | SB(2) | krf, qtzte | surface collection | | Royal Alberta Museum files |
| 301 | GhQx | AB(1) | | surface collection | | Royal Alberta Museum files |
| 302 | Burley (GiQf-4) | ED? | | scatter | beside marsh in glacial spillway | U of Alberta 1989 |
| 303 | GiQq-6 | AB(1) | | campsite, surface collection | | Prov. Museum of Alberta 1969, Kulicki Collection |
| 304 | GiQt-1 | AB(2) | | campsite, surface collection | La Glace | Prov. Museum of Alberta 1969, Richard Dahl Collection |
| 305 | GjQh | SB(1) | cht | scatter | Peavine Creek | Royal Alberta Museum files, Primeau Collection |
| 306 | Henry Taylor Collection (GgQs block) | ED | | surface collection | along Pipestone Creek | Peace River Archaeology Society 1996 |
| 307 | Jerry Cameron Collection (GgQs block) | SB | | surface collection | Wembley | Royal Alberta Museum files |
| 308 | Eric Anderson Collection (GgQs block) | AB(4) SB(3) | | surface collection | Wembley and Belloy | Peace River Archaeology Society 1996 |
| 309 | Ken Lawrence Collection (GgQv block) | AB(1) | | surface collection | Elmworth | Peace River Archaeology Society 1996 |
| 310 | Beaverlodge (GhQu block) | AB(1) SB(1) | AB: krf; SC: qtzte | surface collection | Beaverlodge | Royal Alberta Museum files |
| 311 | Wilson Will Collection (GhQv block) | AB/ SB(3) | | surface collection | Hythe, near a slough | Peace River Archaeology Society 1996 |
| 312 | Richard Primeau Collection (GkQg) | | | | Falher, Peavine Creek drainage near a slough | Arch. Survey Alberta 2011 et seq. |
| 313 | E. H. Littman Collection (GkQo block) | SB | | surface collection | Wanham | Peace River Archaeology Society 1996 |

| | Site Name | Point Type | Lithic Type | Site Type | Notes | Reference |
|---|---|---|---|---|---|---|
| 314 | Nick Poohkay (GlQl block) | SB(2) | cht, obs | surface collection | | Peace River Archaeology Society 1997 |
| 315 | GsQi block (La Glace) | AB(1) | qtzte | surface collection | La Glace | Royal Alberta Museum files |
| 316 | Russell Emerson Collection (GQ block) | SB(1) | | surface collection | | Peace River Archaeology Society 1996 |
| 317 | Thorvald Christensen Collection (GQ block) | AB, SB | | surface collection | | Peace River Archaeology Society 1996 |
| 318 | Otto Woisetchlager Collection (GQ block) | AB(1) SB(2) ED(1) | | surface collection | | Peace River Archaeology Society 1996 |
| 319 | GQ block | AB(1) | prc | surface collection | | Royal Alberta Museum files, unknown collector |
| 320 | Nezu (HhOu-36) | SB(2-4) | brss | campsite; workshop | on ridge | Shortt et al. 1998; Saxberg and Reeves 2003 |
| 321 | Corridor 13 (HhOv-4) | ED | brss | scatter; workshop | raised sandy area | Saxberg et al. 1998; Ball and Kowal 2001; Saxberg and Reeves 2003 |
| 322 | HhOv-65 | CD | brss | scatter; workshop | small elevated dune in muskeg | Ball and Kowal 2001 |
| 323 | HhOv-123 | SB(1) | brss | scatter | raised sandy ridge | Saxberg et al. 1998 |
| 324 | HhOv-159 | ED | brss | workshop | raised sandy area | Saxberg et al. 1998; Saxberg and Reeves 2003 |
| 325 | HhOv-184 | Nezu/ SB(2) | qtzte(2) | scatter | | Clarke and Ronaghan 2000 (ASA Permit 99-073) |
| 326 | HhOv-196 | ED | brss | workshop | small elevated landform in muskeg | Saxberg et al. 1998; Saxberg and Reeves 2003 |
| 327 | HhOw-2 | AB/ Kamut? (1) | brss | scatter; campsite | highway right-of-way | Losey et al. 1974 |
| 328 | Creaky Pine Site (HiOu-56) | SB(1) | qtzte | isolated find | | Somer 2005 (ASA Permit 04-192) |
| 329 | HiOu-69 | Nezu/ SB(1) | lime | subsurface isolated find | elevated landform | Somer 2005 (ASA Permit 04-192) |
| 330 | HQ block (Hines Creek) | AB(1) | prc | surface collection | | Royal Alberta Museum files, unknown collector |
| 331 | Penner/Peace Point Site (IgPc-1) | CK?(1) | | buried campsite | bank of Peace River | Fedirchuk 1973 |

*Point types:* AB, Alberta; CD, Cody; CK, Cody knife; ED, Eden; SC, Scottsbluff.
*Lithic types:* arg, argillite; bas, basalt; brss, Beaver River silicified sandstone; chal, chalcedony; cht, chert; krf, Knife River flint; lime, silicified limestone; mc, Montana chert; mud, mudstone/siliceous mudstone; obs, obsidian; oth, other; porc, porcellanite; prc, Peace River chert; qtzte, quartzite; sand, siliceous sandstone; silt, siltstone/siliceous siltstone; src, Swan River chert; tuff, welded tuff; wood, silicified wood.

## References


Adams, Gary
1976 *Prehistoric Survey of the Lower Red Deer River, 1975*. Archaeological Survey of Alberta Occasional Paper No. 3. Alberta Culture and Multiculturalism, Edmonton.

Agenbroad, Larry D.
1978 *The Hudson-Meng Site: An Alberta Bison Kill in the Nebraska High Plains*. University Press of America, Washington, D.C.

Archaeological Survey of Alberta
2011 Archaeological Sites Inventory Database. Archaeological Survey of Alberta, Historic Resources Management Branch, Alberta Culture and Community Spirit, Edmonton.

Bailey, Jeff
1992 Letter on file at the Royal Alberta Museum.

Balcom, Rebecca J.
1985 *Historical Resources Impact Assessment, Mazeppa Gas Project: Final Report (ASA 85-028)*. Report on file, Archaeological Survey of Alberta, Edmonton.

Ball, Bruce F.
1983 *Archaeology of the Athabasca River Valley between Jasper and Hinton, 1981: Final Report (ASA 81-065)*. Report on file, Archaeological Survey of Alberta, Edmonton.
1986 Site Classification and Prehistoric Settlement Systems in the Upper Athabasca River Valley. In *Final Report of the 1985 and 1986 Field Season at Head-Smashed-In Buffalo Jump*, edited by Brian Ronaghan, pp. 133–159. Archaeological Survey of Alberta Occasional Paper No. 30. Alberta Culture and Multiculturalism, Edmonton.

Ball, Bruce F., and Walter A. Kowal
2001 *Historical Resources Impact Assessment, Proposed Highway 63:14 Upgrade, Athabasca River Crossing to km 10: Final Report (ASA 00-175)*. Report on file, Archaeological Survey of Alberta, Edmonton.

Bamforth, Douglas B.
2002 High-Tech Foragers? Folsom and Later Paleoindian Technology on the Great Plains. *Journal of World Prehistory* 16:55–98.

Beaudoin, Alwynne B., D. S. Lemmen, and D. J. Sauchyn, with W. M. Last, S. A. Wolfe, W. J. Vreeken, J. A. Burns, and I. A. Campbell
2000 *Field-Trip Guide: Late Quaternary History and Geoarchaeology of Southeastern Alberta and Southwestern Saskatchewan*. Post Meeting Field-Trip No. 3. Prepared for GeoCanada 2000 meeting, Calgary.

Beaudoin, Alwynne B., and Gerald A. Oetelaar
2003 The Changing Ecophysical Landscape of Southern Alberta during the Late Pleistocene and Early Holocene. *Plains Anthropologist* 48: 187–207.

Boag, Franca E.
1989 *Project P.A.S.T.: Final Report*. Strathcona Archaeological Society and Canada Employment and Immigration, Edmonton. Report on file, Royal Alberta Museum, Edmonton.

Borden, Charles E.
1952 A Uniform Site Designation Scheme for Canada. *Anthropology in British Columbia* 3:44–48.

Bradley, Bruce A., and George C. Frison
1987 Projectile Points and Specialized Bifaces from the Horner Site. In *The Horner Site*, edited by George C. Frison and L. C. Todd, pp. 199–231. Academic Press, Orlando, Florida.

Brink, Jack
2011 A 9,400 Year Old Stone Tool from Southeastern Alberta. *Alberta Archaeological Review* 52:5–9.

Brink, Jack, and Bob Dawe
1989 *Final Report of the 1985 and 1986 Field Seasons at Head-Smashed-In Buffalo Jump*. Archaeological Survey of Alberta Manuscript Series No. 16. Alberta Culture and Multiculturalism, Edmonton.

Brumley, John H., and Gordon K. Willis
1977 *An Archaeological Inventory of the Suffield Military Reserve, Alberta (ASA CRM 20)*. Report on file, Archaeological Survey of Alberta, Edmonton.

Brumley, Laurie Milne
1977 *Report of Evaluation Excavations Conducted at 7 Sites along the Highway 41:12 Construction Project, New Brigden, East-Central Alberta*. Report on file, Archaeological Survey of Alberta, Edmonton.

Brumley, Laurie Milne, and John H. Brumley
1977 *Report on Evaluation Excavations Conducted at 7 Sites along the Highway 41:12 Construction Project, New Brigden, East Central Alberta (ASA 76-022)*. Report on file, Archaeological Survey of Alberta, Edmonton.

Cameron, Courtney E. G., and Walt Kowal
2007 *Historical Resources Impact Assessment, Proposed Aldritt Development Ltd., Subdivision PT, Section 33-50-26-W4M, Devon, Alberta: Final Report*. Report on file, Archaeological Survey of Alberta, Edmonton.

Christensen, Ole A.
1971 Banff Prehistory: Prehistoric Settlement and Subsistence Technology in Banff National Park. National Historic Sites Service Manuscript Report No. 67. Unpublished Master's

thesis, Department of Archaeology, University of Calgary, Calgary.

Clarke, Grant M., and Brian M. Ronaghan
2000 *Historical Resources Impact Mitigation, Muskeg River Mine Project: Final Report*. Report on file, Archaeological Survey of Alberta, Edmonton.

Cloutier, Riel D.
2006 *Heritage Evaluation of West Fraser Slave Lake (Alberta Plywood Ltd. Division): 2005/2006 Annual Operating Plan, Forest Harvest Developments, Slave Lake, Alberta*. Report on file, Archaeological Survey of Alberta, Edmonton.

Damp, Jonathan E., and B. O. K. Reeves
1981 *Historical Resources Impact Assessment, SR 770 Relocation and Water Intake Access Road, Genesee Power and Mine Project [Volume 1]; Historical Resources Impact Assessment, 1981 Subcrop Coal Drilling Program, Genesee Power and Mine Project (ASA 81-067)*. Report on file, Archaeological Survey of Alberta, Edmonton.

Dau, Barry J., and John H. Brumley
1980 *Heritage Resource Investigations within a Proposed Subdivision in Medicine Hat, Alberta: Final Report*. Report on file, Archaeological Survey of Alberta, Edmonton.

Dawe, Robert J.
1983 Projectile Point Descriptions, Appendix 1. In *Archaeology of the Athabasca River Valley between Jasper and Hinton, 1981: Final Report (ASA 81-065)*, edited by Bruce Ball. Report on file, Archaeological Survey of Alberta, Edmonton.

De Mille, Christy, and Thomas H. Head
2001 *Historical Resources Mitigation, Stonepine Residential Community Development, Portions of NE Sec 1 and SE Sec 12, Twp. 24, Rge. 3, W5M: Final Report (ASA 98-052)*. Report on file, Archaeological Survey of Alberta, Edmonton.

Doll, Maurice F. V.
1980 *The Boss Hill Site (FdPe-4) Locality 1: Report on Project 79-69, Field Season of 1979 (ASA 79-069)*. Report on file, Archaeological Survey of Alberta, Edmonton.

Driver, Jonathan C.
1983 *DjPp-8, a Prehistoric Campsite on the Continental Divide (ASA 76-043)*. Report on file, Archaeological Survey of Alberta, Edmonton.

Duncan, L. R., and E. M. Murray
1971 *Preliminary Archaeological Survey Investigations in the Cremona/Sundre Area, Alberta*. Report on file, Department of Archaeology, University of Calgary, Calgary.

Dyke, Arthur S.
2005 Late Quaternary Vegetation History of Northern North America Based on Pollen, Macrofossil, and Faunal Remains. *Géographie Physique et Quaternaire* 59(2–3):211–262.

Eldridge, Morley, and Duncan McLaren
1998 Site Location Patterning in the Stave Lake Reservoir: Early Period Site Locations. Paper presented at the 31st Annual Canadian Archaeological Association Conference, Victoria, British Columbia.

Elliott, Jack
1970–71 *Jasper National Park and Ya-Ha-Tinda Ranch Archaeological Survey: Preliminary Report, 1970*. National Historic Site Service Manuscript Report No. 44. National and Historic Sites Branch, Department of Indian Affairs and Northern Development, Ottawa, Ontario.

Fedirchuk, Gloria J.
1973 Peace-Athabasca-Slave Archaeological Project — The Penner Site: Salvage Excavation. Manuscript on file, Prairie Regional Office, Parks Canada, Winnipeg, Manitoba.

Fedirchuk, Gloria J., and Allison Bailey
2002 *Historical Resource Studies, Alliance Pipeline Project (2000), Alberta (ASA 00-005)*. Report on file, Archaeological Survey of Alberta, Edmonton.

Fedirchuk, Gloria J., Edward J. McCullough, Les R. Gorham, Wendy J. Unfreed, Barbara J. Kulle, Eugene M. Gryba, and Len V. Hills
1998 *Historical Resources Impact Assessment Report, Alliance Pipeline Limited Partnership, Alliance Pipeline Project, Alberta, Volume I*. Report on file, Archaeological Survey of Alberta, Edmonton.

Fedje, Daryl
1988 *The Norquay and Eclipse Sites: Trans-Canada Highway Twinning Mitigation in Banff National Park*. Environment Canada, Parks Service, Microfiche Report No. 395. Ottawa, Ontario.

Fedje, Daryl, and James M. White
1984 *Vermilion Lakes Archaeology: Interim Report; Trans-Canada Highway Mitigation in Banff National Park*. Parks Canada Microfiche Report Series No. 177. Ottawa, Ontario.

Fenton, Mark M., and John W. Ives
1990 Geoarchaeological Studies of the Beaver River Sandstone, Northeastern Alberta. *Geological Society of America Centennial Special Volume* 4:123–135.

Fisher, Timothy G.
2007 Abandonment Chronology of Glacial Lake

Agassiz's Northwestern Outlet. *Palaeogeography, Palaeoclimatology, Palaeocology* 246: 31–44.

Fisher, T. G., and D. G. Smith

1994 Glacial Lake Agassiz: Its Northwestern Maximum Extent and Outlet in Saskatchewan (Emerson Phase). *Quaternary Science Reviews* 13:845–858.

Forbis, Richard G.

1968 Fletcher: A Paleoindian Site in Alberta. *American Antiquity* 33:1–10.

Forner, Cheryl I., and Bonnie Brenner

2008 *Historical Resources Impact Mitigation, FjPt-2: Atco Pipelines, Wildwood to Keyera Paddle River Pipeline; Final Report (ASA 06-466).* FMA Heritage. Report on file, Archaeological Survey of Alberta, Edmonton.

Frison, George C.

1991 *Prehistoric Hunters of the High Plains.* 2nd ed. Academic Press, San Diego.

Gibson, Terrance H.

1987 *Historical Resources Impact Assessment of Peace Hills Park, Wetaskiwin, Alberta (ASA 87-010).* Report on file, Archaeological Survey of Alberta, Edmonton.

Glenbow Museum

1957 Glenbow Foundation Archaeology, Field Notes. Calgary.

1958 Glenbow Foundation Archaeology, Field Notes. Calgary.

1959 Glenbow Foundation Archaeology, Field Notes. Calgary.

1961 Glenbow Foundation Archaeology, Field Notes. Calgary.

1962 Glenbow Foundation Archaeology, Field Notes. Calgary.

1965 Glenbow Foundation Archaeology, Field Notes. Calgary.

Godfrey-Smith, D. I.

1988 *ASA Obsidian Source Study 1987: Final Report.* Report submitted to the Archaeological Survey of Alberta, Edmonton.

Gordon, Bryan C.

1996 *People of Sunlight, People of Starlight: Barrenland Archaeology in the Northwest Territories of Canada.* Mercury Series, Archaeological Survey of Canada Paper No. 154. Canadian Museum of Civilization, Hull, Quebec.

Gorham, L. R.

1996 *Historical Resources Impact Assessment, Praxair Canada Inc., Fort Saskatchewan to Dupont Plant Hydrogen Pipeline Project (ASA 95-064).* Report on file, Archaeological Survey of Alberta, Edmonton.

1997 *Historical Resources Impact Assessment, Gulf Canada Resources Limited Garrington Line Looping Project: Final Report (ASA 97-097).* Report on file, Archaeological Survey of Alberta, Edmonton.

Gruhn, Ruth

1969 *Preliminary Report on the Muhlbach Site: A Besant Bison Trap in Central Alberta.* National Museums of Canada, Bulletin No. 232, Contributions to Anthropology VII: Archaeology, Paper No. 4. Ottawa, Ontario.

Gryba, Eugene M.

1983a *Sibbald Creek: 11,000 Years of Human Use of the Southern Alberta Foothills.* Archaeological Survey of Alberta Occasional Paper No. 22. Edmonton.

1983b *The 1982 Archaeological Survey of Alberta Highways and Recreation Area Developments: Final Report (ASA 82-072).* Report on file, Archaeological Survey of Alberta, Edmonton.

1988 *An Inventory of Fluted Point Occurrences in Alberta.* Report on file, Royal Alberta Museum, Edmonton.

Gryba, Eugene M., and Kara Stirling

2001 *Historical Resources Impact Assessment, Pointwest Energy Inc., Pointwest Cessford 14-32-27-17 W4M Well and Access Road: Final Report (ASA 01-196).* Report on file, Archaeological Survey of Alberta, Edmonton.

Hanna, Don

2002 *Historical Resource Mitigation, Speargrass Golf Course and Residential Subdivision, Carseland, Parts of 5-22-25-W4M and 32-21-25-W4M: Final Report (ASA 01-032).* Report on file, Archaeological Survey of Alberta, Edmonton.

Hanna, Sharon, and Barbara Neal

1992 *Final Report: Historical Resources Mitigation, North Lateral Extension Loop #2, Sullivan Lake Section (ASA 90-069).* Report on file, Archaeological Survey of Alberta, Edmonton.

Head, Thomas H.

1997 *Historical Resources Impact Assessment, NPS 30 North Lateral Extension Loop No. 3, Heisler and Farrell Sections: Final Report (ASA 96-075).* Report on file, Archaeological Survey of Alberta, Edmonton.

1989 *Historical Resources Impact Assessment, Stanmore Lateral Loop, Youngstown Lateral Loop, Stanmore South Lateral Loop #2: Final Report (ASA 89-060).* Report on file, Archaeological Survey of Alberta, Edmonton.

Heitzmann, Roderick J.

1980 *Historical Resources Inventory and Assessment, Proposed Northern Alberta Highway Construction Projects, 1979 (ASA 79-067).*

Report on file, Archaeological Survey of Alberta, Edmonton.

Hjermstad, Ben
1991 *T.R.A.C.E.: An Artifact Recording Program in South-Central Alberta.* Archaeological Society of Alberta, Calgary Centre and Canada Employment and Immigration, Calgary. Report on file, Royal Alberta Museum, Edmonton.

Huckell, Bruce
1978 Appendix 1: Hudson-Meng Chipped Stone. In *The Hudson-Meng Site: An Alberta Bison Kill in the Nebraska High Plains*, by Larry D. Agenbroad, pp. 153–191. University Press of America, Washington, D.C.

Hughes, Richard E.
2008 *X-ray Fluorescence (Source) Analysis of 14 Obsidian Artifacts from Various Archaeological Sites and Localities in Alberta, Canada.* Geochemical Research Laboratory Letter Report 2008-48. Portolla Valley, California.
2010 *Energy Dispersive X-ray Fluorescence Analysis of Three Broken Obsidian Scottsbluff Projectile Points from Archaeological Site EdPk-3, Located near High River in Alberta, Canada.* Geochemical Research Laboratory Letter Report 2010-81. Portolla Valley, California.

Ives, John W.
2006 13,001 Years Ago — Human Beginnings in Alberta. In *Alberta Formed — Alberta Transformed*, edited by Michael Payne, Don Wetherell, and Cathy Cavanaugh, Vol. 1, pp. 1–34. University of Calgary Press, Calgary; University of Alberta Press, Edmonton.

Johnston, Russell A.
1975 Manuscript, letters, and notes on file from years 1939, 1943, 1954, 1955, 1970, 1971, 1972, 1973, and 1975. Provincial Museum of Alberta, Edmonton.

Kelly, Robert L., and Lawrence C. Todd
1988 Coming into the Country: Early Paleoindian Hunting and Mobility. *American Antiquity* 53:231–244.

Kidd, Robert S.
1978 *Field Season 1977: The Boss Hill Site (FdPe-4), Locality 2 (ASA 77-028).* Report on file, Archaeological Survey of Alberta, Edmonton.

Klein, Richard G.
1989 *The Human Career: Human Biological and Cultural Origin.* University of Chicago Press, Chicago.

Knudson, Ruthann
1971 Fletcher Assemblage Attribute Data. Manuscript on file, Royal Alberta Museum, Edmonton.

Kornfeld, Marcel
2003 *Affluent Foragers of the North American Plains: Landscape Archaeology of the Black Hills.* BAR International Series No. 1106. British Archaeological Reports, Oxford.

Kowal, Walter A., and Courtney E. G. Cameron
2003 *Historical Resources Impact Assessment, Proposed Highway 643:02 Upgrade, Junction Highway 825:02 to Highway 38 (km 6.80 to km 20.66), and Proposed Highway 825:02 Upgrade, Junction Highway 37 to North of Boysdale Road (km 0.00 to km 5.00): Final Report.* Report on file, Archaeological Survey of Alberta, Edmonton.

Kulle, Barbara J., and Barbara Neal
1998 *Historical Resources Mitigation, Cardinal River Coals Ltd., Cheviot Mine Project, Sites FfQh-27 and FfQh-32 (ASA 97-115).* Report on file, Archaeological Survey of Alberta, Edmonton.

Landals, Alison J.
1996 *Historical Resources Impact Assessment, Canadian Occidental Petroleum Limited, Nanton to Cayley Pipeline Project (ASA 95-039).* Report on file, Archaeological Survey of Alberta, Edmonton.

Landals, Alison J., Barbara J. Kulle, Gloria J. Fedirchuk, and Len Hills
1998 *Historical Resources Impact Assessment, Cardinal River Coals Ltd., Cheviot Mine Project (95-025).* Report on file, Archaeological Survey of Alberta, Edmonton.

Langemann, E. Gwyn, and William Perry
2002 *Banff National Park of Canada, Archaeological Resource Description and Analysis.* Parks Canada Agency, Cultural Resources Services, Western Canada Service Centre, Calgary, Alberta.

Le Blanc, Raymond
1983 Site Form. Archaeological Survey of Alberta, Edmonton.

Linnamae, U., and M. R. Corbeil
1993 *Report of the Heron Eden Archaeological Project.* Department of Anthropology and Archaeology, University of Saskatchewan, Saskatoon. Submitted to Heritage Branch, Government of Saskatchewan, Regina.

Losey, Timothy C.
1978 The Prehistoric Cultural Ecology of the Western Prairie-Forest Transition Zone, Alberta, Canada. Unpublished Ph.D. dissertation, Department of Anthropology, University of Alberta, Edmonton.

Losey, Timothy C., R. Freeman, and John Priegert
1974 *Archaeological Reconnaissance, Alberta*

*Highways North, 1974 (ASA Permits 74-010 and 74-014)*. Report on file, Archaeological Survey of Alberta, Edmonton.

Lowell, T. V., T. G. Fisher, G. C. Comer, I. Hajdas, N. Waterson, K. Glover, H. M. Loope, J. M. Schaefer, V. Rinterknecht, W. Broecker, G. Denton, and J. T. Teller

2005 Testing the Lake Agassiz Meltwater Trigger for the Younger Dryas. *Eos* 86(40):365–373.

McCullough, Edward J.

1981 *The Duckett Site (GdOo-16): An Evaluative Study (ASA 80-155)*. Report on file, Archaeological Survey of Alberta, Edmonton.

1988 *Historical Resources Impact Assessment, Singleton Associated Engineering Ltd., Bow River Pipe Lines Ltd., Mainline Looping Program (ASA 88-060)*. Report on file, Archaeological Survey of Alberta, Edmonton.

1991a *Historic Resources Impact Assessment, Amoco Canada Petroleum Company Limited, Wembley Gas Gathering System Expansion Project (ASA 91-025)*. Report on file, Archaeological Survey of Alberta, Edmonton.

1991b *Historical Resources Impact Assessment, IBI Group/Triple Five Corporation, the Range Subdivision (ASA 90-073)*. Report on file, Archaeological Survey of Alberta, Edmonton.

McCullough, Edward J., and Alison J. Landals

1995 *CFD Wainwright Baseline Archaeological Inventory (ASA 94-073)*. Report on file, Archaeological Survey of Alberta, Edmonton.

McCullough, Edward J., and Brian O. K. Reeves

1978 *Historical Resources Impact Assessment, Dome Petroleum Ltd., Waterton–Cochrane Ethane Pipeline (ASA 78-020)*. Report on file, Archaeological Survey of Alberta, Edmonton.

McFee, Ron D.

1979 *Heritage Resources Impact Assessment, Alaska Highway Gas Pipeline, Alberta Segment 7, the Western Leg*. Report on file, Archaeological Survey of Alberta, Edmonton.

McNeil, Paul, L. V. Hills, B. Kooyman, and M. Shayne Tolman

2005 Mammoth Tracks Indicate a Declining Late Pleistocene Population in Southwestern Alberta, Canada. *Quaternary Science Reviews* 24:1253–1259.

Meyer, Daniel A.

2007 *Historical Resources Impact Assessment, Sundance Forest Industries Ltd., Sundance FMA 2005-2006 Developments: Final Report*. Report on file, Archaeological Survey of Alberta, Edmonton.

Meyer, Daniel A., and Brian O. K. Reeves

2002 *Historical Resources Impact Assessment and Mitigation, Weldwood of Canada Limited, Hinton Division Embarras 12, Forestry Unit Haul Roads, Cut Blocks, and Gravel Source: Final Report*. Report on file, Archaeological Survey of Alberta, Edmonton.

Meyer, Dan A., and Jason Roe

2006 *Historical Resources Impact Assessment, Hinton Wood Products, a Division of West Fraser Mills Ltd., Hinton Wood Products FMA 2005 Developments, Volume I: Final Report*. Report on file, Archaeological Survey of Alberta, Edmonton.

Meyer, Daniel A., Nancy Saxburg, Brad Somer, Jason Roe, and Carmen Olson

2007 *Historical Resources Impact Assessment Mitigation, Elk Valley Coal Corporation, Cardinal River Operations, Cheviot Mine 2005 Mitigation Excavations: Final Report 05-396 (Volume 1: Background, Recommendations, and Precontact Site Mitigations; Volume 2: Historic Site Mitigations)*. Report on file, Archaeological Survey of Alberta, Edmonton.

Muñiz, Mark Peter

2005 The Cody Complex Revisited: Landscape Use and Technological Organization on the Northwestern Plains. Unpublished Ph.D. dissertation, Department of Anthropology, University of Colorado, Boulder.

Newton, Barry M., and Gloria J. Fedirchuk

1982 *Historical Resources Impact Assessment, Merland Explorations Limited, Canard Sales Line: Final Report (ASA 82-038)*. Report on file, Archaeological Survey of Alberta, Edmonton.

Peace River Archaeology Society

1996 *Peace Past Project: An Archaeological Survey of the Peace River District*. Peace River Archaeological Society in cooperation with Canada Employment and Immigration. Report on file, Royal Alberta Museum, Edmonton.

Peck, Trevor Richard

2001 Bison Ethology and Native Settlement Patterns during the Old Women's Phase on the Northwestern Plains. Unpublished Ph.D. dissertation, Department of Archaeology, University of Calgary, Calgary.

Pettipas, Leo F.

1980 The Little Gem Complex. *Saskatchewan Archaeology* 1(2):3–81.

Pickard, Roderick J.

1985 Historical Resources Inventory, Jasper National Park (2 volumes). Manuscript on file, Archaeological Research Unit, Western Region, Parks Canada, Calgary.

Provincial Museum of Alberta [name changed to Royal Alberta Museum in 2005]
1969 Provincial Museum of Alberta Archaeological Survey, Edmonton.
1971 Provincial Museum of Alberta Archaeological Survey, Edmonton.
1972 Provincial Museum of Alberta Archaeological Survey, Edmonton.
1973 Provincial Museum of Alberta Archaeological Survey, Edmonton.
1975 Provincial Museum of Alberta Archaeological Survey, Edmonton.
1976 Provincial Museum of Alberta Archaeological Survey, Edmonton.

Quigg, J. Michael
1976a A Note on the Fletcher site. In *Archaeology in Alberta, 1975*, compiled by J. M. Quigg and W. J. Byrne, pp. 108–115. Archaeological Survey of Alberta Occasional Paper No. 1. Alberta Culture and Multiculturalism, Edmonton.
1976b Battle River Valley Survey, 1975. In *Archaeology in Alberta, 1975*, compiled by J. Michael Quigg and W. J. Byrne, pp. 29–34. Archaeological Survey of Alberta Occasional Paper No. 1. Alberta Culture and Multiculturalism, Edmonton.
1978 *Dried Meat Hill Investigations (ASA 77-073)*. Report on file, Archaeological Survey of Alberta, Edmonton.
1980 *A Historical Resource Impact Assessment in Conjunction with the New Trans-Canada Bridge Crossing within Medicine Hat, Alberta (ASA 79-23)*. Report on file, Archaeological Survey of Alberta, Edmonton.

Rayburn, John A., and James T. Teller
2007 Isostatic Rebound in the Northwestern Part of the Lake Agassiz Basin: Isobase Changes and Overflow. *Palaeogeography, Palaeoclimatology, Palaeoecology* 246:23–30.

Red Deer and District Museum
1983 Project Arrowhead. Paper on file, Red Deer Museum, Red Deer, Alberta.

Reeves, Brian O. K.
1964 Glenbow Foundation Archaeology, Field Notes. Calgary.
1972 *The Archaeology of Pass Creek Valley, Waterton Lakes National Park*. National Historic Sites Service Manuscript Report No. 61. Department of Indian Affairs and Northern Development, Ottawa, Ontario.
1976 *Coal Valley Impact on Archaeological Resources, Lifeways of Canada Ltd (ASA 75-050)*. Report on file, Archaeological Survey of Alberta, Edmonton.
1978 Head-Smashed-In: 5500 Years of Bison Jumping in the Alberta Plains. In *Bison Procurement and Utilization: A Symposium*, edited by L. B. Davis and M. Wilson, pp. 151–174. Memoir No. 14. Plains Anthropologist, Lincoln, Nebraska.

Reeves, Brian O. K., and Claire Bourges
2002 *Weldwood (Hinton Division) Forestry Management Area: Historical Resources Overview/Assessment and Proposed Management Plan; Final Report*. Report on file, Archaeological Survey of Alberta, Edmonton.

Reeves, Brian O. K., and Edward J. McCullough
1976 *Archaeological Reconnaissance, Alberta Transportation Highway Construction Program — Transitional Parkland and Boreal Forest [Permit 76-19 and 76-20]*. Report on file, Archaeological Survey of Alberta, Edmonton.
1978 *Historical Resources Overview and Preliminary Assessment, Cold Lake Lease (ASA 77-093)*. Report on file, Archaeological Survey of Alberta, Edmonton.

Ronaghan, Brian M.
1983 *Genesee Power Project: Historical Resources Impact Assessment and Conservation Studies; Final Report (ASA 82-062)*. Report on file, Archaeological Survey of Alberta, Edmonton.
1993 The James Pass Project: Early Holocene Occupation in the Front Ranges of the Rocky Mountains. *Canadian Journal of Archaeology* 17:85–91.

Rutter, Nathaniel W., Andrew J. Weaver, Dean Rokosh, Augustus F. Fanning, and Daniel G. Wright
2000 Data-Model Comparison of the Younger Dryas Event. *Canadian Journal of Earth Science* 37:811–830.

Saxberg, Nancy, and Brian O. K. Reeves
2003 The First 2000 Years of Oil Sands History: Ancient Hunters at the Northwest Outlet of Glacial Lake Agassiz. In *Archaeology in Alberta: A View from the New Millennium*, edited by Jack W. Brink and John F. Dormaar, pp. 290–322. Archaeological Society of Alberta, Medicine Hat.

Saxberg, Nancy, Mack W. Shortt, and Brian O. K. Reeves
1998 *Historical Resources Impact Assessment, Aurora Mine North Highway and Utility and Access Corridors: Final Report (ASA 97-043)*. Report on file, Archaeological Survey of Alberta, Edmonton.

Seebach, John D.
2006 Drought or Development? Patterns of Paleoindian Site Discovery on the Great Plains of North America. *Plains Anthropologist* 51:71–88.

Shortt, Mack W., Nancy Saxberg, and Brian O. K. Reeves
1998 *Aurora Mine North East Pit Opening, Plant Site, Tailings, and Related Workings: HRIA and Mitigation Studies; Final Report (ASA 97-116)*. Report on file, Archaeological Survey of Alberta, Edmonton.

Skinner, Craig E.
2007 *Appendix: Results of X-Ray Fluorescence Analysis*. Northwest Research Obsidian Studies Lab, Corvallis, Oregon, 2007-27. Report submitted to the Royal Alberta Museum, Edmonton.

Smith, Brian J.
1993 *Historical Resources Impact Assessment of Rocky Rapids Lagoon Site Pt. NE 34-49-7-W4M, Rocky Rapids, Alberta: Final Report (ASA 93-058)*. Report on file, Archaeological Survey of Alberta, Edmonton.

Somer, Brad
2005 *Syncrude Aurora Mine North: Historical Resources Impact Assessment and Mitigation Studies; 2004 Field Studies, Volume I*. Report on file, Archaeological Survey of Alberta, Edmonton.

Stryd, Arnold R., and Michael K. Rousseau
1996 The Early Prehistory of the Mid Fraser-Thompson River Area. In *Early Human Occupation in British Columbia*, edited by R. L. Carlson and L. Dalla Bona, pp. 177–204. University of British Columbia Press, Vancouver.

Taylor, E. Fraser
1969 Archaeology of the Peace Hills Area of Central Alberta, Canada. Unpublished Master's thesis, Department of Anthropology, University of Alberta, Edmonton.

Tolman, M. Shayne
2001 DhPg-8: From Mammoths to Machinery; An Overview of 11,000 Years along the St. Mary River. Unpublished Master's thesis, Resources and the Environment Program, University of Calgary.

Unfreed, Wendy J., and Jennifer C. Tischer
2002 *Historical Resources Impact Assessment: Corridor Pipeline Limited, Corridor Pipeline Project (Scotford to Muskeg River Mine); Final Report (ASA 00-073)*. Report on file, Archaeological Survey of Alberta, Edmonton.

University of Alberta
1964 *Alberta Archaeological Survey, 1964*. Report on file, Department of Anthropology, University of Alberta, Edmonton.
1965 *Alberta Archaeological Survey, 1966*. Report on file, Department of Anthropology, University of Alberta, Edmonton.
1966 *Alberta Archaeological Survey, 1966*. Report on file, Department of Anthropology, University of Alberta, Edmonton.
1989 *Alberta Archaeological Survey, 1989*. Report on file, Department of Anthropology, University of Alberta, Edmonton.

University of Calgary
1969 *University of Calgary Archaeological Survey*. Report on file, Department of Archaeology, University of Calgary, Calgary, Alberta.
1971 *University of Calgary Archaeological Survey*. Report on file, Department of Archaeology, University of Calgary, Calgary, Alberta.
1972 *University of Calgary Archaeological Survey*. Report on file, Department of Archaeology, University of Calgary, Calgary, Alberta.

Van Dyke, Stan, and Jon Damp
1981 *Genesee Power Project, Inventory of Historical Resources: Final Report (ASA 81-152)*. Report on file, Archaeological Survey of Alberta, Edmonton.

Van Dyke, Stanley, Thomas Head, and Barbara Neal
1989 *Section 3.0 — 1988 Oldman River Dam Prehistoric Archaeology Mitigation Program — Campsites Component: Final Report (ASA 88-039)*. Report on file, Archaeological Survey of Alberta, Edmonton.

Van Dyke, Stanley, Sharon Lee Hanna, Wendy J. Unfreed, and Barbara Neal
1990 *Section 3.0 — 1989 Oldman River Dam Prehistoric Archaeological Mitigation Program — Campsites Component: Final Report (ASA 89-025)*. Report on file, Archaeological Survey of Alberta, Edmonton.
1991 That Dam Archaeology: Campsites Archaeology in the Oldman River Reservoir. In *Archaeology in Alberta, 1988 and 1989*, edited by Martin Magne, pp. 25–65. Archaeological Survey of Alberta Occasional Paper No. 33. Alberta Culture and Multiculturalism, Edmonton.

Varsakis, Rena
2006 Besant Revisited: The Fincastle Site and Archaeological Cultures on the Northwestern Plains, 2500 BP–1250 BP. Unpublished M.Sc. thesis, Department of Geography, University of Lethbridge, Lethbridge, Alberta.

Vickers, J. Roderick
1986 *Alberta Plains Prehistory: A Review*. Archaeological Survey of Alberta Occasional Paper No. 27. Alberta Culture and Multiculturalism, Edmonton.

Vickers, J. R., and A. B. Beaudoin
1989 A Limiting AMS Date for the Cody Complex Occupation at the Fletcher Site, Alberta, Canada. *Plains Anthropologist* 34:261–264.

Vickers, J. Rod, and Trevor R. Peck
2004 Islands in a Sea of Grass: The Significance of Wood in Winter Campsite Selection on the Northwestern Plains. In *Archaeology on the Edge — New Perspectives from the Northwestern Plains*, edited by Brian Kooyman and Jane H. Kelley, pp. 95–124. Canadian Archaeological Association Occasional Paper No. 4, Vol. 1. University of Calgary Press, Calgary, Alberta.

Vivian, Brian C. C., Dan Meyer, and Murray Lobb
2006 *Historical Resources Impact Assessment for the Talisman Energy Callum Creek Development Area: Final Report.* Report on file, Archaeological Survey of Alberta, Edmonton.

Wettlaufer, Boyd N.
1949 Survey and Excavations at the Maclean Site (Head-Smashed-In). Manuscript and field notes on file, Archaeological Survey of Alberta, Edmonton.

Wilson, Ian R.
1989 The Pink Mountain Site (HhRr-1): An Early Prehistoric Campsite in Northeastern B.C. *Canadian Journal of Archaeology* 13:51–67.
1996 Paleoindian Sites in the Vicinity of Pink Mountain. In *Early Human Occupation in British Columbia*, edited by R. L. Carlson and L. Dalla Bona, pp. 29–34. University of British Columbia Press, Vancouver.

Wilson, Michael Clayton, J. Roderick Vickers, Arthur C. MacWilliams, Alwynne B. Beaudoin, and Ian G. Robertson
1991 New Studies at the Fletcher Palaeo-Indian Bison Kill (Alberta/Scottsbluff), Southern Alberta. In *Archaeology in Alberta, 1988 and 1989*, edited by Martin Magne, pp. 127–133. Archaeological Survey of Alberta Occasional Paper No. 33. Alberta Culture and Multiculturalism, Edmonton.

Wilson, Michael Clayton, John Visser, and Martin P. R. Magne
2011 Microblade Cores from the Northwestern Plains at High River, Alberta, Canada. *Plains Anthropologist* 56:23–36.

Wiseman, Dion, and James Graham
2007 Quantifying Landscape Diversity and Uniqueness in the Prairie Ecozone. *Canadian Journal of Archaeology* 31(3):251–270.

Wondrasek, Rob, Wendy J. Unfreed, Len Hills, and Alison Bailey
1999 *Historical Resources Impact Assessment: Centurion Gas Liquids Inc., Empress Pipeline Project (ASA 98-099).* Report on file, Archaeological Survey of Alberta, Edmonton.

Wood, Barry P.
1991 *Operation Artifact: Artifact Recordation in Southern Alberta of Amateur Collections.* Archaeological Society of Alberta, Lethbridge Centre, in cooperation with Canada Employment and Immigration and the Department of Geography, University of Lethbridge. Report on file, Royal Alberta Museum, Edmonton.

Wood, Barry P., Dale MacDonald-Hauck, and Steven Laubenstein
1993 *SEARCH: South Eastern Alberta Recordation of Cultural Heritage.* Archaeological Society of Alberta, South Eastern Alberta Archaeological Centre, in cooperation with Canada Employment and Immigration. Report on file, Royal Alberta Museum, Edmonton.

Wormington, H. Marie
1957 *Ancient Man in North America.* 4th ed. Popular Series No. 4. Denver Museum of Natural History, Denver, Colorado.

Wormington, H. Marie, and Richard G. Forbis
1965 *An Introduction to the Archaeology of Alberta, Canada.* Denver Museum of Natural History, Proceedings No. 11. Denver, Colorado.

Wright, Bruce W.
1978 *An Historical Resources Inventory and Assessment of the Keephills Study Area: Final Report (ASA 77-057 and 058).* Report on file, Archaeological Survey of Alberta, Edmonton.
1979 *Historical Resource Site Mitigation in the Keephills Area (ASA 78-031).* Report on file, Archaeological Survey of Alberta, Edmonton.

Youell, Alan J.
2007 *Historical Resources Impact Assessment: Petro-Canada Sullivan Field Development Project, 2007 Pipeline Reroutes and 06-15-18-05 W5M Well Site; Final Report.* Report on file (ASA 07-161), Archaeological Survey of Alberta, Edmonton.

7

# Cody in the Rockies

## The Mountain Expression of a Plains Culture Complex?

Matthew E. Hill Jr. and Edward J. Knell

For most of the twentieth century, the Cody complex was viewed as a classic Great Plains Paleoindian complex (Forbis 1968; Irwin and Wormington 1970; Wheat 1972; Wormington 1957). Large Cody kill and processing sites, such as Horner (Frison and Todd 1987), Hudson-Meng (Agenbroad 1978), and Olsen-Chubbuck (Wheat 1972), helped shape the concept that Plains Paleoindians were highly mobile bison hunters. Traditionally associated with the Great Plains, Cody (Eden and Scottsbluff) points and knives have been recovered from a much broader swath of North America, including the Gulf Coast (Aten 1983; Forbis 1968; Johnson 1989; Osborne 1956), the Great Basin (Amick, this volume; Clewlow 1968; Dansie et al. 1991), the Colorado Plateau (Hauck and Hauck 2002; Lipe and Pitblado 1999), Washington state and Alaska (Wormington 1957), and the Rocky Mountains (Bonnichsen et al. 1992; Davis et al. 1991; Forbis and Sperry 1952; Husted 1965; Larson 2012; Pitblado 2003). Points morphologically similar to Eden and Scottsbluff have been recovered from the Great Lakes area (Mason 1962) and even southern Quebec and New England (Cox 2001). Given this regional dispersion, it no longer seems prudent to view the Cody complex as solely a Great Plains culture complex.

If archaeologists accept that Cody is not solely a Great Plains complex, we must then begin the hard work of understanding how (or even if) the Cody lifeway varied in different environments. Doing so requires both an appreciation of how mobile foragers responded to different configurations of biotic and abiotic resources and the identification of key archaeological variables that reflect important changes in land-use strategies. Examining the same cultural tradition in different environmental settings highlights how these foragers shifted adaptive strategies to confront conditions in each environmental zone.

Our chapter addresses regional variation in the Cody complex by exploring differences between Cody complex lifeways in the Rocky Mountains and in the Great Plains (Figure 7.1). Our approach combines faunal and lithic data to develop a more nuanced understanding of Paleoindian lifeways in the Rocky Mountains. We compare our empirical observations from the northern Plains and Rocky Mountain Cody archaeological record with a land-use model inspired by optimal foraging theory and temporal resource predictability theory. We use the same approach as in our prior work on Cody land use in the Great Plains and Rocky Mountains (Knell 2007; Knell and Hill 2012), but here we focus on Cody sites in the Rocky Mountains and Plains grasslands and compare this database with contemporary non-Cody mountains and Plains assemblages. Specifically, we consider how these foragers shifted their land-use and foraging strategies in response to the different structures of biotic and abiotic resources in the Great Plains and Rocky Mountains. Doing so

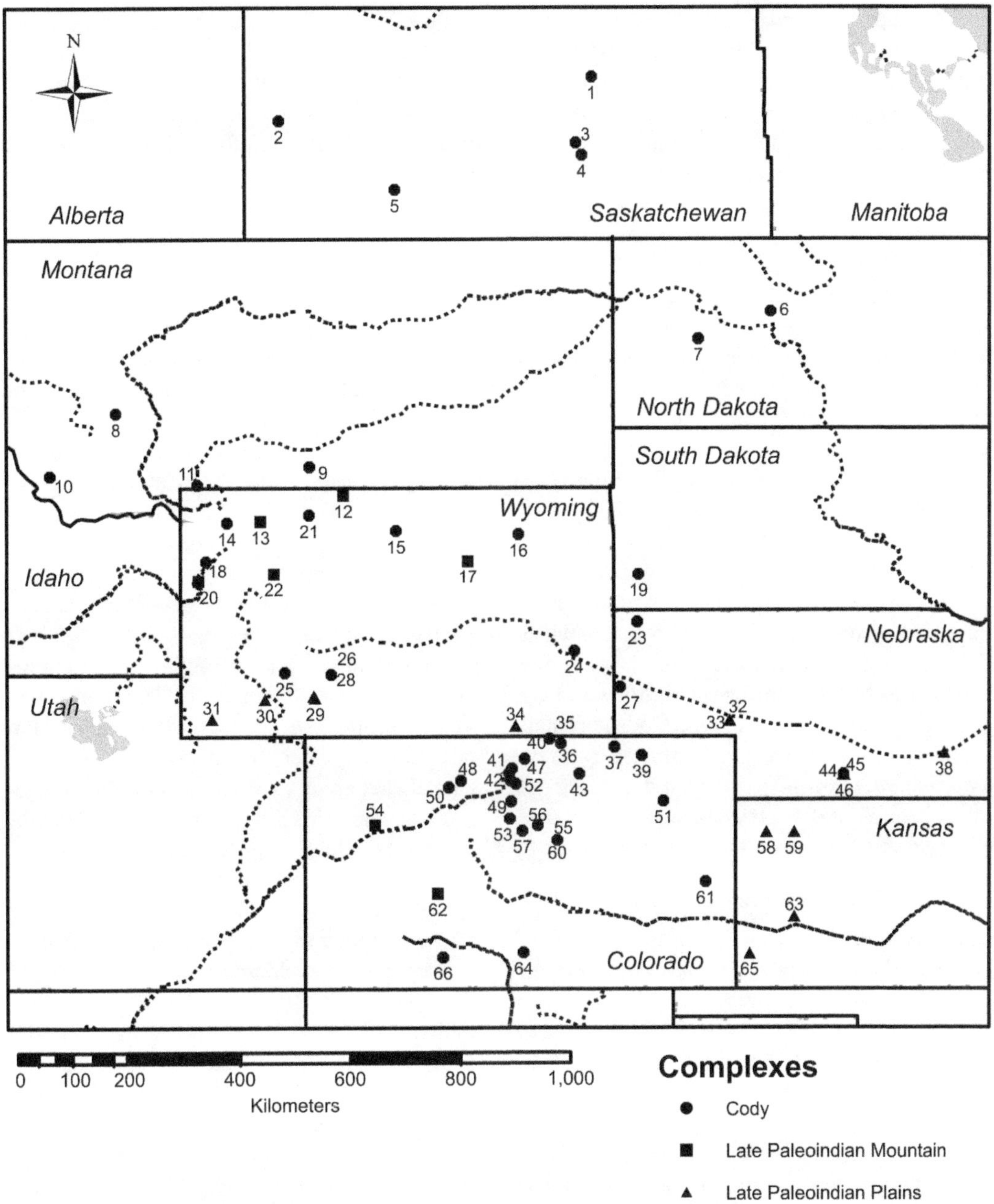


FIGURE 7.1. Late Paleoindian sites mentioned in text and defined by cultural complex. 1. Haskey Area; 2. Heron Eden; 3. Dunn; 4. DjNf-8; 5. Niska; 6. Max; 7. Benz; 8. MacHaffie; 9. Pretty Creek; 10. Mammoth Meadow; 11. Malin Creek; 12. Bottleneck Cave; 13. Mummy Cave; 14. Osprey Beach; 15. Medicine Lodge Creek; 16. Carter/Kerr-McGee; 17. Schiffer Cave; 18. Lawrence; 19. Jim Pitts; 20. 48JO303; 21. Horner; 22. Helen Lookingbill; 23. Hudson-Meng; 24. Hell Gap; 25. Finley; 26. Deadman Wash; 27. Scottsbluff; 28. 48SW13156; 29. 48SW8842; 30. Blue Point; 31. 48UT375; 32. OV Clary; 33. Clary Ranch; 34. James Allen; 35. Lindenmeier; 36. Wilbur Thomas Shelter; 37. Nelson; 38. Meserve; 39. Frasca; 40. Carey Lake; 41. Trail Ridge; 42. Forest Canyon Pass; 43. Jurgens; 44. Red Smoke; 45. Lime Creek; 46. Allen; 47. Flattop Game Drive; 48. 5JA1475; 49. 5BL53; 50. 5JA183; 51. Claypool; 52. Devil's Thumb; 53. Hay Springs; 54. Caribou Lake; 55. Crescent Rockshelter; 56. Barger Gulch Locality A; 57. Jerry Craig; 58. Laird; 59. Burntwood Creek; 60. Lamb Spring; 61. Olsen-Chubbuck; 62. Chance Gulch; 63. Norton; 64. 5HF2108; 65. Winger; 66. 5RN119.

highlights the Cody adaptive strategy in comparison to temporally overlapping Paleoindian cultural complexes.

We begin by briefly discussing the environmental setting of the Rocky Mountains, and then review the Cody complex archaeological record in the Rocky Mountains and its relation to the settlement strategies of other Paleoindians. Next we review prior interpretations of Cody land use in the mountains. Our results section compares the empirical results of our faunal and lithic analyses with the expectations of the land-use model. We conclude by considering whether Cody land-use practices were consistent with our model expectations and discuss the broader implications.

Cody occupation of the Rocky Mountains agrees with many, but not all, of our model predictions. Cody faunal assemblages from mountain sites have a narrower range of prey species, particularly bison, than our model predicts or occurs among non-Cody mountain assemblages. Seasonality data suggest that bison hunting was primarily scheduled during the summer and fall. In keeping with our expectations, Cody mountain flaked stone assemblages are dominated by locally available lithic raw materials and depict regionally restricted land use, but to a lesser degree than among non-Cody mountain assemblages.

### The Rocky Mountain Environment

The Rocky Mountain chain exhibits a high degree of environmental variability across its roughly 5000-km length. We focus on those portions of the mountain range in eastern Idaho, western Montana, western Wyoming, and central Colorado (see approach of Black 1991; Larson 2012; Pitblado 2003).

Elevation is a key variable that strongly influences the nature and structure of the biological (plant and animal) and nonbiological (geology, hydrology, climate) components of the environment (Knight 1994; Wyckoff and Dilsaver 1995). The Rocky Mountains in our project area have five key environmental zones that Paleoindian foragers occupied (Doerner 2007; Mutel and Emerick 1984; Pitblado 2008): foothills (1500–2400 meters above sea level [masl]), park (1800–3000 masl), montane (2400–2900 masl), subalpine (2900–3500 masl), and alpine (>3500 masl).

For simplicity, we combine the foothill and montane zones. These are diverse settings characterized by mixed woodland (e.g., pine, fir juniper, oak), grassland, and shrubland habitats. For this study, we include uplifts and escarpments, such as the Black Hills, Pine Bluffs, and Hartville Uplift, in the foothill-montane zone because they support similar rich biotic communities (see Husted 1974; Knell 2007; Knight 1994). This environmental zone was important to prehistoric foragers because its exposed rock outcrops could serve as shelters, and its surface exposures of high-quality lithic raw materials could be used to make chipped stone tools (e.g., chert, quartzite, obsidian) or ground stone tools (e.g., basalt and quartzite).

At generally the same elevation as the foothill-montane zone are parks. Parks are grassland- or shrubland-covered meadows surrounded by higher mountain peaks (Kornfeld and Frison 2000; Pitblado 2008). Parks usually have a variety of edible plants and sometimes sources of knappable stone (especially chert and quartzite) (Kornfeld and Frison 2000; Naze 1986), and may support considerable populations of large game such as bison, pronghorn, deer, and elk seasonally (and sometimes more permanently) (Pitblado 2008).

In this chapter we distinguish between true mountain parks and lower-elevation intermountain basins, which we associate with Plains environments. We treat these differently because high-elevation parks, such as North (2700 m) and South (3000 m) Parks in Colorado, are considerably higher in elevation than intermountain basins such as the Bighorn (1500 m), Green River (1800 m), and Wind River (1500 m) Basins in Wyoming, and therefore have significantly different climatic and environmental conditions. Additionally, while true high-elevation parks are usually isolated zones bordered by higher forested environments, intermountain basins have more open borders with adjacent plains environments that are connected by alluvial valleys or low rolling hills. This said, we recognize that intermountain basins differ from true plains habitats in several ways. Basins are usually higher in elevation, receive less precipitation, and have slightly different vegetation cover (e.g., intermountain basins have greater sagebrush cover). However, intermountain valleys are similar to plains environments because animals, plants, and people may easily move between zones. We acknowledge that this classification system is imperfect, but we expect human land-use strategies to vary among these settings in response to climatic and ecologic differences.

The subalpine and alpine zones are the highest and harshest. Subalpine environments are a continuation of the woodland habitats of montane settings, but at higher elevation usually have forests with spruce, aspen, and bristlecone pine (Doerner 2007; Pitblado 2008). The subalpine zone can be a source area for edible plants and lithic raw materials (sometimes of poor quality). Foragers were often drawn to subalpine settings to hunt large game (elk, bighorn, mule deer) and fur-bearing animals (black bear, lynx, marmot, hare). This environment also offers a cool refuge from the hot summer conditions of lowland areas.

The alpine zone, found only at the top of the highest mountain ranges, is characterized by tundra or tundra-like conditions. Much of this zone was covered with large mountain glaciers during the late Pleistocene; however, many of these glaciers retreated during the early Holocene (Doerner 2007), thereby opening this environment to human settlement. During the early Holocene, alpine settings were dry, barren, and cold environments, with no trees and limited edible plant life (Brunswig 2007; Doerner 2007). Even though many of the permanent glaciers were gone by the early Holocene, alpine settings were probably closed to human and animal habitation for much of the year because of deep snow and very cold temperatures. However, during the warm summer months, alpine settings likely functioned as migration routes that allowed humans to move between the resource-rich lower-elevation zones on the eastern and western slopes of the mountains. The alpine zone was also used as hunting grounds for various game animals such as elk, bighorn, mountain goat, and mule deer (Benedict 2000; Pitblado 2003, 2008).

## Record of Cody Complex in the Mountains

Until relatively recently, archaeologists often assumed that Cody foragers and other Paleoindians left only a limited archaeological record in the Rocky Mountains (however, see Husted 1965, 1974, 2006; Moomaw 1957; Pitblado 2003, 2008). In fact, as late as the mid-1980s and early 1990s, researchers such as Eddy et al. (1984:19) and York (1991) argued that Paleoindians did not intensively occupy the mountains. The occasional diagnostic Paleoindian artifacts found in mountain settings, including isolated Scottsbluff and Eden points, were often assumed to be curated pieces collected by later prehistoric groups (e.g., Eddy et al. 1984:20; Reed and Metcalf 1999; Wendorf and Miller 1959). This argument appeared reasonable for a time, given the traditional hypothesis that Paleoindians were primarily mammoth- and bison-hunting specialists. Since such prey is preferentially found in lower-elevation grassland environments, there should be little reason for Paleoindians to spend time in the mountains.

Interestingly, even as more Paleoindian sites in the mountains are discovered and archaeologists recognize the use of mountain environments by Cody and other Paleoindian foragers, the extant Paleoindian record in the Rocky Mountains is still described as sparse (Pitblado 2003), meager (Reed and Metcalf 1999:57), or small (Jodry 1999: 49). This is probably because the archaeological record for Cody and other Paleoindian complexes in mountainous environments consist primarily of isolated surface finds of diagnostic projectile points (e.g., Husted 1974; Pitblado 2003; Reed and Metcalf 1999). Fewer intact buried Cody deposits are known from mountainous environments. Table 7.1 lists the key excavated Cody sites known from the Rocky Mountains.

Pitblado (2003:4) correctly notes that archaeological research into the late Paleoindian period in the Rocky Mountains has focused on three areas: rockshelters (found mostly in Wyoming and Montana) in the low foothills, open sites in mountain parks and high-elevation intermountain basins (e.g., Gunnison, San Luis, South Park, Middle Park, and North Park), and open sites in high-elevation subalpine-alpine zones. A number of rockshelter sites contain late Paleoindian archaeological deposits (e.g., Bottleneck Cave, Bush Shelter, Little Canyon Creek, Mangus, Medicine Lodge Creek, Mummy Cave, and Schiffer Cave) throughout the mountains, but this record is dominated by non-Cody cultural complexes (e.g., Angostura, Alder, Hardinger, Lovell Constricted/ Fishtail, James Allen/Frederick, Lusk, and Pryor Stemmed) (Kornfeld et al. 2010; Larson 2012). These localities have a limited early Paleoindian record (Finley et al. 2002; Frison 1992), and most

**TABLE 7.1.** Some Key Cody Complex Sites in Rocky Mountain Settings by Biogeographic Zone.

| Site | Site Type | Reference |
|---|---|---|
| **Foothill-Montane Zone** | | |
| 5HF2108 | unknown | Muñiz et al. 2003; cited in Muñiz 2005 |
| Crescent Rockshelter | rockshelter | Stone and Mendoza 1994 |
| Hell Gap, Loc. I | camp | Knell 2009 |
| Hell Gap, Loc. IIIs/V | camp | Knell et al. 2009 |
| Jim Pitts | camp | Sellet 2009 |
| Lawrence | camp | Wright 1984 |
| MacHaffie II | workshop/camp | Knudson 1983 |
| Malin Fishing Hole | camp | Vivian 2005 |
| Mammoth Meadow I, Level II | camp/workshop | Bonnichsen et al. 1992 |
| Mammoth Meadow I, Level III | camp/workshop | Bonnichsen et al. 1992 |
| Medicine Lodge Creek | rockshelter | Frison and Walker 2007 |
| Osprey Beach | camp | Johnson et al. 2004; Shortt 2002 |
| Pretty Creek | camp | Loendorf et al. 1981 |
| Wilbur Thomas Shelter | rockshelter | Breternitz 1971 |
| **Park Zone** | | |
| 5JA1183 | camp | Brunswig 2007 |
| 5JA1475 | kill/processing? | Brunswig 2007 |
| Barger Gulch, Loc. A | quarry | White 1998; Kornfeld and Frison 2000 |
| Hey Springs | unknown | Kornfeld and Frison 2000 |
| Jerry Craig | kill/processing | Kornfeld et al. 1999 |
| **Alpine Zone** | | |
| 5BL53 | camp | Brunswig 2007 |
| 5RN119 | artifact scatter | Jodry 1999 |
| Carey Lake | hunting camp | Morris 1990 |
| Devil's Thumb Valley | game drive/kill | Brunswig 2007 |
| Flattop Game Drive | game drive/kill | Brunswig 2007 |
| Forest Canyon Pass | game drive/kill | Brunswig 2007 |
| Trail Ridge Game Drive | game drive/kill | Brunswig 2007 |

lack any record of the Cody complex. One of the few rockshelters with a clear Cody occupation is Medicine Lodge Creek, situated along the western slope of the Bighorn Mountains (Frison 1992; Frison and Walker 2007). Other rockshelters have a more limited record of Cody use. A Scottsbluff point base was recovered from the lower levels of the Wilbur Thomas Shelter (Breternitz 1971), near Fort Collins, Colorado. At Crescent Rockshelter (Stone and Mendoza 1994), south of Denver, a Cody knife fragment was recovered in a midden deposit. In both cases, the Cody record includes an isolated artifact from an undated or poorly dated stratigraphic zone. Consequently, few definitive conclusions can be drawn about the nature of these Cody occupations.

A final rockshelter with a potential Cody component is Occupation 1 at the Sorenson site (Davis 1993; Husted 1969). Here two Scottsbluff-like point fragments were recovered in association with two hearths. The resemblance of the Sorenson projectile points with Cody types is vague, and the radiocarbon dates for these deposits are younger than most well-dated Cody sites (Frison 1992; Knell and Muñiz, this volume). The Cody record for the use of rockshelters is very limited, making it difficult to know how Cody foragers used such sites. However, given that the Cody record in rockshelters consists mostly of relatively small artifact assemblages, it is likely that Cody groups utilized these localities for brief periods to process and store plant and animal resources (Kornfeld et al. 2010; Pitblado 2003).

The record for Cody complex occupation is

richest at open-air sites in higher-elevation foothills and parks. A full range of activities occurred in these environments. Long- and short-term camps, such as Hell Gap (Larson et al. 2009), Osprey Beach (Johnson et al. 2004; Shortt 2002), and Pretty Creek (Loendorf et al. 1981), preferentially occur in this setting. The deposits in units II and III of the Mammoth Meadow site, located along the Upper Missouri River valley in the foothills of the Beaverhead Mountains, represent an intensively and repeatedly occupied lithic workshop in this environmental zone. The Jerry Craig site in Middle Park, Colorado, is an example of a Cody bison kill located in a high-elevation park (Hill and Kornfeld 1999; Kornfeld and Frison 2000; Richings-Germain 2002). Here Cody and Cody-like points were recovered along with the remains of five bison killed during the late summer or early fall (Kornfeld and Frison 2000:139). Another potential Cody kill locality in a high-elevation park is 5JA1475, which is located in North Park, Colorado (Brunswig 2007).

Although archaeologists such as E. B. Renaud (1934, 1942), C. T. Hurst (1941), and Betty Yelm (1935) investigated the Paleoindian record from the Rocky Mountains beginning in the 1930s, modern archaeological work on very high elevation (subalpine and alpine) Paleoindian sites really began in earnest in the early 1960s with Wilfred Husted's (1965) work at a James Allen complex site (Fourth of July site) located on top of a terminal moraine in the Southern Rocky Mountains of Colorado (Benedict 2005; see discussion in Pitblado and Brunswig 2007). James Benedict (1979, 1992a, 1992b) and Elizabeth Morris (1990, as cited in Pitblado and Brunswig 2007) spent the next several decades expanding on Husted's (1962, 1965, 1969, 1974) research. Benedict (1985) originally indicated that a Kersey complex point base and a scatter of nondiagnostic lithic debris were associated with a hearth at the Fourth of July site dated 8460 $^{14}$C yr BP (9485 cal BP); however, new excavations and a reanalysis of the original artifacts led Pitblado (2000) to argue that the site is a James Allen/Frederick occupation.

Other sites have produced a limited record of Cody artifacts from very high elevation sites. For example, Morris (1990) recovered numerous Cody point fragments from the high-elevation hunting camp of Carey Lake in Colorado. Brunswig (2007) reports on a Cody knife recovered from an alpine-subalpine ecotone camp (5BL53) in Colorado. Others undoubtedly exist.

Brunswig (2007) reports on a number of high-elevation Cody sites in Colorado that may be game drives. The Devil's Thumb Valley site has a lithic scatter and a surface find of an Eden point in association with low rock walls and rock cairns used for a game drive. Eden points also were associated with game drive features at the Flattop Game Drive site, and a possible Cody point base was recovered from the Trail Ridge Game Drive site (Benedict 2000; Brunswig 2007; Husted 1974).

The limited Cody record at such high-elevation settings makes it hard to reconstruct the nature of these occupations. We can speculate that Cody hunter-gathers preferentially focused on activities near mountain passes (see Benedict 2005). Based on the evidence from the Devil's Thumb Valley site, and potentially Flattop and Trail Ridge, it appears that Cody foragers, like other late Paleoindian foragers and later Archaic and Late Prehistoric groups, also periodically used high-elevation localities for ambush kills of large game animals, probably bighorn sheep and elk (Benedict 2000; Brunswig 2007; Pitblado 2003).

### Comparing Cody Settlement in the Mountains with Other Cultural Complexes

Studies of the distribution of isolated diagnostic points and the occasional buried site in mountain environments suggest that Cody groups regularly used high-elevation localities, especially in comparison with earlier Paleoindian groups. For example, both Husted's (1974) and Brunswig's (2007:283–284) work in the north-central Colorado mountains indicates that Cody and other late Paleoindian foothill-mountain complexes show greater use of high-elevation alpine and subalpine zones than did earlier Paleoindian complexes. Likewise, York's (1991) and Schroeder's (1991) studies in the Dolores Plateau, Colorado and Utah, respectively, conclude that early Paleoindian surface finds more commonly occur in lowland areas (<1800 masl), especially river valleys, than late Paleoindian artifacts. Similarly, Jodry's (1999) overview of the Paleoindian record for Colorado's eastern mountain ranges shows that Eden and Scottsbluff points are found at significantly higher elevations than early Paleoindian points. Amick's (1994) work in New Mexico reports that the mean elevation of Cody finds is 200 m higher than earlier Folsom occurrences.

Despite these findings, we know that early groups occasionally occupied high-elevation sites. Kornfeld and Frison's (2000) work in Middle Park, Colorado, and Jodry's (1999; Jodry et al. 1996) work at the Black Mountain site in southern Colorado uncovered substantial Folsom and Goshen sites above 2500 masl. In addition, Brunswig (2007) reports a series of Clovis, Goshen, and Folsom surface finds in high alpine or subalpine settings in and around Rocky Mountain National Park. However, early Paleoindian groups probably did not intensively use high mountain settings because glaciers and tundra would have limited access to passes and restricted animal migrations, reducing access to important resources and travel corridors.

Not all studies support the contention that Cody and other late Paleoindian complexes preferentially used upland environments. Pitblado's (1998:Table 2) study of the elevation distribution of diagnostic Paleoindian projectile points from the Southern Rockies suggests that Cody complex points were found at lower-elevation localities than most other Paleoindian complexes.

Reed and Metcalf (1999) suggest that early and late Paleoindian use of high-elevation environments varied as a result of different lengths of occupation and during different seasons, thereby resulting in different archaeological expressions of these periods. Specifically, they propose that early Paleoindians occupied the mountains only during warm seasons, whereas later groups made more year-round use of upland environments. York (1991) suggests that the greater use of upland areas by later groups reflects the upward retreat of mountain glaciers during the early Holocene. This suggestion may have merit, but bison tooth and eruption evidence from the Upper Twin Mountain site in Middle Park indicates a likely fall or winter Goshen occupation at over 2500 masl (Kornfeld et al. 1999). Likewise, Pitblado (1998; following the lead of Benedict 1992b) used the predominance of locally available quartzite projectile points from Cody and late Paleoindian sites to suggest that these groups more significantly limited their range to the mountains than did early groups.

Jodry (1999) and others (Brunswig 2007) argue that for mountain zones in Colorado, differential use of high-elevation sites probably relates to climatic shifts during the Paleoindian period. Jodry (1999:60) argues that the lowering of the upper timberline in the Southern Rocky Mountains during the terminal Pleistocene/early Holocene transition accounts for the paucity of Clovis and Folsom sites in very high elevation localities. Paleoecological records (Doerner 2007) suggest that before 10,000 $^{14}$C yrs BP (11,470 cal BP) tundra existed across much of the Rocky Mountains, and tree line was depressed up to 500 m below modern limits. By the late Paleoindian period (10,000–8000 $^{14}$C yrs BP; 11,400–8980 cal BP), rapid warming caused tree lines to move upward and made high-elevation settings more habitable, at least during the warm season.

Jodry (1999) and Benedict (1992b) argue that by late Paleoindian times good campsites could be established in these environments and so these areas were reoccupied repeatedly. It was this reoccupation of late Paleoindian sites that makes them appear more intensively occupied than early Paleoindian sites.

## Prior Models of Cody Land Use in the Mountains

It has been clear for some time that the occupation of mountain settings involves a substantially different kind of lifeway than other areas, especially the plains grasslands/rolling hills (Benedict 1992a; Black 1991; Husted 1969; Pitblado 2003; see discussion in Larson 2012). One of the emerging patterns is that many researchers now accept that Cody complex and other late Paleoindians in mountain environments restricted or tethered their movements to this zone for considerable periods of time (Johnson et al. 2004; Knell and Hill 2012; Richings-Germain 2002; Stanford 1999) (Table 7.2). These interpretations generally rely on the predominance of local toolstone recovered at sites as well as seasonality data depicting a long-term occupation or overwintering strategy (Richings-Germain 2002).

Pitblado (2003) conducted an extensive review of late Paleoindian technological and land-use organization patterning, considering regional patterns in the Great Plains, Southern Rocky Mountains, Colorado Plateau, and Great Basin based on

**TABLE 7.2.** Prior Models of Cody Complex Land Use in Mountain Settings.

| Author | Scale of Analysis | Data Type | Land-Use Strategy | Regionally Restricted? | Causal Pattern |
|---|---|---|---|---|---|
| Amick (1994) | Regional | Projectile point and site distribution | Sites closer to more diverse resource base; isolated points associated with solitary game hunting areas | Not specified | Resource structure: foraging theory |
| Frison (1992) | Regional | Site location, subsistence strategy | Some late Paleoindians were mountains oriented and others plains oriented to monitor resources; Cody doing both | Biome focused, but less so during Cody times | Resource structure: environmental stress |
| Johnson et al. (2004) | Site: Osprey Beach | Toolstone provenance | Warm-season use of high elevations; seasonally transhumant | Regionally restricted long-term/seasonal | Resource structure: cold stress |
| Knell and Hill (2012) | Regional | Toolstone provenance, diet breadth, and bison seasonality | Cody regionally restricted in mountain settings, limited logistical use of plains grasslands | Regionally focused, seasonal | Resource structure: foraging theory |
| Pitblado (2003) | Regional | Projectile points, toolstone provenance | Sporadic use of mountains; plains-oriented lifeway | Not specified | Resource structure: cold stress |
| Richings-Germain (2002) | Site: Jerry Craig | Toolstone provenance, seasonality data | Long-term use of high mountain basin; foothills-montane adapted | Regionally focused, long-term/seasonal | Not specified |
| Stanford (1999) | Regional | Toolstone provenance; climate | Increasing regionalization due to climatic warming and drying | Regionally focused | Resource structure: environmental stress |

projectile point distributions and lithic raw material provenance. Pitblado evaluated all Paleoindian cultural complexes, but here we focus on her conclusions for the Cody complex. She found a higher proportion of Eden/Firstview points on the Plains grasslands than in the Rocky Mountains, leading her to suggest that Cody groups maintained a plains-oriented lifeway in which they logistically hunted big game (see similar views by Black 1991). Conversely, the lower proportion of Eden/Firstview projectile points in the Rocky Mountains indicated sporadic use of this environment, with most points recovered from foothills and parks rather than higher mountain settings. Due to cold-season stresses, both fauna and late Paleoindians preferred lower-elevation foothill or park settings, where they remained logistically oriented. During the warm season, late Paleoindians maintained a "low-intensity, nonwinter, forager-style use of foothills woodlands" (Pitblado 2003:246). Pitblado ultimately interpreted Cody complex and late Paleoindian land use as responses to variations in cold-season versus warm-season resource structure. Benedict (1992b) had previously argued that this relatively simple strategy, in which foragers move up and down elevation gradients based on seasonal conditions, is expected by groups who used the mountains but were unfamiliar with the full range of available ecosystems and resources.

Other research indicates long-term, if not year-round, occupation of mountain environments. In the high-elevation basin of Middle Park, Colorado, the Cody complex Jerry Craig site is a late-summer to early-fall season bison kill with a chipped stone assemblage dominated by local toolstone. Richings-Germain (2002:111) concludes that these Cody complex hunter-gatherers were "a foothills-mountain adapted group inhabiting Middle Park for an extended period, either seasonally as part of a seasonal transhumance system or year-round." Two earlier Paleoindian sites are also suggestive of year-round occupation of Middle Park: Upper Twin Mountain and Barger Gulch. The Goshen complex Upper Twin Mountain site is a winter-season bison kill, which given the high elevation and cold season, suggests that these hunter-gatherers probably intended to remain in the basin rather than leave before snow closed the passes (Kornfeld and Frison 2000).

Similarly, Folsom complex hunter-gatherers occupied the Barger Gulch site (Locality B) from one to three months, possibly during the cold season (Surovell et al. 2003). The pattern in Middle Park may correspond to Pitblado's (2003) inference for Angostura groups, which maintained a full-time occupation strategy in the Southern Rocky Mountains.

The Osprey Beach site, Yellowstone National Park, provides additional clues to Cody complex land-use organization in a high mountain setting (Johnson et al. 2004:142–145). Johnson and her co-authors suggest that Cody complex hunter-gatherers occupied Osprey Beach between summer and early fall, probably summer, based on the high elevation and the warm-dry early Holocene summers but cold winters. They further contend that cold stress led Cody complex groups to overwinter in the foothills rather than the mountains because of the extreme cold and paucity of available resources. The wide variety of sourced lithic raw materials at Osprey Beach is attributed to either (1) trade between seasonally coalesced Cody complex groups in the Yellowstone Plateau or (2) a proposed seasonal round that began in Yellowstone Park during spring-summer, moved south through western Wyoming during fall and northeastern Idaho during winter, and ended with a return to Yellowstone Park via southern Montana (Johnson et al. 2004:243). The seasonal round explanation requires testing but, if true, implies that Cody complex groups maintained a seasonally transhumant land-use strategy. Still requiring consideration is how such a structured transhumant pattern ties into the seasonal resource structure.

Frison (1978, 1988, 1991, 1992, 1993, 1997; Frison and Bonnichsen 1996; Frison and Grey 1980) recognized two distinctive late Paleoindian adaptive strategies: the foothills-mountains-oriented and plains-oriented traditions. Foothills-mountains-oriented groups subsisted on a broad spectrum of plant and animal resources, whereas plains-oriented groups primarily hunted big game. He sees this dichotomous strategy as a response to early Holocene climate fluctuations: late Paleoindians could not adequately monitor resources in both the foothills-mountains and plains grasslands environmental zones (Frison 1992; Frison and Bonnichsen 1996). The dichotomy persisted through late Paleoindian times, but as Frison and Bonnichsen (1996:314; also Frison 1992:339) note, it started breaking down during Cody complex times: "the Cody cultural complex appears in some foothill-mountain Paleoindian sites and seems to be the exception to the dichotomy in subsistence observed between foothill-mountain and open plains groups."

The dichotomy broke down because increased Holocene drying negatively affected bison populations on the plains, which made a late Paleoindian bison-focused subsistence strategy no longer viable (Frison 1992:339). Frison thus cites ecological factors and resource-monitoring concerns as reasons why late Paleoindians maintained the dichotomous foothill-mountain and open-plains strategies. However, at the same time, Frison (1992) notes that compared with other late Paleoindian complexes, Cody groups made limited use of mountain rockshelters, which suggests that while Cody foragers made short trips to upland zones, they may not have intensively occupied these areas.

Knell (2007, this volume; Knell and Hill 2012) has developed a land-use model based on the principles of the patch choice and marginal value theorem, as well as resource availability expectations, which tries to explain the nature of Cody settlement in mountain and plains environments. This model predicts, and analysis of archaeological data supports (Knell 2007; Knell and Hill 2012; Knell, this volume; Root et al., this volume), that foragers will become regionally restricted (i.e., tether or slow down their movements) in environments that are calorie-rich, have seasonally predictable and abundant biotic resources, and have good-quality toolstone. The land-use model predicts that these conditions occur most often in the foothill-montane zone. Moreover, the model predicts that regionally restricted groups in the foothill-montane zone would incorporate a diversity of food resources into their diet (i.e., have a wide diet breadth) and rely on local lithic raw materials for their toolkits.

Conversely, in environmental zones with a low caloric abundance of biotic resources that are temporally unpredictable, and with heterogeneously distributed sources of toolstone, such as large areas of the Great Plains, calorie-maximizing Paleoindians should employ a nonregionally restricted land-use strategy. In these settings foragers would move rapidly through grassland areas in pursuit of mobile game, resulting in narrow diet breadth and high bison use. These groups will use locally available lithic materials when available; however, through high residential and logistical mobility we anticipate a high proportion of nonlocal toolstone in Plains grassland assemblages.

### Test of Existing Models

The current analysis evaluates the utility of some of the prior findings for Cody complex land-use strategies in the mountains. Archaeologists have long noticed a striking parallel between the archaeological record on the Great Plains and in the Rocky Mountains (Frison 1992; Husted 1974), but remaining unknown is the extent to which foragers in these environmental zones practiced similar land-use strategies. To explore this issue, we address two broad questions. First, does Cody land-use organization in mountain settings differ from that evident in plains grassland settings? Second, how similar or different was Cody land-use organization from that of contemporaneous non-Cody late Paleoindian groups living in the same environment?

To investigate these broad objectives, we attempt to answer specific research questions that explore variation in Cody land-use organization:

1. Are the prey choice decisions of Cody foragers in the mountains different from those of Cody foragers in plains settings, and are Cody strategies different from those of other contemporary late Paleoindian groups occupying those same environments?
2. Do Cody foragers occupy different environmental zones at the same time of year as other late Paleoindians?
3. Are the regional lithic raw material use strategies of Cody foragers in the mountains different from those in plains settings, and were Cody strategies different from those of contemporary late Paleoindian groups occupying those same environments?

Test expectations for these research questions are derived from Knell's (2007, this volume; Knell and Hill 2012) land-use model and tested using faunal and lithic information from 64 archaeological sites or components of sites from across the Rocky Mountains and adjacent northern Plains (see Figure 7.1).

The faunal data used in this study come from 45 components: 17 Cody, 14 late Paleoindian Plains (LPP), and 14 late Paleoindian Mountains (LPM) (Table 7.3). Twenty-eight of the sites are from plains grasslands and alluvial valley settings, and 17 are from the mountains (i.e., 16 from foothill-montane and 1 from park zones).

To evaluate the faunal data, we applied three prey-choice measures to residential (i.e., camp) sites. First is the Margalef Index ($D_{mg}$), a richness measure that standardizes the abundance of species by overall sample size (Jones et al. 2008; Magurran 1988). Second is the reciprocal of Simpson's Index, which calculates evenness or relative specialization from the 25 most common taxa (M. E. Hill 2008). Last is the calculation of Abundance Indices for large, medium, and small fauna that capture the effect package size has on diet choice (M. E. Hill 2008). Bison are the predominant large game; cervids and bighorn sheep are the medium game; and lagomorphs, rodents, and canids are the small game. Season of bison mortality is reconstructed using mandibular tooth eruption and occlusal attrition data (Frison 1978, 1982; Todd et al. 1996). Dental age group values are tabulated in 0.1-year increments starting with a presumed middle of spring (i.e., late April) birth pulse (N).

The lithic data used in this study come from 39 components or sites: 29 Cody, 4 LPP, and 6 LPM. The database is split between mountain ($n$ = 14: 1 in park, 2 in subalpine/alpine zone, and 11 in foothill-montane zones) and plains grassland and alluvial valley ($n$ = 25) sites (Table 7.4). The model is tested with two lithic variables: toolstone provenance of projectile points and tools (also see Knell and Hill 2012). Tools were selected as the basis for analysis because they are more often identified to raw material source than is debitage in the literature.

The first lithic variable evaluates the toolstone provenance of projectile points. The proportion of long use-life tools such as projectile points manufactured from local and nonlocal toolstone provides clues to regional procurement systems, as these tools frequently (but not necessarily) remain in toolkits longer than short use-life tools such as utilized flakes. Following this logic, we

**TABLE 7.3.** Summary Statistics for Faunal Data Used in This Study by Cultural Complex and Environmental Zone.

| SITE | Large AI | Medium AI | Small AI | Dental Age Interval | Margalef Index | Simpson D |
|---|---|---|---|---|---|---|
| **Cody in Plains** | | | | | | |
| Carter/Kerr-McGee | | | | 0.6–0.7 | | |
| Finley Station A | 1.00 | 0.00 | 0.00 | 0.6–0.9 | 0.49 | 0.99 |
| Finley Station B | 1.00 | 0.00 | 0.00 | 0.6 | 0.56 | 0.99 |
| Frasca Area 1 | 1.00 | 0.00 | 0.00 | 0.7–0.8 | 0.22 | 1.00 |
| Heron Eden | 1.00 | 0.00 | 0.00 | 0.6–0.7 | 0.20 | 1.00 |
| Horner I | 0.99 | 0.01 | 0.00 | 0.6 | 0.39 | 0.99 |
| Horner II | 1.00 | 0.00 | 0.00 | 0.6 | 0.23 | 1.00 |
| Hudson-Meng | | | | 0.2–0.4 | | |
| Jurgens | 0.97 | 0.02 | 0.01 | 0.4–0.5 | 1.51 | 0.97 |
| Lamb Spring | 1.00 | 0.00 | 0.00 | 0.6–1.0 | 0.31 | 1.00 |
| Lime Creek Zone I | 0.28 | 0.15 | 0.57 | 0.4–0.5 | 1.14 | 0.21 |
| Nelson | 1.00 | 0.00 | 0.00 | 0.7–0.8 | 0.37 | 1.00 |
| Olsen-Chubbuck | 1.00 | 0.00 | 0.00 | 0.4 | 0.23 | 1.00 |
| Scottsbluff | 1.00 | 0.00 | 0.00 | 0.1–0.3 | 0.23 | 1.00 |
| **Cody in Mountains** | | | | | | |
| Hell Gap Locality IIIs/V | 0.99 | 0.00 | 0.01 | 0.1–0.7 | 0.56 | 0.98 |
| Jerry Craig | 1.00 | 0.00 | 0.00 | 0.3–0.5 | 0.35 | 1.00 |
| Medicine Lodge Creek | 0.07 | 0.14 | 0.79 | | 1.50 | 0.36 |
| **Non-Cody Late Paleoindian in Mountains** | | | | | | |
| Helen Lookingbill Level 7/9 | 0.01 | 0.99 | 0.00 | | 0.48 | 0.70 |
| Hell Gap Locality I | | | | 0.3–0.5 | | |
| Medicine Lodge Creek North Paleo. | 0.29 | 0.36 | 0.36 | | 2.27 | 0.12 |
| Medicine Lodge Creek Fire Pit | 0.00 | 0.28 | 0.72 | | 1.98 | 0.17 |
| Medicine Lodge Creek Pryor Stemmed | 0.02 | 0.48 | 0.50 | | 1.77 | 0.22 |
| Mummy Cave Level 1 | 0.00 | 0.14 | 0.86 | | 2.40 | 0.39 |
| Mummy Cave Level 4 | 0.00 | 0.52 | 0.48 | | 2.33 | 0.17 |
| Mummy Cave Level 6 | 0.00 | 0.38 | 0.63 | | 1.90 | 0.16 |
| Mummy Cave Level 8 | 0.00 | 0.98 | 0.02 | | 1.35 | 0.41 |
| Mummy Cave Level 9 | 0.00 | 0.99 | 0.01 | | 1.08 | 0.57 |
| Mummy Cave Level 10 | 0.00 | 0.94 | 0.06 | | 1.62 | 0.56 |
| Mummy Cave Level 11 | 0.00 | 1.00 | 0.00 | | 0.91 | 0.78 |
| Mummy Cave Level 12 | 0.00 | 0.91 | 0.09 | | 1.78 | 0.42 |
| Mummy Cave Level 14 | 0.00 | 0.76 | 0.24 | | 2.12 | 0.36 |
| **Non-Cody Late Paleoindian in Plains** | | | | | | |
| 48SW13156 | 0.00 | 0.02 | 0.98 | | 0.78 | 0.97 |
| 48SW8842 | 0.00 | 0.00 | 1.00 | | 0.60 | 1.00 |
| 48UT375 Component 1 | 0.00 | 0.00 | 1.00 | | 0.59 | 1.00 |
| 48UT375 Component 2 | 0.00 | 0.00 | 1.00 | | 0.62 | 0.98 |
| Allen OL2 | 0.03 | 0.10 | 0.87 | | 2.52 | 0.35 |
| Blue Point Component 1 | 0.10 | 0.25 | 0.65 | | 1.05 | 0.34 |
| Blue Point Component 2 | 0.00 | 0.01 | 0.99 | | 1.16 | 0.83 |
| Burntwood Creek | 1.00 | 0.00 | 0.00 | 0.1–0.2 | 0.27 | 1.00 |
| Clary Ranch | 0.96 | 0.00 | 0.04 | 0.3–0.5 | 0.66 | 0.92 |
| Laird | | | | 0.6–0.9 | | |
| Meserve | 1.00 | 0.00 | 0.00 | | 0.35 | 1.00 |
| Norton Site | | | | 0.6–08 | | |
| OV Clary Middle | 1.00 | 0.00 | 0.00 | 0.3–1.0 | 0.27 | 1.00 |
| Winger | 0.97 | 0.00 | 0.03 | 0.6–0.8 | 0.58 | 0.94 |

*Note:* AI = Artiodactyl Index. Large AI = NISP of size class 4 taxa /total NISP; Medium AI = NISP of size classes 2 and 3 taxa/total NISP; Small AI = NISP of size class 1 taxa /total NISP.

*References:* 48SW13156 (Byers et al. 2005); 48SW8842 (Byers et al. 2005); 48UT375 (Smith et al. 2003); Allen (Bamforth 2007); Blue Point (Johnson and Pastor 2003); Burntwood Creek (Hill et al. 1992); Carter/Kerr-McGee (Frison 1984); Clary Ranch (M. G. Hill 2008); Finley (M. E. Hill 2008; Reynolds and Hill 2010); Frasca (Fulgham and Stanford 1982); Hell Gap (Larson et al. 2009; Knell 2009; Knell et al. 2009); Heron Eden (Corbeil 1995); Horner (Frison and Todd 1987; Muñiz 2005); Hudson-Meng (Agenbroad 1978); Jerry Craig (Richings-Germain 2002); Jurgens (Wheat 1979; Hill and Hill 2002); Laird (Hofman and Blackmar 1997); Lamb Spring (McCartney 1983); Lime Creek (Jones 1999); Medicine Lodge Creek (Frison and Walker 2007); Meserve (Barbour and Schultz 1932); Mummy Cave (Husted and Edgar 2002; Hughes 2003); Nelson (Kornfeld et al. 2007); Norton (Hofman et al. 1995); Olsen-Chubbuck (Wheat 1972); OV Clary (Hill et al. 2011); Scottsbluff (M. E. Hill 2008); Winger (Mandel and Hofman 2003).

**TABLE 7.4.** Summary Statistics for Lithic Variables Used in This Study by Cultural Complex and Environmental Zone.

| Name | Local Tools | Nonlocal Tools | Unknown | TI | Local Points | Nonlocal Points | Unknown Points | PI |
|---|---|---|---|---|---|---|---|---|
| **Cody in Plains** | | | | | | | | |
| Benz | 146 | 0 | 0 | 1.00 | 2 | 0 | 0 | 1.00 |
| Blue Point | 11 | 4 | 0 | 0.73 | 3 | 4 | 0 | 0.43 |
| Carter/Kerr-McGee (Alb) | 3 | | | | 2 | 2 | 1 | 0.50 |
| Carter/Kerr-McGee (Cody) | 0 | 0 | 5 | | 2 | 6 | 16 | 0.25 |
| Claypool | 2 | 8 | 23 | 0.2 | 8 | 21 | 51 | 0.28 |
| DjNf-8 | | | | | 0 | 3 | 8 | 0 |
| Dunn | | | | | 2 | 75 | 0 | 0.026 |
| Frasca Area 1 | 1 | 0 | 0 | | 7 | 0 | 1 | 1.00 |
| Haskey Area | 0 | 0 | 4 | | 14 | 4 | 9 | 0.78 |
| Heron Eden | | | | | 1 | 7 | 5 | 0.13 |
| Horner I | 14 | 119 | 19 | 0.11 | 3 | 44 | 5 | 0.06 |
| Horner II | 3 | 9 | 2 | 0.25 | 1 | 20 | 1 | 0.05 |
| Hudson-Meng | 12 | 9 | 0 | 0.57 | 8 | 13 | 0 | 0.38 |
| Jurgens | 22 | 84 | 42 | 0.21 | 8 | 27 | 32 | 0.23 |
| Lime Creek Zone I | 15 | 0 | 1 | 1.00 | 1 | 0 | 1 | 1.00 |
| Max | 0 | 1 | 0 | | 1 | 44 | 0 | 0.02 |
| Nelson | 6 | 0 | 0 | 1.00 | 3 | 1 | 0 | 0.75 |
| Niska | 5 | 21 | 0 | 0.19 | 0 | 8 | 0 | 0 |
| Olsen-Chubbuck | 0 | 5 | 2 | 0 | 2 | 12 | 13 | 0.14 |
| Scottsbluff | 3 | 1 | 0 | 0.75 | 4 | 0 | 0 | 1.00 |
| **Cody in Mountains** | | | | | | | | |
| Hell Gap Locality I (Alb) | 14 | 3 | 1 | 0.82 | 3 | 0 | 0 | 1.00 |
| Hell Gap Locality I (Cody) | 36 | 2 | 0 | 0.95 | 9 | 0 | 0 | 1.00 |
| Hell Gap Locality IIIs/V | 189 | 1 | 5 | 0.99 | 21 | 0 | 0 | 1.00 |
| Jerry Craig | 14 | 1 | 0 | 0.93 | 64 | 10 | 1 | 0.86 |
| Jim Pitts | | | | | 3 | 1 | 0 | 0.75 |
| MacHaffie | 29 | 3 | 0 | 0.91 | 6 | 3 | 0 | 0.67 |
| Mammoth Meadow | | | | | | | | 1 |
| Osprey Beach | 2 | 35 | 6 | .05 | 2 | 9 | 1 | .18 |
| **Non-Cody Late Paleoindian in Mountain** | | | | | | | | |
| 48JO303 | | | | | 19 | 0 | 0 | 1 |
| Bottleneck Cave Level III | | | | | 14 | 0 | 0 | 1 |
| Caribou Lake | 6 | 1 | 0 | 0.86 | 4 | 0 | 0 | 1 |
| Chance Gulch Locality B | 18 | 0 | 0 | 1 | 19 | 0 | 0 | 1 |
| Hell Gap Locality I (Frederick) | 111 | 0 | 0 | 1 | | | | |
| Schiffer Cave | | | | | 4 | 0 | 0 | 1 |
| **Non-Cody Late Paleoindian in Plains** | | | | | | | | |
| Allen OL2 | 29 | 0 | 0 | 1.00 | 1 | 0 | 0 | |
| Allen IZ | 67 | 0 | 0 | 1.00 | 1 | 0 | 0 | |
| Allen OL1 | 117 | 1 | 0 | 0.99 | 2 | 1 | 1 | 0.67 |
| Red Smoke Zone 88 | | | | | 27 | 7 | 2 | 0.79 |

*Note:* TI = tool index; PI = projectile point index.

*References:* 48JO303 (Frison and Grey 1980); Allen (Bamforth 2007); Benz (Root 1992; Root et al. 1985); Blue Point (Johnson and Pastor 2003); Bottleneck Cave (Husted 1969); Caribou Lake (Pitblado 2000); Carter/Kerr-McGee (Frison 1984; Muñiz 2005); Chance Gulch (Pitblado and Camp 2003); Claypool (Dick and Mountain 1960; Muñiz 2005); DjNf-8 (Ebell 1975); Dunn (Ebell 1988); Frasca (Fulgham and Stanford 1982); Haskey Area (Novecosky 2002); Hell Gap (Byrnes 2003; Irwin-Williams et al. 1973; Knell 2009; Knell et al. 2009; Larson et al. 2009); Heron Eden (Linnamae and Johnson 1999); Horner (Frison and Todd 1987; Muñiz 2005); Hudson-Meng (Agenbroad 1978; Muñiz 2005); Jerry Craig (Richings-Germain 2002); Jim Pitts (Sellet 2009); Jurgens (Wheat 1979; Muñiz 2005); Lime Creek (Davis 1962; Hicks 2002); Max (Root et al., this volume); MacHaffie (Knudson 1983); Mammoth Meadow (Douglas 1991; also Bonnichsen et al. 1992); Nelson (Kornfeld et al. 2007); Niska (Meyer 1985); Olsen-Chubbuck (Wheat 1972; Muñiz 2005); Osprey Beach (Johnson et al. 2004; Shortt 2002); Red Smoke (Knudson 2002); Schiffer Cave (Frison and Grey 1980); Scottsbluff (Knudson, this volume).

interpret sites with a high proportion of projectile points from local sources to reflect regionally restricted land use, and those with a high proportion of points from nonlocal sources to represent nonregionally restricted land use. This proportion is calculated using the projectile point index (PI), which is calculated as follows: PI = Σ Local Lithic Material Projectile Points/(Σ Local Lithic Material Projectile Points + Σ Nonlocal Lithic Material Projectile Points).

The second lithic test expectation uses the tool index (TI), which is similar to the PI but includes only shaped (e.g., scrapers) and unshaped (e.g., utilized flakes) flake tools and nonprojectile point bifaces; projectile points and debitage are excluded. Debitage is excluded because many flakes are typically removed in the production or resharpening of a single tool, which can significantly inflate lithic raw material proportion. The TI assesses the proportion of tools created from local and nonlocal lithic raw material: sites with a high proportion of tools from local sources reflect regionally restricted land use, and those with a high proportion of tools from nonlocal sources reflect nonregionally restricted land use. The TI is calculated as follows: TI = Σ Local Lithic Material Tools/(Σ Local Lithic Material Tools + Σ Nonlocal Lithic Material Tools).

For both indexes, a value closer to 1.0 indicates a high proportion of projectile points or tools from local toolstone and a number closer to 0 indicates a high proportion of points or tools from nonlocal toolstone. For consistency, we roughly adopted the criteria established by Carr (2005; Carr and Boszhardt 2010): PI and TI values ≥.80 represent a high proportion of artifacts from local sources and regionally restricted land use; PI and TI values ≤.25 represent a high proportion of artifacts from nonlocal sources and nonregional land use (Knell and Hill 2012). Values between these thresholds are interpreted as indeterminate evidence for a particular land-use strategy. The cutoff between local and nonlocal toolstone is 40 km (following Gould and Saggers 1985; Meltzer 1989).

### *Prey Choice*

As discussed above, we explore prey choice decisions to determine whether Cody foragers changed land-use strategies based on environment and whether the Cody strategy differed from those of their contemporaries. Our land-use model predicts that strong regional differences should occur in diet choice. Specifically, we expect that populations in mountain settings were regionally restricted foragers who maintained a wide and even diet breadth because they incorporated a wide range of locally available resources into their diet. When in the plains, Paleoindians should have been nonregionally restricted hunter-gatherers who targeted aggregated bison herds, resulting in a narrow and uneven diet breadth. While our model does not explicitly consider differences among cultural groups, nothing in the model suggests that late Paleoindian foragers should vary their land-use approach.

The available data from camp assemblages partially contradict our expectations (Figures 7.2 and 7.3). Among non-Cody late Paleoindian mountain (LPM) sites there is significantly broader diet as measured by the Margalef Index (Mann-Whitney U = 23, $p = .03$) and a more even distribution of prey taxa as measured by the Simpson Index (Mann-Whitney U = 16, $p = .009$) than occurs among late Paleoindian plains (LPP) sites. These results are the expected outcome based on our model, which suggests that hunter-gatherers living in foothill-montane zones practiced a different foraging strategy than foragers in plains grassland settings. Interestingly, Cody sites differ from this pattern, as they show no significant regional difference in prey choice. In fact, mountain Cody sites as a group have diet breadth and evenness values comparable to Cody groups on the plains. Thus, foragers at LPM sites in foothill-montane settings included a wide variety of resources in their diet, whereas Cody foragers in the same environmental zone had a narrow diet breadth focused on bison (i.e., high large-body abundance index).

Comparing the body size abundance indexes between camp assemblages allows us to evaluate how specific prey types were utilized. The broad, generalized diet of LPM sites shows varied use of prey. At only a few of these sites (Medicine Lodge Creek North Paleo and Pryor Stemmed levels; Mummy Cave level 4) was there generally equal use of large, medium, and small game. Instead, it is more common for the assemblages to predominantly consist of either several medium-size artiodactyl taxa (especially bighorn sheep and

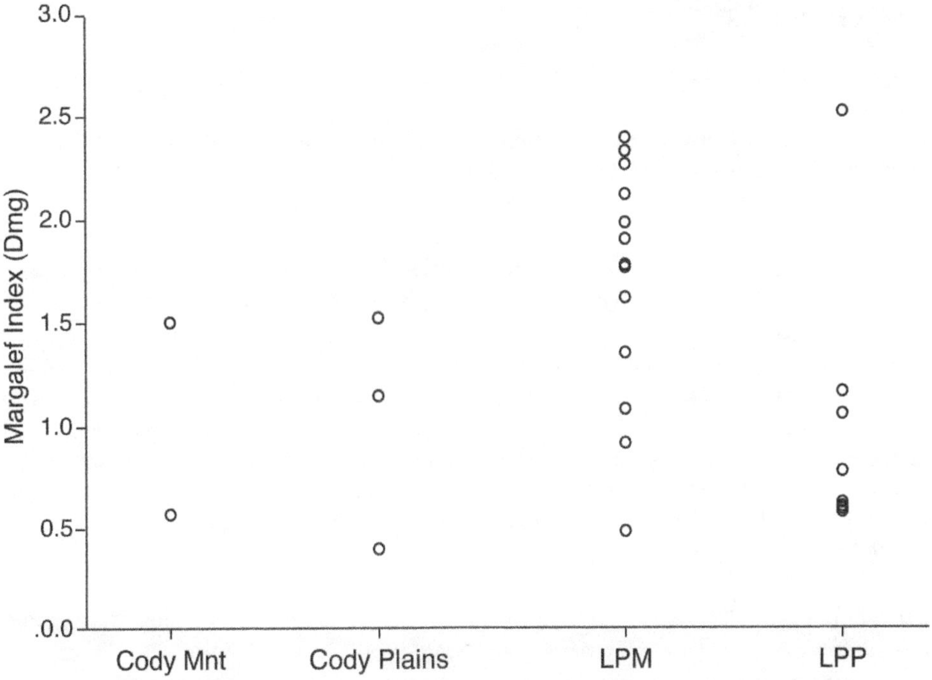


FIGURE 7.2. Margalef Index values by cultural complex and geographic area. Cody Mnt, Cody complex assemblages in mountains; Cody Plains, Cody complex assemblages in plains; LPM, Non-Cody complex assemblages in mountains; LPP, Non-Cody complex assemblages in plains.

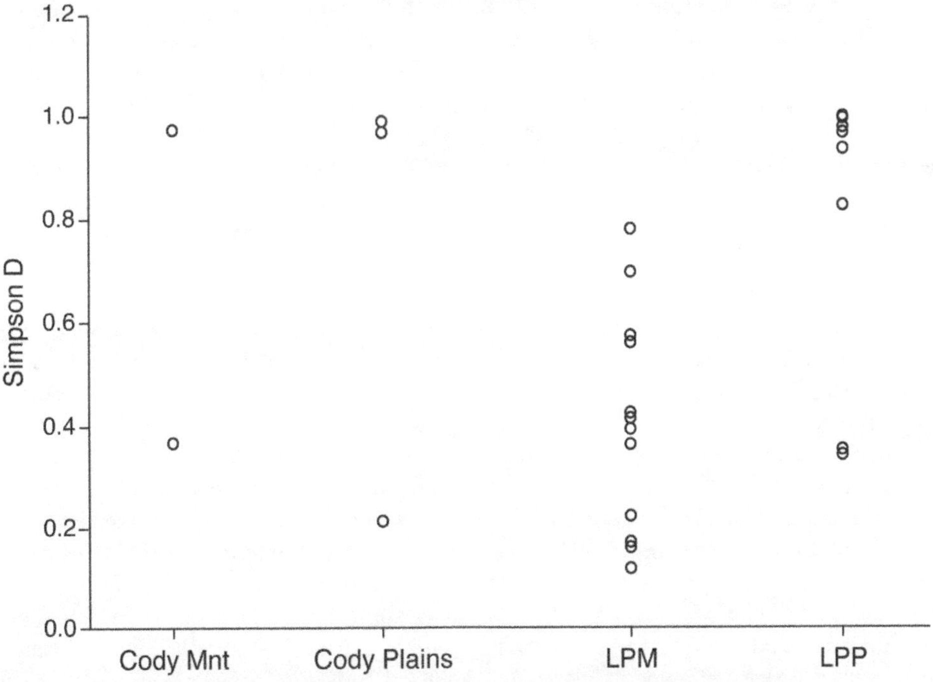


FIGURE 7.3. Simpson D Index values by cultural complex and geographic area. Cody Mnt, Cody complex assemblages in mountains; Cody Plains, Cody complex assemblages in plains; LPM, Non-Cody complex assemblages in mountains; LPP, Non-Cody complex assemblages in plains.

deer, as at Helen Lookingbill and Mummy Cave levels 8, 9, 10, 11, 12, and 14) or a variety of small game (especially lagomorphs and rodents, as at Medicine Lodge Creek Lovell Constricted and Mummy Cave level 6). Conversely, LPP assemblages have relatively narrow diets. Surprisingly, this does not mean that these hunters were specialized big-game hunters; in most cases (e.g., Allen, Blue Point, 48SW8842, 48SW13156, and 48UT375) the narrow diet consisted predominantly of rodent-sized small game. While Allen is located in an alluvial valley, which cuts through a true plains environment that likely supported abundant bison populations, the other sites with this particular focus to their diet are located in the Green River Basin of southwestern Wyoming. During the early Holocene this intermountain basin likely had a dry climate that supported a Great Basin–like arid sagebrush or desert shrubland vegetation. On the surface, it appears that the local environment was probably not suited to supporting large bison populations. This said, however, it should be noted that the Finley site, a contemporary early Holocene site in the Green River Valley, has evidence for one or more kill events that included remains of more than 150 bison. Thus, at roughly the same time that the foragers at Blue Point and 48SW8842 specialized their diet on small prey such as rodents and lagomorphs, the hunters at Finley were able to kill huge numbers of bison in the exact same environment. To us this implies that a simple environmental explanation probably cannot fully explain the patterning we are seeing.

The unanticipated pattern for Cody is likely driven by a couple of factors. First, sample size for Cody camps is small ($n = 3$), making it difficult to demonstrate statistically significant differences. Second, the faunal assemblage from the foothill-montane Cody camp at Hell Gap IIIs/V is dominated by bison remains, which probably results from the fact that this site is situated in a low-elevation uplift that likely supported large, local bison herds or made accessing bison in adjacent plains settings feasible. In contrast, the plains camps of Jurgens and Lime Creek occur along alluvial valleys that offer rich and diverse biotic and abiotic resources, which facilitated increased occupational intensity and exploitation of a greater mixture of small, medium, and large game (Knell and Hill 2012).

### *Seasonality of Kill*

To explore whether Cody foragers occupied different environmental zones at the same time of year as other late Paleoindians, we analyze information on season of bison mortality. Obviously, these data are only a proxy measure for when foragers occupied particular settings, as a lack of evidence for bison hunting during a particular period does not preclude the presence of nonhunting foragers in that environment. Seasonal variability in prey condition may have discouraged hunters from pursuing bison, however. Thus, if different regions have evidence of hunting during the same season, then either the same group of hunters positioned themselves in different environments during the same seasons or different groups of hunters occupied the two areas simultaneously. Despite the lack of precision with seasonality data, it must be recognized that these data are the best available procedure for estimating generalized patterns of seasonal use of different environments.

Our land-use model predicts that because foothills-mountain settings had greater resource abundance throughout much of the year than the plains grasslands, foragers should have been regionally restricted to the foothill-montane zone during summer through winter, when conditions were favorable. During the spring, when only poor-quality resources were available, Cody hunter-gatherers in the mountains optimally employed a nonregionally focused land-use strategy. Because we expect resource abundance to be lower in plains grasslands than mountain settings, foragers in the plains optimally were regionally restricted only during the summer and nonregionally focused during all other times (see Knell 2007 for a full explanation of the expectations).

Figure 7.4 depicts the seasonality estimates for 23 assemblages (see Table 7.3). We lack evidence from LPM sites due to the paucity of bison remains from these assemblages. Therefore, these data allow comparison only between Cody assemblages from plains and mountain settings and among Cody and LPP groups across the plains.

Overall, our model expectations are not fully

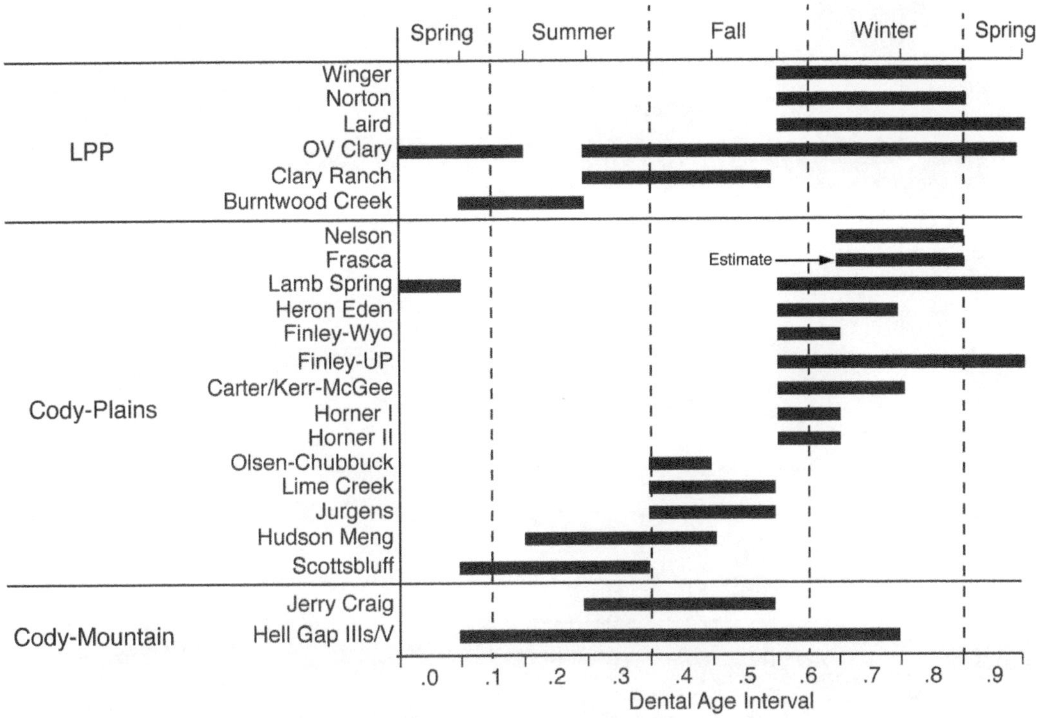


FIGURE 7.4. Dental age interval indicating season of site occupation for bison remains and predicted land-use strategy by cultural complex and environmental zone. Cody Mountain, Cody complex assemblages in mountains; Cody Plains, Cody complex assemblages in plains; LPP, Non-Cody complex assemblages in plains.

met, as the three groups are similar in their seasonal use of bison. In general, there is limited evidence for hunting bison during the spring. All the sites that have evidence for bison hunting during the spring also have evidence of hunting during other seasons. Only at Lamb Spring and OV Clary do spring kills seem quite certain. The paucity of spring kills is probably not surprising given the poor physical condition of bison during this time of year (see Hill, this volume).

All groups intensively preyed on bison during the summer and fall. Thus, Cody hunters clearly utilized plains and both foothill-montane and high-elevation park settings during these periods. In addition, both Cody and LPP groups hunted bison on the plains proper and in slightly higher-elevation intermountain basins (Bighorn Basin, Green River Basin) during much or all of the winter. However, while small sample size is an obvious problem, the lack of evidence for late-winter bison hunting by Cody groups in the foothill-montane zone and high parks is an interesting pattern. The data open the possibility that hunters either abandoned the foothill-montane zone and parks during the coldest months or, (potentially) more likely, shifted their subsistence strategies because of a seasonal decline in the bison population in these parts of the mountains. Either way, future research should consider the degree to which Cody groups were tethered to the mountain environments during the harshest periods of winter.

### Lithic Raw Material Use

The final question considered in this chapter is whether lithic raw material use differed for Cody foragers in different environments and whether Cody complex lithic raw material usage differed from that of their contemporaries. Our model predicts that nonregionally focused foragers who rapidly moved through a region would discard a higher proportion of projectile points and tools of nonlocal material (i.e., low PI and TI) than regionally restricted groups that replenished

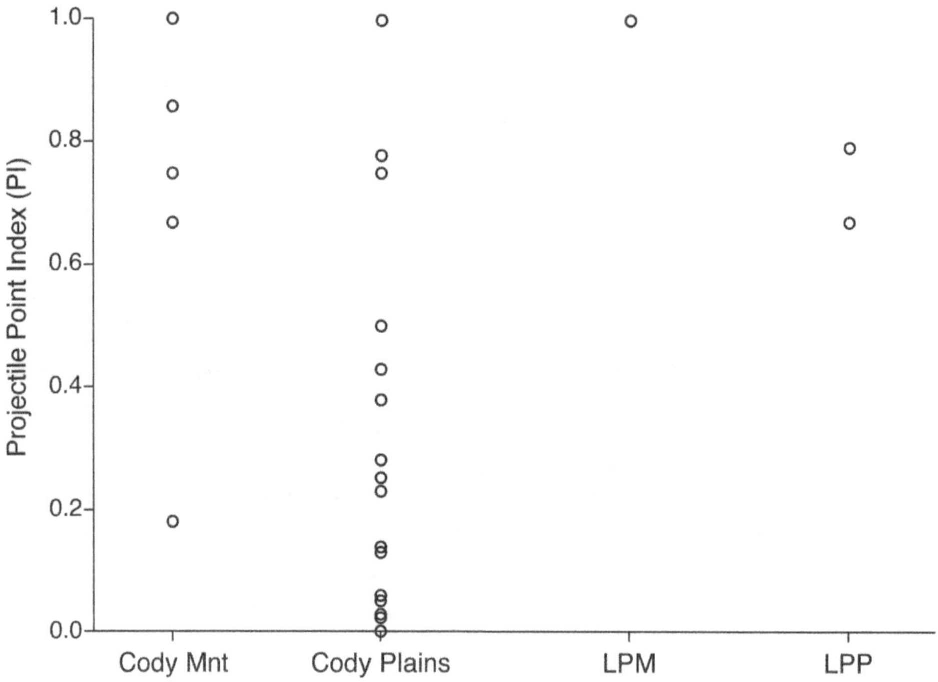


FIGURE 7.5. Projectile point index (PI) values by cultural complex and geographic area. Cody Mnt, Cody complex assemblages in mountains; Cody Plains, Cody complex assemblages in plains; LPM, Non-Cody complex assemblages in mountains; LPP, Non-Cody complex assemblages in plains.

their weaponry and toolkits from local toolstone sources (i.e., high PI and TI). Over time, regionally restricted foragers would discard a high proportion of projectile points and tools of local lithic material.

The sample of sites with PI data includes 8 Mountain Cody, 21 Plains Cody, 5 LPM, and 2 LPP. Figure 7.5 shows the variance in PI values for the four cultural complexes examined in this study. The distribution of PI values across these groups differs significantly (Kruskall-Wallis $\chi^2 = 13.06$, $df = 3$; $p = .005$). PI values for mountain Cody, LPP, and LPM sites are predominantly high and thus indicate regionally restricted land use, whereas Plains Cody PI values are variable but trend toward the lower values (i.e., nonregionally restricted land use).

The very high PI values observed at all LPM assemblages fit our expectations for foragers living in the foothill-montane and higher mountain zones. However, only five of the eight mountain Cody components (Jerry Craig, the three Hell Gap components, and Mammoth Meadow) meet our expectations for regionally restricted land use (PI > .80). The other Cody sites in foothill-montane settings have either a PI value of .18 (Osprey Beach), indicating nonregional land use, or moderately high PI values that fall within the indeterminate land-use strategy category (Jim Pitts and MacHaffie). These data suggest that Cody foragers in the mountains (especially in the foothill-montane zone) practiced a more varied land-use strategy than did other late Paleoindian foragers in the same environment.

The PI values for LPP sites are variable and in some cases do not fit the model expectations. The small sample of LPP sites has moderate PI values that fall within the indeterminate land-use strategy category. The larger sample of Plains Cody sites generally fits the model expectations better than do the LPP sites; however, as discussed below, there are several examples of sites that do not fit our expectations. Overall, for Plains Cody sites it appears that the proximity of a site to its lithic raw material source influences the site's PI values. For example, Plains Cody assemblages with very

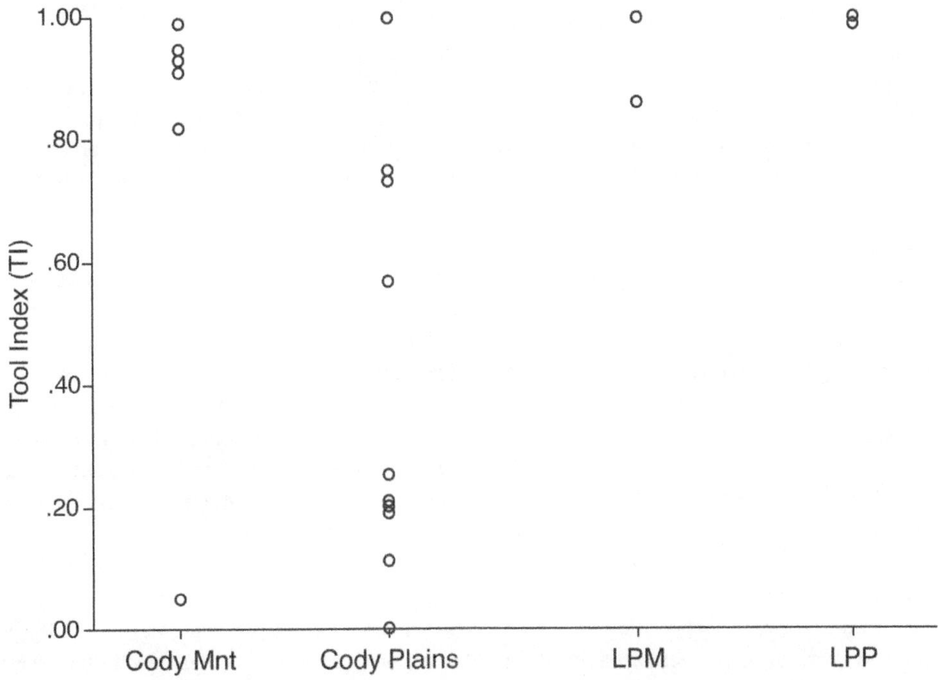


FIGURE 7.6. Tool index (TI) values by cultural complex and geographic area. Cody Mnt, Cody complex assemblages in mountains; Cody Plains, Cody complex assemblages in plains; LPM, Non-Cody complex assemblages in mountains; LPP, Non-Cody complex assemblages in plains.

low PI values (<.25) are preferentially located in regions poor in lithic raw materials, such as the Canadian Prairie ecozone (i.e., DJNF-8, Dunn, Haskey area, Heron Eden, and Niska) or the Prairie Couteau region of North Dakota (i.e., Max site). These sites have point assemblages dominated by nonlocal Knife River flint (also see Root et al., this volume). Conversely, Plains Cody sites (e.g., Benz, Lime Creek, and Scottsbluff) located at or very near high-quality sources of lithic material have an abundance of local stone. Interestingly, the Cody plains sites that do not match expectations generally are large Cody bison kill/processing sites with very low PI values (e.g., Carter/Kerr-McGee, Jurgens, Horner I and II, and Olsen-Chubbuck) but are located in fairly close proximity to lithic raw materials of variable quality. What we see, then, are plains grassland and alluvial valley hunter-gatherers, and those in raw material–poor regions, who planned ahead and procured lithic material from distant sources in anticipation of future hunting/processing activities.

The sample of sites with TI data is smaller than for the PI analysis: 6 Mountain Cody, 13 Plains Cody, 3 LPP, and 3 LPM assemblages. The TI data support the conclusions drawn from the PI analysis (Figure 7.6); however, the differences in the distribution of TI values across groups are not strongly different (Kruskall-Wallis $\chi^2 = 7.55$, $df = 3$; $p = .06$). This could result from the smaller sample sizes for each group.

As with the prior analysis, late Paleoindians living in all parts of the mountains generally have TI values that point to a regionally restricted land-use pattern (TI > .80), as anticipated by the model. The Osprey Beach assemblage in the foothill-montane zone is unusual in that almost all the tools identified to source are from nonlocal sources (TI = .05). Three LPP components—all from the alluvial valley Allen site, which is located near a quarry of high-quality chert—do not meet the model expectations for the plains with very high TI values. The Allen site, however, is in a biotically productive alluvial valley with high-quality toolstone where the model predicts foragers optimally employed a regionally restricted land-use pattern (see Knell 2007; Knell and Hill 2012).

The Plains Cody data are more complex. As previously discussed, Plains Cody sites depicting nonregional land use (TI < .25) are in the lithic raw material–poor Canadian Prairie ecozone (i.e., Djnf-8, Haskey area, Heron Eden, Niska) or are very large bison kills near variable-quality lithic raw material sources (i.e., Jurgens, Horner I and II, and Olsen-Chubbuck). The Plains Cody sites depicting regionally restricted land use (e.g., Benz, Lime Creek, and Nelson) are located at or very near high-quality sources of lithic material.

## Discussion and Conclusions

Our findings generally agree with the land-use model, although some key differences are evident. The most marked area of agreement with our expectations relates to diet choice. At least for the small number of Cody sites in the foothill-montane zone that we consider, diet was narrower and more specialized than our model anticipated. This suggests that Cody diet choice in the mountains might be different from that of non-Cody late Paleoindians who lived in similar settings and whose diets were often very broad and incorporated a mixture of small and medium-sized prey. Surprisingly, the specialization in mountain Cody diets was focused on bison hunting. Our seasonality information indicates that bison hunting across all environments and cultural groups occurred throughout the year, although hunting was probably more limited in spring than during other times of the year.

The paucity of spring bison hunting is not surprising considering that bison in all regions were in very poor condition at this time of the year. However, the lack of bison hunting in the mountains during winter is unexpected because bison were regularly taken in plains grassland settings during this season.

The most obvious difference between Cody and non-Cody groups living in the mountains is the importance of bison hunting in the economy of Cody groups (see also Larson 2012). Given that bison are a large and highly valued resource, it is expected that Cody groups would exploit this species when they encountered it. However, other mountain groups made apparently little or no use of bison. Due to differences in subsistence strategies, it is possible that Cody and non-Cody groups positioned themselves in different parts of the mountains. That is, Cody groups might have preferentially located themselves in low-elevation foothill-montane environments that supported larger congregations of large game (i.e., bison), whereas non-Cody groups in the mountains did not seemingly limit their occupation to these areas but also intensively utilized higher-elevation settings (see discussions in Frison and Grey 1980; Pitblado 2003). However, as Larson's (2012) recent study of 91 Archaic and Paleoindian components demonstrates, Cody and non-Cody late Paleoindian components are both frequently found in foothill-montane settings. In addition, our own limited data suggest that Cody bison hunting in the mountains occurred in the foothills and in higher parks, at least occasionally. So we believe that our data supports the theory that Cody and non-Cody groups had overlapping ranges in the mountains.

Our study of lithic raw material use may help clarify this issue. Results of our lithic raw material use study partially support the idea that Cody groups were more mobile in the mountains (possibly on a seasonal basis) than other late Paleoindian groups (Johnson et al. 2004; Pitblado 1998, 2003). Other late Paleoindians apparently made exclusive use of local raw materials, whereas nonlocal raw material made up a considerable portion of some Cody assemblages in the mountains (e.g., Jim Pitts, 25 percent; MacHaffie, 17 percent; and Osprey Beach, 91.7 percent of the sourced toolstone identified to a known source location). Despite this variability, most Cody mountain sites (the three Hell Gap components, Jerry Craig, Mammoth Meadow, and Medicine Lodge Creek) have a very high proportion of local lithic materials and regionally restricted land use, as anticipated by the model (also see Knell and Hill 2012). We are unsure of the causes of the discrepancy between Cody mountain sites and other late Paleoindian mountain sites (although increased logistical movements into the mountains from parkland and lower foothill/uplift zones is a distinct possibility), but we see the Cody reliance on the mountains as less restrictive than that of the other non-Cody mountain groups. Perhaps it is best to conceptualize Cody groups as less tethered to specific mountain settings than other late Paleoindian groups while nonetheless still making considerable use of the mountains.

This may explain why there is an apparent greater utilization of rockshelters in the foothill-montane zone by non-Cody groups than Cody groups. If non-Cody groups found themselves more tethered to the mountains, the shelter and protection offered by rockshelters made these localities very attractive areas for residence. For Cody groups moving more rapidly through the mountains, however, the adaptive advantage of occupying rockshelters may have been lessened.

Our findings largely agree with prior discussions of Paleoindian use of the mountains but expand our understanding in substantive ways. For example, our results support Pitblado's (2003) contention that Cody groups largely maintained a plains-oriented lifeway in which they logistically hunted big game. Even when occupying mountain settings, Cody groups preferentially focused their occupation on lower-elevation foothill (including prominent uplifts) or park settings, which provided ready access to environments analogous to plains grassland and/or lowland alluvial valleys. In contrast, other late Paleoindian groups that intensively used the foothill-montane zones also intensively used high-elevation mountain zones.

Our results also support the increasingly dominant view that Cody groups were warm-season users of mountain settings (after Johnson et al. 2004:142–145; Pitblado 2003:246; Richings-Germain 2002). The available data suggest that Cody complex bison hunting in the mountains was limited to the summer and fall, and that these hunters presumably spent the cold season in the lower foothill zones, intermountain basins, and/or adjacent plains settings. This Cody seasonal transhumance pattern seemingly differs from the mountain use patterns of other Paleoindians. Both Kornfeld and Frison (2000) and Surovell et al. (2003) contend that earlier Paleoindian Goshen and Folsom groups occupied Middle Park on a nearly year-round basis. Pitblado (2003) argues that Angostura groups maintained a full-time occupation strategy across the Southern Rocky Mountains. Current evidence from Cody sites does not support year-round use of the mountains; however, because of the limited available data, more work on this issue is desperately needed.

In conclusion, our data indicate that Frison's (1992; Frison and Bonnichsen 1996) previously noted dichotomy between the late Paleoindian foothills-mountains and plains-oriented traditions indeed breaks down when it comes to the Cody culture. Cody groups crossed ecological boundaries fairly easily but solved their subsistence and technology problems differently than other late Paleoindian groups. They acted as mobile big-game hunting specialists when in the mountains and sometimes acted as semi-sedentary broad-spectrum foragers in the Plains. It is unclear whether the same Cody groups used both the mountains and the Plains, or whether groups in different environments represented different populations. Our seasonality data suggest that Cody groups regularly hunted bison in both areas during the same season. Whether we are dealing with different groups or group movements between the mountains and the plains, Cody peoples did not follow a fixed seasonal schedule.

## Acknowledgments

Faunal data used in this study came from Matthew Hill's analysis of museum collections: special thanks to Fred Lange, Diana Leonard, and Deborah Confer of the University of Colorado Museum (Jurgens); Larry Martin of the University of Kansas Museum of Natural History (12 Mile Creek and Burntwood Creek); George Corner of the Nebraska State Museum (Finley, Scottsbluff); Jack Hofman of the University of Kansas Department of Anthropology (Norton and Waugh); Jeff Indeck and Rolla Shaller of the Panhandle-Plains Historical Museum (Rex Rodgers); Ernest Lundelius and Melissa Winans of the Texas Archaeological Research Laboratory and the University of Texas Vertebrate Paleontology Laboratory (Bonfire Shelter, Milnesand, and Plainview); and Judy Brown, George Frison, Marcel Kornfeld, Martha Rodgers, and Danny Walker of the University of Wyoming (Finley). Financial support to Matt Hill was provided by the University of Iowa, the Carroll D. Clark Fund of the Department of Anthropology at the University of Kansas, the Haury Fund of the Department of Anthropology at the University of Arizona, and the George C. Frison Institute of Archaeology and Anthropology at the University of Wyoming. Edward Knell thanks for their partial financial support the George C. Frison Institute of Archaeology and Anthropology at the University of Wyoming; the Don E. Crabtree Lithic Technology and Nicholas Michael Scoales scholarships through Washington State University, Department of Anthropology; and California State University–Fullerton for a summer stipend to work on this research. The comments by Margaret Beck, Mary Lou Larson, and an anonymous reviewer on early drafts of this chapter are greatly appreciated.

## References

Agenbroad, Larry D.
1978 *The Hudson-Meng Site: An Alberta Bison Kill in the Nebraska High Plains.* University Press of America, Washington, D.C.

Amick, Daniel S.
1994 *Folsom Diet Breadth and Land Use in the American Southwest.* Ph.D. dissertation, University of New Mexico, Albuquerque. University Microfilms, Ann Arbor, Michigan.

Aten, L.
1983 *Indians of the Upper Texas Coast.* Academic Press, New York.

Bamforth, Douglas B. (editor)
2007 *The Allen Site: A Paleoindian Camp in Southwestern Nebraska.* University of New Mexico Press, Albuquerque.

Barbour, Erwin H., and C. Bertrand Schultz
1932 The Mounted Skeleton of Bison Occidentalis and Associated Dart-Points. *Bulletin of the Nebraska State Museum* 32:263–270.

Benedict, James B.
1979 Getting Away from It All: A Study of Man, Mountains, and the Two-Drought Altithermal. *Southwestern Lore* 45:1–12.
1985 *Arapaho Pass: Glacial Geology and Archaeology at the Crest of the Colorado Front Range.* Research Report No. 3. Center for Mountain Archeology, Ward, Colorado.
1992a Along the Great Divide: Paleoindian Archaeology of the High Colorado Front Range. In *Ice Age Hunters of the Rockies*, edited by D. J. Stanford and J. S. Day, pp. 343–356. Denver Museum of Natural History, Denver; University Press of Colorado, Niwot.
1992b Footprints in the Snow: High-Altitude Cultural Ecology of the Colorado Front Range, U.S.A. *Arctic and Alpine Research* 24:1–16.
2000 Game Drives of the Devil's Thumb Pass Area. In *This Land of Shining Mountains: Archeological Studies in Colorado's Indian Peaks Wilderness Area*, edited by E. Steve Cassells, pp. 18–94. Research Report No. 8. Center for Mountain Archeology, Ward, Colorado.
2005 Rethinking the Fourth of July Valley Site: A Study in Glacial and Periglacial Geoarchaeology. *Geoarchaeology* 20:797–836.

Berman, Jack E.
1959 Bison Bones from the Allen Site, Wyoming. *American Antiquity* 25:116–117.

Black, Kevin D.
1991 Archaic Continuity in the Colorado Rockies: The Mountain Tradition. *Plains Anthropologist* 36:1–29.

Bonnichsen, Robson M., M. D. Beaty, M. D. Turner, and D. Douglas
1992 Paleoindian Lithic Procurement at South Fork of Everson Creek, Southwestern Montana: A Preliminary Statement. In *Ice Age Hunters of the Rockies*, edited by D. J. Stanford and J. S. Day, pp. 285–321. Denver Museum of Natural History, Denver; University Press of Colorado, Niwot.

Breternitz, David A.
1971 Archaeological Investigations at the Wilbur Thomas Shelter, Carr, Colorado. *Southwestern Lore* 36:53–97.

Brunswig, Robert H.
2007 Paleoindian Cultural Landscapes and Archaeology of North Central Colorado's Southern Rockies. In *Frontiers in Colorado Paleoindian Archaeology*, edited by Robert H. Brunswig and Bonnie L. Pitblado, pp. 261–310. University Press of Colorado, Boulder.

Byers, David A., Craig S. Smith, and Jack M. Broughton
2005 Holocene Artiodactyl Population Histories and Large Game Hunting in the Wyoming Basin, USA. *Journal of Archaeological Science* 32:125–142.

Byrnes, Allison M.
2003 Spatial Reconstruction and Flaked Stone Analysis of the Frederick Component, Hell Gap Locality I. Unpublished Master's thesis, Department of Anthropology, University of Wyoming, Laramie.

Carr, Dillon H.
2005 The Organization of Late Paleoindian Lithic Procurement Strategies in Western Wisconsin. *Midcontinental Journal of Archaeology* 30:3–36.

Carr, Dillon H., and Robert Boszhardt
2010 The Organization of Lithic Procurement at Silver Mound, Wisconsin: Source of Hixton Silicified Sandstone. In *Ancient Mines and Quarries: A Transatlantic Perspective*, edited by Margaret Brewer-La Porta, Adrian Burke,

and David Field, pp. 132–141. Oxbow Books, Oxford.

Clewlow, C. W., Jr.
1968 Surface Archaeology of the Black Rock Desert, Nevada. *Reports of the California Archaeological Survey* 73:1–93.

Corbeil, Marcel Ronald
1995 The Archaeology and Taphonomy of the Heron Eden Site, Southwestern Saskatchewan. Unpublished Master's thesis, Department of Anthropology, University of Saskatchewan, Saskatoon.

Cox, S. L.
2001 The Paleo-Indian Period. In *Twelve Thousand Years: American Indians in Maine*, edited by B. J. Bourque, pp. 13–36. University of Nebraska Press, Lincoln.

Dansie, A. J., J. Owen Davis, and Thomas W. Stafford Jr.
1991 The Wizard Beach Recession: Farmdalian (25,000 yr BP) Vertebrate Fossils Co-occur with Early Holocene Artifacts. In *Early Human Occupation in Far Western North America: The Clovis-Archaic Interface*, edited by J. Willig, C. M. Aikens, and J. L. Fagan, pp. 153–200. Nevada State Museum Anthropological Papers No. 21. Carson City, Nevada.

Davis, E. L., C. W. Brott, and D. L. Weide
1991 *The Western Lithic Co-tradition*. San Diego Museum Papers No. 6. San Diego Museum of Man, San Diego.

Davis, E. Mott
1962 *Archaeology of the Lime Creek Site in Southwestern Nebraska*. Special Publication No. 3. University of Nebraska State Museum, Lincoln.

Davis, Leslie B.
1993 Paleo-Indian Archaeology in the High Plains and Rocky Mountains of Montana. In *From Kostenki to Clovis: Upper Paleolithic-Paleo-Indian Adaptations*, edited by O. Soffer and N. D. Praslov, pp. 263–277. Plenum Press, New York.

Dick, Herbert W., and Bert Mountain
1960 The Claypool Site: A Cody Complex Site in Northeastern Colorado. *American Antiquity* 26:223–235.

Doerner, James P.
2007 Late Quaternary Prehistoric Environments of the Colorado Front Range. In *Frontiers in Colorado Paleoindian Archaeology*, edited by Robert H. Brunswig and Bonnie L. Pitblado, pp. 11–38. University Press of Colorado, Boulder.

Douglas, Diane L.
1991 Cultural Variability and Lithic Technology: A Detailed Study of Stone Tools from the Mammoth Meadow Locus, Southwestern Montana. Unpublished Master's thesis, Department of Quaternary Studies, University of Maine, Orono.

Ebell, S. Biron
1975 A Cody Complex Site in South-Central Saskatchewan (DjNf-8). *Saskatchewan Archaeology Newsletter* 49:1–6.
1988 The Dunn Site. *Plains Anthropologist* 33:505–530.

Eddy, Frank W., Allen E. Kane, and Paul R. Nickens
1984 *Southwest Colorado Prehistoric Context: Archaeological Background and Research Directions*. Colorado Historical Society, Denver.

Finley, Judson B., Brian N. Andrews, Marcel Kornfeld, and George C. Frison
2002 Two Moon, a Folsom Rockshelter Occupation in the Bighorn Mountains, Wyoming. *Current Research in the Pleistocene* 19:22–25.

Forbis, R. G.
1968 Fletcher: A Paleo-Indian Site in Alberta. *American Antiquity* 33:1–10.

Forbis, R. G., and J. D. Sperry
1952 An Early Man Site in Montana. *American Antiquity* 18:127–133.

Frison, George C.
1978 Animal Population Studies and Cultural Inference. In *Bison Procurement and Utilization: A Symposium*, edited by Leslie B. Davis and Michael Wilson, pp. 44–52. Memoir No. 14. Plains Anthropologist, Lincoln, Nebraska.
1982 Paleo-Indian Winter Subsistence Strategies on the High Plains. In *Plains Indian Studies: A Collection of Essays in Honor of J. C. Ewers and Waldo Wedel*, edited by D. H. Ubelaker and H. J. Viola, pp. 193–201. Smithsonian Contribution to Anthropology No. 3. Smithsonian Institution, Washington, D.C.
1984 The Carter/Kerr-McGee Paleoindian Site: Cultural Resource Management and Archaeological Research. *American Antiquity* 49: 288–314.
1988 Paleoindian Subsistence and Settlement during Post-Clovis Times on the Northwestern Plains, Adjacent Mountain Ranges, and Intermontane Basins. In *Indians before Columbus: Ice Age Origins*, edited by R. C. Carlisle, pp. 83–106. Ethnography Monographs No. 12. Department of Anthropology, University of Pittsburgh, Pittsburgh, Pennsylvania.
1991 *Prehistoric Hunters of the High Plains*. 2nd ed. Academic Press, San Diego.
1992 The Foothill-Mountains and the Open Plains: The Dichotomy in Paleoindian Subsistence

Strategies between Two Ecosystems. In *Ice Age Hunters of the Rockies*, edited by D. J. Stanford and J. S. Day, pp. 323–342. Denver Museum of Natural History, Denver; University Press of Colorado, Niwot.

1993 The North American Indian: A Wealth of New Data but Still Much More to Learn. In *Prehistory and Human Ecology of the Western Prairies and Northern Plains*, edited by J. A. Tiffany, pp. 5–16. Memoir No. 27. Plains Anthropologist, Lincoln, Nebraska.

1997 The Foothill-Mountain Late Paleoindian and Early Plains Archaic Chronology and Subsistence. In *Changing Perspectives on the Northwestern Plains and Rocky Mountains*, edited by M. L. Larson and J. E. Francis, pp. 84–104. University of South Dakota Press, Vermillion.

Frison, George C., and Robson Bonnichsen

1996 The Pleistocene-Holocene Transition on the Plains and Rocky Mountains of North America. In *Humans at the End of the Ice Age: The Archaeology of the Pleistocene-Holocene Transition*, edited by Lawrence G. Strauss, Berit Valentin Eriksen, Jon Erlandson, and David R. Yesner, pp. 303–318. Plenum Press, New York.

Frison, George C., and Donald C. Grey

1980 Pryor Stemmed: A Specialized Paleo-Indian Ecological Adaptation. *Plains Anthropologist* 25:27–46.

Frison, George C., and Lawrence C. Todd (editors)

1987 *The Horner Site: The Type Site of the Cody Cultural Complex*. Academic Press, Orlando, Florida.

Frison, George C., and Danny N. Walker (editors)

2007 *Medicine Lodge Creek: Holocene Archaeology of the Eastern Big Horn Basin, Wyoming, Volume 1*. Clovis Press, Santa Fe, New Mexico.

Fulgham, Tommy, and Dennis J. Stanford

1982 The Frasca Site: A Preliminary Report. *Southwestern Lore* 48(1):1–9.

Gould, Richard A., and Sherry Saggers

1985 Lithic Procurement in Central Australia: A Closer Look at Binford's Idea of Embeddedness in Archaeology. *American Antiquity* 50:117–136.

Hauck, Forrest Richard, and M. R. Hauck

2002 *KibRidge-Yampa Paleoindian Occupation Site (5MF3687) Preliminary Archaeological Excavations (1993–2001) in Northwestern Colorado*. Archaeological Research Institute General Series No. 4. Bountiful, Utah.

Haynes, C. Vance, Jr., Roelf P. Beukens, A. J. T. Jull, and Owen K. Davis

1992 New Radiocarbon Dates from Some Old Folsom Sites: Accelerator Technology. In *Ice Age Hunters of the Rockies*, edited by D. J. Stanford and J. S. Day, pp. 83–100. Denver Museum of Natural History, Denver; University Press of Colorado, Niwot.

Hicks, Keri

2002 Local Variability in Paleoindian Lifeways: A Comparison of the Lime Creek and Allen Site Worked Stone Assemblages, Southwest, Nebraska. Unpublished Master's thesis, Department of Anthropology, University of Colorado, Boulder.

Hill, Matthew E., Jr.

2008 Variation in Paleoindian Fauna Use on the Great Plains and Rocky Mountains of North America. *Quaternary International* 191: 34–52.

Hill, Matthew E., Jr., and Matthew Glenn Hill

2002 Season of Bison Mortality at the Jurgens Site, Weld County, Colorado. *Current Research in the Pleistocene* 19:104–106.

Hill, Matthew E., Jr., Jack L. Hofman, and Larry D. Martin

1992 A Reinvestigation of the Burntwood Creek Bison Bonebed. *Current Research in the Pleistocene* 9:99–102.

Hill, Matthew G.

2008 *Paleoindian Subsistence Dynamics on the Northwestern Great Plains: Zooarchaeology of the Agate Basin and Clary Ranch Sites*. BAR International Series No. 1756. Archaeopress, Oxford.

Hill, Matthew G., and Marcel Kornfeld

1999 Inferring Season of Kill for a Cody Complex Bison Bonebed in Middle Park Colorado. *Current Research in the Pleistocene* 16: 30–32.

Hill, Matthew G., David J. Rapson, Thomas J. Loebel, and David W. May

2011 Site Structure and Activity Organization at a Late Paleoindian Base Camp in Western Nebraska. *American Antiquity* 76:752–772.

Hofman, Jack L., and Jeanette M. Blackmar

1997 The Paleoindian Laird Bison Bone Bed in Northwestern Kansas. *Kansas Anthropologist* 18:45–58.

Hofman, Jack L., Matthew E. Hill Jr., William C. Johnson, and Dean T. Sather

1995 Norton: An Early-Holocene Bison Bone Bed in Western Kansas. *Current Research in the Pleistocene* 12:19–21.

Hughes, Susan S.

2003 Beyond the Altithermal: The Role of Climate Change in the Prehistoric Adaptation of Northwestern Wyoming. Unpublished Ph.D.

dissertation, Department of Anthropology, University of Washington, Seattle.

Hurst, C. T.

1941 A Folsom Locality in the San Luis Valley, Colorado: A Preliminary Report. *Southwestern Lore* 7:31–34.

Husted, Wilfred M.

1962 A Proposed Archaeological Chronology for Rocky Mountain National Park Based on Projectile Points and Pottery. Unpublished Master's thesis, Department of Anthropology, University of Colorado, Boulder.

1965 Early Occupation of the Colorado Front Range. *American Antiquity* 30:494–498.

1969 *Bighorn Canyon Archaeology*. Smithsonian Institution River Basin Surveys, Publications in Salvage Archeology No. 12. Lincoln, Nebraska.

1974 Prehistoric Occupation of the Alpine Zone in the Rocky Mountains. In *Arctic and Alpine Environments*, edited by J. D. Ives and R. G. Barry, pp. 857–872. Methuen, London.

2006 Accidental Plains (?) Archaeologist: Archaeology in the Heartland. *Plains Anthropologist* 51:745–758.

Husted, Wilfred M., and Robert Edgar

2002 The *Archaeology of Mummy Cave, Wyoming: An Introduction to Shoshonean Prehistory*. Midwest Archeology Center Special Report No. 4. National Park Service, Lincoln, Nebraska.

Irwin, Henry T., and H. Marie Wormington

1970 Paleo-Indian Tool Types in the Great Plains. *Plains Anthropologist* 35:24–34.

Irwin-Williams, Cynthia, Henry Irwin, George Agogino, and C. Vance Haynes

1973 Hell Gap: Paleo-Indian Occupation on the High Plains. *Plains Anthropologist* 18:40–53.

Jodry, Margaret A.

1999 Paleoindian Stage. In *Colorado Prehistory: A Context for the Rio Grande Basin*, edited by M. A. Martorano, T. Hoefer III, M. A. Jodry, Vince Spero, and M. L. Taylor, pp. 45–114. Colorado Council of Professional Archaeologists, Denver.

Jodry, Margaret A., M. D. Turner, V. Spero, J. C. Turner, and Dennis Stanford

1996 Folsom in the Colorado High County: The Black Mountain Site. *Current Research in the Pleistocene* 13:25–27.

Johnson, Ann, Brian Reeves, and Mack Shortt

2004 *Osprey Beach (Site 48YE409/410), Yellowstone National Park, Wyoming*. Lifeways of Canada. Submitted to Yellowstone Center for Resources, Yellowstone National Park, Cooperative Agreement No. CA-1268-1-9017 between Montana State University, Bozeman, and the National Park Service. Copies available from Yellowstone Center for Resources, Mammoth, Wyoming.

Johnson, David, and Jana Pastor

2003 *The Blue Point Site: Paleoindian/Archaic Transition in Southwest Wyoming*. Western Archaeological Services, Rock Springs, Wyoming.

Johnson, LeRoy, Jr.

1989 *Great Plains Interlopers in the Eastern Woodlands during Late Paleo-Indian Times*. Texas Historical Commission, Office of State Archaeologist, Report No. 36. Austin.

Jones, David Chadwick

1999 Late Paleoindian/Early Archaic Archaeology and Subsistence: A Taphonomic Analysis of the Lime Creek Site (25FT41), Southwest Nebraska. Unpublished Master's thesis, Colorado State University, Fort Collins.

Jones, Terry L., Judith F. Porcasi, Jereme W. Gaeta, and Brian F. Codding

2008 The Diablo Canyon Fauna: A Coarse-Grained Record of Trans-Holocene Foraging from the Central California Mainland Coast. *American Antiquity* 73:289–316.

Knell, Edward J.

2007 The Organization of Late Paleoindian Cody Complex Land-Use on the North American Great Plains. Unpublished Ph.D. dissertation, Department of Anthropology, Washington State University, Pullman.

2009 The Locality IIIs/V Eden Complex Component. In *Hell Gap: A Stratified Paleoindian Campsite on the Edge of the Rockies*, edited by Mary Lou Larson, Marcel Kornfeld, and George C. Frison, pp. 157–179. University of Utah Press, Salt Lake City.

Knell, Edward J., and Matthew E. Hill Jr.

2012 Linking Bones and Stones: Regional Variation in Late Paleoindian Cody Complex Land Use and Foraging Strategies. *American Antiquity* 77:40–70.

Knell, Edward J., Matthew G. Hill, and Andrés Izeta

2009 The Locality IIIS/V Eden Complex Component. In *Hell Gap: A Stratified Paleoindian Campsite on the Edge of the Rockies*, edited by Mary Lou Larson, Marcel Kornfeld, and George C. Frison, pp. 157–179. University of Utah Press, Salt Lake City.

Knight, Dennis H.

1994 *Mountains and Plains: The Ecology of Wyoming Landscapes*. Yale University Press, New Haven, Connecticut.

Knudson, Ruthann
1983 *Organizational Variability in Late Paleo-Indian Assemblages.* Washington State University Laboratory of Anthropology Reports of Investigations No. 60. Washington State University, Pullman.
2002 Medicine Creek Is a Paleoindian Cultural Ecotone: The Red Smoke Assemblage. In *Medicine Creek: Seventy Years of Archaeological Investigations*, edited by Donna C. Roper, pp. 84–141. University of Alabama Press, Tuscaloosa.

Kornfeld, Marcel, and George C. Frison
2000 Paleoindian Occupation of the High Country: The Case of Middle Park, Colorado. *Plains Anthropologist* 45:129–153.

Kornfeld, Marcel, George C. Frison, and Mary Lou Larson
2010 *Prehistoric Hunter-Gatherers of the High Plains and Rockies.* 3rd ed. Left Coast Press, Walnut Creek, California.

Kornfeld, Marcel, George C. Frison, Mary Lou Larson, J. C. Miller, and J. Saysette
1999 Paleoindian Bison Procurement and Paleoenvironments in Middle Park, Colorado. *Geoarchaeology* 14:129–153.

Kornfeld, Marcel and Mary Lou Larson
2008 Bonebed and Other Myths: Paleoindian to Archaic Transitions on North American Great Plains and Rocky Mountains. *Quaternary International* 191:18–33.

Kornfeld, Marcel, Mary Lou Larson, Craig Arnold, Adam Wiewel, Mike Toft, and Dennis Stanford
2007 The Nelson Site, a Cody Occupation in Northeastern Colorado. *Plains Anthropologist* 52:257–278.

Larson, Mary Lou
2012 Paleoindian to Archaic Transition: The Northwestern Plains and Central Rocky Mountains. In *From the Pleistocene to the Holocene: Human Organization and Cultural Transformations in Prehistoric North America*, edited by C. Britt Bousman and Bradley J. Vierra, pp. 149–169. Texas A&M Press, College Station.

Larson, Mary Lou, Marcel Kornfeld, and George C. Frison (editors)
2009 *Hell Gap: A Stratified Paleoindian Campsite on the Edge of the Rockies.* University of Utah Press, Salt Lake City.

Linnamae, Urve, and Eldon Johnson
1999 An Analysis of the Lithic Collection from the Heron Eden Site: A Cody Complex Manifestation in Saskatchewan. *Saskatchewan Archaeology* 20:14–32.

Lipe, William D., and Bonnie L. Pitblado
1999 Paleoindian and Archaic Periods. In *Colorado Prehistory: A Context for Southern Colorado River Basin*, edited by W. D. Lipe, M. D. Varien, and R. H. Wilshusen, pp. 95–131. Colorado Council of Professional Archaeologists, Denver.

Loendorf, L. L., J. C. Dahlberg, and L. O. Weston
1981 *The Pretty Creek Archaeological Site, 24CB4 and 5.* Report to the National Park Service. Midwest Archeological Center, Lincoln, Nebraska.

MacKey, J. C., D. Kullen, S. D. Creasman, J. E. Sall, K. Harvey, and C. L. Armitage
1982 Paleoenvironmental reconstruction and Subsistence Change at the Deadman Wash Site in Southwestern Wyoming. *Journal of Intermountain Archaeology* 1:11–65.

Magurran, Anne E.
1988 *Ecological Diversity and Its Measurement.* Princeton University Press, Princeton, New Jersey.

Mandel, Rolfe D., and Jack L. Hofman
2003 Geoarchaeological Investigations at the Winger Site: A Late Paleoindian Bison Bonebed in Southwestern Kansas, U.S.A. *Geoarchaeology* 18:129–144.

Mason, Ronald J.
1962 The Paleo-Indian Tradition in Eastern North America. *Current Anthropology* 3:227–278.

McCartney, Peter Howard
1983 Archaeological Analysis of Bison Remains from the Cody Paleo-Indian Site of Lamb Spring, Colorado. Unpublished Master's thesis, Department of Anthropology, University of Arizona, Tucson.

Meltzer, David J.
1989 Was Stone Exchanged among Eastern North American Paleoindians? In *Eastern Paleoindian Lithic Resource Use*, edited by Christopher J. Ellis and Jonathan C. Lothrop, pp. 11–39. Westview Press, Boulder, Colorado.

Meyer, David
1985 Component of the Scottsbluff Tradition: Excavations at the Niska Site. *Canadian Journal of Archaeology* 9:1–37.

Moomaw, Jack C.
1957 Aborigines of the Colorado Highlands. *Southwestern Lore* 23:35–37.

Morris, Elizabeth A.
1990 Carey Lake, 5LR230, a High Altitude Paleo-Indian Site in Northern Colorado. In *Abstracts of Papers*, 55th Annual Meeting of the Society for American Archaeology, p. 131. Washington, D.C.

Moss, John H. (editor)
1951 *Early Man in the Eden Valley*. University of Pennsylvania Museum Monographs No. 6. Philadelphia.
Mulloy, William
1959 The James Allen Site near Laramie, Wyoming. *American Antiquity* 25:112–116.
Muñiz, Mark P.
2005 The Cody Complex Revisited: Landscape Use and Technological Organization on the Northwestern Plains. Unpublished Ph.D. dissertation, University of Colorado, Boulder.
Muñiz, C. C., S. F. Mehls, and C. C. Chambellan
2003 Addendum to a Class III Cultural Resource Inventory of BLM Parcels within the Wolf Springs Ranch, Huerfano County, Colorado. Prepared by Western Cultural Resource Management for Michael J. Mollerus and the Bureau of Land Management, Canon City District. Manuscript on file, Office of Archaeology and Historic Preservation, Colorado Historical Society, Denver.
Mutel, Connie F., and J. C. Emerick
1984 *From Grasslands to Glaciers*. Johnson Books, Boulder, Colorado.
Naze, Brian
1986 The Folsom Occupation of Middle Park, Colorado. *Southwestern Lore* 25:112–116.
Novecosky, Brad
2002 The Haskey Area, a Cody-Complex Site from the Quill Lakes Region, Saskatchewan, Canada. *Current Research in the Pleistocene* 19:73–74.
Osborne, Douglas
1956 Early Lithic in Pacific Northwest. *Research Studies of the State College of Washington* 24(1):38–44.
Pitblado, Bonnie L.
1998 Peak to Peak in Paleoindian Time: Occupation of Southwestern Colorado. *Plains Anthropologist* 43:333–348.
2000 Living the High Life in Colorado: Late Paleoindian Occupation of the Caribou Lake Site. In *This Land of Shining Mountains: Archaeological Studies in Colorado's India Peaks Wilderness Area*, edited by E. Steve Cassells, pp. 124–158. Research Report No. 8. Center for Mountain Archeology, Ward, Colorado.
2003 *Late Paleoindian Occupation of the Southern Rocky Mountains*. University Press of Colorado, Boulder.
2008 The Rocky Mountains, North America. In *Encyclopedia of Archaeology*, edited by D. M. Pearsall, pp. 318–327. Elsevier Press, Oxford.
Pitblado, Bonnie L., and Robert H. Brunswig
2007 That Was Then, This Is Now: Seventy-Five Years of Paleoindian Research in Colorado. In *Frontiers in Colorado Paleoindian Archaeology*, edited by Robert H. Brunswig and Bonnie L. Pitblado, pp. 39–84. University Press of Colorado, Boulder.
Pitblado, Bonnie L., and Beth A. Camp
2003 *2001–02 Excavations at the Change Gulch Site (5GN817)*. Report submitted to Colorado Historical Society, Denver, and Bureau of Land Management, Denver.
Reed, Alan D., and Michael D. Metcalf
1999 *Colorado Prehistory: A Context for the Northern Colorado River Basin*. Colorado Council of Professional Archaeologists, Denver.
Renaud, E. B.
1934 *The First Thousand Yuma-Folsom Artifacts*. University of Denver Department of Anthropology Archaeological Series Paper No. 1. Denver.
1942 *Reconnaissance Work in the Upper Rio Grande Valley, Colorado and New Mexico*. University of Denver Department of Anthropology Archaeological Series Paper No. 3. Denver.
Reynolds, Cerisa R., and Matthew E. Hill Jr.
2010 Understanding the Relationship between the Bison Bone Beds at the Cody-Aged Finley Site. *Current Research in the Pleistocene* 27: 131–134.
Richings-Germain, Sarah
2002 The Jerry Craig Site: A Paleoindian Bison Bonebed in the Colorado Rocky Mountains. Unpublished Master's thesis, Department of Anthropology, University of Wyoming, Laramie.
Root, Matthew J.
1992 The Knife River Flint Quarries: The Organization of Stone Tool Production. Unpublished Ph.D. dissertation, Department of Anthropology, Washington State University, Pullman.
1997 Production for Exchange at the Knife River Flint Quarries, North Dakota. *Lithic Technology* 22:33–50.
Root, Matthew J., Stanley A. Ahler, Julieann VanNest, Carl R. Falk, and John E. Foss
1985 *Archaeological Investigations in the Knife River Flint Primary Source Area, Dunn County, North Dakota: The Benz Site, 32DU452*. Department of Anthropology, University of North Dakota, Grand Forks, Contribution No. 225. Submitted to the State Historical Society of North Dakota, Bismarck.

Schroeder, Albert R.
1991 Paleo-Indian Occupation in the Eastern Great Basin and Northern Colorado Plateau. *Utah Archaeology* 4:1–15.

Sellet, Frédéric
2009 *The Jim Pitts Site: A Multi-component Paleoindian Campsite in the Black Hills of South Dakota.* University of Northern Colorado School of Social Sciences Anthropology Program. UNC Archaeology Laboratory Technical Series No. 3. South Dakota Archaeological Research Center, Rapid City.

Smith, C. S., T. P. Reust, and R. D. Russell
2003 Site 48UT375: Late Paleoindian Period Subsistence and Land Use Patterns in the Green River Basin, Wyoming. *Plains Anthropologist* 48:133–151.

Shortt, Mack W.
2002 *The Archaeological Inventory of Portions of the South Shore of West Thumb and Testing of the Osprey Beach Locality, Yellowstone National Park: The 2000 Field Season Final Report.* Prepared by Montana State University–Bozeman for Yellowstone National Park.

Stanford, Dennis
1999 Paleoindian Archaeology and Late Pleistocene Environments in the Plains and Southwestern United States. In *Ice Age Peoples of North America: Environments, Origins, and Adaptations*, edited by Robson Bonnichsen and Karen L. Turnmire, pp. 281–339. Center for the Study of the First Americans. Oregon State University Press, Corvallis.

Stone, T., and R. Mendoza
1994 *Excavations at the Crescent Rockshelter: 1993 Field Season.* Cultural Resources Report No. 1. Department of Anthropology, University of Colorado, Denver.

Surovell, T. A., N. M. Waguespack, M. Kornfeld, and G. C. Frison
2003 *The First Five Field Seasons at Barger Gulch, Locality B, Middle Park, Colorado.* Technical Report No. 26. George C. Frison Institute of Archaeology and Anthropology, University of Wyoming, Laramie.

Todd, Lawrence C., David J. Rapson, and Jack L. Hofman
1996 Dentition Studies of the Mill Iron and Other Early Paleoindian Bison Bonebed Sites. In *The Mill Iron Site*, edited by George C. Frison, pp. 145–176. University of New Mexico Press, Albuquerque.

Vivian, Brian C.
2005 Identifying a Cody Component at the Malin Fishing Hole Site (25YE353) in Yellowstone National Park. Paper presented at the 63rd Annual Plains Anthropological Conference, Edmonton, Alberta.

Wendorf, Fred, and J. P. Miller
1959 Artifacts from High Mountain Sites in the Sangre de Cristo Range, New Mexico. *El Palacio* 66:37–52.

Wheat, Joe Ben
1972 *The Olsen-Chubbuck Site: A Paleo-Indian Bison Kill.* Memoirs of the Society for American Archaeology No. 26. Washington, D.C.
1979 *The Jurgens Site.* Memoir No. 15. Plains Anthropologist, Lincoln, Nebraska.

White, Patrice M.
1998 Getting the High Altitude Stone: Lithic Technology at the Barger Gulch Site, Middle Park, Colorado. Unpublished Master's thesis, Department of Anthropology, University of Wyoming, Laramie.

Wormington, H. M.
1957 *Ancient Man in North America.* 4th ed. Popular Series No. 4. Denver Museum of Natural History, Denver, Colorado.

Wright, Gary A.
1984 *People of the High Country: Jackson Hole before the Settlers.* American University Studies Series XI, Vol. 7. Peter Lang, New York.

Wyckoff, W., and L. M. Dilsaver
1995 *The Mountainous West: Explorations in Historical Geography.* University of Nebraska Press, Lincoln.

Yelm, Margaret
1935 Archaeological Survey of Rocky Mountains National Park—Eastern Foothill District. Unpublished Master's thesis, Department of Anthropology, University of Denver, Denver.

York, Robert
1991 Evidence of Paleoindians on the San Juan National Forest, Southwest Colorado. *Southwestern Lore* 57:5–22.

# 8

# Way Out West

## Cody Complex Occupations from the Northwestern Great Basin

Daniel S. Amick

This chapter considers the dispersed evidence for Cody complex occupations west of the Rocky Mountains (Figure 8.1; Table 8.1), and the importance of that evidence for understanding the associated strategies of ecological adaptation among these terminal Pleistocene–early Holocene (TP-EH) foragers in North America. The recognition of Cody complex occupations in far western regions is significant since most of the available evidence suggests that the primary core of the Cody complex ecological adaptation is strongly connected with bison hunting on the Great Plains (Frison and Bonnichsen 1996: 313; also see Hill, this volume). Numerous well-known Cody complex sites are associated with bison kills and processing locations that are 10,000 to 8800 $^{14}$C years BP (11,470–9823 cal BP) and are concentrated on the western High Plains and along the Front Range of the Rocky Mountains and their intermontane basins (Hofman and Graham 1998; Huckell and Judge 2006; Stanford 1999). There are increasing indications, however, that Cody complex groups extended their ranges into the very fringes and even beyond the limits of the prairie-grasslands of the Great Plains. Cody complex groups may have routinely occupied the high altitudes of the Rocky Mountains (Benedict 1992; Brunswig 2007; Hill and Knell, this volume; Pitblado 1998, 2003; Pitblado and Brunswig 2007); the Colorado Plateau (Pitblado 2003; Schroedl 1977); the northern fringes of the prairie-forest steppe (Dawe, this volume; Wormington and Forbis 1965); the cross-timbers woodlands of the eastern Great Plains (Blackmar 2001; Johnson 1989); and the northwoods of the western Great Lakes (Mason 1981, 1997); as well as the far western sagebrush-grasslands (defined by Bailey 1998) of the Snake River Plain, the northern Great Basin (Bryan and Tuohy 1999; Tuohy 1968; Wallmann and Amick 1991), and the Columbia Plateau (Bryan and Tuohy 1999; Butler 1978a; Meatte 1990). Based on the large number of sites and their widespread distribution, Stanford (1999:320) suggests that the Cody complex persisted for a relatively long duration and that these groups maintained higher population levels than the preceding Hell Gap and Agate Basin groups.

Some researchers explain these distributional patterns in terms of either Cody origins or decline. For example, Bryan (1988) suggests that Cody originates in the far northern Plains, with time-transgressive movements toward the Great Plains (but see Dawe, this volume). Others suggest that Cody groups moved outward from the Great Plains with deteriorating climatic conditions that degraded the productivity of the prairie-grassland (e.g., Irwin-Williams and Haynes 1970: 65; Muñiz, this volume [Chapter 2]). Other proposals have Cody groups expanding outward and then returning to the Great Plains with greater diversification of the projectile point assemblage,

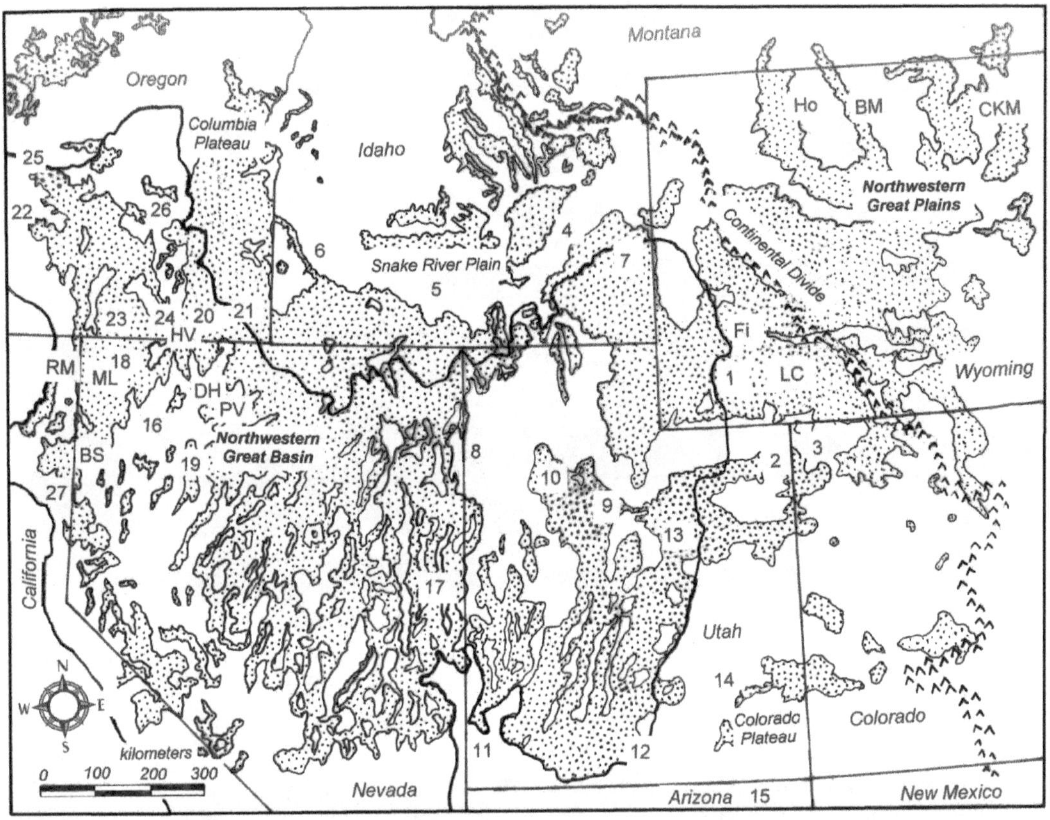


FIGURE 8.1. Distribution of Cody complex finds west of the Rocky Mountains (*numbered*) showing modern sagebrush-grasslands (*stippled*), obsidian sources around the Black Rock Desert, the Continental Divide, the hydrographic boundary of the Great Basin, and Cody complex comparative assemblages. Numbers correspond to site and isolate locations identified in Table 8.1. Locations outside the boundaries of this map include Hell Gap in far eastern Wyoming, Hudson-Meng in far northwestern Nebraska, and the Chase locality (28) on the Thompson River in British Columbia. Key to Cody complex comparative assemblages on this map: BM = Black Mountain; CKM = Carter/Kerr-McGee; Fi = Finley; Ho = Horner; LC = Larson Cache. Key to the obsidian sources identified in this chapter: BS = Bordwell Spring; DH = Double H Mountains; HV = Hawk's Valley; ML = Massacre Lake; PV = Paradise Valley; and RM = Rainbow Mine.

a result of stylistic drift during this geographic and temporal separation (e.g., Greiser 1982:70, 121–122). Throughout the TP-EH, it appears that Cody people were primarily pursuing bison and that their geographic spread tracked the contemporaneous range expansions of bison (Driver 1998; Stanford 1999:325), but Cody subsistence was not exclusively focused on bison (Hill 2008b). In partial contrast to the Folsom evidence, it appears that Cody groups had broader diets and considerably greater flexibility in their subsistence strategies, which allowed geographic expansion beyond the ecological limits of the prairie-grassland. Such patterns raise significant questions about the economic diversity of the Cody complex, as well as its origins and spread.

This chapter addresses several interrelated research questions. Of foremost concern is securing the typological affinity of Cody projectile points/knives from the Great Basin, particularly those from the Black Rock Desert of northwestern Nevada. Investigation of this question focuses on chronological evidence and the typological and technological variability associated with tool breakage patterns, morphometric variation, basal finishing, and raw material preferences. Next are questions of land use, mobility, and subsistence patterns among the Cody finds documented in

**TABLE 8.1.** Cody Complex Finds Reported from Locations West of the Rocky Mountains.

| Location | Site Name/Number | Reference |
|---|---|---|
| (1) Wyoming Basin, WY | Blue Point | Johnson and Pastor 2003 |
| | Pine Springs | Sharrock 1966 |
| | Larson Cache | Ingbar and Frison 1987 |
| | Deadman Wash | Armitage et al. 1982 |
| | Finley | Howard 1943; Howard et al. 1941; Moss et al. 1951; Satterthwaite 1957 |
| (2) Dinosaur NM, CO | Deluge Shelter | Cassells 1983:64 |
| (3) Moffat County, CO | 5MF4334 | Pitblado 2003 |
| | 5MF3687(KibRidge-Yampa) | Hauck and Hauck 2002; Cummings et al. 2007 |
| (4) Upper Snake River, ID | numerous localities | Butler 1973, 1978a |
| (5) Central Snake River, ID | Wilson Butte Cave | Gruhn 1961, 2006 |
| (6) Lower Snake River, ID | numerous localities | Meatte 1990 |
| (7) Caribou County, ID | miniature isolate | this chapter |
| (8) Bonneville Basin, UT | Danger Cave Level II/III | Jennings 1957 (Type W12) |
| (9) Utah Valley, UT | Martin | Janetski 2001 |
| (10) Dugway (DPG), UT | 42TO1872 (Old River Bed) | Schmitt et al. 2007 |
| (11) Washington County, UT | 42WS1553 | Pitblado 2003 |
| (12) Kane County, UT | 42KA35000 | Pitblado 2003 |
| (13) Carbon County, UT | isolate? | Pitblado 2003 |
| (14) Colorado Plateau, UT | numerous isolates | Schroedl 1977 |
| (15) Little Colorado, AZ | Voigt Mesa | Sullivan 1992:108–109 |
| (16) Black Rock Desert, NV | 26HU22 (Wallmann Square-Base) | Clewlow 1968; Tuohy 1968; Wallmann and Amick 1991 |
| | 26HU58 (Wallmann Bison) | Dansie et al. 1988; Dansie and Jerrems 2001, 2004 |
| (17) Great Basin NP, NV | 26WP2018 | Wells 1993:71 |
| (18) Massacre Lake, NV | numerous localities | this chapter |
| (19) Humboldt Sinks, NV | numerous localities | this chapter |
| (20) East Alvord Desert, OR | Coyote Flat | Butler 1970 |
| (21) Owyhee Uplands, OR | Dirty Shame Rockshelter | Hanes 1977, 1988 |
| (22) Cascade Mountains, OR | 35DO161 (Medicine Creek) | Synder 1981 |
| (23) Hart Lake, OR | numerous localities | this chapter |
| (24) Alvord Desert, OR | numerous localities | this chapter |
| (25) Newberry Crater, OR | Paulina Lake (35DS34) | Connolly and Jenkins 1999 |
| (26) Malheur Wetlands, OR | isolate | this chapter |
| (27) Honey Lake, CA | isolate | Riddell 1956 |
| (28) Thompson River, BC | Chase locality | Styrd and Rousseau 1996 |

*Note:* Location numbers correspond to Cody complex finds shown in Figure 8.1.

the northwestern Great Basin. These questions are addressed by studies of lithic raw material movement, faunal associations, and blood residue analysis. Finally, the framework of this interregional investigation of Cody complex variability is designed to be comparative and iterative across the essential archaeological dimensions of time, space, and form. One significant challenge to this effort is the substantial difference in the character of the archaeological record across these diverse regions, resulting in an overall scarcity of dated and buried Cody components west of the Continental Divide.

## Cody Complex Occupations in the Black Rock Desert of Nevada

Several key locations of Cody complex finds occur in the Black Rock Desert of northwestern Nevada, most notably the Wallmann Square-Base site (26HU22) and the Wallmann Bison (26HU58).

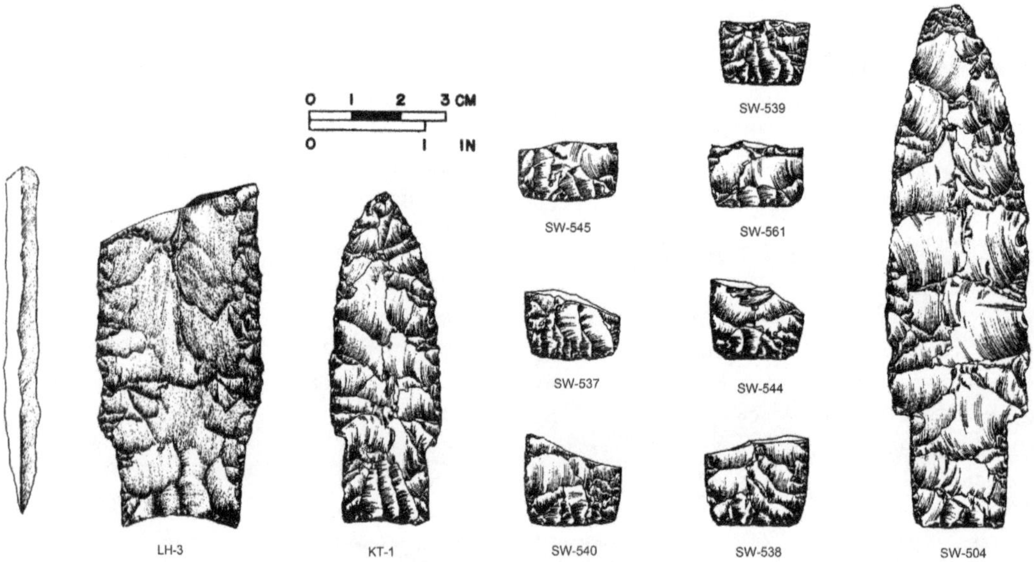


FIGURE 8.2. Cody complex projectile points from the Great Basin. Specimen on the right is associated with the Wallmann Bison (26HU58). It is made from low-silica rhyolite and produced a positive reaction to bison anti-serum. Note the small tip impact fracture and its close morphological and technological resemblance to the Alberta-Cody points from Hudson-Meng. Specimen under the scale is from the Humboldt Sinks and made of Dixie Valley chalcedony.

Dansie et al. (1988:175–178) first reported the Wallmann Bison with an associated projectile point they referred to as "Scottsbluff" (catalog no. SW-504 in Figure 8.2). This point is technologically identical to the Alberta-Cody points from Horner (Bradley and Frison 1987) and Hudson-Meng (Huckell 1978) in its morphology and manufacturing pattern. The depositional context of the Wallmann Bison is interpreted as an eroded remnant of marsh sediment lying immediately above late Pleistocene lake clays. This 10-cm high mound at 1204 meters above sea level (masl) contained the Cody projectile point, a chert flake, and the skeletons of a bison and a waterfowl. Dansie et al. (1988:175) report that the partial *Bison bison* skeleton includes "a disarticulated set of thoracic vertebra dorsal spines, one lumbar vertebra, one cervical vertebra, 15 ribs, and a few small bone fragments." They suggest that "the recovered bones are all high meat-yielding elements, and could represent the deepest elements of a carcass originally buried on its back." Radiocarbon assay of the bone yielded a date of 5240 ± 230 $^{14}$C years BP (UCR-1436) (5479–6495 cal BP), which is inaccurate because the laboratory reported that the bone contained "little organic fraction." Dansie and Jerrems (2004:60) subsequently report a preferred date of 9770 ± 50 $^{14}$C years BP (UCR-3782/CAMS 59156) (11,104–11,260 cal BP) based on purified amino acids (Stafford et al. 1991). This date reliably establishes the age of the Wallmann Bison as contemporaneous with the Cody complex.

Dansie and Jerrems (2004:60) suggest that receding lake levels and the development of marshy conditions characterized the lowland closed basins of the northwestern Great Basin during the early Holocene. The deposits containing the Wallmann Bison are interpreted as direct evidence for a subaerial meadow and slough environment along the ancestral Quinn River (Dansie and Jerrems 2004:60). This paleostream once drained southward into the shallow alkaline lake within the Black Rock playa, where it formed a marshy deltaic environment in the vicinity of the Wallmann Bison. The Quinn River subsequently migrated westward across the playa floor during the Holocene, but its ancestral channel is approximated by the modern arroyo known as Jackson Slough. Geochronological studies of the late Pleistocene and early Holocene paleoshoreline fluctuations in the Black Rock Desert confirm that a nearby shallow lake or marsh environment was contemporaneous with the Wallmann Bison and that this adjacent wetland dropped as low as 1153 masl (51 m below the Wallmann Bison) between 10,000 and 11,000 cal BP (Adams et al. 2008).

The Wallmann Square-Base site (26HU22) is situated about 10 km north of the Wallmann Bison at an elevation of 1212–1215 masl. Clewlow (1968:26–37) formally identified the site and recognized affinities of many projectile points from the site with the Alberta (Cody) type (Clewlow 1968:28–29). This surface scatter has been examined and collected by artifact collectors and professional archaeologists for at least 50 years (Wallmann and Amick 1991). Systematic fieldwork was conducted at 26HU22 in 1990 by the Desert Research Institute and the Bureau of Land Management with the collaboration of local avocational archaeologists. That work had two goals: to verify the surface distribution of Cody artifacts and to test for intact buried deposits of Cody materials. Our investigation centered on a 6400-$m^2$ area of Clewlow's Locality 1, within the larger surface expression that is estimated to be 2 km long and 1 km wide. The site lies primarily on the dune-covered terraces rising above the western side of Jackson Slough. Portions of this landform are as much as 8 m above the surrounding landscape, and provide a significant overview of the adjacent drainage and much of the immediate playa floor.

Subsurface testing consisted of four 1-×-1-m test pits excavated in arbitrary 10-cm levels and screened with 0.64-cm (¼-in.) mesh. The test pits were placed along a low ridge covered by small coppice dunes and blowouts. Two retouch flakes were recovered from the first 10 cm. Excavations continued 45–130 cm below the surface without recovery of additional cultural remains. Stratigraphic profiles documented culturally sterile alluvial clays overlain by a silty eolian mantle. An unusual organic-stained sediment extending 55–130 cm in depth was found in one unit. This deposit was composed of carbonized vegetation lying within an ancient gully. The underlying alluvium was notably oxidized, suggesting the vegetation burned in place and was then capped by alluvium and eolian silts. Nineteen liters of organic residue were collected from this deposit, but the material was too disintegrated for accurate identification of plant species. An uncorrected radiocarbon date of 8810 ± 160 $^{14}C$ years BP (Beta-44758) (9535–10,229 cal BP) was produced on soil humates (0.4 g) obtained from bulk samples prepared by Peter Wigand. While this date is within the minimal age range of Cody chronology (Knell and Muñiz, this volume; Stanford 1999), it remains problematic because of separation from the surface artifacts by 30 cm of eolian deposit and 25 cm of alluvium. In Secret Valley, California, about 100 km west of the Wallmann Square-Base site, West and McGuire (2002) report similar burned marsh deposits of early Holocene age, which they interpret as anthropogenic. The distinctive deposit at 26HU22 may have similar origins, but current subsurface investigations are not adequate for us to draw any firm conclusions about its significance or the potential for subsurface Cody deposits at this locality.

Sixteen lithic artifacts were mapped with an electronic theodolite and collected from the surface of the Wallmann Square-Base site. This assemblage includes 11 Cody projectile point bases, and one of each of the following: complete Cody point, Great Basin Stemmed projectile point base, scraper, flake knife with a graver tip, and flake graver. The number of diagnostic Cody points mapped on the surface confirms the earlier reported association of Cody complex occupations at 26HU22. Stone tools diagnostic of several other time periods also were observed on the surface but not mapped or collected. Clewlow (1968) documents the entire range of prehistoric materials on the surface, and our findings confirm a multicomponent occupational history for this scatter. If this 0.32 percent surface survey sample is representative of the entire scatter, there could be as many as 3750 Cody point fragments at the Wallmann Square-Base site. While this rough calculation may be an overestimate, it nevertheless suggests a substantial Cody occupation. In addition, 161 projectile points and fragments diagnostic of the Cody complex were identified during the documentation of several private artifact collections from the site. These specimens, in combination with the systematically recovered artifacts, provide the majority of materials used for the comparative technological study.

### Typological and Technological Analysis of Square-Based Projectile Points from the Northern Great Basin

A useful summary of the variation in Cody complex projectile point typology and its distributional patterns is provided by Justice (2002a:110–122), who lumps most of these types into what he calls the "Scottsbluff Cluster." Within this cluster he includes what have been called Scottsbluff, Eden, San Jon, Firstview, Kersey, Scottsbluff Eared, Eden Eared, and the Cody Knife, but apparently excludes the Alberta complex (undefined) as distinct from Cody. Justice (2002a:113–114) follows others (e.g., Agenbroad 1978a, 1978b; Bradley 1993:258–260, 2009:268; Bradley and Frison 1987; Frison 1998:14577–14578) in viewing the Cody complex as the probable direct descendant of the Alberta complex. This conclusion is largely based on the intermediate projectile point forms classified as Alberta/Cody from the Horner site. However, based on radiocarbon chronologies and what appears to be a distinctive Alberta component at Hell Gap, Frison and Bonnichsen (1996:313) caution that "the assumption that the Cody complex evolved directly out of the Alberta complex is now open to question." When specific typological attributes are considered, most of the northern Great Basin Cody specimens studied for this analysis are classified as Alberta/Cody I and II, but certain examples conform to specific type descriptions for Alberta, Scottsbluff, and Eden.

The identification and meaning of regional and/or chronological variation in Cody and other early Holocene stemmed point complexes remains a substantial problem that cannot be resolved in this chapter. The extensive disagreements about taxonomic variability and its meaning within the Cody complex have probably produced more heat than light given the limited number of comparative studies. Furthermore, it is becoming increasingly clear that several distinctive cultural complexes overlapped during the TP-EH (Frison 1993; Frison and Bonnichsen 1996: 313; Sellet 2001; Sellet et al. 2009), and these foraging groups may have had regular social interactions.

Consequently, in this chapter Alberta projectile points are included within the broad definition of the Cody complex. This decision is based on the close morphological and technological relationship of these types and the absence of evidence that Alberta can be distinguished spatially or chronologically from the Cody complex (Huckell and Judge 2006:163 provide similar arguments). Whenever possible, typological identifications in this chapter refer to the distinctive types generally recognized within the Scottsbluff cluster (Justice 2002a), but the generic classification as Cody complex is used most commonly, especially for fragmentary artifacts.

Figure 8.3 illustrates typical examples of diagnostic Cody complex projectile points from the Black Rock Desert region of northwestern Nevada. These points almost universally possess edge abrasion of stem margins and the highly patterned sequence of percussion and pressure flaking characteristic of Cody technology. For example, Patten's (1978; 1999:100–103) analysis of techniques likely used in Eden point manufacture illustrates some of its distinctiveness. He describes how the hafting treatment is highly specific and unique with lateral pressure thinning flakes that push past the longitudinal midline, small beveling flakes taken from the base, and a triangular facet at the base resulting in a square stem with a flawless taper from the base to the median ridge in profile. Most successful replicators have advocated the use of a rigid support during the final trimming stage of pressure flaking to produce flake terminations near the midline, the end result of which is the characteristic subdiamond transverse section of Eden-Scottsbluff points (e.g., Bonnichsen and Keyser 1982:141; Bradley and Stanford 1987:416; Patten 1978; 1999: 100–103; also see Bray et al. 1975 for illustration of Don Crabtree's use of this technique). Careful replication experiments also serve as the foundation of Bradley's significant contributions to our understanding of the manufacturing technology of Cody complex projectile points (e.g., Bradley 1991, 1993:258–260, 1998, 2009:267–270; Bradley and Frison 1987; Bradley and Stanford 1987; also see Huckell 1978). Patterning and variation observed in diagnostic Cody complex points from the northern Great Basin conform exactly to these detailed reconstructions of Cody produc-

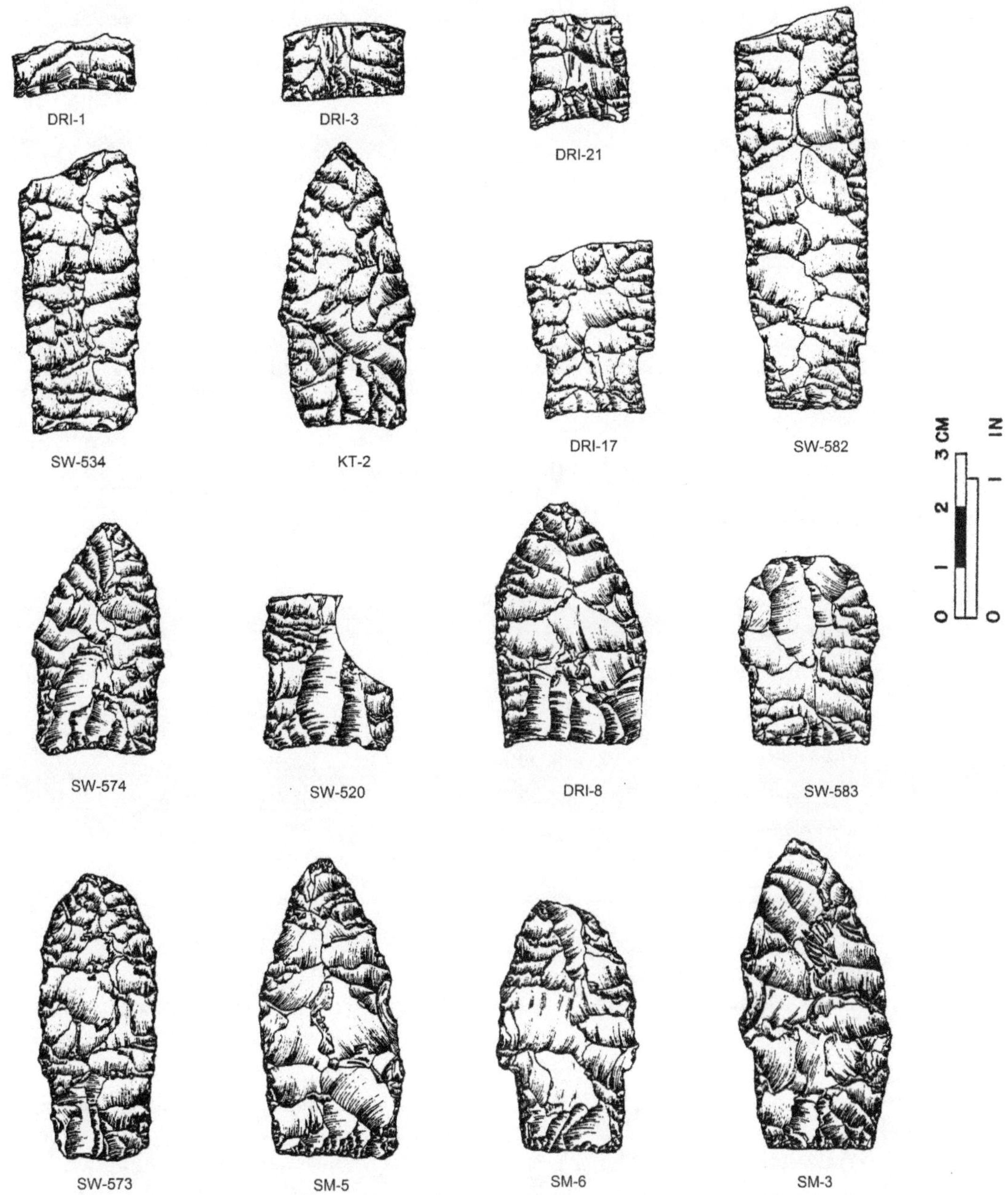


**FIGURE 8.3.** Examples of relatively complete Cody complex projectile points and stem fragments from 26HU22 in the Black Rock Desert, Nevada.

tion grammars; examples of stemmed points that did not match these criteria were excluded from this analysis. I confirmed these typological designations through comparative analysis with Cody complex projectile points from Hudson-Meng (Huckell 1978) in western Nebraska, and the Wyoming sites of Hell Gap (Bradley 2009; Frison 1991; Irwin-Williams et al. 1973; Knell 2009; Knell et al. 2002, 2009; Larson et al. 2009; Muñiz 2009), Horner (Frison and Todd 1987; Jepson 1953), Carter/Kerr-McGee (Frison 1984, 1991), Finley (Frison 1991; Satterthwaite 1957), Larson (Ingbar and Frison 1987), and Black Mountain (Kornfeld et al. 1998).

**TABLE 8.2.** Regional Variation in Cody Projectile Point Basal Finishing (specimen examples in parentheses).

| Production Variant | NW Great Basin | NW High Plains |
|---|---|---|
| Basal beveling: short, abrupt retouch (DRI-1, DRI-8, SW-579) | $n$ = 66; (50.0%) adj res = 2.3 | $n$ = 17; (31.5%) adj res = −2.3 |
| Basal beveling: basal thinning, alternate face (DRI-8, SW-520, SW-574) | $n$ = 32; (24.2%) adj res = −2.5 | $n$ = 23; (42.6%) adj res = 2.5 |
| Basal thinning: characteristic chevron shape (KT-1, SW-163, SW-539) | $n$ = 29; (22.0%) adj res = 0.8 | $n$ = 9; (16.7%) adj res = −0.8 |
| Lateral thinning: over basal beveling (DRI-1, SW-534, SW-583) | $n$ = 5; (3.8%) adj res = −1.0 | $n$ = 4; (7.4%) adj res = 1.0 |
| Lateral thinning: without evidence of basal beveling (Hell Gap, UWI-389) | $n$ = 0; (0.0%) adj res = −1.6 | $n$ = 1; (1.9%) adj res = 1.6 |

*Notes:* NW Great Basin sample includes Black Rock Desert ($n$ = 122), Humboldt Sinks ($n$ = 1), Alvord Desert ($n$ = 2), Hart Lake ($n$ = 5), and Massacre Lake ($n$ = 2). NW High Plains sample includes Black Mountain ($n$ = 7), Hell Gap ($n$ = 21), Carter/Kerr-McGee ($n$ = 8), Finley ($n$ = 1), Larson ($n$ = 1), and Horner ($n$ = 16). adj res = adjusted residual score.

**TABLE 8.3.** Regional Variation in Lithic Raw Material Use.

| Lithic Raw Material | NW Great Basin | NW High Plains |
|---|---|---|
| **Siliceous Volcanic** | | |
| Obsidian | $n$ = 173; (89.6%) adj res = 16.9 | $n$ = 0; adj res = −16.9 |
| Low-silica rhyolite | $n$ = 10; (5.2%) adj res = 3.0 | $n$ = 0; adj res = −3.0 |
| Basalt | $n$ = 2; (1.0%) adj res = −0.2 | $n$ = 2; (1.2%) adj res = 0.2 |
| **Siliceous Sedimentary and Metamorphic** | | |
| Porcellanite, siltstone | $n$ = 0; adj res = −3.0 | $n$ = 4; (2.4%) adj res = 3.0 |
| Quartzite | $n$ = 0; adj res = −6.4 | $n$ = 32; (19.4%) adj res = 6.4 |
| Chert | $n$ = 7; (3.6%) adj res = −7.3 | $n$ = 54; (32.7%) adj res = 7.3 |
| Chalcedony and jasper | $n$ = 1; (0.5%) adj res = −10.2 | $n$ = 73; (44.2%) adj res = 10.2 |

*Notes:* NW Great Basin sample includes Black Rock Desert ($n$ = 178), Humboldt Sinks ($n$ = 1), Alvord Desert ($n$ = 5), Hart Lake ($n$ = 6), and Massacre Lake ($n$ = 3). NW High Plains sample includes Black Mountain ($n$ = 7), Hell Gap ($n$ = 22), Carter/Kerr-McGee ($n$ = 8), Finley ($n$ = 3), Larson ($n$ = 1), Horner ($n$ = 19), Kersey ($n$ = 71), Olsen-Chubbuck ($n$ = 27), and Miscellaneous ($n$ = 5). adj res = adjusted residual score.

### *Diagnostic Basal Thinning and Breakage Patterns*

Two particular aspects of production patterning diagnostic of Cody projectile point technology occur during stem pressure flaking and the rejuvenation of broken tools. Bradley and Stanford (1987:423–426) carefully describe the basal treatments of Cody projectile points, which can involve various combinations of distinctive lateral thinning and basal beveling techniques. Table 8.2 compares these attributes in the study samples from the northern Great Basin and the Great Plains. Both assemblages exhibit an emphasis on basal beveling with short, abrupt retouch, but the Great Plains sample more commonly exhibits that characteristic in combination with basal thinning on the alternate face. It is possible that such minor technological dissimilarities partly represent the effects of raw material differences, which are substantial between these assemblages. Table 8.3 shows that 98.8 percent ($n$ = 163) of the northwestern Great Plains Cody points are made from siliceous sedimentary and metamorphic rocks (especially chert, chalcedony, and jasper), in contrast to the northwestern Great Basin, where 95.9 percent ($n$ = 185) of the Cody points are made from siliceous volcanic rocks (especially obsidian). More importantly, the northwestern Great Basin tools share unique similarities in thinning flake sizes, spacing, and sequencing that are distinctive of Cody technology.

Cody projectile point technology is further distinguished by its design strategy, which results in frequent stem breakage and rejuvenation of the remaining blade fragment through construction of a new stem. These broken points were often re-

**TABLE 8.4.** Sample Variation in Fragment Type Representation.

| Fragment Type | NW Great Basin | NW High Plains |
|---|---|---|
| Stem proximal (broken below shoulders) | $n$ = 130 (67.4%); adj res = 10.2 | $n$ = 23 (13.9%); adj res = −10.2 |
| Corner/Ear/Shoulder (transverse break) | $n$ = 6 (3.1%); adj res = 2.3 | $n$ = 0 (0.0%); adj res = −2.3 |
| Stem/Shoulders proximal (broken above shoulders) | $n$ = 29 (15.0%); adj res = 0.8 | $n$ = 20 (12.1%); adj res = −0.8 |
| Distal with shoulders (broken below shoulders) | $n$ = 4 (2.1%); adj res = −0.2 | $n$ = 4 (2.4%); adj res = 0.2 |
| Tip distal (broken above shoulders) | $n$ = 5 (2.6%); adj res = −1.9 | $n$ = 11 (6.7%); adj res = 1.9 |
| Blade midsection (broken above shoulders) | $n$ = 0 (0.0%); adj res = −4.4 | $n$ = 16 (9.7%); adj res = 4.4 |
| Stem and midsection (broken above midblade) | $n$ = 3 (1.6%); adj res = −4.9 | $n$ = 26 (15.8%); adj res = 4.9 |
| Complete (minor damage allowable) | $n$ = 16 (8.3%); adj res = −7.0 | $n$ = 65 (39.4%); adj res = 7.0 |

*Notes:* NW Great Basin sample includes Black Rock Desert ($n$ = 178), Humboldt Sinks ($n$ = 1), Alvord Desert ($n$ = 5), Hart Lake ($n$ = 6), and Massacre Lake ($n$ = 3). NW High Plains sample includes Black Mountain ($n$ = 7), Hell Gap ($n$ = 22), Carter/Kerr-McGee ($n$ = 8), Finley ($n$ = 3), Larson ($n$ = 1), Horner ($n$ = 19), Kersey ($n$ = 71), Olsen-Chubbuck ($n$ = 27), and Miscellaneous ($n$ = 5). adj res = adjusted residual score.

paired by creating new stems, with the remnant of a bending fracture from this breakage sometimes remaining on the basal end of the rejuvenated stem (Huckell 1978:185). This rejuvenation evidence is present on several of the northwestern Great Basin Cody specimens.

Huckell's (1978:183–188) analysis of the Cody projectile points from Hudson-Meng illustrates the systematic pattern of rebasing on Cody projectile points following stem breakage. He points out (1978:183–185) that the reduction sequence and systematic rebasing of Cody projectile points was intentionally designed to conserve lithic raw material. Interestingly, his arguments anticipated subsequent discussions of technological organization that explored the importance of evaluating stone tool curation and economizing behavior (Binford 1979; Odell 1996; Shott 1996). Regarding Cody projectile point technology, these uniquely designed economizing strategies seem related to risk reduction for groups coping with the functional demands of high mobility.

Substantial evidence exists for stem breakage and the rebasing of Cody projectile points at 26HU22 (Figure 8.4), but the blade portions of these tools are rare. Table 8.4 compares fragment types represented in the northwestern Great Basin and Great Plains assemblages. While the Great Plains sample contains a high percentage of complete points, distal fragments, midsections, and stems with midsections (combining for 74.0 percent of the total), the northwestern Great Basin sample is dominated by stems and proximal fragments (87.1 percent of the total) that are all associated with the large assemblage from 26HU22. The reasons for such strong contrast are difficult to determine and somewhat paradoxical. For example, smaller artifacts like stem fragments are more likely to be recovered from excavated contexts, as occurs among the majority of the Great Plains assemblages in this sample, than from the surface contexts of the northwestern Great Basin sample. Furthermore, it is unlikely that collector bias accounts for these differences because the more fragmentary assemblage of the northwestern Great Basin was produced by unsystematic surface collections rather than the professional excavations characteristic of the Great Plains sample. Finally, the majority of the assemblage from 26HU22 represents the earliest known surface collection of the site and is unbiased from the potential effects of previous historic collections.

The most plausible explanations for the unusually high frequency of stem fragments may be related to the higher rates of tool breakage expected for the more brittle obsidian tools. In addition, most of the large blade fragments originally in the Cody assemblage at 26HU22 may have been rejuvenated following stem breakage and carried away, and many of those that remained on the surface were available for scavenging by later prehistoric occupants. There are numerous Archaic and Late Prehistoric occupations scattered throughout the eastern arm of the Black Rock Desert (Clewlow 1968; Hanes and McGuckian 1987; Smith 2010), including several within the spatial boundaries of 26HU22. Betty's site, a discrete Late Prehistoric campsite that includes substantial evidence of the recycling of earlier lithic debris (e.g., Amick 2007), is one such example.

The playa floor of the Black Rock Desert encompasses 2590 km$^2$, and although limited

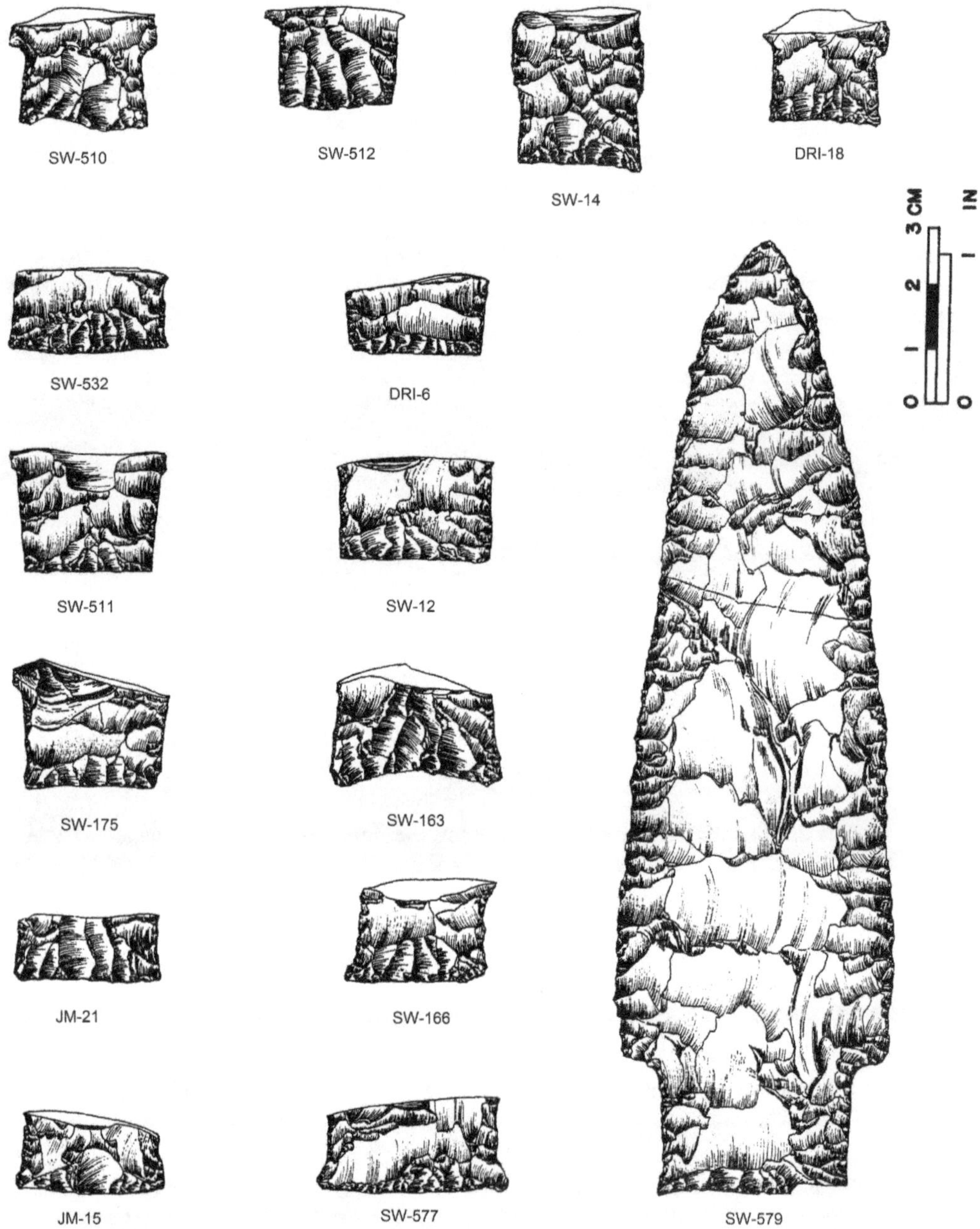


**FIGURE 8.4.** Cody complex projectile points from 26HU22 in the Black Rock Desert, Nevada. SW-579 is made from low-silica rhyolite and best resembles examples assigned to the Alberta type.

secondary sources of microcrystalline silicates occur on adjacent alluvial fans, the playa itself is devoid of chippable toolstone. The nearest toolstone sources lie about 20 km south of 26HU22. Thus, archaeological sites exposed on the surface of the playa often served as important toolstone sources for subsequent itinerants and occupants.

Similar cases of Cody point assemblages dominated by stem fragments are reported at Niska (Meyer 1985) and Quill Lakes (Novecosky 2002) in Saskatchewan, Jurgens (Wheat 1977, 1979) and Claypool (Bradley and Stanford 1987; Dick and Mountain 1960; Stanford and Albanese 1975) in northeastern Colorado, and the Tularosa Basin

**TABLE 8.5.** Size Variation within and between Regional Assemblages.

| Dimension | NW Great Basin | NW High Plains | Dimension | NW Great Basin | NW High Plains |
|---|---|---|---|---|---|
| **Axial maximum length[a] (mm)** | | | **Neck width[e] (mm)** | | |
| Mean | 57.9 | 62.4 | Mean | 23.3 | 18.6 |
| Median | 54.7 | 60.3 | Median | 23.3 | 17.9 |
| Standard deviation | 13.7 | 25.5 | Standard deviation | 3.0 | 3.8 |
| CV | 23% | 41% | CV | 13% | 20% |
| Number of cases | 11 | 65 | Number of cases | 177 | 57 |
| **Blade maximum width[b] (mm)** | | | **Base width[f] (mm)** | | |
| Mean | 29.0 | 21.4 | Mean | 22.9 | 19.1 |
| Median | 27.6 | 21.1 | Median | 22.8 | 18.5 |
| Standard deviation | 6.8 | 4.9 | Standard deviation | 3.6 | 3.4 |
| CV | 23% | 23% | CV | 16% | 17% |
| Number of cases | 35 | 121 | Number of cases | 172 | 131 |
| **Blade maximum thickness[c] (mm)** | | | **Stem maximum length (mm)** | | |
| Mean | 8.2 | 6.5 | Mean | 16.3 | 14.7 |
| Median | 8.2 | 6.4 | Median | 15.5 | 14.4 |
| Standard deviation | 2.0 | 1.2 | Standard deviation | 3.0 | 3.4 |
| CV | 24% | 19% | CV | 18% | 23% |
| Number of cases | 44 | 150 | Number of cases | 43 | 113 |
| **Shoulder width[d] (mm)** | | | **Stem maximum thickness[g] (mm)** | | |
| Mean | 27.9 | 21.0 | Mean | 6.3 | 5.2 |
| Median | 26.6 | 20.8 | Median | 6.5 | 5.1 |
| Standard deviation | 6.5 | 4.8 | Standard deviation | 1.0 | 0.9 |
| CV | 23% | 23% | CV | 15% | 17% |
| Number of cases | 39 | 136 | Number of cases | 185 | 57 |

*Notes:* NW Great Basin sample includes Black Rock Desert ($n$ = 178), Humboldt Sinks ($n$ = 1), Alvord Desert ($n$ = 5), Hart Lake ($n$ = 6), and Massacre Lake ($n$ = 3). NW High Plains sample includes Black Mountain ($n$ = 7), Hell Gap ($n$ = 22), Carter/Kerr-McGee ($n$ = 8), Finley ($n$ = 3), Larson ($n$ = 1), Horner ($n$ = 19), Kersey ($n$ = 71), Olsen-Chubbuck ($n$ = 27), and Miscellaneous ($n$ = 5). CV = coefficient of variation.
[a] Complete specimens only.
[b] Complete points, stems with shoulders, and blade distal and blade midsection portions.
[c] Complete points and blade distal and blade midsection portions.
[d] Complete points, stems with shoulders, and blade distal and blade midsection portions.
[e] Complete points, stems, and certain midsection fragments.
[f] Complete points and stems.
[g] Complete points, stems, and certain midsection fragments.

of southern New Mexico (Amick and Lukowski 2006). While the exact causes of these interassemblage patterns remain uncertain, evidence from analogous Cody assemblages with intrasite spatial data (e.g., Jurgens and Claypool) suggest they may reflect the effects of retooling behavior (e.g., Keeley 1982) in relatively large camps associated with nearby kill sites.

### *Morphometric Variation in Cody Projectile Points*

In addition to its highly unique pattern of manufacture, Cody projectile point technology is characterized by "uniformity of shape" (Huckell 1978: 181). Although there is substantial size variation in Cody projectile points, ranging from miniature (Bonnichsen and Keyser 1982) to jumbo (Wormington 1957:132–135; Wormington and Forbis 1965), there is a strong tendency toward limited variation in shape. There are two main effects of breakage and wear in Cody points: reduction of original length (usually by restemming) and reduction of shoulder width because of blade margin resharpening. Table 8.5 compares the morphological variation in Cody points in the northern Great Basin with those of the Great Plains. In general, Great Basin Cody specimens have slightly broader and thicker blades with stems that are somewhat longer, wider, and thinner, and typically resemble the Alberta/Cody I type of Bradley and Frison (1987:219). This morphological pattern contrasts with the Great Plains sample, which tends to resemble the Alberta/Cody II type of Bradley and Frison (1987:219–220). These

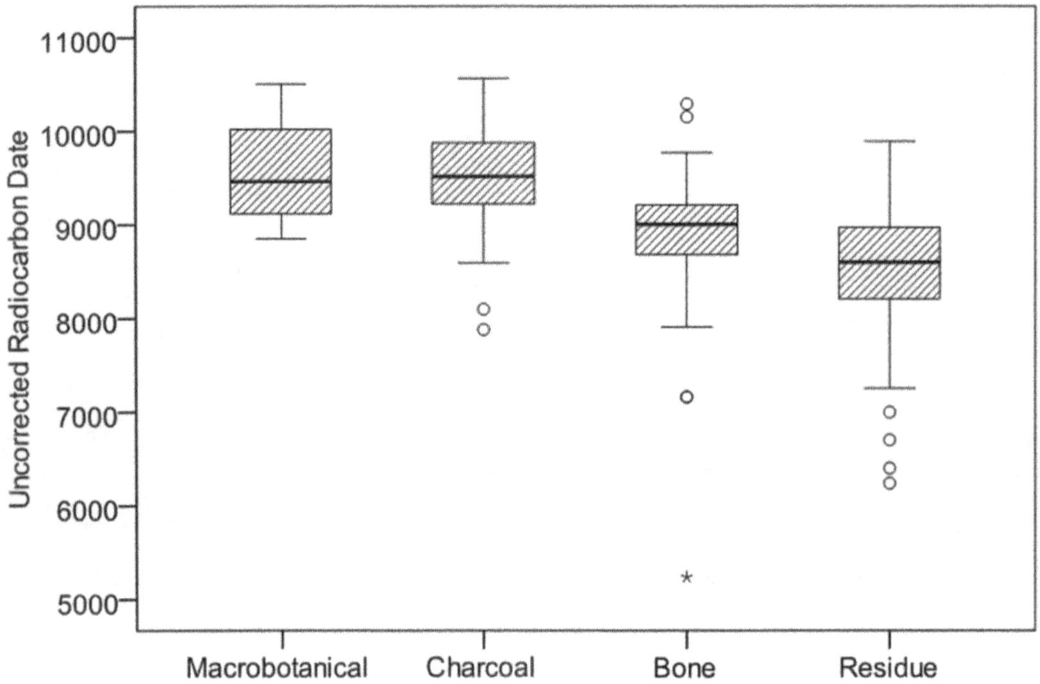


FIGURE 8.5. Box plot of radiocarbon dates ($n$ = 129) associated with archaeological deposits of the Cody complex sorted by the sample materials.

differences may simply reflect the biased and incomplete nature of this sample comparison. They may also represent effects associated with the distinctive flaking properties of the different lithic raw materials characterizing these two regional samples. Most importantly, these morphometric differences can represent contrasts in the reduction phases of these artifacts: the northwestern Great Basin specimens are less reduced. This suggestion seems consistent with the observation that these northwestern Great Basin points are generally less refined than this sample of Great Plains points. Careful analyses of the production technology of Cody projectile points by Bradley and Frison (1987) and Bradley and Stanford (1987) indicate that such morphological differences among Cody variants can be accounted for as the routine effects of repair and resharpening.

### *Chronological Patterning*

As noted above, numerous researchers suggest that patterns of morphometric and technological variation within the Cody cluster projectile point series reflect chronological trends. These hypotheses have not been rigorously tested against the record of radiocarbon dates for the Cody complex, however. A cursory investigation of chronological trends among morphological variants of the Cody cluster was undertaken to evaluate these suggestions and to provide greater temporal context for the Cody complex occupations in the northern Great Basin. A dataset consisting of 129 radiocarbon dates associated with Cody complex occupations at 39 sites is used for this purpose (Table 8.6). These data include 6 dates from the northwestern Great Basin (Nevada and Oregon), 35 from the northern Great Plains (Alberta, Saskatchewan, Montana, North Dakota, and Minnesota), 61 from the central Great Plains (Wyoming, Colorado, and Nebraska), and 27 from the southern Great Plains (Oklahoma, New Mexico, and Texas). The typological association of these dates generally follows the recommendations of the original authors. Figure 8.5 shows a box plot of all 129 dates sorted by the sample materials. This graph illustrates the tendency for bone dates (apatite, collagen, and unspecified) and residue dates (including humates, humins, and humic acids) to

**TABLE 8.6.** Compilation of Cody Associated Radiocarbon Assays Used in This Analysis.

| Site and Location | 14C Date | Lab Number | Component | Material Ref | Dated |
|---|---|---|---|---|---|
| Battle Spring Draw, WY | 9430 ± 40 | n/a | Cody | charcoal | 4 |
| Bayrock, AB | 10,500 ± 200 | GSC-3 | Alberta | willow wood | 19 |
| Benz, ND | 8590 ± 55 | SMU-1488 | Scottsb | humate residue | 23 |
| Benz, ND | 8600 ± 60 | SMU-1390 | Scottsb | humate residue | 23 |
| Benz, ND | 8700 ± 70 | SMU-1282 | Scottsb | humate residue | 23 |
| Benz, ND | 8910 ± 70 | SMU-1271 | Scottsb | humate residue | 23 |
| Benz, ND | 9540 ± 50 | SMU-1488 | Alb-Cody | humate residue | 23 |
| Blackwater Draw, NM | 8640 ± 350 | A-512 | Scottsb | charred bone | 19 |
| Blackwater Draw, NM | 8690 ± 70 | SMU-1671 | Firstvw | humate residue | 12 |
| Blackwater Draw, NM | 8830 ± 160 | Y-2488 | Firstvw | humate residue | 20 |
| Blackwater Draw, NM | 8970 ± 60 | SMU-1672 | Firstvw | humate residue | 12 |
| Blackwater Draw, NM | 8890 ± 290 | A-489 | Firstvw | humate residue | 20 |
| Blue Point, WY | 9540 ± 50 | Beta-133208 | Alb-Cody | charcoal | 19 |
| Bradbury Brook, MN | 9220 ± 75 | Beta-44685 | Alberta | charcoal | 19 |
| Carter/Kerr-McGee, WY | 9130 ± 220 | RL-454 | Cody | bone collagen | 19 |
| Dirty Shame Rockshelter, OR | 8850 ± 75 | SI-2268 | Scottsb | uncharred wood | 19 |
| Dirty Shame Rockshelter, OR | 8905 ± 75 | SI-2268 | Scottsb | charcoal | 19 |
| Dirty Shame Rockshelter, OR | 9500 ± 95 | SI-2268 | Scottsb | charcoal | 19 |
| Finley, WY | 9026 ± 118 | SMU-250 | Eden/SB | bone apatite | 8 |
| Finley, WY | 9030 ± 220 | RL-574 | Eden/SB | n/a | 19 |
| Finley, WY | 9145 ± 88 | AA-74896 | Eden/SB | purified collagen | 10 |
| Finley, WY | 9154 ± 80 | SMU-277 | Eden/SB | n/a | 19 |
| Finley, WY | 9158 ± 84 | AA-74897 | Eden/SB | purified collagen | 10 |
| Finley, WY | 9306 ± 87 | AA-74895 | Eden/SB | purified collagen | 10 |
| Finley, WY | 9333 ± 107 | SMU-276 | Eden/SB | n/a | 19 |
| Fishing Bridge, WY | 8940 ± 60 | Beta-65466 | Cody | charcoal | 19 |
| Fletcher, AB | 9380 ± 110 | TO-1097 | Alberta | *Scirpus* achenes | 25 |
| Fletcher, AB | 9540 ± 110 | CAMS-42980 | Alberta | *Scirpus* achenes | 1 |
| Frasca, CO | 8870 ± 350 | M-1463 | Cody | bison bone | 24 |
| Frasca, CO | 8910 ± 90 | SI-4846 | Cody | bone collagen | 24 |
| Hell Gap, Loc. I, WY | 8590 ± 350 | A-707 | Alberta | charcoal | 20 |
| Hell Gap, Loc. I, WY | 8600 ± 600 | I-245 | Scottsb | charcoal | 8 |
| Hell Gap, Loc. I, WY | 9120 ± 490 | AA-27675 | Eden/SB | charcoal | 16 |
| Hell Gap, Loc. I, WY | 9410 ± 95 | AA-28774 | Alberta | charcoal | 16 |
| Hell Gap, Loc. I, WY | 10,560 ± 80 | AA-20545 | Alberta | charcoal | 16 |
| Hell Gap, Loc. V, WY | 8890 ± 110 | A-753A | Eden/SB | bone collagen | 20 |
| Hell Gap, Loc. V, WY | 9050 ± 160 | A-753C3 | Eden/SB | bone apatite | 20 |
| Heron Eden, SK | 8240 ± 200 | S-3208 | Eden/SB | bone collagen | 19 |
| Heron Eden, SK | 9000 ± 130 | S-3309 | Eden/SB | bone collagen | 19 |
| Heron Eden, SK | 9010 ± 120 | S-3114 | Eden/SB | bone collagen | 19 |
| Heron Eden, SK | 9168 ± 50 | NZA-15745 | Eden/SB | bone collagen | 19 |
| Heron Eden, SK | 9210 ± 110 | S-3308 | Eden/SB | bone collagen | 19 |
| Heron Eden, SK | 10,290 ± 100 | S-3118 | Eden/SB | bone collagen | 19 |
| Horn Shelter No. 2, TX | 9500 ± 200 | TX-1830 | Scottsb | charcoal | 22 |
| Horn Shelter No. 2, TX | 9980 ± 370 | TX-1722 | Scottsb | charcoal | 22 |
| Horner, WY | 7880 ± 1300 | SI-74 | Cody | charcoal | 8 |
| Horner, WY | 8830 ± 120 | UCLA-697A | Cody | bone collagen | 19 |

**TABLE 8.6.** (cont'd.) Compilation of Cody Associated Radiocarbon Assays Used in This Analysis.

| Site and Location | 14C Date | Lab Number | Component | Material Ref | Dated |
|---|---|---|---|---|---|
| Horner, WY | 8840 ± 140 | UCLA-697A | Cody | bone collagen | 8 |
| Horner, WY | 9390 ± 75 | SI-4851 | Cody | charcoal | 8 |
| Horner II, WY | 9875 ± 85 | SI-4851A | Alb-Cody | charcoal | 8 |
| Horner II, WY | 10,060 ± 220 | I-10900 | Alb-Cody | charcoal | 8 |
| Hudson-Meng, NE | 8765 ± 115 | SMU-51 | Alb-Cody | bone apatite | 19 |
| Hudson-Meng, NE | 9220 ± 60 | n/a | Alb-Cody | *Celtis* carbonate | 8 |
| Hudson-Meng, NE | 9235 ± 195 | SMU-52 | Alb-Cody | bone apatite | 19 |
| Hudson-Meng, NE | 9380 ± 70 | Beta-64322 | Alb-Cody | charcoal | 19 |
| Hudson-Meng, NE | 9380 ± 100 | SMU-102 | Alb-Cody | bone apatite | 8 |
| Hudson-Meng, NE | 9570 ± 60 | Beta-64321 | Alb-Cody | charcoal | 19 |
| Hudson-Meng, NE | 9600 ± 60 | Beta-65278 | Alb-Cody | charcoal | 19 |
| Hudson-Meng, NE | 9630 ± 60 | CAMS-10364 | Alb-Cody | charcoal | 19 |
| Hudson-Meng, NE | 9720 ± 80 | CAMS-12841 | Alb-Cody | charcoal | 19 |
| Hudson-Meng, NE | 9820 ± 160 | SMU-224 | Alb-Cody | charcoal | 8 |
| Hudson-Meng, NE | 9890 ± 90 | Beta-64318 | Alb-Cody | charcoal | 19 |
| Hudson-Meng, NE | 9900 ± 60 | Beta-65277 | Alb-Cody | charcoal | 19 |
| Hudson-Meng, NE | 9920 ± 80 | Beta-64320 | Alb-Cody | charcoal | 19 |
| Hudson-Meng, NE | 9970 ± 60 | Beta-65276 | Alb-Cody | charcoal | 19 |
| Hudson-Meng, NE | 10,310 ± 40 | Beta-65280 | Alb-Cody | charcoal | 19 |
| Hudson-Meng, NE | 10,440 ± 80 | Beta-64319 | Alb-Cody | charcoal | 19 |
| Hudson-Meng, NE | 10,540 ± 70 | Beta-65279 | Alb-Cody | charcoal | 19 |
| J-Crossing, AB | 8580 ± 160 | AECV-1198 C | Alberta | bone collagen | 19 |
| J-Crossing, AB | 9600 ± 210 | AECV-746 C | Alberta | bone collagen | 19 |
| Jerry Craig, CO | 9310 ± 50 | Beta-109467 | Cody | charcoal | 11 |
| Jurgens, CO | 9070 ± 90 | SI-3726 | Firstvw | charcoal | 8 |
| Lamb Spring, CO | 8870 ± 350 | M-1463 | Cody | bone collagen | 21 |
| Lime Creek, NE | 9524 ± 450 | C-471 | Scottsb | charcoal | 6 |
| Lindenmeier, CO | 9330 ± 70 | TO-340 | Alb-Cody | charcoal | 9 |
| Lindenmeier, CO | 9880 ± 100 | TO-339 | Alb-Cody | charcoal | 9 |
| Lindenmeier, CO | 10,040 ± 80 | TO-338 | Alb-Cody | charcoal | 9 |
| Lubbock Lake 2B (middle), TX | 8130 ± 80 | SMU-1089 | Firstvw | humic acid residue | 14 |
| Lubbock Lake 2B (middle), TX | 8585 ± 145 | SI-5499 | Firstvw | humin residue | 14 |
| Lubbock Lake 2B (middle), TX | 9330 ± 70 | SMU-759 | Firstvw | humic acid residue | 14 |
| Lubbock Lake 2B (middle), TX | 9550 ± 90 | SMU-1116 | Firstvw | humic acid residue | 14 |
| Lubbock Lake 2B (middle), TX | 9550 ± 100 | SMU-1118 | Firstvw | humic acid residue | 14 |
| Lubbock Lake 2B (middle), TX | 9600 ± 55 | NSRL-10973 | Firstvw | humic acid residue | 14 |
| Lubbock Lake 2B (upper), TX | 6240 ± 40 | SMU-1094 | Firstvw | humic acid residue | 14 |
| Lubbock Lake 2B (upper), TX | 6400 ± 80 | SMU-544 | Firstvw | humic acid residue | 14 |
| Lubbock Lake 2B (upper), TX | 6705 ± 95 | SI-4178 | Firstvw | humin residue | 14 |
| Lubbock Lake 2B (upper), TX | 7255 ± 75 | SI-3204 | Firstvw | humin residue | 14 |
| Lubbock Lake 2B (upper), TX | 7890 ± 100 | SMU-302 | Firstvw | humic acid residue | 14 |
| Lubbock Lake 2B (upper), TX | 7970 ± 80 | SMU-262 | Firstvw | humic acid residue | 14 |
| Lubbock Lake 2B (upper), TX | 8210 ± 240 | SMU-830 | Firstvw | humic acid residue | 14 |
| Lubbock Lake 2B (upper), TX | 8655 ± 90 | SI-4177 | Firstvw | humic acid residue | 14 |
| MacHaffie (stratum 3), MT | 7905 ± 435 | GX-15153-AMS | Scottsb | bone apatite | 7 |
| MacHaffie (stratum 3), MT | 8100 ± 300 | L-578A | Scottsb | charcoal | 7 |
| MacHaffie (stratum 3), MT | 8280 ± 120 | GX-15153-G-AMS | Scottsb | bone gelatin | 7 |

TABLE 8.6. (cont'd.) Compilation of Cody Associated Radiocarbon Assays Used in This Analysis.

| Site and Location | 14C Date | Lab Number | Component | Material Ref | Dated |
|---|---|---|---|---|---|
| MacHaffie (stratum 3), MT | 8403 ± 109 | UGa-6307 | Scottsb | sediment residue | 19 |
| MacHaffie (stratum 3), MT | 8570 ± 40 | Beta-146735 | Scottsb | organic residue | 19 |
| MacHaffie (stratum 3), MT | 8620 ± 200 | GX-15152-AMS | Scottsb | charcoal | 7 |
| MacHaffie (stratum 3), MT | 9270 ± 50 | Beta-105640 | Scottsb | bone collagen | 19 |
| MacHaffie (stratum 3), MT | 9340 ± 120 | GX-15150-A-AMS | Scottsb | bone apatite | 19 |
| MacHaffie (stratum 4), MT | 9210 ± 80 | Tx-7769 | Scottsb | sediment residue | 19 |
| Malin Fishing Hole, MT | 9410 ± 50 | Beta-177460 | Cody | charcoal | 26 |
| Malin Fishing Hole, MT | 9510 ± 50 | Beta-196110 | Cody | charcoal | 26 |
| Malin Fishing Hole, MT | 9530 ± 50 | Beta-196111 | Cody | charcoal | 26 |
| Malin Fishing Hole, MT | 9670 ± 50 | Beta-196112 | Cody | charcoal | 26 |
| Mammoth Meadow I, MT | 9390 ± 90 | TO-1976 | Cody | charcoal | 2 |
| Medicine Lodge Creek, WY | 8830 ± 470 | RL-446 | Cody | charcoal | 8 |
| Medicine Lodge Creek, WY | 9030 ± 260 | RL-382R | Cody | charcoal | 8 |
| Medicine Lodge Creek, WY | 9030 ± 460 | RL-439 | Cody | charcoal | 8 |
| Medicine Lodge Creek, WY | 9160 ± 220 | RL-449 | Cody | bone collagen | 8 |
| Nall (stratum 2), OK | 9640 ± 110 | Beta-121881 | Cody | paleosol residue | 17 |
| Nall (stratum 2), OK | 9790 ± 110 | Beta-121881 | Cody | paleosol residue | 17 |
| Nall (stratum 2/3), OK | 9670 ± 80 | Beta-138041 | Cody | charcoal | 17 |
| Nelson, CO | 7995 ± 80 | SI-4898 | Cody | bone | 3 |
| Niska, SK | 7000 ± 185 | S-2353 | Scottsb | humate residue | 18 |
| Niska, SK | 7165 ± 320 | S-2453 | Scottsb | bone collagen | 18 |
| Niska, SK | 8475 ± 650 | S-2510 | Scottsb | paleosol residue | 19 |
| Olsen-Chubbock | 10,150 ± 500 | A-744 | Firstvw | bison bone | 28 |
| Osprey Beach, WY | 9360 ± 60 | Beta-148567 | Cody | charcoal | 15 |
| San Jon, NM | 8275 ± 65 | A-7438.1 | Firstvw | humate residue | 12 |
| San Jon, NM | 8360 ± 210 | A-7464 | Firstvw | residue | 12 |
| San Jon, NM | 8640 ± 65 | A-7439.1 | Firstvw | humate residue | 12 |
| Scottsbluff, NE | 8680 ± 85 | AA-67442 | Scottsb | purified collagen | 10 |
| Scottsbluff, NE | 8939 ± 85 | AA-67443 | Scottsb | purified collagen | 10 |
| St. Louis (layer 9), SK | 9150 ± 40 | Beta-173611 | Cody | bone collagen | 19 |
| Wallmann Bison, NV | 5240 ± 230 | UCR-1436 | Alb-Cody | bone collagen | 5 |
| Wallmann Bison, NV | 9770 ± 50 | UCR-3782 | Alb-Cody | purified collagen | 5 |
| Wallman Square-Base, NV | 8810 ± 160 | Beta-44758 | Alb-Cody | humate residue | 27 |
| Wetzel, CO | 7160 ± 135 | SI-4849 | Cody | bone | 3 |

*Notes:* All dates refer to original publications and are uncorrected. Component assignments generally follow the recommendations of the primary authors. Inclusion in this database is based on assessment of the relative strength of association. Secondary publication sources have been listed in several cases to reduce the total number of citation listings. Primary sources can be found in these secondary citations.

*Ref:* 1 = Beaudoin 2000; 2 = Bonnichsen et al. 1992; 3 = Cassells 1983:62; 4 = Craven and Eckerle 2005; 5 = Dansie and Jerrems 2004:60; 6 = Davis 1962; 7 = Davis et al. 1991; 8 = Frison 1991:26; 9 = Haynes et al. 1992:89; 10 = Hill 2008a:91; 11 = Hill and Kornfeld 1999:31; 12 = Holliday 1997:126; 13 = Holliday et al. 1983; 14 = Johnson 1987:11; 15 = Johnson et al. 2004:27; 16 = Knell 2007; 17 = LaBelle et al. 2003; 18 = Meyer 1985:28; 19 = Morlan and Betts 2005; 20 = Pitblado 2003:82; 21 = Rancier et al. 1982:12; 22 = Redder 1985:41; 23 = Root et al. 1986:424–425; 24 = Stanford 1999:323; 25 = Vickers and Beaudoin 1989; 26 = Vivian 2005; 27 = Wallmann and Amick 1991; 28 = Wheat 1972:156–158.

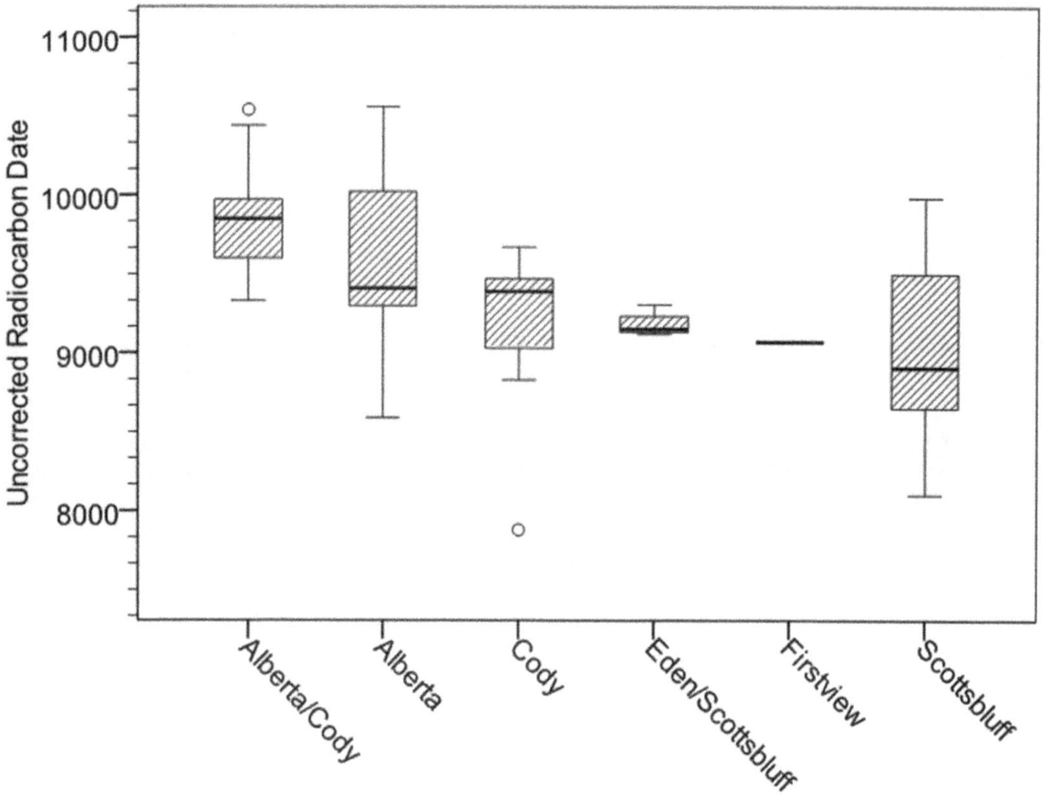


**FIGURE 8.6.** Box plot of radiocarbon dates on paleobotanical materials and purified bone collagen from archaeological deposits of the Cody complex ($n$ = 60), sorted by associated projectile point typological designations. This sample includes dates from Alberta: Bayrock ($n$ = 1) and Fletcher ($n$ = 2); Colorado: Jerry Craig ($n$ = 1), Jurgens ($n$ = 1), and Lindenmeier ($n$ = 4); Minnesota: Bradbury Brook ($n$ = 1); Montana: MacHaffie (Stratum 3) ($n$ = 2), Malin Fishing Hole ($n$ = 4), and Mammoth Meadow I ($n$ = 1); North Dakota: Benz ($n$ = 1); Nebraska: Hudson-Meng ($n$ = 13), Lime Creek ($n$ = 1), and Scottsbluff ($n$ = 2); Nevada: Wallmann Bison ($n$ = 1); Oklahoma: Nall (Stratum 2/3 interface) ($n$ = 1); Oregon: Dirty Shame Rockshelter ($n$ = 3); Texas: Horn Shelter No. 2 ($n$ = 2); and Wyoming: Battle Spring Draw ($n$ = 1), Blue Point ($n$ = 1), Finley ($n$ = 3), Fishing Bridge ($n$ = 1), Hell Gap, Loc. I ($n$ = 5), Horner ($n$ = 4), Medicine Lodge Creek ($n$ = 3), and Osprey Beach ($n$ = 1).

be more variable and generally younger than dates on plant materials (macrobotanical remains and charcoal). Given the generally problematic nature of dates from these materials (Taylor 1987:43–64), they should be excluded from further consideration with the exception of the amino acid dates from purified bone collagen (Stafford et al. 1991).

Removing these problematic materials leaves 60 Cody complex dated associations from 25 sites. Four dates are from the northwestern Great Basin, 12 from the northern Great Plains, 41 from the central Great Plains, and 3 from the southern Great Plains. Figure 8.6 shows a box plot comparing the typological designations for these dates as proposed by the original authors. In general, the associations with Alberta or Alberta/Cody are earliest, with a median age of 9848 $^{14}$C years BP for Alberta/Cody ($n$ = 22) (11,240 cal BP) and 9410 $^{14}$C years BP for Alberta ($n$ = 7) (10,638 cal BP). Cody associations have a median age of 9360 $^{14}$C years BP ($n$ = 15) (10,603 cal BP), and Scottsbluff associations a median age of 8905 $^{14}$C years BP ($n$ = 11) (10,045 cal BP). All other associations have a radiocarbon sample size less than five. The overall median age among the reliable sample materials is 9500 $^{14}$C years BP (10,740 cal BP), with a standard deviation of 546 radiocarbon years. There appears to be a chronological trend for the

Alberta and Alberta/Cody projectile point associations to be earliest, with the associations between the more refined Cody point styles (e.g., Scottsbluff, Eden, Firstview) somewhat later.

This exercise illustrates several problems in the evaluation of the Cody complex radiocarbon chronology. First, rigorous assessments of context and association are challenging when one is conducting a secondary literature review. Second, more than half of the reported dates ($n = 69$, 53.5 percent) come from materials with poor reliability for establishing event dates of the associated archaeological deposits. Finally, these data indicate that geographic trends in Cody chronology are difficult to discern because of sample biases toward the central Great Plains ($n = 41$, 68.3 percent). In particular, more than one-third of the 60 most reliable Cody complex dates ($n = 23$, 38.3 percent) come from only three sites: 13 from Hudson-Meng, Nebraska (Agenbroad 1978b; Frison 1991; Todd and Rapson 1997); 5 from Lindenmeier, Colorado (Haynes et al. 1992); and 5 from Hell Gap, Wyoming (Frison 1991; Knell 2007; Pitblado 2003). Efforts to assess geographic trends in Cody chronology may be hampered until stronger data are available (but see Knell and Muñiz, this volume).

One tentative conclusion from this first approximation of chronological trends is that the Cody occupations of the northern Great Basin may be more closely associated with the early phase of the Cody chronology. This is based on the morphometric tendencies of the majority of these projectile points to be similar to Alberta and Alberta/Cody. It should be noted, however, that there are several examples of Cody complex projectile points in the northern Great Basin that can be classified as members of the highly refined Eden type.

Overall, the Cody projectile points at 26HU22 and 26HU58 bear the most striking resemblance from morphometric and technological standpoints to those from Hudson-Meng in western Nebraska. The average age of the Hudson-Meng site is 9899 $^{14}$C years BP ($n = 13$) (11,280 cal BP), which compares favorably with the date of 9770 $^{14}$C years BP (11,210 cal BP) for the Wallmann Bison (26HU58) and strongly suggests contemporaneity of these two Cody complex sites, which are separated by approximately 1800 km and numerous mountain ranges.

## Economic and Ecological Contexts of Cody Occupations in the Far West

Given the typological and chronological similarities of the Cody complex between the Great Plains and the northwestern Great Basin, critical questions need to be posed about the nature of their potential economic and ecological connections. Approaches to investigating these interrelated questions include analysis of animal protein residues on Cody points from the Black Rock Desert, identification of Cody mobility patterns in the Black Rock Desert through obsidian source analysis, and evaluation of post-Pleistocene records of bison geographic distribution and abundance in the Far West.

### *Blood Residue Analysis*

The documentation of substantial numbers of Cody projectile points in the Black Rock Desert presents nagging questions about the subsistence activities of these groups. Cody groups on the Great Plains are strongly linked with bison hunting, although it is clear that they exploited a variety of other animal and plant species too. The radiocarbon age and Cody projectile point association at the Wallmann Bison (26HU58) indicates that bison were occasionally present in the region during the early Holocene and taken by Cody hunters.

A sample of 25 Cody points from 26HU22 was submitted as a single-blind test for CIEP blood residue analysis. This methodology for the identification of blood residues and its reliability is described by Newman and Julig (1989) and Kooyman et al. (1992). Six specimens produced positive reactions to five different anti-sera.

Table 8.7 lists these positive results, including three points with reactions to more than one antiserum. The most common positive reactions are against human ($n = 5$) and rabbit ($n = 3$) anti-sera. Although research indicates that ancient protein residues can be subject to degradation and false positive identifications (Downs and Lowenstein 1995; Fiedel 1996), these particular results are consistent with the historical frequency of rabbits on this landscape and the known frequent handling

**TABLE 8.7.** Cody Projectile Points with Positive Reactions for Animal Protein Residues.

| Specimen | Animal Protein | | | | | |
|---|---|---|---|---|---|---|
| DRI-8 | | | | | Human | |
| DRI-17 | | | | | | Rabbit |
| SW-504 | | Bison | Bovine | | | |
| SW-535 | | | | | Human | Rabbit |
| SW-574 | | | | Elk | | |
| SW-576 | | | | | | Rabbit |
| SW-579 | Antelope | | | | Human | |
| SW-580 | | Bison | | | Human | |
| SW-582 | | | | | Human | |
| **Totals** | 1 | 2 | 1 | 1 | 5 | 3 |

*Notes:* Tested anti-sera reactions: antelope, bear, bison, bovine, cat, deer, dog, elephant, elk, horse, human, guinea pig, mouse, quail, rabbit, rat, sheep, and turkey.

of these artifacts by humans before protein residue testing.

The blind identification of positive reactions to bison and bovine anti-sera for specimen SW-504 is especially significant because it is the projectile point associated with the Wallmann Bison (26HU58). No provenience information was made available to the lab technician before the CIEP analysis, and there was a 320:1 random chance of associating this particular specimen with the bison anti-serum. Given this artifact's immediate spatial association with a well-dated bison skeleton, the CIEP result appears to be a remarkable confirmation of an apparent Cody bison kill in the Black Rock Desert. Other notable results are the positive identifications of bison residue on SW-580, antelope residue on SW-579, and elk residue on SW-574. These animal species identifications are consistent with faunal assemblages from Cody complex and other Paleoindian sites on the Great Plains (Hill 2008b; also see Knell and Muñiz, this volume), as well as certain TP-EH sites in the northern Great Basin and Columbia Plateau (Ames et al. 1998). It should be noted, however, that faunal assemblages of such age in the northern Great Basin are more commonly dominated by rabbits, hares, fishes, and waterfowl (Beck and Jones 1997).

### *XRF Source Characterization*

The northwestern Great Basin contains numerous secondary sources of obsidian, basalt, low-silica rhyolite (LSR), and microcrystalline silica rocks (e.g., chert, chalcedony, and agate) useful for the production of stone tools. The alluvial fans of the Jackson Range on the eastern side of the Black Rock Desert contain several deposits of microcrystalline silica toolstone that were frequently used by other TP-EH foragers; the Cody occupants of the Black Rock Desert strongly preferred obsidian and LSR from more distant sources (Amick 1995, 1997), however. Substantial alluvial deposits of LSR cobbles are located about 100–150 km to the northwest in California (e.g., Goose Lake and Warner Mountains) and Nevada (e.g., Massacre Lake and Duck Flat), and several obsidian sources are located in the regions surrounding the Black Rock Desert (Figure 8.1).

Table 8.8 presents XRF sourcing results for 21 obsidian and 6 LSR Cody projectile points from the Black Rock Desert (Hughes 1995). Fingerprints of two distinctive LSR sources are identified, but only one is assignable to a specific geologic deposit. Among this selective sample of 27 artifacts, 19 percent ($n$ = 5) are assigned to the Massacre Lake/Nut Mountain source, 15 percent ($n$ = 4) to the Massacre Lake/Guano Valley obsidian sources, 11 percent ($n$ = 3) to the Rainbow Mine source, and 4 percent ($n$ = 1) to the Hawk's Valley source, indicating transport 110–150 km from the north and northwest (the same general region containing abundant LSR sources). Significant toolstone transport from the east and northeast is indicated by assignment of 22 percent ($n$ = 6) of these specimens to the Double H Mountains and 11 percent ($n$ = 3) to Paradise Valley, located about 70–110 km away. One specimen (4 percent) is represented by Bordwell Spring obsidian from

**TABLE 8.8.** XRF Results for Trace and Selected Minor Element Concentrations in 27 Cody Points from the Black Rock Desert, Nevada.

| Specimen | Zn | Ga | Rb | Sr | Y | Zr | Nb | Ba | Ti | Mn | $Fe_2O_3^T$ | Fe/Mn | Source Assignment (Chemical Type) |
|---|---|---|---|---|---|---|---|---|---|---|---|---|---|
| SW-506 | 132 ± 5 | 28 ± 3 | 165 ± 3 | 2 ± 3 | 62 ± 2 | 359 ± 4 | 19 ± 2 | nm | 925 ± 19 | 464 ± 13 | 2.40 ± .12 | 58 | Bordwell Spring |
| JM-9 | 168 ± 5 | 26 ± 3 | 193 ± 3 | 4 ± 3 | 92 ± 2 | 481 ± 4 | 28 ± 2 | nm | 1596 ±2 2 | 540 ± 13 | 3.39 ± .12 | 68 | Double H Mtns |
| JM-20 | 163 ± 5 | 24 ± 3 | 192 ± 3 | 3 ± 3 | 90 ± 2 | 474 ± 4 | 24 ± 2 | nm | 1884 ± 24 | 622 ± 14 | 3.66 ± .12 | nm | Double H Mtns |
| SW-6 | 158 ± 5 | 26 ± 3 | 182 ± 3 | 3 ± 3 | 86 ± 2 | 448 ± 4 | 23 ± 2 | nm | 1697 ± 22 | 587 ± 13 | 3.45 ± .12 | 68 | Double H Mtns |
| SW-9 | 189 ± 6 | 4 ± 4 | 207 ± 4 | 3 ± 3 | 97 ± 2 | 513 ± 5 | 29 ± 2 | nm | 1695 ± 22 | 559 ± 14 | 3.59 ± .12 | 71 | Double H Mtns |
| SW-559 | 147 ± 5 | 22 ± 3 | 191 ± 3 | 4 ± 3 | 85 ± 2 | 449 ± 4 | 22 ± 2 | nm | 1733 ± 21 | 589 ± 13 | 3.39 ± .12 | nm | Double H Mtns |
| SW-597 | 159 ± 5 | 22 ± 4 | 181 ± 4 | 1 ± 3 | 86 ± 2 | 466 ± 5 | 26 ± 2 | m | 1600 ± 23 | 545 ± 14 | 3.50 ± .12 | nm | Double H Mtns |
| SW-590 | 53 ± 4 | 19 ± 3 | 210 ± 3 | 15 ± 3 | 43 ± 2 | 131 ± 3 | 26 ± 2 | nm | 692 ± 16 | 457 ± 13 | 1.03 ± .12 | 22 | Hawk's Valley |
| SW-12 | 124 ± 5 | 17 ± 3 | 209 ±4 | 1 ± 3 | 87 ± 2 | 570 ± 5 | 31 ±2 | nm | nm | nm | nm | 24 | Massacre Lake/Guano Valley |
| SW-568 | 130 ± 5 | 21 ± 3 | 209 ± 4 | 0 ± 3 | 92 ± 2 | 570 ± 5 | 29 ± 2 | nm | nm | nm | nm | 23 | Massacre Lake/Guano Valley |
| SW-569 | 126 ± 5 | 17 ± 3 | 210 ± 4 | 2 ± 3 | 94 ± 2 | 564 ± 5 | 31 ± 2 | nm | nm | nm | nm | 24 | Massacre Lake/Guano Valley |
| SW-570 | 127 ± 5 | 22 ± 3 | 208 ± 4 | 0 ± 3 | 89 ± 2 | 574 ± 5 | 29 ± 2 | nm | nm | nm | nm | 23 | Massacre Lake/Guano Valley |
| SW-555 | 71 ± 4 | 22 ± 3 | 352 ± 4 | 2 ± 3 | 78 ± 2 | 79 ± 3 | 13 ± 2 | nm | nm | nm | nm | 84 | Paradise Valley |
| DRI-5 | 73 ± 4 | 23 ± 3 | 370 ± 3 | 3 ± 3 | 80 ± 2 | 79 ± 3 | 16 ± 2 | nm | nm | nm | nm | 89 | Paradise Valley |
| JM-3 | 69 ± 4 | 20 ± 3 | 376 ± 4 | 0 ± 3 | 84 ± 2 | 79 ± 3 | 18 ± 2 | nm | nm | nm | nm | 83 | Paradise Valley |
| SW-162 | 40 ± 4 | 17 ± 3 | 132 ± 3 | 78 ± 3 | 19 ± 4 | 157 ± 3 | 9 ± 2 | 1015 ±14 | nm | nm | nm | 33 | Rainbow Mine, Warner Mtns |
| SW-169 | 42 ± 4 | 14 ± 3 | 136 ± 3 | 84 ± 3 | 18 ± 2 | 152 ± 4 | 9 ± 2 | 1063 ±13 | nm | nm | nm | 33 | Rainbow Mine, Warner Mtns |
| SW-509 | 40 ± 4 | 12 ± 3 | 122 ± 3 | 73 ± 3 | 20 ± 2 | 133 ± 4 | 10 ± 2 | 955 ±13 | nm | nm | nm | 39 | Rainbow Mine, Warner Mtns |
| SW-594 | 60 ± 4 | 16 ± 3 | 171 ± 3 | 28 ± 3 | 55 ± 2 | 162 ± 4 | 29 ± 2 | 171 ± 12 | 631 ± 16 | 340 ± 13 | 1.45 ± .12 | 49 | Unknown Obsidian |
| SW-511 | 43 ± 4 | 15 ± 3 | 200 ± 3 | 86 ± 3 | 32 ± 2 | 186 ± 4 | 18 ± 2 | 582 ± 12 | nm | nm | nm | 29 | Massacre Lake/Nut Mountain LSR |
| SW-512 | 39 ± 5 | 15 ± 3 | 186 ± 3 | 80 ± 3 | 36 ± 2 | 177 ± 4 | 18 ± 2 | 583 ±13 | nm | nm | nm | 28 | Massacre Lake/Nut Mountain LSR |
| SW-533 | 47 ± 4 | 14 ± 3 | 206 ± 4 | 86 ± 3 | 36 ± 2 | 188 ± 4 | 23 ± 2 | 633 ± 13 | nm | nm | nm | 28 | Massacre Lake/Nut Mountain LSR |
| SW-541 | 44 ± 4 | 19 ± 3 | 190 ± 3 | 79 ± 3 | 35 ± 2 | 177 ± 4 | 19 ± 2 | 621 ±13 | nm | nm | nm | 29 | Massacre Lake/Nut Mountain LSR |
| SW-546 | 46 ± 4 | 16 ± 3 | 190 ± 3 | 85 ± 3 | 34 ± 2 | 175 ± 4 | 18 ± 2 | 573 ± 12 | nm | nm | nm | 29 | Massacre Lake/Nut Mountain LSR |
| SW-529 | 57 ± 4 | 15 ± 3 | 101 ± 3 | 144 ± 3 | 26 ± 2 | 92 ± 3 | 14 ± 2 | 917 ± 13 | nm | nm | nm | 21 | LSR Variety 2 |
| JM-7 | 62 ± 4 | 16 ± 3 | 157 ± 3 | 96 ± 3 | 25 ± 2 | 125 ± 3 | 16 ± 2 | 1072 ± 13 | 652 ± 19 | 655 ± 13 | .95 ± .12 | 13 | Obsidian Var. A |
| SW-166 | 60 ± 4 | 19 ± 3 | 141 ± 3 | 93 ± 3 | 25 ± 2 | 119 ± 3 | 11 ± 2 | 1102 ± 13 | 937 ± 20 | 748 ± 13 | 1.08 ± .12 | 14 | Obsidian Var. A |

*Notes:* Raw data and source assignments provided by Hughes (1995; personal communication 2012). All values in parts per million (ppm) except total iron (in weight percent) and Fe/Mn rations; ± = pooled estimate (in ppm) of x-ray counting uncertainty and regression fitting error at 200–300 seconds livetime; nm = not measured. LSR Variety 2 and Obsidian Variety A have unknown geological source locations.

about 80 km southwest of the Black Rock Desert. Three obsidian specimens (11 percent) and one LSR specimen (4 percent) were not assignable to known sources, which is unusual considering the substantial documentation of geochemical variation in obsidian sources from this region (Hughes 1986, 1995). Overall, these data suggest that Cody groups in the Black Rock Desert procured obsidian from several locations within a radius of at least 125 km, especially utilizing sources in the Massacre Lake region in far northwestern Nevada and the Double H Mountain region in north-central Nevada. This mobility range encompasses roughly 26,000 $km^2$, which is consistent with human foraging economies that emphasize hunting (Kelly 1995:130–132).

### *Bison Distribution and Abundance in the Far West*

The archaeological and paleontological evidence of bison in the Far West is sparse and intermittent following the Last Glacial Maximum (Butler 1978b; Chatters et al. 1995; Graham and Lundelius 1994; Grayson 1982, 1993, 2006; Heaton 1990; Johnson et al. 2005; Lott 2002; Lyman 2004; McDonald 1981; McHugh 1972; Osborne 1953; Plew and Sundell 2000; Reed 1955; Riddell 1952; Schroedl 1973; Van Vuren 1987; Van Vuren and Bray 1985; Van Vuren and Dietz 1993; Wilson 1996). Bison do not appear to have existed in high densities, though the greatest concentrations were in the sagebrush-grasslands of the Snake River Plain, Columbia Plateau, and northern Great Basin. There were several pulses of increased bison and elk populations in these regions during the late Pleistocene, TP-EH, and late Holocene. These intervals correspond with cool-moist climatic conditions that supported increased graminoid biomass. Bison prefer a diet of grasses and sedges, and they are highly mobile and capable of ingesting low-quality forage, which facilitated rapid range extensions in response to relatively brief episodes of grassland expansion (Knapp et al. 1999; Rivals et al. 2007). In particular, western ungulate populations respond most positively to periods of equable, summer-wet climate (Broughton et al. 2008).

Paleoenvironmental records for the TP-EH of the northern Great Basin suggest that conditions were cooler and moister than the present (Grayson 1993; Madsen 2002, 2007; Mehringer 1985; Wigand and Rhode 2002). Reconstructions of the regional patterns of environmental change in the Great Basin are complicated by its topography of mountains and valleys, resulting in high temporal and spatial variability. However, pollen records of the northwestern Great Basin (Mehringer 1985; Minckley et al. 2007; Wigand and Rhode 2002:317–325) show several localized episodes of treeless sagebrush steppe and grass and sedge expansion during the Pre-Boreal Climatic Interval (10,000–9300 $^{14}$C years BP or 11,470–10,530 cal BP). It seems very possible that brief episodes of increased summer moisture supported productive sagebrush-grasslands favorable for bison and elk populations, which in turn attracted Cody hunters to the region. In addition, early Holocene evidence of anthropogenic burning in these sagebrush-grasslands (Minckley et al. 2007; West and McGuire 2002) could reflect intentional efforts to increase ungulate biomass by increasing forage yields. For example, Harniss and Murray (1973) document that controlled burning of sagebrush-grasslands can reduce shrub yields while greatly increasing grass and forb yields for up to 15 years following the burn.

### Discussion and Summary

The poorly recognized evidence for Cody occupations in the northwestern Great Basin is important and provocative. Most notably, it poses difficult questions concerning the origins of the Cody complex and its connections to the Great Basin Stemmed points and the Western Stemmed tradition (WST), which predates and is contemporaneous with the Cody complex (Beck and Jones 1997; Jones and Beck 1999; Smith 2007, 2010). Bryan (1988; also see Bryan and Tuohy 1999) argues that early stemmed projectile point technology originates in the Great Basin and that it even predates Clovis occupations in western North America. Further, he believes it eventually led to the appearance of the Agate Basin and Cody complex projectile point forms on the Great Plains. This suggestion agrees with Bradley's (1993:260) recommendation that Cody technological origins may be related to the preceding Agate Basin cultural complex on the Great Plains. The exact chronological and distributional relationships between the Great Basin Stemmed, Agate Basin, and Cody complex technologies remain poorly studied, however.

Unfortunately, the identification of Cody complex technology in the Far West is further obscured by the tendency of many researchers working west of the Rockies to place any square-stemmed, lanceolate points in the Windust phase, despite the poorly defined nature of this taxon. Windust defines an archaeological phase rather than an artifact type (Leonhardy and Rice 1970; Rice 1972), and thus is inappropriate as a point type designation (Justice 2002b:96–97).

The Windust phase is generally associated with TP-EH occupations of the Columbia Plateau region (Ames 2004; Ames et al. 1998; Beck and Jones 1997; Jones and Beck 1999), and it includes a variety of early stemmed projectile points, some of which are square-based. Rice (1972) associates a wide array of pre-Mazama projectile point categories with what he defined as the Windust phase. In their review of the prehistory of the southern Columbia Plateau, Ames et al. (1998:105) point out that the diversity of projectile point styles found in Windust assemblages seems to suggest a mixture of cultural traditions. Several of the Windust phase projectile points illustrated by Rice (1972: 36–47), which he classifies as Category 1 (Groups 1–3), show general resemblances to Cody complex points (also see Osbun et al. 2004:Figure 8.1) and may benefit from reexamination. Likewise, several of the points illustrated by Connolly and Jenkins (1999:Figure 9.26) from the early Holocene component at the Paulina Lake site in central Oregon conform well to the typological criteria for the Cody complex.

Unfortunately, detailed understanding of Windust projectile point technology and how it may compare with Cody still remains limited at best. In practice, it appears that the term Windust has often been used as a catchall category for any early stemmed projectile points in the Far West that cannot be accommodated within the Great Basin Stemmed cluster. This chapter draws three main conclusions concerning that problem: (1) there is unambiguous evidence that Cody complex technology in the Far West is being obscured by use of this inadequate taxon; (2) evidence of Cody complex occupations in the Far West can be supported on a broad range of technological, typological, chronological, and economic grounds; and (3) detailed study of technological and morphological variation in Windust phase projectile points is needed if we are to resolve questions about the potential relationships of various early stemmed point complexes in the Far West. In any case, it appears that Cody complex occupations are relatively rare and not particularly early in the northern Great Basin, which implies that Cody groups are most likely interlopers in this region (e.g., Johnson 1989).

Beyond these thorny issues of Cody cultural origins and identity, evidence from the Black Rock Desert of Nevada may speak most directly to the adaptive capacity of the people behind the Cody complex. The geographic distribution of Cody sites and projectile points in the Intermountain West suggests that sagebrush grasslands and bison populations served as major ecological corridors guiding the Cody diaspora. The documentation of Cody complex bison hunters in the sagebrush-grasslands of the northwestern Great Basin more than 700 km west of the Rocky Mountains demonstrates that Cody foragers possessed effective economic and social mechanisms for learning landscapes and responding rapidly to the highly dynamic environments of the TP-EH, including the ability to make range extensions when suitable economic opportunities emerged. Such ecological models of early human forager colonization are often referred to as "megapatch" infilling (Beaton 1991). Kelly (2003:54) points out how logistical mobility associated with hunting activities and movement in areas with variable topography (e.g., the Great Basin, Columbia Plateau, and Snake River Plain) can facilitate rapid learning about landscapes. Likewise, Meltzer (2002:42) describes how pursuit of migratory large game (such as bison) can provide a "selective advantage to widespread movement."

Finding effective routes of movement and learning the distribution and character of resource megapatches are often the least challenging aspects for colonists, while gaining knowledge about the more restricted and less predictable locations of lithic resources may have been the most challenging. Here is where establishing and maintaining social networks becomes important. As stated by Meltzer (2002:43) in his discussion of the adaptive strategies of early Paleoindian colonizers, what was most critical was "maintaining vital long-distance links to other groups that could provide mates, resources, and information." Landscape learning is likely to proceed the fastest when colonists are entering occupied lands (Meltzer 2003:224–225). Chronological evidence of TP-EH occupations in the Great Basin (Beck and Jones 1997; Jones and Beck 1999) indicates considerable potential for contemporary occupations by multiple ethnic groups, although the details of these prospective relationships remain murky because of the limitations of the early archaeo-stratigraphic records in this region. In any case, it is highly likely that Cody groups shared the landscapes of the Great Basin and the Great Plains with other ethnic groups, a situation that would have produced opportunities for interaction and information sharing. Knowledge about lithic resource locations would have been a critical source of information needed by newcomers with subsistence practices that demanded high mobility.

Binford (2001:224) presents ethnographic data showing that ethnic area sizes (an estimate of the total land area occupied by a group) are highly variable when population density is low, which is common in arid and semiarid regions and certainly characteristic of the TP-EH populations of the Intermountain West. Interestingly, there seems to be high variability in the scales of land use implied by lithic material procurement in the northwestern Great Basin. For example, at the Sadmat locality, located about 150 km south of the Black Rock Desert, Graf (2001) reports that about half the Great Basin Stemmed points are manufactured from exotic sources of obsidian from 150–240 km away ($n = 18$), which may provide potential support for notions of individual-to-individual exchange among early populations in the Great Basin (e.g., Bamforth 2009). In contrast, at Five Mile Flat, located about 120 km northwest of the Cody sites in the Black Rock Desert, local obsidian sources are abundant and 79 percent ($n = 123$) of the Great Basin Stemmed points were procured from sources within 63 km, with only 7 percent ($n = 9$) transported over minimum distances of 113–229 km (Smith 2007). Material sources used for the Cody points found in the Black Rock Desert of Nevada seem to be confined to a minimum distance of 80–150 km without use of either the limited locally available materials or the more distant sources.

Aside from possible arguments about early projectile point exchange, these distributional patterns of lithic material suggest that TP-EH populations of the northwestern Great Basin likely possessed variable scales of mobility and landscape knowledge (cf. Jones et al. 2003; Smith 2010). After approximately 9000 $^{14}$C years BP (10,203 cal BP), lithic material distributions indicate greatly reduced mobility among human foragers in both the Great Basin (Smith 2007, 2010) and the Great Plains (Larson 1992; Muñiz 2005).

Several factors combine to indicate that the Cody complex was a highly effective foraging adaptation, including the relatively rapid and widespread geographic distribution of Cody occupations across the North American interior; evidence for large-scale land-use patterns, cooperative hunting, and exchange; and theoretical arguments concerning the importance of information sharing and landscape learning. All available economic indicators suggest that these groups pursued relatively small and fragmented populations of bison in these remote, marginal locations, but why? The most likely explanation may be that the core of the Cody adaptive niche was oriented around coping with the variable but gradually declining grassland environments of the TP-EH. This suggestion may require altering our understanding of the Cody complex in some fundamental ways. Instead of viewing the participants in the Cody complex as bison-hunting specialists who benefited from environmental richness and stability, we might more accurately characterize them as highly flexible opportunists who were supremely adapted to coping with environmental uncertainty through highly developed social mechanisms, which can be illustrated by effective strategies such as their impressive range extensions into locations that were already occupied.

When foraging groups are engaged in communal bison hunting, they have greater need for social organization and coordination at larger scales (Bamforth 1988, 1991). This chapter suggests that these social mechanisms may have included special abilities to cooperate with resident ethnic groups as well. Such cooperation may have included sharing information, materials, and individuals between unrelated groups in ways that provided mutual benefit while supporting the survival and geographic expansion of Cody complex lifeways. Documentation of Cody complex adaptations in the Far West and other regions outside the Great Plains provides further evidence of how human migrations are often driven by periods of climatic and environmental instability, and how human colonization of already populated areas can proceed with relative swiftness.

## Acknowledgments

This chapter is dedicated to the memory of Dr. Jonathan O. Davis, who first kindled my interest in the Cody artifacts from the Black Rock Desert and invited me to participate in his research on the paleoenvironmental history of that region. Steve Wallmann originally discovered many of these materials, and this research has been possible only because of his considerable generosity in sharing his personal knowledge and experience. I am sincerely grateful to him for making this study possible and assisting in the donation of many of these artifacts to the Nevada State Museum. Steve also contributed the exceptional line drawings of these artifacts. Fred Nials deserves special thanks for providing geoarchaeological expertise and unwavering support during our fieldwork in the Black Rock. The Desert Research Institute in Reno, Nevada, supported the CIEP blood residue study with research stimulation funding. Funding for the artifact illustrations and the obsidian geochemistry source analyses was provided by a grant from the Robert and Joy Leland Charitable Trust. I sincerely appreciate the technical assistance of Richard Hughes of the Geochemical Research Laboratory and our discussions about this work and its many implications. Peter Wigand contributed the humate sample from the Wallmann site and obtained the radiocarbon date for it. Comparative study of Cody complex points from Wyoming was facilitated by a research fellowship from the George C. Frison Paleoindian Institute at the University of Wyoming. I am especially grateful for the warm hospitality and assistance of Marcel Kornfeld, Mary Lou Larson, and George Frison while conducting my research in Laramie. During early stages of this research, the thoughtful comments on these artifacts by George Frison, C. Vance Haynes, Jack Hofman, Bruce Bradley, Matt Root, Dennis Stanford, David H. Thomas, and Jim Woods were especially helpful. Finally, I am deeply grateful to the editors of this book for their patience and support as well as their careful reading and considerate advice for improving this chapter.

## References

Adams, K. D., T. Goebel, K. Graf, G. M. Smith, A. J. Camp, R. W. Briggs, and D. Rhode
2008 Late Pleistocene and Early Holocene Lake-Level Fluctuations in the Lahontan Basin, Nevada: Implications for the Distribution of Archaeological Sites. *Geoarchaeology* 23(5): 608–643.

Agenbroad, L. D.
1978a Cody Knives and the Cody Complex in Plains Prehistory. *Plains Anthropologist* 23:159–161.
1978b *The Hudson-Meng Site: An Alberta Bison Kill in the Nebraska High Plains.* University Press of America, Washington, D.C.

Ames, K. M.
2004 Review of the Archaeological Data. In National Park Service, *Cultural Affiliation Report on the Kennewick Man.* Accessed online September 27, 2007, from http://www.nps.gov/history/archeology/kennewick/ames2.htm.

Ames, K. E., D. E. Dumond, J. R. Galm, and R. Minor
1998 Prehistory of the Southern Plateau. In *Plateau*, edited by D. E. Walker Jr., pp. 103–119. Handbook of North American Indians, Vol. 12, William C. Sturtevant, general editor. Smithsonian Institution, Washington, D.C.

Amick, D. S.
1995 Raw Material Selection Patterns among Paleoindian Tools from the Black Rock Desert, Nevada. *Current Research in the Pleistocene* 12:55–57.
1997 Geochemical Source Analysis of Obsidian Paleoindian Points from the Black Rock Desert, Nevada. *Current Research in the Pleistocene* 14:97–99.
2007 Behavioral Causes and Archaeological Effects of Lithic Artifact Recycling. In *Tools versus Cores: Alternative Approaches to Stone Tool Analysis*, edited by S. McPherron, pp. 223–252. Cambridge Scholars Publications, Newcastle, U.K.

Amick, D. S., and P. Lukowski
2006 Late Pleistocene and Early Holocene Projectile Points at Fort Bliss, Southern Tularosa Basin, New Mexico and West Texas. *Current Research in the Pleistocene* 23:75–79.

Armitage, C. L., S. D. Creasman, and J. C. Mackey
1982 The Deadman Wash Site: A Multi-component (Paleo-Indian, Archaic, Late

Prehistoric) Site in Southwestern Wyoming. *Journal of Intermountain Archeology* 1:1–10.

Bailey, R. G.

1998 *Ecoregions Map of North America*. 1:15,000,000. Miscellaneous Publication No. 1548. USDA Forest Service, Washington, D.C.

Bamforth, D. B.

1988 *Ecology and Human Organization on the Great Plains*. Plenum Press, New York.

1991 Flintknapping Skill, Communal Hunting, and Paleoindian Point Typology. *Plains Anthropologist* 36:309–322.

2009 Projectile Points, People, and Plains Paleoindian Perambulations. *Journal of Anthropological Archaeology* 28:142–157.

Beaton, J. M.

1991 Colonizing Continents: Some Problems from Australia and the Americas. In *The First Americans: Search and Research*, edited by T. D. Dillehay and D. J. Meltzer, pp. 209–230. CRC Press, Boca Raton, Florida.

Beaudoin, A. B.

2000 Stop 4: The Fletcher Site (DjOw-1). In *Late Quaternary History and Geoarchaeology of Southeastern Alberta and Southwestern Saskatchewan*, edited by A. B. Beaudoin and D. S. Lemmen, pp. 21–23. Field Trip Guidebook No. 3. GeoCanada 2000, Calgary, Alberta.

Beck, C., and G. T. Jones

1997 The Terminal Pleistocene/Early Holocene Archaeology of the Great Basin. *Journal of World Prehistory* 11:161–236.

Benedict, J. B.

1992 Along the Great Divide: Paleoindian Archaeology of the High Colorado Front Range. In *Ice Age Hunters of the Rockies*, edited by D. Stanford and J. Day, pp. 343–360. University Press of Colorado, Boulder.

Binford, L. R.

1979 Organization and Formation Processes: Looking at Curated Technologies. *Journal of Anthropological Research* 35:255–273.

2001 *Constructing Frames of Reference: An Analytical Method for Archaeological Theory Building Using Ethnographic and Environmental Data Sets*. University of California Press, Berkeley.

Blackmar, J. M.

2001 Regional Variability in Clovis, Folsom, and Cody Land Use. *Plains Anthropologist* 46: 65–94.

Bonnichsen, R., M. Beatty, M. D. Turner, and D. Douglas

1992 Paleoindian Lithic Procurement at the South Fork of Everson Creek, Southwestern Montana: A Preliminary Statement. In *Ice Age Hunters of the Rockies*, edited by D. Stanford and J. Day, pp. 285–321. University Press of Colorado, Boulder.

Bonnichsen, B. R., and J. D. Keyser

1982 Three Small Points: A Cody Complex Problem. *Plains Anthropologist* 27:137–144.

Bradley, B. A.

1991 Flaked Stone Technology in the Northern High Plains. In *Prehistoric Hunters of the High Plains*, 2nd ed., by G. C. Frison, pp. 369–395. Academic Press, New York.

1993 Paleo-Indian Flaked Stone Technology in the North American High Plains. In *Kostenki to Clovis: Upper Paleolithic–Paleo-Indian Adaptations*, edited by O. Sofer and N. D. Praslov, pp. 251–262. Plenum Press, New York.

1998 Cody. In *Archaeology of Prehistoric North America: An Encyclopedia*, edited by G. Gibbon, pp. 168–170. Garland, New York.

2009 Bifacial Technology and Paleoindian Projectile Points. In *Hell Gap: A Stratified Paleoindian Campsite at the Edge of the Rockies*, edited by M. L. Larson, M. Kornfeld, and G. C. Frison, pp. 259–273. University of Utah Press, Salt Lake City.

Bradley, B. A., and G. C. Frison

1987 Projectile Points and Specialized Bifaces from the Horner Site. In *The Horner Site: Type Site of the Cody Cultural Complex*, edited by G. C. Frison and L. C. Todd, pp. 199–231. Academic Press, New York.

Bradley, B. A., and D. J. Stanford

1987 Claypool Study. In *The Horner Site: Type Site of the Cody Cultural Complex*, edited by G. C. Frison and L. C. Todd, pp. 405–434. Academic Press, New York.

Bray, W. M., E. H. Swanson, and I. S. Farrington

1975 *The Making of the Past: The New World*. Elsevier, Oxford.

Broughton, J. M., D. A. Byers, A. R. Bryson, W. Eckerle, and D. B. Madsen

2008 Did Climatic Seasonality Control Late Quaternary Artiodactyl Densities in Western North America? *Quaternary Science Reviews* 27:1916–1937.

Brunswig, R. H.

2007 Paleoindian Cultural Landscapes and Archaeology of North-Central Colorado's Southern Rockies. In *Frontiers in Colorado Paleoindian Archaeology: From the Dent Site to the Rocky Mountains*, edited by R. H. Brunswig and B. L. Pitblado, pp. 261–310. University Press of Colorado, Boulder.

Bryan, A. L.

1988 The Relationship of the Stemmed and Fluted

Point Traditions in the Great Basin. In *Early Human Occupation in Far Western North America: The Clovis-Archaic Interface*, edited by J. A. Willig, C. M. Aikens, and J. L. Fagan, pp. 53–74. Anthropological Paper No. 21. Nevada State Museum, Carson City.

Bryan, A. L., and D. R. Tuohy

1999 Prehistory of the Great Basin/Snake River Plain to About 8,500 Years Ago. In *Ice Age Peoples of North America: Environments, Origins, and Adaptations of the First Americans*, edited by R. Bonnichsen and K. L. Turnmire, pp. 249–263. Center for the Study of the First Americans, Texas A&M University, College Station.

Butler, B. R.

1970 A Surface Collection from Coyote Flat, Southeastern Oregon. *Tebiwa* 13:34–57.

1973 Folsom and Plano Points from the Peripheries of the Upper Snake River Country. *Tebiwa* 16: 69–72.

1978a *A Guide to Understanding Idaho Archaeology: The Upper Snake and Salmon River Country*. 3rd ed. Idaho State Museum, Pocatello.

1978b Bison Hunting in the Desert West before 1800: The Paleo-Ecological Potential and Archaeological Reality. In *Bison Procurement and Utilization: A Symposium*, edited by L. B. Davis and M. Wilson, pp. 106–112. Memoir No. 14. Plains Anthropologist, Lincoln, Nebraska.

Cassells, E. S.

1983 *The Archaeology of Colorado*. Johnson Books, Boulder, Colorado.

Chatters, J. C., S. K. Campbell, G. D. Smith, and P. E. Minthorn, Jr.

1995 Bison Procurement in the Far West: A 2,100-Year-Old Kill Site on the Columbia Plateau. *American Antiquity* 60:751–763.

Clewlow, W., Jr.

1968 *Surface Archaeology of the Black Rock Desert, Nevada*. University of California Archaeological Survey Reports No. 73. Berkeley.

Connolly, T. J., and D. L. Jenkins

1999 The Paulina Lake Site (35DS34). In *Newberry Crater: A Ten-Thousand-Year Record of Human Occupation and Environmental Change in the Basin-Plateau Borderlands*, edited by T. J. Connolly, pp. 86–127. University of Utah Anthropological Papers No. 121. University of Utah Press, Salt Lake City.

Craven, C. D., and W. Eckerle

2005 Early Holocene Adaptations at the Battle Spring Draw Paleoindian Site: Evidence for Long-Term Exploitation of Very Small Mammals in the Great Divide Basin, Wyoming. Paper presented at the 63rd meeting of the Plains Anthropological Society, Edmonton, Alberta.

Cummings, L. S., R. A. Varney, and R. A. Bryson

2007 Building a Picture of the Landscape Using Close-Interval Pollen Sampling and Archaeoclimatic Modeling: An Example from the KibRidge-Yampa Paleoindian Site, Northwestern Colorado. In *Frontiers in Colorado Paleoindian Archaeology*, edited by R. H. Brunswig and B. L. Pitblado, pp. 195–217. University Press of Colorado, Boulder.

Dansie, A. J., and W. J. Jerrems

2001 Pleistocene Lake Lahontan: Filling in More Blanks. *Mammoth Trumpet* 17(1):1–20. Center for the Study of the First Americans, Texas A&M University, College Station.

2004 Lahontan Chronology and Early Human Occupation in the Western Great Basin: A New Look at Old Collections. In *New Perspectives on the First Americans*, edited by B. T. Lepper and R. Bonnichsen, pp. 55–63. Center for the Study of the First Americans, Texas A&M University, College Station.

Dansie, A. J., J. O. Davis, and T. W. Stafford Jr.

1988 The Wizards Beach Recession: Farmdalian (25,500 yr BP) Vertebrate Fossils Co-occur with Early Holocene Artifacts. In *Early Human Occupation in Far Western North America: The Clovis-Archaic Interface*, edited by J. A. Willig, C. M. Aikens, and J. L. Fagan, pp. 153–200. Anthropological Paper No. 21. Nevada State Museum, Carson City.

Davis, E. M.

1962 *Archeology of the Lime Creek Site in Southwestern Nebraska*. Special Publication No. 3. University of Nebraska State Museum, Lincoln.

Davis, L. B., J. P. Albanese, L. S. Cummings, and J. W. Fisher Jr.

1991 Reappraisal of the MacHaffie Site Paleoindian Occupational Sequence. *Current Research in the Pleistocene* 8:17–20.

Dick, H. W., and B. Mountain

1960 The Claypool Site: A Cody Complex Site in Northeastern Colorado. *American Antiquity* 26:223–235.

Downs, E. F., and J. M. Lowenstein

1995 Identification of Archaeological Blood Proteins: A Cautionary Note. *Journal of Archaeological Science* 22:11–16.

Driver, J. C.

1998 Human Adaptation at the Pleistocene/Holocene Boundary in Western Canada, 11,000 to 9000 BP. *Quaternary International* 49/50: 141–150.

Fiedel, S. J.

1996 Blood from Stones? Some Methodological and Interpretive Problems in Blood Residue Analysis. *Journal of Archaeological Science* 23:139–147.

Frison, G. C.

1984 Carter/Kerr-McGee Paleoindian Site: Cultural Resource Management and Archaeological Research. *American Antiquity* 49:288–314.

1991 *Prehistoric Hunters of the High Plains*. 2nd ed. Academic Press, New York.

1993 The North American Paleoindian: A Wealth of New Data but Still Much to Learn. In *Prehistory and Human Ecology of the Western Prairies and Northern Plains*, edited by J. Tiffany, pp. 5–16. Memoir No. 27. Plains Anthropologist, Lincoln, Nebraska.

1998 Paleoindian Large Mammal Hunters on the Plains of North America. *Proceedings of the National Academy of Sciences* 95:14576–14583.

Frison, G. C., and R. Bonnichsen

1996 The Pleistocene-Holocene Transition on the Plains and Rocky Mountains of North America. In *Humans at the End of the Ice Age: The Archaeology of the Pleistocene-Holocene Transition*, edited by L. G. Strauss, B. V. Erikson, J. M. Erlandson, and D. R. Yesner, pp. 303–318. Academic Press, New York.

Frison, G. C., and L. C. Todd (editors)

1987 *The Horner Site: The Type Site of the Cody Cultural Complex*. Academic Press, New York.

Graf, K. E.

2001 Paleoindian Technological Provisioning in the Western Great Basin. Unpublished Master's thesis, Department of Anthropology, University of Nevada, Las Vegas.

Graham, R. W., and E. L. Lundelius Jr.

1994 *Faunmap: A Database Documenting Late Quaternary Distributions of Mammal Species in the United States*. Scientific Papers Vol. 25. Illinois State Museum, Springfield.

Grayson, D. K.

1982 Toward a History of Great Basin Mammals during the Past 15,000 Years. In *Man and Environment in the Great Basin*, edited by D. B. Madsen and J. F. O'Connell, pp. 82–101. SAA Papers No. 2. Society for American Archaeology, Washington, D.C.

1993 *The Desert's Past: A Natural History of the Great Basin*. Smithsonian Institution Press, Washington, D.C.

2006 Holocene Bison in the Great Basin, Western USA. *The Holocene* 16(6):913–925.

Greiser, S. T.

1982 *Predictive Models of Hunter-Gatherer Subsistence and Settlement Strategies on the Central High Plains*. Memoir No. 20. Plains Anthropologist, Lincoln, Nebraska.

Gruhn, R.

1961 *The Archaeology of Wilson Butte Cave, South-Central Idaho*. Occasional Papers of the Idaho State College Museum No. 6. Pocatello.

2006 *New Excavations at Wilson Butte Cave*. Occasional Papers of the Idaho Museum of Natural History No. 38. Pocatello.

Hanes, R. C.

1977 Lithic Tools of the Dirty Shame Rockshelter: Typology and Distribution. *Tebiwa* 6:1–24.

1988 *Lithic Assemblages of Dirty Shame Rockshelter: Changing Traditions in the Northern Intermontane*. University of Oregon Anthropological Papers No. 40. Eugene.

Hanes, R. C., and P. McGuckian

1987 Archaeological Survey along the Quinn River, Black Rock Desert, Nevada. *Nevada Archaeologist* 6(1):1–9.

Harniss, R. O., and R. B. Murray

1973 30 Years of Vegetal Change Following Burning of Sagebrush-Grass Range. *Journal of Range Management* 26(5):322–325.

Hauck, F. R., and M. R. Hauck

2002 *KibRidge-Yampa Paleoindian Occupation Site (5MF3687): Preliminary Archaeological Excavations (1993–2001) in Northwestern Colorado*. Archaeological Research Institute, General Studies Series No. 4. Bountiful, Utah.

Haynes, C. V., Jr., R. P. Beukens, A. J. T. Jull, and O. K. Davis

1992 New Radiocarbon Dates for Some Old Folsom Sites: Accelerator Technology. In *Ice Age Hunters of the Rockies*, edited by D. J. Stanford and J. S. Day, pp. 83–100. University Press of Colorado, Boulder.

Heaton, T. H.

1990 Quaternary Mammals of the Great Basin: Extinct Giants, Pleistocene Relicts, and Recent Immigrants. In *Causes of Evolution: A Paleontological Perspective*, edited by R. M. Ross and W. D. Hillman, pp. 422–466. University of Chicago Press, Chicago.

Hill, M. E., Jr.

2008a New Investigations of the Cody-Age Finley and Scottsbluff Bison Bone Beds. *Current Research in the Pleistocene* 25:90–93.

2008b Variation in Paleoindian Fauna Use on the Great Plains and Rocky Mountains of North America. *Quaternary International* 191:34–52.

Hill, M. G., and M. Kornfeld

1999 Inferring Season of Kill for a Cody-Complex Bison Bonebed in Middle Park, Colorado. *Current Research in the Pleistocene* 16:30–32.

Hofman, J. L., and R. W. Graham

1998 The Paleo-Indian Cultures of the Great Plains. In *Archaeology on the Great Plains*, edited by W. R. Wood, pp. 87–139. University of Kansas Press, Lawrence.

Holliday, V. T.

1997 *Paleoindian Geoarchaeology of the Southern High Plains*. University of Texas Press, Austin.

Holliday, V. T., E. Johnson, H. Haas, and R. Stuckenrath

1983 Radiocarbon Ages from the Lubbock Lake Site, 1950–1980: Framework for Cultural and Ecological Change on the Southern High Plains. *Plains Anthropologist* 28:165–182.

Howard, E. B.

1943 The Finley Site Discovery of Yuma Points, in situ, near Eden, Wyoming. *American Antiquity* 3:224–234.

Howard, E. B., L. Satterthwaite Jr., and C. Bache

1941 Preliminary Report on a Buried Yuma Site in Wyoming. *American Antiquity* 1:70–74.

Huckell, B.

1978 Hudson-Meng Chipped Stone. In *The Hudson-Meng Site: An Alberta Bison Kill in the Nebraska High Plains*, by L. D. Agenbroad, pp. 153–189. University Press of America, Washington, D.C.

Huckell, B. B., and W. J. Judge

2006 Paleo-Indian: Plains and Southwest. In *Environment, Origins, and Population*, edited by D. Ubelaker, pp. 148–170. Handbook of North American Indians, Vol. 3, William C. Sturtevant, general editor. Smithsonian Institution, Washington, D.C.

Hughes, R. E.

1986 *Diachronic Variability in Obsidian Procurement Patterns in Northeastern California and Southcentral Oregon*. University of California Publications in Anthropology No. 17. University of California Press, Berkeley.

1995 *X-ray Fluorescence Analysis of Alberta-Cody, Great Basin (Western) Stemmed, and Concave Base Points from the Wallmann and Roland Mudge Localities in the Black Rock Desert, Humboldt County, Nevada*. Geochemical Research Laboratory Letter Report 95-52, July 27. Portola Valley, California.

Ingbar, E. E., and G. C. Frison

1987 The Larson Cache. In *The Horner Site: Type Site of the Cody Cultural Complex*, edited by G. Frison and L. Todd, pp. 461–473. Academic Press, New York.

Irwin-Williams, C., and C. V. Haynes

1970 Climatic Change and Early Population Dynamics in the Southwestern United States. *Quaternary Research* 1:57–71.

Irwin-Williams, C., H. Irwin, G. Agogino, and C. V. Haynes Jr.

1973 Hell Gap: Paleo-Indian Occupation on the High Plains. *Plains Anthropologist* 27:137–144.

Janetski, J. C.

2001 Late Paleoindian Artifacts from Utah Valley. *Utah Archaeology* 14(1):15–26.

Jennings, J. D.

1957 *Danger Cave*. University of Utah Anthropological Papers No. 27. University of Utah Press, Salt Lake City.

Jepson, G. L.

1953 Ancient Buffalo Hunters of Northwestern Wyoming. *Southwestern Lore* 19(3):19–25.

Johnson, A., B. Reeves, and M. Shortt

2004 *Osprey Beach: A Cody Complex Camp on Yellowstone Lake*. Report prepared by Lifeways of Canada. Submitted to the Yellowstone Center for Resources, Yellowstone National Park, Wyoming, and Yellowstone Park Foundation, Bozeman, Montana.

Johnson, D., and J. Pastor (editors)

2003 *The Blue Point Site: Paleo/Archaic Transition in Southwest Wyoming*. Report prepared by Western Archaeological Services, Rock Springs, Wyoming. Submitted to the FMC Corporation, Green River, Wyoming.

Johnson, E. (editor)

1987 *Lubbock Lake: Late Quaternary Studies on the Southern High Plains*. Texas A&M Press, College Station.

Johnson, L., Jr.

1989 *Great Plains Interlopers in the Eastern Woodlands during Late Paleo-Indian Times: The Evidence from Oklahoma, Texas and Areas Close By*. Office of the State Archeologist Report No. 36. Texas Historical Commission, Austin.

Johnson, W. G., S. E. Sharpe, T. F. Bullard, and K. Lupo

2005 Characterizing a First Occurrence of Bison Deposits in Southeastern Nevada. *Western North American Naturalist* 65(1):24–35.

Jones, G. T., and C. Beck

1999 Paleoarchaic Archaeology in the Great Basin. In *Models for the Millennium: Great Basin Anthropology Today*, edited by C. Beck, pp. 83–95. University of Utah Press, Salt Lake City.

Jones, G. T., C. Beck, E. E. Jones, and R. E. Hughes
2003 Lithic Source Use and Paleoarchaic Foraging Territories in the Great Basin. *American Antiquity* 68:5–38.

Justice, N. D.
2002a *Stone Age Spear and Arrow Points of the Southwestern United States*. Indiana University Press, Bloomington.
2002b *Stone Age Spear and Arrow Points of California and the Great Basin*. Indiana University Press, Bloomington.

Keeley, L. H.
1982 Hafting and Retooling: Effects on the Archaeological Record. *American Antiquity* 47:798–809.

Kelly, R. L.
1995 *The Foraging Spectrum: Diversity in Hunter-Gatherer Lifeways*. Smithsonian Institution Press, Washington, D.C.
2003 Colonization of New Land by Hunter-Gatherers: Expectations and Implications Based on Ethnographic Data. In *Colonization of Unfamiliar Landscapes: The Archaeology of Adaptation*, edited by M. Rockman and J. Steele, pp. 44–58. Routledge, New York.

Knapp, A. K., J. M. Blair, J. M. Briggs, S. L. Collins, D. C. Hartnett, L. C. Johnson, and E. G. Towne
1999 The Keystone Role of Bison in North American Tallgrass Prairie. *Bioscience* 49:39–50.

Knell, E. J.
2007 The Organization of Late Paleoindian Cody Complex Land-use on the North American Great Plains. Unpublished Ph.D. dissertation, Department of Anthropology, Washington State University, Pullman.
2009 Cody Complex at Locality I. In *Hell Gap: A Stratified Paleoindian Campsite at the Edge of the Rockies*, edited by M. L. Larson, M. Kornfeld, and G. C. Frison, pp. 180–194. University of Utah Press, Salt Lake City.

Knell, E. J., M. G. Hill, and A. Izeta
2009 The Locality IIIS/V Eden Complex Component. In *Hell Gap: A Stratified Paleoindian Campsite at the Edge of the Rockies*, edited by M. L. Larson, M. Kornfeld, and G. C. Frison, pp. 157–179. University of Utah Press, Salt Lake City.

Knell, E. J., M. G. Hill, A. Izeta, M. Kornfeld, C. V. Haynes Jr., and G. C. Frison
2002 The Cody Complex Component at Locality V of the Hell Gap Site, Wyoming. *Current Research in the Pleistocene* 19:49–52.

Kooyman, B., M. E. Newman, and H. Ceri
1992 Verifying the Reliability of Blood Residue Analysis on Archaeological Tools. *Journal of Archaeological Science* 19:265–269.

Kornfeld, M., J. Finley, J. Kennedy, J. Durr, and G. C. Frison
1998 *The Black Mountain Archaeological District: 1997 Field Study and Summary of Current Investigations*. Technical Report No. 16. Department of Anthropology, University of Wyoming, Laramie.

LaBelle, J. M., V. T. Holliday, and D. J. Meltzer
2003 Early Holocene Paleoindian Deposits at Nall Playa, Oklahoma Panhandle, U.S.A. *Geoarchaeology* 18:5–34.

Larson, M. L.
1992 Site Formation Processes in the Cody and Early Plains Archaic Levels at the Laddie Creek Site, Wyoming. *Geoarchaeology* 7:103–120.

Larson, M. L., M. Kornfeld, and G. C. Frison (editors)
2009 *Hell Gap: A Stratified Paleoindian Campsite at the Edge of the Rockies*. University of Utah Press, Salt Lake City.

Leonhardy, F. C., and D. Rice
1970 A Proposed Cultural Typology for the Lower Snake River Region, Southeastern Washington. *Northwest Anthropological Research Notes* 4(1):1–29.

Lott, D. F.
2002 *American Bison: A Natural History*. University of California Press, Berkeley.

Lyman, R. L.
2004 Late-Quaternary Diminution and Abundance of Prehistoric Bison (*Bison* sp.) in Eastern Washington State, U.S.A. *Quaternary Research* 62:76–85.

Madsen, D. B.
2002 Great Basin Peoples and Late Quaternary Aquatic History. In *Great Basin Aquatic Systems History*, edited by R. Hershler, D. B. Madsen, and D. R. Currey, pp. 387–405. Smithsonian Contributions to the Earth Sciences No. 33. Smithsonian Institution Press, Washington, D.C.
2007 The Paleoarchaic to Archaic Transition in the Great Basin. In *Paleoindian or Paleoarchaic? Great Basin Human Ecology at the Pleistocene-Holocene Transition*, edited by K. E. Graf and D. N. Schmitt, pp. 3–20. University of Utah Press, Salt Lake City.

Mason, R. J.
1981 *Great Lakes Archaeology*. Academic Press, New York.
1997 The Paleo-Indian Tradition. *Wisconsin Archeologist* 78:78–111.

McDonald, J. N.
1981 *North American Bison: Their Classification and Evolution*. University of California Press, Berkeley.

McHugh, T.
1972 *The Time of the Buffalo*. University of Nebraska Press, Lincoln.

Meatte, D. S.
1990 *Prehistory of the Western Snake River Basin*. Occasional Papers of the Idaho Museum of Natural History No. 35. Pocatello.

Mehringer, P. J., Jr.
1985 Late-Quaternary Pollen Records from the Interior Pacific Northwest and Northern Great Basin of the United States. In *Pollen Records of Late-Quaternary North American Sediments*, edited by V. M. Bryant Jr. and R. G. Holloway, pp. 167–190. Contribution Series No. 17. American Association of Stratigraphic Palynologists, Dallas.

Meltzer, D. J.
2002 What Do You Do When No One's Been There Before? Thoughts on the Exploration and Colonization of New Lands. In *The First Americans: The Pleistocene Colonization of the New World*, edited by N. G. Jablonski, pp. 27–58. Memoirs of the California Academy of Sciences No. 27. University of California Press, Berkeley.
2003 Lessons in Landscape Learning. In *Colonization of Unfamiliar Landscapes: The Archaeology of Adaptation*, edited by M. Rockman and J. Steele, pp. 222–241. Routledge, New York.

Meyer, D.
1985 A Component in the Scottsbluff Tradition: Excavations at the Niska Site. *Canadian Journal of Archaeology* 9:1–37.

Minckley, T. A., C. Whitlock, and P. J. Bartlein
2007 Vegetation, Fire, and Climate History of the Northwestern Great Basin during the Last 14,000 Years. *Quaternary Science Reviews* 26:2167–2184.

Morlan, R., and M. Betts (compilers)
2005 *Canadian Radiocarbon Database: CARD*. Available online at http://www.canadianarchaeology.ca/radiocarbon/card/dbase.htm. Accessed March 27, 2005.

Moss, J. H., K. Bryan, G. W. Holmes, L. Satterthwaite Jr., H. P. Hansen, C. B. Schultz, and W. D. Frankforter
1951 *Early Man in the Eden Valley*. University of Pennsylvania Museum Monographs. University Museum, Philadelphia.

Muñiz, M. P.
2005 The Cody Complex Revisited: Landscape Use and Technological Organization on the Northwestern Plains. Unpublished Ph.D. dissertation, Department of Anthropology, University of Colorado, Boulder.
2009 Microwear, Typology, and the Cody Component. In *Hell Gap: A Stratified Paleoindian Campsite at the Edge of the Rockies*, edited by M. L. Larson, M. Kornfeld, and G. C. Frison, pp. 195–215. University of Utah Press, Salt Lake City.

Newman, M. E., and P. Julig
1989 The Identification of Protein Residues on Lithic Artifacts from a Stratified Boreal Forest Site. *Canadian Journal of Archaeology* 13:119–132.

Novecosky, B.
2002 The Haskey Area, a Cody-Complex Site from the Quill Lakes Region, Saskatchewan, Canada. *Current Research in the Pleistocene* 19:73–74.

Odell, G. H.
1996 Economizing Behavior and the Concept of "Curation." In *Stone Tools: Theoretical Insights into Human Prehistory*, edited by G. H. Odell, pp. 51–80. Plenum, New York.

Osborne, D. H.
1953 Archaeological Occurrences of Pronghorn Antelope, Bison, and Horse in the Columbia Plateau. *Scientific Monthly* 77:260–269.

Osbun, T. L., D. O. Stueber, M. Zehendner, and J. L. Fagan
2004 Lithic Debitage and Formed Tools. In *Marmes Rockshelter: A Final Report on 11,000 Years of Cultural Use*, edited by B. A. Hicks, pp. 159–227. Washington State University Press, Pullman.

Patten, B.
1978 The Denver Series, Point #13: Eden. *Flintknappers Exchange* 1(1):18–22. With comments by D. J. Stanford.
1999 *Old Tools — New Eyes: A Primal Primer of Flintknapping*. Stone Dagger Publications, Denver, Colorado.

Pitblado, B. L.
1998 Peak to Peak in Paleoindian Time: Occupation of Southwest Colorado. *Plains Anthropologist* 43:333–348.
2003 *Late Paleoindian Occupation of the Southern Rocky Mountains: Early Holocene Projectile Points and Land Use in the High Country*. University Press of Colorado, Boulder.

Pitblado, B. L., and R. H. Brunswig
2007 That Was Then, This Is Now: Seventy-Five Years of Paleoindian Research in Colorado.

In *Frontiers in Colorado Paleoindian Archaeology: From the Dent Site to the Rocky Mountains*, edited by R. H. Brunswig and B. L. Pitblado, pp. 39–84. University Press of Colorado, Boulder.

Plew, M. G., and T. Sundell
2000 The Archaeological Occurrence of Bison on the Snake River Plain. *North American Archaeology* 21(2):119–137.

Rancier, J., G. Haynes, and D. J. Stanford
1982 1981 Investigations of Lamb Spring. *Southwestern Lore* 48(2):10–17.

Redder, A. J.
1985 Horn Shelter Number 2: The South End; A Preliminary Report. *Central Texas Archeologist* 10:37–65.

Reed, E. K.
1955 Bison beyond the Pecos. *Texas Journal of Science* 7:130–135.

Rice, D. G.
1972 *The Windust Phase in Lower Snake River Prehistory*. Report of Investigations No. 50. Laboratory of Anthropology, Washington State University, Pullman.

Riddell, F. A.
1952 The Recent Occurrence of Bison in Northeastern California. *American Antiquity* 12:168–169.
1956 Archaeological Research in Lassen County, California. *Reports of the University of California Archaeological Survey* 33:44–49. Department of Anthropology, University of California, Berkeley.

Rivals, F., N. Solounias, and M. C. Mihlbachler
2007 Evidence for Geographic Variation in the Diets of Late Pleistocene and Early Holocene *Bison* in North America, and Differences from the Diets of Recent *Bison*. *Quaternary Research* 68:338–346.

Root, M., S. Ahler, C. Falk, J. Foss, H. Haas, and J. Artz
1986 *Archaeological Investigations in the Knife River Flint Primary Source Area, Dunn County, North Dakota: 1982–1986 Program*. Contribution No. 234. Department of Anthropology, University of North Dakota, Grand Forks.

Satterthwaite, L.
1957 *Stone Artifacts at and near the Finley Site, near Eden, Wyoming*. University of Pennsylvania Museum Monograph No. 4. University Museum, Philadelphia.

Schmitt, D. N., D. B. Madsen, C. G. Oviatt, and R. Quist
2007 Late Pleistocene/Early Holocene Geomorphology and Human Occupation of the Old River Bed Delta, Western Utah. In *Paleoindian or Paleoarchaic? Great Basin Human Ecology at the Pleistocene-Holocene Transition*, edited by K. E. Graf and D. N. Schmitt, pp. 105–119. University of Utah Press, Salt Lake City.

Schroedl, A. R.
1977 The Paleo-Indian Period on the Colorado Plateau. *Southwestern Lore* 43(3):1–9.

Schroedl, G. F.
1973 *The Archaeological Occurrence of Bison in the Southern Plateau*. Report of Investigations No. 51. Laboratory of Anthropology, Washington State University, Pullman.

Sellet, F.
2001 A Changing Perspective on Paleoindian Chronology and Typology: A View from the Northwestern Plains. *Arctic Anthropology* 38(2):48–63.

Sellet, F., J. Donohue, and M. G. Hill
2009 The Jim Pitts Site: A Stratified Paleoindian Site in the Black Hills of South Dakota. *American Antiquity* 74:735–758.

Sharrock, F. W.
1966 *Prehistoric Occupation Patterns in Southwestern Wyoming and Cultural Relationships with the Great Basin and Plains Cultural Areas*. University of Utah Anthropological Papers No. 77. University of Utah Press, Salt Lake City.

Shott, M. J.
1996 An Exegesis of the Curation Concept. *Journal of Anthropological Research* 52:259–280.

Smith, G. M.
2007 Pre-Archaic Mobility and Technological Activities at the Parman Localities, Humboldt County, Nevada. In *Paleoindian or Paleoarchaic? Great Basin Human Ecology at the Pleistocene-Holocene Transition*, edited by K. E. Graf and D. N. Schmitt, pp. 139–155. University of Utah Press, Salt Lake City.
2010 Footprints across the Black Rock: Temporal Variability in Prehistoric Foraging Territories and Toolstone Procurement Strategies in the Western Great Basin. *American Antiquity* 75:865–885.

Stafford, T. W., Jr., P. E. Hare, L. A. Currie, A. J. T. Jull, and D. Donahue
1991 Accelerator Radiocarbon Dating at the Molecular Level. *Journal of Archaeological Science* 18:35–72.

Stanford, D.
1999 Paleoindian Archaeology and Late Pleistocene Environments in the Plains and Southwestern United States. In *Ice Age Peoples of North America: Environments, Origins, and Adaptations of the First Americans*, edited by

R. Bonnichsen and K. L. Turnmire, pp. 281–339. Center for the Study of the First Americans, Texas A&M University, College Station.

Stanford, D., and J. Albanese
1975 Preliminary Results of the Smithsonian Institution Excavation at the Claypool Site, Washington County, Colorado. *Southwestern Lore* 41(4):22–28.

Styrd, A. R., and M. K. Rousseau
1996 The Early Prehistory of the Mid Fraser-Thompson River Area. In *Early Human Occupation in British Columbia*, edited by R. L. Carlson and L. Dalla Bona, pp. 177–204. University of British Columbia Press, Vancouver.

Sullivan, A. P., III
1992 Investigating the Archaeological Consequences of Short-Duration Occupation. *American Antiquity* 57:99–115.

Synder, S. L.
1981 Medicine Creek: Pre- and Post-Mazama Occupation in the Cascades. *Tebiwa* 23:1–13.

Taylor, R. E.
1987 *Radiocarbon Dating: An Archaeological Perspective*. Academic Press, New York.

Todd, L. C., and D. J. Rapson
1997 *Hudson-Meng (25SX115): Summary of 1996 Excavations*. Report prepared by Department of Anthropology, Colorado State University, Fort Collins. Submitted to Nebraska National Forests and Grasslands Service, USDA National Forest Service, Chadron.

Tuohy, D. R.
1968 A "Scottsbluff" Point from the Black Rock Desert of Northwestern Nevada. *Nevada Archaeological Survey Reporter* 2(10):6–9.

Van Vuren, D.
1987 Bison West of the Rocky Mountains: An Alternative Explanation. *Northwest Science* 61:65–69.

Van Vuren, D., and M. P. Bray
1985 The Recent Geographic Distribution of *Bison bison* in Oregon. *Murrelet* 66:56–58.

Van Vuren, D., and F. C. Deitz
1993 Evidence of *Bison bison* in the Great Basin. *Great Basin Naturalist* 53:318–319.

Vickers, R. V., and A. B. Beaudoin
1989 A Limiting AMS Date for the Cody Complex Occupation at the Fletcher Site, Alberta, Canada. *Plains Anthropologist* 34:261–264.

Vivian, B. C.
2005 Identifying a Cody Component at the Malin Fishing Hole Site (24YE353) in Yellowstone National Park. Paper presented at the 63rd Plains Anthropological Conference, Edmonton, Alberta.

Wallmann, S., and D. S. Amick
1991 Cody Complex Occupations in the Black Rock Desert, Nevada. *Current Research in the Pleistocene* 8:51–53.

Wells, S. J.
1993 *Archeological Investigations at Great Basin National Park: Testing and Site Recording in Support of the General Management Plan*. Publications in Anthropology No. 64. Western Archeological and Conservation Center, Tucson, Arizona.

West, G. J., and K. R. McGuire
2002 9,500 Years of Burning Recorded in a High Desert Marsh. In *Conference Proceedings: Spring-Fed Wetlands; Important Scientific and Cultural Resources of the Intermountain Region*, edited by D. W. Sada and S. E. Sharpe, pp. 1–10. DHS Publication No. 41210. Desert Research Institute, Las Vegas, Nevada.

Wheat, J. B.
1972 *The Olsen-Chubbuck Site: A Paleo-Indian Bison Kill*. Society for American Archaeology, Memoir No. 26. Washington, D.C.
1977 Technology, Typology, and Use Patterns at the Jurgens Site. In *Paleoindian Lifeways*, edited by E. Johnson, pp. 126–139. *Museum Journal* 17. West Texas Museum Association, Texas Tech University, Lubbock.
1979 *The Jurgens Site*. Memoir No. 15. Plains Anthropologist, Lincoln, Nebraska.

Wigand, P. E., and D. Rhode
2002 Great Basin Vegetation History and Aquatic Systems: The Last 150,000 Years. In *Great Basin Aquatic Systems History*, edited by R. Hershler, D. B. Madsen, and D. R. Currey, pp. 309–367. Smithsonian Contributions to the Earth Sciences No. 33. Smithsonian Institution Press, Washington, D.C.

Wilson, M. C.
1996 Late Quaternary Vertebrates and the Opening of the Ice-Free Corridor, with Special Reference to the Genus *Bison*. *Quaternary International* 32:97–105.

Wormington, H. M.
1957 *Ancient Man in North America*. 4th ed. Popular Series No. 4. Denver Museum of Natural History, Denver, Colorado.

Wormington, H. M., and R. G. Forbis
1965 *An Introduction to the Archaeology of Alberta, Canada*. Proceedings No. 11. Denver Museum of Natural History, Denver, Colorado.

# IV

# Modeling Cody Complex Lifeways and Reevaluating the Cody Complex as an Archaeological Construct

9

# Cody Complex Land-Use Organization on the Northwestern Great Plains

Edward J. Knell

Beginning in earnest with Gordon Willey's (1953) Virú Valley Project, Peru archaeologists have increasingly studied how human settlement and land use correspond to variations in the natural environment. A number of Great Plains researchers have applied this basic premise to studies of the Cody complex (Amick 1994, this volume; Blackmar 2001; Dawe, this volume; Hill and Knell, this volume; Johnson 1989; Johnson et al. 2004; Knell and Hill 2012; Muñiz 2005; Pitblado 2003; Richings-Germain 2002; Root et al., this volume). Through these studies much has been learned about Cody complex land use and lifeways (see Chapter 1, this volume, for a summary), but missing (in most cases) is an overtly theoretical framework to predict, identify, interpret, and explain Cody land-use organization. Amick (1994) and Knell and Hill (2012) have heeded this call on the regional scale, but such a focus is lacking or less well developed at the site or local scale. To begin rectifying the situation, I model, predict, interpret, and explain patterns of Cody land use at the local scale by analyzing three late Paleoindian (one Alberta and two Eden-Scottsbluff) components of the Hell Gap site, Wyoming.

To achieve this goal, I use an optimal foraging–inspired model of land use that predicts and explains variations in Cody land-use organization in relation to resource structure; I test the model using chipped stone and faunal seasonality data from one Alberta and two Eden-Scottsbluff cultural components at Hell Gap. This same model works at the regional scale (see Knell and Hill 2012) and, as is demonstrated below, at the local scale. Beyond merely testing the model, the findings improve our understanding about the ways Cody complex peoples organized land use in relatively small areas, namely, the 65-×-40-km Hartville Uplift, in which the Hell Gap site is located. Between the local-scale test of the model presented here and the regional-scale test in Knell and Hill (2012; summarized here), we gain important insights about the dynamic way that Cody complex peoples organized land use in the northwestern Plains and Rocky Mountains.

## The Land-Use Model

What follows is a shortened description of the land-use model. Longer discussions can be found in Knell and Hill (2012) and Knell (2007).

The land-use model uses general principles of optimal foraging theory and temporal resource predictability theory to assess the conditions of biotic (flora, fauna) and abiotic (lithic raw material) resource structure under which calorie-maximizing hunter-gatherers rapidly passed through an environmental zone (hereafter referred to as "nonregionally focused" land use) or tethered their movements to that environmental zone for one or more seasons using a "regionally restricted" or "core area" land-use strategy. A core area is here defined as a regularly and intensively used part of a group's annual range that has one or more sources of high-quality toolstone and a sufficient balance of desirable biotic resources to support one or more bands of hunter-gatherers for two or more consecutive seasons (sensu E. E. Smith 1990:241, 1991). "Core area" applies to small, well-defined areas such as the Hartville Uplift, in which the Hell Gap site is located; in larger areas or environmental zones, "regionally restricted" is used.

The land-use model is inspired by core principles of optimal foraging theory, but it is not a true optimal foraging model due to limitations of the data available to develop and then test it, difficulties of obtaining data relevant to the early Holocene, and violation of key model assumptions. Instead, the land-use model is a theoretical construct that can help us organize expectations about the ways hunter-gatherers positioned themselves on the landscape.

Three variables are used to create the land-use model: patch caloric return rate, temporal predictability of resource structure, and toolstone availability. The patch caloric return-rate variable relies on general principles of the patch-choice model and marginal value theorem. The patch-choice model (MacArthur and Pianka 1966) predicts when a forager optimally leaves one patch for another (e.g., Bettinger 1991; Kelly 1995; E. A. Smith 1991; Stephens and Krebs 1986; Winterhalder 1981a, b). Individual patches are ranked from most to least productive according to the expected net rate of energy return per unit of foraging time, where search and handling time are included costs. Generally, "foragers should choose the highest-return-rate patches given their environmental knowledge" (Kelly 1995:92).

The patch-choice model does not consider the effects of resource depletion or depression on the length of time a patch is occupied (E. A. Smith 1991). Charnov (1976) developed the marginal value theorem (MVT) to contend with this issue. The MVT recognizes that, over time, foraging depresses the availability of resources within a patch and thus overall harvest rate. The MVT addresses the length of time a forager optimally should remain in a patch before reaching the point of diminishing returns. A point is reached when the harvest rate falls below the average rate for the entire environment when travel time between patches is factored in (e.g., Kelly 1995:91; E. A. Smith 1991). Generally, the MVT predicts that foragers spend more time in high-ranked than low-ranked patches (E. A. Smith 1991:257).

Optimal foraging theory thus provides two important tenets for the land-use model. First, hunter-gatherers prefer patches that provide high caloric returns, and second, they may increase occupation length in high-ranked compared with low-ranked environmental zones. Consequently, the land-use model predicts that hunter-gatherers may increase occupation length in high-ranked patches using a core area land-use strategy. Inversely, because low-ranked patches sustain shorter-term occupations, hunter-gatherers would rapidly move through these areas and employ a nonregional land-use strategy. These expectations are outlined on the vertical axis of Figure 9.1.

To estimate the productivity or ranking of competing resource patches, we can use the kilocalorie per hectare (kcal/ha) abundance measure developed by Kornfeld (1994:96, 101; with modifications by Knell 2007:Appendix B) as a proxy for the patch caloric return-rate variable. The kcal/ha abundance measure provides a quantitative estimate of overall patch productivity and a mechanism for comparing return rates between resource patches. The three resource patches considered here are modeled as large but separate environmental zones: foothills-mountains (FHM; which here serves as a proxy for the Hartville Uplift), plains grasslands (PGR), and alluvial valleys and adjacent plains grasslands (PAV).

Figure 9.2 plots the total kcal/ha abundance of biotic resources by environmental zone and season. Total abundance is a summation of the kcal/ha abundance of 37 floral and faunal resources (see Knell 2007; Knell and Hill 2012). The foothills-mountains consistently have higher total kcal/ha resource abundance throughout the year (particularly during winter and fall) than the plains grasslands and alluvial valleys. Overall, the greatest total kcal/ha abundance or highest ranked resource patch is the foothill-mountain zone, followed by the alluvial valleys and then plains grasslands. The difference in total kcal/ha resource abundance by region and season is not statistically significant, however.

Several reasons probably explain the lack of meaningful differences between the environmental zones. First, relatively few floral and faunal resources were modeled ($n = 37$), representing a

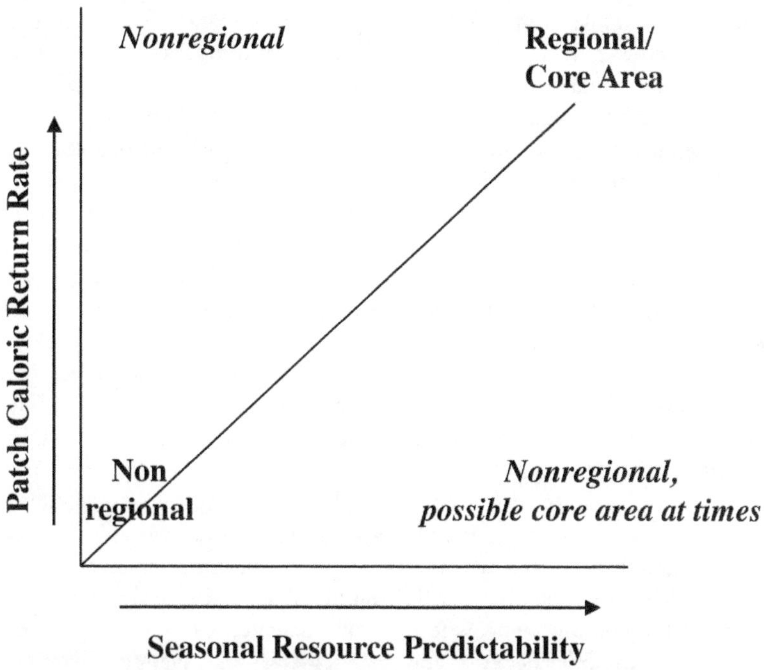


FIGURE 9.1. Land-use model predictions.

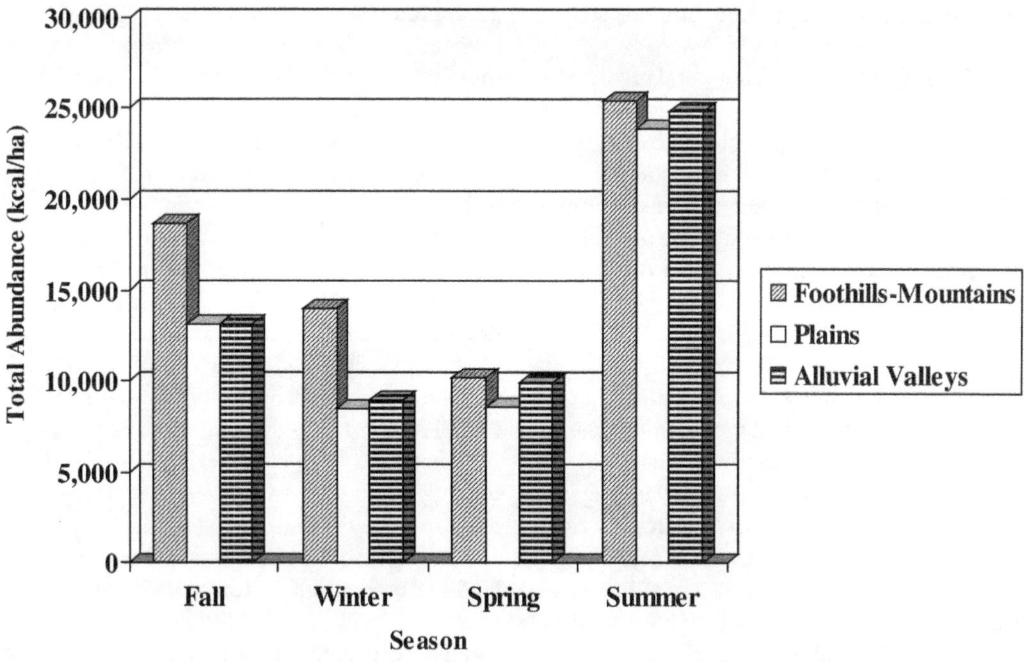


FIGURE 9.2. Total kcal/ha resource abundance by environmental zone and season.

fraction of the possibly available resources. Second, because specific data were lacking for each plant and animal resource, data were obtained from research reports outside the study area and sometimes are educated estimates. Third, and most important, the general nature of the data and method of assigning plants and animals to each environmental zone on a presence-absence basis by season resulted in the proportional inclusion of resources into each environmental zone with the net effect of reducing variability between the zones. Despite the limitations, hunter-gatherers presumably noticed the absolute differences in biotic resource structure and organized land use accordingly.

Another aspect of the land-use model concerns the amount of knowledge or information hunter-gatherers have about the spatial distribution and temporal availability of resources. With information, hunter-gatherers can predict where accumulations of desired resources occur on the landscape and adjust their movements accordingly (e.g., Cashdan 1992; Whallon et al. 2011). Colwell's (1974) concept of resource predictability is the basis for modeling how information about resource structure influenced hunter-gatherer land-use decision-making processes.

Colwell's (1974) model of temporal predictability is based on the variables *constancy* and *contingency*. Constancy is a "measure of the degree to which a resource is continually available" through time (Ebert and Kohler 1988:131). Constancy here serves as a qualitative measure of the predictability that resource availability is high or continuous, or low or discontinuous, in a given patch through time (Bamforth 1988; Ebert and Kohler 1988). Contingency is a "measure of the degree to which the availability of a particular resource can be accurately predicted based on the season, without the need for monitoring that resource" (Ebert and Kohler 1988:131). High contingency occurs when edible plant parts predictably ripen or fauna predictably aggregate in a certain area, and low contingency when edible plant parts are seasonally unavailable or when an animal's presence in an area is unpredictable.

When constancy and contingency are high, hunter-gatherers can predict the availability of desirable resources with high accuracy, enabling them to optimally target these areas. The ability to predict areas of high resource concentrations is key to maintaining a core area land-use strategy. When constancy and contingency are low, resource predictability is low and hunter-gatherers could not reasonably expect to encounter key resources. Under such circumstances they would avoid the patch altogether, monitor (if possible) the patch for desired resources, or rapidly pass through such unpredictable environmental zones using a nonregional land-use strategy. Other variations of constancy and contingency are possible (see italics in Figure 9.1 and discussion in Knell 2007:265), but for an early test of the model, only the two options are considered.

To mesh the resource predictability and patch caloric return-rate variable for model building purposes, one must quantify resource predictability. A numeric resource predictability value was calculated by estimating the degree of constancy and contingency of key resource types: plants, medium-size to small fauna, large fauna, and toolstone (see Knell 2007:268). An ordinal scale value was applied to these estimates such that those resources deemed to have high temporal predictability have a value of 3, those with moderate temporal predictability a value of 2, and those with low temporal predictability a value of 1. These values were summed by resource type and season to determine high and low values of resource predictability (horizontal axis of Figure 9.3).

Figure 9.3 plots the patch caloric return rate (log of kcal/ha abundance) and temporal predictability variable to develop specific expectations regarding the optimal land-use strategy employed by Cody complex hunter-gatherers in each of the modeled environmental zones (i.e., FHM, PGR, PAV). Figure 9.3 is identical to Figure 9.1 except that it has the specific variable thresholds for making the land-use predictions by season and environmental zone.

Using the matrix in Figure 9.3, we can make land-use predictions by season and environmental zone (see Table 9.1). All three environmental zones are expected to have highly predictable and abundant resources during the summer (Figure 9.3, top right), which according to the land-use model should be used by regionally restricted or core area–focused hunter-gatherers seeking to

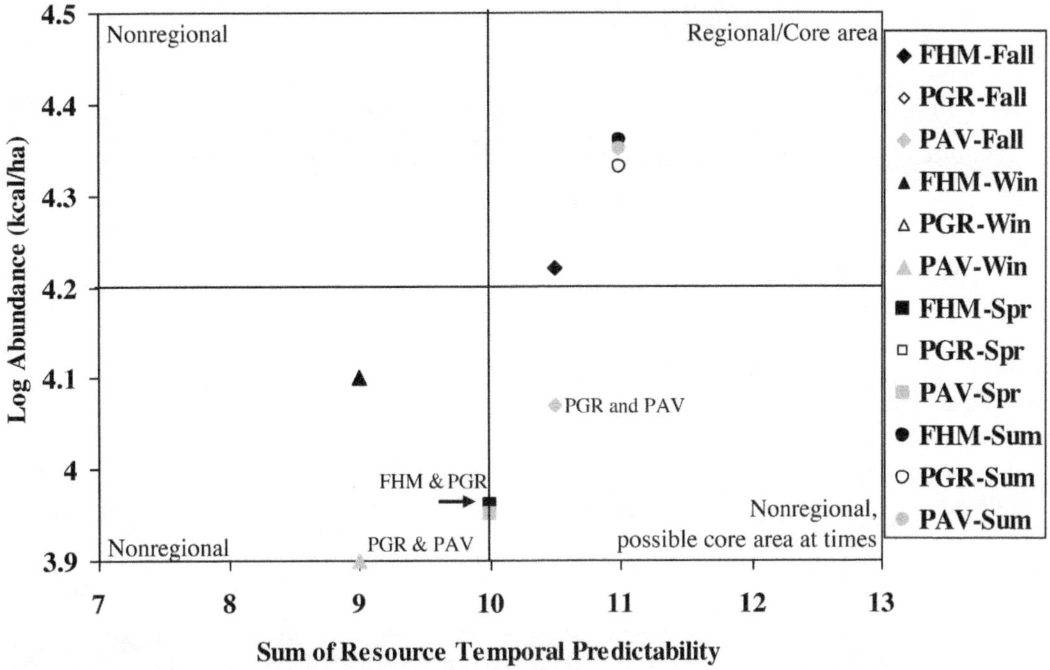


FIGURE 9.3. Cody-specific land-use model predictions. FHM = foothills-mountains; PGR = plains grasslands; PAV = alluvial valleys and adjacent plains grasslands.

maximize their caloric intake. The greater abundance of seasonally predictable and available (i.e., high constancy and contingency) desirable biotic resources and high patch caloric return rate would support a long-term, repetitive occupation. A long-term occupation is defined as consecutive seasons at a site (as determined by bison tooth eruption and wear patterns), given that the smallest temporal unit of study is a single season. A regionally restricted land-use strategy is also expected in the foothills-mountains during the fall (core area strategy in the Hartville Uplift) and winter due to the considerably higher or more favorable (compared with the options) resource structure.

Core area–focused hunter-gatherers are expected to tether subsistence and lithic procurement pursuits to the core area for a relatively long period of time. Recall that a core area is a regularly and intensively used part of a group's annual range with one or more sources of high-quality toolstone and sufficient biotic resources to support one or more bands of hunter-gatherers for two or more consecutive seasons. While core area focused, they should intensively and repetitively use this part of their annual range during the predicted seasons, and in so doing rely on the locally available biotic and toolstone sources. Figure 9.4 schematically portrays what a core area land-use strategy might look like, and how a long-term focus could lead to a reliance on local toolstones. The test expectations used to identify a core area

TABLE 9.1. Land-Use Expectations by Season and Environmental Zone.

| Environmental Zone and Season | Land-Use Expectation |
|---|---|
| **Foothills-Mountains** | |
| Fall | Core Area/Regional |
| Winter | Core Area/Regional |
| Spring | Nonregional |
| Summer | Core Area/Regional |
| **Plains Grasslands** | |
| Fall | Nonregional |
| Winter | Nonregional |
| Spring | Nonregional |
| Summer | Core Area/Regional |
| **Plains Alluvial Valleys** | |
| Fall | Nonregional |
| Winter | Nonregional |
| Spring | Nonregional |
| Summer | Core Area/Regional |

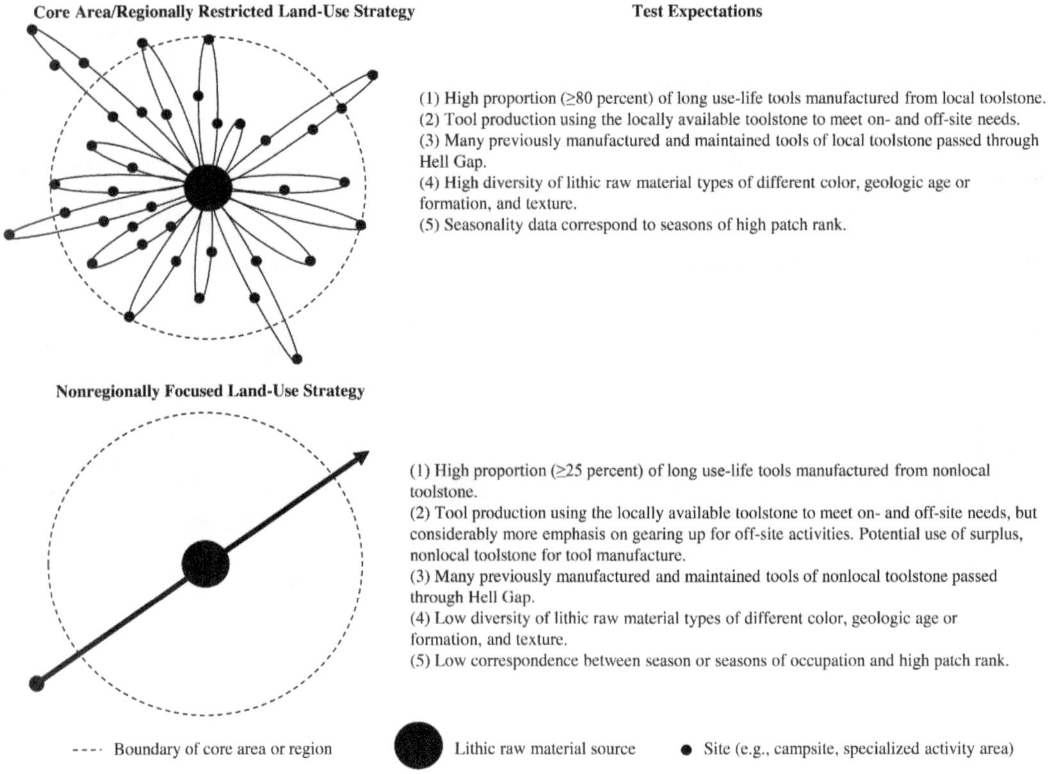


**FIGURE 9.4.** Diagram of core area/regionally restricted and nonregionally focused land-use strategies and test expectations.

land-use strategy archaeologically are summarized in Figure 9.4 and discussed in the next section of the chapter.

Calorie-maximizing hunter-gatherers should be nonregionally focused in low-ranked environmental zones that have low total caloric abundance of seasonally (temporally) unpredictable biotic resources and lack or have heterogeneously distributed toolstone sources (Figure 9.3, bottom left). The presence of high-quality toolstone is insufficient to sustain a long-term, regionally restricted land-use strategy when biotic resource structure is unfavorable; instead, groups should gear up with the toolstone but otherwise rapidly move through such areas using a nonregional strategy. The land-use model predicts that hunter-gatherers would be nonregionally restricted in the plains grasslands and alluvial valleys during all seasons except summer, and in the foothills-mountains during spring, when the resource structure in all environmental zones is poor (Figure 9.3, Table 9.1).

Nonregionally oriented groups would rapidly move between zones as they pursued mobile game or exhausted the resource potential of other nearby zones (Figure 9.4). Sites resulting from nonregionally oriented groups would have chipped stone assemblages dominated by nonlocal toolstone. The test expectations to identify a nonregional land-use strategy are summarized in Figure 9.4; these expectations and those for core area hunter-gatherers are discussed below.

## Testing the Land-Use Model: Hell Gap

The land-use model is tested using chipped stone and faunal seasonality data from one Alberta and two Eden-Scottsbluff components at the Hell Gap site, Wyoming. Specifically tested is whether the Alberta and Eden-Scottsbluff occupants at Hell Gap employed a core area or nonregional land-use strategy when they visited Hell Gap some 9000–10,000 radiocarbon years ago (11,470–10,203 cal BP).

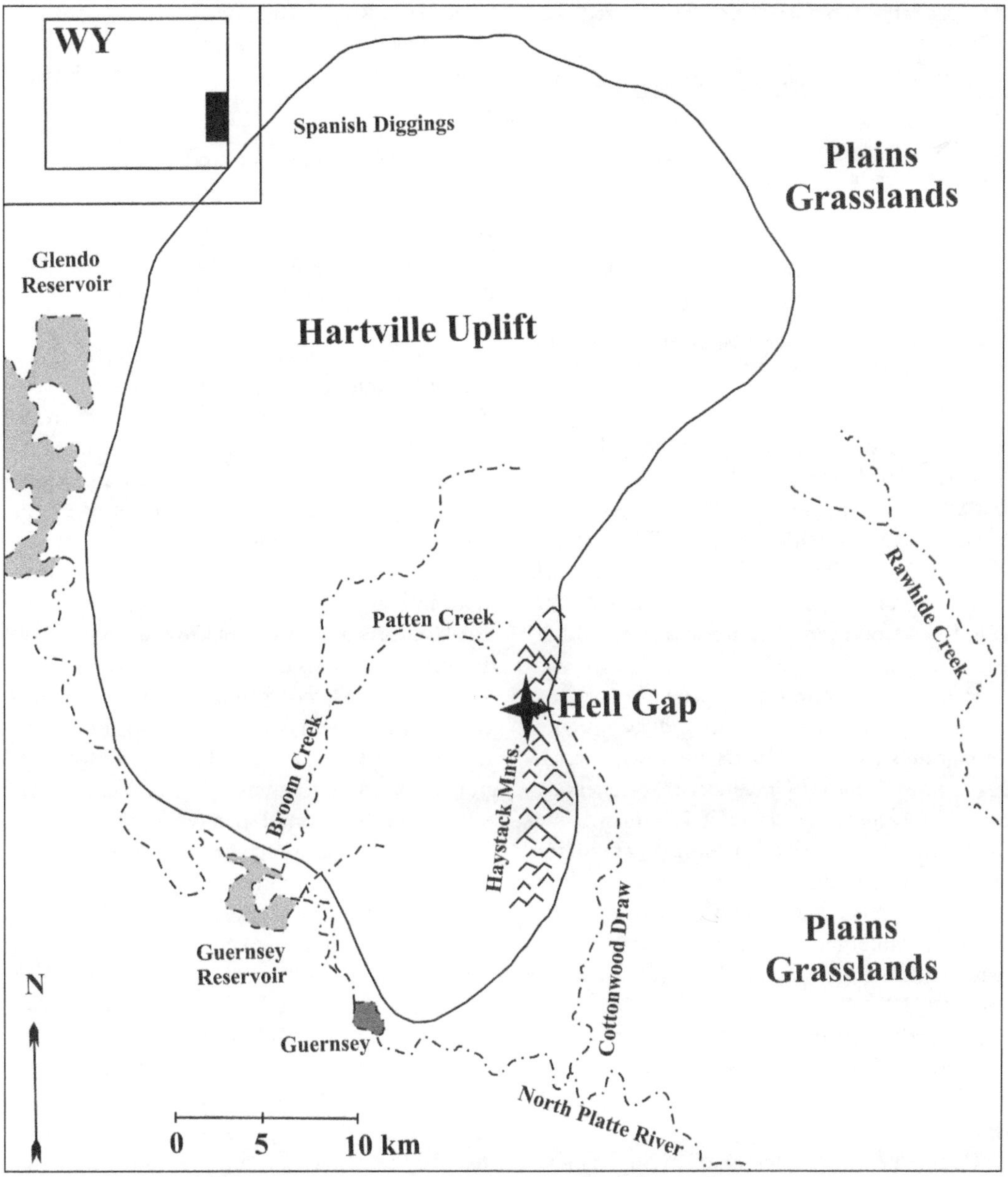


**FIGURE 9.5.** Map of the Hartville Uplift, including the location of Hell Gap. Base map courtesy of Marcel Kornfeld.

Hell Gap is located in the Hartville Uplift, Wyoming, which is a 40-×-65-km (2600 km$^2$) domal uplift located between the Rocky Mountain Front Range and High Plains (Figure 9.5). The site lies at the eastern edge of the Hartville Uplift along the flank of the Haystack Mountains in the Hell Gap Valley, approximately 1500 m (5000 ft.) above sea level.

Hell Gap was an ideal campsite location for hunter-gatherers. The foothills provided protection from the elements and an excellent observation post for monitoring animals in the nearby open plains, and the site itself occurs in an ecotone that supports multiple floral and faunal communities. Water intermittently flows through Hell Gap Creek, a small tributary that runs through the Hell Gap Valley. Nearby trees potentially provided wood for hafting elements, tools, or fire. The Hartville Uplift has many local (within 40 km of Hell Gap), highly knappable formations

**TABLE 9.2.** Artifact Frequency for Each Analyzed Cultural Component at Hell Gap.

| Artifact Type | Alberta | Cody I | Cody V |
|---|---|---|---|
| Core | 0 | 2 | 24 |
| Biface | | | |
| Bifacial tool blank | 0 | 11 | 54 |
| Bifacial tool | 6 | 12 | 28 |
| Flake tool | 15 | 35 | 188 |
| Debitage | 267 | 987 | 3,987 |
| **Total** | 288 | 1,047 | 4,281 |

*Note:* Bifacial tool blank = unfinished/unused biface or projectile point preform; bifacial tool = used biface or projectile point.

and sources of chert and quartzite (Cloverly-Morrison and Fort Union–Wasatch formations, and Mississippian and Miocene age deposits; see Miller 2009 and Knell 2007:99). Hell Gap was an ideal residential campsite location because it is in an ecotone with several floral and faunal communities, wood for fuel, water, and nearby high-quality toolstone.

Hell Gap is a stratified campsite used by Goshen through Lusk Paleoindian and later prehistoric groups (Irwin-Williams et al. 1973; Larson et al. 2009). Harvard University researchers excavated five localities (I–V) at Hell Gap in the 1960s, and University of Wyoming researchers have excavated some of these same localities through the present (Kornfeld and Larson 2009). Only the Alberta and Eden-Scottsbluff component artifacts from Locality I (hereafter Alberta and Cody I; Knell 2007, 2009) and the Eden component artifacts from Locality V (hereafter Cody V; Knell 2007; Knell et al. 2009) that were excavated in the 1960s were analyzed for this study (Figure 9.6).

Chipped stone greater than 1.5 cm was analyzed. The analyzed Alberta and Cody I assemblages come from a 27.9-m$^2$ excavation area and have 288 and 1,047 chipped stone artifacts, respectively (Table 9.2). The Cody V assemblage is from a 47-m$^2$ excavation area and has 4,281 analyzed artifacts (Table 9.2).

The Cody I and V components consist almost entirely of locally procured lithic materials (99.8 and 99.6 percent, respectively). The nonlocal toolstone (>40 km) is White River Group silicate, the closest source of which outcrops east of Hell Gap. Most of the Alberta toolstone is nonlocal Green River formation chert (59.7 percent), which has major outcrops 200 km southwest of Hell Gap. The remainder of the Alberta chipped stone is from sources local to Hell Gap.

*Test Expectation 1: Toolstone Provenance*

The proportion of local to nonlocal toolstone provides a means to distinguish between core area and nonregionally restricted land-use strategies. Researchers commonly suggest that toolstone provenance is a viable variable for distinguishing among land-use practices (e.g., Bamforth 2002a, 2002b; Gardner 1983; Knudson 2002; E. E. Smith 1990, 1991; Stanford 1999), though in reality many recognize that factors such as lithic raw material richness and transport distance (Brantingham 2003, 2006), the number of tool-depleting events (Ingbar 1994), and lithic raw material availability and quality (e.g., Andrefsky 1994; Bamforth 1986) influence the proportion of lithic raw material types recovered at sites. Despite these issues, the underlying message is that a high ratio of local to nonlocal toolstone signifies a tethered or regionally restricted land-use strategy; conversely, a high ratio of nonlocal toolstone signifies nonregionally restricted land use.

Such expectations based on lithic raw material proportions are further weakened because a tool production strategy that results in many flakes will inflate the proportion of artifacts made from local toolstone in a lithic assemblage. Consequently, the proportion of typically long use-life tools (projectile points and end scrapers) manufactured from local and nonlocal toolstone provides a better measure. These artifact classes often remain in toolkits longer than short use-life tools such as utilized flakes, increasing the likelihood that they were transported over long distances and brought to a site from nonlocal sources. Thus, hunter-gatherers who rapidly move through a region are more likely to discard a higher proportion of long use-life tools of nonlocal toolstone than hunter-gatherers who remain tethered to a region.

The proportion-based expectations roughly follow Carr (2005; Carr and Boszhardt 2010; also see Gramly 1980). If 80 percent or more of the long use-life tools are from sources local to the Hartville Uplift, a core area land-use strategy is indicated, whereas if 25 percent or more of the

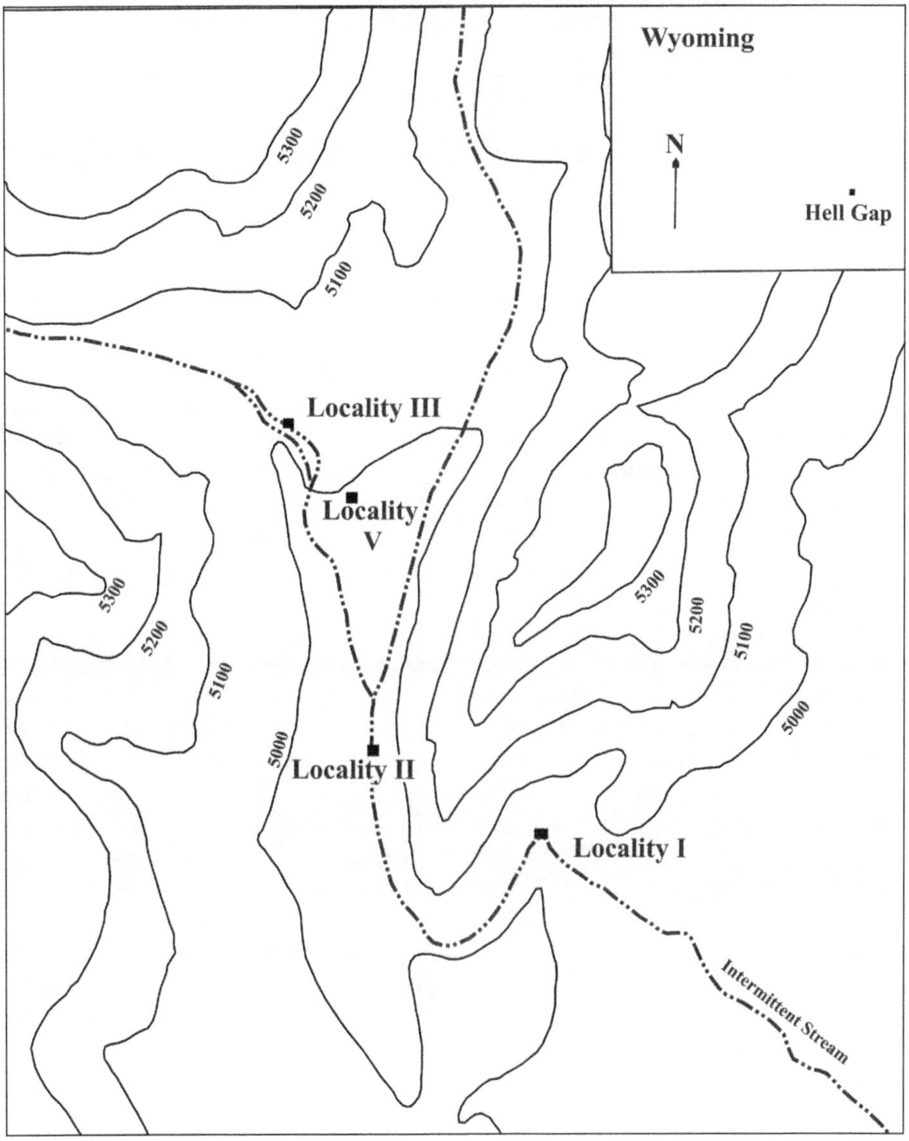


FIGURE 9.6. Hell Gap site location map. Adapted from Irwin-Williams et al. 1973.

long use-life tools come from nonlocal sources, a nonregional land-use strategy is indicated. An indeterminate type of land-use strategy is signified if the percentage falls between these thresholds. The cutoff between local and nonlocal toolstone is 40 km (following Gould and Saggers 1985; Meltzer 1989).

Table 9.3 summarizes the frequency of long use-life tools — here considered to be end scrapers and projectile points — by cultural complex and toolstone provenance at Hell Gap. All the end scrapers and projectile points in the Alberta and Cody I assemblages and all but one (97.4 percent) of the long use-life tools in the Cody V assemblage are from toolstone sources local to the Hartville Uplift. Thus, each cultural component greatly exceeds the 80 percent threshold. This aspect of the technology suggests that Hell Gap was a single location in a core area land-use strategy.

*Test Expectation 2: Tool Production*

The need to replenish toolstone and toolkits influences the way hunter-gatherers moved across the landscape. Where highly knappable toolstone

**TABLE 9.3.** Frequency of Typical Long Use-Life Tools by Cultural Complex and Toolstone Provenance at Hell Gap.

| | Cultural Complex and Toolstone Provenance | | | | | |
|---|---|---|---|---|---|---|
| | Alberta | | Cody I | | Cody V | |
| **Tool Type** | **Local** | **Nonlocal** | **Local** | **Nonlocal** | **Local** | **Nonlocal** |
| End scrapers | 0 | 0 | 2 | 0 | 17 | 1 |
| Projectile points | 3 | 0 | 9 | 0 | 21 | 0 |
| **Total** | 3 | 0 | 11 | 0 | 38 | 1 |

*Note:* Tools from unknown sources are excluded.

is located in close proximity to a site, the expectation is that regionally restricted groups would repetitively replenish their toolkit with this local stone and discard a high proportion of the manufacturing debris to meet their on- and off-site (gearing-up) tool needs (e.g., Andrefsky 1994; Carr 2005; Carr and Boszhardt 2010; Custer et al. 1983). Nonregionally focused hunter-gatherers also would replenish their toolkit with the local stone to meet any on-site and gearing-up needs; however, if uncertainty existed as to when and where they might next replenish their toolkit, they might have emphasized the off-site gearing-up trajectory. During a short-term occupation, it may have been more efficient (in terms of time and energy) for nonregionally focused hunter-gatherers to use any surplus, transported, nonlocal toolstone, resulting in production debris from nonlocal sources.

A number of approaches could be used to assess test expectation 2 or the tool production patterning at Hell Gap. Minimum analytical nodule analysis (MANA; Larson and Kornfeld 1997) was chosen because it results in fine-scale aggregates of toolstone that can be interpreted to distinguish among tool production, tool maintenance, and tool transport strategies.

The premise behind MANA is that analysts separate the lithic raw material from a site or component of a site into aggregated units that vary by raw material type (e.g., chert, quartzite, basalt), source area, and geologic formation or age, as well as by minute variations in color, cortex, texture, fossils, and inclusions. These units are referred to as "minimum analytical nodules," or MANs, and represent individual units of very similar toolstone. MANA analysts reasonably can, and do, assume that MANs include—or potentially include—items removed from the same parent material and thus a limited set of events (Hall 2004; Larson and Kornfeld 1997; Sellet 1999). This assumption renders each MAN, and by extension assemblages of MANs, amenable to further analysis. The identification and interpretation of each MAN was achieved by using the multiple-lines-of-evidence approach described by Knell (2007, 2012).

The MANs depicting tool production are, in part, identified using five technological "scenarios" (which closely follow Sellet 1999, but were slightly modified in Knell 2007, 2012) that portray potential organizational options faced by stone tool–using peoples (Figure 9.7). Scenarios 1, 2, and 3—collectively referred to as the "production scenarios"—model the way that lithic materials to make tools were brought to a site, manufactured into tools or blanks, and the tools either discarded on-site or transported off-site (Figure 9.7, Table 9.4). In scenarios 1 and 2, the entire manufacturing sequence occurred at a site; the main difference was whether the manufactured tools were discarded on-site (scenario 1) or transported off-site (scenario 2). In scenario 3, tool blanks or preforms were transported to a site and the production of the desired tool was *continued* on-site. The solid line in scenario 3 (Figure 9.7) depicts a sequence in which tools or preforms broke or tools were used and then discarded on-site, and the dashed line indicates when tools and preforms were transported off-site. These scenarios capture the procurement of toolstone and production of tools at Hell Gap.

To facilitate test expectation 2, I lumped the technological scenarios into those that portray on-site tool production and those that depict the on-site production of tools for off-site purposes (Table 9.4). The on-site tool production MANs are those resulting from scenario 1 and those

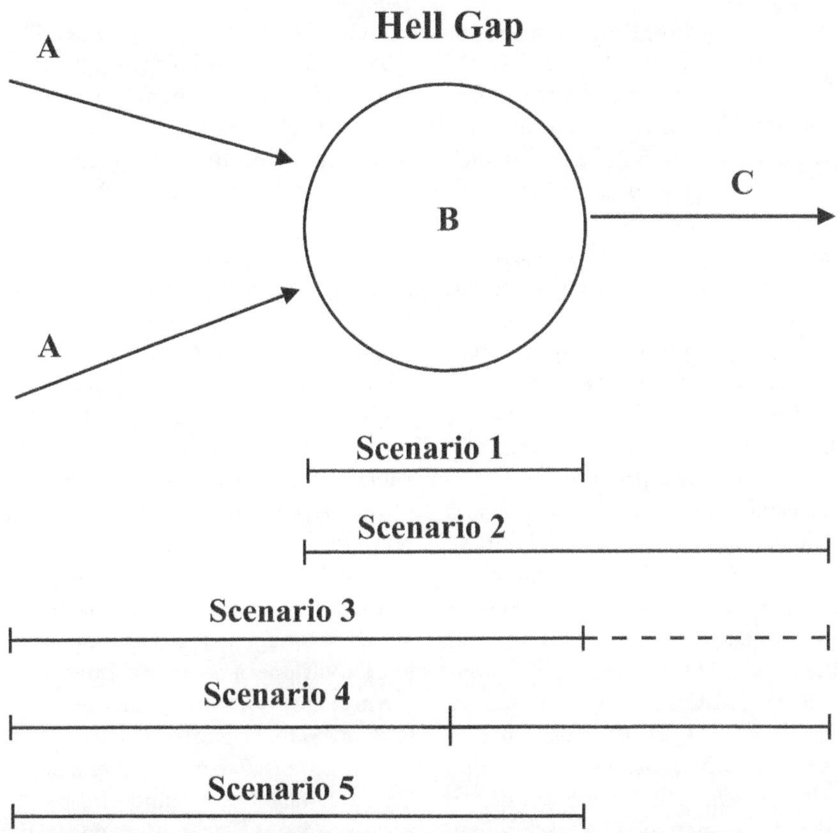


**FIGURE 9.7.** The five MANA scenarios. (A) transport of lithic raw material and tools to Hell Gap, (B) on-site tool manufacture, use, and maintenance, and (C) transport of tools away from Hell Gap.

**TABLE 9.4.** Frequency of On-Site and Off-Site Tool Production Minimum Analytical Nodules (MANs) by Cultural Complex and Toolstone Provenance.

| | Cultural Complex and Toolstone Provenance | | | | | |
|---|---|---|---|---|---|---|
| | Alberta | | Cody I | | Cody V | |
| Scenario | Local | Nonlocal | Local | Nonlocal | Local | Nonlocal |
| **On-Site Tool Production** | | | | | | |
| On-site flake tool production, use, and discard | 0 | 0 | 0 | 0 | 5 | 0 |
| Continued on-site biface production with breakage and discard during manufacture | 0 | 0 | 3 | 0 | 21 | 0 |
| Continued on-site biface production with on-site use and discard | 0 | 0 | 0 | 0 | 1 | 0 |
| Continued on-site flake tool production with on-site use and discard | 0 | 0 | 0 | 0 | 5 | 0 |
| **On-Site Total** | 0 | 0 | 3 | 0 | 32 | 0 |
| **Off-Site Tool Production** | | | | | | |
| On-site flake tool or blank production from a biface core with off-site transport | 0 | 0 | 0 | 0 | 6 | 0 |
| On-site flake tool or blank production from a multidirectional core with off-site transport | 0 | 0 | 2 | 0 | 9 | 0 |
| Continued on-site biface production with off-site transport | 1 | 3 | 6 | 0 | 24 | 0 |
| **Off-Site Total** | 1 | 3 | 8 | 0 | 39 | 0 |

*Note:* Data from Knell 2007:278, 280.

scenario 3 MANs depicting the *continued* on-site manufacture of a tool from a blank that was transported to Hell Gap, broke during manufacture, and was discarded on-site or the tool was used and discarded on-site (Figure 9.7, solid line). Either way, biface tool blanks (unfinished/unused bifaces or projectile point preforms) or tools produced on-site were discarded on-site. The manufacture of blanks or tools that were transported off-site is portrayed by scenario 2 and by scenario 3 (dashed line), in which a blank was transported to Hell Gap, its manufacture *continued* on-site, yet the tool itself was transported off-site. Table 9.4 shows the frequency of MANs by scenario, cultural complex, and toolstone provenance.

The three assemblages have 86 MANs assigned to the tool production scenarios: Alberta ($n = 4$), Cody I ($n = 11$), and Cody V ($n = 71$). Thirty-five MANs from the Cody I and V components fit the criteria for on-site tool production; none of the Alberta MANs meet the criteria. All the on-site tool production MANs consist of toolstones locally available to Hell Gap. This suggests that the Cody I and V occupants relied on local lithic materials to meet their tool production needs, indicating that this aspect of their technology corresponds to the expectations for a core area land-use strategy.

The Cody I and V off-site tool production MANs, like the on-site MANs, depict a complete reliance on local toolstone sources (Table 9.4). This similarly indicates a gearing-up strategy reliant on the local toolstone, and a core area land-use strategy.

The sample of Alberta off-site production MANs is very small ($n = 4$) but indicates that these hunter-gatherers preferentially (75 percent) used lithic materials from nonlocal sources to meet their tool production needs. The seemingly heavy reliance on nonlocal toolstones for tool production suggests that this aspect of the Alberta component technology best reflects a nonregional land-use strategy.

### *Test Expectation 3: Tool Transport and Maintenance*

Test expectation 3 provides direct evidence for whether the Alberta and Cody hunter-gatherers at Hell Gap used the Hartville Uplift as a core area or rapidly passed through it. If these hunter-gatherers restrained their movements to the Hartville Uplift (i.e., core area strategy), they presumably would transport manufactured tools of local toolstone to Hell Gap. That is, if they confined their movements to the Hartville Uplift for long enough, by natural attrition they would discard from the active toolkit many previously manufactured tools of local lithic raw material. Similarly, if they serially cycled through the Hartville Uplift, evidence (debitage) should exist from maintained tools of local lithic material that were not discarded at Hell Gap (i.e., passed through Hell Gap).

If, on the other hand, nonregionally focused Alberta and Cody hunter-gatherers rapidly moved between regions, they presumably transported many tools of nonlocal toolstone to the new region, resulting in a high proportion of discarded nonlocal lithic artifacts transported to but not manufactured at Hell Gap. The nonlocal toolstone assemblage thus would largely consist of previously manufactured, exhausted or broken, technologically complete, long use-life tools transported to but not manufactured at Hell Gap. Debitage from maintained tools that were not discarded at Hell Gap (i.e., passed through the site) should predominantly come from nonlocal sources. MANA scenarios 4 and 5 (Figure 9.7) portray patterns of tool maintenance and transport (Knell 2007, 2012), respectively, and provide a way to identify tool transport and maintenance strategies that can be used to evaluate test expectation 3.

Scenario 4 depicts the transport to Hell Gap of bifacial and flake tools that were maintained (resharpened, refurbished) on-site but transported and discarded off-site. The Cody I and V components have nine scenario 4 MANs; the Alberta assemblage has none. The Cody I component has four and the Cody V component three MANs, indicating that previously finished bifaces were modified at but transported away from Hell Gap (i.e., passed through Hell Gap). Each component has one MAN that depicts modification to a previously finished flake tool that was modified at but transported away from Hell Gap. All the lithic materials are from sources local to Hell Gap, suggesting that tools made elsewhere in the Hell Gap vicinity cycled through the site. This aspect of the technological strategy suggests that the Cody I and V hunter-gatherers used the Hartville Uplift as a core area.

In scenario 5, transported bifacial tools (projectile points, used bifaces) and flake tools are discarded at Hell Gap but not produced or modified there. The three assemblages have 26 MANs with a single bifacial implement: four from the Alberta component and eleven apiece from the Cody I and V components. The majority ($n = 21$) of these MANs have a projectile point, many of which have a haft snap (edge grinding terminating at a lateral snap), indicating that they broke or became exhausted in the haft and were discarded at Hell Gap. All the scenario 5 bifaces were manufactured from lithic material local to the Hartville Uplift.

The three assemblages have 23 scenario 5 MANs that have a transported and discarded flake tool: Alberta ($n = 1$), Cody I ($n = 12$), and Cody V ($n = 10$). The majority (87 percent) of the flake tools in these MANs are from lithic materials local to the Hartville Uplift; three flake tools (two from the Cody I and one from the Cody V assemblage) are nonlocal, White River Group silicate. In each case, more than 80 percent of the scenario 5 biface and flake tool MANs are made from local lithic raw material, suggesting that the transported technology at these sites reflects a core area land-use strategy centered on the Hartville Uplift.

### *Test Expectation 4: Repetitive Use of a Region*

Test expectation 4 addresses the extent to which groups exploited the variety of lithic raw material sources (formations, point sources, color and texture) available to them. The longer a group is tethered to a region with locally available toolstone, the more likely it is to encounter and collect this material from a wider variety of formations and outcrops, thereby increasing not only the frequency of sources represented but also the diversity of toolstone with varying colors and luster (if the raw materials vary) in the assemblage. Nonregionally restricted groups that rapidly passed through these same locales presumably lacked the time to sample the diversity of lithic resources available in that area. Thus, with more time, regionally restricted hunter-gatherers would exploit a wider variety of the locally available bedrock seams or outcrops, resulting in a higher diversity of lithic materials that vary by source, color, and luster than nonregionally restricted groups that spent less time in the uplift.

The Hartville Uplift has a variety of lithic raw material sources that differ by geologic age or formation, color, and luster. The lithic raw material in the Hell Gap assemblages was identified to geologic formation (Cloverly-Morrison, Fort Union–Wasatch, Green River, White River Group) or age (Mississippian, Miocene) following the criteria established by Miller (2009). A color was assigned to each chipped stone specimen using the Munsell soil color chart. Specimens with distinct coloration were identified to a specific hue, value, and chroma (e.g., 10YR 3/1; very dark gray), or if they were less distinct or somewhat mottled, then a single range of Munsell soil colors (e.g., yellowish brown in hue 10YR includes 5/4, 5/6, and 5/8) was assigned. Chert specimens were further subdivided into coarse, dull, and waxy under a tripartite, subjective scheme that considers variations in surface texture and luster. Most of the naturally occurring chert in the Hartville Uplift is of the dull variety. Burned artifacts are in a miscellaneous category, and ultimately were excluded from this analysis because burning affects artifact color and luster (e.g., Domanski and Webb 1992; Rick 1978). Heated artifacts are trickier because of the comparatively moderate color and luster changes, but are included because the changes were generally detectable within the range considered here. The frequency of artifacts assigned to each raw material, color, and luster type by site are in Knell (2007:Appendix D).

The Shannon-Wiener diversity index was used to evaluate the proposition that hunter-gatherers who repetitively exploit a region using a core area land-use strategy encounter and collect toolstone from a more diverse array of point sources than those with less time to encounter and collect the same diversity of toolstone. The Cody I and Cody V assemblages have a higher diversity (H') of lithic raw material type categories (3.239 and 3.148, respectively) than the Alberta complex (1.54) component (Table 9.5). The higher diversity of lithic raw material types in the two Eden-Scottsbluff components suggests that the Eden-Scottsbluff hunter-gatherers more repetitively procured the available toolstone in accordance with a core area land-use strategy. The lower diversity of lithic raw

**TABLE 9.5.** Shannon-Wiener Diversity Index Calculations Used for Test Expectation 4.

| Measure | Alberta | Cody I | Cody V |
|---|---|---|---|
| H′ | 1.54 | 3.24 | 3.15 |
| Richness | 23 | 74 | 103 |
| Evenness ($H'/H'_{max}$) | .49 | .75 | .68 |

*Note:* H′ = index of species diversity. Natural log used in calculations.

material types in the Alberta component suggests nonregional use of the Hartville Uplift.

### *Test Expectation 5: Season of Occupation*

A correspondence should exist between the seasons during which the land-use model predicts that the resource structure in the Hartville Uplift could support a core area strategy and those seasons during which it was optimally used by nonregionally focused hunter-gatherers. The land-use model expectations are as follows: core area focused in fall, winter, and summer, and nonregionally focused in spring (Table 9.1).

Faunal seasonality evidence (based on bison tooth eruption and wear patterns) used to evaluate test expectation 5 is limited to the Cody V component. Dental evidence from the Alberta and Cody I assemblages is either nonexistent or lacks appropriate provenience information. Rapson and Niven (2009:398–399; also see Knell et al. 2009) identified the season of death from two bison mandibles and four bison maxillas in the Cody V assemblage. One specimen indicates a late spring to early summer death, one fall to early winter, one summer, and three summer to early fall. Together these specimens indicate a late spring to early winter occupation.

In comparing the seasonality data with the land-use expectations, we find a good fit between the Cody V evidence and times when the model predicts that the Hartville Uplift (here considered part of the foothill-mountain zone) optimally served as a core area. Most specimens indicate a summer to early fall occupation, which directly corresponds with seasons when the Hartville Uplift was a high-ranked resource patch. The late spring to early summer and fall to early winter specimens both overlap with predicted times of high patch rank. Together the faunal seasonality evidence suggests that the Cody V hunter-gatherers used Hell Gap and the Hartville Uplift during seasons when it was optimally exploited by core area–focused hunter-gatherers.

### *Land-Use Patterning at Hell Gap*

Combining the results of the five test expectations, we can now establish whether the Alberta, Cody I, and Cody V hunter-gatherers were core area focused or nonregionally focused when they occupied Hell Gap, and by extension the Hartville Uplift. Table 9.6 summarizes the test expectations and the inferred land-use strategy.

The Cody I and V components meet all the criteria for a core area land-use strategy. A core area strategy is indicated because (1) each component has a high proportion (>80 percent) of long use-life tools created from local toolstone; (2) the tool production MANs are entirely of local toolstone; (3) the tool transport/maintenance MANs are almost entirely of local toolstone; (4) a wide diversity of the locally available lithic raw material outcrops was used, varying by source/formation, color, and luster; and (5) the season of occupation at Locality V corresponds to the optimal time for using the Hartville Uplift as a core area. The Cody I and V assemblages thus depict a core area land-use strategy at Hell Gap.

The land-use interpretation for the Alberta component is less straightforward. These hunter-gatherers employed a core area strategy, as shown by the high proportion of long use-life tools and transported MANs created from local toolstone (test expectations 1 and 3). The high proportion of tool production MANs of nonlocal lithic material and less repetitive use of the various Hartville Uplift lithic sources (test expectations 2 and 4) indicate a nonregional strategy, however. The discrepancy in land-use signatures results from the emphasis on nonlocal toolstone for tool production but transport and discard of finished tools of local lithic raw material.

Several potential scenarios may account for this discrepancy. One possibility is that Alberta hunter-gatherers geared up with tools (including projectile points) of Hartville Uplift toolstone in anticipation of a long-distance logistical foray to western Wyoming, with a return trip to the Hartville Uplift that included supplies of Green River chert as well as the original, but now exhausted,

**TABLE 9.6.** Inferred Land-Use Strategy for Each Test Expectation and Cultural Component.

| | Inferred Land-Use Strategy | | |
|---|---|---|---|
| **Test Expectation** | **Alberta** | **Cody I** | **Cody V** |
| 1. Long use-life tools: proportion of local to nonlocal toolstone | Core area | Core area | Core area |
| 2. Tool production scenarios | Nonregional | Core area | Core area |
| 3. Tool transport and maintenance scenarios | Core area | Core area | Core area |
| 4. Repetitive use of region (lithic raw material type diversity) | Nonregional | Core area | Core area |
| 5. Season of occupation | NA | NA | Core area |

*Note:* NA indicates not applicable/no data to test the expectation.

projectile points from the Hartville Uplift. Though this scenario is plausible, I would expect more than one transported and discarded Green River chert tool. Another possibility is that the Alberta complex hunter-gatherers maintained a core area land-use strategy centered on the Hartville Uplift, with the Green River chert introduced through trade. Which, if either, of these scenarios best accounts for the noted discrepancies remains uncertain.

To summarize, the Cody I and V hunter-gatherers used Hell Gap as a single location within a broader core area land-use strategy centered on the Hartville Uplift, whereas the signatures for the Alberta component are indeterminate. Though it is tantalizing to expand these inferences and their implications to Cody complex land use outside the Hartville Uplift, the patterning established here provides warranted inferences about land-use only for the Hartville Uplift and particularly Hell Gap. That is, the inferred land-use strategies represent only short slices of time at a single location by a small group of people, and thus provide an inadequate basis for inferring broader land-use trends. When combined with the regional scale analyses, the local-scale patterning identified here provides a framework that we can use to more fully assess how and why resource structure influenced Cody complex land-use organization.

## Cody Land Use Within and Beyond the Hartville Uplift

This section expands the local-scale land-use model findings at Hell Gap both to the Hartville Uplift and to the northern and northwestern Great Plains and Rocky Mountains. This broader context puts the findings at Hell Gap into regional perspective.

### *Hartville Uplift*

The land-use model findings in this chapter are limited to the three Cody complex components at Hell Gap, with the presumption that the findings reflect how Cody peoples organized land use in the Hartville Uplift. The truth is, without testing other Cody sites in the Hartville Uplift, we do not know whether the patterning inferred for Hell Gap applies to the broader Hartville Uplift. Even so, it is instructive to develop a hypothetical model of what a core area land-use strategy — the land-use strategy employed by the Cody I and V hunter-gatherers at Hell Gap — might look like in the Hartville Uplift.

Tests of the land-use model at the local scale (this chapter) and regional scale (Knell and Hill 2012) demonstrate that Cody hunter-gatherers in biotically productive uplifts with high-quality toolstone sources, like the Hartville Uplift, optimally employed a core area land-use strategy. Because of the seasonally predictable and high kcal/ha abundance of biotic resources, as well as abundant and highly knappable toolstone, these hunter-gatherers would have repetitively and intensively exploited the Hartville Uplift resources for a protracted portion of the year. I view it as likely that Cody, and perhaps other, hunter-gatherers established base camps or longer-term residences along the relatively protected flanks of the north-south-trending Haystack Mountains, in which the Hell Gap site is located (Figure 9.8) during the cold season (late fall, early winter). Evidence for Cody period cold-season occupation of the foothill-mountain zone in regions outside the Hartville Uplift comes from the Osprey Beach (Johnson et al. 2004) and Jerry Craig (Hill and Kornfeld 1999; Richings-Germain 2002) sites. From the Haystack Mountains, logistically oriented task groups exploited the interior of the Hartville Uplift and nearby plains grasslands to obtain and bring resources (e.g., food, toolstone, and firewood) back to camp. As more plant resources became available and the ungulate fauna became less aggregated during the warm season (primarily summer and early fall), the need for logistical mobility relaxed and Cody hunter-gatherers more frequently employed a foraging subsistence strategy. In so doing, they frequently moved residential camps as the biotic resources became depleted, while maintaining the option to reuse favorable areas (Figure 9.8). As Cody hunter-gatherers moved through the uplift, they embedded toolstone procurement into their activities, at times sent task groups to procure toolstone when the need arose, or both. Either way, a dominant focus on local toolstone would develop, as is expected in a core area land-use strategy. Nonlocal toolstone potentially entered the system as leftovers from prior land-use practices—as is perhaps indicated in the Alberta component at Locality I—or from occasional short-term logistical activities outside the Hartville Uplift (Figure 9.8, dashed lines) during which Cody hunter-gatherers potentially transported small amounts of nonlocal toolstone back to camp, as may be the case with the White River Group silica recovered from the Cody I and V components. Given that the Hartville Uplift was probably too small to support the annual round of any one Paleoindian group (see Knell 2007), Cody groups presumably left the uplift for long periods (Figure 9.8, dotted lines). The proposed pattern provides a dynamic view of Cody land-use organization in a small region of the Great Plains, and one that could be tested with further research in the Hartville Uplift or with data from other well-studied core areas.

#### *Northern and Northwestern Great Plains*

Knell and Hill (2012) tested the same land-use model presented here but from the regional-scale perspective of the northern and northwestern Great Plains and Rocky Mountains. They obtained faunal and lithic data from 33 Cody complex sites, finding that Cody groups in the comparatively resource-rich foothills-mountains usually tethered their land-use and subsistence exploits to localized regions (i.e., regionally restricted) for a protracted portion of the year. Here Cody groups made spatially limited movements in which they relied on local lithic materials, dispersed bison herds, and a wide variety of plant and animal resources. Conversely, Cody groups in the plains grasslands and the alluvial valleys and adjacent grasslands more often were nonregionally focused, having rapidly moved through and within these regions while making many residential and logistical moves over vast areas. They targeted aggregated bison herds, resulting in many kill and processing sites with high minimum number of individual (MNI) values, and geared up in preparation for kills, resulting in many long use-life tools created from nonlocal lithic materials.

The Hartville Uplift is a domal uplift that is more akin to the foothill-mountain zone than the grassland plains. As such, the patterning at Hell Gap ideally should fit within the regional-scale foothills-mountains pattern. The core area land-use strategy inferred for the Cody I and V components indeed fits within the regional-scale framework of regionally restricted land-use in productive resource areas such as offered by the foothill-mountain zone. It thus appears that the land-use patterning at Hell Gap corresponds to the broader pattern of regionally restricted land use in the foothills-mountains (also see Hill and Knell, this volume), and is fairly representative of overall Cody land-use organization in foothill-mountain zones.

### Conclusion

The land-use model based on optimal foraging, temporal resource predictability, and toolstone availability accurately predicted how variations in biotic and abiotic resource structure influenced Cody complex land use at Hell Gap. Results of the five test expectations suggest that Cody I and V hunter-gatherers used Hell Gap as a single location within a broader core area land-use strategy centered on the Hartville Uplift, whereas the signatures for the Alberta component are indeterminate. The analyses ultimately reveal that the Cody I and V hunter-gatherers at Hell Gap (1) employed the optimal land-use strategy anticipated for the Hartville Uplift and broader foothill-mountain zone, and thereby maximized caloric return-rates, and (2) were core area focused in a productive

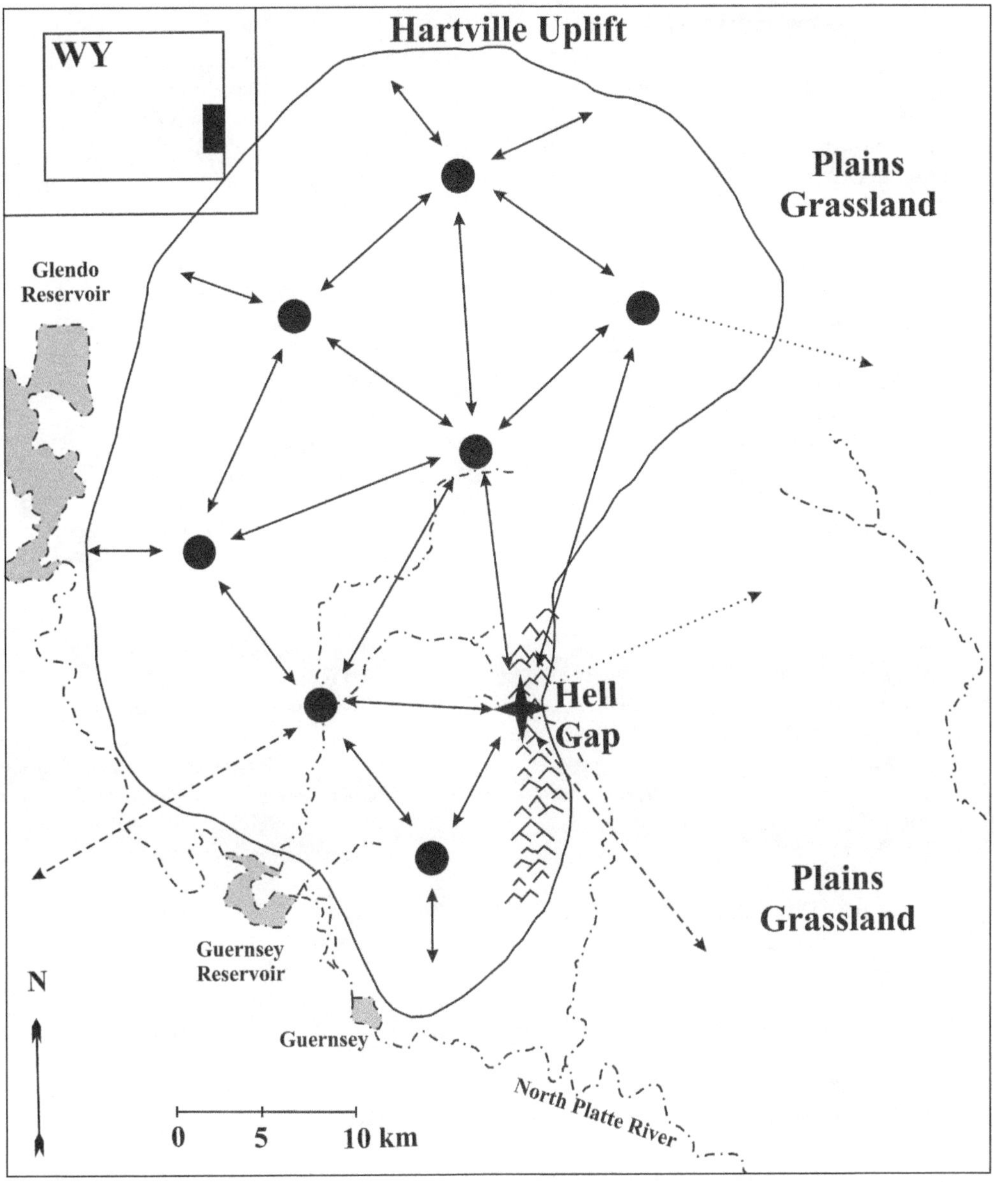


FIGURE 9.8. Map of the Hartville Uplift with a schematic diagram of Hell Gap as a location within a core area land-use strategy centered on the Hartville Uplift. Base map courtesy of Marcel Kornfeld.

resource zone with a high kcal/ha abundance, seasonally predictable biotic resources, and at least one primary source of local, high-quality toolstone. The land-use pattern identified for the Cody I and V components at Hell Gap fits neatly within the regional-scale pattern of land use in the foothills-mountains identified by Knell and Hill (2012). Moreover, Knell and Hill indicate that Cody complex hunter-gatherers were nonregionally restricted in low-productivity resource areas like the plains grasslands and alluvial valleys with adjacent grasslands, which have a low kcal/ha abundance of biotic resources, seasonally unpredictable biotic resources, and no, few, or only secondary deposits of local, high-quality toolstone. These findings not only show heretofore undocumented aspects of Cody complex land use at the local and regional scales but also improve our understanding of Cody land-use organization dynamics.

## Acknowledgments

I thank William Andrefsky, Gary Huckleberry, Tim Kohler, Mary Lou Larson, and Matthew Root for their comments, guidance, and assistance with the dissertation research that led to this chapter, and Mark Muñiz and Matthew E. Hill Jr. for comments on prior drafts of this chapter. Thanks also go to the George C. Frison Institute of Archaeology and Anthropology at the University of Wyoming, which provided partial financial support for this research, as well as to the National Endowment for the Humanities (grant #RK-20187-95), the Wenner-Gren Anthropological Foundation (grant #6311), and the Wyoming Archeological Foundation for their support in curation and analysis of the 1960s Hell Gap material. Partial financial support was also provided by the Don E. Crabtree Lithic Technology and Nicholas Michael Scoales scholarships through Washington State University, Department of Anthropology.

## References

Amick, Daniel S.
1994 *Folsom Diet Breadth and Land Use in the American Southwest.* Ph.D. dissertation, University of New Mexico, Albuquerque. University Microfilms, Ann Arbor, Michigan.

Andrefsky, William, Jr.
1994 Raw-Material Availability and the Organization of Technology. *American Antiquity* 59:21–34.

Bamforth, Douglas B.
1986 Technological Efficiency and Tool Curation. *American Antiquity* 51:38–50.
1988 *Ecology and Human Organization on the Great Plains.* Plenum Press, New York.
2002a High-Tech Foragers? Folsom and Later Paleoindian Technology on the Great Plains. *Journal of World Prehistory* 16:55–98.
2002b The Paleoindian Occupation of the Medicine Creek Drainage, Southwestern Nebraska. In *Medicine Creek: Seventy Years of Archaeological Investigations*, edited by Donna C. Roper, pp. 54–83. University of Alabama Press, Tuscaloosa.

Bettinger, Robert L.
1991 *Hunter-Gatherers: Archaeological and Evolutionary Theory.* Plenum Press, New York.

Blackmar, Jeannette M.
2001 Regional Variability in Clovis, Folsom, and Cody Land Use. *Plains Anthropologist* 46: 65–94.

Brantingham, Jeffrey
2003 A Neutral Model of Stone Raw Material Procurement. *American Antiquity* 68:487–509.
2006 Measuring Forager Mobility. *Current Anthropology* 47:435–459.

Carr, Dillon H.
2005 The Organization of Late Paleoindian Lithic Procurement Strategies in Western Wisconsin. *Midcontinental Journal of Archaeology* 30:3–36.

Carr, Dillon H., and Robert Boszhardt
2010 The Organisation of Lithic Procurement at Silver Mound, Wisconsin: Source of Hixton Silicified Sandstone. In *Ancient Mines and Quarries: A Trans-Atlantic Perspective*, edited by Margaret Brewer-LaPorta, Adrian Burke, and David Field, pp. 132–141. Oxbow Books, Oxford.

Cashdan, Elizabeth
1992 Spatial Organization and Habitat Use. In *Evolutionary Ecology and Human Behavior*, edited by Eric Alden Smith and Bruce Winterhalder, pp. 237–266. Aldine de Gruyter, New York.

Charnov, E. L.
1976 Optimal Foraging, the Marginal Value Theorem. *Theoretical Population Biology* 9:129–136.

Colwell, Robert K.
1974 Predictability, Constancy, and Contingency of Periodic Phenomena. *Ecology* 55:1148–1153.

Custer, Jay F., John A. Cavallo, and R. Michael Stewart
1983 Lithic Procurement and Paleo-Indian Settlement Patterns on the Middle Atlantic Coastal Plain. *North American Archaeologist* 4:263–276.

Domanski, Marian, and John A. Webb
1992 Effect of Heat Treatment on Siliceous Rocks Used in Prehistoric Lithic Technology. *Journal of Archaeological Science* 19:601–614.

Ebert, James I., and Timothy A. Kohler
1988 The Theoretical Basis of Archaeological Predictive Modeling and a Consideration of Appropriate Data-Collection Methods. In *Quantifying the Present and Predicting the Past: Theory, Method, and Application of Archaeological Predictive Modeling*, edited by W. James Judge and Lynne Sebastian, pp. 97–171. U.S. Department of the Interior, Bureau of Land Management, Denver, Colorado.

Gardner, William M.
1983 Stop Me If You've Heard This One Before: The Flint Run Paleoindian Complex Revisited. *Archaeology of Eastern North America* 11:49–64.

Gould, Richard A., and Sherry Saggers
1985 Lithic Procurement in Central Australia: A Closer Look at Binford's Idea of Embeddedness in Archaeology. *American Antiquity* 50: 117–136.

Gramly, Richard Michael
1980 Raw Materials Source Areas and "Curated" Tool Assemblages. *American Antiquity* 45: 823–833.

Hall, Christopher T.
2004 Evaluating Prehistoric Hunter-Gatherer Mobility, Land Use, and Technological Organization Strategies. In *Aggregate Analysis in Chipped Stone*, edited by Christopher T. Hall and Mary Lou Larson, pp. 139–155. University of Utah Press, Salt Lake City.

Hill, Matthew Glenn, and Marcel Kornfeld
1999 Inferring Season of Kill for a Cody-Complex Bonebed in Middle Park, Colorado. *Current Research in the Pleistocene* 16:30–32.

Ingbar, Eric E.
1994 Lithic Raw Material Selection and Technological Organization. In *The Organization of North American Prehistoric Chipped Stone Tool Technologies*, edited by Philip J. Carr, pp. 45–56. International Monographs in Prehistory Archaeological Series No. 7. Ann Arbor, Michigan.

Irwin-Williams, Cynthia, Henry T. Irwin, George A. Agogino, and C. Vance Haynes Jr.
1973 Hell Gap: A Paleo-Indian Occupation on the High Plains. *Plains Anthropologist* 18:40–52.

Johnson, Ann, Brian Reeves, and Mack Shortt
2004 *Osprey Beach (Site 48YE409/410), Yellowstone National Park, Wyoming*. Lifeways of Canada. Submitted to Yellowstone Center for Resources, Yellowstone National Park, Cooperative Agreement No. CA-1268-1-9017 between Montana State University, Bozeman, and the National Park Service. Copies available from Yellowstone Center for Resources, Mammoth, Wyoming.

Johnson, LeRoy, Jr.
1989 *Great Plains Interlopers in the Eastern Woodlands during Late Paleo-Indian Times*. Texas Historical Commission, Office of the State Archeologist, Report No. 36. Austin.

Kelly, Robert L.
1995 *The Foraging Spectrum: Diversity in Hunter-Gatherer Lifeways*. Smithsonian Institution Press, New York.

Knell, Edward J.
2007 The Organization of Late Paleoindian Cody Complex Land-Use on the North American Great Plains. Unpublished Ph.D. dissertation, Department of Anthropology, Washington State University, Pullman.
2009 Cody Complex at Locality I. In *Hell Gap: A Stratified Paleoindian Campsite at the Edge of the Rockies*, edited by Mary Lou Larson, Marcel Kornfeld, and George C. Frison, pp. 180–194. University of Utah Press, Salt Lake City.
2012 Minimum Analytical Nodules and Late Paleoindian Cody Complex Lithic Technological Organization at Hell Gap, Wyoming. *Plains Anthropologist*, in press.

Knell, Edward J., and Matthew E. Hill Jr.
2012 Linking Bones and Stones: Regional Variation in Late Paleoindian Cody Complex Land Use and Foraging Strategies. *American Antiquity* 77:40–70.

Knell, Edward J., Matthew G. Hill, and Andrés D. Izeta
2009 The Locality IIIS/V Eden Complex. In *Hell Gap: A Stratified Paleoindian Campsite at the Edge of the Rockies*, edited by Mary Lou Larson, Marcel Kornfeld, and George C. Frison, pp. 157–179. University of Utah Press, Salt Lake City.

Knudson, Ruthann
2002 Medicine Creek Is a Paleoindian Cultural Ecotone: The Red Smoke Assemblage. In *Medicine Creek: Seventy Years of Archaeological Investigations*, edited by Donna C. Roper, pp. 84–141. University of Alabama Press, Tuscaloosa.

Kornfeld, Marcel
1994 *Pull of the Hills: Affluent Foragers of the Western Black Hills*. Ph.D. dissertation, University of Massachusetts, Amherst. University Microfilms, Ann Arbor, Michigan.

Kornfeld, Marcel, and Mary Lou Larson
2009 Reinvestigation in Context: Paleoindian Prehistory at the Edge of the Rockies. In *Hell Gap: A Stratified Paleoindian Campsite on the Edge of the Rockies*, edited by Mary Lou Larson, Marcel Kornfeld, and George C. Frison, pp. 3–13. University of Utah Press, Salt Lake City.

Larson, Mary Lou, and Marcel Kornfeld
1997 Chipped Stone Nodules: Theory, Method, and Examples. *Lithic Technology* 22:4–18.

Larson, Mary Lou, Marcel Kornfeld, and George C. Frison (editors)
2009 *Hell Gap: A Stratified Paleoindian Campsite at the Edge of the Rockies*. University of Utah Press, Salt Lake City.

MacArthur, R., and E. Pianka
1966 An Optimal Use of a Patchy Environment. *American Naturalist* 100:603–609.

Meltzer, David J.
1989 Was Stone Exchanged among Eastern North American Paleoindians? In *Eastern Paleoindian Lithic Resource Use*, edited by Christopher J. Ellis and Jonathan C. Lothrop, pp. 11–39. Westview Press, Boulder, Colorado.

Miller, James C.
2009 Preliminary Analysis of Lithic Materials. In *Hell Gap: A Stratified Paleoindian Campsite at the Edge of the Rockies*, edited by Mary Lou Larson, Marcel Kornfeld, and George C. Frison, pp. 411–413. University of Utah Press, Salt Lake City.

Muñiz, Mark P.
2005 The Cody Complex Revisited: Landscape Use and Technological Organization on the Northwestern Plains. Unpublished Ph.D. dissertation, Department of Anthropology, University of Colorado, Boulder.

Pitblado, Bonnie L.
2003 *Late Paleoindian Occupation of the Southern Rocky Mountains: Early Holocene Projectile Points and Land Use in the High Country*. University Press of Colorado, Boulder.

Rapson, David J., and Laura B. Niven
2009 Appendix 1: Supplemental Zooarchaeological Tables and Figures. In *Hell Gap: A Stratified Paleoindian Campsite at the Edge of the Rockies*, edited by Mary Lou Larson, Marcel Kornfeld, and George C. Frison, pp. 365–410. University of Utah Press, Salt Lake City.

Richings-Germain, Sarah
2002 The Jerry Craig Site: A Paleoindian Bison Bonebed in the Colorado Rocky Mountains. Unpublished Master's thesis, Department of Anthropology, University of Wyoming, Laramie.

Rick, John Winfield
1978 *Heat-Altered Cherts of the Lower Illinois Valley: An Experimental Study in Prehistoric Technology*. Northwestern University Archaeological Program, Prehistoric Records No. 2. Evanston, Illinois.

Sellet, Frédéric
1999 A Dynamic View of Paleoindian Assemblages at the Hell Gap Site, Wyoming: Reconstructing Lithic Technological Systems. Unpublished Ph.D. dissertation, Department of Anthropology, Southern Methodist University, Dallas.

Smith, Edward Eugene, Jr.
1990 Paleoindian Economy and Settlement Patterns in the Wyandotte Chert Source Area, Unglaciated South-Central Indiana. In *Early Paleoindian Economies of Eastern North America*, edited by Kenneth B. Tankersley and Barrt L. Isaac, pp. 217–258. Research in Economic Anthropology, Supplement No. 5. JAI Press, Greenwich, Connecticut.
1991 *Paleo-Indian Settlement and Lithic Procurement Patterns in the Karstic Region of South-central Indiana*. Ph.D. dissertation, Indiana University, Bloomington. University Microfilms, Ann Arbor, Michigan.

Smith, Eric Alden
1991 *Inujjuamiut Foraging Strategies: Evolutionary Ecology of an Arctic Hunting Economy*. Aldine de Gruyter, New York.

Stanford, Dennis
1999 Paleoindian Archaeology and Late Pleistocene Environments in the Plains and Southwestern United States. In *Ice Age Peoples of North America: Environments, Origins, and Adaptations*, edited by Robson Bonnichsen and Karen L. Turnmire, pp. 281–339. Center for the Study of the First Americans. Oregon State University Press, Corvallis.

Stephens, David W., and John R. Krebs
1986 *Foraging Theory*. Princeton University Press, Princeton, New Jersey.

Whallon, Robert, William A. Lovis, and Robert K. Hitchcock (editors)
2011 *Information and Its Role in Hunter-Gatherer Bands*. Cotsen Institute of Archaeology Press, University of California, Los Angeles.

Willey, Gordon R.
1953 *Prehistoric Settlement Patterns in the Virú Valley, Peru*. Bureau of American Ethnology Bulletin No. 155. Smithsonian Institution, Washington, D.C.

Winterhalder, Bruce
1981a Foraging Strategies in the Boreal Forest: An Analysis of Cree Hunting and Gathering. In *Hunter-Gatherer Foraging Strategies: Ethnographic and Archaeological Analyses*, edited by Bruce Winterhalder and Eric Alden Smith, pp. 66–98. University of Chicago Press, Chicago.
1981b Optimal Foraging Strategies and Hunter-Gatherer Research in Anthropology: Theory and Models. In *Hunter-Gatherer Foraging Strategies: Ethnographic and Archaeological Analyses*, edited by Bruce Winterhalder and Eric Alden Smith, pp. 13–35. University of Chicago Press, Chicago.

10

# Managing Risk on the Western Plains during the Cody Complex

Mark P. Muñiz

The lifeways practiced by the Nunamiut, !Kung, Alyawara, Naskapi, and others offer us a tangible sense of the hard work and uncertainty that goes into living as a hunter-gatherer. Uncertainty and risk pervade attempts to provide food for the family, make and use technology, negotiate social relationships, and deal with outsiders (especially anthropologists). Although hunter-gatherers may have a restricted range of material culture, their social lives are very complex. As such, dealing with risk can often be approached through social mechanisms such as sexual division of labor, relying on extended family (real or fictive), or banking social debt in the form of reciprocal obligations with neighbors who can be called upon in times of trouble (see discussions and examples in Bettinger 1991; Bicchieri 1972; Dahlberg 1981; Ingold et al. 1988; Kelly 1995; Lee and DeVore 1968; Marshall 1998; Panter-Brick et al. 2001). Certainly Paleoindian hunter-gatherers also used social means for managing risk. Unlike the ethnographic hunter-gatherers, however, this side of Paleoindian culture is largely invisible to archaeologists. The evidence we must rely on to understand how Paleoindians dealt with risk is made up of material culture, subsistence remains, and scant traces of how these people moved across a landscape that may seem like a foreign country when viewed from 10,000 years later.

The goal of this chapter is to explore how Cody complex peoples organized lithic technology to manage the risk associated with tool production, hunting, butchery, and hide working at two late Paleoindian sites: Jurgens, Colorado, and Locality V at Hell Gap, Wyoming. To do this, I first define risk, establish how the management of risk is to be evaluated, and then construct a risk management model to predict what Cody people might have done so that we may compare it with what they actually did. In the course of this examination, we will learn more about late Paleoindian human behavior and about the efficacy of the risk management model developed to explore that behavior. The former will enrich our understanding of the human experience on this planet, and the latter will sharpen archaeologists' ability to further explore and describe that experience.

## Thinking about Risk

The study of risk in archaeology has a long but relatively undeveloped history over the past three decades. Elsewhere (Muñiz 2005) I provide an in-depth discussion of the theoretical trajectory of the risk concept for lithic technological organization studies. Early work by Torrence (1983, 1989) and Bleed (1986, 1991, 2001) established basic parameters for how archaeologists began to grapple with the idea that material culture was actively designed to lessen the probability of failure to perform as expected and thus could be used to maximize the extraction of resources. Bamforth and Bleed (1997) refined the earlier approaches to evaluating risk through lithic technology for hunter-gatherer archaeological sites. The critical advance that Bamforth and Bleed provided was to define risk in standard terms that could be tested with archaeological data. To Bamforth and Bleed (1997), risk is composed of (1) the probability of failure, (2) the cost of failure, and (3) the technological costs associated with trying to minimize the probability of failure and thus avoid the costs of failure. Bamforth and Bleed sought to develop quantitative measures for each of these three elements. Muñiz (2005) continued the work of Bamforth and Bleed by modifying the approach for use with qualitative data.

For the research presented here, the *probability of failure* refers to the probability that an actor will fail to successfully complete an activity, and this failure can be affected by the performance of technology and human behavior. The *cost of failure* refers to how much the actor loses if an activity fails. This includes all losses resulting from the failed activity (e.g., lithic raw material wasted during the failed production of a biface, calories lost from spoiled meat, or lives lost from starvation). *Technological costs* are directly aimed at minimizing the probability of failure. Technological costs include all the expenditures required in the pursuit of successfully completing an activity and comprise time, energy, raw materials, knowledge, and social organization.

Significantly, Bamforth and Bleed (1997) also noted that because factors such as methods for acquiring resources and access to alternative resources vary widely, depending on seasonal environmental conditions, group size, social organization, and so on, the decisions a group makes regarding risk may also vary situationally. This is an important component of the risk management analytical framework because it considers the effects of local situational factors on human decision making. The risk management approach is best thought of as a heuristic device that is well suited to explore the continuum of risk management strategies employed in the context of specific site behaviors and resource availability. The risk model predictions developed here do not provide exact probabilities of what Paleoindian hunter-gatherers should have done. They do, however, help us better understand the relationships between the risk variables that structured Paleoindian decision making and the human behavioral processes that responded to those variables.

The approach to evaluating risk management taken here relies on an optimization principle shared throughout human behavioral ecology: people generally wish to maximize the net return for energy expended. For the risk management approach, the energy is spent on technological costs, and the intended maximized return is on the resource acquired, which can be ensured through reducing the probability of failure to zero. Therefore, technological costs provide the primary constraint on a group's ability to reduce the probability of failure in the face of high failure costs (Bamforth and Bleed 1997). While the probability of failure can theoretically be reduced to zero if a high enough technological cost is paid, the degree to which that probability is *actually* reduced is determined by how much the group can afford to pay. Technological costs serve to reduce failure probabilities but also influence behaviors such as long-distance transport, tool manufacture, maintenance and recycling, and discard.

To predict how much a group should invest in technological costs for a specific activity, we need to know the failure costs that are unique to that activity and the range of technological costs that the group can afford. If the cost of failure is low, the model predicts that technological costs should also be low. This condition holds when there are abundant alternative resources that can offset failure. As the cost of failure increases, a proportional increase in the required technological costs to lower the probability of failure (i.e., prevent paying the failure costs) is also expected. The model predicts that a group will pay increasing technological costs until it can no longer afford them.

The probability of failure varies independently from the cost of failure. Both low and very high probabilities of failure result in low technological costs (Figure 10.1). This relationship results from the underlying optimization principle that posits that humans will generally seek the maximum return on their investments. A low probability of failure requires only a low technological cost in response. As that probability rises and eventually becomes moderate, the model predicts that an actor will pay the gradually rising technology costs to decrease the likelihood of failure. However, as the probability of failure continues to increase, it eventually reaches such a high level

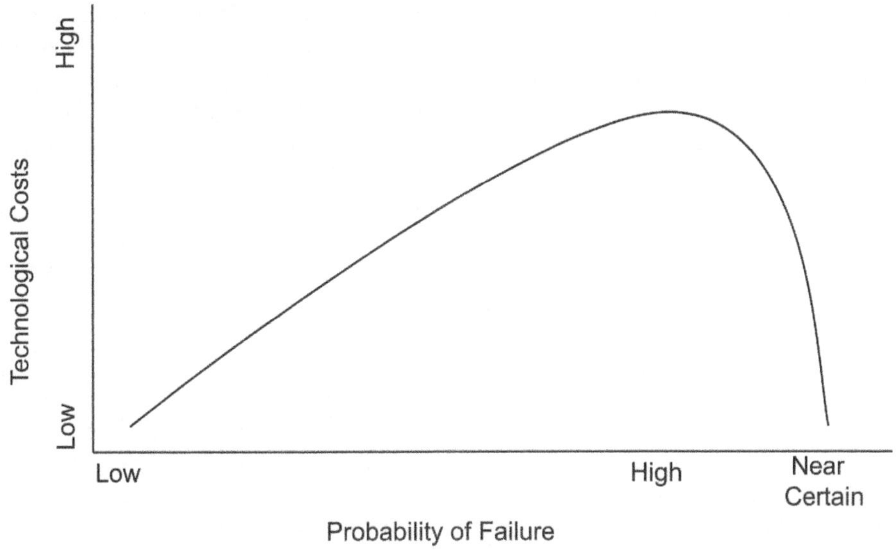


FIGURE 10.1. Proposed relationship between the probability of failure and technological costs.

that a return on any additional technological investment is very improbable and unexpected. At this point the practical (versus theoretical) technological cost drops back to low again because the model predicts that a logical actor recognizes that failure is almost certain and that pursuing the activity does not warrant paying very high technological costs since the expense will almost certainly be wasted.

In real terms, what are the thresholds at which an activity shifts from having a low, to moderate, to high probability of failure or cost of failure, and at what level is the probability of failure too high to warrant additional technological investment? The exact quantitative figures are unknown because of the situational nature of the variability that structures these probabilities. Paleoindians were not likely to figure out the mathematical odds of success before embarking on an activity. Instead, the risk management framework hypothesizes that they most likely estimated the probability of success based on a logical intuitive understanding of the relationships between the three risk variables described above. Therefore, developing risk model predictions based on quantitative estimates for these same variables could be misleading and unnecessary. To get around this apparent impasse, I conduct a comparative analysis of two sites with different risk model predictions in order to evaluate the behaviors at those sites in relation to each other. The outcome of this comparative analysis will indicate if the risk model predictions are consistent with what is empirically observed. When developing relative estimates for the risk model variables, we must avoid circular logic that uses the observable end results of Cody peoples' behavior (e.g., a well-crafted spear point) to predict failure costs that may have initially structured that same behavior (e.g., assuming that only well-made points will effectively kill prey). Such circular logic can be avoided if we use independent geological and paleoenvironmental data to estimate the probability and costs of failure based on the availability of alternative resources.

Even with these limitations, the benefit of using the risk management analytical framework is that the logic and assumptions that structure the approach are simple and straightforward, and the model predictions can be evaluated with empirical observations. Outcomes that are consistent with risk model predictions indicate that Cody peoples employed the same basic logic outlined here, and archaeologists may use this understanding to hypothesize about other aspects of Cody peoples' lives. However, when the model is tested and the outcomes diverge from expectations, we must figure out if the reason for the divergence is a limitation or flaw in the model or if the "risky" behavior is an intentional response unique to Cody culture. It is through identifying such unique cultural responses that we will learn how different groups of people thought about and managed risk, and in so doing, we may also learn something of their cultural priorities.

### Building Risk Management Model Predictions

The underlying principle for developing risk model predictions is that in the face of a high cost of failure for a specific activity, Cody people should try to minimize the probability of failure by paying the required technological costs (Bamforth and Bleed 1997; Muñiz 2005). Two simplifying assumptions are required for developing a relative ranking of the technological costs associated with producing lithic technology.

The first holds that when the same toolstone is used, flake tools are cheaper and less risky to make than unifacial tools, which in turn are less risky and less expensive to make than bifacial tools. For clarity, several definitions are offered to distinguish flake tools from unifaces. If the original flake margins are still intact and the piece lacks significant retouch (defined as generally >2 mm), it is considered an *unmodified flake*. If the original margins are still discernible but the edge exhibits unifacial or bifacial microflaking due to use or light intentional retouch, it is considered an *edge-modified* flake. Both of these conditions are categorized as a "flake tool" for this study. If the original margins are no longer discernible due to patterned unifacial retouch, even if this occurs along a restricted portion of the edge, it is considered a *unifacial tool*. Thus, a flake tool that is resharpened significantly during use can be discarded as a uniface. It is acknowledged that determinations of "flake tool" or "uniface" following these definitions may vary slightly between researchers based on their ability and confidence identifying the original flake morphology. The unifacial tool category also includes more traditional forms such as hafted end scrapers, which are not likely to be mistaken for flake tools.

As one progresses through manufacturing a flake tool, a uniface, and a biface, additional raw material is used and more percussion strokes are required as more mass is removed and more edges are shaped for each respective form. Each additional percussion stroke during manufacture increases the opportunity to break the tool, resulting in failure for the activity. Given this relationship, expectations for the technological costs of certain activities can be ranked based on the range of tools used for those activities.

The second assumption holds that using exotic toolstone (procured from >40 km away, following Meltzer 1989 and Kelly 1995) entails a higher technological cost than using a local source. This relationship applies to direct procurement because as the transport distance increases, associated expenditures in time and energy also increase. The relationship also holds for indirect procurement because as the reliance on trade for toolstone increases, associated social expenditures of time, energy, and material goods required to maintain the trade relationship also increase. Meeting the lowest technological cost results in manufacturing simple flake tools made from local raw materials, while the highest technological costs require making complex bifaces from exotic raw materials (Muñiz 2005).

The risk variables associated with the activities of hunting, butchery, and hide working vary in relation to local situational contexts. The following sections outline risk model expectations for lithic technology in situations with low, medium, and high technological costs for these three activities.

Situations with low technological costs occur for activities with a low probability and cost of failure, typically in settings where there are abundant alternative resources to offset activity failure. In this scenario, the frequency and diversity of specialized tools that are shaped and used for a single, specific function should be low since a greater number of tools with generalized shapes used for multiple tasks meet the minimum functional requirements. For the activity of hunting, low technological cost does not require that brand-new points be made for a specific hunt during a special gearing-up period (cf. Bamforth 1991). Instead, the model predicts that points can be used that are heavily resharpened or recovered from broken fragments and these should make up a large portion of the point assemblage. For butchery, low technological cost allows Cody peoples to rely heavily on flake tools, many of which may be discarded in good condition well before reaching exhaustion. The model predicts that flake butchery tools should significantly outnumber unifacial tools. For hide working, low technological cost allows variability in end scraper morphology because end scrapers may be made in response to situational needs rather than in anticipation of use. As with flakes used for butchery, end scrapers may be discarded in good condition before breaking.

When local conditions lack alternative resources to mitigate failure, or an activity favors a moderate probability of failure, technological costs are ranked moderate. A moderate ranking means that an adequate supply of tools should be ready well before the activity begins, including newly made backups to replace broken or worn tools. In the case of hunting, the point assemblage should have a mix of reworked and newly made points that were produced specifically for an anticipated hunt. The butchery toolkit should still be dominated by flake tools but should also have at least a moderate proportion of unifacial tools that resulted from prolonged maintenance of the original flakes. The butchery toolkit may also include some functionally specialized tools such as Cody knives and ultrathin bifaces made in advance of the activity. Elsewhere, I have noted that Cody ultrathin bifaces were made and used for butchering in an analogous way to older Folsom versions (Muñiz 2004, 2005). Prior research has also identified a very limited range of butchery functions for Cody knives (Muñiz 2005 and additional data in possession of the author). For hide working, a significant portion of the hafted end scrapers should demonstrate morphological regularity as a result of being made in advance of need. A smaller portion of the end scrapers should be discarded before breakage or exhaustion than when technological costs are ranked low.

For situations in which the probability of failure is significant (but not a foregone conclusion) and the cost of failure is high, technological costs are ranked high. Under these conditions, the general well-being of the group may be in danger and lithic tool technology must perform very well to avoid activity failure. A large number of new tools and adequate backups should be made well in advance of need, and tool shape diversity should be the highest among all three scenarios since specialized tools are made to perform specific functions. In this scenario, it is much more important to have a range of specialized tools that perform specific functions very well than a number of generalized tools that perform the same range of functions less efficiently and/or effectively. The model predicts that a hunting toolkit for these conditions will comprise predominantly new points made well in advance of a specific hunt. The butchery toolkit should include flake tools and a large number of unifacial tools that resulted from continued maintenance of the flakes during completion of the activity. Specialized butchery tools, such as Cody knives and ultrathin bifaces, should be present in greater numbers than in the other scenarios. Very few butchery tools should be discarded before breakage or exhaustion, and the specialized tools may be used even after breakage. For the activity of hide working, there should be an abundant number of hafted end scrapers with regular morphologies made well in advance of arriving at the site, and almost all of them should be heavily resharpened or broken before being discarded. To help clarify how these model expectations are applied to actual sites, Table 10.1 presents a summary of the risk model predictions and outcomes for Cody lithic technological organization at Jurgens and Hell Gap Locality V. The specific model predictions for these sites are discussed in more detail below.

## Evaluating the Risk Management Model for Cody Complex Paleoindians

In addition to the paleoenvironmental and geologic data required for evaluating the risk model predictions, independent data are needed for how a group's lithic technology was organized into functionally specific toolkits. For this study, a toolkit is defined as a set of tools that were all used for the same basic activity (e.g., butchery) even though specific tasks may vary within that activity (e.g., removing hide from a carcass, quartering an animal, stripping meat from bone). High-magnification microwear analysis was used to identify diagnostic use-wear traces that were shared by tools within activity-specific toolkits. Microwear analysis plays a key role for this study because it provides an independent line of evidence to identify tools that were used as part of the same toolkit, even though the tools themselves display considerable variability in shape. High-magnification microwear analysis is especially valuable for identifying butchery toolkits

**TABLE 10.1.** Cody Lithic Technology Risk Management Model Predictions and Outcomes.

| Site Activity | Technological Costs | Risk Model Prediction | Analytical Outcome | Points of Divergence from Model Predictions |
|---|---|---|---|---|
| **Tool Manufacture** | | | | |
| Jurgens | Moderate–High | (1) predominant use of exotic toolstone<br>(2) lots of tool recycling | (1) model supported<br>(2) model not supported | (2) very infrequent tool recycling |
| Locality V, Hell Gap | Low | (1) predominant use of local toolstone<br>(2) little tool recycling | (1) and (2) model strongly supported | — |
| **Hunting** | | | | |
| Jurgens | Low | (1) wide range of options for subsistence technology | (1) heavy reliance on exotic toolstone; model support neutral | (1) paid a higher technological cost than model predicted |
| Locality V, Hell Gap | Low | (1) wide range of options for subsistence technology | (1) heavy reliance on local toolstone; model support neutral | — |
| **Light Butchery** | | | | |
| Jurgens | Moderate–High | (1) use exotic stone<br>(2) more unifacial tools than flakes<br>(3) use specialized bifaces | (1) model supported<br>(2) model not supported<br>(3) model supported | (2) more flake tools than predicted |
| Locality V, Hell Gap | Low | (1) use local stone<br>(2) more flake tools than unifaces | (1) model supported<br>(2) model not supported | (2) more unifaces than predicted |
| **Heavy Butchery** | | | | |
| Jurgens | Moderate–High | (1) use exotic stone<br>(2) more unifacial tools than flakes and bifaces | (1) model somewhat supported<br>(2) model somewhat supported | (2) functional role of specialized bifaces somewhat unexpected |
| Locality V, Hell Gap | Low | (1) use local stone<br>(2) more flake tools than unifaces and bifaces | (1) model somewhat supported<br>(2) model supported | (1) use of exotic stone somewhat unexpected |
| **Hide Working** | | | | |
| Jurgens | High | (1) use exotic toolstone<br>(2) regular morphology<br>(3) tools heavily resharpened and/or used to exhaustion | (1) model supported<br>(2) model not supported<br>(3) model not supported | (2) large standard deviation in width:thickness ratio suggests variable haft sizes<br>(3) data suggest discard prior to exhaustion |
| Locality V, Hell Gap | Low–Moderate | (1) use local toolstone<br>(2) variable tool morphology<br>(3) not as heavily resharpened as high technological cost site | (1) model not supported<br>(2) model not supported<br>(3) model somewhat supported | (1) relatively high proportion of exotic raw material<br>(2) morphology more standardized than at Jurgens |

that comprise a wide range of flakes, unifaces, and bifaces. For the purpose of evaluating risk model predictions, a combination of microwear results and site characteristics were used to identify the activities of (1) hunting, indicated by the co-occurrence of projectile points with diagnostic use-wear traces of impact and the faunal remains of prey species; (2) butchery, indicated by the co-occurrence of tools with diagnostic traces of butchery use-wear and the presence of dismembered carcasses; (3) hide working, indicated by end scrapers with diagnostic traces of wet or dry hide wear preserved on their bits; and (4) lithic tool maintenance and manufacture, indicated by debitage that may include a range of production and maintenance strategies.

**TABLE 10.2.** Summary Data for Site Characteristics for Jurgens and Hell Gap Locality V.

| Site Characteristics | Jurgens | Locality V, Hell Gap |
|---|---|---|
| $^{14}C$ date of occupation | 9070 ± 90 | 8890 ± 110; 9050 ± 160 |
| Point style | Kersey | Eden |
| Excavation area | 256 $m^2$ | 47 $m^2$ |
| Seasonality | Fall | Late spring to early winter |
| Artifact assemblage | 528 stone tools, cores, ground stone, etc.; 1656 debitage; 9 organic tools; 1 mineral concretion pipe | 169 tools, cores, ground stone, etc.; 8889 debitage[a] |
| Fauna | 68–74 bison<br>7–8 pronghorn<br>3–4 deer<br>2–4 elk<br>1 moose<br>6 species of small mammals: beaver, marmot, muskrat, pocket gopher, rabbit, and skunk | 7 bison<br>1 deer<br>1 canid<br>1 rabbit |
| Local toolstone | Secondary river cobbles of variable-quality quartzite, chert, and silicified wood | Good-quality chert and fine-grained quartzite from the Hartville Uplift |
| Overall food resource availability | Probably diverse and abundant | Probably abundant |
| Primary references | Hill 2002; Muñiz 2005; Wheat 1979 | Haynes 2009; Irwin 1967; Irwin-Williams et al. 1973; Knell 2007; Knell et al. 2009; Muñiz 2005, 2009 |

[a] Locality V debitage figure differs from Muñiz 2005 to reflect changes in Knell 2007 and Knell et al. 2009.

The risk management analytical framework was applied to the Cody complex occupation at Jurgens, Colorado, and the Eden component from Locality V at Hell Gap, Wyoming (Figure 10.2). The Hell Gap site is located in a valley within the Hartville Uplift and contains several distinct Paleoindian occupation areas (Larson et al. 2009). During the time of the Cody complex, Locality V at Hell Gap was used intermittently between the spring and fall as a camp and lithic workshop by people who made Eden-style projectile points (Knell et al. 2009). The relatively small excavation area (47 $m^2$) uncovered more than 9000 artifacts and a small faunal assemblage (Knell 2007; Knell et al. 2009). The Jurgens site is located on the Kersey Terrace, immediately south of the South Platte River. Wheat's (1979) excavation (256 $m^2$) uncovered three activity areas with more than 2500 artifacts, around 70 bison that were butchered in the fall, and a style of projectile point that he classified as "Kersey."

Jurgens and Locality V have important similarities in the range of activities carried out, making the occupations well suited for a risk management comparison (Table 10.2). Both sites have artifacts, use-wear data, and faunal remains that indicate hunting, animal processing, hide working, and tool maintenance and manufacture. The radiocarbon dates for both sites overlap at one standard deviation and cluster around 9000 $^{14}C$ yr BP (10,220–10,185 cal BP). The Eden occupation at Locality V has been dated to 8890 ± 110 (collagen) (9629–10,235 cal BP) and 9050 ± 160 (apatite) (9675–10,642 cal BP) (Haynes 2009). A combined charcoal sample from Jurgens was dated to 9070 ± 90 (9917–10,495 cal BP) (Wheat 1979).

The two sites also have some differences important to this study (Table 10.2). First, the excavation at Jurgens opened more than five times the area explored at Locality V. Second, there are about ten times as many bison at Jurgens as at Locality V, and Jurgens also contains a much greater diversity of animal species. Third, Locality V has more than four times the amount of debitage than Jurgens, but Jurgens has more than nine times as many end scrapers. Fourth, high-quality lithic raw materials are locally available at Locality V but are very rare to absent at Jurgens. Finally, as I have noted (Muñiz 2005), the condition of the bone (analyzed in Hill 2002), range of artifacts, minimum analytical nodules and raw material distributions, and depositional setting indicate that the Jurgens site most likely represents a single-component occupation rather than three

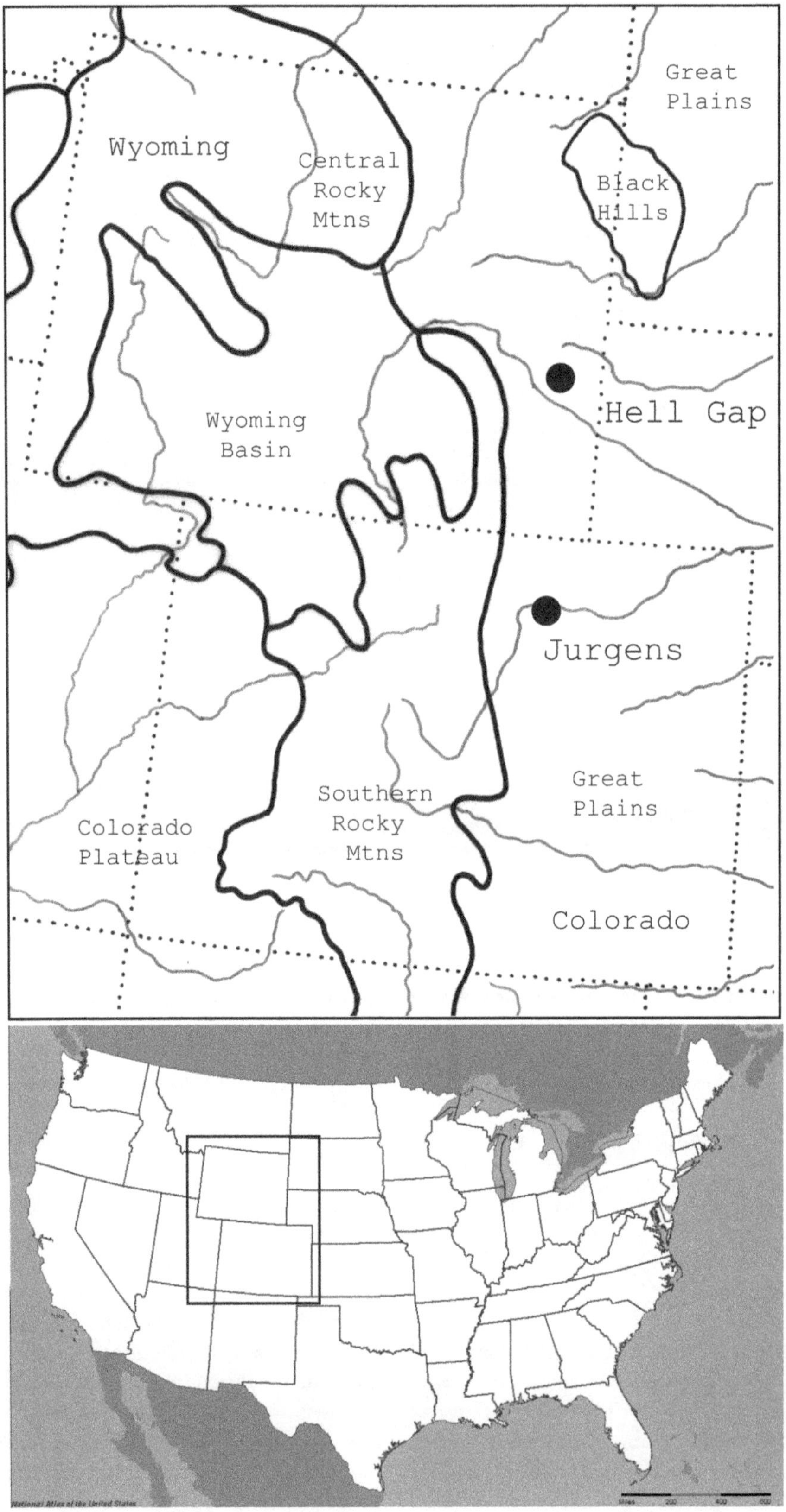


FIGURE 10.2. Location of Jurgens and Hell Gap sites.

distinct occupations as originally proposed by Wheat (1979). Conversely, the wide range in seasonality data (late spring through early winter) at Locality V indicates that this component may include more than one Cody complex occupation and the assemblage may be an aggregate (see Knell 2007; Muñiz 2005).

The assemblages from these two sites were sampled with the goal of conducting high-magnification microwear analysis on every chipped stone tool with formally shaped or intentionally retouched edges (Table 10.3). Several bifacial cores/early stage bifaces were also analyzed. It should be noted that the classification for the Locality V, Hell Gap, sample presented here differs slightly from what is reported by Knell and colleagues (2009; also Knell 2007, this volume; Knell and Hill 2012). This resulted from differences in the taxonomic systems that Knell and I used and a revision to the total amount of reported debitage (e.g., Knell 1999 and 2007). For example, Knell (1999, 2007; Knell et al. 2009) classified many artifacts as flake tools that I classified as debitage, flake tools, or unifaces based on different criteria for determining edge damage, intentional retouch, and use-wear. Some differences also exist in raw material source attributions, with my data including slightly more exotic lithic material than Knell's. I describe the Locality V sample in greater detail elsewhere (Muñiz 2005, 2009).

A sample of 145 artifacts from Locality V and 188 artifacts from Jurgens was selected for this analysis. The sample was made up primarily of formally shaped tools (e.g., bifaces and unifaces) and secondarily of edge-modified flakes that were greater than 9 $cm^2$ in overall size. In Table 10.3 the artifact class "Flakes" is distinct from "Debitage" in that flakes had some indication of patterned edge retouch or damage that distinguished them as having possibly been used. The microwear sample represents 98.6 percent of all the shaped and edge-modified artifacts from Locality V; from Jurgens the sample represents 100 percent of the unifaces and trifaces (i.e., a non-core object with three approximately equally flaked faces), 52.7 percent of the bifaces, and 11.2 percent of the potential flake tools. The remaining unanalyzed Jurgens bifaces are made from raw materials unsuitable for microwear analysis (e.g., quartzite, basalt, silicified sediment). The remaining flakes largely lacked patterned retouch but are included here in the flake tool class for consistency with Wheat (1979). I provide in-depth descriptions of the sampling strategy, cleaning and preparation, and methods used for the microwear analysis elsewhere (Muñiz 2005). Diagnostic traces of use-wear related to hunting, butchery, and hide working were found on 30.3 percent of the Locality V sample and 46.3 percent of the Jurgens sample (Table 10.3).

**TABLE 10.3.** Summary Data for Microwear Samples from Hell Gap Locality V and Jurgens.

| Site | Total Chipped Stone Sample | Microwear Sample | Tools with Diagnostic Use-Wear |
|---|---|---|---|
| **Hell Gap Locality V** | | | |
| Flakes | 53 | 52 | 14 |
| Unifaces | 42 | 41 | 20 |
| Bifaces | 34 | 34 | 3 |
| Points | 13 | 13 | 7 |
| Trifaces[a] | 2 | 2 | 0 |
| Debitage[b] | 8889[c] | 0 | 0 |
| Other | 25 | 3 | 0 |
| **Total** | 9058[c] | 145 | 44 |
| **Jurgens[d]** | | | |
| Flakes | 302–303 | 34 | 14 |
| Unifaces | 93–95 | 95 | 42 |
| Bifaces | 0 | 27 | 15 |
| Points/Hafted knives | 110 | 31 | 15 |
| Trifaces[a] | 1 | 1 | 1 |
| Debitage[b] | 2062–2063 | 0 | 0 |
| Other | 20 | 0 | 0 |
| **Total** | 2588–2592 | 188 | 87 |

[a] A triface is defined as an object flaked on three approximately evenly sized faces that does not appear to be a core.
[b] Debitage figures for Locality V, Hell Gap, from Knell 2007 and Knell et al. 2009; for Jurgens from Wheat 1979.
[c] Debitage and total artifact counts differ from Muñiz 2005 to reflect changes in Knell 2007 and Knell et al. 2009.
[d] Flakes, unifaces, and debitage vary in total number due to discrepancies in original report (see Wheat 1979); all bifaces are included in the category Points/Hafted knives because of overlap in these artifact classes as presented in the original report (see Wheat 1979).

### *Tool Manufacture and Maintenance*

The geologic distribution of good-quality toolstone is very different between the two sites, and this affects the risk model predictions for the activities of tool manufacture and maintenance

(Table 10.1), which are directly related to other activities that use stone tools. Locality V has locally available, high-quality Hartville Uplift chert, while the local raw materials at Jurgens consist of secondary cobbles from the South Platte River that include only sporadic distributions of fine-grained quartzite, various cherts, and silicified wood. The probability of failing to find local, good-quality toolstone at Hell Gap is near zero, resulting in a very low cost of failure and technological cost for lithic tool production at the site. For Jurgens, the probability of failure depends on which river cobbles are exposed at the time of occupation, and thus ranges from moderate to high. It follows that the cost of failing to have an adequate supply of good-quality toolstone on hand on arrival at Jurgens must also rank moderate to high.

If the Cody occupants at Hell Gap knew the quality of the local stone before arriving, they would not be required to spend a great deal of time, energy, or raw material making adequate toolkits ahead of time and their overall technological costs before arriving would be low. At Jurgens the technological costs for obtaining toolstone must rank higher than at Hell Gap in order to reduce the probability of failing to have enough while on site. The model thus predicts that the Jurgens occupants should bring many ready-made tools with them to the site. Following the optimization principle, the model also predicts that to maximize the net return on technological costs, the people at Jurgens should have practiced a greater degree of tool maintenance and recycling than the people at Locality V.

Regarding lithic tool production, the risk management model predictions are well supported at Locality V because the tool assemblage is made up of over 90 percent local Hartville Uplift chert (Knell et al. 2009), and only a single tool in the sample (0.7 percent of the sampled tool assemblage) was recycled from one function to another. Exotic toolstone at Jurgens is a minimum of 68 percent of the assemblage and may be as high as 82 percent if the fine-grained quartzite and unidentified cherts were procured from greater than 40 km away. Because the exact provenience of these materials is unknown, and they could have been locally procured from South Platte River cobbles, minimum and maximum percentages are provided. The exotic source used for most of the tools at Jurgens is White River Group silicate, with the closest source being Flattop Butte, located 115 km away. White River Group silicate was used to make 38 percent of the end scrapers, 21 percent of the projectile points, and 36 percent of the other flake, unifacial, and bifacial tools (Muñiz 2005). Other exotic toolstone includes moderate percentages of Hartville Uplift chert (205 km away) and much smaller proportions of Smoky Hills jasper (305 km away), Alibates agatized dolomite (570 km away), and Knife River flint (775 km away). These data indicate that the Jurgens occupants began collecting raw material and preparing the tools they would eventually use well in advance of occupying the site. This is consistent with the risk management model predictions. Unexpectedly, there is only a single tool at Jurgens that was clearly recycled from one function to another (0.5 percent of the sampled tool assemblage). This lack of recycling is an interesting point of divergence from the risk model predictions. Using the optimization principle outlined above, we would expect that given the lack of local toolstone and large number of bison that were butchered on site, the Jurgens occupants should have maximized the use-life of their toolkits by recycling more frequently. The fact that they did not indicates that they arrived on site with a supply that met or exceeded their minimum requirements, further indicating significant prior planning.

### *Hunting*

Locality V is situated in the Hartville Uplift foothills not far from grasslands to the east and southeast. The Locality V faunal record includes seven *Bison* sp. and at least one canid, *Odocoileus hemionus* (mule deer), and lagomorph (Knell et al. 2009). Jurgens includes a minimum of 68 *Bison* sp., seven *Antilocapra americana* (pronghorn antelope), three *Odocoileus hemionus* (deer), two *Cervus* sp. (elk), and single occurrences of *Alces alces* (moose), *Castor sp.* (beaver), canid, *Sylvilagus* sp. (cottontail), *Lepus* sp. (jackrabbit), *Marmota caligata* (marmot), *Ondatra zibethicus* (muskrat), Mephitidae (skunk), mustelid, and a variety of birds, small mammals (including Cricetidea and *Peromyscus* sp.), turtle, and fish (Wheat 1979). Jurgens is within a kilometer of the South Platte

River channel, placing it within easy access to riparian and grassland resources, as well as being relatively close to the Rocky Mountain foothills.

Site-specific paleoenvironmental studies for Locality V (Fredlund 2009; Miller and Goldberg 2009; Reider 2009; Scott 1979; Walker 2009) and Jurgens (Scott 1979) indicate that around 9000 $^{14}$C yr BP (10,220–10,185 cal BP) the overall conditions were relatively similar to their respective modern environments in terms of moisture regime, plant species, and general productivity. The long-term paleoenvironmental trends (see Muñiz, this volume [Chapter 2]) on the western Plains indicate that the regions surrounding Jurgens and Locality V had adequate forage production to support grazing and browsing animals around 9000 $^{14}$C yr BP (10,220–10,185 cal BP). The paleoenvironmental data suggest that the Jurgens and Locality V inhabitants may not have faced significant costs for failing to successfully hunt large game because alternative food resources were available. In this case, determining the probability of failure for hunting at each site depends on very local environmental conditions (e.g., season, herd movements, effects of recent fires, overgrazing, or erosion). Given that Cody hunters probably gathered information about local conditions and could actively avoid areas that were likely to have poor hunting, the probability of failure for hunting at both sites can be ranked low. Considering the alternative resources that were likely available, the model also predicts that the cost of failure would be low for each site. When the failure cost associated with hunting is low, technological cost should also be low. Thus, Cody groups were not necessarily constrained by heavy technological costs for hunting weaponry and instead may have had a range of options for organizing this technology (Table 10.1).

A comparison of projectile point production and maintenance at each site sheds light on the decisions made to manage the risk associated with hunting (Table 10.4). Just over 80 percent of the projectile points and preforms at Locality V are made from local toolstone, which supports the risk model expectations. Conversely, only 43 percent of the points at Jurgens are made from what may be local quartzite, and if it is not local, this figure drops significantly. The remainder of the Jurgens points originated from between 115 and 775 km away. Although the risk model predicted that technological costs for hunting at Jurgens should be low, the group actually paid high costs for their projectile points in the form of acquiring or otherwise manufacturing and transporting points well in advance of arriving on site. This somewhat unexpected result raises the possibility that the Jurgens occupants were more concerned with conducting a successful bison hunt to procure something other than meat, as edible alternatives were available. While nonbison artiodactyls, small mammals, and other game were clearly available to eat, only bison have bison hides, and the Jurgens hunt occurred in the fall when bison hides are typically in their best condition. Thus, an alternative explanation for why the Jurgens occupants paid such high technological costs is that the cost of failure for procuring bison hides was high because alternative mammal hides would not serve as substitutes.

**TABLE 10.4.** Comparison of Chipped Stone Hunting Technology at Hell Gap Locality V and Jurgens.

| Hunting | Locality V | Jurgens |
|---|---|---|
| Points and preform sample | *n* = 21 | *n* = 67 |
| % Exotic raw material | 19.4% | min. 57% |
| Finished point sample | *n* = 13 | *n* = 59 |
| % Broken points | 92.3% | 64.4% |
| (includes complete and fragmentary points) | | |
| Finished point sample | *n* = 9 | *n* = 41 |
| % Reworked points | 55.6% | 48.8% |
| (does not include base fragments) | | |

The percentage of newly made versus reworked points is very similar for both sites, hovering around half of the total, although it should be noted that evidence of reworking was not always observable on broken points. Even with such potential bias, this is an interesting result considering that the point sample at Jurgens is almost four times larger than the one at Locality V (Table 10.4), the availability of good-quality local toolstone is significantly different at each site, and Jurgens is primarily a kill site while Locality V is a camp-workshop. Could the similarity simply be coincidental and unrelated to adaptive strategies for managing risk?

Knell (2007) demonstrated that projectile point manufacture and replacement was an important component of the occupation activities at Locality V. According to Knell's (2007; Knell et al. 2009) interpretations, the proportion of new and reworked points at Locality V resulted from retooling as people replaced old points with new ones that were made and discarded on site. In this regard, the technological costs being paid at Locality V are in part related to where the group goes after leaving the site and reflect off-site risk management. A kill site such as Jurgens might be expected to produce a mix of new and reworked points for a different reason. Efficient methods for gearing up in anticipation of a large bison kill might result in a new set of points being made for the occasion (Bamforth 1991). If these points supplement reworked points and a sample of each is lost in a kill, then we might end up with similar proportions. In this scenario, it is reasonable to expect technological costs for an important kill site to be paid at a camp-workshop occupied before the kill. In this sense, Locality V and Jurgens represent complementary aspects of a linked risk management strategy. The relationship between these alternative causal mechanisms demonstrates the utility of analyzing technological organization through the risk management framework, as the superficially similar ratios of new and reworked points at seemingly unrelated types of sites can be understood in a broader context.

### *Butchery*

Frison (1991), Jodry (1998, 1999), and Walker (1978) provide detailed descriptions of butchery strategies that avoid meat spoilage as well as replicative experiments designed to evaluate the functional effectiveness of different butchery tool designs. As Frison (1991:298–325) discusses in detail, it is difficult to determine the most efficient application of any specific tool design for butchery, for two reasons. First, a great deal of variability affects each instance of using a specific tool design. Factors such as how recently an animal was killed, the number of people working together, the type of raw material a tool is made from, the incorporation of bone tools, weather conditions, and human fatigue all act to constrain tool efficiency for each step of the process. Second, as a tool is used throughout the butchery process, its optimum application changes depending on edge angle and thickness, degree of retouch, and the required task at hand. Frison (1991:316) provides an excellent example of how an unmodified flake tool is at first best suited to cut open an animal's hide as the initial step in the butchery process but quickly wears from abrasion against skin, hair, and dirt. At this point the flake would need to be resharpened in order to cut open more hide, or it could be used without resharpening to remove the skin from the muscle masses or remove muscle masses from the carcass. As Frison (1991:316) states:

> Butchering covered such a wide range of tool use activity and made so many different demands on a tool that its effects on working edges are next to impossible to separate in a task-specific sense. A tool no longer functional for one kind of butchering use may be perfectly functional for other uses. Certain butchering tasks result in a relatively high attrition of tool working edges whereas others do not. It is suggested from a large body of evidence that the high tool-attrition aspects of butchering were taken care of with special classes of easily made tools that were used up quickly and then discarded. A tool may have a short life in a high-attrition situation, but without modification it may then have a comparatively long life in another situation.

Frison's observations underscore the fact that it is difficult to evaluate a single butchery tool in terms of risk management because it is hard to know the complete use-history of the tool based solely on the archaeological record. While a tool may be recovered in the form of a heavily retouched unifacial flake knife, it may have begun its life as an unmodified flake and moved progressively through different morphological stages as it was used for different tasks. The analysis of entire toolkits helps rectify this problem, as we recognize general patterns of technological organization beyond the single tool.

Replicative experiments by Jodry (1998, 1999) and Walker (1978) document the effectiveness of different tool designs, before subsequent modification, for specific butchery applications. These replicative experiments demonstrate that unmodified and edge-modified flakes are the most efficient tool design for cutting hide and large muscle masses. While unretouched flakes make excellent cutting tools, their edges may be quickly dulled and require resharpening. Unifacially resharpened flake knives (i.e., "unifaces") achieved a similar efficiency rating to unmodified and edge-modified flake tools for cutting meat and connective tissue. When a flake has been significantly retouched to the point where it becomes a unifacial tool, its working edge becomes steeper but also better reinforced, since the thickness and edge angle generally increase. As a result, unifacial flake knives are often better suited than unmodified or edge-modified flake tools for cutting connective tissue away from bone and for separating joints because the edges of the unmodified flake tools are more susceptible to breakage. Frison (1991:307–310) suggests that a unifacially retouched flake knife is probably the best general-purpose butchery tool, and the frequent occurrence of this tool type in kill sites of all ages throughout the Plains supports his observation. Bifacial tools (not including projectile points or point preforms) were very effective at skinning hide and cutting connective tissue, but were not as effective as unifacial knives and flakes at cutting hide or thick muscle masses. However, very thin bifacial knives, such as Jodry's replicated ultrathins, proved to be very effective and efficient at filleting thick muscle masses already removed from the bone in order to make long thin strips of meat for drying. Although these authors did not directly address the effectiveness of different tool designs for processing bone, some estimates can be made based on the basic principles outlined above. In order to process a hard-contact material such as bone or antler, a tool edge needs to be sharp and sturdy enough to withstand the abrasion. Although some unmodified flakes may have a naturally angled edge that is effective for this task, replicative studies made by the author for working bone and antler show that the flake's edge will soon become substantially modified through wear. Bifaces may also provide effective tools for this task, since their edges are reinforced by design. Thus, it is very likely that unifacial and bifacial tools will be the most effective designs for bone processing, regardless of the technological costs that may be associated with their manufacture. Table 10.5 provides a summary of the replicative experiment results conducted by Frison (1991), Jodry (1998, 1999), and Walker (1978).

**TABLE 10.5.** Summary of Tool Designs Best Suited for Specific Butchery Applications.

| Task | Most Effective Tool Design |
|---|---|
| Cutting open hide to begin butchery | Unmodified and edge-modified flake tool |
| Skinning a terrestrial mammal carcass | Biface |
| Cutting through meat masses | Unmodified and edge-modified flake tool and ultrathin biface |
| Cutting meat away from bone | Unifacially retouched flake ("uniface") |
| Cutting tendons and connective tissue | Unifacially retouched flake ("uniface") and biface |
| Separating joints | Large chopper or wedge |

*Note:* Based on replicative studies of Frison (1991), Jodry (1998, 1999), and Walker (1978).

In terms of the risk management predictions for butchery, the primary constraining factor that influences the probability of failure, the cost of failure, and technological costs is the ratio of animals that need butchering to butchers. To simplify the risk model, we must assume from our etic perspective that there is a direct relationship between the number of animals killed and the number of animals that need butchering (however, this need not be a one-to-one correlation). As the latter number increases, the probability of failing to successfully butcher the minimum required amount must also increase. This relationship applies even to conditions of gourmet butchery in which only select muscle elements are harvested. The cost of this failure is situationally dependent on variables such as alternative food resources, season of the year, and desired animal products. If other animals may be hunted or other foods collected, then having meat spoil on the bone may not cost much at all. If a Cody group is more interested in collecting the hides from a herd of bison than the meat, then the cost of spoiled meat may be negligible. The technological costs paid by a Cody group to offset the cost of failure include an adequate number of tools designed for specific butchery tasks and an adequate number of people to use those tools before the desired resources spoil.

Using this simplifying assumption, the risk model predicts that given a high ratio of animals that need butchering to butchers, Cody people should make substantial investments in technological costs designed to reduce the probability of failure. In terms of the failure probability for successfully manufacturing a butchery tool, the model predicts that if an unmodified flake can perform as effectively as a biface for a given task, then the flake should be selected every time because on average it provides a greater net return for the energy and resources expended in its manufacture.

Although we cannot accurately estimate how many butchers were at Jurgens or Locality V, nor what the total need for edible animal products was, we can develop a relative ranking of how much each group should invest in the technological costs associated with butchery (Table 10.1). Given that Jurgens has ten times as many bison as Locality V and about 20 additional nonbison mammals, the risk model predicts that the butchers at Jurgens should invest significantly more in the technological costs needed to offset butchery failure than the butchers at Locality V. Whether the actual technological cost for butchery at Jurgens is ranked moderate or high is less important than the fact that it is significantly higher than at Locality V.

**TABLE 10.6.** Comparison of Chipped Stone Light Butchery Technology at Hell Gap Locality V and Jurgens.

| Light Butchery | Locality V | Jurgens |
|---|---|---|
| Tools with diagnostic microwear | $n = 19$ | $n = 20$ |
| % Exotic raw material | 5.3% | min. 75% |
| % Flake tools | 36.8% | 45% |
| Mean edge angle | 17.4° | 38.2° |
| Standard deviation | 22° | 21.2° |
| $t$-test for 2 independent samples 0.951 (2 tailed, $df = 18, 0.4 < p < 0.2$) | | |
| % Unifacial tools | 52.6% | 30% |
| Mean edge angle | 33.3° | 43.8° |
| Standard deviation | 11.65° | 8.7° |
| $t$-test for 2 independent samples 0.060 (2 tailed, $df = 14, p < 0.9$) | | |
| % Bifaces | 5.3% ($n = 1$) | 5% ($n = 1$) |
| Mean edge angle | 43° | 45° |
| % Specialized bifaces | 5.3% ($n = 1$) | 20% ($n = 4$) |
| Mean edge angle | 33° | 42° |
| Standard deviation | | 15.6° |

Tools with diagnostic traces of butchery use-wear were divided into those used for light and heavy butchery tasks. Light butchery tasks left use-wear traces primarily from soft tissue with only incidental bone or antler contact such as might be produced by skinning and filleting meat masses. Heavy butchery use-wear has soft tissue wear traces but also includes frequent contact with bone or antler such as might result from disarticulating joints and removing sinew, antler, and horn. The total number of tools with diagnostic butchery use-wear is quite similar for the two sites (Table 10.2).

*Light Butchery*

For light butchery tools, the data indicate that at Jurgens a minimum of 75 percent ($n = 20$) were made from exotic toolstone, while at Locality V this figure is around 5 percent ($n = 19$) (Table 10.6). This striking difference demonstrates that the Jurgens occupants invested in the technological costs of preparing and transporting light butchery tools (or the cores to produce them) well before arriving on site. The reliance on local toolstone at Locality V allowed those occupants greater flexibility in the timing of when they made their light butchery tools. These two observations support the respective risk model predictions for each site.

There is also a distinct difference in toolkit composition. The Jurgens toolkit includes a greater proportion of specialized bifaces and flake tools than the Locality V assemblage, while the Locality V assemblage has a greater proportion of unifacial tools. Specialized bifaces at Jurgens include both Cody knives and ultrathin bifaces, while Locality V has only a single ultrathin. I describe the morphology and use-wear data for the Cody knives and ultrathins in more detail elsewhere (Muñiz 2005). A $t$-test for two independent samples evaluated the mean edge angle for flake and unifacial light butchery tools for both sites, and the results failed to reject the null hypothesis in each case, which means that functionally the edges of these two tool classes are the same. The lack of significant difference in mean edge angle between the two sites probably indicates that the difference in tool morphology (flakes at Jurgens and unifaces at Locality V) reflects different degrees of maintenance and resharpening.

The Locality V occupants discarded a greater percentage of unifacial tools than flake tools, even though local supplies of toolstone could have easily been used to produce fresh flake tools that did not require resharpening into unifacial forms. Jurgens residents, who were faced with a finite supply of good-quality exotic toolstone that was brought into the site, discarded more light butchery flake tools without resharpening them to the unifacial stage. These observations are opposite the risk model predictions for the intersite comparison. However, the Jurgens result is internally consistent with model predictions for meeting moderate to high technological costs in that the occupants clearly ensured that a large number of flake tools (and at least four technologically expensive specialized bifaces) were available before arriving on site.

The Locality V result diverges from model predictions because although the occupants had locally available good-quality toolstone, they either preferred the steeper working edges of unifaces to the thinner acute edges of flake tools or resharpened many flake tools to the point that they became unifacial before being discarded. One explanation for this outcome is that functional requirements were perceived as different at the two sites: unifaces were favored over flakes at Locality V and vice versa at Jurgens. This possibility should be explored through comparative faunal analysis that focuses on identifying how different faunal elements were butchered and the relative importance of hide removal at each site. Another explanation is that the Locality V occupants did not discard many flake tools because they removed them from the site when they departed.

*Heavy Butchery*

Heavy butchery tools made on exotic toolstone constitute just over 26 percent of the Locality V toolkit and a minimum of 53 percent of the Jurgens toolkit (Table 10.7). Compared with the light butchery toolkit, the Locality V result is a dramatic increase while the Jurgens figure is a significant decrease. The mean edge angles for flake tools and bifaces at both sites are nearly identical, and a *t*-test for two independent samples found no significant difference between the working-edge angles for unifacial tools at the two sites.

**TABLE 10.7.** Comparison of Chipped Stone Heavy Butchery Technology at Hell Gap Locality V and Jurgens.

| Heavy Butchery | Locality V | Jurgens |
|---|---|---|
| Tools with diagnostic microwear | $n = 19$ | $n = 13$ |
| % Exotic raw material | 26.3% | min. 53.8% |
| % Flake tools | 42.1% | 23.1% |
| Mean edge angle | 52.7° | 53.3° |
| Standard deviation | 35.8° | 19.4° |
| % Unifacial tools | 36.8% | 30.8% |
| Mean edge angle | 64.6° | 48.8° |
| Standard deviation | 20.7° | 22.9° |
| *t*-test for 2 independent samples (2 tailed, $df = 9$, $0.9 < p < 0.5$) | 0.299 | |
| % Bifacial tools | 21.1% | 38.5% |
| Mean edge angle | 68.3° | 66.3° |
| Standard deviation | 47.4° (41° w/o outlier) | 23° |
| % Other (Triface) | 0 | 7.7% |
| Mean edge angle | | 55° |

These results demonstrate that, as before, variability in tool morphology at each site probably results from the effects of a resharpening continuum.

As with the light butchery tools, even though the Jurgens pattern is internally consistent with model predictions, the intersite comparison is opposite what the risk model predicts. The Jurgens butchers most frequently relied on bifaces (38.5 percent) for heavy butchery work, with a decreasing reliance on unifaces (30.8 percent) and flake tools (23.1 percent). The predominance of unifaces over flakes supports the risk model predictions in that flake tools were maintained to the point of becoming unifacial in a toolstone-poor environment. The primary reliance on bifaces indicates that the Jurgens butchers paid high technological costs to make and transport bifaces for heavy butchery tasks, and from this we might infer that the cost of failing to conduct heavy butchery was significant. This supports an interpretation of meat acquisition, rather than primarily hides, as a major goal of the Jurgens occupants.

The heavy butchery toolkit composition at Locality V indicates that flake tools (42.1 percent) were preferred over unifacial tools (36.8 percent) and bifacial tools (21.1 percent). Overall this toolkit is composed of 26.3 percent exotic toolstone, but compared with the Jurgens occupants, the Locality V occupants paid lower technological costs to perform heavy butchery tasks. Given the heavy reliance on flakes, the relatively high proportion of exotic toolstone at Locality V is unexpected and may indicate a kind of use-life succession in which older butchery tools made with exotic stone and with worn and resharpened edges were preferentially used for cutting against hard materials, while new tools with fresh keen edges made from local toolstone were used for light butchery tasks. The preference for flake tools is consistent with the maximization principle of the risk management model, which expects flakes to be selected over bifaces when functional effectiveness is the same and good-quality toolstone is locally available. However, this result is at odds with the replicative experiments that show the effectiveness of bifaces for skinning and disarticulating joints. This discrepancy is intriguing and may indicate that for the Locality V occupants, the ability to make cheap flake tools to perform heavy butchery tasks outweighed the functional benefits of having stouter bifacial edges that perform better but entail a greater technological cost and higher probability of failure to produce.

### *Hide Working*

The failure costs associated with hide working can be estimated as the time, energy, raw materials, and social organization wasted to create a successful hunt that produced the appropriate animal with a hide that was in the proper condition to work *but was not worked.* The season of the year can have a direct impact on both the probability and costs of failure for hide working. In spring, many animals have poor-quality hides because they are fat-depleted and are changing from a winter to a summer coat; in summer, heat can cause untended hides to spoil faster than in cooler months; and frozen winter conditions can make working hides outdoors extremely difficult if not impossible. Fall is often a predictably good time to work hides because animals are in good condition, fur is becoming thicker as winter approaches, and air temperatures are favorable. Hide products such as shelters, clothing, and storage containers are very important technologies for winter survival. Given these conditions,

**TABLE 10.8.** Comparison of Chipped Stone Hide-Working End Scrapers at Hell Gap Locality V and Jurgens.

| Hide Working | Locality V | Jurgens |
|---|---|---|
| End scrapers | $n = 7$ | $n = 65$ |
| % Exotic raw material | 38.5% | min. 57% |
| End scrapers | $n = 7$ | $n = 54$ |
| Mean width: thickness | 3.0 | 3.5 |
| Standard deviation | 0.46 | 1.08 |
| *t*-test for 2 independent samples (2 tailed, $df = 59, p < 0.9$) | 0.024 | |
| End scrapers | $n = 7$ | $n = 59$ |
| Mean edge angle | 53.8° | 67.3° |
| Standard deviation | 12.5° | 14.7° |
| *t*-test for 2 independent samples (2 tailed, $df = 64, p < 0.9$) | 0.018 | |
| End scrapers | $n = 7$ | $n = 63$ |
| % Broken | 12.5% | 12.7% |

*Note:* Jurgens sample sizes vary because measured attributes were not present on all artifacts.

the risk model predicts that Cody people should invest heavily in technological costs in order to have an adequate supply of hide-working tools (and hence worked hides) in the fall (Table 10.1).

A comparison of end scrapers from the two sites provides an indication of how Cody people managed the risk associated with this activity (Table 10.8). The percentage of exotic raw material and the width-to-thickness ratio were evaluated to determine the technological costs paid in advance of using the end scrapers. The mean edge angle and percentage of broken end scrapers were examined for indications of how intensively the tools were used before discard. At Locality V, end scrapers contain the single highest percentage (38.5) of exotic raw material for any tool class, and at Jurgens they tie with projectile points (minimum 57 percent) for this distinction. The long-distance transport of end scrapers supports the risk model predictions that the Jurgens occupants should have paid the technological costs for the important activity of fall hide working. The multiple seasons of occupation at Locality V include the possibility that hides were worked from late spring through early winter, and thus the high proportion of exotic stone is not easily accounted for by the risk model predictions.

A *t*-test for two independent samples using the

width-to-thickness ratios for end scrapers was conducted to evaluate the possibility that different numbers of flintknappers were making end scrapers before arriving at each site. The working assumption for this test is that as the number of flintknappers increases, so too does morphological variability. The results indicate that there is no significant difference between the samples, even though Jurgens has more than nine times the number of end scrapers. The standard deviation in the Jurgens sample is more than twice that for Locality V, which lends some support to the idea that the larger number of end scrapers at Jurgens may have been made by more people. It appears, however, that the basic functional and hafting requirements constraining end scraper morphology outweigh idiosyncratic variation in shape, and thus width-to-thickness ratio may not be a meaningful measure for evaluating technological costs for this tool class.

The final two characteristics regarding intensity of use also show mixed results. Contrary to the risk model predictions, both sites have almost identical percentages of broken end scrapers, and this fails to reflect a difference in intensity of use at the two locations. The average working-edge angle is steeper at Jurgens than at Locality V, which favors the risk model prediction that the Jurgens residents should have maximized the net return on their technological costs by using the scrapers to exhaustion because they paid a higher price than the Locality V residents. However, the difference in mean edge angle at the two sites is not statistically significant.

### Discussion and Conclusions

Overall the results of the risk management analysis of Cody lithic technological organization at Jurgens and Locality V are mixed. Of the 21 risk management model predictions evaluated (Table 10.1), eight were clearly supported, seven were not supported, two can be categorized as neutral, and four received moderate support beyond neutral. When interpreting these results, we must remember that the risk model analysis is intended to be a heuristic device that structures our thinking about lithic technology and identifies important points of divergence from optimally defined behavior that may indicate unique cultural adaptations. Thus, a lack of agreement between the predictions and the empirical observations is not necessarily a failure of the model.

Three of the four risk model predictions for tool manufacture were supported at both sites; however, the lack of recycling at Jurgens did not follow model expectations. This point of divergence highlights the finding that the Jurgens occupants used tools for very specific functions and did not need to convert broken or exhausted tools into new forms. This outcome is contrary to the underlying maximization assumptions used within many of the model predictions, and it has important implications for understanding lithic technology that can be applied outside Cody complex research (see Andrefsky 1994; Bamforth 1986; Binford 1979). Future research stemming from this observation should evaluate under what conditions of mobility, seasonality, and site function hunter-gatherers employed extensive gearing-up strategies that eliminated the need for recycling.

The low technological costs for hunting at both sites did not restrict options for the use of new or reworked projectile points. In this situation, the model allows for multiple, equally effective responses for managing risk. The results of the evaluation neither supported nor failed to support the model predictions, as it was recognized that the two sites could have generated similar point ratios for different reasons. From this evaluation, an important and unexpected outcome arose.

The heavy reliance on exotic toolstone for point production at Jurgens indicated that much higher technological costs were paid than the model predicted was necessary. The technological costs were originally estimated based on the probability of failing to acquire adequate meat when abundant alternative resources were available. If, however, the cost of failure is assessed in terms of lost bison *hides* rather than bison *meat*, the cost of failure increases significantly and raises the technological costs. Under these conditions, the heavy use of exotic toolstone for points supports the model predictions. Given that the results of the hide-working analysis indicated that the Jurgens occupants paid relatively high technological costs for making end scrapers, we should consider the fact that Cody groups and other Paleoindians may have been conducting large fall bison kills as much for the hides and animal by-products (e.g., sinew, bone) as for the edible meat. If hunting primarily for hides was truly an important function of fall bison kills (e.g., Frison et al. 1987), then many of our taphonomic expectations regarding cutmarks, butchery patterns, and estimates of pounds of meat consumed by Cody camp occupants (e.g., Agenbroad 1978; Todd and Rapson 1999; Wheat 1972, 1979) will need to be significantly revised. However, the heavy butchery toolkit at Jurgens also indicated that high technological costs were paid in advance of the kill, supporting an interpretation that meat acquisition was still an important goal. Future research on Paleoindian fall bison kills should reexamine the role of end scrapers in the technological organization with an eye toward hide (and bone and sinew) procurement being at least as important as meat.

Model predictions regarding the use of local and exotic stone for light butchery tools were supported at both sites, and the prediction for the use of specialized bifaces at Jurgens also received empirical support. The greater reliance on flakes than unifaces at Jurgens, and the converse at Locality V, went against model predictions. Analysis of the edge angles indicates that this divergence may represent differential resharpening at each site. Future research should evaluate the role of gearing up and discard in relation to large-scale Cody complex seasonal land-use patterns as a potential causal mechanism structuring these observations (see Root et al. and Knell, this volume).

Risk management model predictions for the use of local stone and reliance on flake tools for heavy butchery tasks at Locality V received strong empirical support and indicate that the Cody occupants employed a strategy that managed risk in an optimized way that is analogous to how it is conceived here. Predictions regarding the heavy butchery toolkit at Jurgens were somewhat supported in terms of the use of exotic toolstone and the reliance on unifaces, but the role of bifaces was unexpected. The use of expensive tools to conduct a task that is likely to incur tool failure combined with a lack of recycling suggests that (1) the Jurgens occupants had such an abundant supply of bifaces that they could absorb any losses incurred; (2) bifaces performed a function that could not be matched by other tool shapes or edge morphologies; or (3) the bifaces were handled with such adroit skill that the users did not incur a significant increase in the probability of breakage during the task. Evaluating which of these options accounts for the observations at Jurgens must await future research that incorporates replicative experiments and additional analyses of similar Cody complex sites.

The six risk model predictions regarding hide working were generally not well supported. Although the use of exotic toolstone at Jurgens was expected, the irregular morphology and discard before tool exhaustion did not support model predictions. At Locality V the relatively high percentage of exotic toolstone and consistent end scraper morphology went against model predictions; however, the lack of heavy resharpening offered some support. These points of divergence indicate that the functional and maintenance requirements of end scrapers may constrain variability in how they are treated such that the morphological attributes selected here are insufficient to test the risk management model as currently developed. Even so, the fact that Jurgens has a larger standard deviation in width-to-thickness ratio than Locality V indicates more variability in the dimensions of the hafts used at Jurgens and may also indicate a concomitant increase in the number of individuals scraping hides. Bamforth (1991) suggests that Cody flintknappers decreased morphological variability in point dimensions because incipient craft specialists made most of the points before a large-scale bison hunt during a gearing-up period. The results of the risk management analysis indicate that morphological variability in end scrapers may actually increase during the same gearing-up period preceding communal bison hunts. If this trend holds across other sites similar to Jurgens, future research might investigate if different forms of social organization (e.g., gender roles) are structuring this variability.

An important outcome of evaluating the risk management strategies at Jurgens and Locality V through qualitative measures of technological costs is that we are able to think about these two sites in a structured theoretical framework relative to each other. Rather than treat these sites as stand-alone entities with different functional roles within the adaptive Cody cultural system, we can begin to think about how they relate to each other at a larger scale of technological organization. Placing the Jurgens and Locality V assemblages on a continuum leads us to a more comprehensive understanding of the large-scale strategies Cody people used for organizing lithic technology. Sites like Jurgens, where functionally useful toolkits were discarded in good condition, would not exist without sites like Locality V, where new toolkits were manufactured and replenished. Locations like Locality V that were repeatedly occupied by groups who used them as a hub for retooling (Knell 2007; Knell et al. 2009) include a mix of debris from (1) making new tools to replenish toolkits brought into the site, (2) the remnants of old toolkits discarded during the occupation, (3) tools made and used specifically during the on-site occupation, and (4) blanks and tools made for future use that may or may not fit into cohesive toolkits. In such a situation, it is very difficult to isolate which tools or portions of toolkits were affected by past off-site factors, active on-site factors, and future factors that could be predicted only by the makers and users of the toolkits. This has significant implications for our ability to test the risk management model with sites such as Locality V. At Cody complex sites such as Jurgens, Carter/Kerr-McGee, Horner II, and Olsen-Chubbuck (Frison 1984; Frison and Todd 1987; Wheat 1972, 1979), the assemblages reflect a relatively restricted set of activities that most likely resulted from single (or temporally restricted) occupations focused largely on processing bison kills. In such cases the relationship between risk management and the activities that occurred on site can be more directly addressed.

This application of the risk management analytical framework has demonstrated that even if risk variables cannot be mathematically quantified, provided that circular reasoning is avoided, a qualitative evaluation of model predictions can identify previously unrecognized aspects of technological organization. While this study has also shown some of the limits of the risk management approach, it has identified important aspects of Cody behavior that diverged from model predictions. Exploring and understanding the function of such divergences in future research will lead us to a greater understanding of Cody adaptive strategies and social organization.

## Acknowledgments

I thank the Anthropology Department at the University of Colorado for a Predissertation Research Grant and Graduate Fellowship that helped support me while I conducted the analyses. Thanks to the University of Colorado Museum for loaning the Jurgens material and to the George C. Frison Institute at the University of Wyoming for making accessible the Hell Gap material. I am also grateful to Mary Lou Larson and Marcel Kornfeld for their hospitality while I was at the University of Wyoming. Thanks to Doug Bamforth, Bob Kelly, and Ed Knell for commenting on earlier versions of this chapter. My family also deserves thanks for their patience while I worked on this project. Any misinterpretation of the data presented here is solely the responsibility of the author.

## References

Agenbroad, Larry D.

1978 *The Hudson-Meng Site: An Alberta Bison Kill in the Nebraska High Plains.* University Press of America, Washington, D.C.

Andrefsky, William, Jr.

1994 Raw-Material Availability and the Organization of Technology. *American Antiquity* 59:21–34.

Bamforth, Douglas B.

1986 Technological Efficiency and Tool Curation. *American Antiquity* 51:38–50.

1991 Flintknapping Skill, Communal Hunting, and Paleoindian Point Typology. *Plains Anthropologist* 36:309–322.

Bamforth, Douglas B., and Peter Bleed

1997 Technology, Flaked Stone Technology, and Risk. In *Rediscovering Darwin: Evolutionary Theory and Archeological Explanation*, edited by C. M. Barton and G. A. Clark, pp. 109–139. Archeological Papers of the American Anthropological Association No. 7. Arlington, Virginia.

Bettinger, Robert L.

1991 *Hunter-Gatherers: Archaeological and Evolutionary Theory.* Plenum Press, New York.

Bicchieri, M. G. (editor)
1972 *Hunters and Gatherers Today: A Socioeconomic Study of Eleven Such Cultures in the Twentieth Century*. Waveland Press, Prospect Heights, Illinois.

Binford, Lewis R.
1979 Organization and Formation Processes: Looking at Curated Technologies. *Journal of Anthropological Research* 35:255–273.

Bleed, Peter
1986 The Optimal Design of Hunting Weapons: Maintainability or Reliability. *American Antiquity* 51:737–747.
1991 Operations Research and Archaeology. *American Antiquity* 56:19–35.
2001 Trees or Chains, Links or Branches: Conceptual Alternatives for Consideration of Stone Tool Production and Other Sequential Activities. *Journal of Archaeological Method and Theory* 8:101–127.

Dahlberg, Frances (editor)
1981 *Woman the Gatherer*. Yale University Press, New Haven, Connecticut.

Fredlund, Glen
2009 Phytolith Evidence for Vegetation and Climate Change during the Pleistocene-Holocene Transition. In *Hell Gap: A Stratified Paleoindian Campsite at the Edge of the Rockies*, edited by M. L. Larson, M. Kornfeld, and G. C. Frison, pp. 90–98. University of Utah Press, Salt Lake City.

Frison, George C.
1984 The Carter/Kerr-McGee Paleoindian Site: Cultural Resource Management and Archaeological Research. *American Antiquity* 49: 288–314.
1991 *Prehistoric Hunters of the High Plains*. 2nd ed. Academic Press, San Diego.

Frison, George C., and Lawrence C. Todd (editors)
1987 *The Horner Site: The Type Site of the Cody Cultural Complex*. Academic Press, Orlando, Florida.

Frison, George C., Lawrence C. Todd, and Bruce A. Bradley
1987 Summary and Concluding Remarks. In *The Horner Site: The Type Site of the Cody Cultural Complex*, edited by G. C. Frison and L. C. Todd, pp. 361–369. Academic Press, Orlando, Florida.

Haynes, C. Vance, Jr.
2009 Geochronology. In *Hell Gap: A Stratified Paleoindian Campsite at the Edge of the Rockies*, edited by M. L. Larson, M. Kornfeld, and G. C. Frison, pp. 39–52. University of Utah Press, Salt Lake City.

Hill, Matthew E.
2002 Seasonality and Site Structure at the Jurgens Paleoindian Bison Bonebed. Paper presented at the 60th Plains Anthropological Conference, Oklahoma City, Oklahoma.

Ingold, Tim, David Riches, and James Woodburn (editors)
1988 *Hunters and Gatherers, Volume 2: Property, Power, and Ideology*. Berg, Oxford.

Irwin, Henry T.
1967 The Itama: Late Pleistocene Inhabitants of the Plains of the United States and Canada and the American Southwest. Unpublished Ph.D. dissertation, Department of Anthropology, Harvard University, Cambridge, Massachusetts.

Irwin-Williams, Cynthia, Henry T. Irwin, George A. Agogino, and C. Vance Haynes Jr.
1973 Hell Gap: A Paleo-Indian Occupation on the High Plains. *Plains Anthropologist* 18: 40–52.

Jodry, Margaret A.
1998 The Possible Design of Folsom Ultrathin Bifaces as Fillet Knives for Jerky Production. *Current Research in the Pleistocene* 15:75–77.
1999 Folsom Technological and Socioeconomic Strategies: Views from Stewart's Cattle Guard and the Upper Rio Grande Basin, Colorado. Unpublished Ph.D. dissertation, Department of Anthropology, American University, Washington, D.C.

Kelly, Robert L.
1995 *The Foraging Spectrum: Diversity in Hunter-Gatherer Lifeways*. Smithsonian Institution Press, Washington, D.C.

Knell, Edward J.
1999 Late Paleoindian Cody Period Mobility Patterns. Unpublished Master's thesis, Department of Anthropology, University of Wyoming, Laramie.
2007 The Organization of Late Paleoindian Cody Complex Land-Use on the North American Great Plains. Unpublished Ph.D. dissertation, Department of Anthropology, Washington State University, Pullman.

Knell, Edward J., and Matthew E. Hill Jr.
2012 Linking Bones and Stones: Regional Variation in Late Paleoindian Cody Complex Land Use and Foraging Strategies. *American Antiquity* 77:40–70.

Knell, Edward J., Matthew G. Hill, and Andrés D. Izeta
2009 The Locality IIIS/V Eden Complex Component. In *Hell Gap: A Stratified Paleoindian Campsite at the Edge of the Rockies*, edited by M. L. Larson, M. Kornfeld, and G. C. Frison,

pp. 157–179. University of Utah Press, Salt Lake City.
Larson, Mary Lou, Marcel Kornfeld, and George C. Frison (editors)
2009 *Hell Gap: A Stratified Paleoindian Campsite at the Edge of the Rockies*. University of Utah Press, Salt Lake City.
Lee, Richard B., and Irven DeVore (editors)
1968 *Man the Hunter*. Aldine, Chicago.
Marshall, Lorna
1998 Sharing, Talking, and Giving: Relief of Social Tensions among the !Kung. In *Kalahari Hunter-Gatherers: Studies of the !Kung San and Their Neighbors*, edited by R. B. Lee and I. DeVore, pp. 349–371. Harvard University Press, Cambridge, Massachusetts.
Meltzer, David J.
1989 Was Stone Exchanged among Eastern North American Paleoindians? In *Eastern Paleoindian Lithic Resource Use*, edited by C. J. Ellis and J. C. Lothrop, pp. 11–39. Westview Press, Boulder, Colorado.
Miller, Christopher E., and Paul Goldberg
2009 Micromorphology and Paleoenvironments. In *Hell Gap: A Stratified Paleoindian Campsite at the Edge of the Rockies*, edited by M. L. Larson, M. Kornfeld, and G. C. Frison, pp. 72–89. University of Utah Press, Salt Lake City.
Muñiz, Mark P.
2004 The Role of Ultrathin Bifaces in Folsom and Cody Butchering Technology and Implications for Understanding Cultural Continuity in the Paleoindian Period. Paper presented at the 62nd Annual Meeting of the Plains Anthropological Society, Billings, Montana.
2005 The Cody Complex Revisited: Landscape Use and Technological Organization on the Northwestern Plains. Unpublished Ph.D. dissertation, Department of Anthropology, University of Colorado, Boulder.
2009 Microwear, Typology, and the Cody Component. In *Hell Gap: A Stratified Paleoindian Campsite at the Edge of the Rockies*, edited by M. L. Larson, M. Kornfeld, and G. C. Frison, pp. 195–215. University of Utah Press, Salt Lake City.
Panter-Brick, Catherine, Robert H. Layton, and Peter Rowley-Conwy (editors)
2001 *Hunter-Gatherers: An Interdisciplinary Perspective*. Cambridge University Press, Cambridge.
Reider, Richard G.
2009 Soil Development. In *Hell Gap: A Stratified Paleoindian Campsite at the Edge of the Rockies*, edited by M. L. Larson, M. Kornfeld, and G. C. Frison, pp. 53–71. University of Utah Press, Salt Lake City.
Scott, Linda
1979 Appendix 1: Jurgens Site Palynological Analysis. In *The Jurgens Site*, by Joe Ben Wheat, pp. 149–151. Memoir No. 15. Plains Anthropologist, Lincoln, Nebraska.
Todd, Lawrence C., and David J. Rapson
1999 Formational Analysis of Bison Bonebeds and Interpretation of Paleoindian Subsistence. In *Le bison: Gibier et moyen de subsistance des hommes du Paléolithique aux Paléoindiens des Grandes Plaines*, edited by J.-Ph. Brugal, F. David, J. G. Enloe, and J. Jaubert, pp. 479–499. Editions APDCA, Antibes, France.
Torrence, Robin
1983 Time Budgeting and Hunter-Gatherer Technology. In *Hunter-Gatherer Economy in Prehistory: A European Perspective*, edited by Geoff Bailer, pp. 11–22. Cambridge University Press, Cambridge.
1989 Retooling: Towards a Behavioral Theory of Stone Tools. In *Time, Energy, and Stone Tools*, edited by Robin Torrence, pp. 57–66. Cambridge University Press, Cambridge.
Walker, Danny N.
2009 Small Mammals from Locality I: A Paleoenvironmental Reassessment. In *Hell Gap: A Stratified Paleoindian Campsite at the Edge of the Rockies*, edited by M. L. Larson, M. Kornfeld, and G. C. Frison, pp. 429–434. University of Utah Press, Salt Lake City.
Walker, Philip L.
1978 Butchering and Stone Tool Function. *American Antiquity* 43:710–715.
Wheat, Joe Ben
1972 *The Olsen-Chubbuck Site: A Paleo-Indian Bison Kill*. Society for American Archaeology Memoir No. 26. Washington, D.C.
1979 *The Jurgens Site*. Memoir No. 15. Plains Anthropologist, Lincoln, Nebraska.

11

# The Scottsbluff Bison Quarry Site

## Its Place in the Cody Complex

Ruthann Knudson

Projectile point typology begins with the description of artifacts from a specific site. Over the years those typological descriptions and names become entities in and of themselves, sometimes without much reference to the specific attributes of the "type" assemblage and its included artifacts. They become more of an archaeological idea than a historical reality. It is important for Paleoindian scholars to understand the original Scottsbluff Bison Quarry assemblage attributes as compared with the early twenty-first-century Scottsbluff "type."

After eight decades of American Paleoindian research we know that only a few basic shapes of flaked stone lanceolate bifacial points exist that are ballistically functional as killing tools and/or useful as cutting or butchering tools. Variations focus on the haft and the facial flaking. There are a limited number of ways one can make a projectile point for use as a spear. Spear points have to be put on a haft, with the proximal end of the biface fluted, stemmed, straight, constricted, or notched (see Musil 1988). Moreover, the facial flaking can be enough to shape a symmetrical tool but not be highly patterned, or it can be horizontally parallel or obliquely flaked with varying regimentation of the patterned flaking. Within that variation, the bilaterally initiated facial flaking may meet at the tool midpoint or roll over the median. Individual knapping artisans varied the spacing of the facial flake scars, and variations in knapping materials may determine the final artistry of the tool. Frison (2004:110) notes that he has not found any specific Paleoindian point style more lethal than any other but that individual hunters undoubtedly had individual preferences.

During the life of the tool it may be reworked, either resharpened or recycled (Wyckoff 1999:46). Within all this categorization, there can be either a limited range or wide number of point "types," depending whether the analyst is a splitter or a lumper.

Over the past eight decades archaeologists and collectors have often assumed that a parallel exists between a single unified point "type" and a sociocultural group of people. This may or may not be true. Addressed here is how all this fits with the Scottsbluff Bison Quarry assemblage, type site for the Scottsbluff projectile point, a diagnostic of the Cody complex.

### The Evolution of the Scottsbluff Point Type

Marie Wormington reported the Scottsbluff artifacts in 1939 (p. 27) as "three Yumas (1 Collateral, 2 Indeterminates) and five other artifacts. Of the latter, one which may have been used as a dart point or as a knife, had a flaring stem not normally characteristic of Yuma forms.... The remainder of the artifacts were knives or scrapers."

In 1944 (p. 30) Wormington referred to these artifacts as

> a parallel flaked point, two of the type formerly called Indeterminate Yuma, and five other ar-

> tifacts. Of the latter, one which may have been used as a dart point or knife, had a flaring stem not normally characteristic of Yuma forms.... The remainder of the artifacts were knives or scrapers. The parallel flaked point exhibited Collateral flaking; it is wide relative to the length and stem indentations are rather deep. Howard [1943:232, Pl. XIb, c] has suggested that the name *Scottsbluff Yuma* be assigned to this type since it was first found at this site and in order to differentiate it from the typical Eden Yuma which is long and narrow with less strongly marked stem and shoulders. A further difference between the two types of points lies in the fact that the Scottsbluff Yuma is flatter and the median ridge has practically disappeared.

Wormington's 1949 Paleoindian compendium was a significant revision of her earlier publications. She had a section called "Scottsbluff Points" (p. 58), in which she observed that the first Scottsbluff point had been found by Barbour and Schultz at the Scottsbluff site. She noted that it "usually has horizontal parallel flaking, is fairly wide relative to its length and has rather marked stem indentations. It is relatively flat and median ridges are not marked." This is apparently Scottsbluff artifact A7073 (see Figure 11.4b below). She also commented that one of the points (apparently also artifact A7073) "has a somewhat flaring stem," and she remarked that the other four artifacts could be classified as scrapers. She noted that Scottsbluff points had been found at San Jon (Roberts 1942; also see Knudson 1995), the Clovis gravel pit (Blackwater Draw [Hester et al. 1972]), and a "deeply buried site near Cambridge, Nebraska" (apparently the Lime Creek [Davis 1962] site). In her discussion of the Eden point, Wormington (1949:60) said that a point similar to the Finley Eden tools (Howard 1943) had been found at Scottsbluff (artifact A7071; see Figure 11.4d below) and that they must both be part of the same horizontal parallel flaking complex. Wormington (1949:61–62) also discussed the Lime Creek site assemblage, noting that it had two and perhaps three Scottsbluff points.

In 1957 Wormington published the fourth edition of *Ancient Man in North America*, which became her final revision. Here she discussed the Scottsbluff Bison Quarry in a major section titled "Scottsbluff and Eden Points." She described the assemblage (p. 118) as follows:

> One [of the Scottsbluff artifacts] was a plano-convex end scraper and three were modified flakes that have no diagnostic value; but there were also three fragmentary points and one complete specimen. The latter is the one which has provided the name for the Scottsbluff type. There is another specimen, with only the tip missing, which resembles the former but has a more triangular blade, a more deeply inset stem, and is thinner. Another point, which lacks only a small portion of the base, is a lanceolate form with somewhat convex sides, and can be classified as a Plainview. The flaking is essentially oblique. The fourth point lacks the basal portion and cannot be identified.

The accompanying illustration (Wormington 1957:Figure 38) includes, from left to right, facial views of Scottsbluff artifacts A7071, A7073, and A7072. Artifact A7071, which is relatively long, is the named Scottsbluff point. Wormington goes on to discuss Scottsbluff points as having been found at Lime Creek, MacHaffie (Forbis and Sperry 1952; see also Knudson 1983), and San Jon, and in surface collections in northwestern Louisiana and eastern Texas as well as in Washington, British Columbia, Alberta, Saskatchewan, and Ontario. Her "Artifacts of the Cody Complex" on pages 266–267 includes Scottsbluff Types I and II, Eden with collateral flaking, Eden with transverse flaking, and a Cody knife. None of these drawings is of the Scottsbluff Bison Quarry artifacts.

Thus was the Paleoindian Scottsbluff point type created. Since 1957 most North American Paleoindian typological compendia (e.g., Frison 1991; Irwin 1968; Justice 1987; Taylor 2006) have built on Wormington's structure with little assessment of the data and assumptions behind the original model. There is undoubted value and validity in the Wormington model, but the specific sites and collections merit reconsideration and the unilineal nature of the 1950s paradigm definitely needs modification. The evolution of the Scottsbluff type over 20 years is evident in Wormington's writing. The evolution of these concepts and the new information about the involved assemblages and their complexity has certainly changed over the half century since 1957! The Scottsbluff point type and the Scottsbluff site assemblage need to be reviewed in their own right, and the individual knappers and materials, as well as the associated societies, taken into consideration.

Prehistoric systematics (Binford 1972; Dunnell 1971) are not as exciting as understanding what archaeological evidence means in terms of what people were doing at a specific site, what they ate, or speculations about how many people were living together and what they were doing at different seasons of the year. However, the definition and organization of culture-historically significant tool types and time units is critical to the related interpretation of changing human adaptations. If we do not know how things relate in time and space, we cannot study their patterning over time and space. Thus, attention is paid here to the Scottsbluff type and its place within the Cody complex, and its relativity to other Paleoindian culture-historical units.

Wormington (1957:3–4) discussed her concerns about typology for her readers:

> It should be noted that not all archaeologists would classify these points in exactly the same way. Ideally, an archaeological type should have "demonstrable historical meaning in terms of behavior patterns" (Krieger [1944], p. 272). Actually, however, a projectile point type is essentially an artificial construct, and in typology there are no eternal verities. An individual or a group of individuals may feel that certain traits characterize a sufficiently large number of points that a recurring pattern, believed to be culturally significant and delimited in time and space, can be recognized. In order to be able to communicate with others, it is necessary to assign a name to this group, and a type is thus created.
>
> Not all archaeologists create types in the same way, however. Some are "lumpers" who recognize only few types and allow a great variation within each category. Others are "splitters" who recognize a large number of types and insist on greater uniformity because they believe that certain relatively small differences may be significant. Even though archaeologists try to avoid both extremes, they must, if they are honest, admit that they tend toward one end of the scale or the other. The tendencies of the writer [Wormington] are, admittedly, on the splitting side.
>
> If type names are to serve as a means of communication, it is essential that the reader and writer attach the same meaning to the words. On pages 261 to 271 [of the 1957 publication] will be found pictures and definitions of certain key types. The purpose of this section is not to set up immutable categories but simply to indicate what the writer has in mind when using a type name in the following discussion. Obviously, not every point placed in a given category will be an exact replica of the point shown; there are too many variations as regards individual initiative, skill, materials used, etc. What is involved is that, when a type name is used, the specimen under discussion will, in the writer's opinion, conform to the definition and be more nearly like the specimen illustrated than like any of the others.

### The Scottsbluff Site

The Scottsbluff Bison Quarry (25SF2) was on the north bank of Spring Creek about 15 m east of its junction with Kiowa Creek, on the south side of the North Platte River valley in far western Nebraska (Figures 11.1–11.3). The site was found and excavated during a Nebraska State Museum paleontological recovery project in 1932 (Barbour and Schultz 1932; Bell and Van Royen 1934:60–62; MacClintock 1935). The quarry is located just northeast of and below Signal Butte west of Gering, Nebraska, in Scotts Bluff County. During the fossil collection project, eight flaked stone artifacts (see Figures 11.4 and 11.5 below) were found within the bison bonebed, and Barbour and Schultz (1932:Figure 169 caption) noted that five of the pieces "were found far back and deep in the quarry." The deposit "var[ied] in thickness from two to four feet [0.6–1.2 m], and having a length of thirty feet [9 m], was a solid mass of skulls, jaws, and bones" (Barbour and Schultz 1932:283). These were found under 16–30 feet (4.9–9 m) of sand and silt. The deposit was in the coarse gravels of an old Spring Creek river channel incised into a floor of Oligocene Brule clay, left by a stream with "a considerable volume of water with a strong current" (Barbour and Schultz 1932:284).

**FIGURE 11.1.** Great Plains map locating the Hell Gap, Hudson-Meng, James Allen, Scottsbluff, Signal Butte, and Medicine Creek (Allen, Lime Creek, and Red Smoke) sites.

Several eminent geologists and anthropologists, including Earl H. Bell of the University of Nebraska, Etienne B. Renaud of Denver University, and Jesse Dade Figgins of the Colorado Museum of Natural History (now the Denver Museum of Nature and Science), visited the site during the investigations. It was the consensus of the excavators and site visitors that the artifacts were in their original deposition locations within the bone mass.

Bell and Van Royen (1934:61) noted that the fossil channel into which the gravels and bone had been deposited "does not appear to be very much wider than the present canyon of Spring Creek. A study of this little canyon and the neighboring territory indicates that the general course of the old channel closely corresponds to that of the present creek. All the visible evidence seems to point toward the occurrence of long range changes in the life of essentially one and the same creek, Spring Creek."

Haynes (1960) noted that the fossil channel (in which he illustrated Section B) was about six feet (1.8 m) wide across the whole stream incision. Spring Creek is a minor tributary to Kiowa Creek, minor enough that it is not even named in the Scotts Bluff County soil survey (Soil Conservation Survey 1968:Sheet 39).

FIGURE 11.2. The Scottsbluff site landscape in 1936, with the site upstream to the left and Signal Butte in the background. Courtesy of the Archives, University of Nebraska State Museum.

The artifacts were found in situ in the top of the gravel layer below the dense bonebed, which included articulated bone units (Schultz and Eiseley 1935:310, 1936:524). The bison species was identified as *Bison occidentalis* by Schultz and Eiseley (1935:311), and the bones were in association with now-extinct *Succinea ovalis pleistocenica* and *S. grosvenori gelida*, as well as *Fossaria parva tazewelliana* (freshwater snails; Schultz and Eiseley 1935:316). The site was revisited in 1933, 1934, and 1935 (Barbour and Schultz 1936:438), when it was paleontologically and geologically restudied. At that time several other land and freshwater invertebrate species were identified in the bonebed level, considered to be a typical middle to late Pleistocene fauna. The several publications on the site excavation (Barbour and Schultz 1932, 1936; Lugn 1934:353; Schultz and Eiseley 1935, 1936) do not specify that the site was so thoroughly excavated that nothing remained, but when Vance Haynes visited the site in 1960 (Haynes 1960), he could not find any archaeological evidence. I found no site remnants when I visited the locality in 1970.

In 2005 Matthew E. Hill (2008; Hill and Knudson 2006) inventoried the entire Scottsbluff site bison assemblage and recorded 1461 specimens. Most of the bones were major limb bones, crania, and cervical vertebrae. Very small and easily disarticulated bone elements, as well as the originally reported bone fragments, were noticeably missing in the extant collection. The bones were generally whole and showed little carnivore damage or evidence of subaerial weathering or root etching. Hill judged that the bones represented 26 animals, probably in a cow-calf herd.

The skeletal array supported the inference that water action culled the smaller, lighter bones from the deposit and that much of the original deposit may be away from the excavated site. The presence of artifacts at the top of the gravels below the bonebed suggests that there had been some winnowing of the bonebed. However, the presence of skeletal articulations reported by the original investigators, as well as stone "chips" (flakes) in the deposit, indicates that the original activity area was not very far from the final site area. Given the area's topography, it is likely that the original kill/butchering location was within a quarter kilometer or less from the final archaeological site. The site has recently been radiocarbon dated by Hill (2008) to 8680 ± 85 (10,115–9500 cal BP) and 8938 ± 85 (10,239–9744 cal BP) (Table 11.1).

The Scottsbluff site is located several hundred meters northeast and downslope from the Signal Butte site (25SF1; Forbis et al. n.d.; Strong 1933,

**FIGURE 11.3.** Loren Eiseley and Bertrand Schultz at the Scottsbluff site in 1932. Courtesy of the Archives, University of Nebraska State Museum.

**TABLE 11.1.** Radiocarbon Dates from Scottsbluff and Related Sites.

| Site | $^{14}$C Years BP | Cal BP[a] | Lab Number | Dated Material | Reference |
|---|---|---|---|---|---|
| Allen Occ. Level 2 | 8680±460 | 11,095–8540 | Tx-6595 | Charcoal | May 2007:Table 3.3 |
| Clary Ranch | 9040±45 | 10,255–10,160 | CAMS-105849 | Bison bone collagen, AMS[b] | Hill 2005 |
| Hell Gap | | | | | |
| Loc. 1 Scottsbluff level | 8600±600 | 11,230–8180 | I-245 | Charcoal | Haynes 2009:47 |
| | 9120±490 | 11,760–9020 | AA-27675 | Charcoal | |
| Loc. IIIS/V Cody | 8890±110 | 10,250–9550 | A-753A | Bone collagen | |
| | 9050±160 | 10,600–9630 | A753C8 | Bone apatite | |
| Loc. I Frederick | 8600±380 | 10,585–8595 | A-501 | Charcoal + burned earth | |
| James Allen | 8405±25 | 9495–9310 | UCI-AMS-19330 | Bone fragment, AMS | Knudson and Kornfeld 2007 |
| Lime Creek Zone 1 | 10,040±270 | 12,620–10,710 | Tx-6777 | Humates | May 2007:Table 3.6; zone lies between these two dates |
| | 9120±510 | 11,830–9010 | Tx-6778 | Humates | |
| Red Smoke | 8830±130 | 10,245–9535 | Tx-7558a | Charcoal + burned bone | Knudson 2002:Table 7.2; May 2007:Table 3.8 |
| | 8910±130 | 10,295–9550 | Tx-7558b | Charcoal + burned bone | |
| Scottsbluff | 8938±85 | 10,250–9690 | AA-67443 | *Bison* humerus | Hill 2008; Hill and Knudson 2006 |
| | 8680±85 | 10,115–9495 | AA-67442 | *Bison* humerus | Hill 2008; Hill and Knudson 2006 |

[a] Correlated with INTCAL09 dataset (Reimer et al. 2009).

[b] AMS = accelerated mass spectrometry.

1935; also see Knudson 2002:125–129). Though Signal Butte's Lowermost Level 1 was relatively thin, at least one of its flaked stone artifact midsections (Knudson 2002:Figure 7.17e) exhibits parallel-collateral flaking that may represent the Eden-Scottsbluff flaking pattern. Another Level 1 artifact (Knudson 2002:Figure 7.17g) had oblique flaking. As discussed below, most of the Scottsbluff artifacts are made of White River Group silicates (WRGS; Hoard et al. 1993; Miller 2009). Most of the Signal Butte Level 1 artifacts were also flaked from this material. Signal Butte is a WRGS bedrock source, with chalcedony veins in its caprock (Bliss 1950), and there are other WRGS outcrops within 5–10 km.

### The Scottsbluff Site Flaked Stone Assemblage

Eight flaked stone tools were found in the Scottsbluff Bison Quarry (Barbour and Schultz 1932: Figure 169; Barbour and Schultz 1936:Figure 202A, B, E; Bell and Van Royen 1934:Plate facing p. 49; this chapter, Figures 11.4 and 11.5 and Table 11.2). Additionally, "a number of small chips of flinty chalcedony in direct association" with the bonebed (Barbour and Schultz 1936:434) were recorded; however, none of those "chips" remains today with the eight Scottsbluff artifacts in the University of Nebraska State Museum collection. The following description of the tools is based on macroscopic analysis; no microscopic review has been made of any of the artifacts.

#### *A7071 (Figure 11.4d, Table 11.2)*

This long (length:width ratio of 4.4:1) WRGS lanceolate point has facial flaking with horizontal parallel flake scars that terminate at a strong midline ridge; they are relatively collateral. The width:thickness ratio is nearly 3:1. The piece has a 16-mm-long straight stem that is inset only ~1.5 mm on each side and is moderately to heavily ground; the inset appears to be from grinding rather than flaking. There is a suggestion of light edge rounding on a 1.5-mm length along each of the lateral edges just above the stem, perhaps from hafting abrasion or prehension. There is no suggestion of beveling on the point, but a very fine serration occurs on the lateral edges (a similar pattern occurs on some of the Jurgens site points [Greiser 1977; Wheat 1979]). The piece has a luster and hue (dark red gray, 5YR4/1 [Munsell Color Company 1954]) that suggest it may have been heat-treated (Crabtree and Butler 1964; Odell 2000; Purdy 1974) before flaking.

By the time of Wormington's 1957 publication (compare with her 1944 discussion), this piece had become the model of the Scottsbluff Type I point (Wormington 1957:Figure 38 left). Note, however, that this artifact is not the one illustrated in Figure 70 (left) of that publication.

#### *A7072 (Figure 11.4c, Table 11.2)*

This WRGS biface was the first piece found during the Scottsbluff site excavations, and was described by Wormington (1957:118, Figure 38 right) as "a lanceolate form with somewhat convex sides, and can be classified as a Plainview. The flaking is essentially oblique." There is no significant convexity to the proximal portion of the tool. Heavy edge grinding exists along the proximal 25 mm of each lateral edge above the broken corners. The tool has alternate edge thinning but no noticeable beveling. It has a dark red gray hue (10R4/1-2 to 10R5-6/1) and slight luster, suggesting that it may have been heat-treated.

The tool bears little resemblance to the tools from the Plainview assemblage in Texas (Knudson 1983; Krieger 1947). In 1957 Wormington had few models of Plains Paleoindian points with which to compare collections; hence any unfluted, unstemmed lanceolate point with unpatterned facial flaking tended to be called "Plainview" (Knudson 2009b). She did not compare it with the obliquely flaked Angostura (Hughes 1949; Hannus et al. 1986), Browns Valley (Jenks 1937), or James Allen collections described and illustrated in her 1957 volume.

Barbour and Schultz (1932:286) commented, "All concerned think it impossible that these artifacts could have been buried intrusively." Bell and Van Royen (1934:60) noted that "it was found to be fairly certain that the point [A7072] was not intrusive to the fossils. The later finds of three more dart points and a snub nosed scraper bear out this conclusion and we do not need to consider this possibility further." Subsequent discussions of the site (e.g., Schultz and Eiseley 1935) refute the suggestion in the (poorly phrased) initial sentence of the Bell and Van Royen quotation, noting that the point was clearly in situ.

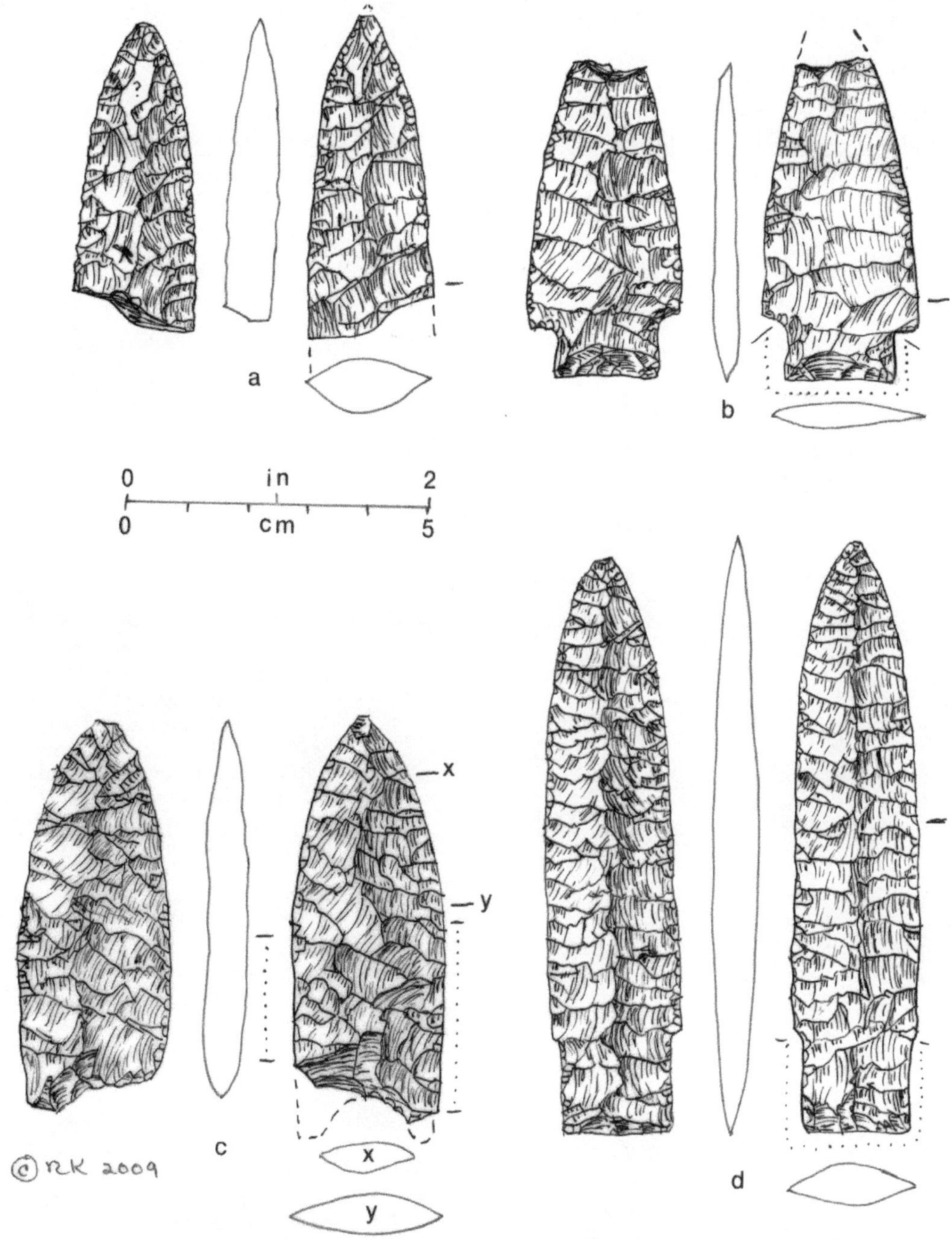


**FIGURE 11.4.** Scottsbluff site (25SF2) projectile points: nos. 7074 (a), 7073 (b), 7072 (c), and 7071 (d).

### *A7073 (Figure 11.4b, Table 11.2)*

This thin WRGS stemmed point was found well into the site, and over the years has come to be the model for Wormington's (1957:Figure 70 second from left) Scottsbluff Type II. Wormington (1939: 27, 1944:30, 1949:58) referred to this tool as having a "flaring stem," but by 1957 she had deleted that description. The stem clearly has a squared proximal form, flaked into the piece and moderately ground on all edges. There is no evidence that the piece was reworked. One edge of the stem extends farther up the lateral edge than the other, making

**TABLE 11.2.** Scottsbluff Site (25SF2) Artifact Dimensions.

| Nebraska State Museum Catalog No. | Barbour and Schultz 1932 Artifact No. | Barbour and Schultz 1932 Fig. 169 | Fig. No. in This Chapter | Artifact Description: Material, form | Length (cm) | Width (cm) | Thickness (cm) | Deposition |
|---|---|---|---|---|---|---|---|---|
| A7071 | 1-30-8-32 | d | 11.4d | WRGS collaterally flaked stemmed point | 96 | 22 | 8 | Fourth artifact found; 4'–6' back from the original bank face at ~17' depth in the top of the gravels below the bonebed (Schultz & Eiseley 1935:308) |
| A7072 | 1-4-8-32 | a | 11.4c | WRGS unstemmed point | >66 | 26 | 7 | First artifact found (Barbour & Schultz 1932:Figure 169a); toward bottom of the bonebed ~10" above the floor of Brule clay & buried under 14' (Schultz & Eiseley 1935:308) |
| A7073 | 1-4-9-32 | e | 11.4b | WRGS asymmetrical stemmed point | >53 | 26 | 4.5 | Fifth artifact found; 4'–6' back from the original bank face at ~17' depth in the top of the gravels below the bonebed (Schultz & Eiseley 1935:308) |
| A7074 | 1-12-8-32 | c | 11.4a | WRGS point missing base | >51 | 21 | 9 | Third artifact found; 4'–6' back from the original bank face at ~17' depth in the top of the gravels below the bonebed (Schultz & Eiseley 1935:308) |
| A7075 | 1-8-9-32 | h | 11.5b | Hartville chert end scraper | 37 | 29 | 8 | Last artifact found; 4'–6' back from the original bank face at ~17' depth in the top of the gravels below the bonebed (Schultz & Eiseley 1935:308) |
| A7076 | 1-10-8-32 | b | 11.5c | WRGS flake tool | >45 | 26 | 15 | Second artifact found; 4'–6' back from the original bank face at ~17' depth in the top of the gravels below the bonebed (Schultz & Eiseley 1935:308) |
| A7077 | 1-5-9-32 | g | 11.5a | WRGS biface flake, perhaps used | 40 | 31 | 4 | Seventh artifact found; 4'–6' back from the original bank face at ~17' depth in the top of the gravels below the bonebed (Schultz & Eiseley 1935:308) |
| A7078 | 2-4-9-32 | f | 11.5d | WRGS used flake | 54 | 36 | 7 | Sixth artifact found; 4'–6' back from the original bank face at ~17' depth in the top of the gravels below the bonebed (Schultz & Eiseley 1935:308) |

*Note:* WRGS = White River Group silicates (Hoard et al. 1993).

it appear "asymmetrical" to some viewers. This apparently was the basis for Irwin's (1968:104) belief that the piece was a knife rather than a projectile point.

The artifact has horizontal parallel flaking from both faces of one edge, and very flat flaking that did not create a medial ridge. The tool's blade edges all appear to have been lightly abraded to remove the arris tips between flake scars along those edges, or perhaps they were scrubbed through cutting use. There is no suggestion of beveling on the tool, and it has a pinkish gray (7.5YR6-7/2) hue that suggests heat treatment. Light edge rounding on the proximal 5 and 3 mm,

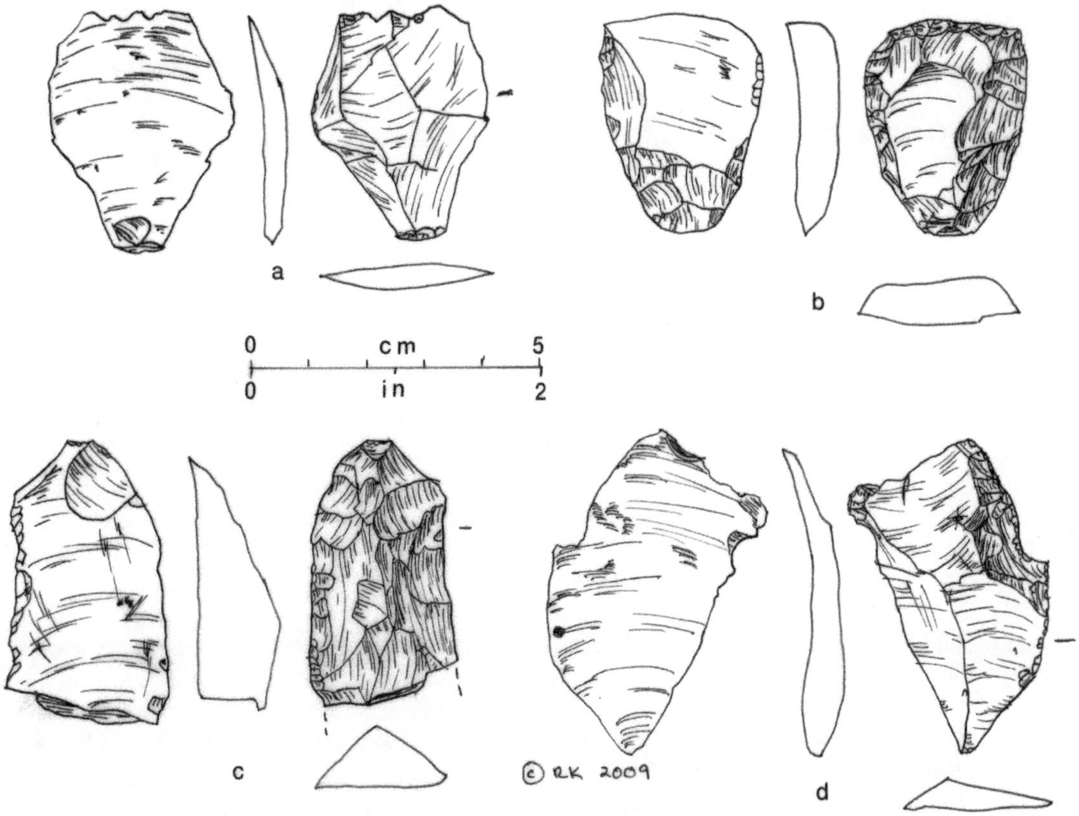


FIGURE 11.5. Scottsbluff site (25SF2) flake tools: nos. 7077 (a), 7075 (b), 7076 (c), and 7078 (d).

respectively, of the proximal ends of the two lateral edges suggest hafting or prehension abrasion.

*A7074 (Figure 11.4a, Table 11.2)*

This distal segment of a WRGS point is snapped off at the base and has no stem or proximal lateral abrasion. The piece is relatively thick, lacks any patterned facial flaking, and is roughly serrated with a bevel flaked into one lateral edge. It has a dark gray brown (9YR4/2) hue that suggests it could have been heat-altered.

*A7075 (Figure 11.5b, Table 11.2)*

This Hartville chert (my identification) flake tool is unifacially flaked on its distal edge to form an end scraper, and its lateral edges have been minimally flaked. There is evidence of heavy abrasion on both lateral edges, from tool use, haft abrasion, or prehension wear. I have observed that Hartville chert frequently occurs in North Platte River gravels in the Scottsbluff area, and hence it can be considered a local lithic resource. Bell and Van Royen (1934:62) noted that this tool is a "type frequently encountered in western Nebraska, especially in the lower stratum of Signal Butte." The tool's luster and hue (5YR5/3 [red brown]) suggest that it may have been heat-treated.

*A7076 (Figure 11.5c, Table 11.2)*

This thick broken flake tool may have been removed from a larger WRGS biface, and it has been hinge-fractured at its proximal end. It has been worked along at least one lateral edge, and the other edge is spalled on the ventral face as if from heavy use. The tool is oriented parallel to the original flake axis. The tool is light red brown (5YR6/3) in hue, and that combined with its luster and potlidding on the dorsal face suggest it was heat-altered or burned. There is some rounding of the arris on the proximal portion of the dorsal face, suggesting abrasion by wear, hafting, or prehension.

### *A7077 (Figure 11.5a, Table 11.2)*

This thin, unused, and unmodified WRGS flake appears to have been removed from a biface. Its hue (10R5/4 [weak red]) and slight luster suggest that it was heat-treated.

### *A7078 (Figure 11.5d, Table 11.2)*

This relatively thin WRGS flake was finely retouched or exhibits use-wear along one lateral edge. Its hue (7.5YR6/2-4 [pinkish gray to light brown]) and luster suggest that it has been heat-treated.

Muñiz's (2005:427) microwear analysis of Cody-ascribed artifact collections concluded that "projectile points and end scrapers...were almost always used for only single functions." Frison (1991:289–325, 2004:198–202) says that cutting into animal hide, the first step in butchering, dulls a tool edge quickly because of the grit in the hide. Subsequent cutting of animal muscle and fat, and frequent encounters with bone and tough sinew, will also quickly modify an edge. The original Scottsbluff excavators commented that there were small stone flakes in the bone mass, which suggests that some tool resharpening took place during the butchering process. None of the extant artifacts shows much evidence of reworking, however. It appears that the four points in the Scottsbluff assemblage were used to kill rather than butcher the carcasses, and may have been lost in the bone mass or discarded because they were broken. The scraper does not exhibit heavy use-wear, nor do the other three flake tools; however, they could have been used for lighter work. Numerous killing and/or butchering tools were probably taken away from the site when the occupants left.

The entire assemblage of flaked stone tools or debitage from the Scottsbluff site is made of locally available lithic material, mostly WRGS with one Hartville chert item. All of these artifacts have evidence of heat treatment, if not burning.

The geological evidence indicates that the *Bison* bone mass and its associated artifacts may have been moved from the original kill and butchery site (Hill 2008), but the presence of articulated bone units and small flakes suggests that it was not moved far enough to have significantly reorganized itself. It is my opinion that the Scottsbluff assemblage, as recovered in 1932, is a single component.

Recent study of the Hudson-Meng bonebed and artifacts (Agenbroad 1978; Largent 2007) demonstrates that multiple events can be reflected in what appears to be a single-event deposition of bone and artifacts. Today's Scottsbluff collection consists of the artifacts and bones, minimal catalog records, the published articles, and no site remnants in situ. These do not demonstrate significant site complexity.

## Scottsbluff Assemblage Comparisons

If the Scottsbluff assemblage represents a single human bison kill and butchering event, it reflects several tool facial flaking patterns that have been considered separate Paleoindian artifact types over the past 80 years. Alberta, Scottsbluff, and perhaps James Allen points were found at the Hudson-Meng bison kill site (Agenbroad 1978), 120 km north of Scottsbluff (Figure 11.1). Both unpatterned and parallel horizontal and oblique facial flaking patterns are found within the Medicine Creek site (Allen, Lime Creek, Red Smoke) assemblages from southern Nebraska, some 320 km southeast of the Scottsbluff site. These varying designs or "types" have also been found in proximity at the Hell Gap sites, some 105 km northwest up the North Platte valley (see Figure 11.1). In essence, the variety of technologies represented at Scottsbluff is not unique among Great Plains Paleoindian sites.

In the 1950s-excavated Medicine Creek sites, it appears that the various facial flaking patterns may be found together within individual components as well as distributed between defined components. In the 1960s-excavated Hell Gap sites, it appears that each flaking style has its own unique component. Given the historic nature of both sets of excavation data, it is unclear whether either or both patterns reflect prehistoric technological, social, and/or cultural reality. What follows is a review of western Plains sites that played important roles in defining the Cody complex, with special attention to variation in point styles.

### *Lime Creek*

Lime Creek (25FT41) is a multicomponent site in the Medicine Creek drainage, Frontier County, Nebraska (Davis 1953, 1954, 1962; Figure 11.1).

The site was excavated by the University of Nebraska State Museum from 1947 to 1950, led by E. Mott Davis. Lime Creek is a tributary of Medicine Creek, which is in turn a tributary of the Republican River, which flows east across southern Nebraska and northern Kansas to debouch into the Kansas River and eventually into the Missouri River. Lime Creek was one of three major sites excavated by the museum in the Medicine Creek drainage; its companion sites were Red Smoke, also excavated by Davis (1953, 1954; Knudson 2002), and Allen, excavated by Preston Holder and Joyce Wike (1949, 1950; Bamforth 2002; Bamforth, ed. 2007). All three sites are considered to be combination workshop/camp areas.

Lime Creek yielded more than 200 artifacts distributed across three defined cultural zones (Davis 1962; May 2007:25–31). Zone I (lowermost; Table 11.2) had five points (Davis 1962:77): a "Scottsbluff" point, a "Milnesand" point, a midsection with transverse flaking (no. 7602; Davis 1962:Figure 19A, p. 77) of Smoky Hill jasper (Davis 1962:Table II) that Davis noted may have broken in manufacture (Davis as quoted in Hicks 2002:71), and two simple flake points (Davis 1962:77).

The "Scottsbluff" point (Wormington 1957:120–121) appears to be reworked and has stem edge grinding (no. 7554; Davis 1962:Figures 10A and 24; this chapter, Figure 11.6 [left]). Its design has similarities to the Scottsbluff A7071 piece (Figure 11.4d), though A7071 has more strikingly parallel horizontal flaking. The projectile point is made of Hartville chert (my identification). In my experience the Hartville materials found in North Platte River gravels are not large enough to have been serially reduced to produce a Scottsbluff-like projectile point. Thus, it is assumed that the point was made at the Hartville bedrock quarries in southeastern Wyoming (some 550–575 km northwest of Medicine Creek), someplace between there and Lime Creek, or at Medicine Creek itself from a large preform. Without detailed analysis of the Lime Creek debitage, it is impossible to state where the tool was produced.

The "Milnesand" point has alternate beveling (no. 7551; Davis 1962:Table II, Figures 10B and 23, pp. 63 and 77; this chapter, Figure 11.6 [right]), and was considered by Hicks (2002:69–71) to be a manufacturing by-product. The point is of gray and black flint (Wormington 1957:120–121), possibly Nehawka flint (Blackman 1907), as were a few of the Red Smoke artifacts (Knudson 2002:Table 7.3).

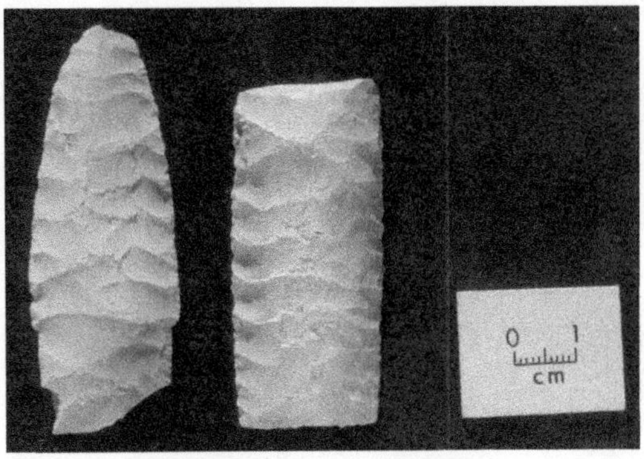

**FIGURE 11.6.** Lime Creek (25FT41) Zone I points: nos. 7554 (*left*) and 7551 (*right*).

The rest of the Zone I assemblage is predominantly (Davis 1962:Figures 10–16) Smoky Hill jasper (Knudson 2002), which outcrops along the Lime Creek valley. May (2007:29) says that Cultural Zone I includes two discrete occupation surfaces. If that is the case, these distinctive artifacts may have been left during separate camping episodes at the site.

Cultural Zone I includes 17 Lime Creek knives as identified by Davis (1962:Figures 11 and 12, pp. 76–77), which were included within Hicks's Lime Creek lithic analysis as Cody point preforms (Hicks 2002:Figures 4.13–14). These Smoky Hill jasper artifacts have parallel margins and a squared base (Hicks 2002:15). A comparison of Lime Creek Zone I Cody point preforms with an experimental Cody point production data set (Bradley and Stanford 1987) suggested that "flintknappers at the Lime Creek site had a different mental template than the Claypool study flintknappers" and that the Lime Creek inhabitants "were not trying to make Eden points" (Hicks 2002:111–112).

Davis's Lime Creek Zone III included at least three points, one of which he labeled "Plainview" (no. 7605; Davis 1962:Figures 20A and 30; this chapter, Figure 11.7 [left]) and another "Milnesand" (no. 7604; Davis 1962:Figures 20B and 29; this chapter, Figure 11.7 [center]), while noting that a third (no. 7607; Davis 1962:Figures 20C and 28; this chapter, Figure 11.7 [right]) was obliquely flaked. Based on the latter point, Irwin (1968:107)

FIGURE 11.7. Lime Creek (25FT41) Zone III points: nos. 7605 (*left*), 7604 (*center*), and 7607 (*right*).

assigned Zone III to the Frederick Complex (see Hell Gap site discussion below). All of these are made of Smoky Hill jasper. Davis's Table II description of Lime Creek site points notes that the pieces from Zone III included one of gray-pink Morrison quartzite (Hicks 2002:39), which is found in the Hartville Uplift where the Hell Gap sites lie (Miller 2009:412), and the rest of yellow, orange-yellow, green-brown, or brown (Smoky Hill) jasper. Zone III has not been radiocarbon dated, but it lies several stratigraphic units above the Zones I and II cultural material (May 2007; Table 11.1).

Wormington (1957:120–122) illustrated the Zone I "Scottsbluff" and "Milnesand" points with her discussion of the Lime Creek site, which she included under the "Scottsbluff and Eden Points" heading. However, despite having Davis's (1954) dissertation available, she did not discuss or describe the entire large Lime Creek assemblage, including the Lime Creek knives and other tools. At the end of this major section she discussed categorizing Scottsbluff and Eden points as "Cody" points, stating that there was evidence in the western U.S. and Canadian plains that these were used by the same people (p. 136). Thus, the Lime Creek site came to be subsumed under the Cody rubric.

Despite the application of the "Scottsbluff" appellation to a projectile point from Lime Creek as well as one from Red Smoke (see below), I am more comfortable identifying Lime Creek, Red Smoke, and Allen with their own Medicine Creek complex (Irwin 1968:66, 108–109; Knudson 2002:134–135), which emphasizes their reliance on Smoky Hill jasper and common designs characterized by relatively unpatterned facial flaking. When Wormington assigned Lime Creek to the Cody complex in 1957, there was no information from Hell Gap, minimal information from Medicine Creek, and a slim set of Plains Paleoindian sites with which then-known materials could be compared. Irwin's (1968:66–70) assignment of the Lime Creek site to Cody and Frederick labels did not consider the large amount of Smoky Hill points/fragments and other production debris, or the exotic nature of the few points that reflected a Cody design, and generally followed Wormington's model. Hicks's (2002) problems in correlating the Lime Creek knives production pattern with the Claypool Cody pattern suggest that the Medicine Creek site occupants were involved in a different reduction technology—one adapted to the Smoky Hill jasper. There are not an infinite number of ways one can reduce a raw material, whether tabular or blocky, to a biface or to a specific bifacial point design. I would definitely assign a couple of individual points from Lime Creek and Red Smoke to the Cody pattern, but would assign the overall archaeological components at each site to the local Medicine Creek complex. Trade and exchange were undoubtedly a part of the Medicine Creek drainage site occupants' lives.

### *Red Smoke*

The Red Smoke site (25FT42) is also located in the Lime Creek valley within the Medicine Creek drainage (Davis 1953, 1954; Knudson 2002; Figure 11.1, Table 11.1). The site was tested in 1946 and excavated in 1949 through 1952. Wormington (1957: 117–118) treated the Red Smoke assemblage as a complex separate from her discussion of Scottsbluff and Eden points.

Davis recognized eight cultural occupation zones at Red Smoke (May 2007:31–37), most of which reflected Smoky Hill jasper workshops and related camps. Many of the bifacial tools were beveled but had relatively undistinguished facial flaking, and consequently were put under the Plainview rubric (Knudson 2009b) by Wormington and Davis.

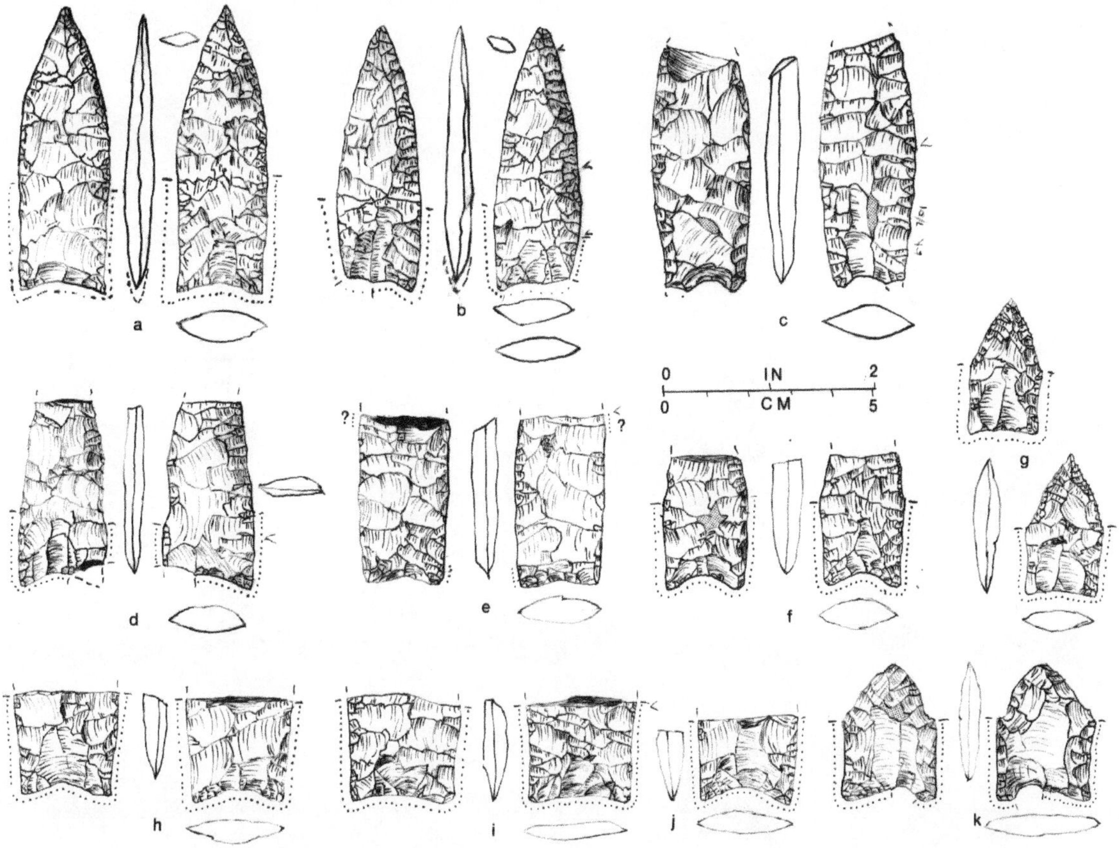


FIGURE 11.8. Red Smoke (25FT42) points of Smoky Hill jasper: nos. A8787 (a), 2295-52 (b), 2121-52 (c), A8262 (d), A8793 (e), A8252 (f), 1167-52 (g), A8263 (h), A8253 (i), A8251 (j), and 1869-52 (k).

Two horizontal parallel flaked point midsections were found in Red Smoke's main occupation, labeled Zone V or 88. One of these is of Alibates agatized dolomite (no. A8256; Knudson 2002:Figure 7.11a; this chapter, Figure 11.9a), and the other is of Cloverly-Morrison orthoquartzite from Spanish Diggings in the Hartville Uplift (no. 1529-52; Knudson 2002:Figure 7.11b; this chapter, Figure 11.9b). These were accompanied by more than 30 points from that level made of Smoky Hill jasper (Figure 11.8), including two that are obliquely flaked (no. A8801, Figure 11.9e; and no. 1829-52, Figure 11.9f). It was probably because of the preponderance of the Smoky Hills lithic material in the unit, accompanied by the horizontally flaked pieces made of nonlocal material, that Wormington declined to include the Red Smoke material within her Cody designation. Irwin (1968) and Knudson (2002:133) have suggested that the Red Smoke Zone V people had ties to the Meserve and Dalton technologies in the Mississippi-Missouri drainage. The site's association with Smoky Hill jasper and design affinities with (1) western Plains oblique and parallel flaked assemblages, (2) more nonpatterned "Plainview"-like artifacts, and (3) beveled "Dalton"-like tools support its inclusion within its own Medicine Creek complex.

### *Allen*

The Allen site (25FT50; Holder and Wike 1949; Bamforth, ed. 2007; Figure 11.1, Table 11.1), located in the Lime Creek valley, was excavated from 1947 to 1949 and has recently been extensively analyzed (Bamforth, ed. 2007). The site has two major occupation levels. The earlier, lower unit lacks artifacts stylistically related to the Scottsbluff site points, though the Intermediate Zone may be contemporary with Cody materials (May

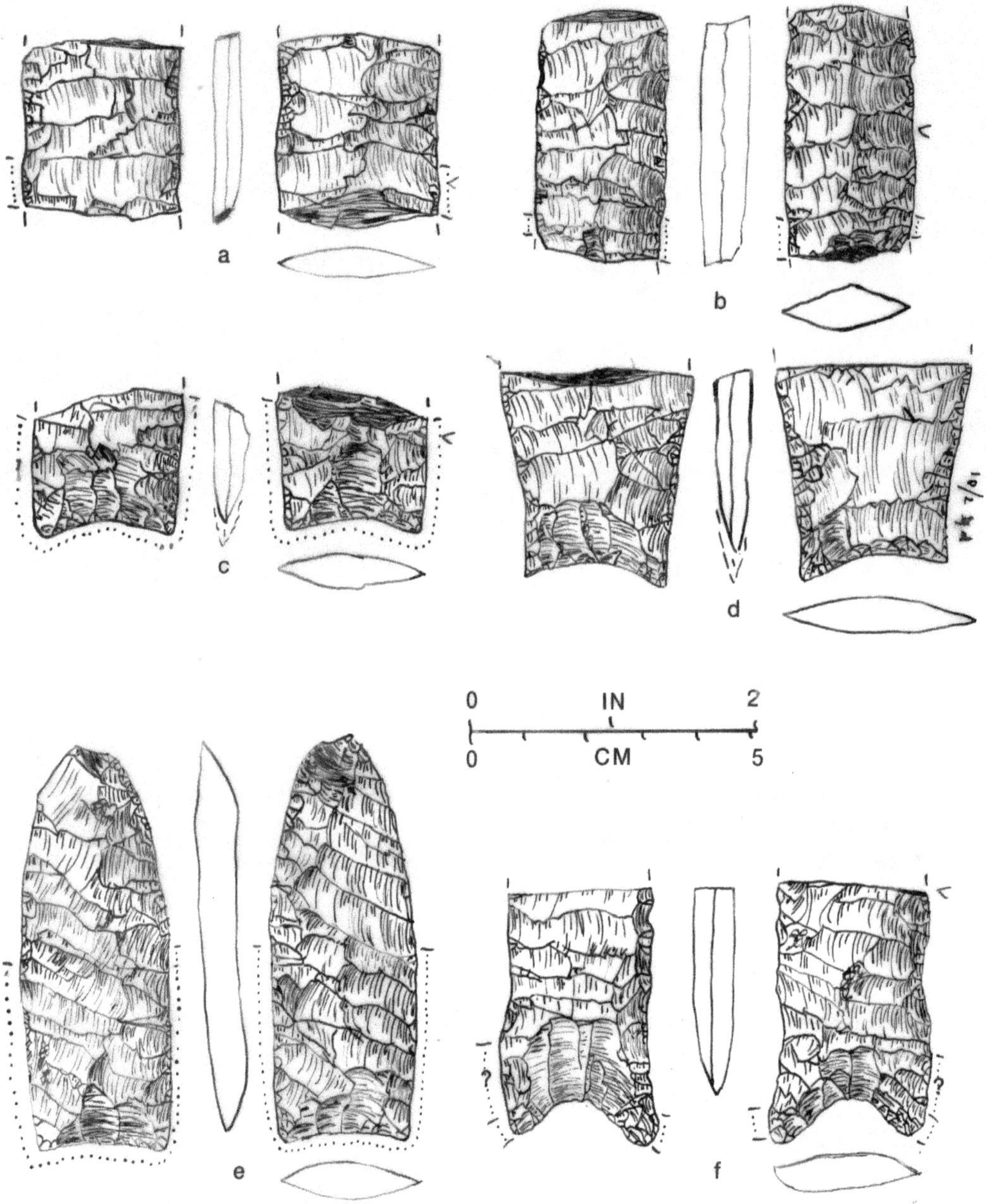


FIGURE 11.9. Red Smoke (25FT42) points of Alibates agatized dolomite (a, A8256, and c, A8261), Hartville quartzite (b, 1529-52), chert (d, 2294-52), and probably high-quality obliquely flaked Smoky Hill jasper (e, A8801, and f, 1829-52).

2007:20–25). The site is considered to be a camp area in which significant chipped stone tool production took place.

Occupation Level 2 may have had two obliquely flaked points associated with it; unfortunately, both are now unprovenienced (Bamforth 2007:161). Bradley (2009:271) has recently subsumed the obliquely flaked tools from Allen, Hell Gap, Frederick and Lusk components, Brown's Valley, and Angostura under the historic Frontier complex rubric proposed by Holder and Wike in 1949 on the basis of the obliquely flaked artifacts. However, the missing provenience data for the two Allen points make their use in defining any archaeological unit questionable.

### Hell Gap Localities I and IIIS/V Cody

The Hell Gap site (48GO306) is located in Goshen County in southeastern Wyoming, in the upper reaches of Cottonwood Creek, which drains south 20 km to the North Platte River (Knell 2007, 2009; Knell et al. 2009; Figure 11.1, Table 11.1). The site is surrounded by bedrock Hartville chert and quartzite outcrops. The site was excavated in the 1960s (Irwin-Williams et al. 1973; also see Knudson 2009a; Larson et al. 2009) and then reopened by the University of Wyoming in the 1990s. Most of the current published analyses make primary use of the 1960s data, supplemented by information acquired in the 1990s and early twenty-first century (see Larson et al. 2009). Locality I is a major multicomponent unit in the southern portion of the Hell Gap excavations, and Locality IIIS/V is in the upper valley. Both have yielded Cody material, though each assemblage has a different character.

Knell, Hill, and Izeta (2009) include all the Hell Gap Locality V material under the Eden typological rubric, whereas the Locality I assemblage (Knell 2009) is classified as a combination of Eden and Scottsbluff forms; Irwin (1968) referred to them all as *Cody* points. At both of these locations the occupants relied on the local Hartville cherts and quartzites for their flaked stone tool production, and they apparently hunted individual bison or small bison herds from the local area. Both of these localities are interpreted as camp/workshop areas.

Several of the Locality I artifacts illustrated in Knell (2009:Figure 12.9) are very slightly shouldered and appear similar to Scottsbluff point A7071 (this chapter, Figure 11.4d); apparently the facial flaking may be more or less parallel horizontal on the Locality I pieces. Bradley (2009:268) comments that Eden points have "highly patterned serial flaking" and a median ridge. Given that the Hell Gap archaeological (and presumed cultural) sequence was defined in the 1960s, recent studies have been concerned with socioeconomic/sociocultural issues rather than artifact classification criteria. The illustrations available in Knell (2007, 2009), Knell et al. (2009), and Bradley (2009) do not include many lateral or cross sections, but it appears that few of these tools resemble Scottsbluff A7073 (Figure 11.4b). Certainly none of the Cody-assigned materials reflects Scottsbluff artifacts A7072 (Figure 11.4c) or A7074 (Figure 11.4a).

Haynes (2009:47, 49) notes that across the Hell Gap localities Stratum F is a sedimentary mix of Eden, Frederick, and Lusk material left as people occupied the flat Hell Gap valley floor. This mix is comparable to the variety of point forms at the Scottsbluff site; in the overlapping palimpsests of many late Paleoindian sites, including Hell Gap, it may be inappropriate to separate out "components" based on point forms.

### Hell Gap Locality I Frederick

Locality I has a component with obliquely flaked projectile points labeled *Frederick* after the landowner (Byrnes 2009; Figures 11.1 and 11.10, Table 11.1). The component included more than 3000 artifacts, two-thirds of which are debitage and only 34 of which are bifaces or biface fragments (Bradley 2009:270–271). The points are made of local Hartville chert and Cloverly-Morrison formation orthoquartzite (Miller 2009), and Dakota quartzite (Banks 1990:89–90). The unit is relatively small, and difficult to separate out from other Locality I components. Irwin (1968:46, 106–108) described this as a "rich living surface" that included a stone circle, suggesting that a primitive shelter was erected at the site. He noted that comparable points were found at the James Allen (see below), Lime Creek (Irwin 1968:67–69), and Scottsbluff (Irwin 1968:76) sites.

### James Allen

The James Allen site, located at the southern end of the Laramie Basin in Wyoming, was excavated in 1951 (Mulloy 1959; Figure 11.1, Table 11.1). The site is approximately 250 km northwest of the Scottsbluff site over the Rocky Mountains. This apparently was a single bison kill butchering event, with the remains of about 15 animals recovered from the excavations. As at the Scottsbluff site, there is no apparent associated camping area. The associated points (Figure 11.11) were predominantly obliquely flaked; I am currently

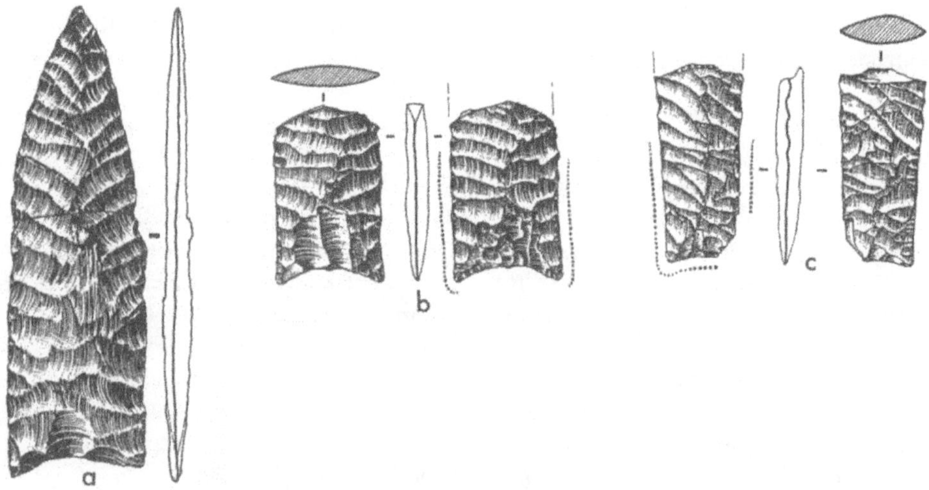


FIGURE 11.10. Hell Gap Frederick and Lusk points. From Knudson 2009a:Figure 2.8.

analyzing 70 tools from the site. Most of the tools are made from what is presumed to be a relatively local quartzite, though a specific source area has not been identified. The oblique flaking on these points is not highly regimented, being more like the flaking pattern on the Scottsbluff A7072 point (Figure 11.4c).

### *Clary Ranch*

The Clary Ranch site (Hill et al. 2002; Hill 2005; Knudson 2002:124–125) is just off the North Platte River, about 160 km southeast of the Scottsbluff site and 280 km northwest of the Medicine Creek Valley. This bison kill, butchering, and camp site is 9000 $^{14}$C years old (Table 11.1) (ca. 10,200 cal BP); its lithic assemblage is not yet well documented or analyzed. However, Myers's (1997) illustration of some of the points from this site exhibits a facial flaking pattern similar to the oblique, parallel flaked points from the James Allen and other sites but with beveling similar to the Red Smoke artifacts. The flaking has some similarities to the Scottsbluff A7072 point and to one face of the Scottsbluff A7074 point. When analysts move beyond a "traditional" Plains point typology to look at the technology and style of individual tools while comparing multiple assemblages, the Clary Ranch assemblage could well be a key to understanding the complexity of early Holocene cultures.

## Discussion and Conclusion

### *Where Does the Scottsbluff Site Fit?*

The Scottsbluff site is a Plains Paleoindian site whose artifact-derived "type" definitions have been used as archetypes for many archaeologists and most collectors without reference to the original tools and their association within a single-event assemblage. Consideration of the projectile points from Scottsbluff demonstrates the issue.

Artifact A7071 (Figure 11.4d), Wormington's (1957) model Scottsbluff I Cody-related point type, would in 2012 probably be identified as "Eden" by most people and assigned to the Cody complex (Frison 1991:66; Wormington 1957). That is, it has affinities with points from Horner (Frison and Todd 1987), Finley (Moss et al. 1951), Hell Gap, Claypool (Bradley and Stanford 1987; Dick and Mountain 1960), Olsen-Chubbuck (Wheat 1972), and Jurgens (Wheat 1979).

Artifact A7072 (Figure 11.4c), with its oblique flaking, would probably be assigned in 2012 to an Alder (Davis et al. 1989), Angostura, Frederick, James Allen, or Lusk type. I see more similarities between Scottsbluff artifact A7072 and the James Allen assemblage than I do between the Scottsbluff point and the materials from the Hell Gap (Frederick) or Ray Long (Angostura) collections. My practice is to carefully document and illustrate the collection from any single component, analyze its technology and function, and then

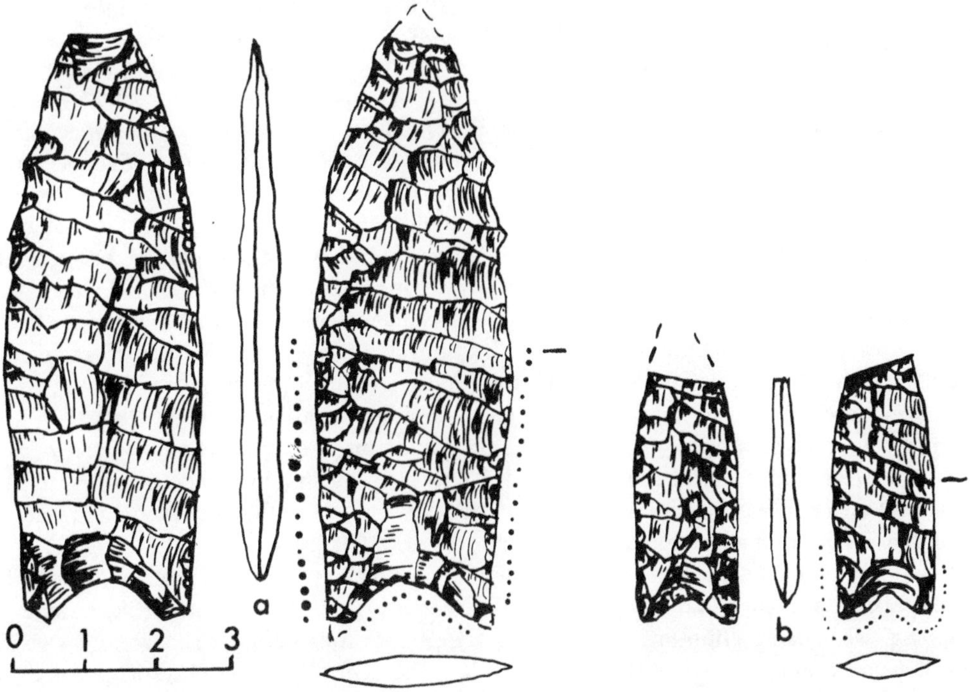


FIGURE 11.11. James Allen site points: nos. 60436 (a) and 60434 (b). From Knudson and Kornfeld 2007:Figure 1.

describe comparable patterns in other assemblages before assigning a culture-historical label to it. Only when there are many such descriptions and analyses can we suggest valid relationships among these various collections and their associated people.

Artifact A7073 (Figure 11.4b) is the model for Wormington's (1957) Scottsbluff II Cody-related point. Its thin form and lack of a marked medial ridge seems to have few direct counterparts in Cody-assigned assemblages other than the "Cody knives" (Blackmar 1998; Frison 1991; Wormington 1957:267). I have not had firsthand experience with all those assemblages, and a review of them could identify counterparts. At the Horner site there are a few points whose planar outline is similar to that of Scottsbluff artifact A7073; however, none of them is as thin. At present, this form appears to be relatively unique to the Scottsbluff site, and may reflect a single artisan and a specific piece of material more than a wider technological or sociocultural "type."

Artifact A7074 (Figure 11.4a) has counterparts all over the Plains given its nondiagnostic facial flaking, except for its bevel. It is similar to many of the artifacts from Red Smoke, Lime Creek, and the Allen site. It is of local material, relatively thick, beveled, and roughly serrated. Again, it may represent one artisan's design and skill product rather than a specific "type."

Table 11.1 shows that even given their wide variations in error ranges, there are four dates (Allen Level 2, Hell Gap [Frederick], Hell Gap [Scottsbluff], and Scottsbluff) that center at about 8600 radiocarbon years ago (ca. 9543 cal BP). The others (Clary Ranch, Hell Gap Cody [as in Knell 2009], Lime Creek 1, Red Smoke) tend to date a couple of hundred years earlier. These appear to be all roughly contemporary over an ovoid 500-km area that ranges from the Black Hills to Hell Gap (lithic source area) to James Allen to Scottsbluff (lithic source area) to Medicine Creek (lithic source area). Most of these dates are less than precise, though the more recently dated Hell Gap and Clary Ranch component assessments are more reliable. The data suggest that a more lanceolate form was being produced before the Scottsbluff site was created and that the Scottsbluff materials represent a younger style within the identified Cody continuum.

### *Who Were the Scottsbluff People?*

After the bison were dispatched by the Scottsbluff site hunters, it must have been urgent to process the meat before there was much spoilage (Brink 2008:168–178; Frison 2004:114). Hill has identified a minimum of 26 bison in a mixed herd (13 percent bulls, 35 percent adult cows, 52 percent calves) in the kill/butchering event. Based on carcass weight data, Jack Brink (personal communication 2009) estimates that these animals would have yielded 5700 to 7500 kg of meat and fat (e.g., 12,500–16,500 lbs). There is little evidence of significant carnivore predation of the Scottsbluff site bone assemblages.

Brink (personal communication 2009) believes that the kill may have been (1) by male hunters out on a hunting expedition, (2) near an existing camp, or (3) in a location away from an existing camp, so that people had to move to the kill site once the animals had been dispatched. If the killing was done by a hunting party, he estimates that 20–30 adult males could have directed the kill and butchered the animals. However, it is likely that the hides were needed by their larger family group(s). Additional people then would have scraped and tanned the hides, as well as dried the meat. A great deal of work to process the hides and meat, much less the marrow-yielding bone, was involved! Brink suggests that the processing could have taken 8–10 days if only 20–30 men were available, but a camp of 100 people could have processed the meat and hides more quickly. However, the hide tanning would have still taken a full week of work by the larger group.

While the people conducting the kill/butchering event could have camped on Signal Butte, it is unlikely that they moved all the kill products up there. It is more likely that whatever number of people were involved, they camped elsewhere along the North Platte Valley. If there were indeed 100 people associated with this event, this must have been a relatively large congregation of men, women, and children during the early Holocene period. Could this have been an annual congregation that combined the obtaining of food, hide, and bone with seasonal socializing and ritual?

If there were this many people, perhaps there were multiple kin groups or other social groups, and perhaps the various bifacial flaking patterns on the four points represent different social groups and/or different knappers. However, these tools are all made of local material and likely were made by only one or a few knappers. Specific designs could have been preferred by certain individuals and/or had links to specific functions or even specific ritual activities. The Hell Gap, Scottsbluff, and Medicine Creek localities could have had excess local stone material for trading and exchanging, perhaps in negotiations over mates or because of personal preference for specific materials. There are no answers to questions about design-social links in this assemblage, much less about the number of knappers.

These people left only eight artifacts in the kill. That seems to have been conservative behavior, especially when lithic material for new tools was locally available in bedrock seams and Platte Valley gravels. It may be that the water action that seems to have winnowed some of the bone from the site also removed some flaked stone tools from the probable butchering area.

The Scottsbluff site creators appear to have forgotten to follow the typology manuals when they created their stone tools. Assuming that the Scottsbluff assemblage represents a single point in time, it would appear that the points made of local materials have design connections to the north and west (Cody complex, Frederick complex [Irwin 1968:69, 106–108]), south and east (Medicine Creek complex), and beyond (Dalton in the Mississippi Valley, Plainview in the southern Plains). This clearly represents prehistoric technological and cultural reality, but how does that fit with twenty-first-century archaeological interpretations of what ought to go with what?

### *Scottsbluff, Cody, and Cultural Historical Units*

I have tremendous admiration for anyone who takes on the task of compiling archaeological data and presenting it in a synthesis of knowledge (e.g., Kornfeld et al.'s 2010 compendium on northwestern Great Plains and Rocky Mountain prehistory). Such compendia must have named culture-historical units to make sense of the cultural (including technological) complexity involved in synthesizing more than 13,000 years of data in an area perhaps 800 km in each direction. The culture-historical units must be based on synthesized named categories of artifacts, since that is the most basic dataset we have that apparently reflects cultural diversity (e.g., in the choices of reduction technology, shape design, hafting technique, life cycle). Yet there are not an infinite number of variations on the shape and facial flaking of most of these tools. Hunters must have created ballistically appropriate throwing and thrusting spear points that could reliably be attached to a shaft. The tools had to have sharp edges for piercing hide, and perhaps for cutting through skin, sinew, and muscle as well as for disjointing bones. I believe they also created tools that were personally satisfying (i.e., were art pieces) that may or may not have represented specific social groups. Flintknapping is not an intuitive skill; significant knowledge is required to reduce a piece of stone into a usable and desirable form. Production of balanced and stylized pieces requires teaching by an expert; the sharing of this learned information may have resulted in as much design consistency as any ascribed set of cultural rules.

It is important to understand the relationship of prehistoric knowledge, skill, functional requirements, information sharing, aesthetic preference, and perhaps also some group standards to the archaeological task of explaining these ancient patterns. To fulfill that explanatory task, we propose tool types and culture-historical units that we must continually recognize as artificial units created in modern minds to try to explain prehistoric cultural patterns. The models created by Wormington, Jepsen (1951, 1953), and others in the past have been critical to the evolving understanding of the past. However, the analytical categories must evolve to meet our new data and new analytical processes.

In 2012 I would define the "Cody complex" as a set of northern Plains and perhaps northern Great Basin sites and assemblages characterized by bifacial points with parallel collateral flaking. These locations were environmentally similar during the time period in which we think people used these materials. The greatest concentration of "Cody" assemblages probably dates from about 9200 to 8800 radiocarbon years ago (10,340–9823 cal BP), though the dates of materials in the Canadian Plains are not well understood. There are parallel collaterally flaked points from earlier assemblages, such as Plainview (Knudson 1983:Figure 12a, b) at 10,000 radiocarbon years BP (ca. 11,470 cal BP) and Hudson-Meng (Muñiz 2010) at about 9500 radiocarbon years BP (ca. 10,740 cal BP) (see also Knell and Muñiz, this volume). The distribution of point styles probably is best displayed as a series of battleship frequency curves following traditional seriation methods (Irwin 1971; O'Brien and Lyman 1999) with tails that precede and follow the greatest concentration of known sites characterized by parallel collateral flaking.

Sites and assemblages from this period have had more analysis than younger materials from these areas, and there appears to be a stylistic accord to many of the assemblages now assigned to a "Cody" category. However, the people who made, used, traded, inherited, and lost those tools were very fluid, and the archaeological use and understanding of those categories must recognize that fluidity. "Cody" people probably did not recognize themselves as a tightly bound sociocultural unit (i.e., the tools should not be interpreted too tightly). But insofar as they had some sociocultural unit recognition, their territory had boundaries and neighbors with whom they shared information, mates, and resources (food, raw materials). That sharing would result in differences in the materials, shapes, uses, and life cycles of stone tools, whose variability may be difficult to recognize and interpret in the archaeological record; that, however, is the exciting task of the archaeologist!

In the meantime, I would call the Scottsbluff site assemblage "Scottsbluff." I would then look at its culture-historical relationships, noting both the Cody pattern and the Medicine Creek pattern, and similarities to the later parallel-oblique material. I am comfortable with ambiguity at this stage of our slim knowledge of Plains prehistory, and I think one can still develop synthesizing models with such ambiguity built into them.

Again, in 2012, I would use Irwin's historical concept of the Medicine Creek complex to understand the sites focused on the Smoky Hill jasper resource, and their trade and exchange systems with other areas and people who used other lithic resources. I would look at the parallel-oblique flaked tool assemblages in the northern Plains (e.g., James Allen, Hell Gap, Ray Long, Barton Gulch) as an overlapping but generally younger technological pattern which may represent another sociocultural unit or units but which is presently still very poorly known.

In historic times, when much pressure existed on Native American territories, subsistence, and lifeways, a few young men (usually males in the stories) traveled from the Rio Grande to the Canadian Rockies and from the Dalles on the Columbia River to the Ohio River valley, but they were rare individuals. Before Indians had the horse, most of them lived in a very prescribed annual round to procure enough food to eat, mates to grow a new generation, and social occasions to relax and celebrate. They probably did not move over much more than 300 km in any year, all within a well-known territory. Paleoindian people were probably equally restricted in their range, with a few people (males or females) moving more widely to trade and explore. Our Paleoindian culture-historical units and cultural interpretations should probably reflect comparable lifestyles.

The future rests first of all on careful understanding of individual sites and assemblages and careful construction of the synthesizing units on which we base our cultural explanations. The Scottsbluff site and assemblage is a small example of the need for sophisticated anthropological understanding of the people who butchered those bison and celebrated their lives in company with family and friends.

## Acknowledgments

I thank Ed Knell and Mark Muñiz for inviting me to participate in the symposium that led to this book and for providing useful comments that contributed to the final form of the chapter. Marie Wormington first taught me to be concerned about Paleoindian typology, and W. Raymond Wood introduced me to the Scottsbluff site in 1970. Many years ago Jim Gunnerson, then director of the University of Nebraska State Museum, provided me access to the Scottsbluff and Lime Creek collections, and the museum's Susan Curtis recently helped with Scottsbluff artifact site numbers. Mott Davis was irreplaceable in his contributions to the Red Smoke analysis and my understanding of the site, and Trisha Nelson recently helped check out Red Smoke catalog numbers at the Nebraska State Historical Society. George Frison, Marcel Kornfeld, Jim Duguid, and Danny Walker provided assistance with work on the James Allen material, and with Henry Irwin and Mary Lou Larson helped inform my understanding of the Hell Gap localities and assemblages. Jack Brink was invaluable in helping me think about the activities and people involved in the prehistoric Scottsbluff bison kill event. I could not have written this chapter without help from Montana State University–Great Falls College of Technology interlibrary loan librarians Beth Cooper and Kirsten Bryson. Thank you!

## References

Agenbroad, Larry D.
1978 *The Hudson-Meng Site. An Alberta Bison Kill in the Nebraska High Plains*. University Press of America, Washington, D.C.

Bamforth, Douglas B.
2002 The Paleoindian Occupation of the Medicine Creek Drainage, Southwestern Nebraska. In *Seventy Years of Archaeology in the Medicine Creek Valley of Nebraska*, edited by Donna Roper, pp. 54–83. University of Alabama Press, Tuscaloosa.
2007 The Allen Site Lithic Assemblage. In *The Allen Site: A Paleoindian Camp in Southwestern Nebraska*, edited by Douglas B. Bamforth, pp. 148–183. University of New Mexico Press, Albuquerque.

Bamforth, Douglas B. (editor)
2007 *The Allen Site: A Paleoindian Camp in Southwestern Nebraska*. University of New Mexico Press, Albuquerque.

Banks, Larry D.
1990 *From Mountain Peaks to Alligator Stomachs: A Review of Lithic Sources in the Trans-Mississippi South, the Southern Plains, and Adjacent Southwest*. Oklahoma Anthropological Society Memoir No. 4. Norman.

Barbour, Erwin Hinckley, and C. Bertrand Schultz
1932 The Scottsbluff Bison Quarry and Its Artifacts. *Bulletin of the Nebraska State Museum* 1(34):283–286.
1936 Palaeontologic and Geologic Considerations of Early Man in Nebraska. *Bulletin of the Nebraska State Museum* 1(45):432–449.

Bell, Earl H., and William Van Royen
1934 An Evaluation of Recent Nebraska Finds Sometimes Attributed to the Pleistocene. *Wisconsin Archaeologist* 13(3):49–70.

Binford, Lewis R.
1972 Archaeological Systematics and the Study of Culture Process. In *Contemporary Archaeology*, edited by Mark P. Leone, pp. 125–132. Southern Illinois University Press, Carbondale.

Blackman, E. E.
1907 Nehawka Flint Quarries. *Records of the Past* 6(4):103–110.

Blackmar, Jeanette M.
1998 The Distribution of Cody Knives: A Distinctive Trait of the Cody Complex. *Current Research in the Pleistocene* 15:6–9.

Bliss, Wesley L.
1950 Early and Late Lithic Horizons in the Plains. *Proceedings of the Sixth Plains Archeological Conference of 1948*, edited by Jesse D. Jennings, pp. 108–116. Anthropological Papers No. 11. Department of Anthropology, University of Utah, Salt Lake City.

Bradley, Bruce A.
2009 Bifacial Technology and Paleoindian Projectile Points. In *Hell Gap: A Stratified Paleoindian Campsite at the Edge of the Rockies*, edited by Mary Lou Larson, Marcel Kornfeld, and George C. Frison, pp. 243–258. University of Utah Press, Salt Lake City.

Bradley, Bruce A., and Dennis J. Stanford
1987 The Claypool Study. In *The Horner Site: The Type Site of the Cody Cultural Complex*, edited by George C. Frison and Lawrence C. Todd, pp. 405–434. Academic Press, New York.

Brink, Jack W.
2008 *Imagining Head-Smashed-In: Aboriginal Buffalo Hunting on the Northern Plains.* AU Press, Athabasca University, Edmonton, Alberta.

Byrnes, Allison M.
2009 Frederick Component at Locality I. In *Hell Gap: A Stratified Paleoindian Campsite at the Edge of the Rockies*, edited by Mary Lou Larson, Marcel Kornfeld, and George C. Frison, pp. 216–228. University of Utah Press, Salt Lake City.

Crabtree, Don E., and B. Robert Butler
1964 Notes on Experiments in Flint-knapping: I. Heat Treatment of Silica Minerals. *Tebiwa* 7:106.

Davis, E. Mott
1953 Recent Data from Two Paleo-Indian Sites on Medicine Creek, Nebraska. *American Antiquity* 18:380–386.
1954 The Culture History of the Central Great Plains Prior to the Introduction of Pottery. Unpublished Ph.D. dissertation, Harvard University, Cambridge, Massachusetts.
1962 *Archeology of the Lime Creek Site in Southwestern Nebraska.* University of Nebraska State Museum Special Publication No. 3. Lincoln.

Davis, Leslie B., Stephen A. Aaberg, William P. Eckerle, John W. Fisher Jr., and Sally T. Greiser
1989 Montana Paleoindian Occupation of the Barton Gulch Site, Ruby Valley, Southwestern Montana. *Current Research in the Pleistocene* 6:7–9.

Dick, Herbert W., and Bert Mountain
1960 The Claypool Site: A Cody Complex Site in Northeastern Colorado. *American Antiquity* 26:223–235.

Dunnell, Robert C.
1971 *Systematics in Prehistory.* Free Press, New York.

Forbis, Richard G., and J. D. Sperry
1952 An Early Man Site in Montana. *American Antiquity* 18:127–133.

Forbis, Richard G., William Duncan Strong, and Maurice E. Kirkby
n.d. Signal Butte and MacHaffie: Two Stratified Sites on the Northern Great Plains. Manuscript on file, University of Calgary Archives, Calgary, Alberta.

Frison, George C.
1991 *Prehistoric Hunters of the High Plains.* 2nd ed. Academic Press, New York.
2004 *Survival by Hunting: Prehistoric Human Predators and Animal Prey.* University of California Press, Berkeley.

Frison, George C., and Lawrence C. Todd (editors)
1987 *The Horner Site: The Type Site of the Cody Cultural Complex.* Academic Press, New York.

Greiser, Sally T.
1977 Micro-analysis of Wear-Patterns on Projectile Points and Knives from the Jurgens Site, Kersey, Colorado. *Plains Anthropologist* 22:107–116.

Hannus, L. Adrien, with John Albanese, Linda J. Scott, and Rhoda Owen Lewis
1986 Report on 1985 Test Excavations at the Ray Long Site (39FA65) Angostura Reservoir, Fall River County, South Dakota. *South Dakota Archaeology* 10:48–104.

Haynes, C. Vance, Jr.
1960 Scottsbluff Bison Quarry Field Notes Taken 2 October 1960. Manuscript in possession of the author, Department of Anthropology, University of Arizona, Tucson.
2009 Geochronology. In *Hell Gap: A Stratified Paleoindian Campsite at the Edge of the Rockies*, edited by Mary Lou Larson, Marcel Kornfeld, and George C. Frison, pp. 39–52. University of Utah Press, Salt Lake City.

Hester, James J., with Ernest L. Lundelius Jr. and Roald Fryxell
1972 *Blackwater Locality No. 1: A Stratified Early*

*Man Site in Eastern New Mexico*. Fort Burgwin Research Center, Southern Methodist University, Rancho de Taos, New Mexico.

Hicks, Keri
2002 Local Variability in Paleoindian Lifeways: A Comparison of the Lime Creek and Allen Site Worked Stone Assemblages, Southwest Nebraska. Unpublished Master's thesis, Department of Anthropology, University of Colorado, Boulder.

Hill, Matthew E., Jr.
2008 New Investigations of the Cody-Age Finley and Scottsbluff Bison Bone Beds. *Current Research in the Pleistocene* 25:90–93.

Hill, Matthew E., Jr., and Ruthann Knudson
2006 A New Look at the Scottsbluff Bison Quarry (25SF2). Paper presented at the 64th Annual Plains Anthropological Conference, Topeka, Kansas.

Hill, Matthew G.
2005 Late Paleoindian (Allen/Frederick Complex) Subsistence Activities at the Clary Ranch Site, Ash Hollow, Garden County, Nebraska. *Plains Anthropologist* 50:249–263.

Hill, Matthew Glenn, Matthew E. Hill Jr., David W. May, Thomas P. Myers, David J. Rapson, Frédéric Sellet, James L. Theler, and Lawrence C. Todd
2002 Palaeoindian Subsistence Behavior at the Clary Ranch Site, Nebraska, USA. *Antiquity* 76:311–312.

Hoard, Robert J., John R. Bozell, Steven R. Holen, Michael D. Glascock, Hector Neff, and J. Michael Elam
1993 Source Determination of White River Group Silicates from Two Archaeological Sites in the Great Plains. *American Antiquity* 58:698–710.

Holder, Preston, and Joyce Wike
1949 The Frontier Culture Complex: A Preliminary Report on a Prehistoric Hunter's Camp in Southwestern Nebraska. *American Antiquity* 24:260–266.
1950 The Allen Site (FT-50): Archeological Evidence of an Early Hunter's Camp on Medicine Creek, Frontier County, Nebraska. In *Proceedings of the Sixth Plains Archeological Conference, 1948*, edited by Jesse Jennings, pp. 105–108. Anthropological Papers No. 11. Department of Anthropology, University of Utah, Salt Lake City.

Howard, Edgar B.
1943 The Finley Site: Discovery of Yuma Points, *in situ*, near Eden, Wyoming. *American Antiquity* 8:224–241.

Hughes, Jack T.
1949 Investigations in Western South Dakota and Northeastern Wyoming. *American Antiquity* 14:266–277.

Irwin, Henry T.
1968 The Itama: Late Pleistocene Inhabitants of the Plains of the United States and Canada. Unpublished Ph.D. dissertation, Department of Anthropology, Harvard University, Cambridge, Massachusetts.
1971 Effects of Excavation on Seriation at a Palaeo-Indian Site. In *Mathematics in the Archaeological and Historical Sciences: Proceedings of the Anglo-Romanian Conference, Mamaia 1970*, edited by F. R. Hodson, D. G. Kendall, and P. Tăutut, pp. 209–214. Edinburgh University Press, Edinburgh.

Irwin-Williams, Cynthia, Henry T. Irwin, George Agogino, and C. Vance Haynes
1973 Hell Gap: Paleo-Indian Occupation on the High Plains. *Plains Anthropologist* 18:40–53.

Jenks, A. E.
1937 *Minnesota's Browns Valley Man and Associated Burial Artifacts*. Memoirs of the American Anthropological Association No. 49. Menasha, Wisconsin.

Jepson, Glenn L.
1951 Ancient Buffalo Hunters in Wyoming. *Archeological Society of New Jersey Newsletter* 24:22–24.
1953 Ancient Buffalo Hunters. *Princeton Alumni Weekly* 53(25):cover, 10–12.

Justice, Noel D.
1987 *Stone Age Spear Points of the Midcontinental and Eastern United States: A Modern Survey and Reference*. Indiana University Press, Bloomington.

Knell, Edward J.
2007 The Organization of Late Paleoindian Cody Complex Land-Use on the North American Great Plains. Unpublished Ph.D. dissertation, Department of Anthropology, Washington State University, Pullman.
2009 Cody Complex at Locality I. In *Hell Gap: A Stratified Paleoindian Campsite at the Edge of the Rockies*, edited by Mary Lou Larson, Marcel Kornfeld, and George C. Frison, pp. 180–194. University of Utah Press, Salt Lake City.

Knell, Edward J., Matthew G. Hill, and Andrés D. Izeta
2009 The Locality IIIS/V Eden Complex Component. In *Hell Gap: A Stratified Paleoindian Campsite at the Edge of the Rockies*, edited by Mary Lou Larson, Marcel Kornfeld, and George C. Frison, pp. 157–179. University of Utah Press, Salt Lake City.

Knudson, Ruthann
1983 *Organizational Variability in Late Paleo-*

*Indian Assemblages*. Washington State University, Laboratory of Anthropology, Reports of Investigation No. 60. Pullman.

1995 The San Jon Points and Paleoindian Typology. *Plains Anthropologist* 40:391–397.

2002 Medicine Creek Is a Paleoindian Cultural Ecotone: The Red Smoke Assemblage. In *Seventy Years of Archaeology in the Medicine Creek Valley of Nebraska*, edited by Donna Roper, pp. 84–141. University of Alabama Press, Tuscaloosa.

2009a The Early Expeditions: University of Wyoming, Harvard University, and the Peabody Museum. In *Hell Gap: A Stratified Paleoindian Campsite at the Edge of the Rockies*, edited by Mary Lou Larson, Marcel Kornfeld, and George C. Frison, pp. 14–35. University of Utah Press, Salt Lake City.

2009b Plainview Technology and Typology in Plain View. Paper presented at the 67th Annual Plains Anthropological Conference, Norman.

Knudson, Ruthann, and Marcel Kornfeld

2007 A New Date for the James Allen Site, Laramie Basin, Wyoming. *Current Research in the Pleistocene* 24:112–114.

Kornfeld, Marcel, George C. Frison, and Mary Lou Larson

2010 *Prehistoric Hunter-Gatherers of the High Plains and Rockies*. 3rd ed. Left Coast Press, Walnut Creek, California.

Krieger, Alex D.

1944 The Typological Concept. *American Antiquity* 9:271–288.

1947 Artifacts from the Plainview Bison Bed. In "Fossil Bison and Associated Artifacts from Plainview, Texas," by E. H. Sellards, Glen L. Evans, and Grayson E. Meade, with Alex D. Krieger, pp. 938–952. *Bulletin of the Geological Society of America* 58:927–954.

Largent, Floyd

2007 Is It or Isn't It? The Quiet Controversy over the Hudson-Meng Site. *Mammoth Trumpet* 22(3):14–16, 20.

Larson, Mary Lou, Marcel Kornfeld, and George C. Frison (editors)

2009 *Hell Gap: A Stratified Paleoindian Campsite at the Edge of the Rockies*. University of Utah Press, Salt Lake City.

Lugn, A. L.

1934 Outline of Pleistocene Geology of Nebraska [The Geology and Mammalian Fauna of the Pleistocene of Nebraska, Part 1]. *Nebraska State Museum Bulletin* 41: 294– 319.

MacClintock, Paul

1935 Investigation of the Geology of the Yuma-Folsom Sites in Western Nebraska. *Carnegie Institution of Washington Year Book* 34:318–319. Washington, D.C.

May, David W.

2007 Landforms, Alluvial Stratigraphy, and Radiocarbon Chronology at Selected Paleoindian Sites around Medicine Creek Reservoir. In *The Allen Site: A Paleoindian Camp in Southwestern Nebraska*, edited by Douglas B. Bamforth, pp. 17–46. University of New Mexico Press, Albuquerque.

Miller, James C.

2009 Preliminary Analysis of Lithic Materials. In *Hell Gap: A Stratified Paleoindian Campsite at the Edge of the Rockies*, edited by Mary Lou Larson, Marcel Kornfeld, and George C. Frison, pp. 411–413. University of Utah Press, Salt Lake City.

Moss, John H., Kirk Bryan, G. William Holmes, Linton Satterthwaite Jr., Henry P. Hansen, C. Bertrand Schultz, and W. D. Frankforter

1951 *Early Man in the Eden Valley*. University of Pennsylvania, Museum Monographs No. 6. Philadelphia.

Mulloy, William

1959 The James Allen Site, near Laramie, Wyoming. *American Antiquity* 25:112–116.

Muñiz, Mark Peter

2005 The Cody Complex Revisited: Landscape Use and Technological Organization on the Northwestern Plains. Unpublished Ph.D. dissertation, Department of Anthropology, University of Colorado, Boulder.

2010 *Results of 2008 Archaeological Investigations at the Hudson-Meng Site (25SX115), Sioux County, Nebraska*. Report submitted to Heritage Resources Program, Nebraska National Forest, Chadron.

Munsell Color Company

1954 *Munsell Soil Color Charts*. Munsell Color Company, Baltimore, Maryland.

Musil, Robert R.

1988 Functional Efficiency and Technological Change: A Hafting Tradition Model for Prehistoric America. In *Early Human Occupation in Far Western North America: The Clovis-Archaic Interface*, edited by Judith A. Willig, C. Melvin Aikens, and John L. Fagan, pp. 373–387. Nevada State Museum Anthropological Papers No. 21. Carson City.

Myers, Thomas P.

1997 Reduction Sequence at the Clary Ranch Site. *Current Research in the Pleistocene* 14:61–68.

O'Brien, Michael J., and R. Lee Lyman

1999 *Seriation, Stratigraphy, and Index Fossils: The*

*Backbone of Archaeological Dating*. Kluwer Academic/Plenum Publishers, New York.

Odell, George H.

2000 Stone Tool Research at the End of the Millennium: Procurement and Technology. *Journal of Anthropological Research* 8:269–331.

Purdy, Barbara A.

1974 Investigations Concerning the Thermal Alteration of Silica Minerals: An Archaeological Approach. *Tebiwa* 17:37–66.

Reimer, P., M. Baillie, E. Bard, A. Bayliss, J. W. Beck, C. Bertrand, P. Blackwell, C. Buck, G. Burr, K. B. Cutler, P. E. Damon, R. L. Edwards, R. G. Fairbanks, M. Friedrich, T. P. Guilderson, A. G. Hogg, K. A. Hughen, B. Kromer, G. McCormack, S. Manning, C. Ramsey, R. Reimer, S. Remmelle, J. Southon, M. Stuiver, S. Talamo, F. Taylor, J. Van der Plicht, and C. Weyhenmeyer

2009 IntCal09 and Marine09 Radiocarbon Age Calibration Curves, 0–50,000 years cal BP. *Radiocarbon* 51:1111–1150.

Roberts, Frank H. H., Jr.

1942 *Archeological and Geological Investigations in the San Jon District, Eastern New Mexico*. Smithsonian Miscellaneous Collections 103(4). Smithsonian Institution, Washington, D.C.

Schultz, C. Bertrand

1932 Association of Artifacts and Extinct Mammals in Nebraska. *Nebraska State Museum Bulletin* 33(1):271–282.

Schultz, C. Bertrand, and Loren C. Eiseley

1935 Paleontological Evidence of the Antiquity of the Scottsbluff Basin Quarry and Its Associated Artifacts. *American Anthropologist* 37:306–318.

1936 An Added Note on the Scottsbluff Quarry. *American Anthropologist* 38:521–524.

Soil Conservation Service

1968 *Soil Survey, Scotts Bluff County, Nebraska*. U.S. Department of Agriculture Soil Conservation Service in cooperation with the University of Nebraska Conservation and Survey Division, Washington, D.C.

Strong, William Duncan

1933 Signal Butte, a Prehistoric Narrative in the High Plains. In *Exploration and Field-Work of the Smithsonian Institution in 1932*, pp. 69–72. Smithsonian Institution, Washington, D.C.

1935 Recent Discoveries of Human Artifacts Associated with Extinct Mammals in Nebraska and Closely Adjacent Regions. In *An Introduction to Nebraska Archeology*, by William Duncan Strong, pp. 220–239. Smithsonian Miscellaneous Collections 93(10). Smithsonian Institution, Washington, D.C.

Taylor, Jeb

2006 *Projectile Points of the High Plains: New Perspectives on Typology Based on Examinations of Original Type Site Specimens*. Jeb Taylor Artifacts, Buffalo, Wyoming.

Wheat, Joe Ben

1972 *The Olsen-Chubbuck Site: A Paleo-Indian Bison Kill*. Memoirs of the Society for American Archaeology No. 26. Washington, D.C.

1979 *The Jurgens Site*. Memoir 15. Plains Anthropologist, Lincoln, Nebraska.

Wormington, H. M.

1939 *Ancient Man in North America*. Popular Series No. 4. Denver Museum of Natural History, Denver, Colorado.

1944 *Ancient Man in North America*. 2nd ed. Popular Series No. 4. Denver Museum of Natural History, Denver, Colorado.

1949 *Ancient Man in North America*. 3rd ed. Popular Series No. 4. Denver Museum of Natural History, Denver, Colorado.

1957 *Ancient Man in North America*. 4th ed. Popular Series No. 4. Denver Museum of Natural History, Denver, Colorado.

Wyckoff, Don G.

1999 Southern Plains Folsom Lithic Technology: A View from the Edge. In *Folsom Lithic Technology: Explorations in Structure and Variation*, edited by Daniel S. Amick, pp. 39–64. International Monographs in Prehistory, Ann Arbor, Michigan.

# V

# Perspectives on the Cody Complex

# 12

# A Cody Future

## Comments

Douglas B. Bamforth

Paleoindian archaeology is in the midst of a conceptual sea change, and the chapters in this book make important contributions to that change. For decades, archaeological approaches to the terminal Pleistocene/early Holocene ways of life on the Great Plains have been dominated by a single idea: Kelly and Todd's (1988) hypothesis regarding the adaptations of the initial colonizers of North America, uncritically extended to periods of time dating thousands of years after that colonization. Our approaches have further been limited by a near-total focus on two aspects of the archaeological record: projectile points and bison bone. Discussions of Paleoindian archaeology have often downplayed all but the most obvious regional variations in settlement and subsistence and have tended to observe temporal changes in the environment that Paleoindian groups lived in without considering how those changes might have affected the lives those groups led. There are exceptions to these generalizations, but the dominant pattern is unambiguous; to take only one example, Dixon (1999:213) notes that non-Paleoindian archaeologists often refer to Plains Paleoindian studies as "projectile point archaeology."

Recent work challenging traditional perspectives (e.g., Andrews et al. 2008; Bamforth 2002, 2009, 2011b; Hill 2007; LaBelle 2005) does not reject the contributions that points and bison kills can make but instead emphasizes more holistic syntheses of as much of the available data as possible. The results of this work are, unsurprisingly, that such syntheses change what we see in the Paleoindian past: the Paleoindian diet was rich and diverse, projectile points do not by themselves tell us much about overall Paleoindian technological patterns, and no single site (or single kind of site) documents a general pattern of Paleoindian settlement.

This book continues this newer stream of work, both by expanding our attention beyond the Folsom period, which has so dominated recent publications (and particularly beyond Folsom projectile points), and by overtly emphasizing large-scale synthesis. A number of chapters here exploit the information potential of projectile points, and exploit it productively, but the book as a whole offers important information on the broader human contexts that points are only a small part of. Many, and perhaps most, of the revisions of long-standing reconstructions of Paleoindian ways of life rest on the recognition that past studies have overinterpreted a limited array of evidence, and revisionists have therefore worked hard to expand the information they examine. But while turning to broader syntheses of whole assemblages and integrating all of the available data over large regions are essential to expanding our knowledge of the Paleoindian period, it remains true that the Paleoindian database, Cody and otherwise, is sparse, fragmentary, and unevenly distributed in time and space. My goal here, then, is less to assess what these chapters say about Cody than to suggest some of the important issues that Cody archaeology needs to grapple with to continue moving in the direction this volume has taken it.

### What Is Cody?

As Knell and Muñiz's introduction makes clear, "Cody" refers to an archaeological construct spanning some 2000 years over nearly half the area of North America that was not covered in ice during the early Holocene. This is an immense length of time and a breathtakingly large area. What are we talking about when we consider a set of archaeological sites scattered across this span of time and space?

First and foremost, we are talking about a particular style, or set of styles, of projectile points. The term "Cody" subsumes at least 11 more or less explicitly named varieties of spear points (I enumerate them elsewhere [Bamforth 1991:315]) that share a basic set of characteristics (see Knell and Muñiz, this volume). Assessing what Cody is depends, in part, on how we make sense of this variety of forms. As Knudson (this volume) notes, we often divide ourselves into "lumpers," who identify smaller numbers of more variable groups based on relatively general morphological and/or technological similarities, and "splitters," who identify larger numbers of more homogeneous groups differentiated on the basis of more specific characteristics. Many Cody archaeologists have been splitters, some explicitly so (i.e., Wormington 1957:3), and the array of categories of Cody points reflects this. This simple dichotomy, though, masks the deeper issue of how we choose the variables on which we base our classifications.

No two handcrafted objects are exactly alike, and a creative and committed splitter could devise separate and empirically verifiable "types" for every artifact in any given collection of objects. As this suggests, there is no absolute and universally relevant way to classify a given set of objects. The deeper issue, then, is to specify what a particular classification is supposed to help us to do and which characteristics of a set of objects we have to look at in order to do that. If we are interested in identifying individual artisans in the past, and if every object in a particular collection was made by a different person, we need a classification that puts each object in its own category and we need to record information that is relevant to identifying a particular individual's particular products. In contrast, if we are interested in finding widely useful culture-historical markers, we need a classification that transcends patterns that result from idiosyncratic variation among individual artisans and focuses instead on traits shared by many artisans.

Bradley and Stanford (1987:411) confronted this issue directly in the context of Cody archaeology, contrasting "major features" of Cody points, which they argue reflect community-level standards of artifact design, and "minor features," which they argue reflect idiosyncratic, possibly individual-level, variation in craft production. In effect, their major features are the kinds of traits that we need to search for in order to define useful culture-historical markers, and the search for such markers is the single overarching research question that drove archaeological analyses of Paleoindian points, including Cody points, for most of the twentieth century. The features that subsume the many varieties of points that we refer to generally as "Cody" are exactly the features that Bradley and Stanford identify: size, shape, and basic reduction technology (particularly general patterns of finishing flaking). Cody points have square bases and slightly indented shoulders, and often show fairly precise patterns of parallel collateral finishing flaking directed straight in from the edge toward the midline. Knappers who lived over much of North America liked this general style of point, and for two millennia they taught their descendants how to make it. For better or for worse, then, in archaeological practice, Bradley and Stanford's major features tell us how to see Cody and when and where we see it: the distribution of these features in space and time justifies both the groupings of sites in many of the chapters here and the arguments that we can track Cody into the boreal forest in Canada and nearly to the slopes of the Sierra Nevada. They do not, though, tell us in human terms what we are looking at when we do this.

I have so far avoided, and will continue to avoid, the term "Cody complex." Knell and Muñiz trace this term to Jepsen (1951) and note Wormington's (1957:275) definition of "complex." Wormington's definition, though, has deep roots in early and mid-twentieth-century archaeological thought. Tellingly, although Wormington did not cite McKern (1939), she specifically linked her concept of a complex — "a group of related traits or characteristics" — to one of McKern's taxonomic constructs, the concept of a "focus." In defining these constructs, McKern discussed what he referred to as "trait complexes," by which he meant sets of archaeologically visible characteristics that occurred together in groups of sites. He used the term to refer both to extensive sets of traits that make groups of individual archaeological sites essentially identical in culture-historical terms (and thus define a focus) and to shorter and more generalized sets of traits that he hoped would let us arrange the culture-historical units we construct into increasingly inclusive hierarchical units ("aspects," "phases," etc.). McKern explicitly viewed his taxa as socially meaningful: he hoped that the term Wormington appealed to (the "focus") would often "correspond closely to the local tribe in ethnology," although he recognized the problems with this assumption (McKern 1939:308). By the time Wormington was writing, though, Willey and Phillips (1958) were developing a second approach to culture history. Although this approach replicated much of McKern's general framework using different terminology (for example, McKern's "focus" is Willey and Phillips's "phase"), it added more general concepts ("tradition" and "horizon") that cross-cut taxonomic units, concepts based more on general artifact styles than on detailed trait-list similarities. Significantly, Willey and Phillips did not mean these cross-cutting concepts to have the kind of social reality that foci and phases were thought to have; they were markers of interaction and historical connection instead of social boundaries.

The story of archaeological approaches to culture-historical taxonomy is not an inherently interesting topic, but it is important here because the deep history of these approaches constrains and directs the way we think in the present. Wormington's implicit link to McKern's Midwest Taxonomic System highlights a significant difference between the actual practice of Cody archaeologists and the original concept of a complex (or "techno-complex," which is fundamentally the same concept applied when the traits linking sites together consist largely of stone tools). McKern sought holistic, comprehensive sets of different traits that linked sites together in detail; in contrast, archaeologists define "Cody" sites by recognizing the presence of a single *fossile directeur*, the Cody-style projectile point (and, much more rarely, the stylistically similar Cody knife). The list of artifacts that archaeologists use to define the Cody "complex" (or techno-complex) is little more than a modestly diverse set of projectile points, which does some violence to the approach McKern had in mind and is far closer to Willey and Phillips's idea of a horizon. Hill and Knell (this volume) exemplify this problem: noting the extraordinary geographic distribution of Cody-style projectile points, with no reference to any other kind of artifact, they explicitly wonder whether we can view the Cody "complex" as "solely a Great Plains culture complex."

This issue matters in this general context, but not because we need an extended debate about what taxonomic terms to use when we talk about Cody; there are few better ways to avoid talking about ancient human beings than to focus a conversation on culture-historical taxonomy. Rather, it is important because different kinds of terms carry with them different kinds of implicit meanings, and these implicit meanings shape our inferences. The distinction between taxonomic units that we hope have social meaning (foci or phases, recognized on the basis of trait complexes) and stylistic patterns that mark some kind of shared community standards of artifact production (horizons and traditions) gets more complicated in the Cody case if we take account of the span of time and geographic range of Cody points. Eighmy and LaBelle (1996) observed that the cultural-historical taxa defined on the Plains for the Ceramic period have temporal spans and geographic distributions that we might plausibly think of in terms of the kinds of social units McKern and others had in mind, units something like ethnographically defined tribes (although whether Ceramic period taxa actually refer to real social units is another question entirely; they almost certainly do not). The immensely longer temporal spans and spectacularly larger geographic distributions of units like Cody, though, suggest that they reflect social or other forces that operated at spatial and temporal scales for which we lack historical or ethnographic models.

This is important here because all the archaeological chapters in this book include and exclude sites for analysis or comparison depending on whether or not those sites are "Cody," and it is worth being clear about what this might mean. How we think about Cody-ness in the face of a limited archaeological database affects what we see, and it does this in more than one way. On one hand, the idea of a "complex" leads us to contemplate the expansion and contraction of social groups with particular ways of life, while the idea of a "horizon" suggests we might consider the circumstances under which diverse local groups adopted or rejected particular canons of artifact style and production (also see Blackmar 2001). On the other hand, and at a more practical level, classifying sites as Cody because they have produced a Cody point (or preform or knife), and as non-Cody if they have not produced such a point, excludes all sites occupied by Cody people who either happened not to throw a point away or who happened to throw one away in a place where archaeologists happen not to have looked. Using projectile points to identify Cody sites also inevitably directs our attention to hunting and away from sites that have nothing to do with hunting. These latter sites, no matter how many of them there may be in the world and no matter how important they might have been to Cody ways of life, are likely to be effectively invisible given current archaeological practice: they are, by implicit definition, non-Cody sites.

With these issues as background, I consider the chapters here in three groups. The first are Muñiz's and Widga's studies of the Cody environment, which provide an important background to the archaeological chapters. I then divide the archaeological chapters into two groups on the basis of geography, one set (by Hill, Knudson, Hill and Knell, Knell, and Muñiz) focused on sites in the Cody "heartland" (that is, the western and northwestern Plains, where Cody has been studied most intensively) and a second (by Root et al., Dawe, and Amick) on Cody outside this area.

### Cody Landscape(s)

In practice, then, what we mean when we identify the time/space distribution of the "Cody complex" is the range of times and places in which ancient people made Cody-style spear points. The chapters in this volume leave no doubt that the spatial distribution of Cody point-makers extended far beyond the northern/northwestern Plains region that I refer to as the "heartland." The environmental data this book presents, though, focus particularly on this region, and document both the complexity of the changes that occurred over the course of the Cody period and some of the important problems involved in studying those changes.

The environmental chapters differ in geographic coverage and, importantly, in the lines of evidence they examine: Muñiz concentrates on the heartland and synthesizes a wide array of evidence, while Widga extends his focus geographically much farther to the east and builds climatic reconstructions only on microfauna. These differences may account for some of the contrasting conclusions these chapters present. For example, Muñiz sees overall trends from cooler/wetter early to warmer/drier conditions, consistent with most accounts of early Holocene climatic trends, while Widga sees a shift from cooler/drier to warmer/wetter. Perhaps most important here, though, both analyses identify significant patterns of change, over time, and Muñiz documents important geographic variation in environmental conditions. To take only one aspect of this variation, the drying trend he sees appears to have had more severe effects in more western areas than in more eastern areas, as indicated by dune activation on the western Plains but not farther to the east. General trends in precipitation and temperature, important as they are, have predictably different effects in different places, and Cody people had to cope with these differences.

In addressing variation like this, though, we need to be careful to ensure that our reconstructions do not exceed the refinement of our tools, particularly radiocarbon dating. It is very likely that some of the complexity in the patterns that these studies propose reflects the ways in which plateaus in the radiocarbon calibration curve collapse long periods of calendar years into short periods of radiocarbon years: there are multiple episodes in the section of the curve dated to Cody times when short spans of radiocarbon time correspond to centuries in real time (see Reimer et al. 2009:Figure 2; Reimer et al. 2004:Figures A-8 and A-9). This means that observations that appear to document variation at a moment in time may actually document centuries of change, that there are intervals during which it is difficult to distinguish temporal change from spatial variation, and that no amount of analysis of the $^{14}$C record will fix either of these problems. Both of the paleoenvironmental chapters here are susceptible to this: data derived from a single physically stratified sequence can document patterns of change in a given locality and can help to control this problem, but linking sets of localities together into larger regional sequences inevitably depends on radiocarbon. There is no obvious way to evade radiocarbon calibration issues without some kind of chronometric control that is independent of $^{14}$C. However, it is worth contemplating the possibility that the overall pattern of change may be less complex than it seems because some of the variation that appears to be simultaneous may actually represent change over time.

Nevertheless, Widga's analysis of bison size and horn configuration illustrates the benefits of finer-grained chronology particularly well: his data strongly support my (Bamforth 1988) chronologically extremely coarse-grained arguments about long-term changes in bison dominance behavior, showing concretely how those changes occurred over the course of the Paleoindian period, and they amplify Smiley's (1979) analysis and arguments as well. Widga's explanation for the post-Pleistocene reduction in bison body size, though, merits comment. He argues that increased forage production raised bison density—presumably overall population size—producing poor nutrition and thus smaller animals. This does not fit well with much of the research on ungulate ecology. Increasing forage production raises ungulate populations because it enhances their nutritional status, resulting in better calf survival, better resistance to predation, and more extensive seasonal storage of body fat that increases animals' ability (in temperate climates) to survive the food-poor period of late winter and early spring. Poor nutrition does the opposite, resulting in population declines. An alternative explanation might be that the changing character of the Plains grasslands, with a shift to shorter and more warm-season grasses, selected for smaller animals that were better able to forage over large areas; in fact, at the same time that bison became smaller, they became proportionately more long-legged, implying selection for more efficient runners (Bamforth 1988).

I focus on bison ecology not because it is useful to conceive of Cody groups (or any other Paleoindian groups) as specialized bison hunters (it is not useful, as more than one chapter here documents). However, inferences about bison adaptations highlight an essential implication of the work that Widga and Muñiz present. Changing climate over the two millennia of the Cody period did not just mean that people had to have warmer winter clothes sometimes; it meant that the resources on which people depended were distributed across the landscape in different ways over time. Furthermore, more severe late Cody aridity on the western Plains would have had effects on hunter-gatherers there that would likely not have been evident to the east. Changing the numbers and herding/migration behavior of prey animals alters the ways in which humans can prey on them (Bamforth 1988), and varying the length and severity of the winter affects the choices humans have to make to get through that difficult time of year. Understanding variation and temporal change in the kinds, distributions, and densities of resources across the vast area discussed here is essential to understanding something about how Cody groups lived their lives, the subject of the second group of chapters.

### Cody in the Heartland

I use the term "Cody heartland" to refer to the heartland of intensive investigation on richly productive archaeological sites, not to an area that we can convincingly show to have been the original source of some classic Cody way of life. This usage reflects the quality and detail of the evidence available for analysis: archaeologists have spent more time working on Cody sites on the western/northwestern Plains and adjacent areas than elsewhere, offering more opportunities to see Cody lives more clearly. The heartland chapters here move us well down the road to doing just that.

First and foremost, these chapters document substantial and important diversity in every aspect of the archaeological record that they consider, including the styles of points used in single bison kills, the kinds of prey Cody hunters took and the ways in which they took that prey, and the organization of the technology that Cody people used to support their ways of life. People who made Cody points used different parts of the landscape in different ways (also see Bamforth and Becker 2000), hunted a wide variety of species in addition to bison, and relied heavily on local raw material to make their tools. The richness of the variation that the authors document here is particularly significant because it is so fundamentally incompatible with the long-dominant view of Paleoindian lifeways in general, Kelly and Todd's (1988) model of big-game specialists wandering unpredictably over huge areas. Despite being developed to account for the earliest ways of life in North America, this model relied primarily on data from much later Paleoindian sites, and particularly depended on Todd's (1987) analysis of the Horner site, a Cody bison kill and the Cody type site. The work presented here leaves no doubt that sites like Horner were *not* part of the kind of homogeneous way of life that archaeologists have so often reconstructed for early periods in North America. If the Cody-age Horner site pattern has any implications at all for earlier occupations in North America, then, it implies that those occupations were as complex and diverse as Cody.

The multiple discussions of Cody faunal exploitation here are particularly important in this context: like other Paleoindian groups, Cody groups as a whole were not just specialized bison hunters (also see Hill 2007). It is difficult to overestimate the importance of this observation. The traditional view of post-Clovis Paleoindian lifeways is founded in an inference of specialized big-game hunting, with this hunting requiring constant unpredictable movement in search of herds and such movement determining technology. Recognizing structured seasonal patterns of Paleoindian bison hunting along with systematic exploitation of a wide range of other species does not just modify this view; it eviscerates it. We can describe Paleoindians as "part-time" specialists (as Hofman and Todd [2001] do for Folsom hunters), but we can describe any number of hunter-gatherer groups on the Plains over the last 13,000 years essentially the same way. Furthermore, as soon as we retreat from the idea that Paleoindian groups needed to search constantly for herds of bison to slaughter, the conceptual basis for the traditional view of Paleoindian mobility, and thus of Paleoindian technology, evaporates.

Moreover, the two technologically focused chapters show how much more interesting and complex Paleoindian technology is than traditional perspective would have it. There are many reasons for this, but one that is surely at the top of the list is that these two chapters look beyond projectile points: Knell considers whole assemblages, and Muñiz samples all artifact classes other than debitage. These chapters emphasize different aspects of flaked stone technology—Knell's analytical nodules provide more information on production, and Muñiz's microwear data provide more information on use—but document both the kinds of patterns and the ambiguities that focused and temporally nuanced studies are likely to offer in the future. If any research shows us that it is past time to abandon the monolithic views of Paleoindian technology that linger sadly in the literature, this is it.

But while recognizing diversity in faunal and lithic assemblages is fundamentally important, our ultimate goal is to make meaning of this diversity. And the devil of making meaning is where it always is, in the details. The work here refutes many existing ideas about Cody archaeology, but we should be wary of putting any of this work into the same kind of absolute, unchallenged position these ideas have occupied in the past. A few examples illustrate this.

Most generally, these chapters blur the importance of time and change and sometimes underplay regional differences in the conditions Cody groups had to respond to. For decades, Paleoindian archaeologists have aggregated sites to make up for the scarcity of evidence we have to work with, but we need to do this with our eyes open. For this book, such aggregation means that there is a near total disconnect between the pronounced patterns of environmental change so clearly documented by the two paleoenvironmental chapters and the regionally and temporally broad archaeological syntheses that put this volume on the cutting edge of recent developments in Paleoindian studies. We can do little to expand our sample of dated sites except hope to discover and investigate more sites in the future. However, summaries of such topics as how groups altered their activities with the seasons need to note that Cody seasons changed substantially over time; so, too, must seasonal Cody activities have changed. Long-term changes in winter severity have nontrivial implications for hunting, residential, and travel habits. The large-scale overviews here tie together large amounts of data, but they basically average those data over millennia of substantial environmental change. The sites they consider may all be Cody, but they were Cody sites produced by people living under, and presumably responding to, a wide range of environmental regimes.

Future work on Cody that builds on these chapters needs to take this into account, and closer analysis of the details of the sites we currently know something about may offer a way to expand on these important but time-averaged generalizations. However, looking in more detail at known sites requires us to be cautious both about how we classify those sites into functional and other kinds of groups for our analyses and about how we classify them into culture-historic units. The Medicine Creek Paleoindian sites in southwestern Nebraska illustrate both of these issues.

These sites (Allen, Lime Creek, and Red Smoke; Bamforth 2002, 2007; Davis 1954, 1962; Hicks 2002; Jones 1999; Knudson 2002) are located within a tiny area along Medicine Creek and its tributary, Lime Creek, and were all occupied and reoccupied throughout Paleoindian times. Allen was used and reused, apparently at very short intervals, for the entire post-Clovis Paleoindian period, including during Cody times, while Lime Creek shows a major concentration of material (Zone I) dated to Cody times, and Red Smoke shows limited Cody-era accumulation and a major concentration of material dated to the latest parts of the Paleoindian period. Significantly, these sites are not all the same. Allen (on the main course of Medicine Creek itself) is a generalized residential base, while Lime Creek and Red Smoke (along a tributary of Medicine Creek) are located immediately adjacent to raw material sources and are predominantly workshops with limited evidence of other kinds of activity. This matters: Paleoindian groups did different things in different parts of the Medicine Creek landscape, producing sites that are collectively integrated but functionally distinct. Archaeological material from each of those sites, then, does not monitor comparable sets of activities with comparable implications for our overall view of Paleoindian ways of life. In particular, people probably "camped" (slept, ate, built a fire now and then, sat around and talked) at Red Smoke and Lime Creek, but the archaeology they left behind tells us in no uncertain terms that these sites are not "camps" in the same sense that the Allen site is. This is particularly relevant to studies of Cody diet: provisioning work groups on short trips to a quarry is not the same as provisioning families, and collapsing the fauna generated by such groups together with that discarded at residential sites, as Hill (this volume) and Hill and Knell (this volume) do, makes it difficult to assess variability that we know exists. In passing, and with this in mind, it seems unusual for Hill to classify the Lime Creek site as a 137-$m^2$ "bison bonebed"; I would classify it as a 137-$m^2$ workshop/midden area that produced a small collection of bison bone (along with the bones of beaver, antelope, deer, elk, etc.; Jones 1999; Knell and Muñiz, this volume). Including this kind of a site with Olsen-Chubbuck in an analysis of numbers of bison per square meter of excavation seems more likely to blur patterning than to reveal it.

Classifying the Medicine Creek sites as Cody or not-Cody is also problematic. Paleoindians unambiguously used all three of the Medicine Creek sites, albeit for different purposes, during the time interval in which Cody points were made. However, they left diagnostic Cody artifacts only at Lime Creek, where excavations recovered one finished point, a second nearly finished point that likely would have been Cody style (both made from nonlocal stone), and 22 unfinished and discarded Cody point preforms, all in local Smoky Hill jasper (Hicks 2002; these are Davis's [1962] "Lime Creek knives"). For most archaeologists, this makes Lime Creek a Cody site, one that was apparently used almost entirely to carry out early stages of stone tool production by groups that lived most of their lives and carried out most of their other activities elsewhere (for example, at the nearby Allen site). Red Smoke, used for exactly the same purposes as Lime Creek at exactly the same time, and located about a 10-minute walk upstream from Lime Creek, did not produce a Cody point; it is thus not a Cody site.

Similarly, in this view, the Allen site is not a Cody site, despite the fact that it is about a 20-minute walk downstream from the Lime Creek site and that, throughout the course of the entire Cody period, it was a place where Paleoindians carried out the wide range of residential activities that are *not* represented at Lime Creek and Red Smoke. Taking Lime Creek as a "Cody" site comparable to other Cody sites — for example, Hell Gap — then, requires us (1) to treat data from one of two contemporary and demonstrably nonresidential limited-activity quarry/workshop sites as directly comparable to widely scattered camps and kill sites and (2) to ignore (or classify as not-Cody) the data from the undoubted Cody-age levels at a residential site located an easy half-hour walk away from these two sites.

But could Red Smoke and Allen be Cody sites? The Cody-era stratum at Allen (the Intermediate Zone, or IZ) produced only one point (which is not a Cody point, but which also does not fall obviously into any other defined Paleoindian type) and three preforms, none of which is clearly diagnostic of any specific kind of finished point. As it happens, the IZ point from Allen (University of Nebraska State Museum number 9215-48 [Bamforth 2007:Figure 10.4]) is extremely similar to a Cody-age, but not Cody-style, point from Zone 83 at Red Smoke (University of Nebraska State Museum number 1937-52 [Knudson 2002:Figure 7.10]). Both of these are small and relatively poorly made lanceolate points with slightly convex edges and concave bases, and both are finished with irregular but generally oblique flaking. Knudson's emphasis here on the diversity of points within the single bonebed at the Scottsbluff site — a classic and undoubted Cody site — is particularly significant in this context: despite its status as the type site for Scottsbluff points, one of the points it produced (A7072) is clearly not in a Cody style and is essentially a slightly larger and somewhat better-made version of the points from the Cody-era levels at Red Smoke and Allen.

Scottsbluff and Lime Creek are "Cody" sites; Allen and Red Smoke are "non-Cody" sites. But Scottsbluff, Allen, and Red Smoke produced a similar style of non-Cody point that dates to Cody times and, in the case of the Scottsbluff bonebed, was apparently used alongside Cody points in a single bison kill. At Medicine Creek, sites like Allen — used continuously throughout the entire Paleoindian period — are the places where the miners and stoneworkers who used sites like Red Smoke and Lime Creek actually lived (cf. Bamforth and Hicks 2008). This means that the faunal remains at Lime Creek represent the procurement activities of special-purpose task groups ranging out from residential bases for short periods of time, and do not necessarily tell us much about the way that everyday Cody-era residential groups provisioned themselves. Do they provide information comparable to the information from Allen (or Hell Gap) on overall "Cody" subsistence practices? Similarly, the highly specialized nonresidential lithic assemblages from Lime Creek and Red Smoke, consisting primarily of discarded industrial debris, do not necessarily tell us about overall Cody-era technology.

Knudson (this volume) argues that none of the Medicine Creek sites should be called Cody. Discard of unfinished Cody-style point preforms at Lime Creek, though, may not be consistent with this. As Hicks (2002) notes, the Lime Creek preforms most likely differ from Bradley and Frison's (1987) experimental preforms because these latter pieces were successful experimental pieces directed at producing Eden-style points, while the specimens from Lime Creek were archaeological production failures rejected by their makers and probably directed at other Cody forms. But Knudson's arguments regarding Medicine Creek and the other sites she considers speak *directly* to the question of what it means to group archaeological sites together on the basis of projectile point style (also see Knudson 2002). Knell and Muñiz's introduction notes the paucity of work on Cody social relations, but analyses focused on topics like subsistence and land use — the kinds of things we hope we are good at looking at — depend, at least in part, on assumptions about society and interregional interaction that generally go unmentioned and unchallenged. We may or may not want to follow Knudson (this volume) or Bradley (2009) and define a new Medicine Creek complex, or resurrect Holder and Wike's (1949) Frontier complex (or Davis's [1954, 1962] Lime Creek or Dutcher complexes). But we do need to take seriously the likelihood that regionally distinct groups with local social identities and ways of life sometimes shared common patterns of point production, as Blackmar (2001:66) suggested.

Discussions of these kinds of taxonomic issues may seem like antiques in our processual/post-processual/agency-theoretic twenty-first-century world. However, the social issues that, as Knell and Muñiz note, are so sorely neglected in Cody archaeology are not just an important topic for future investigation; they are fundamental to underlying assumptions that are central to this book. The notion of a "Cody complex" here imposes a problematic assumption of social boundaries on the data examined in this volume, and this assumption structures both the data analyses and the interpretation of the patterns these analyses document. This is clearest in the most ambitious synthesis here, Hill and Knell's overview of Cody in the Rockies, which systematically compares sites with and without Cody points in them in the grasslands and high country. This entire analysis depends on attributing direct social meaning to differences in projectile point style: present evidence (including differing geographic distributions of point styles and overlapping sets of radiocarbon dates [Grund 2009; Holliday 2000; Kornfeld et al. 2010; Pitblado 2003]) leaves little doubt that Cody-period knappers scattered widely across the American West did not all make Cody-style points. Hill and Knell's systematic comparison of Cody and non-Cody data rests on this fact, and Will McKern's ghost is restless.

As I noted above, McKern was explicitly cautious about whether or not complexes of archaeological traits defined real social units. By and large, implicitly or explicitly, the authors in this book are not cautious: much of the discussion here assumes that shared point styles imply shared socio-cultural relations that make it useful to try to define shared and distinctive subsistence, mobility, and technological patterns. Weissner (1983) demonstrated that differences in point styles can reflect some kinds of social group differences, but it is important that these differences were among groups with distinct and minimally overlapping or non-overlapping ranges, a very different situation than the one we see here. Is it plausible that Cody people did not live at the Allen site over the 1000 years or so that the aggregate assemblage recovered from the Intermediate Zone accumulated? If Cody points define a bounded social group with distinctive dietary preferences and land-use patterns, why do the myriad of point styles lumped together as non-Cody define a single pattern of diet and land use that stands in contrast to the Cody pattern? The variation in subsistence practices that Hill and Knell document is interesting and important, but an analysis that searches for differences between datasets defined by projectile point styles more or less *requires* us to interpret differences in terms of distinctive lifeways led by distinctive groups.

The analyses here also often incorporate more specific unchallenged, perhaps implicit, assumptions as well. I have noted that the specifically technological chapters particularly document how much richer our views of Paleoindian archaeology become when we look beyond projectile points, and how much more complex the relations between technology and land-use patterns are than much of the existing literature suggests. But they leave important questions unsettled. Muñiz notes problems of equifinality in his inferences that will be difficult to solve, for example, and both his and Knell's larger theoretical arguments require detailed knowledge of many aspects of tool production and use that we do not have, at least at present. To take only one example, Knell classifies points and end scrapers as "long use-life tools" but offers no support for this. Spears and scraping *tools* certainly did have long use-lives, but this does not imply that the stone points and blades that came and went in those larger implements lasted very long. Spear points made for a large bison kill—used and then discarded when the kill was over—likely had use-lives of less than a day, and experimental data (i.e., Cheshier and Kelly 2006; Hunzicker 2008) indicate that even points used in smaller-scale day-to-day hunting broke on average in a few casts. Schultz (1992) shows that scraping a single bison hide requires 100 or more episodes of resharpening, leaving no doubt that the use-lives of the end scrapers used for this purpose were likely often on the order of an hour or two. Both Muñiz and Knell take Paleoindian lithic analysis in profoundly important new directions, but they raise as many questions for research as they answer.

Paleoindian use of raw material is also very variable, and both Knell's and Hill and Knell's chapters examine it, documenting substantial differences in material use within and between regions. But like most Paleoindian archaeology, these studies use quarry locations as measures of the scale of movement across the landscape, which necessarily assumes that people acquired all their raw material directly at its geologic source. Paleoindians surely did this, but they just as surely moved this material across the landscape in more than one way and made decisions about how to move it that varied according to the kind of artifact they were moving. Post-Clovis Paleoindians systematically cached finished and unfinished projectile points, but not other kinds of tools, and these caches often included points and preforms made of stone from great distances away (Bamforth 2009). Cody people did this, too: the Harmon cache, from south-central Nebraska, includes 36 Cody preforms and three finished Cody points, made from Smoky Hill jasper, which is local to the area, as well as from Flint Hills and Burlington cherts, which are not (Bamforth 2011a). Getting access to distant stone used for points, then, often simply required knowing cache locations or, perhaps, knowing the people who were carrying material on its way to or from a cache location.

Frequencies of projectile points made from local versus nonlocal stone, used by chapters in this book to monitor mobility, are thus just as likely to monitor social networks. And this opens questions that we have barely begun to ask. What kinds of social forces produced shared templates of artifact design over large areas and long spans of time? How do regional patterns of raw material distribution map onto more subtle kinds of variation — Bradley and Stanford's (1987) minor features — in point styles (cf. Knudson, this volume)? Can we link long-distance transport of small amounts of material to the kinds of social interactions we need to think about to answer either of these questions (Bamforth 2009)?

We can see similar implicit but important assumptions in some of the faunal studies as well. For example, Hill addresses the role of bison hunting in Cody ways of life, undoubtedly the classic topic for this period, and shows that it was diverse. But at least one of his fundamental questions — whether or not Cody hunters took bison year-round — is not now, and never has been, at issue. Phrased in that way, the answer is simple: of course Cody people hunted bison year-round, and, probably, so did every other indigenous society that ever lived on the Plains. The questions that have been at the center of the debate over Paleoindian (including Cody) lifeways have to do with whether or not the *organization* of bison hunting changed seasonally. Fundamentally, these questions are, first, whether or not there was a particular period of the year when people hunted communally (in Driver's [1990] sense of a hunt in which specific people carry out specific roles in a preorganized plan), and, second, whether or not Paleoindians formed social aggregations to carry out this kind of hunting. Asking these latter questions suggests that searching for ways of identifying communal and other kinds of hunts should be central to *any* discussion of Cody bison hunting: not all bison kills are the same just because they have dead bison in them. This issue is closely linked to the argument that *large* Paleoindian bison kills were fortuitous rather than carefully planned, anticipated, and organized — that is, that Paleoindian groups just happened to be ready to slaughter and process herds of 100 or more bison when they somehow managed to stumble onto them at sites like Horner or Olsen-Chubbuck. This claim (also made by Wheat [1972]) is dubious in the extreme; certainly, Hofman's (1994) arguments in support of it have more to do with the limited conceptual framework archaeologists have brought to this debate than to the way ancient people hunted on the Great Plains (Bamforth 2011b).

### Cody at the Edges

The relative richness of the database that defines the area I am calling the Cody heartland lets us see diverse kinds of regional land-use patterns, dietary and technological complexity, and seasonal change at the same time that it highlights how complex and difficult it can be to make sense of this diversity. This level of detail is hard to find outside this region, though. The Cody edge chapters have three important traits in common. The first is their obvious attention to regions that extend the range of Cody far beyond the areas where archaeologists have traditionally seen it (that is, beyond the Cody heartland). Second, where the chapters in the previous group systematically integrate assemblage-level data on stone tools, had access to good data on faunal collections, or relied on both approaches, the chapters in this group focus largely (but, importantly, not quite entirely) on the distribution of Cody-style projectile points. Finally, and linked to this second trait, these chapters show the clearest reliance on the concept of Cody as a marker for a particular social group.

The Cody edge chapters tell us unambiguously how widespread Cody-style points are in North America. Just as Blackmar (2001) documented the extent of the Cody presence in the woodlands east of the central and southern Plains, so too do all three of these chapters document it in the far north of the Plains and in the northern portions of the intermontane west. Amick's meticulous analysis is particularly important in showing the Cody presence far beyond the Great Plains. Archaeology's traditional regional divisions can obscure this kind of distribution, often by applying distinctive regional type names to identical objects. We may need more work to decide if Windust points are different from Cody points, but we definitely know that Cody is one of the most widely distributed sets of projectile point types that was ever made in native North America.

But understanding what this means brings us directly back to the question of what Cody is, and particularly back to the difference between points made in the same style and points made by the same people (that is, to the culture-historical difference between horizons and complexes). All three of the Cody edge chapters offer us a kind of Cody Nation, planting the flag, or the spear, in new lands. These new lands are very different from one another, though, and they have produced archaeological evidence of Cody occupations that differs to some extent as well.

The far northern early Holocene Great Plains, hemmed in by ice and flanked on the east by immense glacial lakes, may have been a fairly brutal place to live during the probably colder interval of the Younger Dryas, as the rare finds of pre-Cody points there that Dawe notes perhaps imply (although the details and chronology of glacial retreat and environmental change in the region are known imprecisely [Beaudoin and Oetelaar 2003; Yansa 2007]). A rapid end to the Younger Dryas might have offered a largely uninhabited expanse of grassland that became increasingly productive over time and that was open to Cody groups from the south. And we know that Cody groups from the south were connected to this region: both Dawe and Root and his colleagues identify substantial amounts of southern raw material in Cody-age assemblages from Canada. What is most important about this identification, though, is *not* that Cody-style projectile points of southern material found their way onto the northern Plains. Paleoindian groups uniformly seem to have preferred to use stone from distant sources for their points, and they supplied themselves with such stone in a variety of ways: reconstructing Paleoindian range sizes only on the basis of the raw materials used to produce points is a fundamentally problematic exercise (Bamforth 2009). What is truly important is that Root and his colleagues show that *whole assemblages* made from southern stone moved north. This is a different matter altogether; this is what we should see with movements of people. The numbers of sites and artifacts other than points that underlie these chapters are fairly small, and we can hope for more data in the future, but this is an intriguing pattern.

The northern Great Basin, in contrast, appears to have been both well suited to human occupation and extensively occupied before Cody times (Beck and Jones 1997; Jones et al. 2003). The Cody period here corresponds to an interval of climate change that, as Amick suggests, may have increased bison populations (although this is not certain — bison were present there before Cody times, and we simply do not have enough data to assess their numbers empirically). But, in contrast to the northern Plains case, we have no evidence of an actual presence of Plains people in the Great Basin. Rather, we have only Plains-style points. Non-Cody Paleoindian/Paleoarchaic hunters in the Great Basin appear to have been quite capable of hunting bison and other large mammals (Beck and Jones 1997), and the evidence of Cody prey selection there, limited as it is, documents exploitation of an array of large and small species that is very similar to that seen in non-Cody sites. It is not clear that the available data show us a change in anything other than projectile point style.

I raise this issue not because it demonstrates that Cody groups did not expand into the northern Great Basin, but because it documents that we do not yet have an archaeological signature that can really tell us that they did; the contrast with the northern Cody edge evidence in this sense is intriguing. Archaeologists and others have argued that movements of people between the Plains and the Great Basin were important throughout human history in North America and that these occurred along exactly the route that Amick proposes (i.e., Aikens 1967; Ambrose 2000; Beck and Jones 2010; Wheeler 2002). But how do we demonstrate rigorously that they occurred in a past that we can see only through archaeological data? What is Cody?

## Looking to the Future

There is no doubt that building on the research in this book will require more work on new Cody sites as well as continued digging through existing museum resources. New data will expand the number of sites we can consider, shine new light on collections we already know something about, and refine the broad-scale patterns documented here. Some of this work will involve studies of projectile points. What is the range of variation in point styles in well-documented Cody sites? How many multiple-point-style sites like Scottsbluff are out there, and why, where, and how often do distinct Cody and non-Cody point types overlap in time or occur in the same site? Expanding analyses like Hill and Knell's — analyses that gather data from sites dated to Cody times rather than only from sites defined as being Cody because they have a Cody-style point in them — has the potential to address many important but largely neglected aspects of Paleoindian archaeology. Other work will expand the range of Cody lithic and faunal assemblages that are known in detail, with projectile points a minor emphasis (as they should be more often in Paleoindian research).

Future work also needs to deal with geographic variation at a finer scale of analysis. For example, the chapters here leave no doubt that Cody populations in different areas exploited different suites of animals: there is no such thing as a single "Cody" way of life. But this kind of regional variation implies that explanations of prey choice have to take account of what animals are available for the choosing. Did hunters on the open grasslands take bison because they were the highest-ranked species available or because they were almost the only species available? We should not be surprised to find a wider range of prey in sites located in habitats — the mountains, for example — that supported a wider range of prey species. And the environmental chapters here show that even seemingly homogeneous environmental zones — open grasslands, for example — were anything but homogeneous in time or space. Carving adjacent environmental zones into completely separate analytic units can also mask interrelations between them: Paleoindians living in the sheltered Medicine Creek valley, for example, surely hunted into the open grasslands right next to them, leaving archaeological traces of their activities in both places.

What, then, is "Cody"? Was there a "Cody people" who led a particular kind of Cody life, in the bounded social sense of an archaeological complex? Or were there just widespread and perhaps quite diverse groups of people who chose to make Cody points, in the sense of an archaeological horizon? I have noted that the assumption of some kind of more or less homogeneous Cody social entity lurks behind most of the chapters in this volume, and this assumption requires closer attention in the future than it has received to date. Certainly, the diversity of ways of life documented over and over again here is more consistent with Cody as a horizon than with Cody as a complex, and we need to work harder to sort this problem out. But there are many, many questions that profoundly influence the ways in which we think about the patterns in our data, questions that often arise only because of the kind of synthetic efforts presented here. These require not just more data but different perspectives brought to the data, like the perspectives in this book, and new approaches to thinking about Paleoindian ways of life. What is Cody, anyway?

## Acknowledgments

Thanks to Ed Knell and Mark Muñiz for inviting me to participate in this project. Tom Westfall let me know about the Harmon cache, and Jack Harmon let me work with it. And a particular thank-you to Gary Wilson for catching problems with my references and to Kim Vivier for meticulous copyediting.

## References

Aikens, C. M.
1967 Plains Relationships of the Fremont Culture: A Hypothesis. *American Antiquity* 32:198–209.

Ambrose, S. E.
2000 *Nothing Like It in the World: The Men Who Built the Transcontinental Railroad, 1863–1869*. Simon and Schuster, New York.

Andrews, B., J. LaBelle, and J. Seebach
2008 Spatial Variability in the Folsom Archaeological Record: A Multiscalar Approach. *American Antiquity* 73:464–490.

Bamforth, D. B.
1988 *Ecology and Human Organization on the Great Plains*. Plenum Press, New York.
1991 Flintknapping Skill, Communal Hunting, and Paleoindian Projectile Point Typology. *Plains Anthropologist* 36:309–322.
2002 High-Tech Foragers? Folsom and Later Paleoindian Technology on the Great Plains. *Journal of World Prehistory* 16:55–98.
2009 Projectile Points, People, and Plains Paleoindian Perambulations. *Journal of Anthropological Archaeology* 28:142–157.
2011a Paleoindian Perambulations and the Harmon Cache. Paper presented at the 69th Annual Meeting of the Plains Anthropological Society, Tucson, Arizona.
2011b Origin Stories, Archaeological Evidence, and Post-Clovis Paleoindian Bison Hunting on the Great Plains. *American Antiquity* 76:24–40.

Bamforth, Douglas B. (editor)
2007 *The Allen Site: A Paleoindian Camp in Southwestern Nebraska*. University of New Mexico Press, Albuquerque.

Bamforth, D. B., and M. Becker
2000 Core/Biface Ratios, Mobility, Refitting, and Artifact Use-Lives: A Paleoindian Example. *Plains Anthropologist* 45:273–290.

Bamforth, D. B., and K. Hicks
2008 Production Skill and Paleoindian Work Group Organization in the Medicine Creek Drainage, Southwestern Nebraska. In *Skilful Stones: Approaches to Knowledge and Practice in Lithic Technology*, edited by N. Finlay and D. Bamforth. *Journal of Archaeological Method and Theory* 15:132–153.

Beaudoin, A., and G. Oetelaar
2003 The Changing Ecophysical Landscape of Southern Alberta during the Late Pleistocene and Early Holocene. *Plains Anthropologist* 48:187–207.

Beck, C., and G. Jones
1997 The Terminal Pleistocene/Early Holocene Archaeology of the Great Basin. *Journal of World Prehistory* 11:161–236.
2010 Clovis and Western Stemmed: Population Migration and the Meeting of Two Technologies. *American Antiquity* 75:81–116.

Blackmar, J.
2001 Regional Variability in Clovis, Folsom, and Cody Land-Use. *Plains Anthropologist* 46:65–94.

Bradley, B.
2009 Bifacial Technology and Paleoindian Projectile Points. In *Hell Gap: A Stratified Paleoindian Campsite at the Edge of the Rockies*, edited by M. Larson, M. Kornfeld, and G. Frison, pp. 243–258. University of Utah Press, Salt Lake City.

Bradley, B., and G. Frison
1987 Projectile Points and Specialized Bifaces from the Horner Site. In *The Horner Site*, edited by G. Frison and L. Todd, pp. 199–232. Academic Press, New York.

Bradley, B., and D. Stanford
1987 The Claypool Study. In *The Horner Site*, edited by G. Frison and L. Todd, pp. 405–434. Academic Press, New York.

Cheshier, J., and R. Kelly
2006 Projectile Point Shape and Durability: The Effect of Thickness:Length. *American Antiquity* 71:353–364.

Davis, E. M.
1954 The Culture History of the Central Great Plains Prior to the Introduction of Pottery. Unpublished Ph.D. dissertation, Department of Anthropology, Harvard University, Cambridge, Massachusetts.
1962 *Archeology of the Lime Creek Site in Southwestern Nebraska*. Special Publication No. 3. University of Nebraska State Museum, Lincoln.

Dixon, J.
1999 *Bones, Boats, and Bison*. University of New Mexico Press, Albuquerque.

Driver, J.
1990 Meat in Due Season: The Timing of Communal Hunts. In *Hunters of the Recent Past*,

edited by L. Davis and B. Reeves, pp. 11–33. Unwin Hyman, Boston.

Eighmy, J., and J. LaBelle
1996 Radiocarbon Dating of Twenty-Seven Plains Complexes and Phases. *Plains Anthropologist* 41:53–69.

Grund, B.
2009 Paleoindian Projectile Points of the Great Plains: Typology, Chronology, and the Implications of Radiocarbon Dating. Senior honors thesis, Department of Anthropology, University of Colorado, Boulder.

Hicks, K.
2002 Local Variability in Paleoindian Lifeways: A Comparison of the Lime Creek and Allen Site Worked Stone Assemblages, Southwestern Nebraska. Unpublished Master's thesis, Department of Anthropology, University of Colorado, Boulder.

Hill, M. E.
2007 A Moveable Feast: Variation in Faunal Resource Use among Central and Western North American Paleoindian Sites. *American Antiquity* 72:417–438.

Hofman, J.
1994 Paleoindian Aggregations on the Great Plains. *Journal of Anthropological Archaeology* 13:341–370.

Hofman, J., and L. Todd
2001 Tyranny in the Archaeological Record of Specialized Hunters. In *People and Wildlife in Northern North America: Essays in Honor of R. Dale Guthrie*, edited by S. Craig Gerlach and Maribeth S. Murray, pp. 200–215. BAR International Series No. 944. British Archaeological Reports, Oxford.

Holder, P., and J. Wike
1949 The Frontier Culture Complex: A Preliminary Report on a Prehistoric Hunter's Camp in Southwestern Nebraska. *American Antiquity* 24:260–266.

Holliday, V.
2000 The Evolution of Paleoindian Geochronology and Typology on the Great Plains. *Geoarchaeology* 15:227–290.

Hunzicker, D.
2008 Folsom Projectile Technology: An Experiment in Design, Effectiveness and Efficiency. *Plains Anthropologist* 53:291–311.

Jepsen, G.
1951 Ancient Buffalo Hunters in Wyoming. *Archaeological Society of New Jersey Newsletter* 24:22–24.

Jones, D. C.
1999 Late Paleoindian/Early Archaic Archaeology and Subsistence: A Taphonomic Analysis of the Lime Creek Site (25FT41), Southwest Nebraska. Unpublished Master's thesis, Colorado State University, Fort Collins.

Jones, G., C. Beck, E. Jones, and R. Hughes
2003 Lithic Source Use and Paleoarchaic Foraging in the Great Basin. *American Antiquity* 68: 5–38.

Kelly, R., and L. Todd
1988 Coming into the Country: Early Paleoindian Hunting and Mobility. *American Antiquity* 53:231–244.

Knudson, R.
2002 Medicine Creek Is a Paleoindian Cultural Ecotone: The Red Smoke Assemblage. In *Medicine Creek: Seventy Years of Archaeological Investigations*, edited by D. Roper, pp. 84–141. University of Alabama Press, Tuscaloosa.

Kornfeld, Marcel, George C. Frison, and Mary Lou Larson
2010 *Prehistoric Hunter-Gatherers of the High Plains and Rockies*. 3rd ed. Left Coast Press, Walnut Creek, California.

LaBelle, J.
2005 Hunter-Gatherer Foraging Variability during the Early Holocene of the Central Plain of North America. Unpublished Ph.D. dissertation, Department of Anthropology, Southern Methodist University, Dallas, Texas.

McKern, W.
1939 The Midwestern Taxonomic Method as an Aid to Archaeological Culture Study. *American Antiquity* 4:301–313.

Muñiz, M.
2005 The Cody Complex Revisited: Landscape Use and Technological Organization on the Northwestern Plains. Unpublished Ph.D. dissertation, Department of Anthropology, University of Colorado, Boulder.

Pitblado, B. L.
2003 *Late Paleoindian Occupation of the Southern Rocky Mountains*. University Press of Colorado, Boulder.

Reimer, P., M. Baillie, E. Bard, A. Bayliss, J. W. Beck, C. Bertrand, P. Blackwell, C. Buck, G. Burr, K. B. Cutler, P. E. Damon, R. L. Edwards, R. G. Fairbanks, M. Friedrich, T. P. Guilderson, A. G. Hogg, K. A. Hughen, B. Kromer, G. McCormack, S. Manning, C. Ramsey, R. Reimer, S. Remmelle, J. Southon, M. Stuiver, S. Talamo, F. Taylor, J. Van der Plicht, and C. Weyhenmeyer
2004 IntCal04 Terrestrial Radiocarbon Age Calibration, 26-0 ka BP. *Radiocarbon* 46:1029–1058.

Reimer, P., M. Baillie, E. Bard, A. Bayliss, J. W. Beck, C. Bertrand, P. Blackwell, C. Buck, G. Burr, K. B. Cutler, P. E. Damon, R. L. Edwards, R. G. Fairbanks, M. Friedrich, T. P. Guilderson, A. G. Hogg, K. A. Hughen, B. Kromer, G. McCormack, S. Manning, C. Ramsey, R. Reimer, S. Remmelle, J. Southon, M. Stuiver, S. Talamo, F. Taylor, J. Van der Plicht, and C. Weyhenmeyer

2009 IntCal09 and Marine09 Radiocarbon Age Calibration Curves, 0–50,000 Years cal BP. *Radiocarbon* 51:1111–1150.

Schultz, J.

1992 The Use-Wear Generated by Processing Bison Hides. *Plains Anthropologist* 37:333–352.

Smiley, F.

1979 An Analysis of Cursorial Aspects of the Biomechanics of the Forelimb in Wyoming Holocene Bison. Unpublished Master's thesis, Department of Anthropology, University of Wyoming, Laramie.

Todd, L. C.

1987 Taphonomy of the Horner II Bone Bed. In *The Horner Site: The Type Site of the Cody Cultural Complex*, edited by G. C. Frison and L. C. Todd, pp. 107–198. Academic Press, New York.

Weissner, P.

1983 Style and Social Information in Kalahari San Projectile Points. *American Antiquity* 48:253–276.

Wheat, J. B.

1972 *The Olsen-Chubbuck Site: A Paleo-Indian Bison Kill*. Memoirs of the Society for American Archaeology No. 26. Washington, D.C.

Wheeler, C.

2002 Culture Change on the Great Basin–Great Plains Frontier: The Archaic of Southwestern Wyoming. Unpublished Ph.D. dissertation, Department of Anthropology, University of Colorado, Boulder.

Willey, G., and P. Phillips

1958 *Method and Theory in American Archaeology*. University of Chicago Press, Chicago.

Wormington, H. M.

1957 *Ancient Man in North America*. 4th ed. Denver Museum of Natural History Popular Series No. 4. Denver, Colorado.

Yansa, C.

2007 Lake Records of Northern Plains Paleoindian and Early Archaic Environments: The Park Oasis Hypothesis. *Plains Anthropologist* 52:109–144.

# Contributors

Daniel S. Amick
Department of Anthropology
Loyola University
Chicago, Illinois

Douglas Bamforth
Department of Anthropology
University of Colorado
Boulder, Colorado

Robert J. Dawe
Royal Alberta Museum
Edmonton, Alberta, Canada

Matthew E. Hill Jr.
Department of Anthropology
University of Iowa
Iowa City, Iowa

Edward J. Knell
Department of Anthropology
California State University
Fullerton, California

Ruthann Knudson
Knudson Associates
Great Falls College
Montana State University
Great Falls, Montana

Mark P. Muñiz
Department of Sociology and Anthropology
St. Cloud State University
St. Cloud, Minnesota

Matthew J. Root
Rain Shadow Research
Department of Anthropology
Washington State University
Pullman, Washington

Jeb Taylor
Buffalo, Wyoming

Chris Widga
Landscape History Program
Illinois State Museum
Springfield, Illinois

# Index